Munich, Bavaria
& the Black Forest

Bavaria
p89

Stuttgart & the
Black Forest
p197

Munich
p42
◉

Salzburg
◉ & Around
p169

Marc Di Duca, Kerry Christiani

PLAN YOUR TRIP

ON THE ROAD

OKTOBERFEST P28

Contents

TRIBERGER WASSERFÄLLE
P246

Welcome to Munich, Bavaria & the Black Forest

Hilltop castles and green energy, beer halls and luxury cars, Alps and edgy art – southern Germany blends thigh-slapping tradition with clear-headed modernity like nowhere else on earth.

Alpine Air & Munich Flair

Bavaria is definitely a place for those who prefer their air fresh rather than freshened. Though the Alps only tickle Germany's underbelly, locals know how to get the most out of their peaks, stringing cable cars up the vertical reality of the Alps; marking out entire atlases of cycling, hiking and cross-country skiing trails; even running a train up the inside of the Zugspitze, Germany's highest mountain. Yet all this is just a short ride from the urban *joie de vivre* of Munich, a sassy, sophisticated and self-confident city with a nonchalant, slightly Mediterranean feel.

King of the Castle

Southern Germany is famed for its castles, from medieval fortresses to the 19th-century follies commissioned by Bavaria's most celebrated king, Ludwig II. Mad about Versailles (and some claim just plain mad) he 'single-handedly' launched Bavaria's tourist industry and even stirred Walt Disney with his story-book Schloss Neuschwanstein. You could spend a month zigzagging between sugary palaces, stuccoed baroque residences, wind-cracked Gothic ruins and vista-rich chateaux. Palace fatigue? Then retreat to a cosy tavern and raise a tankard to this marvellous corner of Europe.

Cuckoo Clocks & Lederhosen

If you're in search of strapping Alpine types in Lederhosen, buxom wenches juggling platters of pork, tipsy oompah bands and lanes of Hänsel-and-Gretel cottages, you'll be pleased to hear that Germany's south keeps all its clichéd promises. Nowhere is this truer than on the Romantic Road, a 350km route from Würzburg to the Alps stringing centuries of quaint walled towns along a ribbon of history and tweeness. And if you think the folksy fuss is just for the tourists you'd be wrong – many Bavarians keep a pair of Lederhosen or a Dirndl in their closets for special occasions.

Southern Comfort

The Germans have a word for it – *Gemütlichkeit* – that untranslatable blend of cosiness, well-being and a laid-back attitude. Nowhere does this mood permeate deeper than in the prosperous south where it awaits you in a region of fairy-lit beer gardens, Alpine views, medieval towns and rousing hilltop castles. But there's another facet to *Gemütlichkeit*: it's also a marble-smooth autobahn of luxury cars speeding to gourmet restaurants and chic Alpine spas, Munich's high-brow cultural scene robed in black, and cappuccinos at dawn on intercity expresses. The two southern Germanys coexist side-by-side, an incongruous mix but reassuringly predictable.

Why I Love Southern Germany

By Marc Di Duca, Writer

Is it the sap-scented hills and trails in forests Black and Bavarian, the Franconian beer and dark tourism of Nuremberg or the emotions stirred by the tragic Ludwig II story? Or is it a mildly envious admiration for southern Germany's knack of producing cars that work, its galleries packed with modern art or the awe I feel for the German intellect as I face yet another devilishly complex Deutsche Bahn ticket machine (perhaps not)? I suppose it's all the above and heaps more that has me returning time and again to this quirky yet level-headed corner of Europe.

For more about our writers, see p328

Above: Nuremberg (p127)

Munich, Bavaria & the Black Forest

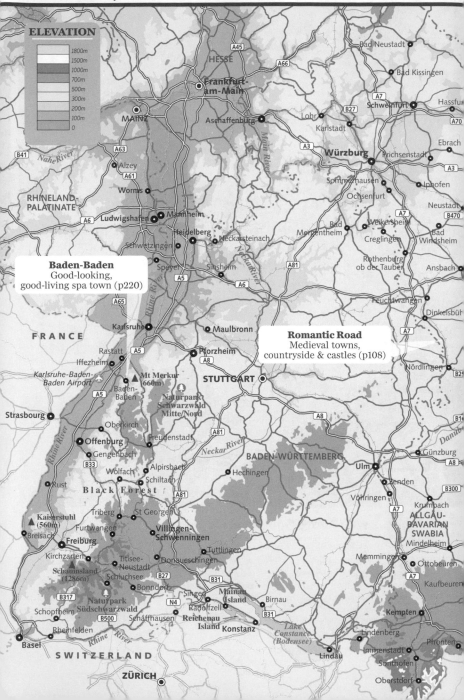

ELEVATION

1800m
1500m
1000m
700m
500m
300m
200m
100m
0

Baden-Baden
Good-looking,
good-living spa town (p220)

Romantic Road
Medieval towns,
countryside & castles (p108)

Nuremberg
The south's most kid-friendly city (p127)

Munich
Explore Bavaria's exciting capital city (p42)

Salzburg
Visit Mozart and Maria's Alpine home (p169)

Bavarian Alps
Picturesque hiking amids mountain peaks (p92)

Schloss Neuschwanstein
Explore the world's most famous castle (p92)

Munich, Bavaria & the Black Forest's
Top 10

Munich

1 Confident and cutting edge, traditional and twee, Bavaria's capital (p42) takes all the state's quirky variety and condenses it into one of Europe's most intriguing destinations. The 'city of art and beer' wows with its world-beating collections of old masters, Gothic sculpture and pop art; but when the high-brow day ends, Munich retreats to the beer hall to savour a hop-infused culture like no other. Factor in some intense nightlife, world-class museums and easy-going locals and it's plain to see there's much more to Munich than just Oktoberfest. Below left: Neues Rathaus and Marienplatz (p46)

Oktoberfest

2 Social barriers evaporate, strangers become friends and everybody sings too loudly, drinks in excess and has way too much fun at the world's biggest beer bash (p28) in Munich. The event lures a global posse of hedonists, but there's a quieter, folksier side, with less raucous beer tents and time-honoured traditions teleporting visitors back to its early 19th-century beginnings. So squeeze into your Lederhosen or Dirndl and get on down to the Theresienwiese – it's an experience you won't forget, if you can remember it at all, that is.

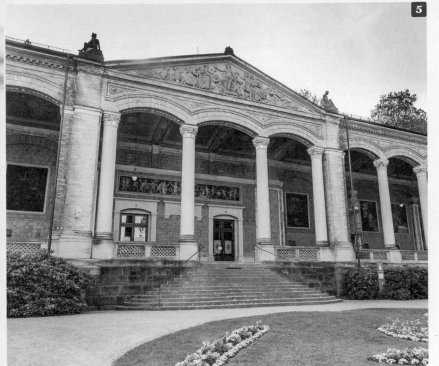

Beer Halls & Gardens

3 Munich and Bavaria are synonymous with the beer hall, a time-warped institution of towering tankards, tightly trussed, strong-armed waitresses, and resident oompah bands. The (grand)daddy of all beer halls is central Munich's Hofbräuhaus (p76; pictured left), but there are plenty of equally characterful, and perhaps less touristy, spots throughout the south. If you prefer your watering holes alfresco, Munich's beer gardens have been plonking down wet ones for over 200 years, and this summertime passion certainly has another two centuries' worth of elbow bending to come.

Romantic Road

4 As roads go, western Bavaria's Romantic Road (p108) is something pretty special – a 350km-long ribbon of higgledy-piggledy walled towns and soothing countryside. However, it's not all medieval quaintness; the route passes blockbuster Schloss Harburg (pictured left), the Unesco-listed baroque Wieskirche and Ludwig II's Neuschwanstein. Yes, it's tourist-clogged, and yes, the renovation can be more Technicolor than Teutonic, but come in the snow, stroll after the tourist buses depart or tackle the route by bike, and the Romantic Road begins to live up to its name.

Baden-Baden

5 Some 2000 years ago the Romans raved about *baden* (bathing) in the therapeutic waters of Baden-Baden (p220), and the spring-fed town still hasn't lost its touch. Royalty and celebrities from Queen Victoria to Victoria Beckham have put this classy Black Forest spa town on the global map, but its merits speak for themselves. Nestled snugly at the foot of thickly wooded hills, this is a good-looking, good-living town of pristine belle époque villas and sculpture-strewn gardens, cupola-crowned spas, and ritzy boutiques, cafes and restaurants. Above: Trinkhalle (p220)

Hiking

6 If you're a fan of *wandern* (hiking), boy, are you in for a treat – the hiking in southern Germany is about as good as it gets. Whether you want to ramble among the mythical mountains of Berchtesgaden, splashed with jewel-coloured lakes; crest the country's highest peak, 2962m Zugspitze (p98); or trek from hut to hut in the Alps, there is a trail with your name on it. Edging west brings you to the wonderful solitude, bristling spruce forests and mile after glorious mile of footpaths in the Black Forest. Below: Berchtesgaden National Park (p106)

Nuremberg

7 The beer is as dark as the tourism in buzzing Nuremberg (p127), where some of the region's most evocative Nazi heritage sites, including the mammoth rally grounds (pictured below) where the faithful came en masse to Heil Hitler, draw those on the Third Reich trail. So with all its Nazi and WWII associations, you may be surprised to hear that Bavaria's second city is also its most child-friendly, with heaps for the kids to do. It's also a magnet for Renaissance art fans, enticed to the city by Dürer, who was born here.

Schloss Neuschwanstein

8 Bavaria's best-known castle (p92) emerges from hilltop woodland above Füssen like a bed-time story-book vision. Commissioned by Ludwig II, 19th-century king of Bavaria, Neuschwanstein is top of the league when it comes to Germany's tourist attractions and it's easy to see why. What would have been a private royal residence is a reflection of Ludwig II's longing to retreat into his own cloistered fantasy world, a secluded realm in which the operas of Richard Wagner played a pivotal role. No wonder Walt found inspiration here for his Disney World creations.

Salzburg

9 At times Salzburg (p169) can feel like a Hollywood film set, with its theatrical Alpine back-drop, exuberant baroque architecture, and Mozart and Maria everywhere. But here's the good news: it's real. History seeps through the Altstadt's maze of narrow lanes, crowned by a formidable fortress and sprinkled with churches and abbeys. Pathways thread along river banks and cliff ridges, allowing you to survey the city from every photogenic angle. By night, locals pour into palatial concert halls for chamber concerts, and chestnut-canopied beer gardens for monastic brews.

Christmas Markets

10 It's Advent so pull on your woollies, grab a mug of mulled wine and a wedge of fes-tive gingerbread and set out to discover southern Germany's fabled Yuletide markets. Sprawled across ancient town squares in a Christmassy ruck of fairy lights, handmade orna-ments, live nativity scenes and irresistible treats, they arouse a bagful of sea-son's cheer as you hunt down those not-made-in-China (though look to make sure) gifts for folks back home. Nuremberg has the biggest fair (p133; pictured above), but Mu-nich and Freiburg also get in on the act.

Need to Know

For more information, see Survival Guide (p301)

Currency
Euro (€)

Language
German

Visas
Generally not required for stays of up to 90 days; some nationalities will need a Schengen visa.

Money
ATMs are ubiquitous, accessible 24/7 and the easiest and quickest way to obtain cash. But not all machines take all cards. Check with your bank or credit-card company about fees. Credit and debit cards accepted at most hotels and shops but not all restaurants.

Mobile Phones
Phones from other countries work in Germany but if they contain a non-EU SIM they attract roaming charges. Local SIM cards cost as little as €10.

Time
Central European Time (GMT/UTC plus one hour)

When to Go

Warm to hot summers, mild winters
Warm to hot summers, cold winters
Mild summers, cold winters
Cold climate

Nuremberg
GO Apr–Oct

Stuttgart
GO Apr–Oct

Munich
GO Year-Round

Freiburg
GO Apr–Oct

Salzburg
GO Year-Round

High Season
(May–Sep)

➡ The best time to travel: skies are bright and temperatures comfortable.

➡ Good for hiking and other outdoor pursuits; hanging out in beer gardens; attending festivals.

Shoulder
(Mar–May & Oct)

➡ Fewer tourists means lower prices and less-crowded sights.

➡ Surprisingly pleasant weather and a riot of colour: wildflowers in spring, foliage in autumn.

Low Season
(Nov–Feb)

➡ With the exception of winter sports, activities focus more on culture and city life.

➡ Reduced opening hours or seasonal closures at museums, other sights and smaller guesthouses.

Useful Websites

City of Munich (www. muenchen.de) Official tourism site.

Bavarian Tourism Association (www.bayern.by) Bavaria's official tourism site.

Black Forest Tourism (www. blackforest-tourism.com) Black Forest's official tourism site.

Castles in Bavaria (www. schloesser.bayern.de) Bavaria's palaces and castles.

State of Bavaria (www.bayern. de) Official Bavarian government site.

Important Numbers

Omit the area code if you are inside that area. Drop the initial 0 if calling from abroad.

Country code	☎+49
International access code	☎00
Emergency (police, fire, ambulance, mountain rescue)	☎112

Exchange Rates

Australia	A$1	€0.63
Canada	C$1	€0.64
Japan	¥100	€0.76
New Zealand	NZ$1	€0.60
UK	UK£1	€1.13
USA	US$1	€0.80

For current exchange rates see www.xe.com

Daily Costs

**Budget:
Less than €70**

➡ Dorm beds: €15–30

➡ Lots of relatively cheap supermarkets for self-caterers

➡ In Munich, visit museums and galleries on Sunday when many charge €1 admission

**Midrange:
€70–200**

➡ Double room in a midrange hotel: around €80

➡ Main course in a midrange restaurant: €12–22

➡ Economy car rental: from around €30 per day (less if booked online in advance)

**Top End:
More than €200**

➡ Luxury hotel room: from €120

➡ Three-course meal in a good restaurant: around €50

Opening Hours

Opening hours don't vary much across the year.

Banks 8.30am–4pm Mon-Fri, limited opening Sat

Restaurants 11am-11pm

Cafes 7.30am–7pm

Bars and clubs 6pm–1am minimum

Shops 9.30am–8pm Mon-Sat

Arriving in the Region

Munich Airport Shuttle bus every 20 minutes to the Hauptbahnhof from 5am to 8pm. S-Bahn every 20 minutes, almost 24 hours. Taxi to city centre €50 to €70.

Nuremberg Airport U-Bahns run every few minutes to the city centre. Taxi to city centre about €20.

Salzburg Airport City bus every 10 to 15 minutes to the Hauptbahnhof from 5.30am to 11pm. Taxi to city centre €15 to €20.

Getting Around

Getting around Bavaria and the Black Forest is most efficient by car or by train. Regional bus services fill the gaps in areas not well served by the rail network.

Train The most efficient way of getting around with a dense network of lines and stations.

Car Good for travelling at your own pace and without the ticket and time constraints of the public transport system. Motorways are good; things can slow down considerably off the autobahn.

Bus Most journeys in the Alps and some on the Romantic Road are by bus. Otherwise this is the least efficient way of seeing the region.

Bike A cheap and green way of touring the region's cities. Bike paths are plentiful in Munich and Nuremberg.

For much more on **getting around**, see p309

PLAN YOUR TRIP NEED TO KNOW

First Time Munich, Bavaria & the Black Forest

For more information, see Survival Guide (p301)

Checklist

➡ Ensure your passport is valid for another four months after arrival in Germany

➡ Check budget airline baggage restrictions carefully

➡ Inform your bank-/credit-card company you'll be travelling in Germany

➡ Make sure your travel insurance covers all planned activities

➡ Find out what you need to provide to hire a car

What to Pack

➡ Hiking boots and other walking gear for Alpine trails

➡ Phrasebook or translation app

➡ European plug adaptors for charging gadgetry – they will be harder to come by in Germany

➡ A sweater or fleece even in summer for evenings in the Alps

Top Tips for Your Trip

➡ Holidays such as Easter or Christmas aren't good times to travel to Germany. Things are often completely dead.

➡ Schedule some time away from southern Germany's big cities to sample life at a slower, more traditional pace.

➡ If you are not going to Oktoberfest, don't even think about going to Munich in late September when the city is booked up.

➡ Make sure you are insured for any extreme activities such as winter sports in the Alps.

➡ When travelling around Bavaria and Baden-Württemberg by train, put off your journey until after 9am when you can use a Land ticket giving you unlimited travel in either region all day for €24 (Baden-Württemberg) or €25 (Bavaria).

What to Wear

Bavarians (and their counterparts in the Black Forest) are a culturally conservative bunch. Smart casual will do for the vast majority of evening occasions, and outside of more fashion-conscious Munich, you may be surprised how informally Germans dress for smart restaurants and the theatre. Only the most upmarket establishments may insist on jackets for men.

For sightseeing take sturdy shoes for all those cobbled streets and a waterproof coat; walking boots or trail shoes are essential if you are heading to the Alps. Even in summer long sleeves are a must in the evenings, especially at altitude.

Sleeping

➡ If heading to the region in late September (during Oktoberfest) accommodation may be very difficult to book at short notice.

➡ Rooms with air-con are rare. Wherever you stay, breakfast always appears on price lists as a separate item, not included in room rates.

➡ Another extra charge is the Kurtaxe (resort tax), particularly common in the Alps. Between €1 and €3, it's not included in the room rate but often gains you a discount card for local transport and sights.

➡ Wi-fi at every standard of accommodation is virtually guaranteed and almost always free.

Money

Southern Germany is an expensive place to visit, but there are ways of preventing your stash of euros from being depleted too rapidly.

➡ Germany's public transport systems offer myriad ways of saving cash – hardly anyone pays full fare. The best place to start is www.bahn.de.

➡ Making accommodation reservations on popular booking websites can save you a lot, especially at quiet times in large cities.

➡ Take advantage of generous buffet breakfasts and inexpensive lunch menus to fill up on the cheap.

Bargaining

Bargaining is not acceptable anywhere at any time in Germany's south.

Tipping

When to tip You could get through an entire trip around southern Germany without giving a single tip. Few service industry employees expect them these days, though most still appreciate a little extra when it comes their way.

Hotels Generally €1 per bag.

Pubs Leave a little small change for the bar staff.

Restaurants Round up the bill to the nearest €5 (or €10) if you were satisfied with service.

Taxis Round up to the nearest €5 so the driver doesn't have to hunt for change.

Toilet attendants €0.50 usually keeps these guys happy unless a price list states exact rates.

Language

It's just about possible to get by in Germany's south without speaking any German whatsoever, but learning a few simple words and phrases will pay dividends in all kinds of situations from the restaurant table to the booking office. In big cities, such as Munich and Nuremberg, English is spoken by those who come into regular contact with foreigners, but this may not be the case in rural locations.

 Do you accept credit cards?
Nehmen Sie Kreditkarten?
nay·men zee kre·deet·kar·ten

Cash is still king in Germany, so don't assume you'll be able to pay by credit card – it's best to enquire first.

 Which beer would you recommend?
Welches Bier empfehlen Sie?
vel·khes beer emp·fay·len zee

Who better to ask for advice on beer than the Germans, whether at a beer garden, hall, cellar or on a brewery tour?

 Can I get this without meat?
Kann ich das ohne Fleisch bekommen?
kan ikh das aw·ne flaish be·ko·men

In the land of *Wurst* and *Schnitzel* it may be difficult to find a variety of vegetarian meals, especially in smaller towns.

 Do you speak English?
Sprechen Sie Englisch?
shpre·khen zee eng·lish

Given Berlin's cosmopolitan tapestry, the answer will most likely be 'yes' but it's still polite not to assume and to ask first.

 Do you run original versions?
Spielen auch Originalversionen?
shpee·len owkh o·ri·gi·nahl·fer·zi·aw·nen

German cinemas usually run movies dubbed into German – look for a cinema that runs subtitled original versions.

Etiquette

Southern Germans are a pretty rigid bunch, with elderly people in particular expecting lots of set behaviour and stock phrases. It's easy to make a mistake, but the following should help you avoid red-faced moments.

Greetings Until noon say *'Guten Morgen'*; from noon until early evening this becomes *'Grüss Gott'*. *'Guten Abend'* is used from around 6pm onwards until it's time to say *'Gute Nacht'*. Use the formal *'Sie'* with strangers, and the informal *'du'* and first names if invited to. If in doubt, use *'Sie'*.

At the table Tucking in before the *'Guten Appetit'* starting gun is fired is regarded as bad manners. When drinking wine, the toast is *'Zum Wohl'*, with beer it's *'Prost'*.

When meeting up Punctuality is appreciated – never arrive more than 15 minutes late.

What's New

Vespa Munich

The vespa scooter is a common sight in Munich – join in the low-cc fun on a new Vespa tour of the Bavarian capital guided by a GPS unit. (p63)

Testturm

Rottweil's futuristic, 246m-high Testturm, open to the public since late 2017, has Germany's highest lookout platform and ravishing views of the Black Forest. (p249)

Museum of Bavarian History

In 2019, Regensburg will open a major new attraction, the Museum of Bavarian History, which will inhabit an ultra-modern structure right on the banks of the Danube.

Swabian Alps

This oft-overlooked region now has a major new draw – in 2017 its caves and ice art gained it much-deserved and long-awaited Unesco World Heritage status. (p209)

Weissenhof Estate

Architecture enthusiasts are thrilled by the recent opening of this estate, built in 1927 for the Deutscher Werkbund exhibition. Two of Le Corbusier's houses here have Unesco World Heritage status. (p200)

Munich's new infrastructure projects

Showing Munich's commitment to sustainable green development, the city is adding a new S-Bahn line to relieve congestion in the city centre and drilling a tunnel under the English Garden which will reunite the two halves of the city's green lung.

Stuttgart's Kraftpaule

With knowledgeable bartenders and a wide range of ales, Stuttgart's cool new microbrewery and bar is a sign of the city's growing thirst for craft beer. (p206)

Amphibious Splash Tours

A cruise along the Salzach River in this new boat-bus amphibious vehicle is an enjoyable and pretty unique way of seeing Salzburg from the river. (p180)

Weinhaus Neuner

One of Munich's best and most traditional places to enjoy Bavarian dishes and wine, Weinhaus Neuner has reopened in the city centre. (p73)

For more recommendations and reviews, see lonelyplanet.com/germany/munich-bavaria-the-black-forest

If You Like...

Castles & Palaces

Love castles? Then Bavaria is your place with some blockbuster piles hugging hilltops and hogging city-centre plots.

Schloss Neuschwanstein King Ludwig's – and the world's – most celebrated castle is Bavaria's top must-see. (p92)

Munich Residenz The former residence of the Bavarian royal family is essential viewing in the Bavarian capital. (p43)

Schloss Linderhof Versailles-inspired Linderhof occupies a remote site surrounded by snowcapped peaks and moody pine forests. (p97)

Schloss Herrenchiemsee Another of Ludwig II's 'Versailles in miniature' located on an island in the Chiemsee. (p104)

Schloss Nymphenburg Munich's grandest pile is famous for its 'Gallery of the Beauties' and stately gardens. (p59)

Würzburg Residenz Home to the local prince-bishops and the world's largest ceiling fresco. (p109)

Lakes & Mountains

Bavaria claims just a sliver of the Alps but packs a lot into its mountains. Between the peaks glisten glacier-fed lakes providing stop-and-stare vistas and ample opportunities for water-borne fun.

Zugspitze You won't need crampons to tackle Germany's highest peak – just a ticket for the train! (p98)

Starnberger See A watery weekend destination for Munich folk and the place King Ludwig II met his mysterious end. (p88)

Garmisch-Partenkirchen The German Alps' premier resort has the state's longest skiing season and heaps of hiking possibilities. (p97)

Königssee Bavaria's most picturesque lake is a great starting point for flits into the Alpine backcountry. (p106)

Lake Constance Shared between Germany, Switzerland and Austria, and by millions of snap-happy tourists. (p250)

WWII Heritage

Southern Germany certainly has its fair share of sites made infamous by the Nazis during their rise to power and subsequent demise at the hands of the Allies.

Hitler's Eagle's Nest Soar into the Alps to this high perch built as Hitler's mountain retreat. (p106)

Dachau Concentration Camp The Nazis' first concentration camp is a moving memorial to the inmates that suffered and died here. (p86)

Memorium Nuremberg Trials Visit the courtroom where many top-ranking Nazis were tried and sentenced for their crimes against humanity. (p129)

Reichsparteitagsgelände Ever wondered where all that footage of a ranting Hitler and Sieg-Heiling masses was filmed? (p129)

Dokumentation Obersalzberg Learn how Obersalzberg in the Berchtesgadener Land became the Nazis' headquarters. (p106)

White Rose Memorial This small memorial in Munich's Ludwig-Maximilians-Universität commemorates students executed for anti-Nazi activities. (p53)

Museums

Bavaria's ruling Wittelsbach family certainly liked their art and their world-class collections now pack Munich's museums and galleries. Countless other repositories of the past tell southern Germany's tale with imagination and flair.

Münchner Stadtmuseum An innovatively conceived overview of Munich's past created in

2008 to mark the city's 850th birthday. (p46)

Alte Pinakothek The finest art from the Wittelsbachs' extensive collections and the high-brow highlight of Munich's Kunstareal. (p54)

Pinakothek der Moderne Chunky retro design and artwork, plus temporary shows, pack out this minimalist, purpose-built Munich museum. (p54)

Deutsches Museum This great museum has experiments and demonstrations that bring out the boffin in everyone, especially kids. (p61)

Germanisches Nationalmuseum Nuremberg's contribution to the Bavarian museum scene is this journey through Germany's cultural past. (p128)

Museum der Bayerischen Könige A stunning location on the Alpsee and a must for all Bavarian royalty fans. (p94)

Local Food & Drink

It would seem southern Germany has a beer and a sausage for every day of the year. And you can round off a Teutonic feast with possibly the world's most scrumptious type of cake.

Beer Every tipple has its home – whisky belongs to Scotland, wine to France, beer to Bavaria. (p290)

Sausages You could easily put together a sausage-themed tour of southern Germany. (p287)

Snowballs & Gingerbread Rothenburg's sugar-dusted snowballs and Nuremberg's peppery gingerbread are just two of the region's tooth-rotters. (p288)

Black Forest gateau A mouthwatering combination of chocolate sponge, whipped cream and black cherries, infused with cherry brandy. (p288)

Top: Frauenkirche (p47), Munich

Bottom: DenkStätte Weisse Rose (p53), Munich

Wine Southern Germany's finest wines come from the south-facing slopes around Würzburg. (p292)

Churches

From baroque riots to Gothic restraint, round-arched Romanesque to red-brick marvels, southern Germany's steadfast Catholic tradition has bequeathed the region a posse of trip-stopping churches, often bejewelled with exquisite works of art.

Freiburger Münster A sandstone colossus presiding over Freiburg's historical core. The tower affords views as far as France. (p236)

Wieskirche This Unesco-listed barrage of baroque ornamentation enjoys a pretty setting amid idyllic Alpine meadows. (p125)

Asamkirche Munich's baroque masterpiece created by the Asam brothers as their private chapel. (p47)

Frauenkirche No building in the city centre may rise higher than the spires of Munich's famous church. (p47)

St Martin Church The spire of Landshut's basilica is the world's tallest brick structure at 130m. (p161)

Cars & Trains

Germany and Bavaria are synonymous with high-tech industries, particularly when it comes to cars. Explore the past and present of Bavaria's motor industry and discover its railway heritage at high-velocity museums.

BMW Welt & Museum Experience BMW's high-octane present then cross the bridge to the company's exciting car museum. (p58)

Deutsche Bahn Museum A wonderful repository of Germany's choo-choo past containing some of its best-known locos. (p127)

Audi Forum Ingolstadt is home to Audi and the company's museum will get a petrolhead's pulse racing. (p158)

Bayerisches Eisenbahnmuseum Nördlingen's railway museum is a retirement home for Deutsche Bahn's steam locos of yesteryear. (p120)

Mercedes-Benz Museum Complete your luxury car museum collection at this shrine to the Mercs of yesterday in Stuttgart. (p201)

Shopping

For every chain store and out-of-town megamall in Germany's south there's an independent boutique or family-run emporium selling those special items you just won't find back home.

Christmas Markets Packing the centres of Munich, Nuremberg and Salzburg, among others, the region's Yuletide bazaars are Europe's best. (p133)

Dirndl & Lederhosen If you're planning a session in a beer tent, you may as well look the part. (p284)

Käthe Wohlfahrt Weihnachtsdorf It's Christmas every day of the year at Rothenburg's Christmas Village. (p117)

Cuckoo clocks Triberg is cuckoo central, though these inimitable timepieces are available across the region. (p246)

Toys Southern Germany has given mankind Ravensburger jigsaws, the world of Playmobil and Käthe-Kruse dolls. (p135)

Music & Literature

Some of the biggest heavyweights of the Germanic musical and literary worlds hail from this neck of the *Wald*.

Wagner Germany's most controversial composer had Bayreuth's Festspielhaus built specially for his operas. (p143)

Mozart Salzburg is Mozart central, though associations do pop up in several other places across southern Germany. (p176)

Goethe Drop into Tübingen's Cottahaus, once the home of Goethe's first publisher. (p210)

Sound of Music Take a *Sound of Music* film location tour around Salzburg's city centre. (p169)

Brecht Visit the Augsburg house where Germany's greatest 20th-century playwright and poet was born. (p123)

Spas & Pools

Perhaps not instantly synonymous with spas and pools, southern Germany offers a surprising number of places to get pampered.

Baden-Baden The grand dame of central Europe's spa towns and still a magnet for royalty and celebrity. (p220)

Watzmann Therme Berchtesgaden's spa complex offers wellness, sport and saunas galore against a pristine Alpine backdrop. (p107)

Badeparadies Palm trees in the Black Forest? Not the only surprise at this spa and water park. (p244)

Müller'sches Volksbad Munich's most characterful swimming pool still bedecked in original *Jugendstil* decoration. (p63)

Month by Month

January

With the last corks of New Year popped, it's time to clear your head on the ski slopes of the Alps. Winter bites coldest in January so wrap up snug while sightseeing.

☆ Mozartwoche

Since 1956 Salzburg has held a Mozart Week in late January to mark the great composer's birthday on the 27th of the month. The event lures a spectacular list of internationally renowned conductors, soloists and orchestras. (p180)

February

The skiing season reaches its zenith with clogged pistes and queues at the ski lifts. Down in the valleys and on the plains you can usually kiss goodbye to the snow as the very first hints of spring appear.

★ Fasching (Carnival)

During the six-week pre-Lent period (January to February) preceding Ash Wednesday, many towns celebrate with silly costumes, waving parades, incomprehensible satirical shows and drunken revelry, especially in Munich (www.munich-touristinfo.de). Rio it ain't.

May

Spring has well and truly *gesprungen!* Cable cars are heaving hikers instead of skiers up the mountainsides, the beer garden season kicks off under flowering chestnut trees and asparagus features on just about every menu.

★ Maifest

On the eve of 1 May, the May Festival celebrates the end of winter with villagers chopping down a tree to make a *Maibaum* (maypole), painting it, carving and decorating it, then partying around it.

★ Africa Festival

Bongo drums, hot rhythms and fancy costumes turn the banks of the Main River in Würzburg into Europe's largest international festival of African-origin music. The event is held in late May and draws around 100,000 visitors. (p112)

July

Fleeing the city heat is as easy as buying a train ticket to the cooler air of the Alps. Return to an urban setting in the evenings as the festival season swings into action.

★ Christopher Street Day

Gay, lesbian, straight or transgender – everybody comes out to party at Munich's flashy gay parade held over two days in mid-July and attracting 50,000 revellers. Provocative costumes, rainbow flags, techno music and naked torsos guaranteed. (p64)

★ Samba Festival

This unlikely orgy of song and dance in mid-July draws a quarter of a million people to normally sedate Coburg for three days of exotically colourful carnival costumes, high-energy music and a procession of gyrating backsides. (p147)

St Annafest

The enormously popular St Anna Festival (www.alladooch-annafest.de) is an 11-day beer party taking over an enchanted forest near Forchheim. Held between late July and early August.

Tollwood Festival

Crowds flock to Munich's Olympiapark for this popular month-long world-culture festival with concerts, theatre, circus acts, readings and other fun events. It's held from late June to late July, and attracts huge international acts. (p64)

Wagner Festival

This prestigious festival held in Bayreuth from late July to August is *the* Wagner event of the year attracting opera-goers from every continent. Tickets are hard to come by. (p143)

August

Summer is at its peak, the kids are off school, camping grounds fill with an international fleet of campervans, and the Alpine meadows reach their floral peak.

Gäubodenfest

Second in size only to Oktoberfest this mass booze-up is an occasion for much red-faced revelry. It draws around 1.2 million people to little Straubing for 11 days

from the second Friday of August. (p168)

Salzburg Festival

One of Europe's most important classical-music festivals, this premier event runs from late July to the end of August and features everything from Mozart to contemporary music, opera and theatre. (p182)

Sommerfest

In early August join in four days of gigs, food and partying by the River Neckar in Stuttgart. If the weather is hot the event attracts half a million revellers. (p199)

Stuttgarter Weindorf

Beginning on the last weekend in August, this 12-day event sees winemakers from the region sell the year's vintages from hundreds of booths in Schlossplatz, Kirchstrasse and Marktplatz. (p203)

September

Autumn delivers its first nip, especially at altitude. Pupils return to their schools, students to uni and small-town Germany reverts to its reassuringly predictable central European normality.

Cannstatter Volksfest

Very similar to Oktoberfest, Stuttgart's biggest beer festival takes place for two weeks from late September to mid-October and features processions, a fairground and a huge firework

display to round things off. (p203)

Oktoberfest

Oktoberfest should be under October, right? Wrong. It actually takes place more in September than October. The world's most celebrated guzzle fest is Bavaria's top event with five million raising a tankard or 10. *Prost!* (p28)

October

Munich Marathon

Bavaria's top mass-participation running event wisely takes place just after Oktoberfest, keeping at least the runners sober in the weeks leading up to the race. It ends in a grandstand finish at the Olympiastadion. (p64)

December

An eventful month with the ski season beginning in earnest and the 5 December visit by St Nick. Bavarian New Year's Eve celebrations see fireworks launched by thousands of amateur (pyro)maniacs.

Christmas Markets

Celebrate the holidays at glittery Christmas markets with mulled wine, gingerbread cookies and shimmering ornaments. The markets in Munich, Nuremberg, Freiburg and Salzburg are the most famous. Open from late November to 24 December. (p133)

Itineraries

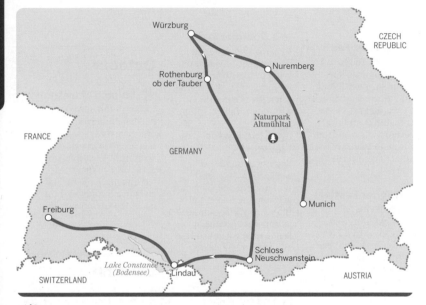

10 DAYS Southern Germany Highlights

This itinerary takes in the best of the region in a whistle-stop tour of southern Germany's must-sees. You could spend months exploring the region but 10 days is just enough to tick off the essentials.

Kick off your southern odyssey in **Munich** where three days is barely enough time to sample the Bavarian capital's art and beer. A short hop north by train brings you to **Nuremberg**, the bustling capital of Franconia and a major draw for fans of both dark tourism and dark beer. Another train, another historic city, this time university town **Würzburg**, famous for its wines and the prince-bishop's residence. You're now at the northern terminus of the 350km-long Romantic Road. The most engaging stop along the route is **Rothenburg ob der Tauber**, a labyrinth of medieval streets and lanes with heaps of sugary architecture. The Romantic Road ends at the gates of **Schloss Neuschwanstein**, Bavarian king Ludwig II's fairy-tale pad and one of the world's most iconic 19th-century follies. Stop off at **Lindau** on the shores of Lake Constance en route to **Freiburg** in the southern Black Forest, where you can follow a tour of the Münster with a slab of the famous local gateau.

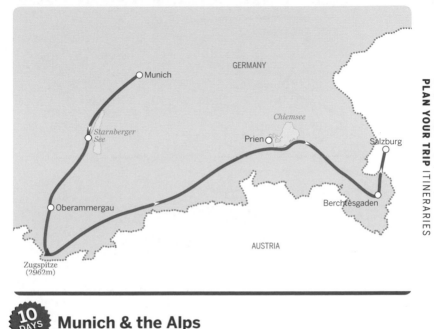

10 DAYS Munich & the Alps

The Alps are a definite highlight of Bavaria and almost every visitor makes at least one trip to these famous peaks. This itinerary includes the best stop-offs and features everything from lakes in the foothills to a train ride to the top of the highest peak.

The route can be tackled as a point-to-point trip or as day trips from Munich; the German Alps are easily reachable by train from there. Beginning in **Munich**, you'll need at least three days to cover the essential viewing in this vibrant metropolis, perhaps reserving time for a spot of shopping and to visit some of the city's lesser-known sights such as the Olympiapark and BMW Welt. If there's time, the incredibly beautiful **Starnberger See** is an S-Bahn ride away. Pretty **Oberammergau**, famous for its once-a-decade passion play, is just over two hours (with changes) on the train from Munich Hauptbahnhof and makes a superb base for visiting King Ludwig II's Schloss Linderhof, an easy 12km hike. Then it's time to stand on the roof of Germany: the **Zugspitze** above Garmisch-Partenkirchen, the Bundesrepublik's highest peak. If you don't have your own wheels you'll have to backtrack all the way to Munich to reach the **Chiemsee**. Water sports are one of the big draws here, though most come for another of Ludwig II's palaces, Schloss Herrenchiemsee, set on an island (the Herreninsel) in the lake and accessible by ferry from the town of **Prien**. After a day of messing around on the *Wasser,* it's back into the mountains, this time the ranges around **Berchtesgaden** in Germany's extreme southeastern tip. Some intriguing Nazi history can be found here, particularly Hitler's mountain perch, the Eagle's Nest, now a seasonal restaurant that draws many visitors. For an equally photogenic escapade, take one of the electric boats from Berchtesgaden along the stunningly picturesque Königssee, surrounded by the Berchtesgaden National Park. From Berchtesgaden it's a short bus ride into Austria and a day or two of *Sound of Music*–mania in achingly beautiful **Salzburg**.

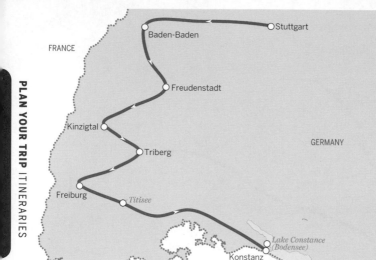

Stuttgart & the Black Forest

This zigzagging canter through Germany's southwest is for those who like a varied time on their travels – the route is a mix of cuckoo clocks and state-of-the art luxury car museums, half-timbered villages and the big-city vibe of Stuttgart.

Begin with a couple of days exploring the galleries, stately plazas and vibrant nightlife of regional capital **Stuttgart**. High on your agenda should be the city's regal heart, Schlossplatz, the Staatsgalerie's art treasures and evenings spent sampling local Rieslings in a *Weinstube* (wine tavern) or hanging out in Theodor-Heuss-Strasse's lounge bars. Car fans should race to the space-age Mercedes-Benz and Porsche museums. On day three, head west to **Baden-Baden**, a swish art nouveau spa town picturesquely nestled at the foot of the Black Forest's spruce-cloaked hills. Here you can wallow in thermal waters, saunter through the sculpture-speckled Lichtentaler Allee gardens and try your luck in the casino. Day four takes you south along the serpentine Schwarzwald-Hochstrasse (B500), with tremendous forest and mountain panoramas at every bend. Stop to glimpse Germany's largest square in **Freudenstadt** on your way to the curving **Kinzigtal**, the prettiest valley in this neck of the woods, with its orchards, vineyards and cluster of half-timbered villages. Your fifth day takes you to the Black Forest's most storied town, **Triberg**, where Germany's highest waterfall flows, the world's biggest cuckoo clock calls, and Claus Schäfer bakes *the* best Black Forest gateau using the original 1915 recipe. Work off the cake with a walk or cross-country ski in the wooded heights of Martinskapelle or Stöcklewaldturm. A scenic hour's drive from Triberg brings you to the sunny university city of **Freiburg**, close to the French border. Spend the day absorbing its easygoing flair in the Altstadt's quaint lanes, watched over by a monster of a medieval minster. Wind out your final day by the lake. Swinging east brings you to forest-rimmed **Titisee** en route to the watery expanse of **Lake Constance**, Central Europe's third-largest lake, flanked by quaint villages, vineyards, wetlands and beaches. An afternoon in **Konstanz** is just long enough to get a taste of this Roman-rooted city, where the historic alleys of the Altstadt wend down to a relaxed lakefront promenade.

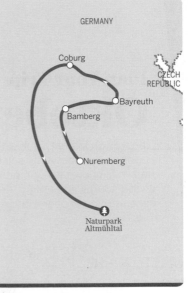

Romantic Road

1 WEEK

Germany's most popular tourist route winds its way for 350km through Bavaria's western reaches.

The Romantic Road begins at **Würzburg** where two days are enough to tour the impressive baroque Residenz and sample the region's wines. From here head south to magical **Rothenburg ob der Tauber** where you can lose yourself in the medieval lanes and celebrate Christmas every day. Your next destination is quaint little **Dinkelsbühl**, a medieval gem ringed by a complete set of town walls. More medieval defences ring **Nördlingen**, a less touristy but equally attractive stopover. Set aside some time to check out the story-book castle guarding the half-timbered village of **Harburg**, and to stroll through twee **Donauwörth** before hitting the city of **Augsburg**, the Romantic Road's biggest settlement boasting several worthwhile attractions. Many a church graces the Romantic Road but, to Augsburg's south, the one packing the mightiest punch is the luminous **Wieskirche**, a true baroque masterpiece. Contemplate King Ludwig II's flights of fancy at his whimsical castle, **Schloss Neuschwanstein**, where Germany's most popular tourist route comes to a fittingly fairy-tale climax.

Nuremberg & Franconia

1 WEEK

Franconia has quite a different feel to it than southern Bavaria. Some of Bavaria's most intriguing museums, historical centres and cultural associations are in its north and this trip covers all the essentials.

The lively capital of Franconia, **Nuremberg** has bags to see and do – including the Nuremberg trials courtroom, the Germanisches Nationalmuseum and the Deutsche Bahn Museum – and an embarrassment of eateries to choose from when you return from exploring the region. A close second in Franconia's pecking order is Unesco-listed **Bamberg**, a confusion of ancient bridges, winding cobbled streets and riverside cottages, the air perfumed by numerous breweries producing the town's unique *Rauchbier* (smoked beer). An hour's train ride brings you to **Bayreuth**, famous for its annual Wagner Festival but a pleasant place to stroll any time of year. Around 100km north of Nuremberg, **Coburg** is memorable for its fortress, its British royal family connections and the longest sausages you'll ever eat served in the smallest bread buns. Round off your time in Franconia with a hike, bike or canoe trip (requiring more time) through the glorious **Altmühltal Nature Park**.

Plan Your Trip
Oktoberfest

The world's largest drink-a-thon and the traditional highlight of Bavaria's annual events calender, Oktoberfest is one of the best-known fairs on earth. No other event manages to mix such a level of crimson-faced humour, drunken debauchery and excessive consumption of beer with so much tradition, history and oompah music.

Need to Know

Where
At the Theresienwiese to the west of the city centre. Poccistrasse and Theresienwiese are the nearest U-Bahn stations.

When
For 16 days up to the first (or occasionally second) Sunday in October.

2019: 21 September to 6 October

2020: 19 September to 4 October

2021: 18 September to 3 October

Opening Hours
Beer is served from 10am to 10.30pm Monday to Friday, 9am to 10.30 Saturday and Sunday.

Other attractions and facilities open longer hours.

Cost
Admission: free

Price of a 1L *Mass* of beer: around €11

Half a roast chicken: around €10

Numbers
Visitors: between six and seven million

Amount of beer consumed: between six and seven million litres

Beer tents: 35

Mass Hysteria

As early as mid-July the brewery crews move in to start erecting the tents which almost fill the Theresienwiese, a gravelly open space in the western reaches of Munich city centre known locally as the Wiesn. When the canvas is taut, the space-age technology is in place to deliver millions of litres of beer to the taps, the Ferris wheel is ready to roll and tens of thousands of chickens are rotating on grills, the Wiesn is ready to welcome the millions of people who arrive annually to toast Germany's 'city of beer'.

During the 16 days of festivities, most travellers dip in for a few days or perhaps a week, taking time off from the *Mass* (the towering 1L mugs of beer) to see Munich's sights and perhaps a castle or two. Whatever you decide to do, be sure to book everything up to a year in advance. And if you can't make it for Oktoberfest, fear not. Throughout the summer and autumn the region hosts countless other fests, often with more traditional, less commercial atmospheres (and cheaper beer). Erding and Straubing have particularly good events.

A Bit of History

The world's biggest foam fest has its origins in a simple horse race. In 1810 Bavarian crown prince Ludwig, later King

TOP 10 TIPS

➡ No cash changes hands within the beer tents – to be served beer, buy special metal tokens (Biermarken) from outside the tents. If you have tokens left over at the end of your session, you can spend them in some Munich pubs.

➡ No glass bottles are allowed at the Oktoberfest due to countless injuries over the years.

➡ Food at Oktoberfest is as pricey as the beer, so bring your own snacks. These can be consumed on the outside terraces of the beer tents but not inside.

➡ Beer tents are elbow to elbow all day on Saturday and Sunday, but for lighter traffic try a weekday afternoon. Until Friday of the first week the evenings tend to be slightly less swamped as well. If you pop out of a beer tent during the busy times, don't expect your seat to be free when you return.

➡ Most tents have table service, but some have areas where you get the beer yourself. Tents usually employ a sufficient number of wait staff to make service swift.

➡ Don't even think of lighting up in any of the beer tents. Anti-smoking laws mean your time in the tent will be up and you could face a fine.

➡ Don't drink in excess – the beer at Oktoberfest is strong stuff, and probably much more potent than your local brew back home.

➡ The vast majority of the beer tents have their last call at 10.30pm.

➡ The Wiesn has its own post office, left-luggage office and childcare centre.

➡ You can reserve a seat at some of the beer tents up to a year in advance – see the tents' individual websites to find out how.

Ludwig I, married Princess Therese of Saxe-Hildburghausen, and following the wedding a horse race was held at the city gates. The six-day celebration was such a galloping success that it became an annual event, was extended and moved forward to start in September so that visitors could enjoy warmer weather and lighter nights. The horse race, which quickly became a sideshow to the suds, ended in 1960, but an agricultural show is still part of the Oktoberfest, albeit a minor one.

Ozapft ist's!

Starting at 10.45am on the first day, the brewer's parade (the Festzug) travels through the city centre from the River Isar to the fairgrounds. This involves many old, brightly decorated horse-drawn carriages once used to transport kegs from brewery to pub and countless felt-hatted tagalongs. When the procession reaches the Wiesn, focus switches to the Schottenhamel beer tent and the mayor of Munich who, on the stroke of noon, takes a mallet and knocks the tap into the first keg. As the beer flows forth and the thirsty crowds cheer, the mayor exclaims: 'Ozapft ist's!' (literally 'It's

tapped' in Bavarian dialect). If you want to witness this ceremonial opening of the Oktoberfest, be sure to get there as early as 9am to bag a seat.

The Beer

Let's get down to the real reason most come to Oktoberfest – the beer. All the suds pulled at Oktoberfest must have been brewed within Munich's city limits which restricts the number of breweries permitted to wet your whistle to six: Hofbräu-München (of Hofbräuhaus fame), the world-famous Paulaner, Löwenbräu, Augustiner, and the less well-known Hacker-Pschorr and Spatenbräu.

The famous 1L Mass brought to your table by a Dirndl-trussed waitress contains pretty strong stuff as the breweries cook up special concoctions for the occasion (usually known as Oktoberfestbier). The percentage of alcohol starts at around 5.8% which makes a single Mass the equivalent of almost 3.5 pints of most regular ales in Britain, Australia and the US. Traditionally the most potent brews are piped to the Wiesn by Hofbräu, the weakest by Hacker-Pschorr.

Not Just Beer

The Oktoberfest is not called the world's biggest fair for nothing, and while most visitor's focus is on the *Bier,* there's quite a lot going on away from the tents.

The funfair with its big wheel, ye-olde test-your-strength booths and scarier 21st-century rides are obvious attractions but magic performances, an agricultural show (more interesting than it sounds) and stalls selling everything from Oktoberfest souvenirs to waffles constitute other minor diversions. The first Sunday sees an impressive costumed procession wend its way through Munich city centre, a tradition going back to 1835, and the customary religious Oktoberfest mass is held in the Hippodrom beer tent on the first Thursday. A brass band concert huffs and puffs beneath the Bavaria statue on the morning of the second Sunday near the spot from where the gun salute is fired on the last Sunday. These events are mostly attended by locals, but give a more traditional insight into the origins and customs of this blockbuster fair for those with a deeper, less inebriated interest.

Sleeping It Off

Your chances of scoring a room in Munich once the mayor has driven the tap into the famous first keg are next to nil, and even a bed in the dingiest of dorms will come with an absurd price tag. However, with Munich's excellent transport links to the rest of Bavaria, and the proximity of the Hauptbahnhof to the Theresienwiese, commuting in from Augsburg, Garmisch-Partenkirchen or Ingolstadt, or even Salzburg and Nuremberg, is feasible. This secret got out long ago, and accommodation providers across Bavaria hitch up their rates from mid-September, but not as much as in Munich. Book accommodation just as the previous Oktoberfest is finishing if possible. If you do stay out of town, make sure you know when the last train back is, or you'll be spending a night at the Hauptbahnhof!

Camping is a fun and relatively inexpensive way to get around the accommodation shortage. **Wies'n Camp** (www.munich-oktoberfest.com) sets up shop every year at the Olympic Equestrian Centre in München-Riem, a 20-minute S-Bahn ride from the Hauptbahnhof. The site has pitches for €14 a night. A place you won't need your own rustling nylon is **The Tent** (www.the-tent.com) where you can bed down in the communal FloorTent for as little as €15 a night!

Family Fun

The two Tuesday afternoons (from noon to 6pm) are dedicated family days with reduced charges for funfair rides, special family oriented events, and lots of balloons and roasted almonds. Away from these days, the Augustiner Festhalle is regarded as the most family-friendly beer tent, but children are allowed into all the others. All tots under six must be out by 8pm every day. The tents have become better places for children since the music was turned down (until 6pm) and smoking was banned.

Dirndl & Lederhosen

Part of the fun at the Wiesn is looking the part: traditional Bavarian Dirndl for the gals, Lederhosen and felt hat for the guys. Dirndl consists of a figure-squeezing bodice, a frilly blouse, a skirt that ends just

IMPORTANT OKTOBERFEST NUMBERS

Don't forget that when calling from a mobile, the dialling code for Munich is ☏089.

WHAT YOU'RE LOOKING FOR	NUMBER
Security point	☏5022 2366
First-aid post	☏5022 2424
Oktoberfest police station	☏500 3220
Guided tours of Oktoberfest	☏232 3900
Oktoberfest Lost & Found office	☏2338 2825
Taxi	☏21 610

Top: Oktoberfest crowds

Bottom: Festzug (brewer's parade; p29)

OKTOBERFEST'S ASTOUNDING STATS

➡ The biggest ever beer tent was the Bräurosl of 1913 which held a whopping 12,000 drinkers.

➡ Munich's biggest bash of the year has been cancelled an amazing 24 times, mostly due to cholera epidemics and war. There was no Oktoberfest during either world wars and in 1923 and 1924 inflation put paid to the festivities.

➡ If you are your party's nominated driver, don't think you're getting off lightly when it comes to the bill. A litre of water costs almost as much as a *Mass* of beer!

➡ Some 90,000L of wine is supped over the 16 days of Wiesn frolics.

➡ It takes around 10 weeks to erect the beer tents and five weeks to dismantle them.

➡ Around 12,000 waiters and waitresses are employed at Oktoberfest.

➡ Around 75% of the Munich Red Cross' annual workload occurs during Oktoberfest.

➡ Around 900 passports are handed into the lost property office each year.

below the knee and an apron. The real deal costs a tiger-economy-size bailout of euros but Munich has countless discount *Trachten* (folk costume) shops, some which pop up specially for Oktoberfest, where vastly cheaper versions can be bought or even hired. For real-deal, secondhand Dirndl and Lederhosen, try Holareidulijö (p84).

Top Beer Tents

Here is our selection of the Wiesn's finest marquees:

Hippodrom (www.hippodrom-oktoberfest.de) Seating 3200 inside, this popular tent attracts a young crowd and the occasional German celebrity. Spatenbräu and Löwenbräu beers and top-notch Bavarian food, plus lots of pricey champagne.

Hofbräu-Festzelt (www.hb-festzelt.de) Including the beer garden and standing room, this tent can accommodate almost 10,000 drinkers. A favourite among English-speaking visitors.

Schottenhamel (www.festzelt.schottenhamel. de) Where Munich's mayor kicks off the whole caboodle with a little mallet.

Käfers Wiesen Schänke (www.facebook.com/ kaeferwiesnschae) Excellent food, longer opening hours (to 1am) and Paulaner beer make this a popular tent with partying celebs and wannabes.

Glöckle Wirt (www.gloeckle-wirt.de) If you fancy something a bit different, this is one of the most attractive, most intimate and smallest of the beer tents, bedecked with antiques and knick-knacks of yesteryear.

Online Resources

Oktoberfest (www.oktoberfest.de) The definitive website containing facts, figures and maps.

City of Munich (www.oktoberfest.eu, www. oktoberfest.info) Official pages from the City of Munich website.

Oktoberfest-TV (www.oktoberfest-tv.de) Webcam coverage of the event plus heaps of info.

Dangers & Annoyances

The approximately seven million litres of strong Oktoberfest beer equates to a lot of intoxicating ethanol and, as you might expect, drunkenness is the main source of danger during Oktoberfest. Things tend to be pretty calm within the beer tents themselves, but it's late at night, when the elbow bending is over, that trouble can flare up as the inebriated masses stagger to the Hauptbahnhof and other stations.

For problems at the Wiesn, Oktoberfest has its own dedicated police force, lost and found office, first-aid post and fire brigade.

Aktion Sichere Wiesn für Mädchen und Frauen (www.sicherewiesn.de) offers free multilingual assistance at Oktoberfest to women who have been sexually harassed or feel otherwise unsafe. It's behind the Schottenhamelzelt and is open from 6pm to 1am, from 3pm Sat.

There have been rare cases of drink spiking at Oktoberfest.

Plan Your Trip
Activities

Bavaria and the Black Forest certainly live up to their reputations as first-rate outdoor destinations. There's plenty to do year-round, with each season offering its own special delights, be it hiking among spring wildflowers, swimming in an Alpine lake warmed by the summer sun, biking among a kaleidoscope of autumn foliage or celebrating winter by skiing through deep powder.

Hiking & Mountaineering

Der Weg ist das Ziel (the journey is the reward) could be the perfect strapline for Bavaria and the Black Forest. No matter whether you want to peak-bag in the Alps, stroll gently among fragrant spruce and pine with the kids or embark on multiday treks over hill and forested dale, this region is brilliant for exploring on foot.

Trails are usually well signposted, sometimes with symbols quaintly painted on tree trunks. To find a route matching your fitness level and time frame, pick the brains of local tourist office staff, who may also be able to supply you with maps and tips. Some offer multiday 'hiking without luggage' packages that include accommodation and luggage transfer between hotels.

The sky-scraping peaks of the Bavarian Alps are Germany's mountaineering heartland. Here you can pick between day treks and multiday hut-to-hut clambers, though you'll need to be reasonably fit and come equipped with the right gear and topographic maps or GPS. Trails can be steep and narrow, with icy patches lingering well into early summer. Before heading out, seek local advice on routes, equipment and weather. If you're inexperienced, ask tourist offices about local outfitters offering instruction, equipment rental and guided tours.

Best...

Skiing
Garmisch-Partenkirchen – A holy grail for downhill skiers, with titanic peaks, groomed slopes and an impeccable snow record.

Hiking
Black Forest National Park – Mile after pine-scented mile of trails weaving through forests, mist-enshrouded valleys and half-timbered villages that look like something from a bedtime story-book.

Mountaineering
Bavarian Alps – Grapple with limestone peaks in this mountaineering wonderland.

Windsurfing
Walchensee – Let your sail catch the breeze on this jewel-coloured, mountain-rimmed lake.

Cycling
Altmühltal Radweg – A 'Best of Bavaria' bike ride, taking in river bends and dense forests, ragged limestone cliffs and castle-topped villages.

The **Deutscher Alpenverein** (DAV; www.alpenverein.de) is a mine of information on hiking and mountaineering, and has local branches in practically every town. It maintains hundreds of Alpine mountain huts, where you can spend the night and get a meal. Local DAV chapters also organise courses (climbing, mountaineering etc), as well as guided treks. If you're planning multiday treks, becoming a member of the organisation can yield a 30% to 50% discount on Alpine huts and other benefits, including insurance.

For climbing routes, gear, walls and more, visit www.dav-felsinfo.de, www.klettern.de and www.climbing.de (all in German).

When to Walk

The summer months are the best for walking in the Alps, when snow retreats to the highest peaks, and wildflowers carpet the slopes. Rush hour is from July to August when you'll need to book hut accommodation well in advance. Autumn has its own charm, with fewer crowds and a riot of colour in deciduous forests. Snow makes it impossible to undertake high-altitude walks during the rest of the year. Many of the big resorts, however, are criss-crossed with winter walking trails, and crunching through snow with a crisp blue sky overhead certainly has its own magic.

Resources

German National Tourist Office (www.germany.travel) Your first port of call, with information in English on walking in Bavaria and the Black Forest.

Kompass (www.kompass.de, in German) Has a reliable series of 1:25,000 scale walking maps, which come with booklets listing background information on trails.

Wanderbares Deutschland (www.wanderbares-deutschland.de) Features the lowdown on dozens of walking trails and has a handy interactive map. Some routes are also detailed in English.

Wandern ohne Gepäck (www.wandern-ohne-gepaeck-deutschland.de, in German) Touch base with the 'hiking without luggage' specialists.

Winter Sports

Modern lifts, primed ski runs from easy-peasy blues to death-wish blacks, solitary cross-country trails, log huts, steaming mulled wine, hearty dinners by a crackling fire – these are the hallmarks of a German skiing holiday.

The Bavarian Alps, only an hour's drive south of Munich, offer the best downhill slopes and most reliable snow conditions. The most famous and ritzy resort is Garmisch-Partenkirchen (p97), a snowball's throw from Germany's highest peak, 2962m Zugspitze. The resort has 60km of slopes to pound, mostly geared towards intermediates.

Picture-book pretty Oberstdorf (p102) in the Allgäu Alps forms the heart of the Oberstdorf-Kleinwalsertal ski region, where 125km of slopes are covered by a single ski pass. It's a good pick for boarders, with snow parks and a half-pipe to play on, and cross-country skiers who come to huff 75km of classic and 55km of skating tracks. For low-key skiing and stunning scenery, there is Jenner (p107) near Berchtesgaden, with vertical drops up to 600m and truly royal vistas of the emerald Königssee, and family-magnet Kranzberg in Mittenwald (p101).

Elsewhere in the country, the mountains may not soar as high as in the Alps, but assets include cheaper prices, smaller crowds, and resorts with a low-key atmosphere suited to families. The Bavarian Forest and the Black Forest have the most reliable snow levels, with moderate downhill action on the Grosser Arber and Feldberg mountains respectively.

At higher elevations, the season generally runs from late November/early December to March. Resorts have equipment-hire facilities. Skis, boots and poles cost around €20/15 for downhill/cross-country gear. Group lessons cost €35 to €50 per day.

Resources

Bergfex (www.bergfex.com) A handy website with piste maps, snow forecasts of the Alps and details of German ski resorts.

On the Snow (www.onthesnow.co.uk) Reviews of Germany's ski resorts, plus snow reports, webcams and lift pass details.

Skiresort (www.skiresort.de) Ski resorts searchable by map and region, with piste details, pass prices and more.

Cycling & Mountain Biking

Strap on your helmet! Bavaria and the Black Forest are superb cycling territory, whether you're off on a leisurely lakeside spin or a multiday bike touring adventure. Practically every town and region has a network of signposted bike routes. For day tours, staff at the local tourist offices can supply you with ideas, maps and advice.

Mountain biking is hugely popular in the Black Forest and in the Alpine region, especially around Garmisch-Partenkirchen (p98), Berchtesgaden (p106) and Freudenstadt (p228). The Bavarian Forest is another top destination for mountain bikers with more than 450km of challenging routes and climbs. The mountain-bike elite comes to the Black Forest for several international MTB races, including the Black Forest **Ultra Bike Marathon** (www.ultra-bike.de; ☉mid-Jun), the Worldclass MTB Challenge (July) and the **Vaude Trans Schwarzwald** (www.rothaus-bike-giro.de; ☉mid-Aug).

Southern Germany is criss-crossed by dozens of long-distance trails, making it ideal for *Radwandern* (bike touring). Routes are well signposted and typically are a combination of lightly travelled back roads, forestry tracks and paved highways with dedicated bike lanes.

TOP FIVE BIKE TOURING TRAILS

Altmühltal Radweg (166km) Easy to moderate route from Rothenburg to Beilngries, following the Altmühl River through the Altmühltal Nature Park.

Donauradweg (434km) Travelling from Neu-Ulm to Passau, this is a delightful, easy to moderate riverside trip along one of Europe's great streams.

Romantic Road (350km) Würzburg to Füssen; this easy to moderate route is one of the nicest ways to explore Germany's most famous holiday route, though it can get busy during the summer peak season.

Bodensee-Königssee Radweg (418km) Lindau to Berchtesgaden; a moderate route running along the foot of the Alps with magnificent views.

Bodensee Radweg (273km) Mostly flat, well-marked, tri-country route, which does a loop of Europe's third-largest lake, taking in vineyards, meadows, orchards, wetlands, historic towns and Alpine vistas.

STEAM & SOAK

If climbing mountains or whizzing down slopes has left you frazzled and achy, a trip to a day spa may be just the ticket. Every place has its own array of massages and treatments. Not a stitch of clothing is worn in German saunas, so leave your modesty in the locker, and always bring or hire a towel.

Friedrichsbad (p223) The crown jewel of Baden-Baden's spas, with its Roman Irish bath and Carrera marble pool.

Watzmann Therme (p107) Perfect for a soak in the Bavarian Alps.

Sanitas Spa (p247) Snuggled in the Black Forest, this Triberg spa has first-class treatments, a pool with views of forest-draped hills and, ahhh, blissfully few crowds.

Kaiser-Friedrich-Therme (0611-318 078; www.wiesbaden.de; Langgasse 38-40; per hour adult/child May-Aug €5/3, Sep-Apr €6.50/4.50; 10am-10pm, to midnight Fri & Sat Sep-Apr, women only Tue) Splash around as the Romans once did at this regal-looking spa in Wiesbaden, where spring water bubbles up at 66.4°C.

Rupertustherme (01805-606 706; www.rupertustherme.de; Friedrich-Ebert-Allee 21, Bad Reichenhall; 4hr ticket €14, incl sauna €19; 9am-10pm) Saline-spring day spa with big Alpine views.

Bike Rental

Most towns have at least one bike-hire station (often at or near the train station), usually with a choice of city, mountain, electric and children's bikes. Depending on the model, you'll pay between €10 to €40 per day or €50 to €120 per week, plus a deposit.

Route Planning

For inspiration and route planning, check out www.germany-tourism, which provides (in English) an overview of routes, helpful planning tips, a route finder and free downloads of route maps and descriptions. For more detailed route descriptions German readers can consult www.schwarzwald-bike. de, www.blackforest-tourism.com and www. bayernbike.de. The Galli Verlag (www.galli-verlag.de) publishes a variety of bike guides sold in bookshops and by the publisher.

Maps & Resources

For basic route maps, order or download the free *Bayernnetz für Radler* (Bavarian Cycling Network) from www.bayerninfo. de. For on-the-road navigating, the best maps are those published by the national cycling organisation Allgemeiner Deutscher Fahrrad Club (www.adfc.de). They indicate inclines, track conditions and the location of repair shops. GPS users should find the UTM grid coordinates useful.

ADFC also publishes a useful online directory called Bett & Bike (www.bett undbike.de) that lists thousands of bicycle-friendly accommodations. Bookstores stock the printed version.

Water Sports

There's no sea for miles but southern Germany's lakes and rivers offer plenty of water-based action. The water quality is high, especially in the glacier-fed Alpine lakes, but the swimming season is relatively short (June to September) since water temperatures rarely climb above 21°C. Steady breezes, deep water and good visibility attract windsurfers and divers to the dazzlingly turquoise, mountain-backed Walchensee in Tölzer Land. Starnberger See, Lake Constance, the fjordlike Schluchsee and Chiemsee offer great windsurfing, sailing and boating in lovely surroundings.

Kayaking and canoeing are great fun and easy to get the hang of. One of the most popular areas to absorb the slow, soothing rhythm of waterways is the Altmühltal Nature Park, where the mellow Altmühl River meanders past steep cliffs, willow-fringed banks and little beaches.

Canyoning is growing in popularity across Europe and southern Germany is no exception. Suitable sites have been identified across the region – contact **Xconcepts** (0151-1143 6890; www.xconcepts.de) near Oberstdorf for guided canyoning excursions.

Plan Your Trip
Travel with Children

With its tradition of lager, beer halls, Lederhosen and tipsy oompah ensembles, you'd be excused for thinking southern Germany is a wholly unsuitable place to bring the little'uns. But you'd be wrong. Germany's south, especially its larger cities, lays on lots of tot-focused activities. In fact, having kids on board can make your holiday a more enjoyable experience and bring you closer to the locals than a few tankards of ale ever could.

On the Ground
In Transit

Trains are preferable to buses when travelling with toddlers as they can leave their seats and wander around quite safely. All trains have at least half a carriage dedicated to carrying prams (and bikes and wheelchairs) and copious amounts of luggage.

Most forms of city transport – such as Munich's trams, trains and underground – are pram-friendly and lifts are ubiquitous. Various discounts are available for families.

Most car hire companies provide child booster and baby seats. They are often free but must be reserved in advance.

Feeding Frenzy

When it comes to feeding the pack, Germany's south is one of Europe's easier destinations. Most restaurants welcome young diners with smaller portions, special menus and perhaps even a free balloon.

Youngsters under 16 are allowed into pubs and bars at any time, as long as they are accompanied by a parent. This includes beer halls and gardens, the latter being particularly popular with families who

Best Places for Kids

Nuremberg
Bavaria's most child-friendly city with attractions as diverse as the Deutsche Bahn Museum, a school museum and a zoo.

Munich
Plenty of hands-on and high-octane diversions as well as a classic toy museum and fantastic trams to ride all day.

Rothenburg ob der Tauber
Edible snowballs and Christmas tree lights in the heat of the summer holidays – pure magic if you're six.

Europa-Park
Europe in miniature and Welt der Kinder (Children's World) at Germany's biggest theme park.

Ulm
Most kids love Lego and most adults love the fact Legoland keeps them occupied for a few hours.

can bring their own picnics. Thanks to the region's smoking ban, fume-filled premises are a thing of the past.

Breastfeeding in public is perfectly acceptable.

All Change

City centres can be a headache for parents of nappy-wearing children – your best bet is to pop into a department store, though these usually position their toilets as far away from the entrance as possible, on the very top floor, and some now charge (thanks, Sanifair!). Things are better at places of interest, and at child-centric attractions nappy-changing amenities are first-rate. In emergencies you can go into the nearest pub or restaurant – staff rarely object.

Discounts

Family tickets are available at the vast majority of sights. It's always worth asking if there's a discount, even if none is advertised.

Bayerisches Eisenbahnmuseum, Nördlingen (p120) Retired locos to clamber around on and seasonal steam-train rides.

Fresh-Air Fun

Playground of the Senses, Nuremberg (p135) Education by stealth at this large open-air experiment park.

Englischer Garten, Munich (p51) Large playground, ice creams, boat rides and acres of grass.

Tierpark Hellabrunn, Munich (p69) Themed playgrounds, a cafe, feeding sessions and a special children's zoo.

Rainy-Day Sights

Playmobil, Nuremberg (p135) Headquartered in Zindorf just outside Nuremberg, the adjoining fun park is one of the city's best family attractions.

Münchner Marionettentheater, Munich (p83) Bavaria's top puppet theatre.

BMW Welt, Munich (p58) Kids can grip the wheel of BMW's latest models and wish they were old enough to have a driver's licence.

Children's Highlights

Museums

Deutsches Museum, Munich (p61)The Kinderreich at Munich's science museum is hands-on fun for kids.

Deutsche Bahn Museum, Nuremberg (p127) Germany's top railway museum has a huge interactive section for choo-choo enthusiasts.

Children & Young People's Museum, Nuremberg (p135) Heaps of hands-on experiments.

Weihnachtsdorf, Rothenburg ob der Tauber (p117) This Romantic Road institution houses a hands-off museum meaning kids are usually more interested in the adjacent Yuletide superstore.

Spielzeugmuseum, Munich (p69) An 'I had that in 1974' kinda museum, so not just for kids.

Planning

When to Go

The best times to visit are spring and early autumn. Summer temperatures see the niggle factor climb and central Europe's sub-zero winters are no fun.

Sleeping

The majority of hotels and guesthouses are pretty kid-friendly and the higher up the hotel food chain you ascend, the more facilities (babysitting, laundry) there are likely to be. Small-hotel and guesthouse owners are generally willing to supply extra beds and even cots for babies. Of course campsites are the most entertaining places to stay; some have playgrounds and kids' clubs.

Regions at a Glance

Munich

History
Museums
Beer

Historic Sights

Losing yourself in the House of Wittelsbach's opulent Residenz, taking a guided tour of Nazi-related sites or discovering the city's recent sporting past at the Olympiapark and Allianz Arena are just some of the history-rich experiences on offer.

Well-Rounded Culture

From the hands-on fun of the Deutsches Museum to the high-brow, hands-off masterpieces of the Alte Pinakothek, and the outrageous pop art of the Museum Brandhorst to the waxed classics of the BMW Museum, Munich has a repository of the past for every rainy day, and one for most sunny ones, too.

Ale Capital

Mammoth beer halls swaying to the oompah beat; chestnut-canopied beer gardens and Oktoberfest; proud breweries striving to out-brew their rivals and breakfasts of *Weissbier* and *Weisswurst* – Munich is the unchallenged beer capital of the world.

p42

Bavaria

Castles
Romance
Mountains

Fairy-Tale Palaces

From spectacular hilltop follies such as Neuschwanstein to medieval strongholds like Nuremberg's Kaiserburg, visits to castles and palaces provide some of Bavaria's most memorable days out.

Romantic Scenery

Whether it be the panorama from an Alpine peak or a lazy cruise along the Danube, Bavaria packs in a lot of dreamy encounters. But the biggest chunk of romance comes in the form of the Romantic Road, a mostly rural route meandering from one time-warped medieval town to the next.

Alpine Magic

Compared to its neighbours, Bavaria possesses but a scant sliver of the Alps. But there's still bags of dramatic scenery out there to enjoy, clearly visible and easily reachable from Munich. Winter skiing and summer hiking are the main draws.

p89

Salzburg & Around

Music
Architecture
Outdoor Activities

Mozart & Maria

The city that sired Mozart has music in its blood. *The Sound of Music* bike tours rattle through the tangled lanes, while classical music climaxes during August's Salzburg Festival.

Baroque Treasures

They broke the baroque mould when they refashioned Salzburg following the counter-reformation, and it's all thanks to some high-minded prince-archbishops. Ramble among architectural riches like the lordly Residenz and Dom in the Unesco World Heritage–listed Altstadt.

Mountain Action

Mother Superior sang about climbing every mountain, but now cable cars zip up Salzburg's peaks. Take in the full sweep of the city from Mönchsberg and Kapuzinerberg, hike, ski and paraglide at Untersberg and Gaisberg, or delve into the Alps for serious outdoor action.

p169

Stuttgart & the Black Forest

Landscapes
Outdoor Activities
City Life

Lyrical Landscapes

The Black Forest is fairy-tale Germany in a nutshell. This forested patchwork of hills and valleys, where waterfalls and brooks run swift and clear, is one of the region's greatest escapes. Tiptoe off the beaten track to half-timbered villages and tucked-away farmhouses.

Trails Galore

Big views, bracing air and well-marked trails lure you outdoors here. Strap on boots for some of Germany's best hiking or swish through snowy woodlands on cross-country skis. Lake Constance is perfect cycling terrain.

Cultured Cities

Stuttgart woos with outstanding galleries, concert halls and high-tech temples to the automobile, but there's more. Soak in the spas of Baden-Baden, hang out in Roman-rooted Konstanz, and spy the world's tallest steeple in Ulm.

p197

On the Road

Bavaria
p89

Stuttgart & the
Black Forest
p197

Munich
p42
◉

Salzburg
◉ & Around
p169

Munich

♪ 089 / POP 1.46 MILLION

Best Places to Eat

➡ Weinhaus Neuner (p71)

➡ Königsquelle (p69)

➡ Tantris (p73)

➡ Prinz Myshkin (p69)

➡ Esszimmer (p73)

Best Places to Stay

➡ Bayerischer Hof (p63)

➡ Flushing Meadows (p62)

➡ Hotel Laimer Hof (p65)

➡ Hotel Mandarin Oriental Munich (p63)

➡ Louis Hotel (p63)

Why Go?

The natural habitat of well-heeled power dressers and Lederhosen-clad thigh-slappers, Mediterranean-style street cafes and Mitteleuropa beer halls, highbrow art and high-tech industry, Germany's unofficial southern capital is a flourishing success story that revels in its own contradictions. If you're looking for Alpine clichés, they're all here, but the Bavarian metropolis has many an unexpected card down its Dirndl.

But whatever else this city is, it's popular. Statistics show Munich is enticing more visitors than ever, especially in summer and during Oktoberfest, when the entire planet seems to arrive to toast the town.

Munich's walkable centre retains a small-town air but holds some world-class sights, especially art galleries and museums. Throw in royal Bavarian heritage, an entire suburb of Olympic legacy and a kitbag of dark tourism, and it's clear why southern Germany's metropolis is such a favourite among those who seek out the past but like to hit the town once they're done.

When to Go

Shoulder seasons (April–June and September–October) are best, avoiding the heat of summer and the bitter winter temperatures. However, avoid late September and early October unless visiting Oktoberfest.

The Christmas market season is a good time to come, as is festival season over the summer.

History

It was Benedictine monks, drawn by fertile farmland and the closeness to Catholic Italy, who settled in what is now Munich. The city derives its name from the medieval Munichen (monks). In 1158 the Imperial Diet in Augsburg sanctioned the rule of Heinrich der Löwe, and Munich the city was born.

In 1240 the city passed to the House of Wittelsbach, which would govern Munich (and Bavaria) until the 20th century. Munich prospered as a salt-trading centre but was hit hard by plague in 1349. The epidemic subsided only after 150 years, whereupon the relieved Schäffler (coopers) initiated a ritualistic dance to remind burghers of their good fortune. The Schäfflertanz is performed every seven years but is re-enacted daily by the little figures on the city's Glockenspiel (carillon) on Marienplatz.

By the 19th century an explosion of monument building gave Munich its spectacular architecture and wide Italianate avenues. Things got out of hand after King Ludwig II ascended the throne in 1864, as spending for his grandiose projects (such as Schloss Neuschwanstein) bankrupted the royal house and threatened the government's coffers. Ironically, today they are the biggest money-spinners of Bavaria's tourism industry.

Munich has seen many turbulent times, but none like the first half of the 20th century. WWI practically starved the city to death, while the Nazis first rose to prominence here and WWII nearly wiped Munich off the map.

The 1972 Olympic Games began as a celebration of a new democratic Germany but ended in tragedy when 17 people were killed in a terrorist hostage-taking incident. In 2006 the city won a brighter place in sporting history when it hosted the opening game of the FIFA World Cup.

Today Munich's claim to being the 'secret capital' of Germany is well founded. The city is recognised for its high living standards – with more millionaires per capita than any other German city except Hamburg – and for a cultural scene that rivals that of larger more important European capitals. Looking towards its 900th birthday, this great metropolis is striding affluently forward in the 21st century.

◎ Sights

Munich's major sights cluster around the Altstadt, with the main museum district just north of the Residenz. However, it will take another day or two to explore bohemian Schwabing, the sprawling Englischer Garten, and trendy Haidhausen to the east. Northwest of the Altstadt you'll find cosmopolitan Neuhausen, the Olympiapark, and another of Munich's royal highlights – Schloss Nymphenburg.

◎ Altstadt & Residenz

★ **Residenzmuseum**   MUSEUM
(Map p48; ☑ 089-290 671; www.residenz-muenchen. de; Residenzstrasse 1; adult/concession/under 18yr €7/6/free; ⊙ 9am-6pm Apr–mid-Oct, 10am-5pm mid-Oct–Mar, last entry 1hr before closing; Ⓤ Odeonsplatz) Home to Bavaria's Wittelsbach rulers from 1508 until WWI, the Residenz is Munich's number-one attraction. The amazing treasures, as well as all the trappings of the Wittelbachs' lifestyle over the centuries, are on display at the Residenzmuseum, which takes up around half of the palace. Allow at least two hours to see everything at a gallop.

Tours are in the company of a rather long-winded audioguide (free), and gone are the days when the building was divided into morning and afternoon sections, all of which means a lot of ground to cover in one go. It's worth fast-forwarding a bit to where the prescribed route splits into short and long tours, taking the long route for the most spectacular interiors. Approximately 90 rooms are open to the public at any one time, but as renovation work is ongoing, closures are inevitable, and you may not see all the highlights.

When wandering the Residenz, don't forget that only 50 sq metres of the building's roof remained intact at the end of WWII. Most of what you see today is a Wittelsbach postwar reconstruction.

The tours start at the Grottenhof (Grotto Court), home of the wonderful Perseusbrunnen (Perseus Fountain), with its namesake holding the dripping head of Medusa. Next door is the famous Antiquarium, a barrel-vaulted hall smothered in frescoes and built to house the Wittelsbachs' enormous antique collection. It's widely regarded as the finest Renaissance interior north of the Alps.

Further along the tour route, the neo-Byzantine Hofkirche was built for Ludwig I in 1826. After WWII only the red-brick walls were left; it reopened as an atmospheric concert venue in 2003.

Upstairs are the Kurfürstenzimmer (Electors Rooms), with some stunning Italian portraits and a passage lined with two dozen views of Italy, painted by local romantic artist Carl Rottmann. Also up here are François Cuvilliés' Reiche Zimmer (Rich Rooms), a

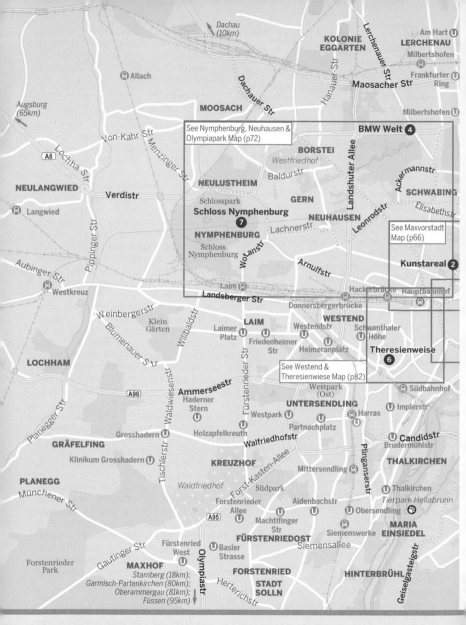

Munich Highlights

1 Hofbräuhaus (p76) Raising a 1L stein at the mothership of authentic beer halls.

2 Kunstareal (p58) Hitting up the south's leading art museums in one compact area.

3 Residenzmuseum (p43) Revelling in the pomp and splendour of this top museum.

4 BMW Welt (p58) Getting under the high-octane hood of BMW's latest models.

5 Englischer Garten (p51) Watching daredevil surfers

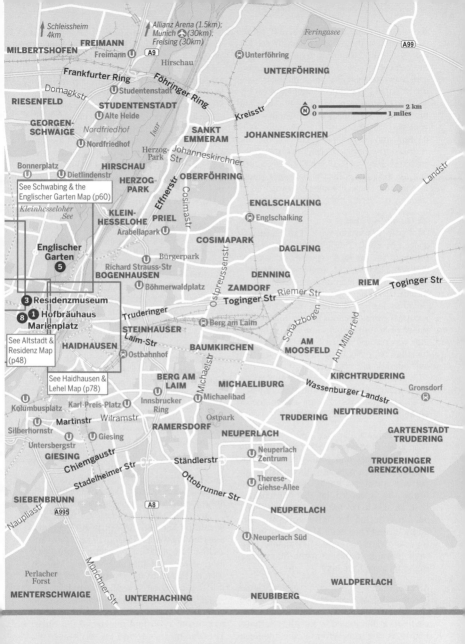

negotiate an urban wave on the artificial stream.

6 Oktoberfest (p64) Raising several steins to a truly Munich experience.

7 Schloss Nymphenburg (p59) Revelling in the utter grandeur of this commanding palace.

8 Marienplatz (p46) Taking in the heart and soul of the Altstadt, the city's busiest spot.

six-room extravaganza of exuberant rococo carried out by the top stucco and fresco artists of the day; they're a definite highlight. More rococo magic awaits in the *Ahnengallery* (Ancestors Gallery), with 121 portraits of the rulers of Bavaria in chronological order.

The *Hofkapelle*, reserved for the ruler and his family, fades quickly in the memory when you see the exquisite *Reichekapelle*, with its blue-and-gilt ceiling, inlaid marble and 16th-century organ. Considered the finest rococo interiors in southern Germany, another spot to linger is the *Steinzimmer* (Stone Rooms), the emperor's quarters, awash in intricately patterned and coloured marble.

★ **Cuvilliés-Theater**　　　THEATRE
(Map p48; Residenzstrasse 1; adult/concession/ under 18yr €3.50/2.50/free; ⊙2-6pm Mon-Sat, 9am-6pm Sun Apr-Jul & Sep–mid-Oct, 9am-6pm daily Aug, 2-5pm Mon-Sat, 10am-5pm Sun Nov-Mar; ⓐ Nationaltheater) Commissioned by Maximilian III in the mid-18th century, François Cuvilliés fashioned one of Europe's finest rococo theatres. Famous for hosting the premiere of Mozart's opera *Idomeneo,* the theatre was restored in the mid-noughties, and its stage regularly hosts high-brow musical and operatic performances.

Access is limited to the auditorium, where you can take a seat and admire the four tiers of loggias (galleries), dripping with rococo embellishment, at your leisure.

★ **Marienplatz**　　　SQUARE
(Map p48; ⓢ Marienplatz, ⓤ Marienplatz) The epicentral heart and soul of the Altstadt, Marienplatz is a popular gathering spot and packs a lot of personality into a compact frame. It's anchored by the Mariensäule, built in 1638 to celebrate victory over Swedish forces during the Thirty Years' War. This is the busiest spot in all Munich, throngs of tourists swarming across its expanse from early morning till late at night. Many walking tours leave from here.

Altes Rathaus　　　HISTORIC BUILDING
(Old Town Hall; Map p48; Marienplatz; ⓢ Marienplatz, ⓤ Marienplatz) The eastern side of Marienplatz is dominated by the Altes Rathaus. Lightning got the better of the medieval original in 1460 and WWII bombs levelled its successor, so what you see is really the third incarnation of the building designed by Jörg von Halspach of Frauenkirche fame. On 9 November 1938 Joseph Goebbels gave a hate-filled speech here that launched the nationwide *Kristallnacht* pogroms.

★ **Münchner Stadtmuseum**　　　MUSEUM
(City Museum; Map p48; www.muenchner-stadt museum.de; St-Jakobs-Platz 1; adult/concession/ child €7/3.50/free, audioguide free; ⊙10am-6pm Tue-Sun; ⓢ Marienplatz, ⓤ Marienplatz) Installed for the city's 850th birthday (2008), the Münchner Stadtmuseum's Typisch München (Typically Munich) exhibition – taking up the whole of a rambling building – tells Munich's story in an imaginative, uncluttered and engaging way. Exhibits in each section represent something quintessential about the city; a booklet/audioguide relates the tale behind them, thus condensing a long and tangled history into easily digestible themes.

Set out in chronological order, the exhibition kicks off with the monks who founded the city and ends with the postwar-boom decades. The first of five sections, Old Munich, contains a scale model of the city in the late 16th century (one of five commissioned by Duke Albrecht V; the Bayerisches Nationalmuseum (p53) displays the others), but the highlight here is the *The Morris Dancers,* a series of statuettes gyrating like 15th-century ravers. It's one of the most valuable works owned by the city.

Next comes New Munich, which charts the Bavarian capital's 18th- and 19th-century transformation into a prestigious royal capital and the making of the modern city. The *Canaletto View* gives an idea in oil paint of how Munich looked in the mid-18th century, before the Wittelsbachs (the German noble family that ruled Bavaria) launched their makeover. The section also takes a fascinating look at the origins of Oktoberfest and Munich's cuisine, as well as the phenomenon of the 'Munich Beauty' – Munich's womenfolk are regarded as Germany's most attractive.

City of Munich examines the weird and wonderful late 19th and early 20th century, a period known for *Jugendstil* (art nouveau) architecture and design, Richard Wagner, and avant-garde rumblings in Schwabing. Munich became known as the 'city of art and beer', a title that many agree it still holds today.

The fourth hall, Revue, becomes a little obscure, but basically deals with the aftermath of WWI and the rise of the Nazis. The lead-up to war and the city's suffering during WWII occupy the Feuchtwangersaal, where a photo of a very determined Chamberlain stands next to the other signatories to the 1938 Munich Agreement, which created parts of Czechoslovakia to Nazi Germany. This is followed by a couple of fascinating rooms that paint a portrait of the modern city, including nostalgic TV footage from the last 40 years.

Though the Typical Munich exhibition touches on the period, the rise of the Nazis has been rightly left as a powerful separate exhibition called Nationalsozialismus in München. This occupies an eerily windowless annexe.

★ Asamkirche CHURCH

(Map p48; Sendlinger Strasse 32; ⊙9am-6pm; 🚇Sendlinger Tor, ⓤSendlinger Tor) Though pocket sized, the late-baroque Asamkirche, built in 1746, is as rich and epic as a giant's treasure chest. Its creators, the brothers Cosmas Damian Asam and Egid Quirin Asam, dug deep into their considerable talent box to swathe every inch of wall space with gilt garlands and docile cherubs, false marble and oversized barley-twist columns.

The crowning glory is the ceiling fresco illustrating the life of St John Nepomuk, to whom the church is dedicated (lie down on your back in a pew to fully appreciate the complicated perspective). The brothers lived next door and this was originally their private chapel; the main altar could be seen through a window from their home.

Frauenkirche CHURCH

(Church of Our Lady; Map p48; www.muenchnerdom.de; Frauenplatz 1; ⊙7.30am-8.30pm; ⓢMarienplatz) The landmark Frauenkirche, built between 1468 and 1488, is Munich's spiritual heart and the Mt Everest among its churches. No other building in the central city may stand taller than its onion-domed twin towers, which reach a skyscraping 99m. The south tower can be climbed, but has been under urgent renovation for several years.

The church sustained severe bomb damage in WWII; its reconstruction is a soaring passage of light but otherwise fairly spartan. Of note are the epic cenotaph (empty tomb) of Ludwig the Bavarian, just past the entrance, and the bronze plaques of Pope Benedict XVI and his predecessor John Paul II affixed to nearby pillars.

Heiliggeistkirche CHURCH

(Church of the Holy Spirit; Map p48; Tal 77; ⊙7am-6pm; ⓢMarienplatz, ⓤMarienplatz) Gothic at its core, this baroque church on the edge of the Viktualienmarkt has fantastic ceiling frescoes created by the Asam brothers in 1720, depicting the foundation of a hospice that once stood next door. The hospice was demolished to make way for the new Viktualienmarkt.

Michaelskirche CHURCH

(Church of St Michael; Map p48; www.st-michaelmuenchen.de; Kaufingerstrasse 52; crypt €2; ⊙crypt 9.30am-4.30pm Mon-Fri, to 2.30pm Sat & Sun; 🚇Karlsplatz, ⓢKarlsplatz, ⓤKarlsplatz) It stands quiet and dignified amid the retail frenzy out on Kaufingerstrasse, but to fans of Ludwig II, the Michaelskirche is the ultimate place of pilgrimage. Its dank crypt is the final resting place of the Mad King, whose humble tomb is usually drowned in flowers.

Completed in 1597, St Michael's was the largest Renaissance church north of the Alps when it was built. It boasts an impressive unsupported barrel-vaulted ceiling, and the massive bronze statue between the two entrances shows the archangel finishing off a dragon-like creature, a classic Counter Reformation–era symbol of Catholicism triumphing over Protestantism. The building has been fully renovated and has never looked more impressive.

Viktualienmarkt MARKET

(Map p48; ⊙Mon-Fri & morning Sat; ⓤMarienplatz, ⓢMarienplatz) Fresh fruit and vegetables, piles of artisan cheeses, tubs of exotic olives, hams and jams, chanterelles and truffles – Viktualienmarkt is a feast of flavours and one of central Europe's finest gourmet markets.

The market moved here in 1807 when it outgrew the Marienplatz, and many of the stalls have been run by generations of the same family. Put together a picnic and head for the market's very own beer garden for an alfresco lunch with a brew and to watch the traders in action.

St Peterskirche CHURCH

(Church of St Peter; Map p48; Rindermarkt 1; church free, tower adult/child €3/2; ⊙tower 9am-6pm Mon-Fri, from 10am Sat & Sun; ⓤMarienplatz, ⓢMarienplatz) Some 306 steps divide you from the best view of central Munich from the 92m tower of St Peterskirche, central Munich's oldest church (1150). Inside awaits a virtual textbook of art through the centuries. Worth a closer peek are the Gothic St-Martin-Altar, the baroque ceiling fresco by Johann Baptist Zimmermann and rococo sculptures by Ignaz Günther.

Jüdisches Museum MUSEUM

(Jewish Museum; Map p48; www.juedischesmuseum-muenchen.de; St-Jakobs-Platz 16; adult/child €6/3; ⊙10am-6pm Tue-Sun; 🚇Sendlinger Tor, ⓤSendlinger Tor) Coming to terms with its Nazi past has not historically been a priority

Altstadt & Residenz

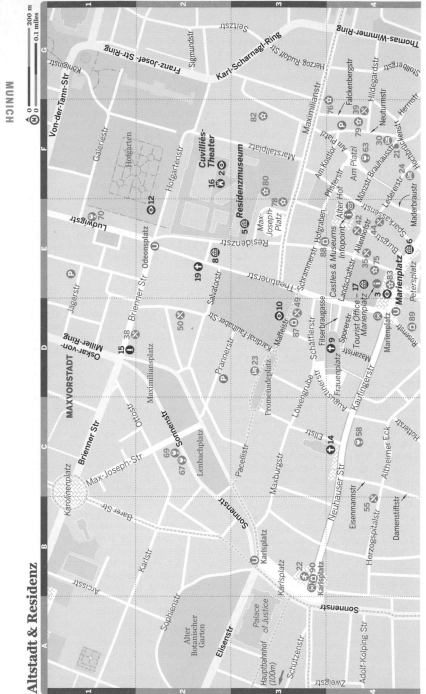

200 m
0.1 miles

MAXVORSTADT

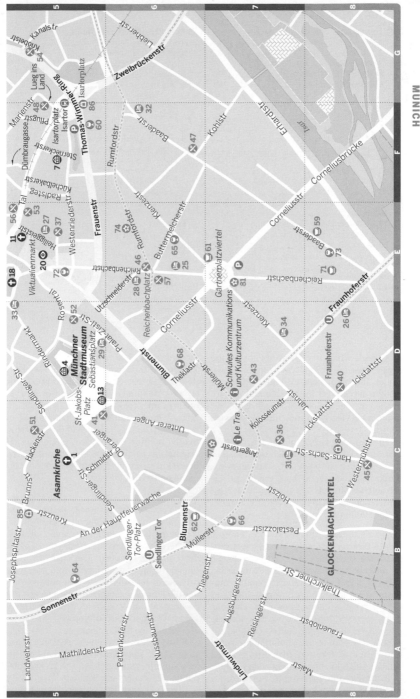

Altstadt & Residenz

in Munich, which is why the opening of the Jewish Museum in 2007 was hailed as a milestone. The permanent exhibition offers an insight into Jewish history, life and culture in the city. The Holocaust is dealt with, but the focus is clearly on contemporary Jewish culture.

The museum is part of the Jewish complex on St-Jakobs-Platz, which also includes a community centre with a restaurant and a bunker-like synagogue that's rarely open to the public. Munich has the second-largest Jewish population in Germany after Berlin's: around 9000 people.

Bier & Oktoberfestmuseum MUSEUM
(Beer & Oktoberfest Museum; Map p48; www.bier-und-oktoberfestmuseum.de; Sterneckerstrasse 2; adult/concession €4/2.50; ⊙1-6pm Tue-Sat; 🚊Isartor, Ⓢ Isartor) Head to this popular museum to learn all about Bavarian suds and the world's most famous booze-up. The four floors heave with old brewing vats, historic photos and some of the earliest Oktoberfest regalia. The 14th-century building has some fine medieval features, including painted ceilings and a kitchen with an open fire.

If during your tour you've worked up a thirst, the museum has its very own pub.

Monument to the Victims of National Socialism MONUMENT
(Map p48; Brienner Strasse; Ⓤ Odeonsplatz) This striking monument is made up of four Ts holding up a block-like cage in which an eternal flame gutters in remembrance of those who died at the hands of the Nazis due to their political beliefs, race, religion, sexual orientation or disability. Moved to this spot in 2014, it's a sternly simple reminder of Munich's not-so-distant past.

Feldherrnhalle HISTORIC BUILDING
(Field Marshalls Hall; Map p48; Residenzstrasse 1; Ⓤ Odeonsplatz) Corking up Odeonsplatz' southern side is Friedrich von Gärnter's Feldherrnhalle, modelled on the Loggia dei Lanzi in Florence. The structure pays homage to the Bavarian army and positively drips with testosterone; check out the statues of General Johann Tilly, who kicked the Swedes out of Munich during the Thirty Years' War; and Karl Philipp von Wrede, an ally turned foe of Napoléon.

It was here on 9 November 1923 that police stopped the so-called Beer Hall Putsch, Hitler's attempt to bring down the Weimar Republic (Germany's government after WWI). A fierce skirmish left 20 people, including

16 Nazis, dead. A plaque in the pavement of the square's eastern side commemorates the police officers who perished in the incident.

Hitler was subsequently tried and sentenced to five years in jail, but he ended up serving a mere nine months in Landsberg am Lech prison, where he penned his hate-filled manifesto, *Mein Kampf.*

Theatinerkirche　　　　　　　CHURCH
(Map p48; Theatinerstrasse 22; ⏰7am-9pm; Ⓢ Odeonsplatz) FREE The mustard-yellow Theatinerkirche, built to commemorate the 1662 birth of Prince Max Emanuel, is the work of Swiss architect Enrico Zuccalli. Also known as St Kajetan's, it's a voluptuous design with massive twin towers flanking a giant cupola. Inside, an ornate dome lords it over the Fürstengruft (royal crypt), the final destination of several Wittelsbach rulers, including King Maximilian II (1811–64).

⊙ Schwabing & the Englischer Garten

⭐ **Englischer Garten**　　　　　　PARK
(English Garden; Map p60; Ⓤ Universität) The sprawling English Garden is among Europe's biggest city parks – it even rivals London's Hyde Park and New York's Central Park for size – and is a popular playground for locals and visitors alike. Stretching north from Prinzregentenstrasse for about 5km, it was commissioned by Elector Karl Theodor in 1789 and designed by Benjamin Thompson, an American-born scientist working as an adviser to the Bavarian government.

Paths meander around in dark stands of mature oak and maple before emerging into sunlit meadows of lush grass. Locals are mindful of the park's popularity and cyclists, walkers and joggers coexist amicably. Street musicians dodge balls kicked by children and students sprawl on the grass to chat about missed lectures.

Sooner or later you'll find your way to the Kleinhesseloher See, a lovely lake at the centre of the park. Work up a sweat while taking a spin around the lake's three little islands, then quaff a well-earned foamy one at the Seehaus beer garden (p79).

Several historic follies lend the park a playful charm. The wholly unexpected Chinesischer Turm (p79), now at the heart of Munich's oldest beer garden, was built in the 18th century during a pan-European craze

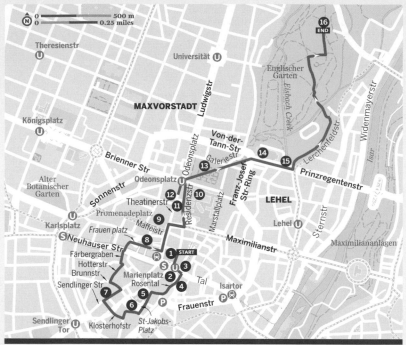

🏃 City Walk
Historic Centre & the Englischer Garten

START MARIENPLATZ
FINISH ENGLISCHER GARTEN
LENGTH 6KM, TWO HOURS

Kick off at central Marienplatz where the glockenspiel chimes from the ❶ **Neues Rathaus**, the impressive Gothic town hall. The steeple of the ❷ **St Peterskirche** (p47) affords great views of the old town, including the ❸ **Altes Rathaus** (p46). Turn left as you leave St Peters and walk down Petersplatz to the ❹ **Viktualienmarkt** (p47). Then head south to Sebastiansplatz and the ❺ **Münchner Stadtmuseum** (p46). The big cube opposite on St-Jakobs-Platz is Munich's synagogue, flanked by the ❻ **Jüdisches Museum** (p47).

From here follow Unterer Anger, turn right on Klosterhofstrasse, which continues as Schmidstrasse and reaches Sendlinger Strasse. Turn right for a peek inside the ❼ **Asamkirche** (p47). Backtrack a few steps on Sendlinger Strasse, turn left on Hackenstrasse, right on Hotterstrasse, past the tiny Hundskugel, the city's oldest restaurant, left

on Altheimer Eck and right on Färbergraben. This takes you to Kaufinger Strasse, the Altstadt's shopping strip. Continue on Augustinerstrasse to the twin-onion-domed ❽ **Frauenkirche** (p47) with great views from the top. Lanes behind the church lead to Weinstrasse; turn left and continue on Theatinerstrasse, taking a break at the ❾ **Fünf Höfe** shopping arcade. Backtrack a few steps on Theatinerstrasse, then turn left on tiny Perusastrasse, which brings you to the ❿ **Residenz** (p43).

Continue north on Residenzstrasse to reach Odeonsplatz, dominated by the ⓫ **Feldherrnhalle** (p50), a shrine to war heroes. The mustard-yellow ⓬ **Theatinerkirche** (p51) contains the Wittelsbachs' crypt. Cross the ⓭ **Hofgarten** and take the underpass, then turn right on Prinzregentenstrasse and proceed past the ⓮ **Haus der Kunst** (p53). Just beyond, don't miss the ⓯ **surfers** (p51) riding the artificial wave on the Eisbach creek. Across the creek, turn left into the Englischer Garten and the multi tiered ⓰ **Chinesischer Turm** (p79) for a well-deserved beer.

for all things oriental. Further south, at the top of a gentle hill, stands the heavily photographed Monopteros (1838), a small Greek temple whose ledges are often knee-to-knee with dangling legs belonging to people admiring the view of the Munich skyline.

Another hint of Asia awaits further south at the Japanisches Teehaus, built for the 1972 Olympics next to an idyllic duck pond. The best time to come is for an authentic tea ceremony celebrated by a Japanese tea master, though it's only open two days a month.

★ **Bayerisches Nationalmuseum** MUSEUM
(Map p60; www.bayerisches-nationalmuseum.de; Prinzregentenstrasse 3; adult/concession/child €7/6/free, Sun €1; ⊘10am-5pm Tue, Wed & Fri-Sun, to 8pm Thu; 🚋 Nationalmuseum/Haus Der Kunst, 🚊 Nationalmuseum/Haus Der Kunst) Picture the classic 19th-century museum, a palatial neoclassical edifice overflowing with exotic treasure and thought-provoking works of art, a repository for a nation's history, a grand purpose-built display case for royal trinkets, church baubles and state-owned rarities – this is the Bavarian National Museum, a good old-fashioned institution for no-nonsense museum lovers. As the collection fills 40 rooms over three floors, there's a lot to get through here, so be prepared for at least two hours' legwork.

Most visitors start on the 1st floor, where hall after hall is packed with baroque, mannerist and Renaissance sculpture, ecclesiastical treasures (check out all those wobbly Gothic 'S' figures), Renaissance clothing and one-off pieces such as the 1000-year-old St Kunigunde's chest fashioned in mammoth ivory and gold. Climb to the 2nd floor to move up in history to the rococo, *Jugendstil* and modern periods, represented by priceless collections of Nymphenburg and Meissen porcelain, Tiffany glass, Augsburg silver and precious items used by the Bavarian royal family. Also up here is a huge circular model of Munich in the first half of the 19th century, shortly after it was transformed into a capital fit for a kingdom.

It's easy to miss, but the building's basement also holds an evocatively displayed collection of Krippen (nativity scenes), some with a Cecil B DeMille–style cast of thousands. Retold in paper, wood and resin, there are Christmas-story scenes here from Bohemia, Moravia and Tyrol, but the biggest contingent hails from Naples. Also here is the excellent museum shop.

DenkStätte Weisse Rose MEMORIAL
(Map p60; www.weisse-rose-stiftung.de; Geschwister-Scholl-Platz 1; ⊘10am-5pm Mon-Fri, 11am-4.30pm Sat; Ⓤ Universität) **FREE** This memorial exhibit to the Weisse Rose (White Rose; a nonviolent resistance group led by Munich University students Hans and Sophie Scholl to oppose the Nazis) is within the Ludwig-Maximilians-Universität. It's a moving story, and one of Munich's most heroic, told in photographs and exhibits from the period.

Haus der Kunst MUSEUM
(House of Art; Map p60; www.hausderkunst.de; Prinzregentenstrasse 1; adult/concession €12/5; ⊘10am-8pm Fri-Wed, to 10pm Thu; 🚋 National museum/Haus Der Kunst, 🚊 Nationalmuseum/Haus Der Kunst) This austere fascist-era edifice was built in 1937 to showcase Nazi art, but now the Haus der Kunst presents works by exactly the artists whom the Nazis rejected and deemed degenerate. Temporary shows focus on contemporary art and design.

Ludwig-Maximilians-Universität UNIVERSITY
(LMU; Map p60; www.uni-muenchen.de; Geschwister-Scholl-Platz 1; Ⓢ Universität) The oldest university in Bavaria Ludwig-Maximilians-Universität started out as a political football for its rulers. Founded in Ingolstadt in 1472, it moved to Landshut in 1800 before being lassoed to Munich in 1826 by newly crowned King Ludwig I. It has produced more than a dozen Nobel Prize winners, including Wilhelm Röntgen in 1901 (Physics) and Theodor Hänsch in 2005 (Physics).

The main building, by Friedrich von Gärtner of course, has cathedral-like dimensions and is accented with sculpture and other artworks. A flight of stairs leads to a light court with a memorial to *Die Weisse Rose,* the Nazi resistance group founded by Hans and Sophie Scholl. To get the full story, visit the small DenkStätte in the vaulted space behind.

Ludwigskirche CHURCH
(Church of St Ludwig; Map p60; Ludwigstrasse 20; ⊘8am-8pm; Ⓢ Universität) The sombre twin-towered Ludwigskirche, built by Friedrich von Gärtner between 1829 and 1844, is a highly decorative, almost Byzantine, affair with one major showpiece: the *Last Judgment* fresco by the Nazarene painter Peter Cornelius in the choir. It's one of the largest in the world and an immodest – and thoroughly unsuccessful – attempt to outdo Michelangelo's version.

MAXIMILIANSTRASSE

It's pricey and pretentious, but no trip to Munich would be complete without a wander along Maximilianstrasse, one of the city's swishest boulevards. Starting at Max-Joseph-Platz, it's a 1km-long ribbon of style where well-heeled shoppers browse for Breguet and Prada and bored bodyguards loiter by Bentleys and Rolls Royces. It's also a haunt for Munich's many beggars. Several of the city's finest theatrical venues, including the Nationaltheater, the Kammerspiele and the GOP Varieté Theater, are also here.

Built between 1852 and 1875, Maximilianstrasse was essentially an ego trip for King Max II. He harnessed the skills of architect Friedrich von Bürklein to create a unique stylistic hotchpotch ranging from Bavarian rustic to Italian Renaissance and English Gothic. It even became known as the Maximilianic Style. That's the king gazing down upon his boulevard from his perch at the centre of the strip. Clinging to the base are four rather stern-looking children holding the coats of arms of Bavaria, Franconia, Swabia and the Palatinate.

◉ Maxvorstadt

★ Alte Pinakothek   MUSEUM

(Map p66; ☑ 089-238 0516; www.pinakothek.de; Barer Strasse 27; adult/concession/child €7/5/free, Sun €1, audioguide €4.50; ⊙ 10am-8pm Tue, to 6pm Wed-Sun; ☐ Pinakotheken, ☐ Pinakotheken) Munich's main repository of Old European Masters is crammed with all the major players who decorated canvases between the 14th and 18th centuries. This neoclassical temple was masterminded by Leo von Klenze and is a delicacy even if you can't tell your Rembrandt from your Rubens. The collection is world famous for its exceptional quality and depth, especially when it comes to German masters.

The oldest works are altar paintings, among which the standouts are Michael Pacher's *Four Church Fathers* and Lucas Cranach the Elder's *Crucifixion* (1503), an emotional rendition of the suffering Jesus.

A key room is the Dürersaal upstairs. Here hangs Albrecht Dürer's famous Christ-like *Self-Portrait* (1500), showing the gaze of an artist brimming with self-confidence. His final major work, *The Four Apostles,* depicts John, Peter, Paul and Mark as rather humble men, in keeping with post-Reformation ideas. Compare this to Matthias Grünewald's *Sts Erasmus and Maurice,* which shows the saints dressed in rich robes like kings.

For a secular theme, inspect Albrecht Altdorfer's *Battle of Alexander the Great* (1529), which captures in great detail a 6th-century war pitting Greeks against Persians.

There's a choice bunch of works by Dutch masters, including an altarpiece by Rogier van der Weyden called *The Adoration of the Magi,* plus *The Seven Joys of Mary* by Hans Memling, *Danae* by Jan Gossaert and *The Land of Cockayne* by Pieter Brue-gel the Elder. At 6m in height, Rubens' epic *Last Judgment* is so big that Klenze custom-designed the hall for it. A memorable portrait is *Hélène Fourment* (1631), a youthful beauty who was the ageing Rubens' second wife.

The Italians are represented by Botticelli, Rafael, Titian and many others, while the French collection includes paintings by Nicolas Poussin, Claude Lorrain and François Boucher. Among the Spaniards are such heavy hitters as Murillo and Velázquez, and Greece's El Greco also features.

★ Pinakothek der Moderne   MUSEUM

(Map p66; ☑ 089-2380 5360; www.pinakothek. de; Barer Strasse 40; adult/child €10/free, Sun €1; ⊙ 10am-6pm Tue, Wed & Fri-Sun, to 8pm Thu; ☐ Pinakotheken, ☐ Pinakotheken) Germany's largest modern-art museum unites four significant collections under a single roof: 20th-century art, applied design from the 19th century to today, a graphics collection and an architecture museum. It's housed in a spectacular building by Stephan Braunfels, whose four-storey interior centres on a vast eye-like dome through which soft natural light filters throughout the blanched-white galleries.

The State Gallery of Modern Art has some exemplary modern classics by Picasso, Klee, Dalí and Kandinsky and many lesser-known works that will be new to most visitors. More recent big shots include Georg Baselitz, Andy Warhol, Cy Twombly, Dan Flavin and the late enfant terrible Joseph Beuys.

In a world obsessed by retro style, the New Collection is the busiest section of the museum. Housed in the basement, it focuses on applied design from the industrial revolution via art nouveau and Bauhaus to today. VW Beetles, Eames chairs and early Apple Macs stand alongside more obscure interwar items that wouldn't be out of place in a Kraftwerk video. There are lots of 1960s furniture, the latest spool tape recorders and an exhibition of the weirdest jewellery you'll ever see.

The State Graphics Collection has 400,000 pieces of art on paper, including drawings, prints and engravings by such artists as Leonardo da Vinci and Paul Cézanne. Because of the light-sensitive nature of these works, only a tiny fraction of the collection is shown at any given time.

Finally, there's the Architecture Museum, with entire studios of drawings, blueprints, photographs and models by such top practitioners as baroque architect Balthasar Neumann, Bauhaus maven Le Corbusier and 1920s expressionist Erich Mendelsohn.

★ **Museum Brandhorst**   GALLERY
(Map p66; www.museum-brandhorst.de; Theresienstrasse 35a; adult/concession/child €7/5/ free, Sun €1; ☉10am-6pm Tue, Wed & Fri-Sun, to 8pm Thu; 🚊 Maxvorstadt/Sammlung Brandhorst, 🚇 Pinakotheken) A big, bold and aptly abstract building, clad entirely in vividly multihued ceramic tubes, the Brandhorst jostled its way into the Munich Kunstareal in a punk blaze of colour mid-2009. Its walls, its floor and occasionally its ceiling provide space for some of the most challenging art in the city, among it some instantly recognisable 20th-century images by Andy Warhol, whose work dominates the collection.

Pop Art's 1960s poster boy pops up throughout the gallery and even has an entire room dedicated to pieces such as his punkish *Self-Portrait* (1986), *Marilyn* (1962) and *Triple Elvis* (1963).

The other prevailing artist at the Brandhorst is the lesser-known Cy Twombly. His arrestingly spectacular splash-and-dribble canvases are an acquired taste, but this is the place to acquire it if ever there was one.

Elsewhere Dan Flavin floodlights various corners with his eye-watering light installations and other big names such as Mario Merz, Alex Katz and Sigmar Polke also make an appearance. Damien Hirst gets a look-in here and there.

Neue Pinakothek   MUSEUM
(Map p66; ☎089-2380 5195; www.pinakothek. de; Barer Strasse 29; adult/child €7/free, Sun €1; ☉10am-6pm Thu-Mon, to 8pm Wed; 🚊 Pinakotheken, 🚇 Pinakotheken) The Neue Pinakothek harbours a well-respected collection of 19th- and early-20th-century paintings and sculpture, from rococo to *Jugendstil* (art nouveau). All the world-famous household names get wall space here, including crowd-pleasing French

impressionists such as Monet, Cézanne and Degas as well as Van Gogh, whose boldly pigmented *Sunflowers* (1888) radiates cheer.

Perhaps the most memorable canvases, though, are by Romantic painter Caspar David Friedrich, who specialised in emotionally charged, brooding landscapes. There are also works by Gauguin, including *Breton Peasant Women* (1894), and Manet, including *Breakfast in the Studio* (1869). Turner gets a look-in with his dramatically sublime *Ostende* (1844).

Local painters represented in the exhibition include Carl Spitzweg and Wilhelm von Kobell of the Dachau School and Munich society painters such as Wilhelm von Kaulbach, Franz Lenbach and Karl von Piloty. Another focus is work by the Deutschrömer (German Romans), a group of neoclassicists centred on Johann Koch, who stuck mainly to Italian landscapes.

★ **Königsplatz**   SQUARE
(Map p66; 🚊 Königsplatz, 🚇 Königsplatz) Nothing less than the Acropolis in Athens provided the inspiration for Leo von Klenze's imposing Königsplatz, commissioned by Ludwig I and anchored by a Doric-columned Propyläen gateway and two temple-like museums. The Nazis added a few buildings of their own and used the square for their mass parades. Only the foundations of these structures remain at the eastern end of the square, rendered unrecognisable by foliage. Peaceful and green today, the square comes alive in summer during concerts and open-air cinema.

NS Dokuzentrum   ARCHIVES
(National Socialism Documentation Centre; Map p66; ☎089-2336 7000; www.ns-dokuzentrummuenchen.de; Max-Mannheimer-Platz 1; adult/concession €5/2.50; ☉10am-7pm Tue-Sun; 🚊100, Königsplatz, 🚇 Königsplatz) The mission of the NS Dokuzentrum, located right at the heart of what was once Nazi central in Munich, is to educate locals and visitors alike about the Nazi period and Munich's role in it. The excellent exhibition looks to find the answers to questions such as how did Hitler come to power, what led to the war, and why did democracy fail. Period documents, artefacts, films and multimedia stations help visitors form their own opinions on these questions.

Antikensammlungen   MUSEUM
(Map p66; www.antike-am-koenigsplatz.mwn.de; Königsplatz 1; adult/child €6/free, Sun €1; ☉10am-5pm Tue & Thu-Sun, to 8pm Wed; 🚊 Königsplatz, 🚇 Königsplatz) This old-school museum is an

(Continued on page 58)

A Historical Journey

To sample the region's history is essentially the main reason most head to Germany's south and there really is something for everyone here. Churches, palaces, Nazi sights and whole medieval towns preserved in historical aspic are the main draws.

Nazi Past

Despite all the chocolate box scenery, Bavaria hides a dark past. From Dachau concentration camp to Hitler's Eagle's Nest, Nuremberg's courthouse and Reichsparteitagsgelände to Berchtesgaden's Dokumentation Obersalzberg, there are plenty of opportunities across the state to reflect upon this most sinister chapter in history.

Romantic Road

If you like your history quaint, efficiently well-preserved, varied and drawn up into an orderly queue, get yourself onto the Romantic Road, Germany's most popular touring route. From Würzburg to the Alps, this 350km route takes in medieval walled towns, baroque churches and palaces, a thousand half-timbered houses and some of Germany's best castles.

The House of Wittelsbach

They ruled for well over 700 years, bequeathed modern Bavaria a wealth of architecture, art and other trinkets, and one of their number, 'mad' King Ludwig II, launched the state's tourist industry with his architectural flights of fancy and Wagner obsession – the Wittelsbachs did more to shape Bavaria than any other family.

Magnificent Churches

Whether you are fan of stern Romanesque, flowery rococo, sugary baroque or pompous neo-Gothic, southern Germany has a church for you. Top temples to include on any ecclesiastically themed itinerary include the remote Wieskirche, Munich's Asamkirche, the Münsters of Freiburg and Ulm and Landshut's brick colossus.

1. Rothenburg ob der Tauber (p114) **2.** Eagle's Nest (p106), Berchtesgaden **3.** Wieskirche (p125)

MUNICH'S KUNSTAREAL

The **Kunstareal** (Map p64; www.kunst areal.de; 🚇 Pinakotheken, 🚇 Pinakotheken) is the compact Maxvorstadt area, roughly defined by Türkenstrasse, Schellingstrasse, Luisenstrasse and Karlstrasse, which is packed with southern Germany's finest art museums. These include the Alte Pinakothek (p54), the Museum Brandhorst (p55), the Neue Pinakothek (p55) and the Pinakothek der Moderne (p54).

(Continued from page 55)

engaging showcase of exquisite Greek, Roman and Etruscan antiquities. The collection of Greek vases, each artistically decorated with gods and heroes, wars and weddings, is particularly outstanding. Other galleries present gold and silver jewellery and ornaments, figurines made from terracotta and more precious bronze, and superfragile glass drinking vessels. Tickets for the museum are also valid for the Glyptothek.

Glyptothek MUSEUM
(Map p66; www.antike-am-koenigsplatz.mwn.de; Königsplatz 3; adult/child €6/free, Sun €1; ⏱ 10am-5pm Fri-Sun, Tue & Wed, to 8pm Thu; 🚇 Königsplatz, Ⓤ Königsplatz) If you're a fan of classical art or simply enjoy the sight of naked guys without noses (or other pertinent body parts), make a beeline for the Glyptothek. One of Munich's oldest museums, it's a feast of art and sculpture from ancient Greece and Rome amassed by Ludwig I between 1806 and 1830, and it opens a surprisingly naughty window onto the ancient world. Tickets for the museum are also valid for the Antikensammlungen.

Lenbachhaus MUSEUM
(Municipal Gallery; Map p66; ☎ 089-2333 2000; www.lenbachhaus.de; Luisenstrasse 33; adult/child incl audioguide €10/5; ⏱ 10am-8pm Tue, to 6pm Wed-Sun; 🚇 Königsplatz, Ⓤ Königsplatz) With its fabulous wing added by noted architect Norman Foster, this glorious gallery is the go-to place to admire the vibrant canvases of Kandinsky, Franz Marc, Paul Klee and other members of ground-breaking modernist group Der Blaue Reiter (The Blue Rider), founded in Munich in 1911.

Contemporary art is another focal point. An eye-catcher is a glass-and-steel sculpture by Olafur Eliasson in the soaring atrium. Many other big names are also represented, including Gerhard Richter, Sigmar Polke, Anselm Kiefer, Andy Warhol, Dan Flavin, Richard Serra and Jenny Holzer.

Tickets are also valid for special exhibits at the nearby Kunstbau, a 120m-long tunnel above the Königsplatz U-Bahn station.

Alter Botanischer Garten PARK
(Map p66; Sophienstrasse 7; ⏱ 24hr; Ⓢ Karlsplatz, 🚇 Karlsplatz, 🚊 Karlsplatz) The Old Botanical Garden is a pleasant place to soothe your soles and souls after an Altstadt shopping spree or to see out a long wait for a train away from the Hauptbahnhof. Created under King Maximilian in 1814, most of the tender specimens were moved in the early 20th century to the New Botanical Garden behind Schloss Nymphenburg, leaving this island of city-centre greenery.

The Neptunbrunnen (Neptune Fountain), on the south side, dates from the Nazi period when the garden was turned into a public park. The neoclassical entrance gate is called the Kleine Propyläen and is a leftover from the original gardens. The Old Botanical Gardens are also home to one of Munich's lower-profile beer gardens, Park-Cafe (p77).

⊙ Nymphenburg, Neuhausen & Olympiapark

★**BMW Welt** NOTABLE BUILDING
(BMW World; Map p72; ☎ 089-125 016 001; www.bmw-welt.de; Am Olympiapark 1; tours adult/child €7/5; ⏱ 7.30am-midnight Mon-Sat, from 9am Sun; Ⓤ Olympiazentrum) **FREE** Next to the Olympia park, the glass-and-steel, double-cone tornado spiralling down from a dark cloud the size of an aircraft carrier holds BMW Welt, truly a petrolhead's dream. Apart from its role as a prestigious car pick-up centre, this king of showrooms acts as a shop window for BMW's latest models and a show space for the company as a whole.

Straddle a powerful motorbike, marvel at technology-packed saloons and estates (no tyre kicking, please), browse the 'lifestyle' shop or take the 80-minute guided tour. On the Junior Campus, kids learn about mobility, fancy themselves car engineers and even get to design their own vehicle in workshops. Hang around long enough and you're sure to see motorbike stunts on the staircases and other petroleum-fuelled antics.

★**Olympiapark** SPORTSGROUND
(Olympic Park; Map p70; www.olympiapark.de; stadium tour adult/concession €8/6; ⏱ stadium

tours 11am, 1pm & 4pm Apr-Oct; Ⓤ Olympiazentrum) The area to the north of the city where soldiers once paraded and the world's first Zeppelin landed in 1909 found a new role in the 1960s as the Olympiapark. Built for the 1972 Olympic Summer Games, it has quite a small-scale feel, and some may be amazed that the games could once have been held at such a petite venue.

The complex draws people year-round with concerts, festivals and sporting events, and its swimming hall and ice-skating rink are open to the public. A good first stop is the Info-Pavilion, which has information, maps, tour tickets and a model of the complex. You can also rent a self-guided audio tour.

Olympiapark has two famous eye-catchers: the 290m **Olympiaturm** (Olympic Tower; adult/child €7/5; ◎9am-midnight) and the warped **Olympiastadion** (Olympic Stadium; ◎9am-8pm mid-May–mid-Sep, shorter hr rest of yr). Germans have a soft spot for the latter because it was on this hallowed turf in 1974 that the national soccer team – led by 'the Kaiser', Franz Beckenbauer – won the FIFA World Cup.

When the sky is clear, you'll quite literally have Munich at your feet against the breathtaking backdrop of the Alps from the top of the Olympiaturm.

★**Schloss Nymphenburg**   PALACE
(Map p72; www.schloss-nymphenburg.de; castle adult/child €6/free, all sites €11.50/free; ◎9am-6pm Apr–mid-Oct, 10am-4pm mid-Oct–Mar; ⬛Schloss Nymphenburg) This commanding palace and its lavish gardens sprawl around 5km northwest of the Altstadt. Begun in 1664 as a villa for Electress Adelaide of Savoy, the stately pile was extended over the next century to create the royal family's summer residence. Franz Duke of Bavaria, head of the once royal Wittelsbach family, still occupies an apartment here.

The main palace building consists of a large villa and two wings of creaking parquet floors and sumptuous period rooms. Right at the beginning of the self-guided tour comes the high point of the entire Schloss, the Schönheitengalerie, housed in the former apartments of Queen Caroline. Some 38 portraits of attractive females chosen by an admiring King Ludwig I peer prettily from the walls. The most famous image is of Helene Sedlmayr, the daughter of a shoemaker, wearing a lavish frock the king gave her for the sitting. You'll also find Ludwig's beautiful, but notorious, lover Lola Montez, as well as 19th-century gossip-column celebrity Lady Jane Ellenborough and English beauty Lady Jane Erskine.

Further along the tour route comes the Queen's Bedroom, which still contains the sleigh bed on which Ludwig II was born, and the King's Chamber, resplendent with three-dimensional ceiling frescoes.

Also in the main building is the **Marstallmuseum** (adult/child €4.50/free), displaying royal coaches and riding gear. This includes Ludwig II's fairy tale–like rococo sleigh, ingeniously fitted with oil lamps for his crazed nocturnal outings. Upstairs is the world's largest collection of porcelain made by the famous Nymphenburger Manufaktur. Also known as the Sammlung Bäuml, it presents the entire product palette from the company's founding in 1747 until 1930.

The sprawling **palace grounds** (combined ticket for all 4 park buildings adult/child €4.50/3.50) behind Schloss Nymphenburg is a favourite spot with Münchners and visitors for strolling, jogging or whiling away a lazy afternoon. It's laid out in grand English style and accented with water features, including a large lake, a cascade and a canal, which is popular for feeding swans and for ice skating and ice curling when it freezes over in winter.

The park's chief folly, the Amalienburg, is a small hunting lodge dripping with crystal and gilt decoration; don't miss the amazing Spiegelsaal (hall of mirrors). The two-storey Pagodenburg was built in the early 18th century as a Chinese tea house and is swathed in ceramic tiles depicting landscapes, figures and floral ornamentation. The Badenburg is a sauna and bathing house that still has its original heating system. Finally, the Magdalenenklause was built as a mock hermitage in faux-ruined style.

BMW Museum   MUSEUM
(Map p72; www.bmw-welt.de; Am Olympiapark 2; adult/child €10/7; ◎10am-6pm Tue-Sun; Ⓤ Olympiazentrum) This silver, bowl-shaped museum comprises seven themed 'houses' that examine the development of BMW's product line and include sections on motorcycles and motor racing. Even if you can't tell a head gasket from a crankshaft, the interior design – with its curvy retro feel, futuristic bridges, squares and huge backlit wall screens – is reason enough to visit.

The museum is linked to two more architecturally stunning buildings: the BMW headquarters (closed to the public) and the BMW Welt showroom.

Schwabing & the Englischer Garten

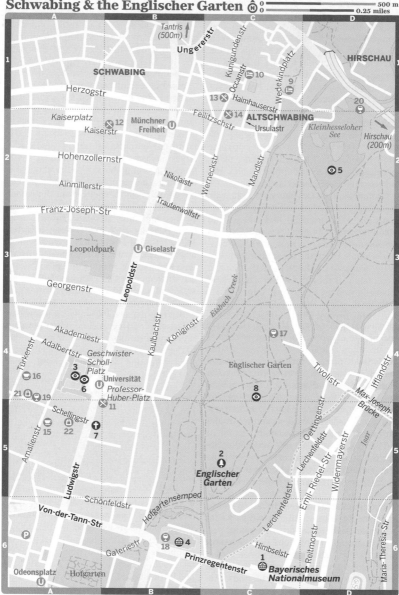

Museum Mensch und Natur MUSEUM
(Museum of Humankind & Nature; Map p72; www.mmn-muenchen.de; Schloss Nymphenburg; adult/child €3.50/2.50; ⊙9am-5pm Tue, Wed & Fri, to 8pm Thu, 10am-6pm Sat & Sun; ⌂Schloss Nymphenburg) Kids will have plenty of ooh and aah moments in the Museum of Humankind & Nature, in the Schloss Nymphenburg north wing. Anything but old school, it puts a premium on interactive displays, models, audiovisual presentations and attractive animal dioramas. It's all in German, but few

Schwabing & the Englischer Garten

language skills are needed to appreciate the visuals.

◉ Haidhausen & Lehel

★**Deutsches Museum** MUSEUM
(Map p78; ☎089-217 9333; www.deutsches-museum.de; Museumsinsel 1; adult/child €12/4; ⊗9am-5pm; ⓢDeutsches Museum) If you're one of those people for whom science is an unfathomable turn-off, a visit to the Deutsches Museum might just show you that physics and engineering are more fun than you thought. Spending a few hours in this temple to technology is an eye-opening journey of discovery, and the exhibitions and demonstrations will certainly be a hit with young, sponge-like minds.

There are tonnes of interactive displays (including glass-blowing and paper making), live demonstrations and experiments, model coal and salt mines, and engaging sections on cave paintings, geodesy, microelectronics and astronomy. In fact, it can be pretty overwhelming after a while, so it's best to prioritise what you want to see.

The place to entertain children aged three to eight is the fabulous Kinderreich, where 1000 activities await, from a kid-sized mouse wheel to interactive water fun. Get the littlies to climb all over a fire engine, build things with giant Lego, construct a waterway with canals and locks, or bang on a drum all day in a – thankfully – soundproof instrument room. Note that Kinderreich closes at 4.30pm.

Museum Fünf Kontinente MUSEUM
(State Museum of Ethnology; Map p78; www.museum-fuenf-kontinente.de; Maximilianstrasse 42; adult/child €5/free, Sun €1; ⊗9.30am-5.30pm Tue-Sun; ⓢMaxmonument) A bonanza of art and objects from Africa, India, the Americas, the Middle East and Polynesia, the State Museum of Ethnology has one of the most prestigious and complete ethnological collections anywhere. Sculpture from West and Central Africa is particularly impressive, as are Peruvian ceramics, Indian jewellery, mummy parts, and artefacts from the days of Captain Cook.

Museum Villa Stuck MUSEUM
(Map p78; ☎089-455 5510; www.villastuck.de; Prinzregentenstrasse 60; adult/concession €9/4.50; ⊗11am-6pm Tue-Sun; ⓢFriedensengel/Villa Stuck) Around the turn of the 20th century, Franz von Stuck was a leading light on Munich's art scene, and his residence is one of the finest *Jugendstil* homes you're ever likely to see. Stuck came up with the intricate design, which forges tapestries, patterned floors, coffered ceilings and other elements into a harmonious work of art. Today his glorious pad is open as a museum with changing exhibitions.

Sammlung Schack MUSEUM
(Map p78; www.sammlung-schack.de; Prinzregentenstrasse 9; adult/concession €4/3; ⊗10am-6pm Wed-Sun; ⓢReitmorstrasse/Sammlung Schack) Count Adolf Friedrich von Schack (1815–94) was a great fan of 19th-century Romantic painters such as Böcklin, Feuerbach and von Schwind. His collection is housed in the former Prussian embassy, now the Schack-Galerie. A tour of the intimate space is like an escape into the idealised fantasy worlds created by these artists.

THE WHITE ROSE

Open resistance to the Nazis was rare during the Third Reich; after 1933, intimidation and the instant 'justice' of the Gestapo and SS served as powerful disincentives. One of the few groups to rebel was the ill-fated Weisse Rose (White Rose), led by Munich University student siblings Hans and Sophie Scholl.

The nonviolent White Rose began operating in 1942, its members stealing out at night to smear 'Freedom!' and 'Down with Hitler!' on the city's walls. Soon they were printing anti-Nazi leaflets on the mass extermination of the Jews and other Nazi atrocities. One read: 'We shall not be silent – we are your guilty conscience. The White Rose will not leave you in peace'.

In February 1943, Hans and Sophie were caught distributing leaflets at the university. Together with their best friend, Christoph Probst, the Scholls were arrested and charged with treason. After a summary trial, all three were found guilty and beheaded the same afternoon. Their extraordinary courage inspired the award-winning film *Sophie Scholl – Die Letzten Tage* (Sophie Scholl – The Final Days; 2005).

A memorial exhibit to the White Rose, DenkStätte (p53), is within Ludwig-Maximilian-Universität.

⊙ Westend & Theresienwiese

Deutsches Museum – Verkehrszentrum   MUSEUM

(Transport Museum; Map p82; www.deutsches-museum.de/verkehrszentrum; Am Bavariapark 5; adult/child €7/3; ⊙9am-5pm; ⓤTheresienwiese) An ode to the Bavarian obsession with getting around, the Transport Museum explores the ingenious ways humans have devised to transport things and each other. From the earliest automobiles to famous race cars and high-speed ICE trains, the collection is a virtual trip through transport history.

The exhibit is spread over three historic trade-fair halls near Theresienwiese, each with its own theme – Public Transportation, Travel, and Mobility & Technology. It's a fun place even if you can't tell a piston from a carburettor. Classic cars abound, vintage bikes fill an entire wall and there's even an old petrol station.

Theresienwiese   PARK

(Map p82; ⓤTheresienwiese) The huge Theresienwiese (Theresa Meadow), better known as Wies'n, southwest of the Altstadt, is the site of the Oktoberfest. At the western end of the 'meadow' is the Ruhmeshalle (Hall of Fame) FREE guarding solemn statues of Bavarian leaders, as well as the Bavariastatue (Statue of Bavaria; adult/child €3.50/2.50; ⊙9am-6pm Apr-mid-Oct, to 8pm during Oktoberfest), an 18m-high Amazon in the Statue of Liberty tradition, oak wreath in her hand and lion at her feet.

This iron lady has a cunning design that makes her seem solid, but actually you can climb via the knee joint up to the head for a great view of the Oktoberfest. At other times, views are not particularly inspiring.

🏃 Activities

Boating

A lovely spot to take your sweetheart for a spin is on the Kleinhesseloher See (p51) in the Englischer Garten. Rowing or pedal boats cost around €8 per half-hour for up to four people. Boats may also be hired at the Olympiapark (p58).

Cycling

Munich is an excellent place for cycling, particularly along the Isar River. Some 1200km of cycle paths within the city limits make it one of Europe's friendliest places for two-wheelers.

Skating

Iceskaters can glide alongside future medallists in the Olympia-Eissportzentrum (Map p72; ☑089-306 70; www.olympiapark.de; Spiridon-Louis-Ring 21; adult/child per session €4.50/3; ⊙check website for times), hit the frozen canals in Nymphenburg (free) or twirl around at the Münchner Eiszauber (Map p48; www.muenchnereiszauber.de; adult €5-8.50, child €3.50-6; ⊙late Nov-late Jan; 🚊Karlsplatz, Ⓢ Karlsplatz, ⓤKarlsplatz) ice rink on Karlsplatz.

Swimming

Bathing in the Isar River isn't advisable, due to strong and unpredictable currents (especially in the Englischer Garten), though many locals do. Better to head out of town to one of the many nearby swimming lakes, including the popular Feringasee (by car, take the S8 to Unterföhring, then follow signs), where the party never stops on hot summer days; the pretty Feldmochinger See (**S** Feldmoching), which is framed by gentle mounds and has a special area for wheelchair-bound bathers (by car, take the S1 to Feldmoching); and the Unterföhringer See (Poschinger Weihen), which has warm water and is easily reached by bicycle via the Isarradweg cycele path or via the S8 to Unterföhring.

The best public-swimming-pool options, both indoors, are the **Olympia Schwimmhalle** (Map p72; www.swm.de; Coubertinplatz 1; 3hr pass adult/child €4.80/3.80; ⊗10am-7pm Mon, to 10pm Tue-Sun; **S** Olympiazentrum), where Mark Spitz famously won seven gold medals in 1972, and the spectacular **Müller'sches Volksbad** (Map p78; www.swm.de; Rosenheimer Strasse 1; adult/child €4.50/3.40; ⊗7.30am-11pm; 🚊Am Gasteig), where you can swim in art nouveau splendour.

🐾 Tours

For a budget tour of Munich's high-brow collections, hop aboard **bus 100 Museenlinie** (Map p82; www.mvv-muenchen.de), which runs from the Hauptbahnhof to the Ostbahnhof (east station) via 21 of the city's museums and galleries, including all the big hitters. As this is an ordinary bus route, the tour costs no more than a public-transport ticket.

⭐ **Radius Tours & Bike Rental**   TOURS
(Map p82; ☑089-543 487 7740; www.radius tours.com; Arnulfstrasse 3, Hauptbahnhof; ⊗8.30am-8pm; 🚊Hauptbahnhof, Ⓤ Hauptbahnhof, **S** Hauptbahnhof) Entertaining and informative English-language tours include the two-hour Discover Munich walk (€15), the fascinating 2½-hour Third Reich tour (€17.50), and the three-hour Bavarian Beer tour (€36). The company also runs popular excursions to Neuschwanstein, Salzburg and Dachau and has hundreds of bikes for hire (€14.50 per day).

⭐ **Walk on the Roof**   WALKING
(Map p72; adult/concessions €43/33; ⊗2.30pm Apr-Oct) Can't make it to the Alps for a high-altitude clamber? No matter. Just head to the Olympic Stadium for a walk on the roof. Yup, the roof; that famously contorted steel and Plexiglas confection is ready for its close-up. Just like in the mountains, you'll be roped and hooked up to a steel cable as you clamber around under the eagle-eyed super-

vision of an experienced guide showering you with fascinating details about the stadium's architecture and construction.

SightRunning Munich   RUNNING
(☑0151-6136 5099; www.muenchen-sightrunning. de; Edelweissstrasse 6; 1hr tours €25-50) Hit the ground running with this novel way of seeing the sights in the company of an experienced guide-runner. There are running tours of Nymphenburg, the English Garden, Olympiapark and the Isar, or you can have one tailor made. All you need is a pair of trainers and the ability to run for an hour – so it's not for everyone.

Street Art Tour   CULTURAL
(☑089-4613 9401; www.streetarttour.org) Operated by an agency called Positive Propaganda, these fascinating street-art tours will show you a completely different side to Munich.

Mike's Bike Tours   CYCLING
(Map p48; ☑089-2554 3987; www.mikesbike tours.com; Bräuhausstrasse 10; classic tour €29; **S** Marienplatz, Ⓤ Marienplatz) This outfit runs various guided bike tours of the city as well as a couple of other themed excursions. The classic tour is around four hours long; the deluxe tour goes for five hours.

Munich Walk Tours   WALKING
(Map p66; ☑089-2423 1767; www.munich walktours.de; tours from €14; 🚊Hauptbahnhof, **S** Hauptbahnhof, Ⓤ Hauptbahnhof) In addition to running an almost identical roster to Munich's other tour companies and acting as an agent for them (see website for times and prices), this place also runs cycling tours of the English Garden.

Vespa Munich   TOURS
(Map p72; ☑0151-517 251 69; www.vespa munich.com; Dom-Pedro-Strasse 26; full-day tour €59; ⊗office 10am-2pm daily, pick-ups 9am-6pm; 🚊Leonrodplatz) Book in advance, pick up your vespa and spend the day bombing around Munich guided by the GPS unit provided. It's the latest fun way to see the city, but good luck on those freeways!

Grayline Hop-On-Hop-Off Tours   BUS
(Map p82 ; www.grayline.com/munich; adult/child from €20/11; ⊗hourly; Ⓤ Hauptbahnhof, **S** Hauptbahnhof) This well-known tour-bus company offers a choice of three tours, from one-hour highlights to the 2½-hour grand tour, as well as excursions to Ludwig II's castles, the Romantic Road, Dachau, Berchtesgaden, Zugspitze and Salzburg. All tours can be booked

online, and the buses are new. The main departure point is outside the Karstadt department store opposite the Hauptbahnhof.

✴ Festivals & Events

★ Starkbierzeit
BEER

(☺Feb-Apr) Salvator, Optimator, Unimator, Maximator and Triumphator are not the names of gladiators but potent *Doppelbock* brews de-kegged only between Shrovetide and Easter. Many Bavarian breweries take part.

Frühlingsfest
BEER

(www.fruehlingsfest-muenchen.de; ☺late Apr-early May) This mini-Oktoberfest kicks off the outdoor-festival season with two weeks of beer tents and attractions at the Theresienwiese.

★ Tollwood Festival
CULTURAL

(www.tollwood.de; ☺late Jun-late Jul) Major world-culture festival with concerts, theatre, circus, readings and other fun events at the Olympiapark.

Filmfest München
FILM

(www.filmfest-muenchen.de; ☺late Jun) This festival presents intriguing and often high-calibre fare by newbies and masters from around the world. Held at the Gasteig and cinemas around the city centre.

Opernfestspiele
MUSIC

(Opera Festival; www.muenchner-opern-festspiele. de; ☺ Jul) The Bavarian State Opera brings in top-notch talent from around the world for this month-long festival, which takes place at numerous venues around the city

Christopher Street Day
LGBT

(www.csd-munich.de; ☺mid-Jul) Gay festival and parade culminating in a big street party on Marienplatz. Usually held on the second weekend in July.

Tanzwerkstatt Europa
PERFORMING ARTS

(www.jointadventures.net; ☺mid-Aug) Performances and workshops for modern dance, drama and readings held over 10 days

Hans Sachs Strassenfest
LGBT

(www.hans-sachs-strassenfest.de; ☺mid-Aug)This street party is held along Hans-Sachs-Strasse in the Glockenbachviertel.

★ Oktoberfest
BEER

(www.oktoberfest.de; ☺mid-Sep-early Oct) Legendary beer-swilling party. Held on the Theresienwiese.

Munich Marathon
SPORTS

(www.generalimuenchenmarathon.de; ☺mid-Oct) More than 10,000 runners from around the world take to the streets, finishing after just over 42km at the Olympiastadion.

★ Christkindlmarkt
CHRISTMAS MARKET

(www.christkindlmarkt.de; ☺late Nov-Christmas Eve) Traditional Christmas market on Marienplatz, one of Germany's best.

🛏 Sleeping

Munich has the full range of accommodation options you would expect from a major city in Western Europe. Luxury hotels dot the centre, midrange places gather near the Hauptbahnhof. Room rates tend to be higher than in the rest of Bavaria, and they skyrocket during the Oktoberfest. However, midrange accommodation is cheaper here than in other major European cities.

🛏 Altstadt & Residenz

★ Flushing Meadows
DESIGN HOTEL €€

(Map p48; ☑089-5527 9170; www.flushing meadowshotel.com; Fraunhoferstrasse 32; studios around €150; P ❄ 🛜; Ⓢ Fraunhoferstrasse) Urban explorers keen on up-to-the-minute design cherish this new contender on the top two floors of a former postal office in the hip Glockenbachviertel. Each of the 11 concrete-ceilinged lofts reflects the vision of a locally known personality, while three of the five penthouse studios have a private terrace. Breakfast costs €10.50.

The panorama bar has quickly become the darling of the local in-crowd.

H'Otello B'01 München
BOUTIQUE HOTEL €€

(Map p48; ☑089-4583 1200; www.hotello.de; Baaderstrasse 1; s/d from €90/110; ❄🛜; 🚇Isartor, Ⓢ Isartor) Though now not as excitingly different as it once was, Munich's first boutique hotel is all about understated retro design and amiable service. Rooms won't fit a tonne of luggage but are nicely dressed in creamy hues, tactile fabrics and subtle lighting. Guests rave about the breakfast: a smorgasbord of fresh fruit, deli salads, smoked salmon and organic cheeses.

Hotel am Markt
HOTEL €€

(Map p48; ☑089-225 014; www.hotel-am-markt. eu; Heiliggeiststrasse 6; s/d from €90/122; 🛜; Ⓢ Marienplatz, Ⓤ Marienplatz) As supercentral as you could wish, this slender, medieval-style hotel occupies a gabled and turreted building overlooking the Viktualienmarkt.

Bedrooms are midrange business standard, some with cheap flatpack, others with vaguely antique-style furniture and wood-panelling. Bathrooms have been spruced up recently, and standards are generally good. There's a restaurant on-site.

Pension Gärtnerplatz GUESTHOUSE **€€**
(Map p48; ☎089-202 5170; www.pensiongaert nerplatz.de; Klenzestrasse 45; s/d €86/142; ☎; Ⓤ Fraunhoferstrasse) Flee the urban hullabaloo to an Alpine fantasy land with alluring rooms boasting carved wood, painted bedsteads, woollen rugs and crisp, quality bedding. In one room a portrait of Ludwig II watches you as you slumber; breakfasts are organic.

Hotel am Viktualienmarkt HOTEL **€€**
(Map p48; ☎089-231 1090; www.hotel-am-vik tualienmarkt.de; Utzschneiderstrasse 14; s/d from €59/139; ☎; Ⓢ Marienplatz, Ⓤ Marienplatz) Elke and her daughter Stephanie run this good-value property with panache and a sunny attitude. The best of the 26 up-to-date rooms have wooden floors and framed poster art. All this, plus the city-centre location, makes it a superb deal.

★ Bayerischer Hof HOTEL **€€€**
(Map p48; ☎089-212 00; www.bayerischerhof. de; Promenadeplatz 2-6; r €250-450; ❄☎❄; ☐ Theatinerstrasse) Around since 1841, this is one of the grande dames of the Munich hotel world. Rooms come in a number of styles, from busy Laura Ashley to minimalist cosmopolitan. The supercentral location and pool come in addition to impeccably regimented staff. Marble, antiques and oil paintings abound, and you can dine till you burst at any of the five fabulous restaurants.

★ Louis Hotel HOTEL **€€€**
(Map p48; ☎089-411 9080; www.louis-hotel.com; Viktualienmarkt 6/Rindermarkt 2; r €179-320; ☎; Ⓢ Marienplatz) An air of relaxed sophistication pervades the scene-savvy Louis, where 72 good-sized rooms are furnished in nut and oak, natural stone and elegant tiles. Rooms come equipped with the latest technology. All have small balconies facing either the courtyard or the Viktualienmarkt. Views are also terrific from the rooftop bar and restaurant.

Breakfast costs a yodelling €28.50 extra, more than a room near the Hauptbahnhof.

Cortiina HOTEL **€€€**
(Map p48; ☎089-242 2490; www.cortiina.com; Ledererstrasse 8; s/d from €199/231; P❄☎; Ⓤ Marienplatz, Ⓢ Marienplatz) Tiptoeing be-

tween hip and haute, this hotel scores best with trendy, design-minded travellers. The street-level lounge usually buzzes with cocktail-swigging professional types, but all traces of hustle evaporate the moment you step into your minimalist, feng shui–inspired room.

★ Hotel Mandarin Oriental Munich HOTEL **€€€**
(Map p48; ☎089-290 980; www.mandarin oriental.com; Neuturmstrasse 1; d from €650; P❄@☎❄; Ⓢ Marienplatz, Ⓤ Marienplatz) These magnificent neo-Renaissance digs lure the world's glamorous, rich, powerful and famous with opulently understated rooms and top-notch service. Paul McCartney, Bill Clinton and Prince Charles have crumpled the sheets here. Service is polite almost to a fault.

Deutsche Eiche HOTEL **€€€**
(Map p48; ☎089-231 1660; www.deutsche-eiche.com; Reichenbachstrasse 13; s/d from €79/169; ☎; ☐ Reichenbachplatz) The rainbow flag flutters brightly alongside the usual national pennants outside this traditionally gay outpost that invites style junkies of all sexual orientations to enjoy the slick rooms and first-class restaurant. There's a well-known sauna on the premises.

Hotel Blauer Bock HOTEL **€€€**
(Map p48; ☎089-231 780; www.hotelblauer bock.de; Sebastiansplatz 9; s/d from €89/153; ☎; Ⓢ Marienplatz, Ⓤ Marienplatz) A pretzel's throw from the Viktualienmarkt, this simple hotel has cunningly slipped through the net of Altstadt gentrification to become one of the city centre's best deals, though prices have risen in recent years. It has a superb restaurant on the premises and parking in nearby garages.

Hotel Olympic HOTEL **€€€**
(Map p48; ☎089-231 890; www.hotel-olympic. de; Hans-Sachs-Strasse 4; s €95-180, d €160-250; P@☎; ☐ Müllerstrasse) If you're looking for a well-run place that's also small, friendly and peaceful with understated style, then this guesthouse-type hotel in a funky location might be for you. Rooms double up as mini art galleries and staff couldn't be more accommodating. Parking costs €15 a night.

🛏 Haidhausen & Lehel

Hotel Splendid-Dollmann HOTEL **€€**
(Map p78; ☎089-238 080; www.hotel-splendid-dollmann.de; Thierschstrasse 49; s/d from

Maxvorstadt

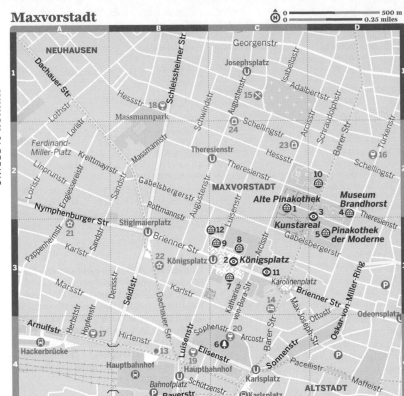

€100/120; 🛜; 🚇Lehel, Ⓤ Lehel) This small but posh Hotel Splendid-Dollmann delivers old-world charm and is sure to delight the romantically inclined. The mood is set at check-in where fresh orchids, classical music and friendly staff welcome you. Retire to antique-furnished rooms, the idyllic terraced garden or the regally furnished lounge. Rooms in front must deal with tram noise.

Hotel am Nockherberg
HOTEL €€

(🗕089-623 0010; www.nockherberg.de; Nockherstrasse 38a; s/d from €74/109; Ⓟ 🛜; Ⓢ Kolumbusplatz) Located south of the Isar, this charming base puts you close to the Deutsches Museum, the bar- and restaurant-filled Gärtnerplatzviertel and the Gasteig Cultural Centre. The decor of the 48 rooms and suites is pleasingly modern in a generic kind of way, and all major modcons are accounted for. Booking directly with the hotel guarantees the best rates.

★ Hotel Ritzi
HOTEL €€€

(Map p78; 🗕089-414 240 890; www.hotel-ritzi.de; Maria-Theresia-Strasse 2a; s/d from €100/159; 🛜; 🚇Maxmilianeum) At this charming art hotel next to a little park, creaky wooden stairs (no lift) lead to 25 rooms that transport you to the Caribbean, Africa, Morocco and other exotic lands. But it's the *Jugendstil* features of the building that really impress, as does the much-praised restaurant downstairs, with its Sunday brunch and well-chosen wine list.

Hotel Opéra
HOTEL €€€

(Map p78; 🗕089-210 4940; www.hotel-opera.de; St-Anna-Strasse 10; r €105-350; Ⓟ 🛜; 🚇Lehel) Like the gates to heaven, a white double door opens at the touch of a tiny brass button at the Hotel Opéra. Beyond awaits a smart, petite cocoon of quiet sophistication with peaches-and-cream marble floors, a chandelier scavenged from the Vatican and uniquely decorated rooms. Parking is €20 extra.

Maxvorstadt

🛏 Maxvorstadt

Hotel Marienbad   HOTEL €€
(Map p66; ☑089-595 585; www.hotelmarien
bad.de; Barer Strasse 11; s €55-155, d €120-160;
🅿🛜; 🚇Ottostrasse) Back in the 19th century,
Wagner, Puccini and Rilke shacked up at the
Marienbad, which once ranked among Munich's finest hotels. The place is still friendly and well maintained, and the 30 rooms
flaunt an endearing jumble of styles, from
playful art nouveau to floral country Bavarian to campy 1960s utilitarian. Amenities are
of more recent vintage.

🛏 Nymphenburg, Neuhausen & Olympiapark

⭐Hotel Laimer Hof   HOTEL €€
(Map p72; ☑089-178 0380; www.laimerhof.de;
Laimer Strasse 40; s/d from €65/85; 🅿🛜; 🚇Ro-
manplatz) A mere a five-minute aristocratic
amble from Schloss Nymphenburg, this commendably tranquil refuge is run by a friendly team who take time to get to know their
guests. No two of the 23 rooms are alike, but
all boast antique touches, oriental carpets
and golden beds. Free bike rental, and coffee
and tea in the lobby. Breakfast costs €12.

🛏 Schwabing & the Englischer Garten

⭐La Maison   DESIGN HOTEL €€
(Map p60; ☑089-3303 5550; www.hotel-la-mai
son.com; Occamstrasse 24; r from €109; 🅿✳🛜;
🚇Münchner Freiheit) Situated in the cool area
of Schwabing, this discerningly retro hotel
comes immaculately presented in shades of
imperial purple and ubercool grey. Rooms
at this sassy number wow with heated oak
floors, jet-black washbasins and starkly contrasting design throughout – though the operators can't resist putting a pack of gummy
bears on the expertly ruffed pillows! Cool
bar on ground level.

Gästehaus Englischer Garten   GUESTHOUSE €€
(Map p60; ☑089-383 9410; www.hoteleng
lischergarten.de; Liebergesellstrasse 8; s/d/apt
from €81/95/108; 🅿🛜; 🚇Münchner Freiheit)
Cosily inserted into a 200-year-old ivy-clad
mill, this small guesthouse on the edge of
the Englischer Garten offers a Bavarian
version of the British B&B experience. Not
all rooms are en suite, and those with their
own facilities are considerably more expensive. The breakfast is a wallet-clouting
€10.50 extra.

🛏 Westend & Theresienwiese

⭐Hotel Cocoon   DESIGN HOTEL €
(Map p82; ☑089-5999 3907; www.hotel-cocoon.
de; Lindwurmstrasse 35; s/d from €57/65; 😊🛜;
🚇Sendlinger Tor, 🚇Sendlinger Tor) Fans of retro design will strike gold in this central
lifestyle hotel. Things kick off in reception,
with its faux-'70s veneer and dangling '60s
ball chairs, and continue in the rooms. All
are identical, decorated in retro oranges and
greens and fully technologically equipped.

The glass showers stand in the sleeping area, with only a kitschy Alpine-meadow scene veiling life's vitals.

Wombats City Hostel Munich HOSTEL €

(Map p82; ☑ 089-5998 9180; www.wombats-hostels.com; Senefelderstrasse 1; dm/d from €25/95; P @ �
; ☐ Hauptbahnhof, U Hauptbahnhof) Munich's top hostel is a professionally run affair with a whopping 300 dorm beds plus private rooms. Dorms are painted in cheerful pastels and outfitted with wooden floors, en-suite facilities, sturdy lockers and comfy pine bunks, all in a central location near the train station.

Pension Westfalia B&B €

(Map p82; ☑ 089-530 377; www.pension-westfalia.de; Mozartstrasse 23; s/d from €45/60; �
; U Goetheplatz) Only a stumble away from the Oktoberfest meadow, this stately four-storey house conceals a cosy, family-run guesthouse that makes a serene base for sightseeing (outside the beer fest). Rooms are reached by lift; the cheaper ones have corridor facilities.

Hotelissimo Haberstock HOTEL €€

(Map p82; ☑ 089-557 855; www.hotelissimo.com; Schillerstrasse 4; s/d from €74/104; �
; ☐ Hauptbahnhof, S Hauptbahnhof, U Hauptbahnhof) The cheery decor at this value-for-money pick reflects the vision of the owners, a husband-and-wife team with a feel for colour, fabrics and design. Easy-on-the-eye gold, brown and cream tones dominate the good-sized rooms on the lower floors, while upper rooms radiate a bolder, Mediterranean palette.

Hotel Mariandl HOTEL €€

(Map p82; ☑ 089-552 9100; www.mariandl.com; Goethestrasse 51; s €69-98, d €88-175; �
; ☐ Sendlinger Tor, U Sendlinger Tor) If you like your history laced with quirkiness, you'll simply be delighted with this rambling neo-Gothic mansion. It's an utterly charming place where rooms convincingly capture the *Jugendstil* period with hand-selected antiques and ornamented ceilings. Breakfast is served until 4pm in the Vienna-style downstairs cafe, which also hosts frequent live jazz or classical-music nights.

Demas City Hotel HOTEL €€

(Map p82; ☑ 089-693 3990; www.demas-city.de; Landwehrstrasse 19; s/d from €102/122; �
; ☐ Karlsplatz, S Karlsplatz, U Karlsplatz) The 44 rooms at this quiet sleeper near the Hauptbahnhof are done out in trendy greys and blacks, accentuated by flashes of bold colour. Bathrooms are a snug fit and the location is uninspiring, but it's a decent, if vibe-less, place for centrally based snoozing, breakfasting and web-surfing.

Hotel Müller HOTEL €€

(Map p82; ☑ 089-232 3860; Fliegenstrasse 4; s/d from €79/109; �
; S Sendlinger Tor) This friendly hotel has big, bright, business-standard rooms and a good price-to-quality ratio, with five-star breakfasts and polite staff. Despite the city-centre location, the side-street position is pretty quiet.

Hotel Eder HOTEL €€

(Map p82; ☑ 089-554 660; www.hotel-eder.de; Zweigstrasse 8; s €55-180, d €65-230; P ☐
; ☐ Hauptbahnhof, S Hauptbahnhof, U Hauptbahnhof) A slice of small-town Bavaria teleported to the slightly seedy area south of the Hauptbahnhof, this rustic oasis has its chequered curtains, carved-wood chairs and Sisi/Ludwig II portraits firmly in place for those who didn't come all this way for the cocktails. The unevenly sized rooms are slightly vanilla, but given the pricing, this is a good deal.

Alpen Hotel HOTEL €€

(Map p82; ☑ 089-559 330; www.alpenhotel-muenchen.de; Adolf-Kolping-Strasse 14; s/d from €119/139; ☐
; S Hauptbahnhof, ☐ Hauptbahnhof, ☐ Hauptbahnhof) Don't be fooled by the slightly gloomy corridors here – rooms are of a very high business standard, parading big bathrooms and every amenity you could need. The downstairs restaurant is a lively spot.

Hotel Uhland HOTEL €€

(Map p82; ☑ 089-543 350; www.hotel-uhland.de; Uhlandstrasse 1; s/d incl breakfast from €99/129; P ☐
; U Theresienwiese) Crisp, professionally run operation with well-maintained business-standard rooms, big breakfasts and attentive staff. Little touches such as musical instruments and real art on the walls mean bedrooms are far from bland. Parking is €5, but spaces are limited.

Meininger's HOSTEL, HOTEL €€

(Map p82; ☑ 089-5499 8023; www.meininger-hostels.de; Landsbergerstrasse 20; dm/s/d without breakfast from €30/75/95; ☐
; ☐ Holzapfelstrasse) About 800m west of the Hauptbahnhof, this energetic hostel-hotel has basic, clean, bright rooms with big dorms divided into two for a bit of privacy. Room rates vary depending on

MUNICH FOR CHILDREN
....

(Tiny) hands down, Munich is a great city for children, with plenty of activities to please tots with even the shortest attention span. There are plenty of parks for romping around, swimming pools and lakes for cooling off, and family-friendly beer gardens with children's playgrounds for making new friends.

Deutsches Museum Many of the city's museums have special kid-oriented programs, but the highly interactive Kinderreich at the Deutsches Museum (p61) specifically lures the single-digit set.

Tierpark Hellabrunn Petting baby goats, feeding pelicans, watching falcons and hawks perform or even riding a camel should make for some unforgettable memories at the **city zoo** (Hellabrunn Zoo; ☑089-625 080; www.tierpark-hellabrunn.de; Tierparkstrasse 30; adult/child €15/6; ⊙9am-6pm Apr-Sep, to 5pm Oct-Mar; ☒52 from Marienplatz, ☒Tiroler Platz, ⓤThalkirchen).

SeaLife München For a fishy immersion, head to this **attraction** (Map p72; www.visit-sealife.com; Willi-Daume-Platz 1; adult/child gate prices €17.95/14.50; ⊙10am-5pm Mon-Fri, to 6pm Sat & Sun; ⑤Olympiazentrum) in the Olympiapark.

Paläontologisches Museum Dino fans will gravitate **here** (Palaeontological Museum; Map p66; www.palmuc.de; Richard-Wagner-Strasse 10; ⊙8am-4pm Mon-Thu, to 2pm Fri; ☒Königsplatz, ⓤKönigsplatz) **FREE**.

Museum Mensch und Natur Budding scientists will find plenty to marvel at in this museum (p60) within the Schloss Nymphenburg.

Spielzeugmuseum The **Spielzeugmuseum** (Toy Museum; Map p48; www.toymuseum.de; Marienplatz 15; adult/child €4/1; ⊙10am-5.30pm; ⑤Marienplatz, ⓤMarienplatz) is of the look-but-don't-touch variety, but kids might get a kick out of seeing what toys grandma used to pester her parents for.

Münchner Marionettentheater The adorable singing and dancing marionettes performing here (p83) have enthralled generations of wee ones.

Münchner Theater für Kinder This theatre (p83) offers budding thespians a chance to enjoy fairy tales and children's classics in the style of *Pinocchio* and German children's classic *Max & Moritz*.

---

the date, events taking place in Munich, and occupancy. Breakfast is an extra €6.90; bike hire costs from €8 per day.

Hotel Königshof
HOTEL €€€

(Map p82; ☑089-551 360; www.koenigshof-hotel.de; Karlsplatz 25; d from €250; ❈☎; ☒Karlsplatz, ⑤Karlsplatz, ⓤKarlsplatz) Over-the-top luxury and obsessive attention to detail make the 'King's Court' a real treat if you like that sort of thing. Rooms range from better-than-average business standard to sumptuous belle époque–style quarters. A Michelin-starred restaurant and a stylish bar are on the premises, and some of the rooms have views of busy Karlsplatz (Stachus), giving the place a heart-of-the-action feel.

Anna Hotel
DESIGN HOTEL €€€

(Map p82; ☑089-599 940; www.geisel-privat hotels.de; Schützenstrasse 1; r from €165; ❈☎;

☒Karlsplatz, ⓤKarlsplatz, ⑤Karlsplatz) Urban sophisticates love this well-positioned designer den, where you can retire to rooms dressed in sensuous furniture and regal colours, or tempered by teak, marble and mosaics and offering a more minimalist feel. The swanky restaurant-bar is a hive of dining activity.

Schiller 5
HOTEL €€€

(Map p82; ☑089-515 040; www.schiller5.com; Schillerstrasse 5; s/d from €119/163; ℗❈☎; ⑤Hauptbahnhof, ☒Hauptbahnhof, ☒Hauptbahnhof) Not only are the pads at this semiapartment hotel smartly trimmed, you also get a lot for your euro here in the shape of a well-equipped kitchenette, sound system, coffee machine and extra large bed in every room. Some guests complain of street noise, so try to bag a room away from the hustle below.

Sofitel Munich Bayerpost
HOTEL €€€

(Map p82; ☑089-599 480; www.sofitel-munich. com; Bayerstrasse 12; r from €240; P➔❄@❄; S Hauptbahnhof, ⏚ Hauptbahnhof) The restored Renaissance facade of a former post office hides this high-concept jewel, which wraps all that's great about Munich – history, innovation, elegance, the art of living – into one neat and appealing package. Be sure to make time for the luxurious spa, where the grotto-like pool juts into the atrium lobby lidded by a tinted glass roof.

✗ Eating

Munich has southern Germany's most exciting restaurant scene. The best dishes make use of fresh regional, seasonal and organic ingredients. The Bavarian capital is also the best place between Vienna and Paris for internationally flavoured dining, especially for Italian, Afghan, Vietnamese and Turkish food, and even vegetarians can look forward to something other than noodles and salads.

✗ Altstadt & Residenz

Bratwurstherzl
FRANCONIAN €

(Map p48; Dreifaltigkeitsplatz 1; mains €7-12; ⏰10am-11pm Mon-Sat; S Marienplatz, U Marienplatz) Cosy panelling and an ancient vaulted brick ceiling set the tone of this Old Munich tavern with a Franconian focus. Homemade organic sausages are grilled to perfection on an open beechwood fire and served on heart-shaped pewter plates. They're best enjoyed with a beer from the Hacker-Pschorr brewery.

Götterspeise
CAFE €

(Map p48; Jahnstrasse 30; snacks from €3.50; ⏰8am-7pm Mon-Fri, to 6pm Sat; ⏚ Müllerstrasse) The name of this cafe translates as 'food of the gods' and the food in question is that most addictive of treats, chocolate. Here it comes in many forms, both liquid and solid, but there are also teas, coffees and cakes and little outside perches for when the sun shines.

Küche am Tor
GERMAN, ITALIAN €

(Map p48; Lueg Ins Land 1; mains around €9.50; ⏰noon-5pm Mon-Fri; ✐; ⏚Isartor, S Isartor) No-nonsense, blink-and-you'd-miss-it lunch stop for local office workers. The comfortingly short menu contains mostly German fare, but also includes Mediterranean touches such as pesto, tuna and *salsiccia* (Italian sausage). Mostly a tourist-free zone.

Wiener Cafe
CAFE €

(Map p48; cnr Reichenbachstrasse & Rumfordstrasse; snacks €2-5; ⏰8.30am-6pm Mon-Fri, 8am-5pm Sat; ⏚Reichenbachplatz) The only cool thing about this delightfully oldfashioned coffeehouse, which serves cakes, snacks and drinks, is the marble tabletops.

Cordo Bar
TAPAS €

(Map p48; www.cordo-bar.de; Ickstattstrasse 1a; tapas €2.90-10, mains €4.50-15; ⏰4pm-1am Mon-Thu, to 2am Fri & Sat, to midnight Sun; ☎; U Fraunhoferstrasse) Choose between the raw-wood streetside seats or the darkwood-and-tiles interior at this atmospheric tapas bar. The small plates ooze with Iberian imagination and can be paired with any of 13 cocktails for a refined night out.

Schmalznudel
CAFE €

(Cafe Frischhut; Map p48; Prälat-Zistl-Strasse 8; pastries €2.10; ⏰8am-6pm Mon-Sat; S Marienplatz, U Marienplatz) This incredibly popular institution serves just four traditional pastries, one of which, the *Schmalznudel* (an oily type of doughnut), gives the place its local nickname. All baked goodies you munch here are crisp and fragrant, as they're always fresh off the hotplate. They're best eaten with a steaming pot of coffee on a winter's day.

★ Weisses Brauhaus
BAVARIAN €€

(Map p48; ☑089-290 1380; www.weisses-brau haus.de; Tal 7; mains €7-20; ⏰8am-12.30am; S Marienplatz, U Marienplatz) One of Munich's classic beer halls, this place is charged in the evenings with red-faced, ale-infused hilarity, with Alpine whoops accompanying the rabble-rousing oompah band. The *Weisswurst* (veal sausage) here sets the standard; sluice down a pair with the unsurpassed Schneider *Weissbier*, but only before noon. Understandably very popular and reservations are recommended after 7pm.

★ Fraunhofer
BAVARIAN €€

(Map p48; ☑089-266 460; www.fraunhofertheat er.de; Fraunhoferstrasse 9; mains €5-20; ⏰4.30pm-1am; ✐; ⏚ Müllerstrasse) With its screechy parquet floors, stuccoed ceilings, wood panelling and virtually no trace that the last century even happened, this wonderfully characterful inn is perfect for exploring the region with a fork. The menu is a seasonally adapted checklist of southern German favourites but also features at least a dozen vegetarian dishes and the odd exotic ingredient. Cash only.

The tiny theatre at the back stages great shows and was among the venues that pioneered a modern style of *Volksmusik* (folk music) back in the '70s and '80s.

★ Prinz Myshkin
VEGETARIAN €€

(Map p48; ☑ 089-265 596; www.prinzmyshkin.com; Hackenstrasse 2; mains €9-20; ☺ 11am-12.30am; ☑; Ⓢ Marienplatz, Ⓤ Marienplatz) This place is proof, if any were needed, that the vegetarian experience has well and truly left the sandals, beards and lentils era. Ensconced in a former brewery, Munich's premier meat-free dining spot occupies a gleamingly whitewashed, vaulted space where health-conscious eaters come to savour imaginative dishes such as curry-orange-carrot soup, unexpectedly good curries and 'wellness desserts'.

Königsquelle
EUROPEAN €€

(Map p48; ☑ 089-220 071; www.koenigsquelle. com; Baaderplatz 2; mains €10-27; ☺ 5pm-1am Sun-Fri, from 7pm Sat; Ⓡ Isartor, Ⓡ Isartor, Ⓢ Isartor) This wood-panelled Munich institution is well loved for its attentive service, expertly prepared food and dark, well-stocked hardwood bar containing what must be the Bavarian capital's best selection of malt whiskies, stacked high behind the bar. The only-just decipherable handwritten menu hovers somewhere mid-Alps, with anything from schnitzel to linguine and goat's cheese to cannelloni to choose from.

Cafe Luitpold
CAFE €€

(Map p48; www.cafe-luitpold.de; Briennerstrasse 11; mains €10-19; ☺ 8am-7pm Mon, to 11pm Tue-Sat, 9am-7pm Sun; ☎; Ⓤ Odeonsplatz) A cluster of pillarbox-red streetside tables and chairs announces you've arrived at this stylish but not ubercool retreat. It offers a choice of three spaces: a lively bar, a less boisterous columned cafe and a cool palm-leaved atrium. Good for a daytime coffee-and-cake halt or a full evening blowout with all the trimmings.

Les Deux Brasserie
INTERNATIONAL €€

(Map p48; ☑ 089-710 407 373; www.les deux-muc.de; Maffaistrasse 3a; mains €7-17; ☺ noon-10pm; Ⓢ Marienplatz) Below the eponymous fine-dining restaurant, Les Deux's ground-floor brasserie is perfect for taking a tasty break without breaking the budget. Choose from such classics as miniburgers, club sandwich or Icelandic cod and chips, or go for one of the more elaborate weekly specials. If the weather permits, tables spill into the courtyard.

Tegernseer Tal
BAVARIAN €€

(Map p48; ☑ 089-222 626; www.tegernseer-tal8. com; Tal 8; mains €10-20; ☺ 9.30am-1am Sun-Wed, to 3am Thu-Sat; ☎; Ⓢ Marienplatz, Ⓤ Marienplatz) A blond-wood interior illuminated by a huge skylight makes this a bright alternative to Munich's dark-panelled taverns. And with Alpine Tegernseer beer on tap and an imaginative menu of regional food, this is generally a lighter, calmer more refined beer-hall experience with a less raucous ambience.

Bamyan
AFGHANI €€

(Map p48; www.bamyan.de; Hans-Sachs-Strasse 3; mains €9.50-20; ☺ 5pm-1am Sun-Fri, from 11.30am Sat; Ⓡ Müllerstrasse) The terms 'happy hour', 'cocktail' and 'chilled vibe' don't normally go together with the word 'Afghan', but that's exactly the combination you get at this exotic hang-out, named after the Buddha statues infamously destroyed by the Taliban in 2001. The gastro-award-winning Central Asian soups, kebabs, rice and lamb dishes, and big salads are eaten at handmade tables inlaid with ornate metalwork.

OskarMaria
INTERNATIONAL €€

(Map p48; www.oskarmaria.com; Salvatorplatz 1; mains €9-23; ☺ 10am-midnight Mon-Sat, to 7pm Sun; ☑; Ⓤ Odeonsplatz) The bookish cafe at the Literaturhaus cultural centre is a commendably stylish spot, with high ceilings, rows of small central European cafe tables and sprightly waiters. The more highbrow atmosphere will be appreciated by those who prefer their eateries (virtually) tourist free, and the menu features international staples plus several Bavarian favourites.

Fedora
ITALIAN €€

(Map p48; www.fedorabar.de; Ledererstrasse 3; mains around €10, pizzas €10-15; ☺ 11.30am-11pm Mon-Thu, to midnight Fri & Sat, 5-10pm Sun; ☎; Ⓢ Marienplatz, Ⓤ Marienplatz) Occupying the vaulted spaces of the 13th-century Zerwirkgewölbe, this Italian job named after the famous hat does a decent pizza and has an open kitchen where you can watch cooks load it up. Tables bearing chequered tablecloths spread out from a big bar, and there's plenty of sunny street-side seating.

Vegelangelo
VEGETARIAN €€

(Map p48; ☑ 089-2880 6836; www.vegelangelo.de; Thomas-Wimmer-Ring 16; mains €13-19, set menu €22-34; ☺ noon-2pm Tue-Thu, 6pm-late Mon-Sat; ☑; Ⓡ Isartor, Ⓢ Isartor) Reservations are compulsory at this petite vegie spot, where Indian odds and ends, a piano and a small Victorian fireplace distract little from the superb meat-free cooking, all of which can be converted to suit vegans. There's a set-menu-only policy Friday

Nymphenburg, Neuhausen & Olympiapark

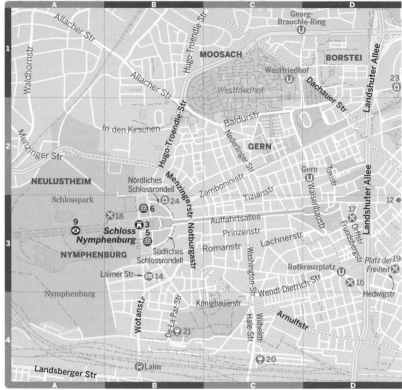

Nymphenburg, Neuhausen & Olympiapark

Alois Dallmayr FOOD HALL €€

(Map p48; ☑ 089-213 50; www.dallmayr.de; Dienerstrasse 14; ⊙ 9.30am-7pm Mon-Sat; ⑤ Marienplatz, ⓤ Marienplatz) A pricey gourmet delicatessen right in the thick of the Altstadt action, Alois Dallmayr is best known for its coffee but has so much more, including cheeses, ham, truffles, wine, caviar and exotic foods from every corner of the globe.

Einstein JEWISH €€

(Map p48; ☑ 089-202 400 332; www.einstein-restaurant.de; St-Jakobs-Platz 18; mains €19-20; ⊙ noon-3pm & 6pm-midnight Sat-Thu, 12.30-3pm Fri; 🐾; 🚇 Marienplatz, ⓤ Marienplatz) Reflected in the plate-glass windows of the Jewish Museum, this is the only kosher eatery in the city centre. The ID-and-bag-search entry process is worth it for the restaurant's uncluttered lines, smartly laid tables, soothing ambience and menu of well-crafted Jewish dishes. Reservations online only.

Conviva im Blauen Haus INTERNATIONAL €€

(Map p48; www.conviva-muenchen.de; Hildegardstrasse 1; 3-course lunch €8-10, dinner mains €10-22; ⊙ 11am-1am Mon-Sat, from 5pm Sun; 🍴; 🚇 Kammerspiele) The industrially exposed interior and barely dressed tables mean nothing distracts from the great food at this theatre restaurant. The daily-changing menus make the most of local seasonal ingredients and are reassuringly short. The lunch menu is a steal.

★**Weinhaus Neuner** BAVARIAN €€€

(Map p48; ☑ 089-260 3954; www.weinhaus-neuner.de; Herzogspitalstrasse 8; mains €20-25; ⊙ noon-midnight; ⑤ Karlsplatz, ⓤ Karlsplatz) This Munich institution has been serving Bavarian-Austrian classics and a long wine list for well over 100 years. Take a break from the hop-infused frenzy and pork knuckle to enjoy schnitzel and *Tafelspitz* (boiled veal or beef), helped along with a Franconian Riesling or a Wachau Grüner Veltiner amid the understated surroundings. Reservations advised.

Galleria ITALIAN €€€

(Map p48; ☑ 089-297 995; www.ristorante-galleria.de; Sparkassenstrasse 11; mains €17.50-30; ⊙ noon-2.30pm & 6-11pm; ⑤ Marienplatz, ⓤ Marienplatz) Munich has a multitude of Italian eateries, but Galleria is a cut above the rest. The compact interior hits you first, a multihued, eclectic mix of contemporary art and tightly packed tables. The menu throws up a few surprises – some dishes contain very un-Italian ingredients, such as

and Saturday. No prams allowed and no tap water served, but it does accept Bitcoin.

Kochspielhaus INTERNATIONAL €€

(Map p48; ☑ 089-5480 2738; www.kochspiel haus.de; Rumfordstrasse 5; breakfast €7.50-16, mains €8.50-17; ⊙ 7am-6pm Sun-Tue, to 10pm Wed-Sat; ⑤ Fraunhoferstrasse) Attached to a gourmet bakery called Backspielhaus, this modern country-style lair accented with massive candles packages only superfresh, top-quality ingredients into clever pasta, meat and fish dishes. Also a great spot for breakfast.

Deutsche Eiche INTERNATIONAL €€

(Map p48; ☑ 089-231 1660; www.deutsche-eiche.com; Reichenbachstrasse 13; mains €9-17; ⊙ 7am-1am; 🚇 Reichenbachplatz) A Munich institution and gay central, this was once filmmaker Rainer Werner Fassbinder's favourite hang-out. It's still a popular spot and packs in a mixed crowd for its schnitzels, salads and prompt service.

curry and coconut. Reservations are pretty much essential in the evening.

✖ Haidhausen & Lehel

Wirtshaus in der Au
BAVARIAN €€

(Map p78; ☑089-448 1400; www.wirtshaus inderau.de; Lilienstrasse 51; mains €10-22; ⊗5pm-midnight Mon-Fri, from 10am Sat & Sun; ⓐDeutsches Museum) This Bavarian tavern's simple slogan is 'Beer and dumplings since 1901', and it's this time-honoured staple – dumplings – that's the speciality here (the tavern even runs a dumpling-making course in English). Once a brewery, the space-rich dining area has chunky tiled floors, a lofty ceiling and a crackling fireplace in winter. When spring springs, the beer garden fills.

Sir Tobi
BAVARIAN €€

(Map p78; ☑089-3249 4825; www.sirtobi-muenchen.de; Sternstrasse 16; mains €9-20; ⊗11.30am-3pm Mon-Fri, 5.30pm-midnight Thu-Sat; ⓢ; ⓐLehel) This Bavarian bistro serves delicious, slow-food versions of southern German and Austrian dishes in an environment of crisp white tablecloths and fresh flowers. The service here is particularly good.

Fischhäusl
SEAFOOD €€

(Map p78; Wiener Platz; mains €7-15; ⊗9.30am-6pm Tue-Fri, 9am-2.30pm Sat; ⓐWiener Platz) Part of the food market on Wiener Platz, this kiosk with a few seats is one of the best spots in Munich to lunch on fish, which is prepared simply on a grill and served with salad, potatoes and white wine.

Dreigroschenkeller
BAVARIAN €€

(Map p78; Lilienstrasse 2; mains €10-20; ⊗5pm-1am Sun-Thu, to 3am Fri & Sat; ⓐDeutsches Museum) A quirky, labyrinthine brick-cellar pub with rooms – based upon Bertolt Brecht's *Die Dreigroschenoper* (The Threepenny Opera) – ranging from a prison cell to a red satiny salon. There are several types of beer to choose from and an extensive menu of hearty Bavarian favourites.

✖ Maxvorstadt

Il Mulino
ITALIAN €€

(Map p66; www.ristorante-ilmulino.de; Görresstrasse 1; mains €6-20; ⊗11.30am-midnight; ⓢJosephsplatz) This much-loved neighbourhood classic has been feeding Italophiles and immigrants from the beautiful country for over three decades. All the expected pastas and pizzas are present and correct, though the daily specials will likely tickle the palate of more curious eaters. Somewhat surprisingly 'The Mill' was declared Bavarian restaurant of the year in 2017.

✖ Nymphenburg, Neuhausen & Olympiapark

Ruffini
CAFE €

(Map p72; www.ruffini.de; Orffstrasse 22; meals €7-10; ⊗10am-midnight Tue-Sun; ⓢ; ⓐNeuhausen) Well worth the effort of delving deep into Neuhausen to find it, this cafe is a fun place to be no matter where the hands of the clock are. On sunny days the self-service rooftop terrace gets busy with locals – few tourists make it out here. Regular music events, from rock to classical.

Eiscafé Sarcletti
GELATO €

(Map p72; www.sarcletti.de; Nymphenburger Strasse 155; ⊗9am-11.30pm May-Aug, shorter hours Sep-Apr; ⓤRotkreuzplatz) Ice-cream addicts have been getting their gelato fix at this Munich institution since 1879. Choose from more than 50 mouth-watering flavours, from not-so-plain vanilla to buttermilk and mango.

Zauberberg
INTERNATIONAL €€

(Map p72; Hedwigstrasse 14; 3-course dinner menu around €45; ⊗6.30pm-1am Tue-Sat; ⓐAlbrechtstrasse) Far off the tourist track, this 40-seat locals' favourite will put your tummy into a state of contentment with its elegant, well-composed international creations. Single plates are available, but in order to truly sample the chef's talents, you should order a multicourse menu.

Chopan
AFGHANI €€

(Map p72; ☑089-1895 6459; www.chopan.de; Elvirastrasse 18a; mains €8-20; ⊗6pm-midnight; ⓤMaillingerstrasse) Munich has a huge Afghan community, whose most respected eatery is this much-lauded restaurant done out in the style of a Central Asian caravanserai, with rich fabrics, multihued glass lanterns and geometric patterns. In this culinary Aladdin's cave, you'll discover an exotic menu of lamb, lentils, rice, spinach and flatbread in various combinations. No alcohol.

Schlosscafé im Palmenhaus
CAFE €€

(Map p72; ☑089-175 309; www.palmenhaus.de; Schloss Nymphenburg 43; mains €10-17; ⊗11am-6pm Tue-Fri, from 10am Sat & Sun; ⓐSchloss Nymphenburg) The glass-fronted 1820 palm house where Ludwig II used to keep his exotic house plants warm in winter is now a high-ceilinged and pleasantly scented cafe serving soups, salads, sandwiches and other light meals. It's just behind Schloss Nymphenburg.

★ **Esszimmer**   MEDITERRANEAN €€€
(Map p72; ☑ 089-358 991 814; www.bmw-welt. com; BMW Welt, Am Olympiapark 1; 4/5 courses €130/145; ☺ from 7pm Tue-Sat; ❄ ☎; Ⓤ Olympiazentrum) It took Bobby Bräuer, head chef at the gourmet restaurant at BMW World, just two years to gain his first Michelin star. Munich's top dining spot is the place to sample high-octane French and Mediterranean morsels, carnivore and wholly vegetarian, served in a trendily dark and veneered dining room above the i8s and 7 Series. Life in the gastronomic fast lane.

✖ Schwabing & the Englischer Garten

Cafe an der Uni   CAFE €
(Map p60; Ludwigstrasse 24; mains around €9; ☺ 8am-1am Mon-Fri, from 9am Sat & Sun; ☎ ☑; Ⓢ Universität) Anytime is a good time to be at charismatic CADU. Enjoy breakfast (served until a hangover-friendly 10pm!), a cuppa Java or a Helles in the lovely garden hidden by a wall from busy Ludwigstrasse.

★ **Cochinchina**   ASIAN €€
(Map p60; ☑ 089-3898 9577; www.cochinchina.de; Kaiserstrasse 28; mains around €20; ☺ 11.30am-2.30pm & 6pm-midnight; ☎; Ⓤ Münchner Freiheit) Bearing an old name for southern Vietnam, this cosmopolitan Asian fusion restaurant is Munich's top place for Vietnamese and Chinese concoctions. The food is consumed in a dark, dramatically exotic space devoted to the firefly and splashed with colour in the shape of Chinese vases and lamps. The traditional *pho* soup is southern Germany's best.

Potting Shed   BURGERS €€
(Map p60; www.thepottingshed.de; Occamstrasse 11; mains €5-18; ☺ from 6pm Tue-Sat; Ⓤ Münchner Freiheit) This relaxed hang-out serves tapas, gourmet burgers and cocktails to an easygoing evening crowd. The burger menu whisks you round the globe, but it's the 'Potting Shed Special', involving an organic beef burger flambéed in whisky, that catches the eye on the simple but well-concocted menu.

Ruff's Burger & BBQ   BURGERS €€
(Map p60; Occamstrasse 4; burgers €5.50-16, other mains €9-19; ☺ 11.30am-11pm Mon-Wed, to midnight Thu-Sat, to 10pm Sun; ☎; Ⓤ Münchner Freiheit) Munich's obsession with putting a bit of fried meat between two buns is celebrated at this Schwabing joint, where the burgers are 100% Bavarian beef – except, of course, for the token veggie version. Erdinger and Tegernseer beer and mostly outdoor seating.

★ **Tantris**   INTERNATIONAL €€€
(☑ 089-361 9590; www.tantris.de; Johann-Fichte-Strasse 7; menu from €100; ☺ noon-3pm & 6.30pm-1am Tue-Sat Oct-Dec, closed Tue Jan-Sep; ☎; Ⓤ Dietlindenstrasse) Tantris means 'the search for perfection' and here, at one of Germany's most famous restaurants, it's not far off it. The interior design is full-bodied '70s – all postbox reds, truffle blacks and illuminated yellows. The food is sublime and the service is sometimes as unobtrusive as it is efficient. The wine cellar is probably Germany's best. Reservations essential.

✖ Westend & Theresienwiese

★ **Marais**   CAFE €
(Map p82; www.cafe-marais.de; Parkstrasse 2; dishes €5-13; ☺ 8am-8pm Tue-Sat, 10am-6pm Sun; ☑; 🚆 Holzapfelstrasse) Is it a junk shop, a cafe or a sewing shop? Well, Westend's oddest coffeehouse is in fact all three, and everything you see in this converted haberdashery – the knick-knacks, the cakes and the antique chair you're sitting on – is for sale.

Bodhi   VEGAN €€
(Map p82; ☑ 089-4114 2458; www.bodhivegan.de; Ligsalzstrasse 23; mains €9.50-17; ☺ 5pm-midnight; ☑; Ⓤ Schwanthalerhöhe) This vegan restaurant has an uncluttered, wood-rich interior where health-conscious diners feast on meat-and-dairy-free pastas, burgers, salads, soya steaks and tofu-based dishes. Whether those same wellness fanatics swill it all down with the large selection of cocktails and whisky is something you'll have to see for yourself.

La Vecchia Masseria   ITALIAN €€
(Map p82; Mathildenstrasse 3; mains €10-20, pizzas €7.50-12; ☺ 11.30am-11.30pm; 🚆 Sendlinger Tor, Ⓢ Sendlinger Tor) In an area traditionally settled by Italians, this is one of Munich's longest-established Italian *osterie*. Choose between the small beer garden out front or the earthy, rurally themed dining room with its chunky wood tables, antique tin buckets, baskets and clothing irons, all conjuring up the ambience of an Apennines farmhouse. All pizzas are €5.99 on Sundays.

Dinner Hopping   MULTICUISINE €€€
(Map p82; www.dinnerhopping.de; Arnulfstrasse 1, departure & arrival point next to the Hauptbahnhof;

dinner experience from €129; ⊙6.30-10.15pm; 🚇Hauptbahnhof, 🚇Hauptbahnhof, 🚊Hauptbahnhof) Be driven around Munich in an old yellow US schoolbus as you enjoy either an Italian, American or Bavarian three-course dinner accompanied by a live act. It may sound gimmicky, but the food gets rave reviews.

🍺 Drinking & Nightlife

Munich is truly a great place for boozers. Raucous beer halls, snazzy hotel lounges, chestnut-canopied beer gardens, DJ bars, designer cocktail temples – the variety is huge. And no matter where you are, you won't be far from an enticing cafe to get a caffeine-infused pick-me-up. Munich has some of Europe's best nightclubs with exciting venues for almost every musical taste.

🍺 Altstadt & Residenz

★Hofbräuhaus   BEER HALL
(Map p48; 📞089-2901 36100; www.hofbraeuhaus.de; Am Platzl 9; ⊙9am-midnight; 🚇Kammerspiele, 🚊Marienplatz, 🚇Marienplatz) Even if you don't like beer, every visitor to Munich should make a pilgrimage to the mothership of all beer halls, if only once. Within this major tourist attraction, you'll discover a range of spaces in which to do your *Mass* lifting: the horse chestnut–shaded garden, the main hall next to the oompah band, tables opposite the industrial-scale kitchen and quieter corners.

One unusual feature is that you can buy your beer with prepaid beer tokens, just like during Oktoberfest. There's an interesting gift shop on the premises, and the Hofbräuhaus prides itself on being open every day of the year, even Christmas day.

★Pacha   CLUB
(Map p48; www.pacha-muenchen.de; Maximiliansplatz 5; ⊙7pm-6am Thu, 11pm-6am Fri & Sat; 🚊Lenbachplatz) One of a gaggle of clubs at Maximiliansplatz 5, this nightspot with its cherry logo is one of Munich's hottest nights out, with the DJs spinning their stuff till well after sunrise.

★Schumann's Bar   BAR
(Map p48; 📞089-229 060; www.schumanns.de; Odeonsplatz 6-7; ⊙8am-3am Mon-Fri, 6pm-3am Sat & Sun; 🚊Odeonsplatz) Urbane and sophisticated, Schumann's shakes up Munich's nightlife with libational flights of fancy in an impressive range of concoctions. It's also good for weekday breakfasts. Cash only.

Augustiner-Grossgaststätte   BEER HALL
(Map p48; 📞089-2318 3257; www.augustinerrestaurant.com; Neuhauser Strasse 27; ⊙9am-11.30pm) This sprawling beer hall has a less raucous atmosphere and superior food to the usual offerings. Altogether it's a much more authentic example of an old-style Munich beer hall, but with the added highlight of a tranquil arcaded beer garden out back.

★MilchundBar   CLUB
(Map p48; www.milchundbar.de; Sonnenstrasse 27; ⊙10pm-7am Mon-Thu, 11pm-9am Fri & Sat; 🚇Sendlinger Tor, 🚇Sendlinger Tor) One of the hottest addresses in the city centre for those who like to spend the hours between supper and breakfast boogieing to an eclectic mix of nostalgia hits during the week and top DJs at the weekends.

Viktualienmarkt   BEER GARDEN
(Map p48; Viktualienmarkt 6; ⊙9am-10pm; 🚇Marienplatz, 🚊Marienplatz) After a day of sightseeing or stocking up on tasty nibbles at the Viktualienmarkt (p47), find a table at this chestnut-shaded beer garden surrounded by stalls, a Munich institution since 1807. All of Munich's breweries take turns serving here, so you never know what's on tap.

Rote Sonne   CLUB
(Map p48; www.rote-sonne.com; Maximiliansplatz 5; ⊙from 11pm Thu-Sun; 🚊Lenbachplatz) Named for a 1969 Munich cult movie starring it-girl Uschi Obermaier, the Red Sun is a fiery nirvana for fans of electronic sounds. A global roster of DJs keeps the dance floor packed and sweaty until the sun rises.

Braunauer Hof   BEER HALL
(Map p48; www.wirtshaus-im-braunauer-hof.de; Frauenstrasse 42; ⊙10am-midnight Mon-Sat, to 10pm Sun; 🚇Isartor, 🚊Isartor) Near the Isartor, drinkers can choose between the traditional Bavarian interior or the beer garden out the back, which enjoys a surprisingly tranquil setting despite its city-centre location. Most come for the Paulaner beer in the evening, but the €8.50 lunch menu is commendable value for money.

Trachtenvogl   CAFE
(Map p48; www.trachtenvogl.de; Reichenbachstrasse 47; ⊙9am-10pm; 🖥; 🚊Fraunhoferstrasse) At night you'll have to shoehorn your way into this buzzy lair favoured by a chatty, boozy crowd of scenesters, artists and students. Daytimes are mellower – all the better to sample its seasonal menu and check out

the incongruous collection of knick-knacks left over from the days when this was a traditional garment shop.

Baader Café
CAFE

(Map p48; www.baadercafe.de; Baaderstrasse 47; ⏱9.30am-1am Sun-Thu, to 2am Fri & Sat; 🛜; 🚇Fraunhoferstrasse) Around since the mid-'80s, this literary think-and-drink place lures all sorts, from short skirts to tweed jackets, who linger over daytime coffees and nighttime cocktails. It's normally packed, even on winter Wednesday mornings, and is popular among Brits who come for the authentic English breakfast.

Cafe Pini
CAFE

(Map p48; www.cafepini.de; Klenzestrasse 45; ⏱8am-11pm Mon-Fri, from 9am Sat, 9am-7pm Sun; 🇺Fraunhoferstrasse) *Bibite, panini, giornali* (drinks, sandwiches, newspapers) is the holy trinity served up at this Italian cafe, which takes you back to the days of the *Wirtschaftswunder* when Italian *gastarbeiter* (foreign workers) flooded into Munich to rebuild the city after WWII. Take a break, pull up a vintage seat and enjoy the area's most authentic Italian coffee.

Niederlassung
BAR

(Map p48; ☑089-3260 0307; www.niederlassung.org; Buttermelcherstrasse 6; ⏱7pm-1am Tue-Thu, to 3am Fri & Sat, to midnight Sun; 🇸Fraunhoferstrasse, 🚇Isartor) From Adler Dry to Zephyr, this gin joint stocks an impressive 80 varieties of juniper juice in an unpretentious setting filled with books and sofas and humming with indie sounds. There's even a selection of different tonic waters to choose from. Happy hour from 7pm to 9pm and after midnight.

Zephyr Bar
COCKTAIL BAR

(Map p48; www.zephyr-bar.de; Baaderstrasse 68; ⏱8pm-1am Sun-Thu, to 3am Fri & Sat; 🇸Fraunhoferstrasse) At one of Munich's best bars, Alex Schmaltz whips up courageous potions with unusual ingredients such as homemade cucumber-dill juice, sesame oil or banana-parsley puree. Cocktail alchemy at its finest, and a top gin selection to boot.

Del Fiore
CAFE

(Map p48; www.delfiore.de; Gärtnerplatz 1; ⏱10am-midnight; 🛜; 🚇Reichenbachplatz) Come to this buzzing Italian coffeehouse, the only one with outdoor seating on the Gärtnerplatz, where there's standing room only from the first rays of late winter to the

last of autumn. Great people-watching possibilities all day long.

📍 Haidhausen & Lehel

Biergarten Muffatwerk
BEER GARDEN

(Map p78; www.muffatwerk.de; Zellstrasse 4; ⏱from noon mid-Mar–mid-Oct; 🚇Am Gasteig) Think of this one as a progressive beer garden with reggae instead of oompah, civilised imbibing instead of brainless guzzling, organic meats, fish and vegetables on the grill, and the option of chilling in lounge chairs. Opening hours are open-ended, meaning some very late finishes.

Hofbräukeller
BEER HALL

(Map p78; ☑089-459 9250; www.hofbraeukeller.de; Wiener Platz; ⏱10am-midnight; 🚇Wiener Platz) One of the original beer halls, this wood-panelled, staunchly traditional tavern serves nine different types of the finest Hofbräu, including two alcohol-free versions and always a seasonal brew. Out back is what was, many claim, Munich's first beer garden.

📍 Maxvorstadt

★Alter Simpl
PUB

(Map p66; ☑089-272 3083; www.altersimpl.com; Türkenstrasse 57; ⏱11am-3am Mon-Fri, to 4am Sat & Sun; 🚇Schellingstrasse) Thomas Mann and Hermann Hesse used to knock 'em back at this well-scuffed and wood-panelled thirst parlour. A bookish ambience still pervades, making this an apt spot at which to curl up with a weighty tome over a few Irish ales. The curious name is an abbreviation of the satirical magazine *Simplicissimus*.

Augustiner Keller
BEER GARDEN

(Map p66; www.augustinerkeller.de; Arnulfstrasse 52; ⏱10am-1am Apr-Oct; 🛗; 🚇Hopfenstrasse) Every year this leafy 5000-seat beer garden, about 500m west of the Hauptbahnhof, buzzes with fairy-lit thirst-quenching activity from the first sign that spring may have *gesprungen*. The ancient chestnuts are thick enough to seek refuge under when it rains, or else lug your mug to the actual beer cellar. Small playground.

Park-Cafe
BEER GARDEN

(Map p66; www.parkcafe089.de; Sophienstrasse 7; ⏱11am-11pm; 🚇Lenbachplatz) A hidden gem, this typical Munich beer garden in the Alter Botanischer Garten serves Hofbräu suds and lots of filling food.

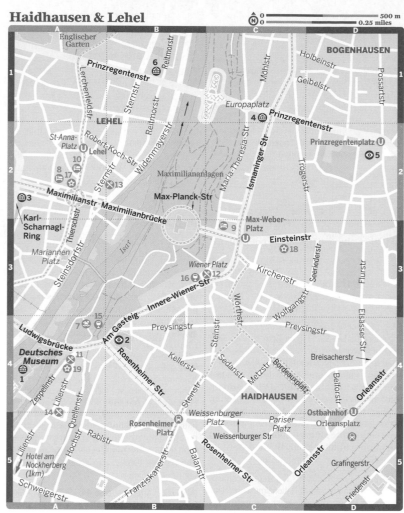

Eat the Rich   BAR
(Map p66; www.eattherich.de; Hessstrasse 90; ⊙7pm-1am Thu, to 4am Fri & Sat; ⓤ Theresienstrasse) Strong cocktails served in half-litre glasses quickly loosen inhibitions at this sizzling nightspot, a great place to crash when the party's winding down everywhere else. Food is served till 3am on weekends.

🍷 Nymphenburg, Neuhausen & Olympiapark

Hirschgarten   BEER GARDEN
(Map p72; www.hirschgarten.de; Hirschgarten 1; ⊙11.30am-1am; 🚋 Kriemhildenstrasse, Ⓢ Laim)

The Everest of Munich beer gardens can seat up to 8000 Augustiner lovers, making it Bavaria's biggest – an accolade indeed. It's in a lovely spot in a former royal hunting preserve and rubs up against a deer enclosure and a carousel. Steer here after visiting Schloss Nymphenburg – it's only a short walk south of the palace.

Backstage   CLUB
(Map p72; www.backstage.eu; Reitknechtstrasse 6; Ⓢ Hirschgarten) Refreshingly nonmainstream, this groovetastic club has a chilled night beer garden and a shape-shifting line-up of punk, nu metal, hip-hop, dance hall

Haidhausen & Lehel

Top Sights
1 Deutsches Museum A4

Sights
2 Kulturzentrum Gasteig B4
3 Museum Fünf Kontinente A2
4 Museum Villa Stuck C1
5 Prinzregententheater D2
6 Sammlung Schack B1

Activities, Courses & Tours
7 Müller'sches Volksbad A4

Sleeping
8 Hotel Opéra A2
9 Hotel Ritzi C3
10 Hotel Splendid-Dollmann A2

Eating
11 Dreigroschenkeller A4
12 Fischhäusl C3
13 Sir Tobi B2
14 Wirtshaus in der Au A5

Drinking & Nightlife
15 Biergarten Muffatwerk A4
16 Hofbräukeller B3

Entertainment
17 GOP Varieté Theater A2
18 Jazzclub Unterfahrt im Einstein C3
Münchner Philharmoniker .... (see 2)
19 Museum-Lichtspiele A4

and other alternative sounds, both canned and live.

Schwabing & the Englischer Garten

★ Chinesischer Turm BEER GARDEN

(Map p60; 089-383 8730; www.chinaturm.de; Englischer Garten 3; 10am-11pm late Apr-Oct; Chinesischer Turm, Tivolistrasse) This one's hard to ignore because of its English Garden location and pedigree as Munich's oldest beer garden (open since 1791). Camera-toting tourists and laid-back locals, picnicking families and businesspeople sneaking a sly brew clomp around the wooden pagoda, showered by the strained sounds of possibly the world's drunkest oompah band.

P1 CLUB

(Map p60; www.p1-club.de; Prinzregentenstrasse 1; 11pm-4am Tue-Sat; Nationalmuseum/Haus der Kunst) If you make it past the notorious face control at Munich's premier late spot, you'll encounter a crowd of Bundesliga reserve players, Q-list celebs and quite a few Russian speakers too busy seeing and being seen to actually have a good time. But it's all part of the fun, and the decor and summer terrace have their appeal.

Hirschau BEER GARDEN

(www.hirschau-muenchen.de; Gysslingstrasse 15; noon-11pm Mon-Fri, from 11am Sat & Sun; U Dietlindenstrasse) This mammoth beer garden in the northern half of the English Garden can seat 1700 quaffers and hosts live music almost every day in the summer months. When the picnic is over, dispatch the kids to the large playground while you indulge in some tankard caressing.

Cafe Zeitgeist CAFE

(Map p60; Türkenstrasse 74; 9am-1am Sun-Thu, to 3am Fri & Sat; Schellingstrasse) Go with the zeitgeist and take a pew at this perfect spot where you can enjoy a hearty breakfast or pore over coffee and cake as you watch, from a shady courtyard, the steady flow of students and hipsters wandering along Türkenstrasse.

Seehaus BEER GARDEN

(Map p60; Kleinhesselohe 3; 10am-1am; S Münchner Freiheit) On the shores of the English Garden's Kleinhesseloher See, Seehaus has a family-friendly beer garden with an attached restaurant that can be described as almost-upmarket.

Black Bean CAFE

(Map p60; Amalienstrasse 44; 7am-7pm Mon-Fri, from 8am Sat & Sun; ; U Universität) If you thought the only decent brew Bavarians could mash was beer, train your Arabica radar to this regional retort to Starbucks. The organic coffee gets tops marks, as do the muffins.

Schall & Rauch BAR

(Map p60; Schellingstrasse 22; 10am-1am Sun-Thu, to 3am Fri & Sat; ; U Universität) The few battered cafe chairs and vintage barstools get bagged quickly at this small, friendly, open-fronted bar, meaning drinkers often spill out onto Schellingstrasse even during the day. With a long menu of drinks and an easygoing feel, this is a relaxing place for lunch or a last weekend drink at 2am.

OUT & ABOUT IN MUNICH

Homosexuality is legal in Bavaria, but the scene, even in Munich, is tiny compared to, say, Berlin or Cologne. Homosexuality is widely accepted, and gays will experience no hostility in the capital. There are websites aplenty, but most are in German only. Try www.gay-web.de or, for women, www.lesarion.de. The **Schwules Kommunikations und Kulturzentrum** (Map p48; ☎089-856 346 400; www.subonline.org; Müllerstrasse 14; ◷7-11pm Sun-Thu, to midnight Fri, 8pm-1am Sat; ⊜Müllerstrasse) in the city centre is a gay information agency. Lesbians can also turn to **Le Tra** (Map p48; ☎089-725 4272; www.letra.de; Angertorstrasse 3; ◷2.30-5pm Mon & Wed; ⊜Müllerstrasse).

The main street parties of the year are Christopher Street Day (p64), held on Marienplatz on the second weekend in July, and the Hans Sachs Strassenfest (p64), held in mid-August along Hans-Sachs-Strasse in the Glockenbachviertel.

Bars & Clubs

Ochsengarten (Map p48; www.ochsengarten.de; Müllerstrasse 47; ◷8pm-3am Sun-Thu, 8pm-late Fri & Sat; ⊜Müllerstrasse) The first bar to open in the Bavarian capital where you have to be clad in leather, rubber, lycra, neopren or other kinky attire to get in. Gay men only.

Edelheiss (Map p48; www.edelheiss.de; Pestalozzistrasse 6; ◷3pm-1am Mon-Thu, to 3am Fri & Sat; ⊜Sendlinger Tor, Ⓤ Sendlinger Tor) A laid-back cafe by day, Edelheiss has vibrant gay party nights, especially at weekends.

Prosecco (Map p48; www.prosecco-munich.de; Theklastrasse 1; ◷from 10pm; ⊜Müllerstrasse) Fun venue for dancing, cruising and drinking that attracts a mixed bunch of party people with quirky decor and a cheesy mix of music (mostly '80s and charts).

NY Club (Map p66; www.nyclub.de; Elisenstrasse 3; ◷11pm-7am Thu-Sat; ⊜Hauptbahnhof, Ⓤ Hauptbahnhof, Ⓢ Hauptbahnhof) After a move to near the Old Botanical Gardens, it's again 'Raining Men' at Munich's hottest gay dance temple, where you can party away with Ibiza-style abandon on the cool, main floor.

🍷 Westend & Theresienwiese

★**Augustiner Bräustuben** BEER HALL
(Map p82; ☎089-507 047; www.braeustuben.de; Landsberger Strasse 19; ◷10am-midnight; ⊜Holzapfelstrasse) Depending on the wind direction, the bitter-sweet aroma of hops envelops you as you approach this traditional beer hall inside the Augustiner brewery. The Bavarian fare is superb, especially the *Schweinshaxe* (pork knuckle). Due to the location, the atmosphere in the evenings is slightly more authentic than that of its city-centre cousins, with fewer tourists at the long tables.

★**Harry Klein** CLUB
(Map p82; ☎089-4028 7400; www.harryklein club.de; Sonnenstrasse 8; ◷from 11pm; ⊜Karlsplatz, Ⓢ Karlsplatz, Ⓤ Karlsplatz) Follow the gold-lined passageway off Sonnenstrasse to what some regard as one of the best *Elektro-clubs* in the world. Nights here are an amazing alchemy of electro sound and visuals, with live video art projected onto the walls Kraftwerk-style and blending to awe-inspiring effect with the music.

Strom Club CLUB
(Map p82; www.strom-muc.de; Lindwurmstrasse 88; ◷from 8pm, see website for dates; Ⓤ Poccistrasse) Indie rock, postpunk, and underground are the speciality of this industrial club near the Theresienwiese. Live bands, both local and international, and DJs keep the crowd jumping till the early hours.

☆ Entertainment

As you might expect from a major metropolis, Munich's entertainment scene is lively and multifaceted, though not particularly edgy. You can hobnob with high society at the opera or the chic P1 disco, hang with the kids at an indie club, catch a flick alfresco or watch one of Germany's best soccer teams.

Tickets to cultural and sporting events are available at venue box offices and official ticket outlets, such as Zentraler Kartenvorverkauf (p82). Outlets are also good for online bookings, as is München Ticket (p82), which shares premises with the tourist office.

Cinemas

For show information check any of the listings publications. Movies presented in their original language are denoted in listings by the acronym OF *(Originalfassung)* or OV *(Originalversion);* those with German subtitles are marked OmU *(Original mit Untertiteln).*

Museum-Lichtspiele
CINEMA

(Map p78; ☑ 089-482 403; www.museum-lichtspiele.de; Lilienstrasse 2; 🚇 Deutsches Museum) Cult cinema with wacky interior and screenings of the *Rocky Horror Picture Show* (11.10pm Friday and Saturday nights). Shows English-language movies.

Cinema
CINEMA

(Map p66; ☑ 089-555 255; www.cinema-muenchen.de; Nymphenburger Strasse 31; 🇺 Stiglmaierplatz) Cult cinema with all films in English.

Classical & Opera

Bayerische Staatsoper
OPERA

(Bavarian State Opera; Map p48; ☑ 089-2185 1025; www.staatsoper.de; Max-Joseph-Platz 2; 🚇 Nationaltheater) One of the world's best opera companies, the Bavarian State Opera performs to sell-out crowds at the **Nationaltheater** (Map p48) in the Residenz and puts the emphasis on Mozart, Strauss and Wagner. In summer it hosts the prestigious Opernfestspiele (p64). The opera's house band is the Bayerisches Staatsorchester, in business since 1523 and thus Munich's oldest orchestra.

Münchner Philharmoniker
CLASSICAL MUSIC

(Map p78; ☑ 089-480 985 500; www.mphil.de; Rosenheimer Strasse 5; ⊘ mid-Sep–Jun; 🚇 Am Gasteig) Munich's premier orchestra regularly performs at the **Gasteig Cultural Centre** (Map p76; ☑ tickets 089-548 181 81; www.gasteig.de). Book tickets early, as performances usually sell out.

BR-Symphonieorchester
CLASSICAL MUSIC

(☑ 089-590 001; www.br-so.com) Charismatic Lithuanian maestro Mariss Jansons has rejuvenated this orchestra's playlist and often performs with its choir at such venues as the Gasteig and the **Prinzregententheater** (Map p76; ☑ 089-218 502; www.theaterakademie.de; Prinzregentenplatz 12; 🇸 Prinzregentenplatz).

Staatstheater am Gärtnerplatz
PERFORMING ARTS

(Map p48; ☑ 089-2185 1960; www.gaertnerplatztheater.de; Gärtnerplatz 3; 🚇 Reichenbachplatz) Spruced up to southern German standards for its 150th birthday in November 2015, this grand theatre specialises in light opera, musicals and dance.

Jazz

Jazzclub Unterfahrt im Einstein
LIVE MUSIC

(Map p78; ☑ 089-448 2794; www.unterfahrt.de; Einsteinstrasse 42; ⊘ from 9pm; 🇺 Max-Weber-Platz) Join a diverse crowd at this long-established, intimate club for a mixed bag of acts ranging from old bebop to edgy experimental. The Sunday open-jam session is legendary.

Jazzbar Vogler
JAZZ

(Map p48; www.jazzbar-vogler.com; Rumfordstrasse 17; €2-6; ⊘ 7pm-midnight Mon-Thu, to 1am Fri & Sat; 🚇 Reichenbachplatz) This intimate watering hole brings some of Munich's baddest cats to the stage. You never know who'll show up for Monday's jam session, and Tuesday to Thursday are live piano nights, but the main acts take to the stage on Friday and Saturday. Cash only.

Café am Beethovenplatz
JAZZ

(Map p82; ☑ 089-552 9100; Goethestrasse 51; ⊘ 9am-1am; 🇸 Sendlinger Tor) Downstairs at the Hotel Mariandl (p66), this is Munich's oldest music cafe. It has an eclectic menu of sounds ranging from bossa nova to piano to Italian *canzoni* (songs). Reservations advised.

Theatre

Bayerisches Staatsschauspiel
THEATRE

(☑ 089-2185 1940; www.residenztheater.de) This leading ensemble has gone alternative in recent years, staging Shakespeare, Schiller and other tried-and-true playwrights in 21st-century garb and the like. Performances are in the **Residenztheater** (Map p48; Max-Joseph-Platz 2; 🚇 Nationaltheater), the **Theater im Marstall** (Map p48; Marstallplatz 4; 🚇 Kammerspiele) and the Cuvilliés-Theater (p46).

Münchner Kammerspiele
THEATRE

(Map p48; ☑ 089-2339 6600; www.muenchnerkammerspiele.de; Maximilianstrasse 26; 🚇 Kammerspiele) A venerable theatre with an edgy bent, the Kammerspiele delivers provocative interpretations of the classics as well as works by contemporary playwrights. Performances are in a beautifully refurbished art nouveau theatre at Maximilianstrasse 26 and in the **Neues Haus** (Map p48; Falckenbergstrasse 1; 🚇 Kammerspiele), a 21st-century glass cube nearby.

Deutsches Theater
THEATRE

(Map p82; ☑ 089-5523 4444; www.deutsches-theater.de; Schwanthalerstrasse 13; 🇺 Hauptbahnhof, 🇸 Hauptbahnhof) On wide and bustling Schwanthalerstrasse, Munich's answer to

Westend & Theresienwiese

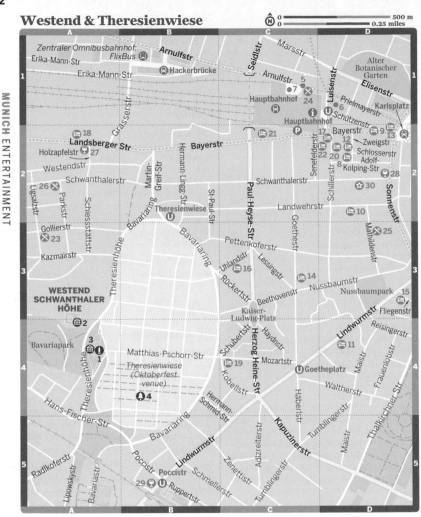

London's West End hosts touring road shows such as *Dirty Dancing*, *The Gruffalo* and *Mamma Mia*.

GOP Varieté Theater
THEATRE

(Map p78; ☎089-210 288 444; www.variete.de; Maximilianstrasse 47; ⊠Maxmonument) Hosts a real jumble of acts and shows, from magicians to light comedies to musicals.

Zentraler Kartenvorverkauf – Marienplatz
BOOKING SERVICE

(Map p48; ☎089-5450 6060; www.zkv-muenchen.de; Marienplatz; ⊘9am-8pm Mon-Sat; ⓊMarienplatz) One of the best places to buy tickets to cultural and sporting events. Located in the entrance to the U·STYLE Galeria Kaufhof clothes shop in Marienplatz U-Bahn station.

München Ticket
BOOKING SERVICE

(Map p48; ☎089-5481 8181; www.muenchen ticket.de; Marienplatz; ⊘10am-8pm Mon-Sat; ⓊMarienplatz, ⓈMarienplatz) Tickets for cultural and sporting events in Munich are available from this office within the Neues Rathaus. Enter from Dienerstrasse.

Westend & Theresienwiese

Puppet & Children's Theatre

Münchner Theater für Kinder   THEATRE
(Map p66; ☑ 089-594 545; www.mtfk.de; Dachauer Strasse 46; ⊘ 3pm daily, 10am Sat, Sun & school holidays; ⊠ Stiglmaierplatz) At the Münchner Theater für Kinder budding thespians can enjoy fairy tales and children's classics à la *Max & Moritz* and *Pinocchio*.

Münchner Marionettentheater   PUPPET THEATRE
(Map p48; ☑ 089-265 712; www.muema-theater. de; Blumenstrasse 32; ⊘ 3pm Mon, Wed & Fri, 8pm Sat; ⊠ Müllerstrasse) The adorable singing and dancing marionettes performing at the Münchner Marionettentheater have enthralled generations of wee ones.

Spectator Sports

★ FC Bayern München   FOOTBALL
(☑ 089-6993 1333; www.fcbayern.de; Allianz Arena, Werner-Heisenberg-Allee 25, Fröttmaning; ⓤ Fröttmaning) Germany's most successful team both domestically and on a European level plays home games at the impressive Allianz Arena, built for the 2006 World Cup. Tickets can be ordered online.

EHC München   ICE HOCKEY
(Map p72; www.ehc-muenchen.de; Olympia Eishalle, Olympiapark; ⓤ Olympiazentrum) It's not one of Germany's premier ice-hockey outfits, but EHC München's games at the Olympic ice rink are exciting spectacles nonetheless; the team features several Canadian and American players.

🔒 Shopping

Munich is a fun and sophisticated place to shop that goes far beyond chains and department stores. If that's what you want, head to Neuhauser Strasse and Kaufingerstrasse. Southeast of there, Sendlinger Strasse has smaller and somewhat more individual stores. The Glockenbachviertel and Schwabing have many intriguing stores specialising in vintage clothing, books and antiques.

★ Globetrotter   SPORTS & OUTDOORS
(Map p48; www.globetrotter.de; Isartorplatz 8-10; ⊘ 10am-8pm Mon-Sat; ⓤ Isartor, Ⓢ Isartor) Munich's premier outdoors and travel stockist is worth a browse even if you've never pulled on a pair of hiking boots. The basement boasts a lake for testing out kayaks and there's a travel agent and even a branch of the Alpenverein, as well as every travel and outdoor accessory you could ever possibly need. Stocks the best range of maps and guides in the city.

★ Munich Readery   BOOKS
(Map p66; www.readery.de; Augustenstrasse 104; ⊘ 11am-8pm Mon-Fri, 10am-6pm Sat; ⓤ Theresienstrasse) With Germany's biggest collection of secondhand English-language titles, the Readery is the place to go in Bavaria for holiday reading matter. In fact we think this may be the only such secondhand bookshop

between Paris and Prague. The shop holds events such as author readings, and there's a monthly book club. See the website for details.

Pick & Weight
CLOTHING

(Map p60; Schellingstrasse 24; ☉noon-8pm Mon-Sat; Ⓤ Universität) Part of a small national chain, Pick & Weight sells top-notch vintage clothing for between €25 and €95 per kilo. The men's and women's attire, plus accessories, are of the highest quality, and the shop is crammed with exquisite yesteryear pieces.

★ Holareidulijö
CLOTHING

(Map p66; www.holareidulijoe.com; Schellingstrasse 81; ☉noon-6.30pm Tue-Fri, 10am-1pm Sat May-Sep, 2-6pm Thu & Fri, 11am-1pm Sat Oct-Apr; Ⓢ Schellingstrasse) This rare secondhand traditional-clothing store (the name is a phonetic yodel) is worth a look even if you don't intend buying. Apparently, wearing hand-me-down Lederhosen greatly reduces the risk of chafing.

Loden-Frey
CLOTHING

(Map p48; ☏089-210 390; www.lodenfrey.com; Maffeistrasse 5-7; ☉10am-8pm Mon-Sat; Ⓢ Theatinerstrasse) The famous cloth producer stocks a wide range of Bavarian wear and other top-end clothes. The Lederhosen and Dirndl outfits are a cut above the discount nightout versions and prices are accordingly high.

Porzellan Manufaktur Nymphenburg
CERAMICS

(Map p72; ☏089-1791 970; www.nymphenburg.com; Nördliches Schlossrondell 8; ☉10am-5pm Mon-Fri; Ⓢ Schloss Nymphenburg) Traditional and contemporary porcelain masterpieces by the royal manufacturer. Prices are high.

Manufactum
HOMEWARES

(Map p48; www.manufactum.de; Dienerstrasse 12; ☉9.30am-7pm Mon-Sat; Ⓢ Marienplatz; Ⓢ Marienplatz) Anyone with an admiration for top-quality design from Germany and further afield should make a beeline for this store. Last-a-lifetime household items compete for shelf space with retro toys, Bauhaus lamps and times-gone-by stationery. The stock changes according to the season.

Words' Worth Books
BOOKS

(Map p60; www.wordsworth.de; Schellingstrasse 3; ☉9am-8pm Mon-Fri, 10am-4pm Sat; Ⓢ Schellingstrasse) You will find tonnes of English-language books, from secondhand novels to the latest bestsellers, at this excellent and long-established bookstore.

7 Himmel
CLOTHING

(Map p48; www.siebterhimmel.com; Hans-Sachs-Strasse 17; ☉11am-7pm Mon-Fri, 10am-6pm Sat; Ⓢ Müllerstrasse) Couture cool-hunters will be in seventh heaven (a translation of the boutique's name) when browsing the assortment of fashions and accessories by indie labels sold at surprisingly reasonable prices.

Schuster
SPORTS & OUTDOORS

(Map p48; Rosenstrasse 1-5; ☉10am-8pm Mon-Sat; Ⓢ Marienplatz, Ⓤ Marienplatz) Get tooled up for the Alps at this sports megastore boasting seven shiny floors of equipment, including cycling, skiing, travel and camping paraphernalia.

Bottles & Glashaus
GLASS

(Map p48; www.bottles.de; Josephspitalstrasse 1; ☉10am-7pm Mon-Fri, to 6pm Sat; Ⓢ Sendlinger Tor, Ⓤ Sendlinger Tor) If it's made of glass, this wonderfully stocked backstreet shop sells it, from jam jars to wine glasses, marbles to vases, paperweights to Venetian-style beads.

Flohmarkt im Olympiapark
MARKET

(Map p72; Olympiapark; ☉7am-4pm Fri & Sat; Ⓢ Olympiapark West) Large flea market held outside the Olympiastadion.

Stachus Passagen
MALL

(Map p48; www.stachus-passagen.de; Karlsplatz/Stachus; ☉9.30am-8pm Mon-Sat; Ⓢ Karlsplatz, Ⓢ Karlsplatz, Ⓤ Karlsplatz) Europe's biggest underground shopping mall, with 36 escalators and 250,000 shoppers a day wandering its 58 mainstream shops.

ⓘ Information

DANGERS & ANNOYANCES

During Oktoberfest crime and staggering drunks are major problems, especially around the Hauptbahnhof. It's no joke: drunks in a crowd trying to make their way home can get violent, and there are around 100 cases of assault every year. Leave early or stay cautious – if not sober – yourself.

Strong and unpredictable currents make cooling off in the Eisbach creek in the Englischer Garten more dangerous than it looks. Exercise extreme caution; there have been deaths.

Fast-moving bikes in central Munich are a menace. Make sure you don't wander onto bike lanes, especially when waiting to cross the road and when alighting from buses and trams.

EMERGENCY

Ambulance	☏192 22
Fire	☏112
Police	☏110

INTERNET ACCESS

As across the rest of Europe, internet cafes are generally a thing of the past. Wi-fi is widespread and often free. Most public libraries offer internet access to nonresidents. Check www. muenchner-stadtbibliothek.de (in German) for details.

MEDICAL SERVICES

The US and UK consulates can provide lists of English-speaking doctors.

Ärztlicher Hausbesuchdienst (☑ 089-555 566; www.ahd-hausbesuch.de; ⊘ 24hr) Doctor for home and hotel visits.

Bereitschaftsdienst der Münchner Ärzte (☑ 116 117; ⊘ 24hr) Evening and weekend nonemergency medical services with English-speaking doctors.

Emergency dentist (☑ 089-3000 5515; ⊘ 24hr)

Emergency pharmacy (www.apotheken.de) Online referrals to the nearest open pharmacy. Most pharmacies have employees who speak passable English, but there are several designated international pharmacies with staff fluent in English, including **Internationale Ludwigs-Apotheke** (☑ 089-550 50/0; www. ludwigsapo.de; Neuhauser Strasse 11; ⊘ 9am-8pm Mon-Sat; Ⓤ Marienplatz).

Schwabing Hospital (☑ 089-30 680; Kölner Platz 1; Ⓤ Scheidplatz) Accident and Emergency department.

MONEY

ATMs abound in the city centre, though not all take every type of card. All major credit cards are widely accepted.

Reisebank (Bahnhofplatz 2; ⊘ 7am-10pm; ⓡ Hauptbahnhof, Ⓤ Hauptbahnhof, Ⓢ Hauptbahnhof) Best place to change and withdraw money at the Hauptbahnhof.

POST

Post office (Map p48; Alter Hof 6-7; ⊘ 9am-6.30pm Mon-Fri, 9.30am-12.30pm Sat; Ⓤ Marienplatz, Ⓢ Marienplatz) For additional branches, search www.deutschepost.de.

TOURIST INFORMATION

There are branches of the tourist office at the **Hauptbahnhof** (Map p82; ☑ 089-21 800; www. muenchen.de; Bahnhofplatz 2; ⊘ 9am-8pm Mon-Sat, 10am-6pm Sun; ⓡ Hauptbahnhof, Ⓤ Hauptbahnhof, Ⓢ Hauptbahnhof) and on the **Marienplatz** (Map p48; ☑ 089-2339 6500; www.muenchen.de; Marienplatz 2; ⊘ 9am-7pm Mon-Fri, to 4pm Sat, 10am-2pm Sun; Ⓤ Marienplatz, Ⓢ Marienplatz).

Castles & Museums Infopoint (Map p48; ☑ 089-2101 4050; www.infopoint-museen-bayern.de; Alter Hof 1; ⊘ 10am-6pm Mon-Sat; Ⓤ Marienplatz, Ⓢ Marienplatz) is the central information point for museums and palaces throughout Bavaria.

ℹ MUNICH CITY TOUR CARD

The **Munich City Tour Card** (www. citytourcard-muenchen.com; 1/3 days €12.90/24.90) includes all public transport in the *Innenraum* (Munich city – zones 1 to 4, marked white on transport maps) and discounts of between 10% and 50% for over 80 attractions, tours, eateries and theatres. These include the Residenz, the BMW Museum and the Bier & Oktoberfestmuseum. It's available at some hotels, tourist offices, Munich public transport authority (MVV) offices and U-Bahn, S-Bahn and DB vending machines.

ℹ Getting There & Away

AIR

Munich Airport (MUC; ☑ 089-975 00; www. munich-airport.de), aka Flughafen Franz Josef Strauss, is second in importance only to Frankfurt for international and domestic connections. The main carrier is Lufthansa, but over 80 other companies operate from the airport's two runways, from major carriers such as British Airways and Emirates to minor operations such as Luxair and Air Malta.

Only one major airline from the UK doesn't use Munich's main airport – Ryanair flies into Memmingen's **Allgäu Airport** (FMM; ☑ 08331-984 2000; www.allgaeu-airport.de; Am Flughafen 35, Memmingen), 125km to the west.

BUS

The **Zentraler Omnibusbahnhof** (Central Bus Station, ZOB; Map p82; www.muenchen-zob.de; Arnulfstrasse 21; Ⓢ Hackerbrücke) next to the Hackerbrücke S-Bahn station handles the vast majority of international and domestic coach services. There's a Eurolines/Touring office, a supermarket and various eateries on the 1st floor; buses depart from ground level.

The main operator out of the ZOB is now low-cost coach company **Flixbus** (Map p82; ☑ 030 300 137 300; www.flixbus.com; Zentraler Omnibusbahnhof, Arnulfstrasse 21), which links Munich to destinations across Germany and beyond.

A special Deutsche Bahn express coach leaves for Prague (€70, 4¾ hours, three daily) from the ZOB.

TRAIN

Train connections from Munich to destinations in Bavaria are excellent and there are also numerous services to more distant cities within Germany and around Europe. All services leave from the **Hauptbahnhof** (Central Station).

Staffed by native English speakers, **Euraide** (www.euraide.de; Desk 1, Reisezentrum,

Hauptbahnhof; ⊙ 10am-7pm Mon-Fri Mar-Apr & Aug-Dec, 9.30am-8pm May-Jul; ⓐ Hauptbahnhof, Ⓤ Hauptbahnhof, Ⓢ Hauptbahnhof) is a friendly agency based at the Hauptbahnhof that sells all DB (Deutsche Bahn) products, makes reservations and creates personalised rail tours of Germany and beyond.

Connections from Munich:

Augsburg €14.60 to €20, 30 to 50 minutes, thrice hourly

Baden-Baden €80, four hours, hourly (change in Mannheim)

Berlin €150, 5¼ hours, hourly

Cologne €147, 4½ hours, hourly

Frankfurt €105, 3¼ hours, hourly

Freiburg €100, 4½ hours, hourly (change in Mannheim or Karlsruhe)

Nuremberg €40-€60, one hour, twice hourly

Regensberg €29.70, 1½ hours, hourly

Vienna €99, four hours, every two hours

Würzburg €74, two hours, twice hourly

Zürich €84, 4¾ hours, thrice daily

❶ Getting Around

Central Munich is compact enough to explore on foot. The outlying suburbs are easily reachable by public transport, which is extensive and efficient.

TO/FROM THE AIRPORT

Munich Airport Linked by S-Bahn (S1 and S8) to the Hauptbahnhof. The trip costs €10.80, takes about 40 minutes and runs every 20 minutes almost 24 hours a day. The Lufthansa Airport Bus shuttles at 20-minute intervals between the airport and Arnulfstrasse, next to the Hauptbahnhof, between 5.15am and 7.55pm. The trip takes about 45 minutes and costs €10.50 (return €17). A taxi from Munich Airport to the Altstadt costs €50 to €70.

Allgäu Airport The Allgäu Airport Express also leaves from Arnulfstrasse at the Hauptbahnhof, making the trip up to seven times a day. The journey takes one hour 40 minutes and the fare is €13 (return €19.50).

CAR & MOTORCYCLE

Driving in central Munich can be a nightmare; many streets are one-way or pedestrian only, ticket enforcement is Orwellian and parking is a nightmare. Car parks (indicated on the tourist-office map) charge about €1.70 to €2.20 per hour.

PUBLIC TRANSPORT

Munich's efficient public-transport system is composed of buses, trams, the U-Bahn and the S-Bahn. It's operated by MVV (www.mvv-muenchen.de), which maintains offices in the U-Bahn stations at Marienplatz, the Hauptbahnhof, Sendlinger Tor, the Ostbahnhof and Poccistrasse. Staff hand out free network maps and timetables, sell tickets and answer questions.

Automated trip planning in English is best done online. The U-Bahn and S-Bahn run almost 24 hours a day, with perhaps a short gap between 2am and 4am. Night buses and trams operate in the city centre.

Tickets & Fares

The city-of-Munich region is divided into four zones, with most places of visitor interest (except Dachau and the airport) conveniently clustering within the white *Innenraum* (inner zone).

Single tickets cost €2.70. Children aged between six and 14 pay a flat €1.40 regardless of the length of the trip. Day passes are €6.70 for individuals and €12.80 for up to five people travelling together; a weekly pass called an IsarCard costs €15.40. Bikes cost €3 to take aboard and may only be taken on *U-Bahn* and S-Bahn trains, but not during the 6am to 9am and 4pm to 6pm rush hours.

Bus drivers sell single tickets and day passes, but tickets for the U-Bahn and S-Bahn and other passes must be purchased from vending machines at stations or MVV offices. Tram tickets are available from vending machines on board. Most tickets must be stamped (validated) at station platform entrances and on board buses and trams before use. The fine for getting caught without a valid ticket is €40.

TAXI

Taxis cost €3.70 at flag fall plus €1.90 per kilometre and are not much more convenient than public transport. Luggage is sometimes charged at €1.50 per piece. Ring a taxi on 216 10 or 194 10. Taxi ranks are indicated on the city's tourist map.

AROUND MUNICH

Dachau

📋 08131 / POP 46,900

Officially called **KZ-Gedenkstätte Dachau** (Dachau Concentration Camp Memorial Site; 📋 08131-669 970; www.kz-gedenkstaette-dachau. de; Peter-Roth-Strasse 2a, Dachau; ⊙ 9am-5pm) FREE, this was the Nazis' first concentration camp, built by Heinrich Himmler in March 1933 to house political prisoners. All in all, it 'processed' more than 200,000 inmates, killing at least 43,000, and is now a haunting memorial. Expect to spend two to three hours here to fully absorb the exhibits. Note that children aged under 12 may find the experience too disturbing.

The place to start is the **visitors centre**, which houses a bookshop, a cafe and a tour-booking desk where you can pick up an audioguide (€4). It's on your left as you enter the main gate. Two-and-a-half-hour tours (€3.50) also run from here at 11am and

1pm (extra tours run at 12.15pm on Sunday between July and September).

You pass into the compound itself through the **Jourhaus**, originally the only entrance. Set in wrought iron, the infamous, chilling slogan 'Arbeit Macht Frei' (Work Sets You Free) hits you at the gate.

The **museum** is at the southern end of the camp. Here, a 22-minute English-language documentary runs at 10am, 11.30am, 12.30pm, 2pm and 3pm and uses mostly postliberation footage to outline what took place here. Either side of the small cinema extends an exhibition relating the camp's harrowing story, from a relatively orderly prison for religious inmates, leftists and criminals to an overcrowded concentration camp racked by typhus, and its eventual liberation by the US Army in April 1945.

Disturbing displays include photographs of the camp, its officers and prisoners (all male until 1944), and of horrifying 'scientific experiments' carried out by Nazi doctors. Other exhibits include a whipping block, a chart showing the system of prisoner categories (Jews, homosexuals, Jehovah's Witnesses, Poles, Roma and other 'asocial' people) and documents on the persecution of 'degenerate' authors banned by the party. There's also a lot of information on the rise of the Nazis and other concentration camps around Europe, a scale model of the camp at its greatest extent and numerous uniforms and everyday objects belonging to inmates and guards.

Outside, in the former roll-call square, is the **International Memorial** (1968), inscribed in English, French, Yiddish, German and Russian, which reads 'Never Again'. Behind the exhibit building, the bunker was the notorious camp prison where inmates were tortured. Executions took place in the prison yard.

Inmates were housed in large barracks, now demolished, which used to line the main road north of the roll-call square. In the camp's northwestern corner is the crematorium and gas chamber, disguised as a shower room but never used. Several religious shrines, including a timber Russian Orthodox church, stand nearby.

ⓘ Getting There & Away

Dachau is about 16km northwest of central Munich. The S2 makes the trip from Munich Hauptbahnhof to the station in Dachau in 22 minutes. You'll need a two-zone ticket (€5.80) or four strips of a *Streifenkarte* (multiple-journey ticket). Here change to bus 726 alighting at the KZ-Gedenkstätte stop (with almost everyone else).

Schleissheim

🔊 089 / POP 11,600

When you've exhausted all possibilities in central Munich, the northern suburb of Schleissheim is well worth the short S-Bahn trip for its three elegant palaces and a high-flying aviation museum, a great way to entertain the kids on a rainy afternoon.

⦿ Sights

★**Neues Schloss Schleissheim**　　PALACE
(New Palace; www.schloesser-schleissheim.de; Max-Emanuel-Platz 1; adult/concession €4.50/3.50, all 3 palaces €8/6; ⊙9am-6pm Tues-Sun Apr-Sep, 10am-4pm Oct-Mar; 🚇Mittenheimer Strasse) The crown jewel of Schleissheim's palatial trio is the Neues Schloss Schleissheim. This pompous pile was dreamed up by Prince-Elector Max Emanuel in 1701 in anticipation of his promotion to emperor. It never came. Instead he was forced into exile for over a decade and didn't get back to building until 1715. Cash-flow problems required the scaling back of the original plans, but given the palace's huge dimensions and opulent interior, it's hard to imagine where exactly the cuts fell.

Some of the finest artists of the baroque era were called in to create such eye-pleasing sights as the ceremonial staircase, the Victory Hall and the Grand Gallery. There are outstanding pieces of period furniture, including the elector's four-poster bed, intricately inlaid tables, and a particularly impressive ceiling fresco by Cosmas Damian Asam.

The palace is home to the Staatsgalerie (State Gallery), a selection of European baroque art drawn from the Bavarian State Collection, including works by such masters as Peter Paul Rubens, Anthony van Dyck and Carlo Saraceni. The most impressive room here is the Grand Galerie.

Schloss Lustheim　　PALACE
(www.schloesser-schleissheim.de; adult/concession €3.50/2.50, all 3 palaces €8/6; ⊙9am-6pm Tues-Sun Apr-Sep, 10am-4pm Oct-Mar; 🚇Mittenheimer Strasse) While construction of Prince-Elector Max Emanuel's Neues Schloss Schleissheim was going on, the elector and his retinue resided in the fanciful hunting palace of Schloss Lustheim, on a little island in the eastern Schlosspark. It now provides an elegant setting for porcelain masterpieces from Meissen belonging to the Bayerisches Nationalmuseum.

Altes Schloss Schleissheim PALACE
(www.schloesser-schleissheim.de; Maximilian-shof 1; adult/concession €3/2, all 3 palaces €8/6; ⊙9am-6pm Tues-Sun Apr-Sep, 10am-4pm Oct-Mar; 🚉Mittenheimer Strasse) The Altes Schloss Schleissheim is a mere shadow of its Renaissance self, having been altered and refashioned in the intervening centuries. It houses paintings and sculpture depicting religious culture and festivals all over the world, including an impressive collection of more than 100 nativity scenes.

Flugwerft Schleissheim MUSEUM
(www.deutsches-museum.de/flugwerft; Ferdinand-Schulz-Allee; adult/child €7/3; ⊙9am-5pm; 🚉Mittenheimerstrasse) The Flugwerft Schleissheim, the aviation branch of the Deutsches Museum, makes for a nice change of pace and aesthetics from Schleissheim's regal palaces. Spirits will soar at the sight of the lethal Soviet MiG-21 fighter jet, the Vietnam-era F-4E Phantom and a replica of Otto Lilienthal's 1894 glider, with a revolutionary wing shaped like Batman's cape. Kids can climb into an original cockpit, land a plane and even get their pilot's licence.

🚗 Getting There & Away

To get to Schleissheim, take the S1 (direction Freising) to Oberschleissheim (€5.80), then walk along Mittenheimer Strasse for about 15 minutes towards the palaces. On weekdays only, bus 292 goes to the Mittenheimer Strasse stop.

By car, take Leopoldstrasse north until it becomes Ingolstädter Strasse. Then take the A99 to the Neuherberg exit, at the southern end of the airstrip.

Starnberger Fünf-Seen-Land

Once a royal retreat and still a popular place of residence for the rich and famous, the Fünf-Seen-Land (Five Lakes District) is set in a glacial plain and makes a fast and easy escape from the urban bustle of Munich. Organised tourism in these parts is very much a seasonal affair, but any time is good for hiking and cycling.

Starnberg is the biggest and most famous body of water here. The other lakes – Ammersee, Pilsensee, Wörthsee and Wesslinger See – are smaller and offer more secluded charm. Swimming, boating and windsurfing are popular activities on all lakes, and the area is also riddled with a whopping

493km of bike paths and 185km of hiking trails.

◎ Sights & Activities

★**Kloster Andechs** MONASTERY
(📞08152-3760; www.andechs.de; Bergstrasse 2, Andechs; ⊙8am-6pm Mon-Fri, 9am-6pm Sat, 9.45am-6pm Sun) FREE Founded in the 10th century, the gorgeous hilltop monastery of Andechs has long been a place of pilgrimage, though today more visitors come to slurp the Benedictines' fabled ales.

Marienmunster ABBEY
(📞08807-948 940; Klosterhof 10a, Diessen) FREE A real gem in the baroque architectural style, Diessen's Marienmunster was built between 1732 and 1739 by the famous architect of the period, Johann Michael Fischer. The highlights are the stucco and fresco decoration as well as altarpieces by Tiepolo and Straub.

Buchheim Museum MUSEUM
(www.buchheimmuseum.de; Am Hirschgarten 1, Bernried; adult/concession €8.50/4; ⊙10am-6pm Tue-Sun Apr-Oct, to 5pm Nov-Mar) Art fans should make a special trip to this museum on the western shore of Starnberger See, espcially if they have an interest in expressionism. The Buchheim collection features expressionist paintings as well as folk items. The building is set in parkland on the water's edge.

Bike It CYCLING
(📞08151-746 430; www.bikeit.de; Bahnhofstrasse 1, Starnberg) This all-things-bike company runs guided bike tours from around €25.

🛈 Information

Starnberger Fünf-Seen-Land Tourist Office (📞08151-906 00; www.sta5.de; Hauptstrasse 1, Starnberg; ⊙8am-6pm Mon-Fri, 9am-1pm Sat May-Oct, 9.30am-5pm Mon-Fri Nov-Apr) Tourist office covering the entire lakes region.
Tourist Office – Herrsching (📞08151-906 040; www.sta5.de; Bahnhofsplatz 3, Herrsching; ⊙9am-1pm & 2-6pm Mon-Fri, 9am-1pm Sat May-Sep, 10am-1pm Mon-Fri Oct-Apr) Tourist office for the Ammersee area.

🚗 Getting There & Away

Starnberg is a half-hour ride on the S6 train from Munich Hauptbahnhof (€5.80).

From Easter to mid-October **Bayerische-Seen-Schifffahrt** (📞08151-8061; www.seen-schifffahrt.de) runs boat services from Starnberg to other lakeside towns as well as offering longer cruises. Boats dock behind the S-Bahn station in Starnberg.

Bavaria

POP 12.4 MILLION

Best Places to Eat

➡ Bürgerspital Weinstube
(p113)

➡ Gaststätte St Bartholomä
(p108)

➡ Albrecht Dürer Stube
(p136)

➡ Perlacht Acht (p124)

➡ Mittermeier (p117)

Best Places
to Stay

➡ Bayerischer Hof (p157)

➡ Hotel Schloss Ort (p164)

➡ Elements Hotel (p154)

➡ Dinkelsbühler Kunst-
Stuben (p118)

Why Go?

From the cloud-shredding Alps to the fertile Danube plain, the Free State of Bavaria is a place that keeps its clichéd promises. Story-book castles bequeathed by an oddball king poke through dark forest, cowbells tinkle in flower-filled meadows, the thwack of palm on Lederhosen accompanies the clump of frothy stein on timber bench, and medieval walled towns go about their time-warped business.

But diverse Bavaria offers much more than the chocolate-box idyll. Learn about Bavaria's state-of-the-art motor industry in Ingolstadt, discover its Nazi past in Nuremberg and Berchtesgaden, sip world-class wines in Würzburg, get on the Wagner trail in Bayreuth or seek out countless kiddy attractions across the state. Destinations are often described as possessing 'something for everyone', but in Bavaria's case this is no exaggeration.

And, whatever you do in Germany's southeast, every occasion is infused with that untranslatable feel-good air of *Gemütlichkeit* (cosiness) that makes exploring the region such an easygoing experience.

When to Go

A winter journey along an off-season, tourist-free Romantic Road really sees the snow-bound route live up to its name. Come the spring, tuck into some seasonal fare as Bavaria goes crazy for asparagus during *Spargelzeit* (from late March). The summer months are all about the beer garden, and this is obviously the best time to savour the region's unsurpassed brews in the balmy, fairy-lit air. Autumn is the time to experience the dreamy haze of the Bavarian Forest and the bustle of Bavaria's cities, revived after the summer's time out.

Bavaria Highlights

❶ Schloss Neuschwanstein (p92) Indulging your romantic fantasies at this fairy-tale castle.

❷ Zugspitze (p98) Rack-and-pinioning your way to the top of Germany's highest peak.

❸ Berchtesgaden (p106) Perching at the Eagle's Nest to enjoy show-stopping Alpine vistas.

❹ Bavarian Forest (p165) Striking a trail through the tranquil wilds of this national park.

❺ Dinkelsbühl (p118) Going full circle around the town walls of this quaint town.

❻ Königssee (p106) Messing around on the waters of this achingly picturesque lake.

❼ Nuremberg (p127) Revisiting Bavaria's Nazi past.

❽ Beer Savouring a cold one in some of the hundreds of superb beer gardens, breweries and brewpubs across the region.

History

For centuries Bavaria was ruled as a duchy in the Holy Roman Empire, a patchwork of nations that extended from Italy to the North Sea. In the early 19th century, a conquering Napoleon annexed Bavaria, elevated it to the rank of kingdom and doubled its size. The fledgling nation became the object of power struggles between Prussia and Austria and, in 1871, was brought into the German Reich by Bismarck.

Bavaria was the only German state that refused to ratify the Basic Law (Germany's near constitution) following WWII. Instead, Bavaria's leaders opted to return to its prewar status as a 'free state', and drafted their own constitution. Almost ever since, the *Land* (state) has been ruled by the Christlich-Soziale Union (CSU), the arch-conservative party that is peculiar to Bavaria. Its dominance of the politics of a single *Land* is unique in postwar Germany, having ruled for all but five of the last 50 years without the need to form a coalition with anyone else. Its sister party, the CDU, operates in the rest of the country by mutual agreement.

❶ Getting There & Around

Munich is Bavaria's main transport hub, second only to Frankfurt in flight and rail connections. Rail is the best way to reach Munich from other parts of Germany, and the best means of getting from the Bavarian capital to other parts of Bavaria. Air links within Bavaria are much less extensive.

Without your own set of wheels in Eastern Bavaria and the Alps, you'll have to rely on bus services, which peter out in the evenings and at weekends. Trips along the Romantic Road can be done by tour bus, although again a car is a better idea. Several long-distance cycling routes cross Bavaria and the region's cities are some of the most cycle friendly in the world, so getting around on two wheels could not be easier.

BAVARIAN ALPS

Stretching west from Germany's remote southeastern corner to the Allgäu region near Lake Constance, the Bavarian Alps (Bayerische Alpen) form a stunningly beautiful natural divide along the Austrian border. Ranges further south may be higher, but these mountains shoot up from the foothills so abruptly that the impact is all the more dramatic.

The region is pocked with quaint frescoed villages, spas and health retreats, and possibilities for skiing, snowboarding, hiking, canoeing and paragliding – much of it year-round. The ski season lasts from about late December until April, while summer activities stretch from late May to November.

One of the largest resorts in the area is Garmisch-Partenkirchen, one of urban Bavaria's favourite getaways. Berchtesgaden, Füssen and Oberstdorf are also good bases.

❶ Getting Around

There are few direct train routes between main centres, meaning buses are the most efficient method of public transport in the Alpine area. If you're driving, sometimes a short cut via Austria works out to be quicker (such as between Garmisch-Partenkirchen and Füssen or Oberstdorf).

Füssen

📌 08362 / POP 15,400

Nestled at the foot of the Alps, tourist-busy Füssen is the southern climax of the Romantic Road, with the nearby castles of Neuschwanstein and Hohenschwangau the highlight of many a southern Germany trip. But having 'done' the country's most popular tourist route and seen Ludwig II's fantasy palaces, there are several other reasons to linger longer in the area. The town of Füssen is worth half a day's exploration and, from here, you can easily escape from the crowds into a landscape of gentle hiking trails and Alpine vistas.

◉ Sights

★ **Schloss Neuschwanstein** CASTLE
(📌 tickets 08362-930 830; www.neuschwanstein.de; Neuschwansteinstrasse 20; adult/child €13/free, incl Hohenschwangau €25/free; ⊘ 9am-6pm Apr–mid-Oct, 10am-4pm mid-Oct–Mar) Appearing through the mountaintops like a mirage, Schloss Neuschwanstein was the model for Disney's *Sleeping Beauty* castle. King Ludwig II planned this fairy-tale pile himself, with the help of a stage designer rather than an architect. He envisioned it as a giant stage on which to recreate the world of Germanic mythology, inspired by the operatic works of his friend Richard Wagner. The most impressive room is the Sängersaal (Minstrels' Hall), whose frescos depict scenes from the opera *Tannhäuser*.

Built as a romantic medieval castle, work started in 1869 and, like so many of Ludwig's grand schemes, was never finished. For all the coffer-depleting sums spent on it, the king spent just over 170 days in residence.

Completed sections include Ludwig's Tristan and Isolde–themed bedroom, dominated by a huge Gothic-style bed crowned with intricately carved cathedral-like spires; a gaudy artificial grotto (another allusion to Tannhäuser); and the Byzantine-style Thronsaal (Throne Room) with an incredible mosaic floor containing over two million stones. The painting opposite the (throneless) throne platform depicts another castle dreamed up by Ludwig that was never built (he planned many more). Almost every window provides tour-halting views across the plain below.

The tour ends with a 20-minute film on the castle and its creator, and there's a reasonably priced cafe and the inevitable gift shops.

For the postcard view of Neuschwanstein and the plains beyond, walk 10 minutes up to Marienbrücke (Mary's Bridge), which spans the spectacular Pöllat Gorge over a waterfall just above the castle. It's said Ludwig enjoyed coming up here after dark to watch the candlelight radiating from the Sängersaal.

★ **Schloss Hohenschwangau** CASTLE
(☑ 08362-930 830; www.hohenschwangau.de; Alpseestrasse 30; adult/child €13/free, incl Neuschwanstein €25/free; ☉ 8am-5pm Apr–mid-Oct, 9am-3pm mid-Oct–Mar) King Ludwig II grew up at the sun-yellow Schloss Hohenschwangau and later enjoyed summers here until his death in 1886. His father, Maximilian II, built this palace in a neo-Gothic style atop 12th-century ruins left by Schwangau knights. Far less showy than Neuschwanstein, Hohenschwangau has a distinctly lived-in feel where every piece of furniture is a used original. After his father died, Ludwig's main alteration was having stars, illuminated with hidden oil lamps, painted on the ceiling of his bedroom.

It was at Hohenschwangau where Ludwig first met Richard Wagner. The Hohenstaufensaal features a square piano where the hard-up composer would entertain Ludwig with excerpts from his latest creation. Some rooms have frescos from German mythology, including the story of the Swan Knight, *Lohengrin*. The swan theme runs throughout.

Hohes Schloss CASTLE, GALLERY
(Magnusplatz 10; adult/child €6/free; ☉ galleries 11am-5pm Tue-Sun Apr-Oct, 1-4pm Fri-Sun Nov-Mar) The Hohes Schloss, a late-Gothic confection and one-time retreat of the bishops of Augsburg, towers over Füssen's compact historical centre. The north wing of the palace contains the Staatsgalerie (State Gallery), with regional paintings and sculpture from the 15th and 16th centuries. The Städtische Gemäldegalerie (City Paintings Gallery) below is a showcase of 19th-century artists.

Tegelbergbahn CABLE CAR
(www.tegelbergbahn.de; one-way/return €13.30/20.60; ☉ 9am-5pm) For fabulous views of the Alps and the Forggensee, take this cable car to the top of the Tegelberg (1730m), a prime launching point for hang-gliders and parasailers. From here it's a wonderful hike down to the castles (two to three hours); follow the signs to Königsschlösser). To get to the valley station, take RVO bus 73 or 78 (www.rvo-bus.de) from Füssen Bahnhof.

Museum Füssen MUSEUM
(Lechhalde 3; adult/child €6/free; ☉ 11am-5pm Tue-Sun Apr-Oct, 1-4pm Fri-Sun Nov-Mar) Below the Hohes Schloss, and integrated into the former Abbey of St Mang, this museum highlights Füssen's heyday as a 16th-century violin-making centre. You can also view the abbey's festive baroque rooms, Romanesque cloister and the St Anna Kapelle (AD 830) with its famous 'Dance of Death' paintings.

🛏 Sleeping

Old Kings Hostel HOSTEL €
(☑ 08362-883 4090; www.oldkingshostel.com; Franziskanergasse 2; dm €22, d from €44; 🛜) This great design hostel tucked away in the mesh of lanes in the old town has two dorms and three doubles, all with a different quirky, but

---

CASTLE TICKETS & TOURS

Schloss Neuschwanstein and Schloss Hohenschwangau can only be visited on guided tours (in German or English), which last about 35 minutes each (Hohenschwangau is first). Strictly timed tickets are available from the **Ticket Centre** (☑ 08362-930 830; www. hohenschwangau.de; Alpenseestrasse 12; ☉ 7.30am-5pm Apr–mid-Oct, 8.30am-3pm mid-Oct–Mar) at the foot of the castles. In summer, come as early as 8am to ensure you get in that day.

Enough time is left between tours for the steep 30- to 40-minute walk between the castles. Alternatively, you can take a horse-drawn carriage, which is only marginally quicker.

Tickets for the Museum of the Bavarian Kings (p94) can be bought at the Ticket Centre and at the museum itself.

All Munich's tour companies run day excursions out to the castles.

DON'T MISS

MUSEUM DER BAYERISCHEN KÖNIGE

Palace-fatigued visitors often head straight for the bus stop, coach park or nearest beer after a tour of the castles, most overlooking this worthwhile **museum** (Museum of the Bavarian Kings; www.museumderbayerischenkoenige.de; Alpseestrasse 27; adult/child €11/free; ⊙9am-5pm), installed in a former lakeside hotel 400m from the castle ticket office (heading towards Alpsee lake). The architecturally stunning museum is packed with historical background on Bavaria's former first family and well worth the extra legwork.

The big-window views across the stunningly beautiful lake (a great picnic spot) to the Alps are almost as stunning as the Wittelsbach bling on show, including Ludwig II's famous blue-and-gold robe.

not overplayed, theme. Kitchen, continental breakfast, laundry service and local beer are all available and the whole place is kept very neat and tidy.

Bavaria City Hostel　　　　HOSTEL €
(☑08362-926 6980; www.hostelfuessen.com; Reichenstrasse 15; dm/d from €18/44; ☞) The BCH is a colourful, well-run place created out of a part of the Zum Goldenen Posthorn Hotel. Dorms hold four to six people, and while bright, the themes will be a touch 'in-your-face' for some. The nine-bed dorm has a smooth, Japanese-Oriental thing going on, while the Mountain Lodge is an Alpine dream. Staff can help with most things such as tours and tickets.

★Hotel Sonne　　　　DESIGN HOTEL €€
(☑08362-9080; www.hotel-fuessen.de; Prinzregentenplatz 1; s/d from €90/110; ⓟ☞) Although traditional looking from outside, this Altstadt favourite offers an unexpected design-hotel experience within. Themed rooms feature everything from swooping bed canopies to big-print wallpaper, huge pieces of wall art to sumptuous fabrics. The public spaces are littered with pieces of art, period costumes and design features – the overall effect is impressive and slightly unusual for this part of Germany.

Altstadthotel Zum Hechten　　HOTEL €€
(☑08362-916 00; www.hotel-hechten.com; Ritterstrasse 6; s €60-85, d €95-120; ⓟ☞) This is one of Füssen's oldest hotels and one of its friendliest. Public areas are traditional in style, while the bedrooms are bright and modern with beautifully patterned parquet floors, large beds and sunny colours. The small but classy spa is great for relaxing after a day on the trail.

Fantasia　　　　DESIGN HOTEL €€
(☑08362-9080; www.hotel-fantasia.de; Ottostrasse 1; s €40-80, d €50-100; ☞) This late-19th-century former holiday home for nuns and monks has been converted into a quirky design hotel. The lounge is straight out of a design magazine; the rooms are slightly less wild, but still boast huge ceiling prints of Schloss Neuschwanstein and idiosyncratic furniture. There's a pleasant garden in which to unwind after a hard day's castle hopping.

Steakhaus　　　　GUESTHOUSE €€
(☑08362-509 883; www.steakhouse-fuessen. de; Tiroler Strasse 31; s/d €30/85; ⓟ☞) These budget rooms above a restaurant a 10-minute walk south of Füssen town centre, towards the border with Austria, will win no prizes for decor or character, but the location at the Lechfall gorge, with uncluttered views of the Alps, River Lech and surrounding forests, can be pure magic.

✖ Eating

Vinzenzmurr　　　　BAVARIAN €
(Reichenstrasse 35; all dishes under €6; ⊙8am-6pm Mon-Fri, 7.30am-1pm Sat) Füssen branch of the Munich butcher and self-service canteen offering no-nonsense portions of *Leberkäse* (meatloaf) in a bun, goulash soup, *Saures Lüngerl* (goat or beef lung with dumplings), bratwurst and schnitzel as well as something for those crazy vegetarians. No coffee or desserts.

Restaurant Ritterstub'n　　GERMAN €€
(☑08362-7759; www.restaurant-ritterstuben.de; Ritterstrasse 4; mains €10-18.50; ⊙11.30am-10pm Tue-Sun) This convivial pit stop has value-priced salads, snacks, lunch specials, fish, schnitzel and gluten-free dishes, and even a cute kids' menu. The medieval knight theme can be a bit grating but does little to distract from the filling food when you arrive hungry from the peaks.

Beim Olivenbauer AUSTRIAN, ITALIAN €€
(☑ 08362-6250; www.beim-olivenbauer.de; Ottostrasse 7; mains €8-19; ☺ 11.30am-11.30pm) The
Tyrol meets the Allgäu at this fun eatery,
its interior a jumble of Doric columns, mismatched tables and chairs, multihued paint
and assorted rural knick-knackery. Treat
yourself to a wheel of pizza and a glass of
Austrian wine, or go local with a plate of
Maultaschen (pork and spinach ravioli) and
a mug of local beer.

Zum Franziskaner BAVARIAN €€
(Kemptener Strasse 1; mains €6.50-18; ☺ 11.30am-
10pm) This popular restaurant specialises in
Schweinshaxe (pork knuckle) and schnitzel, prepared in more varieties than you
can imagine. There's some choice for noncarnivores such as *Käsespätzle* (rolled

cheese noodles) and salads. When the sun
shines the outdoor seating shares the pavement with the 'foot-washing' statue.

Zum Hechten BAVARIAN €€
(Ritterstrasse 6; mains €8-19; ☺ 10am-10pm) Füssen's best hotel restaurant has six different
spaces to enjoy and keeps things regional
with a menu of Allgäu staples like schnitzel
and noodles, Bavarian pork-themed favourites, and local specialities such as venison
goulash from the Ammertal.

ⓘ Information

Tourist Office (☑ 08362-938 50; www.
fuessen.de; Kaiser-Maximilian-Platz; ☺ 9am-
5pm Mon-Fri, 9.30am-3.30pm Sat) Very
professionally run operation where staff field
questions about the castles with a smile. Can
also help find rooms.

LUDWIG II, FAIRY-TALE KING
···

Every year on 13 June, a stirring ceremony takes place in Berg, on the eastern shore of
Lake Starnberg. A small boat quietly glides towards a cross just offshore and a plain wreath
is fastened to its front. The sound of a single trumpet cuts the silence as the boat returns
from this solemn ritual in honour of the most beloved king ever to rule Bavaria: Ludwig II.

The cross approximately marks the spot where Ludwig died under mysterious cir-
cumstances in 1886. His early death capped the life of a man at odds with the harsh
realities of a modern world no longer in need of a romantic and idealistic monarch.

Prinz Otto Ludwig Friedrich Wilhelm was a sensitive soul, fascinated by romantic epics, architecture and music, but his parents, Maximilian II and Marie, took little interest in
his musings and he suffered a lonely and joyless childhood. In 1864, at 18 years old, the
prince became king. He was briefly engaged to the sister of Elisabeth (Sisi), the Austrian
empress, but, as a rule, he preferred the company of men. He also worshipped composer
Richard Wagner, whose Bayreuth opera house was built with Ludwig's funds.

Ludwig was an enthusiastic leader initially, but Bavaria's days as a sovereign state
were numbered, and he became a puppet king after the creation of the German Reich
in 1871 (which had its advantages, as Bismarck gave Ludwig a hefty allowance). Ludwig
withdrew completely to drink, draw up castle plans and view concerts and operas in
private. His obsession with French culture and the Sun King, Louis XIV, inspired the fantastical palaces of Neuschwanstein (p92), Linderhof (p97) and Herrenchiemsee (p104)
– lavish projects that spelt his undoing.

Contrary to popular belief, it was only Ludwig's purse – and not the state treasury – that
was being bankrupted. However, by 1886 his evergrowing mountain of debt and erratic behaviour had put him at odds with his cabinet. The king, it seemed, needed to be 'managed'.

In January 1886, several ministers and relatives arranged a hasty psychiatric test that
diagnosed Ludwig as mentally unfit to rule (this was made easier by the fact that his
brother had been declared insane years earlier). That June, he was removed to Schloss
Berg on Lake Starnberg. A few days later the dejected bachelor and his doctor took a
Sunday evening lakeside walk and were found several hours later, drowned in just a few
feet of water.

No one knows with certainty what happened that night. There was no eyewitness
nor any proper criminal investigation. The circumstantial evidence was conflicting and
incomplete. Reports and documents were tampered with, destroyed or lost. Conspiracy
theories abound. That summer the authorities opened Neuschwanstein to the public to
help pay off Ludwig's huge debts. King Ludwig II was dead, but the myth, and a tourist
industry, had been born.

ℹ️ Getting There & Away

BUS

The **Deutsche Touring** (www.touring.de, www.romantic-road.com) **Romantic Road Coach** (p109) leaves from outside Füssen train station (stop 3) at 8am. It arrives in Füssen at 8.30pm.

TRAIN

If you want to do the castles in a single day from Munich, you'll need to start very early. The first train leaves Munich at 4.48am (€28.40, change in Kaufbeuren), reaching Füssen at 6.49am. Otherwise, direct trains leave Munich once every two hours throughout the day.

ℹ️ Getting Around

BUS

RVO buses 78 and 73 (www.rvo-bus.de) serve the castles from Füssen Bahnhof (€4.40 return, eight minutes, at least hourly). Buy tickets from the driver.

Oberammergau

📞 08822 / POP 5400

Quietly quaint Oberammergau occupies a wide valley surrounded by the dark forests and snow-dusted peaks of the Ammergauer Alps. The centre is packed with traditional painted houses, woodcarving shops and awestruck tourists who come here to learn about the town's world-famous Passion Play. It's also a great budget base for hikes and cross-country skiing trips into easily accessible Alpine backcountry.

⊙ Sights

Passionstheater THEATRE
(📞 08822-941 36; www.passionstheater.de; Othmar-Weis-Strasse 1; tour adult/child €6/2, combined tour & Oberammergau Museum entry €8/3; ⊙ 10am-5pm Tue-Sun) The Passionstheater, where the Passion Play is performed, can be visited as part of a guided tour. The tour provides ample background on the play's history and also lets you peek at the costumes and

sets. Ask the tourist office about music, plays and opera performances that take place here over the summer.

Oberammergau Museum MUSEUM
(📞 08822-941 36; www.oberammergaumuseum.de; Dorfstrasse 8; adult/child €3.50/1.50, combined museum entry & Passiontheater tour adult/concession €6/5; ⊙ 10am-5pm Tue-Sun Apr-Oct) This is one of the best places to view exquisite examples of Oberammergau's famously intricate woodcarving art. The village has a long tradition of craftspeople producing anything from an entire nativity scene in a single walnut shell to a life-size Virgin Mary. If you get the urge to take some home, plenty of specialist shops around town sell pricey pieces.

Pilatushaus NOTABLE BUILDING
(📞 08822-949 511; Ludwig-Thoma-Strasse 10; ⊙ 1-6pm Tue-Sun mid-May–mid-Oct) FREE Aside from the Passion Play, Oberammergau's other claim to fame is its Lüftmalerei, the eye-popping house facades painted in an illusionist style. The pick of the crop is the amazing Pilatushaus, whose painted columns snap into 3D as you approach. It contains a gallery of glass traditional painting on the 1st floor and several workshops where you can watch demonstrations of local crafts.

🎭 Festivals & Events

⭐ **Passion Play** THEATRE
(www.passionplay-oberammergau.com) A blend of opera, ritual and Hollywood epic, the Passion Play has been performed every year ending in a zero (plus some extra years for a variety of reasons) since the late 17th century as a collective thank you from the villagers for being spared the plague.

Half the village takes part, sewing amazing costumes and growing hair and beards for their roles (no wigs or false hair allowed). The next performances will take place between May and October 2020, but tours of

---

WORTH A TRIP

KLOSTER ETTAL

Ettal would be just another bend in the road were it not for this famous **monastery** (www.kloster-ettal.de; Kaiser-Ludwig-Platz 1, Ettal; ⊙ 8.30am-noon & 1.15-5.45pm Mon-Sat, 9-10.45am & 2.30-5.30pm Sun). The highlight here is the sugary rococo basilica housing the monks' prized possession, a marble Madonna brought from Rome by Ludwig der Bayer in 1330. However, some might argue that the real high point is sampling the monastically distilled Ettaler Klosterlikör, an equally sugary herbal digestif.

Ettal is 5km south of Oberammergau, an easy hike along the Ammer River. Otherwise take bus 9606 from Garmisch-Partenkirchen or Oberammergau.

SCHLOSS LINDERHOF

A pocket-sized trove of weird treasures, Schloss Linderhof (www.schlosslinderhof.de; adult/child €8.50/free; ⊙9am-6pm Apr–mid-Oct, 10am-4.30pm mid-Oct–Mar) was Ludwig II's smallest but most sumptuous palace, and the only one he lived to see fully completed. Finished in 1878, the palace hugs a steep hillside in a fantasy landscape of French gardens, fountains and follies. The reclusive king used the palace as a retreat and hardly ever received visitors here. Linderhof was inspired by Versailles and dedicated to Louis XIV, the French 'Sun King'.

Linderhof's myth-laden, jewel-encrusted rooms are a monument to the king's excesses that so unsettled the governors in Munich. The private bedroom is the largest, heavily ornamented and anchored by an enormous 108-candle crystal chandelier weighing 500kg. An artificial waterfall, built to cool the room in summer, cascades just outside the window. The dining room reflects the king's fetish for privacy and inventions. The king ate from a mechanised dining board, whimsically labelled 'Table, Lay Yourself', that sank through the floor so that his servants could replenish it without being seen.

Created by the famous court gardener Carl von Effner, the gardens and outbuildings, open April to October, are as fascinating as the castle itself. The highlight is the oriental-style Moorish Kiosk, where Ludwig, dressed in oriental garb, would preside over nightly entertainment from a peacock throne. Underwater light dances on the stalactites at the Venus Grotto, an artificial cave inspired by a stage set for Wagner's *Tannhäuser*. Now sadly empty, Ludwig's fantastic conch-shaped boat is moored by the shore.

Linderhof is about 13km west of Oberammergau and 26km northwest of Garmisch-Partenkirchen. Bus 9622 travels to Linderhof from Oberammergau nine times a day. If coming from Garmisch-Partenkirchen change in Ettal or Oberammergau. The last service from Linderhof is just before 6pm but, if you miss it, the 13km vista-rich hike back to Oberammergau is an easygoing amble along the valley floor through shady woodland.

the Passionstheater enable you to take a peek at the costumes and sets any time.

The theatre doesn't lie dormant in the decade between Passion Plays – ask the tourist office about music, plays and opera performances that take place here over the summer.

🛏 Sleeping & Eating

Gästehaus Richter B&B €
(☎08822-935 765; www.gaestehaus-richter.de; Welfengasse 2; s €36-42, d €70-85; 🔊) The best deal in Oberammergau, this family-run guesthouse offers well-maintained rooms with some traditional Alpine elements, guest kitchen and a hearty breakfast.

DJH Hostel HOSTEL €
(☎08822-4114; www.oberammergau.jugendher berge.de; Malensteinweg 10; dm from €23) This oddly wood-clad hostel provides immaculate en suite rooms, a guest kitchen and a filling Alpine breakfast.

Hotel Turmwirt HOTEL €€
(☎08822-926 00; www.turmwirt.de; Ettalerstrasse 2; s/d from €90/115; 🔊) This well-maintained hotel next to the church has pristine business-standard rooms, some with Alpine views from the balconies and bits of woodcarving art and traditional Alpine furniture throughout.

Mundart BAVARIAN €€
(☎08822-949 7565; www.restaurant-mundart.de; Bahnhofstrasse 12; mains €13-21; ⊙5-11pm Wed-Fri, from 11am Sat & Sun; 🔊) Mouth-wateringly light, 21st-century versions of Bavarian classics await at this trendy, baby-blue and grey themed restaurant near the train station. The menu is reassuringly brief, prices reasonable and the service the best in the village. Always a choice of dishes for noncarnivores.

❶ Information

Tourist Office (☎08822-922 740; www. ammergauer-alpen.de; Eugen-Papst-Strasse 9a; ⊙9am-6pm Mon-Fri, to 1pm Sat & Sun, closed Sat & Sun Nov-Mar)

❶ Getting There & Away

Hourly trains connect Munich with Oberammergau (change at Murnau; €22, 1¾ hours). Hourly RVO bus 9606 goes direct to Garmisch-Partenkirchen via Ettal; change at Echelsbacher Brücke for Füssen.

Garmisch-Partenkirchen

☎08821 / POP 27,150

The double-barrelled resort of Garmisch-Partenkirchen is blessed with a fabled setting just a snowball's throw from the Alps and is a top hang-out for outdoorsy types, skiing fans and day-trippers from Munich. To say you 'wintered in Garmisch' still has an aristocratic ring, and the area offers some of the best skiing in the land, including runs on Germany's highest peak, the Zugspitze (2962m).

The towns of Garmisch and Partenkirchen were merged for the 1936 Winter Olympics and, to this day, host international skiing events. Each retains its own distinct character: Garmisch has a more 21st-century feel, while Partenkirchen has retained its old-world Alpine village vibe.

Sights

★Zugspitze MOUNTAIN

(Map p99; www.zugspitze.de; return adult/child €56/32; ⌚train 8.15am-2.15pm) On good days, views from Germany's rooftop extend into four countries. The round trip starts in Garmisch aboard a cogwheel train (Zahnradbahn) that chugs along the mountain base to the Eibsee, an idyllic forest lake. From here, the Eibsee-Seilbahn, a supersteep cable car, swings to the top at 2962m. When you're done admiring the views, the Gletscherbahn cable car takes you to the Zugspitze glacier at 2600m, from where the cogwheel train heads back to Garmisch.

Partnachklamm CANYON

(Map p99; www.partnachklamm.eu; adult/child €5/2; ⌚8am-6pm May & Oct, 6am-10pm Jun-Sep, 9am-6pm Nov-Apr) A top attraction around Garmisch is this narrow and dramatically beautiful 700m-long gorge with walls rising up to 80m. The trail hewn into the rock is especially spectacular in winter when you can walk beneath curtains of icicles and frozen waterfalls.

Jagdschloss Schachen CASTLE

(Map p99; ☎08822-920 30; adult/child €4.50/free; ⌚tours 11am, 1pm, 2pm & 3pm Jun-Sep) A popular hiking route is to King Ludwig II's hunting lodge, Jagdschloss Schachen, which can be reached via the Partnachklamm in about a four-hour hike (10km). A plain wooden hut from the outside, the interior is surprisingly magnificent; the Moorish Room is something straight out of *Arabian Nights*.

Kirchdorf Wamberg VILLAGE

(Map p99; Wamberg) For an easy hike accompanied by achingly quaint, chocolate-box views head to Germany's highest Kirchdorf (basically a hamlet with a church where services are held). You can walk from near the hospital (around 45 minutes) or take the Eckbauerbahn lift then walk along the path heading northeast through some exquisite Alpine scenery. The views from the village are worth the effort.

Activities

★Zugspitzbahn RAIL

(Map p100; www.zugspitze.de; return adult/concession €56/32) You can climb Germany's highest mountain on foot…or you can take the train! Trains leave from a special station next to G-P's main train terminus. The first train in the morning departs at 8.15am, the last service from the top at 4.30pm with hourly trains in between.

Deutscher Alpenverein HIKING

(Map p100; ☎08821-2701; www.alpenverein-gapa.de; Carl-Reiser-Strasse 2; ⌚4-6pm Tue, 10am-noon Wed & Fri, 4-7pm Thu) The German Alpine Club offers guided hikes and courses and its website is a mine of detailed, expertly updated local information, albeit in German only.

Bergsteigerschule Zugspitze HIKING

(Map p99; ☎08821-589 99; www.bergsteiger-schule-zugspitze.de; Am Kreuzeckbahnhof 12a; ⌚8am-noon & 1-5pm Mon-Fri) A mountaineering school offering guided hikes and courses. Located at the lower station of the Alpspitzbahn, southwest of the town.

Skischule SKIING

(Map p100; ☎08821-4931; www.skischule-gap.de; Am Hausberg 8) Offers a high standard of skiing courses as well as equipment hire.

Alpensport Total SKIING

(Map p100; ☎08821-1425; www.alpensporttotal.de; Marienplatz 18; ⌚8am-6pm) Winter ski school and hire centre that organises other outdoor activities in the warmer months.

Sleeping

DJH Hostel HOSTEL €

(Map p99; ☎08821-967 050; www.garmisch.jugendherberge.de; Jochstrasse 10; dm from €26; P@📶) The standards at this smart, immaculately maintained hostel are as good as at some chain hotels. Rooms have Ikea-style furnishings and fruity colour schemes, and there are indoor and outdoor climbing walls if the Alps are not enough. Located 4.5km north of the town.

Transfers from the train station cost a whopping €65 so either walk or catch bus 3 or 4 from outside the train station to Burgrain.

Around Garmisch-Partenkirchen

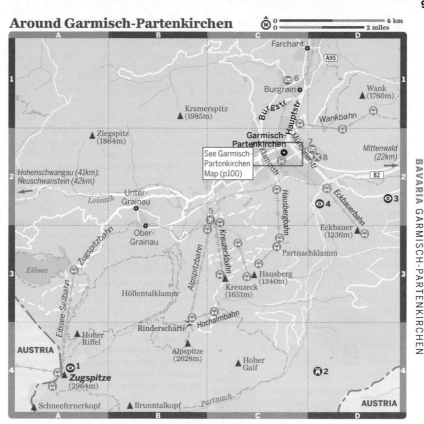

Around Garmisch-Partenkirchen

◎ Top Sights
1 Zugspitze..A4

◎ Sights
2 Jagdschloss Schachen........................D4
3 Kirchdorf Wamberg D2
4 Partnachklamm..................................D2

◯ Activities, Courses & Tours
5 Bergsteigerschule Zugspitze C2

◯ Sleeping
6 DJH Hostel...C1
7 Gasthof zum Rassen D2

◯ Eating
8 Gasthof Fraundorfer D2

★ **Reindl's Partenkirchner Hof**   HOTEL €€
(Map p100; ☏ 08821-943 870; www.reindls.de; Bahnhofstrasse 15; s/d €100/150; Ⓟ 🛜) Reindl's may not look worthy of its five stars from street level, but this elegant, tri-winged luxury hotel is stacked with perks, a wine bar and a top-notch gourmet restaurant. Renovated to perfection on a rolling basis, the rooms are studies in folk-themed elegance and some enjoy gobsmacking Alpine views to get you in the mood.

Gasthof zum Rassen   HOTEL €€
(Map p99; ☏ 08821-2089; www.gasthof-rassen. de; Ludwigstrasse 45; s/d from €70/90; Ⓟ 🛜) This beautifully frescoed 14th-century building is home to a great option in this price bracket, where the simply furnished, contemporary rooms contrast with the traditionally frilly styling of the communal areas. The cavernous event hall, which was formerly a brewery, houses Bavaria's oldest folk theatre.

Garmisch-Partenkirchen

Garmisch-Partenkirchen

Activities, Courses & Tours
1 Alpensport Total.................................A2
2 Bikecenter...D1
3 Deutscher Alpenverein.......................C1
4 Skischule...A2
5 Zugspitzbahn......................................C2

Sleeping
6 Hostel 2962.......................................C2
7 Hotel Garmischer Hof.........................B1
8 Reindl's Partenkirchner Hof...............C2

Eating
9 Bräustüberl..A1
10 Hofbräustüberl.................................B1
11 Zirbel..A2
12 Zum Wildschütz.................................A2

Hotel Garmischer Hof   HOTEL €€
(Map p100; ☎ 08821-9110; www.garmischer-hof.de; Chamonixstrasse 10; s €75-85, d €85-200; 🖧🖳) Owned by the Seiwald family since 1928, many a climber, skier and Alpine adventurer has creased the sheets at this welcoming inn. Rooms are elegant and cosy with some traditional Alpine touches, the buffet breakfast is served in the vaulted cafe-restaurant, and there's a spa and sauna providing après-ski relief.

Hostel 2962   HOSTEL €€
(Map p100; ☎ 08821-909 2674; www.hostel 2962-garmisch.com; Partnachauenstrasse 3; dm/d from €25/70; 🖧) Touted as a hostel, the somewhat vibe-less 2962 is essentially a typical Garmisch hotel with seven dorms, but a good choice nonetheless. If you can get into one of the four- or five-bed rooms, it's the cheapest sleep in town. Breakfast is an extra €6 if you stay in a dorm.

Eating

★ Gasthof Fraundorfer   BAVARIAN €€
(Map p99; ☎ 08821-9270; www.gasthof-fraun dorfer.de; Ludwigstrasse 24; mains €5-23; ⏱ 7am-midnight Thu-Mon, from 5pm Wed) If you've travelled to the Alps to experience yodelling, knee slapping and beetroot-faced locals squeezed into Lederhosen, you just arrived at the right address. Steins of frothing ale fuel the increasingly raucous atmosphere as the evening progresses and monster portions of plattered pig meat push belt buckles to the limit. Decor ranges from baroque cherubs to hunting trophies and the 'Sports Corner'. Unmissable.

Zum Wildschütz   BAVARIAN €€
(Map p100; Bankgasse 9; mains €9-20; ⏱ 11.30am-11pm) The best place in town for fresh venison, rabbit, wild boar and other seasonal game dishes, this place is, not surprisingly, popular with hunters. The Tyrolean and south Bavarian takes on schnitzel aren't bad either. If you prefer your victuals critter free, look elsewhere.

Zirbel   PUB FOOD €€
(Map p100; www.zirbel-stube.de; Promenadestrasse 2; mains €8-20; ⏱ 5pm-1am) A bit away from the tourist promenade and guarded by a grumpy-looking woodcarved bear, this locally popular, low-beamed and rustically themed pub serves noodle dishes, salads and schnitzel, all helped down with Hofbräu beer. Sadly, it's only open in the evenings.

Bräustüberl
GERMAN €€

(Map p100; ☑ 08821-2312; www.braeustueberl-garmisch.de; Fürstenstrasse 23; mains €6-19; ☺ from 5pm Mon-Fri, from 10am Sat & Sun) This quintessentially Bavarian tavern dating from 1663 is the place to cosy up with some local nosh, served by Dirndl-trussed waitresses, while the enormous enamel coal-burning stove revives snow-chilled extremities. Live music and theatre take place in the upstairs hall.

Hofbräustüberl
BAVARIAN, CROATIAN €€

(Map p100; Chamonixstrasse 2; mains €11-20; ☺11.30am-3pm & 5-11pm; ☎) Balkan spice meets south German heartiness at this Bavarian-Yugoslav restaurant right in the thick of things. Despite the seemingly *echt-Bayern* (authentic Bavarian) name, the long menu is a mixed bag of Alps and Adriatic, the interior understated and quite formal, the service top notch. The wines from the former Yugoslavia are a rare treat.

ⓘ Information

Mountain Rescue (☑ 08821-3611, 112; www.bergwacht-bayern.de; Auenstrasse 7) Mountain rescue station.

Post Office (Map p100; Bahnhofstrasse 30; ☺8am-6pm Mon-Fri, to 1pm Sat)

Tourist Office (Map p100; ☑ 08821-180 700; www.gapa.de; Richard-Strauss-Platz 2; ☺9am-5pm Mon-Fri, to 3pm Sat) Friendly staff hand out maps, brochures and advice.

ⓘ Getting There & Around

Garmisch-Partenkirchen has hourly connections from Munich (€22, one hour 20 minutes); special packages, available from Munich Hauptbahnhof, combine the return trip with a Zugspitze day ski pass (around €60).

RVO bus 9606 (www.rvo-bus.de) leaves from the **bus station** (Map p100; Bahnhofstrasse) at 9.40am, reaching the Füssen castles at Neuschwanstein and Hohenschwangau two hours later. On the way back take the 4.18pm bus 9651 and change onto the 9606 at Echelsbacher Brücke. The same connection runs at 5.18pm for those who want more time. The 9606 also runs hourly to Oberammergau (40 minutes).

For bike hire, try **Bikecenter** (Map p100; ☑ 08821-549 46; www.bikeverleih.de; Ludwigstrasse 90; ☺9am-6.30pm Mon-Fri, to 6pm Sat).

Mittenwald

☑ 08823 / POP 7400

Nestled in a cul-de-sac under snowcapped peaks, sleepily alluring Mittenwald, 20km southeast of Garmisch-Partenkirchen, is the most natural spot imaginable for a resort.

Known far and wide for its master violin makers, the citizens of this drowsy village seem almost bemused by its popularity. The air is ridiculously clean, and on the main street the loudest noise is a babbling brook.

⊙ Sights & Activities

Geigenbaumuseum
MUSEUM

(www.geigenbaumuseum-mittenwald.de; Ballenhausgasse 3; adult/child €5.50/2; ☺10am-5pm Tue-Sun Feb–mid-Mar & mid-May–mid-Oct, shorter hours rest of year) Matthias Klotz (1653–1743) is the man credited with turning Mittenwald into an internationally renowned centre of violin making. Learn more about him, his craft and the instrument itself in the engagingly organised Geigenbaumuseum. There's still a violin-making school in town today and the film showing the many steps required in fashioning the instrument is truly fascinating. The museum is also the venue for occasional concerts.

Erste Skischule Mittenwald
SKIING

(☑ 08823-3582; www.skischule-mittenwald.de; Bahnhofsplatz 14; ☺8am-6pm) Equipment hire and ski/snowboard instruction.

🛏 Sleeping & Eating

Hotel-Gasthof Alpenrose
HOTEL €€

(☑ 08823-927 00; www.alpenrose-mittenwald.de; Obermarkt 1; s €34-63, d €80-105; ☎) A purely Alpine affair, the friendly Hotel-Gasthof Alpenrose has cosy, old-style rooms, a folksy restaurant and live Bavarian music almost nightly. Staff can arrange horse-riding trips for all ages.

Gaststätte Römerschanz
BAVARIAN €€

(Innsbrucker Strasse 30; mains €7-17; ☺10am-midnight Wed-Mon; ☎) A short walk from the Obermarkt, the much-lauded Gaststätte Römerschanz has a cosy, seasonally decorated interior and Mittenwald's tastiest food served gourmet-style on odd-shaped plates.

🍺 Drinking

Postkeller
PUB

(www.brauereigaststaette-postkeller.de; Innsbrucker Strasse 13; ☺10am-late Fri-Tue, from 5pm Thu) This modern pub belongs to Mittenwald's very own brewery, and is hence the best place to try the local lager. It claims to be Germany's highest altitude brewery.

ⓘ Information

Tourist Office (☑ 08823-339 81; www.mittenwald.de; Dammkarstrasse 3; ☺8.30am-6pm

Mon-Fri, 9am-noon Sat, 10am-noon Sun mid-May–mid-Oct, shorter hours rest of the year) The professional team here keeps a well-maintained website and can help out with just about anything in the Mittenwald area.

ℹ Getting There & Away

Mittenwald is served by trains from Garmisch-Partenkirchen (€4.90, 20 minutes, hourly), Munich (€22, 1¾ hours, hourly) and Innsbruck (€11.10, one hour, every two hours), across the border in Austria. Otherwise RVO bus 9608 connects Mittenwald with Garmisch-Partenkirchen (30 minutes) several times a day.

Oberstdorf

📞 08322 / POP 9700

Spectacularly situated in the western Alps, the Allgäu region feels a long, long way from the rest of Bavaria, both in its cuisine (more *Spätzle* than dumplings) and the dialect, which is closer to the Swabian of Baden-Württemberg. The Allgäu's chief draw is the car-free resort of Oberstdorf, a major skiing centre that's just a short hop from Austria.

🎿 Activities

Oberstdorf is almost ringed by towering peaks and offers some top-draw hiking. In-the-know skiers value the resort for its friendliness, lower prices and less-crowded pistes. The village is surrounded by 70km of well-maintained cross-country trails and three ski fields: the Nebelhorn, Fellhorn/Kanzelwand and Söllereck. For ski hire and tuition, try **Alpin Skischule** (📞08322-952 90; www.alpinskischule.de; Bahnhofplatz 1a; ⊙8.30am-6pm) opposite the train station or **Erste Skischule Oberstdorf** (📞08322-3110; www.skischule-oberstdorf.de; Freiherr-von-Brutscher-Strasse 4).

Eissportzentrum Oberstdorf ICE SKATING
(📞08322-700 5003; www.eissportzentrum-oberstdorf.de; Rossbichlstrasse 2-6) The Eissportzentrum Oberstdorf, behind the Nebelhorn cable-car station, is the biggest ice-skating complex in Germany, with three separate rinks. Check the website for public skating session times.

🛏 Sleeping

Oberstdorf is chock-full of private guesthouses, but owners are usually reluctant to rent rooms for just a single night, even in the quieter shoulder seasons.

Oberstdorf Hostel HOSTEL €
(📞08322-987 8400; www.oberstdorf-hostel.de; Mühlbachstrasse 12; dm/s/d from €20/20/65; P🛜) This very family-friendly hostel in the village of Tiefenbach is around 10 minutes by car from Oberstdorf train station. Rooms with up to six beds are spotless, there's a playground for the kiddies and lots of activities going on. Prices include breakfast and there's a very good-value family package that includes dinner, too.

DJH Hostel HOSTEL €
(📞08322-987 50; www.oberstdorf.jugendherberge.de; Kornau 8; dm €24; 🛜) A relaxed, 200-bed chalet-hostel with commanding views of the Allgäu Alps. Take bus 1 from the bus station in front of the Hauptbahnhof to the Reute stop; it's in the suburb of Kornau, near the Söllereck chairlift.

Haus Edelweiss APARTMENT €€
(📞08322-959 60; www.edelweiss.de; Freibergstrasse 7; apt €50-145; P🔄🛜) As crisp and sparkling as freshly fallen alpine snow, this recently completed apartment hotel just a couple of blocks from the tourist office has 19 pristine, self-contained flats with fully equipped kitchens, ideal for stays of three nights or more. Generally the longer you tarry, the fewer euros per night you spend.

Weinklause GUESTHOUSE €€
(📞08322-969 30; www.weinklause.de; Prinzenstrasse 10; s/d from €75/100; P🛜) Willing to take one-nighting hikers at the drop of a felt hat, this superb lodge offers all shapes and sizes of room and apartment, some with kitchenettes, others with jaw-dropping, spectacular alpine views. A generous breakfast is served in the restaurant, which comes to life most nights with local live music.

🍴 Eating & Drinking

Restaurant-Cafe Allgäu BAVARIAN €€
(📞08322-809 657; www.restaurant-cafe-allgäu.de; Pfarrstrasse 10; mains €12-20; ⊙11.30am-10pm Wed-Sun; 🛜) For the best local Allgäu dishes, head to this long-established, knick-knack-filled restaurant where the pork knuckle, schnitzel, *Kartoffelrösti* (potato fritter) and of course signature *Käsespätzle* all come in Alpine portions. There are plenty of vegetarian dishes and superb local beer on tap.

⭐**Oberstdorfer Dampfbierbrauerei** BREWERY
(www.dampfbierbrauerei.de; Bahnhofplatz 8; ⊙11am-1am Wed-Sun) Knock back a few 'steamy ales' at

Germany's southernmost brewery, right next to the train station. The brewery runs free tours in German at 11am every Wednesday.

ℹ Information

Tourist Office (☑ 08322-7000; www.oberst dorf.de; Prinzregenten-Platz 1; ☺ 9am-5pm Mon-Fri, 9.30am-noon Sat) The tourist office and its **branch office** (☑ 08322-7000; Bahnhofplatz; ☺ 10am-5pm) at the train station runs a room-finding service.

ℹ Getting There & Away

There are direct Alex trains from Munich (€22.70, 2½ hours, every two hours), otherwise change in Buchloe or Kempten. The train station is a short walk north of the town centre on Bahnhofstrasse.

Bad Tölz

☑ 08041 / POP 18,500

Situated some 40km south of central Munich, Bad Tölz is a pretty spa town straddling the Isar River. The town's gentle inclines provide a delightful spot for its attractive, frescoed houses and the quaint shops of the old town. At weekends city folk flock here to wander the streets and for hiking trips along the river. Bad Tölz is also the gateway to the Tölzer Land region and its emerald-green lakes, the Walchensee and the Kochelsee.

◉ Sights & Activities

Cobblestoned and car-free, Marktstrasse is flanked by statuesque townhouses with ornate overhanging eaves that look twice as high on the sloping street.

Kalvarienberg   LANDMARK
(Cavalry Church; Kalvarienberg) Above the town, on Kalvarienberg, looms Bad Tölz' landmark, the twin-towered Kalvarienbergkirche. This enormous baroque structure stands side by side with the petite Leonhardikapelle (Leonhardi Chapel; 1718), the destination of the town's well-known Leonhardifahrt (Leonardi pilgrimage).

Stadtmuseum   MUSEUM
(☑ 8041-504 688; Marktstrasse 48; adult/child €2/1.50; ☺ 10am-5pm Tue-Sun) The Stadtmuseum covers all aspects of local culture and history, with a fine collection of painted armoires (the so-called Tölzer Kasten), a 2m-tall, single-stringed *Nonnengeige* (marine trumpet), examples of traditional glass painting and a cart used in the Leonhardifahrt.

Blomberg   HIKING
Southwest of Bad Tölz, the Blomberg (1248m) is a family-friendly mountain that has easy hiking and a fun Alpine slide in summer and a natural toboggan track in winter. Unless you're walking, getting up the hill involves, weather permitting, a chairlift ride aboard the **Blombergbahn** (www.blombergbahn.de; top station adult/child return €11/5; ☺ 9am-5pm).

Over 1km long, the fibreglass Alpine toboggan track snakes down the mountain from the middle station. You zip down at up to 50km/h through the 17 hairpin bends on little wheeled bobsleds with a joystick to control braking. A long-sleeved shirt and jeans are recommended to provide a little protection. To reach Blomberg, take RVO bus 9612 from the train station to the Blombergbahn stop.

✸ Festivals & Events

Leonhardifahrt   CULTURAL
(www.toelzer-leonhardifahrt.bayern; ☺ 6 Nov) Every year on 6 November, residents pay homage to the patron saint of horses, Leonhard. The famous Leonhardifahrt is a pilgrimage up to the Leonhardi chapel on Kalvarienberg, where townsfolk dress up in traditional costume and ride dozens of garlanded horse carts to the strains of brass bands.

🛏 Sleeping & Eating

Posthotel Kolberbräu   HOTEL €€
(☑ 08041-768 80; www.kolberbraeu.de; Marktstrasse 29; s/d from €50/90; ☏) Posthotel Kolberbräu is a very well-appointed, 30-room inn set amid the bustle of the main street, with hefty timber furniture, a classic Bavarian restaurant and a tradition going back four centuries.

Gasthof Zantl   BAVARIAN €€
(www.gasthof-zantl.de; Salzstrasse 31; mains €8-18; ☺ 5pm-late Fri-Mon, plus 11am-2.30pm Sat & Sun) One of Bad Tölz' oldest buildings, this convivial tavern has a predictably pork-heavy menu, with ingredients sourced from local villages as much as possible. There's a sunny beer garden out front.

ℹ Information

Tourist Office (☑ 08041-793 5156; www.bad-toelz.de; Marktstrasse 48; ☺ 10am-5pm Tue-Sun)

ℹ Getting There & Away

The private **Bayerische Oberlandbahn** (BOB; ☑ 08024-997 171; www.meridian-bob-brb. de) runs trains between Bad Tölz and Munich

BAVARIA BAD TÖLZ

Hauptbahnhof (€13.90, 50 minutes, at least hourly). Alternatively, take the S2 from central Munich to Holzkirchen, then change to the BOB. In Holzkirchen make sure you board the Bad Tölz–bound portion of the train.

Chiemsee

📞 08051

The Chiemsee is Bavaria's biggest lake (if you don't count Bodensee which is only partially in the state) and its natural beauty and water sports make the area popular with de-stressing city dwellers – many affluent Munich residents own weekend retreats by its shimmering waters. However, the vast majority of foreign visitors arrive at the shores of the Bavarian Sea – as Chiemsee is often called – in search of King Ludwig II's Schloss Herrenchiemsee.

The towns of Prien am Chiemsee and, about 5km south, Bernau am Chiemsee (both on the Munich–Salzburg rail line) are good bases for exploring the lake. Of the two towns, Prien is by far the larger and livelier.

◎ Sights

★ **Schloss Herrenchiemsee**   CASTLE
(📞 08051-688 70; www.herren-chiemsee.de; adult/child €11/free; ⊙ tours 9am-6pm Apr-Oct, 9.40am-4.15pm Nov-Mar) An island just 1.5km across the Chiemsee from Prien, Herreninsel is home to Ludwig II's Versailles-inspired castle. Begun in 1878, it was never intended as a residence, but as a homage to absolutist monarchy, as epitomised by Ludwig's hero, Louis XIV. Ludwig spent only 10 days here and even then was rarely seen, preferring to read at night and sleep all day. The palace is typical of Ludwig's creations, its design the product of his romantic obsessions and unfettered imagination.

Ludwig splurged more money on this palace than on Neuschwanstein and Linderhof combined, but when cash ran out in 1885, one year before his death, 50 rooms remained unfinished. Those that were completed outdo each other in opulence. The vast Gesandtentreppe (Ambassador Staircase), a double staircase leading to a frescoed gallery and topped by a glass roof, is the first visual knock-out on the guided tour, but that fades in comparison to the stunning Grosse Spiegelgalerie (Great Hall of Mirrors). This tunnel of light runs the length of the garden (98m, or 10m longer than that in Versailles). It sports 52 candelabra and 33 great glass chandeliers with 7000 candles, which took 70 servants half an hour to light.

In late July it becomes a wonderful venue for classical concerts.

The Paradeschlafzimmer (State Bedroom) features a canopied bed perching altarlike on a pedestal behind a golden balustrade. This was the heart of the palace, where morning and evening audiences were held. But it's the king's bedroom, the Kleines Blaues Schlafzimmer (Little Blue Bedroom), that really takes the cake. The decoration is sickly sweet, encrusted with gilded stucco and wildly extravagant carvings. The room is bathed in a soft blue light emanating from a glass globe at the foot of the bed. It supposedly took 18 months for a technician to perfect the lamp to the king's satisfaction.

Admission to the palace also entitles you to a spin around the König-Ludwig II-Museum, where you can see the king's christening and coronation robes, more blueprints of megalomaniac buildings and his death mask.

To reach the palace, take the hourly or half-hourly ferry from Prien-Stock or from Bernau-Felden. From the boat landing on Herreninsel, it's about a 20-minute walk through pretty gardens to the palace. Palace tours (in German or English) last 30 minutes.

Fraueninsel   ISLAND
A third of this tiny island is occupied by **Frauenwörth Abbey** (www.frauenwoerth. de; Fraueninsel; admission free, tours €4) `FREE`, founded in the late 8th century, making it one of the oldest abbeys in Bavaria. The 10th-century church, whose free-standing campanile sports a distinctive onion-dome top (11th century), is worth a visit. Opposite the church is the AD 860 Carolingian **Torhalle** (admission €2; ⊙ 10am-6pm May-Oct). It houses medieval objets d'art, sculpture and changing exhibitions of regional paintings from the 18th to the 20th centuries.

🏃 Activities

The swimming beaches at Chieming and Gstadt (both free) are the easiest to reach, on the lake's eastern and northern shores respectively. A variety of boats are available for hire at many beaches. In Prien, **Bootsverleih Stöffl** (📞 08051-2000; www.stoeffl.de; Seestrasse 120, Prien; ⊙ Easter-Oct) is possibly the best company to approach.

Prienavera   SWIMMING
(📞 08051-609 570; www.prienavera.de; Seestrasse 120, Prien; 4hr pass adult/child €12/7, day pass

€14/8; ⊙10am-10pm Mon-Fri, 9am-10pm Sat & Sun) The futuristic-looking glass roof by the harbour in Prien-Stock shelters Prienavera, a popular pool complex with a wellness area, water slides and a restaurant.

🛏 Sleeping

Panorama Camping Harras
CAMPGROUND €

(☑08051-904 613; www.camping-harras.de; Harrasser Strasse 135; per person/tent/car from €9.40/5.80/3.40) This camping ground is scenically located on a peninsula 3km south of Prien with its own private beach. There is water-sports equipment for hire and the restaurant-beer garden has a delightful lakeside terrace.

Hotel Bonnschlössl
HOTEL €€

(☑08051-961 400; www.bonnschloessl.de; Ferdinand-Bonn-Strasse 2, Bernau; s €50-75, d €85-180; ℗🐾) Built in 1477, this pocket-size 21-room palace hotel with faux turrets once belonged to the Bavarian royal court. Rooms are stylish, if slightly overfurnished, and there's a wonderful terrace with a rambling garden. There's a small spa area, a library and a lobby bar, but no restaurant.

Luitpold am See
HOTEL €€

(☑08051-609 100; www.luitpold-am-see.de; Seestrasse 101, Prien; s €60-80, d €115-155; 🐾) Right on the lake shore in Prien, the 54 rooms at this excellent hotel offer a good price to standard ratio, with their pristine bathrooms, wood-rich furnishings and pretty views. There's an on-site restaurant and *Konditorei* (cafe-bakery) and reception can help out with travel arrangements, tours and the like.

🍴 Eating

Alter Wirt
BAVARIAN €€

(www.alter-wirt-bernau.de; Kirchplatz 9, Bernau; mains €10-19; ⊙8am-11pm Tue-Sun) This massive half-timbered inn with seven centuries of history, situated on Bernau's main street, plates up south German meat slabs and international standards to a mix of locals and tourists. For dessert why not try *Heisse Liebe* ('Hot Love') – vanilla and chocolate ice cream with hot raspberry sauce and cream.

Westernacher am See
BAVARIAN €€

(☑08051-4722; www.westernacher-chiemsee.de; Seestrasse 115, Prien; mains €5.50-18.50; ⊙8am-11pm) This busy lakeside dining haven has multiple personalities, with a cosy restaurant, cocktail bar, cafe, beer garden and glassed-in winter terrace. The long menu is an eclectic affair combining pizzas, Bavarian favourites, Italian pasta, Thai curries and Chiemsee fish dishes.

Sallers Badehaus
BAVARIAN €€

(☑08051-966 3450; www.sallers-badehaus.de; Rathausstrasse 11; mains €8-20; ⊙11am-11pm Mon-Fri, from 9am Sat & Sun; 🐾) Near the Chiemsee Tourist Office and the lake shore, this fancy restaurant, contemporary beer hall and garden has quirky decor and gourmet-style fare priced for all wallet capacities.

❶ Information

Bernau Tourist Office (☑08051-986 80; www.bernau-am-chiemsee.de; Aschauer Strasse 10, Bernau; ⊙9am-6pm Mon-Fri, 9am-noon Sat, slightly shorter hours mid-Sep–mid-Jul)
Chiemsee Tourist Office (☑08051-965 550; www.chiemsee-alpenland.de; Felden 10; ⊙10am-12.30pm & 1.30-6.30pm Mon-Fri) On the southern lake shore, near the Bernau-Felden autobahn exit.
Prien Tourist Office (☑08051-690 50; www.tourismus.prien.de; Alte Rathausstrasse 11, Prien; ⊙8.30am-6pm Mon-Fri, to 4pm Sat, closed Sat Oct-Apr)

❶ Getting There & Away

If you're day tripping to Herrenchiemsee, conveniently interconnecting transport is available. To explore more, you'll need a set of wheels.

Meridian trains run from Munich to Prien (€20.50, 55 minutes, hourly) and Bernau (€21.50, one hour, hourly). Hourly RVO bus 9505 connects the two lake towns.

❶ Getting Around

Local buses run from Prien Bahnhof to the harbour in Stock. You can also take the historic **Chiemseebahn** (www.chiemsee-schifffahrt.de; return €4), one of the world's oldest narrow-gauge steam trains (1887).

Chiemsee-Schifffahrt (☑08051-6090; www.chiemsee-schifffahrt.de; Seestrasse 108) operates half-hourly to hourly ferries from Prien with stops at Herreninsel, Fraueninsel, Seebruck and Chieming on a schedule that changes seasonally. You can circumnavigate the entire lake and make all these stops (getting off and catching the next ferry that comes your way) for €13. Children aged six to 15 get a 50% discount.

Chiemgau Biking (☑08051-961 4973; www.chiemgau-biking.de; Chiemseestrasse 84, Bernau; per day from €9; ⊙8.30am-6pm Mon-Fri, 9am-1pm Sat) and **Bike Rental Fritz Müller** (☑08051-961 4948; www.fahrradverleih-chiemsee.de; Felden 12, Bernau; per day from €9), both in Bernau, hire out bikes and run bike tours of the lake area.

Berchtesgaden

📞 08652 / POP 7800

Plunging deep into Austria and framed by six high-rise mountain ranges, the Berchtesgadener Land is a drop-dead-gorgeous corner of Bavaria steeped in myths and legends. Local lore has it that angels given the task of distributing the earth's wonders were startled by God's order to get a shift on and dropped them all here by accident. These most definitely included the Watzmann (2713m), Germany's second-highest mountain, and the pristine Königssee, perhaps Germany's most photogenic body of water.

Much of the area is protected by law within the Berchtesgaden National Park, which was declared a biosphere reserve by Unesco in 1990. The village of Berchtesgaden is the obvious base for hiking circuits into the park.

Away from the trails, the area has a more sinister aspect – the mountaintop Eagle's Nest was a lodge built for Hitler and is now a major dark-tourism destination while the Dokumentation Obersalzberg chronicles the region's Nazi past.

◉ Sights

★ Eagle's Nest   HISTORIC SITE

(Kehlsteinhaus; 📞 08652-29 69; www.kehlstein haus.de; Obersalzberg; tour €30.50; ⊙ buses 8.30am-4.50pm mid-May–Oct) Located at 1834m above sea level, the Eagle's Nest was built as a mountaintop retreat for Hitler, and gifted to him on his 50th birthday. It took around 3000 workers a mere two years to carve the precipitous 6km-long mountain road, cut a 124m-long tunnel and a brass-panelled lift through the rock, and build the lodge itself (now a restaurant). It can only be reached by special shuttle bus from the Kehlsteinhaus bus station.

On clear days, views from the top are breathtaking. If you're not driving, bus 838 makes the trip to the shuttle bus stop from the Berchtesgaden Hauptbahnhof every half-hour.

At the mountain station, you'll be asked to book a spot on a return bus. Allow at least two hours to get through lines, explore the lodge and the mountaintop, and perhaps have a bite to eat. Tours including the bus and guide can be booked online in advance.

★ Königssee   LAKE

(Schönau am Königsee) Gliding serenely across the wonderfully picturesque, emerald-green Königssee makes for some unforgettable memories and photo opportunities. Cradled by steep mountain walls some 5km south of Berchtesgaden, the Königssee is Germany's highest lake (603m), with drinkably pure waters shimmering into fjordlike depths. Bus 841/843 makes the trip out here from the Berchtesgaden train station roughly every hour.

Escape the hubbub of the bustling lakeside tourist village of Schönau by taking an electric boat tour (p108) to St Bartholomä, a quaint onion-domed chapel on the western shore. At some point, the boat will stop while the captain plays a horn towards the Echo Wall – the sound will bounce seven times. From St Bartholomä, an easy trail leads to the wondrous Eiskapelle (ice chapel) in about one hour.

You can also skip the crowds by meandering along the lake shore. It's a nice and easy 3.5km return walk to the secluded Malerwinkel (Painter's Corner), a lookout famed for its picturesque vantage point.

★ Dokumentation Obersalzberg   MUSEUM

(📞 08652-947 960; www.obersalzberg.de; Salzbergstrasse 41, Obersalzberg; adult/child €3/free, audioguide €2; ⊙ 9am-5pm daily Apr-Oct, 10am-3pm Tue-Sun Nov-Mar, last entry 1hr before closing) In 1933 the tranquil Alpine settlement of Obersalzberg (3km from Berchtesgaden) in essence became the second seat of Nazi power after Berlin, a dark period that's given the full historical treatment at this superb exhibition. Various rooms document the forced takeover of the area, the construction of the compound and the daily life of the Nazi elite. All facets of Nazi terror are dealt with, including Hitler's near-mythical appeal, his racial politics, the resistance movement, foreign policy and the death camps.

Berchtesgaden National Park   NATIONAL PARK

(www.nationalpark-berchtesgaden.de) Forty years old in 2018, the wilds of this 210-sq-km park still offer some of the best hiking in Germany. A good introduction is a 2km trail up from St Bartholomä beside the Königssee to the notorious Watzmann-Ostwand, where scores of mountaineers have met their deaths. Another popular hike goes from the southern end of the Königssee to the Obersee.

For details of routes visit the **national park office** (Haus der Berge; 📞 08652-979 0600; www.haus-der-berge.bayern.de; Hanielstrasse 7; exhibition €4; ⊙ 9am-5pm), or buy a copy of the Berchtesgadener Land (sheet 794) map in

HITLER'S MOUNTAIN RETREAT
....

Of all the German towns tainted by the Third Reich, Berchtesgaden has a burden heavier than most. Hitler fell in love with nearby Obersalzberg in the 1920s and bought a small country home, later enlarged into the imposing Berghof.

After seizing power in 1933, Hitler established a part-time headquarters here and brought much of the party brass with him. They bought, or often confiscated, large tracts of land and tore down farmhouses to erect a 7ft-high barbed-wire fence. Obersalzberg was sealed off as the fortified southern headquarters of the NSDAP (National Socialist German Workers' Party). In 1938, British prime minister Neville Chamberlain visited for negotiations (later continued in Munich), which led to the infamous promise of 'peace in our time' at the expense of Czechoslovakia's Sudetenland.

Little is left of Hitler's Alpine fortress today. In the final days of WWII, the Royal Air Force levelled much of Obersalzberg, though the Eagle's Nest, Hitler's mountaintop eyrie, was left strangely unscathed. The historical twist and turns are dissected at the impressive Dokumentation Obersalzberg.

the Kompass series, available across Germany or online.

Salzbergwerk   HISTORIC SITE
(www.salzzeitreise.de; Bergwerkstrasse 83; adult/child €17/9.50; ☺9am 5pm Apr-Oct, 11am-3pm Nov-Mar) Once a major producer of 'white gold', Berchtesgaden has thrown open its salt mines for fun-filled 1½-hour tours. Kids especially love donning miners' garb and whooshing down a wooden slide into the depths of the mine. Down below, highlights include mysteriously glowing salt grottoes and crossing a 100m-long subterranean salt lake on a wooden raft. Take hourly bus 840 from Berchtesgaden train station.

🏃 Activities

Jenner-Königssee Area   SKIING
(www.jennerbahn.de; daily pass €33) The Jenner-Königssee area at Königssee is the biggest and most varied of five local ski fields. For equipment hire and courses, try **Skischule Treff-Aktiv** (✆08652-66710; www.skischule-treffaktiv.de; Jennerbahnstrasse 16).

Watzmann Therme   SPA
(✆08652-946 40; www.watzmann-therme.de; Bergwerkstrasse 54; 2hr/4hr/day €11.70/15.40/17.70; ☺10am-10pm) The Watzman Therme is Berchtesgaden's thermal wellness complex, with several indoor and outdoor pools and various hydrotherapeutic treatment stations, a sauna and inspiring Alpine views.

👉 Tours

Eagle's Nest Tours   TOURS
(✆08652-649 71; www.eagles-nest-tours.com; Königsseer Strasse 2; €55; ☺1.15pm mid-May–Oct) This highly reputable outfit offers a fascinat-

ing overview of Berchtesgaden's Nazi legacy. Guest are taken not only to the Eagle's Nest but around the Obersalzberg area and into the underground bunker system. The four-hour English-language tour departs from the tourist office, across the roundabout opposite the train station. Booking ahead is advisable in July and August.

🛏 Sleeping

DJH Hostel   HOSTEL €
(✆08652-943 70; www.berchtesgaden.jugendherberge.de; Struberberg 6; dm from €23; ☜) This 265-bed hostel is situated in the suburb of Strub, and has great views of Mt Watzmann. It's a 25-minute walk from the Hauptbahnhof or a short hop on bus 839.

KS Hostel Berchtesgaden   HOSTEL €
(✆08652-979 8420; www.hostel-berchtesgaden.de; Bahnhofplatz 4; dm from €23; P☜) This basic hostel above a Burger King is actually attached to the railway station, making it good for arrival and departure as well as for accessing buses to the sights. Rooms are spartan but there's cycle storage, free parking and common rooms on all floors.

★**Hotel Reikartz
Vier Jahreszeiten**   HOTEL €€
(✆08652-9520; www.hotel-vierjahreszeiten-berchtesgaden.de; Maximilianstrasse 20; r from €70; ☺reception 7am-11pm; P☜☈) For a taste of Berchtesgaden's storied past, stay at this traditional lodge where Bavarian royalty once crumpled the sheets. Rooms are very well kept and the south-facing (more-expensive) quarters offer dramatic views of the peaks. After a day's sightseeing, dinner in the hunting lodge–style Hubertusstuben restaurant is a real treat.

Hotel Edelweiss HOTEL €€
(🖉08652-979 90; www.edelweiss-berchtesgaden. com; Maximilianstrasse 2; d incl breakfast €110-200; 🛜🖵) In the heart of town, the Edelweiss is a sleek affair. The style could be described as modern Bavarian, meaning a combination of traditional woodsy flair and factors such as a luxe spa, a rooftop terrace restaurant-bar with widescreen Alpine views and an outdoor infinity pool. Rooms are XL-sized and most have a balcony.

Hotel Bavaria HOTEL €€
(🖉08652-966 10; www.hotelbavaria.net; Sunklergässchen 11; s/d from €50/110; 🅿) Belonging to the same family for well over a century, this professionally run hotel offers a romantic vision of Alpine life with rooms bedecked in frilly curtains, canopied beds, heart-shaped mirrors and knotty wood galore. Five of the pricier rooms have private whirlpools. Breakfast is a gourmet affair, with sparkling wine and both hot and cold delectables.

Hotel Krone HOTEL €€
(🖉08652-946 00; www.hotel-krone-berchtes gaden.de; Am Rad 5; s €45-55, d €80-120; @🛜🖵) Within ambling-distance of Berchtesgaden centre, this family-run gem provides almost unrivalled views of the valley and the Alps beyond. The timber-rich cabin-style rooms are generously cut affairs, with carved ceilings, niches and bedsteads all in aromatic pine. Take breakfast on the suntrap terrace for a memorable start, and end the day with a sauna or Roman steam bath.

🍴 Eating

⭐**Gaststätte St Bartholomä** BAVARIAN €€
(🖉08652-964 937; www.bartholomae-wirt.de; St Bartholomä; mains €10-20; ⊙open according to the boat tour timetable) Perched on the shore of the Königssee, and accessible by **boat tour** (🖉08652-963 60; www.seenschifffahrt.de; Schönau; return boat €15; ⊙boats 8am-5.15pm mid-Jun–mid-Sep, shorter hours rest of the year), this is a tourist haunt that actually serves delicious food made with ingredients picked, plucked and hunted from the surrounding forests and the lake. Savour generous platters of venison in mushroom sauce with dumplings and red sauerkraut in the large beer garden or indoors.

⭐**Bräustübl** BAVARIAN €€
(🖉08652-976 724; www.braeustueberl-bercht esgaden.de; Bräuhausstrasse 13; mains €7-17;

⊙10am-midnight) Past the vaulted entrance painted in Bavaria's white and blue diamonds this lively but cosy beer hall–beer garden is run by the local brewery. Expect a carnivorous feast with favourites such as pork roast and the house speciality: breaded calf's head (tastes better than it sounds). On Friday and Saturday, an oompah band launches into knee-slapping action.

Le Ciel INTERNATIONAL €€€
(🖉08652-975 50; www.restaurant-leciel.de; Hintereck 1; mains €30-40; ⊙6.30-10.30pm Wed-Sat; 🛜) Don't let the Hotel InterConti location turn you off: Le Ciel really is as heavenly as its French name suggests and it has the Michelin star to prove it. Testers were especially impressed by Ulrich Heimann's knack for spinning regional ingredients into inspired gourmet compositions. Service is smooth and the circular dining room is magical.

ℹ Information

Post Office (Franziskanerplatz 2; ⊙9am-noon & 2-5pm Mon-Fri, 9am-noon Sat)

Tourist Office (🖉08652-896 70; www.bercht esgaden.com; Königsseer Strasse 2; ⊙8.30am-6pm Mon-Fri, 9am-5pm Sat, shorter hours mid-Oct–Mar) Near the train station, this helpful office has information on the entire region.

ℹ Getting There & Around

Berchtesgaden is south of the Munich–Salzburg A8 autobahn. Travelling from Munich by train involves a change from Meridian to BLB (Berchtesgadener Land Bahn) trains at Freilassing (€36.40, 2½ hours, at least hourly connections). The best option between Berchtesgaden and Salzburg is RVO bus 840 (45 minutes), which leaves from the train station in both towns roughly hourly.

The train station in Berchtesgaden is around 15 minutes' walk from the village centre. The Eagle's Nest, Königssee and Dokumentation Obersalzberg all require trips by bus if you don't have your own transport. Seeing all the sights in a day without your own transport is virtually impossible.

THE ROMANTIC ROAD

From the vineyards of Würzburg to the foot of the Alps, the almost 400km-long Romantic Road (Romantische Strasse) draws two million visitors every year, making it by far the most popular of Germany's holiday routes. This well-trodden trail cuts through a cultural and historical cross-section of southern Germany as it traverses Franconia and clips Baden-Württemberg in the north before plunging into Bavaria proper to end at Ludwig II's crazy castles. Expect lots of Japanese signs and menus, tourist coaches and kitsch galore, but also a fair wedge of *Gemütlichkeit* and geniune hospitality from those who earn their living on this most romantic of routes.

ℹ Getting There & Away

Though Frankfurt is the most popular gateway for the Romantic Road, Munich is a good choice as well, especially if you decide to take the bus.

With its gentle gradients between towns, the Romantic Road is ideal for the holidaying cyclist. Bikes can be hired at many train stations; tourist offices keep lists of bicycle-friendly hotels that permit storage, or check out Bett und Bike (www.bettundbike.de) predeparture.

Direct trains run from Munich to Füssen every two hours, more often if you change in Buchloe. Rothenburg is linked by train to Würzburg, Munich, Augsburg and Nuremberg, with at least one change needed in Steinach to reach any destination.

ℹ Getting Around

It is possible to do this route using train connections and local buses, but the going is complicated, tedious and slow on weekdays, virtually impossible at weekends. The ideal way to travel is by car, though many foreign travellers prefer to take Deutsche Touring's **Romantic Road Coach** (www.romanticroadcoach.de), which can get incredibly crowded in summer. From April to October the special coach runs daily in each direction between Frankfurt and Füssen (for Neuschwanstein); the entire journey takes around 12 hours. There's no charge for breaking the journey and continuing the next day.

Tickets are available for short segments of the trip, and reservations are only necessary during peak-season weekends. Reservations can be made through travel agents, **Deutsche Touring** (www.touring.de, www.romantic-road.com) and Deutsche Bahn's Reisezentrum offices in the train stations. If you stayed on the coach all the way from Frankfurt to Füssen (a pointless exercise), the total fare would be €158. The average fare from one stop to the next is around €5.

Coaches can accommodate bicycles but you must give three working days' notice. Students, children, pensioners and rail-pass holders qualify for discounts of between 10% and 50%.

For detailed schedules and prices, see www.romanticroadcoach.de.

Würzburg

📞 0931 / POP 126,000

Straddling the Main River, scenic Würzburg is renowned for its art, architecture and delicate wines. The definite highlight is the Residenz, one of Germany's finest baroque buildings, though there's plenty more to see besides. A large student population guarantees a lively scene, and plenty of hip nightlife pulsates through its cobbled streets. The city is also the northern terminus of the Romantic Road, Germany's most popular tourist route.

History

Würzburg was a Franconian duchy when, in 686, three Irish missionaries tried to persuade Duke Gosbert to convert to Christianity, and ditch his wife. Gosbert was mulling it over when his wife had the three bumped off. When the murders were discovered decades later, the martyrs became saints and Würzburg was made a pilgrimage city, and, in 742, a bishopric.

For centuries the resident prince-bishops wielded enormous power and wealth, and the city grew in opulence under their rule. Their crowning glory is the Residenz, one of the finest baroque structures in Germany and a Unesco World Heritage Site.

In WWII 90% of the city centre was flattened. Authorities originally planned to leave the ruins as a reminder of the horrors of war, but a valiant rebuilding project saw the city restored almost to its pre-war glory.

◉ Sights

★ **Würzburg Residenz** PALACE
(www.residenz-wuerzburg.de; Balthasar-Neumann-Promenade; adult/child €7.50/free; ☉ 9am-6pm Apr-Oct, 10am-4.30pm Nov-Mar, 45min English tours 11am & 3pm, plus 1.30pm & 4.30pm Apr-Oct) The vast Unesco-listed Residenz, built by 18th-century architect Balthasar Neumann as the home of the local prince-bishops, is one of Germany's most important and beautiful baroque palaces. Top billing goes to the brilliant zigzagging *Treppenhaus* (Staircase) lidded by what still is the world's largest fresco, a masterpiece by Giovanni Battista Tiepolo depicting allegories of the four then-known continents (Europe, Africa, America and Asia).

The structure was commissioned in 1720 by prince-bishop Johann Philipp Franz von Schönborn, who was unhappy with his old-fashioned digs up in Marienberg Fortress, and took almost 60 years to complete. Today the 360 rooms are home to government institutions, university faculties and a museum, but the grandest 40 have been restored for visitors to admire.

Besides the Grand Staircase, you can feast your eyes on the ice-white stucco-adorned

BAVARIA WÜRZBURG

Würzburg

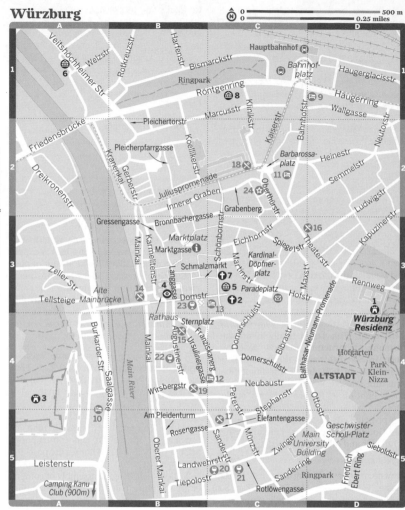

Weisser Saal (White Hall) before entering the *Kaisersaal* (Imperial Hall), canopied by yet another impressive Tiepolo fresco. Other stunners include the gilded stucco *Spiegelkabinett* (Mirror Hall), covered with a unique mirror-like glass painted with figural, floral and animal motifs (accessible by tour only).

In the residence's south wing, the *Hofkirche* (Court Church) is another Neumann and Tiepolo co-production. Its marble columns, gold leaf and profusion of angels match the Residenz in both splendour and proportions.

Entered via frilly wrought-iron gates, the *Hofgarten* (Court Garden; open until dusk, free) is a smooth blend of French- and English-style landscaping teeming with whimsical sculptures of children, mostly by court sculptor Peter Wagner. Concerts, festivals and special events take place here during the warmer months.

The complex also houses collections of antiques, paintings and drawings in the Martin-von-Wagner Museum (no relation to Peter) and, handily, a winery in the atmospheric cellar, the Staatlicher Hofkeller Würzburg, that is open for tours with tasting.

Würzburg

◎ Top Sights
1 Würzburg Residenz D3

◎ Sights
2 Dom St Kilian C3
3 Festung Marienberg A4
4 Grafeneckart B3
5 Museum am Dom C3
6 Museum im Kulturspeicher A1
7 Neumünster C3
8 Röntgen Gedächtnisstätte C1

◎ Sleeping
9 Babelfish D1
10 DJH Hostel A5
11 Hotel Poppular C2
12 Hotel Rebstock C4
13 Hotel Zum Winzermännle C3

◎ Eating
14 Alte Mainmühle B3
15 Backöfele B4
16 Bürgerspital Weinstube D3
17 Capri & Blaue Grotto C5
18 Juliusspital C2
    Juliusspital Bäckerei .... (see 18)
19 Uni-Café B4

◎ Drinking & Nightlife
20 Kult C5
21 MUCK C5
22 Odeon Lounge B4
23 Sternbäck B3

◎ Entertainment
24 Standard C2

BAVARIA WÜRZBURG

Festung Marienberg   FORTRESS
(tour adult/child €3.50/free; ⊙tours 11am, 2pm, 3pm & 4pm Tue-Sun, plus 10am & 1pm Sat & Sun mid-Mar–Oct, 11am, 2pm & 3pm Sat & Sun Nov–mid-Mar) Enjoy panoramic city and vineyard views from this hulking fortress whose construction was initiated around 1200 by the local prince-bishops who governed here until 1719. Dramatically illuminated at night, the structure was only penetrated once, by Swedish troops during the Thirty Years' War, in 1631. Inside, the Fürstenbaumuseum (closed November to mid-March) sheds light on its former residents' opulent lifestyle, while the Mainfränkisches Museum presents city history and works by local late-Gothic master carver Tilman Riemenschneider and other famous artists.

Neumünster   CHURCH
(www.neumuenster-wuerzburg.de; Schönbornstrasse; ⊙6am-6.30pm Mon-Sat, from 8am Sun) In the Altstadt, this satisfyingly symmetrical church stands on the site where three ill-fated Irish missionaries who tried to convert Duke Gosbert to Christianity in 686 met their maker. Romanesque at its core, it was given a thorough baroque restyle by the Zimmermann brothers and is typical of their work. The interior has busts of the three martyrs (Kilian, Colonan and Totnan) on the high altar and the tomb of St Kilian lurks in the well-lit crypt.

Dom St Kilian   CHURCH
(www.dom-wuerzburg.de; Domstrasse 40; ⊙8am-7pm Mon-Sat, to 8pm Sun) FREE This highly unusual cathedral has a Romanesque core that has been altered many times over the centuries. The elaborate stucco work of the chancel contrasts starkly with the bare whitewash of the austere Romanesque nave that is capped with a ceiling that wouldn't look out of place in a 1960s bus station. The whole mishmash creates quite an impression and is possibly Germany's oddest cathedral interior. The Schönbornkapelle by Balthasar Neumann returns a little baroque order to things.

Museum im Kulturspeicher   MUSEUM
(☑0931-322 250; www.kulturspeicher.de; Veitshöchheimer Strasse 5; adult/child €3.50/2; ⊙1-6pm Tue, 11am-6pm Wed & Fri-Sun, 11am-7pm Thu) In a born-again historic granary right on the Main River, you'll find this absorbing art museum with choice artworks from the 19th to the 21st centuries. The emphasis is on German impressionism, neorealism and contemporary art, but the building also houses the post-1945 constructivist works of the Peter C Ruppert collection, a challenging assembly of computer art, sculpture, paintings and photographs.

Grafeneckart   MEMORIAL
(Domstrasse) FREE Adjoining the Rathaus, the 1659-built Grafeneckart houses a scale model of the WWII bombing. It starkly depicts the extent of the damage to the city following the night of 16 March 1945, when 1000 tons of explosives were dropped on the city and 5000 citizens lost their lives in just 20 minutes. Viewing it and reading the potted history of events before you climb up to the fortress overlooking the city gives you an appreciation of Würzburg's astonishing recovery.

Museum am Dom   MUSEUM
(www.museum-am-dom.de; Kiliansplatz; adult/child €4/free; ⊙10am-5pm Tue-Sun) Housed in a beautiful building by the cathedral, this worthwhile

museum displays collections of modern art on Christian themes. Works of international renown by Joseph Beuys, Otto Dix and Käthe Kollwitz are on show, as well as masterpieces of the Romantic, Gothic and baroque periods.

Röntgen Gedächtnisstätte MUSEUM
(www.wilhelmconradroentgen.de; Röntgenring 8; ⊙ 8am-7pm Mon-Fri, to 5pm Sat) FREE Wilhelm Conrad Röntgen discovered X-rays in 1895 and was the winner of the very first Nobel Prize in 1901. His preserved laboratory forms the heart of this small exhibition that is complemented by a film on Röntgen's life and work in English.

⚡ Festivals & Events

Mozart Fest MUSIC
(✆ 0931-372 336; www.mozartfest-wuerzburg.de; ⊙ mid-May–late Jun) Germany's oldest Mozart festival takes place at the Residenz, the Kiliansdom, the Mainfranken Theater and several other venues including some of the city's wine taverns.

Africa Festival CULTURAL
(✆ 0931-150 60; www.africafestival.org; ⊙ early Jun) Held on the meadows northwest of the river at Mainwiesen, this is Germany's best festival of Afro music with acts from almost 60 countries across Africa and the Caribbean taking part.

Hoffest am Stein WINE
(www.hoffest-am-stein.de; ⊙ Jul) Popular wine and music festival held in the first half of July at the Weingut am Stein.

Stramu MUSIC
(www.stramu-wuerzburg.de; ⊙ Sep) This street music festival claims to be Europe's largest stage-free music event attracting over 400 acts from all over the world.

🛏 Sleeping

Babelfish HOSTEL €
(✆ 0931-304 0430; www.babelfish-hostel.de; Haugerring 2; dm €25, s/d €65/80; ⊙ reception 8am-midnight; 🛜) With a name inspired by a creature in Douglas Adams' *The Hitchhiker's Guide to the Galaxy,* this uncluttered and spotlessly clean hostel has 74 beds spread over two floors and a sunny rooftop terrace. The communal areas are an inviting place to down a few beers in the evening and there's a well-equipped kitchen. Breakfast costs €5.90.

DJH Hostel HOSTEL €
(✆ 0931-467 7860; www.wuerzburg.jugendherberge.de; Fred-Joseph-Platz 2; dm from €25) At

the foot of the fortress, this well-equipped, wheelchair-friendly hostel has room for over 230 snoozers in three- to eight-bed dorms.

Camping Kanu Club CAMPGROUND €
(✆ 0931-725 36; www.kc-wuerzburg.de; Mergentheimer Strasse 13b; per person/tent €4/3) Around 2km to the south of Würzburg, this is the closest camping ground to the town centre. Take tram 3 or 5 to the Judenbühlweg stop, which is on its doorstep.

Hotel Zum Winzermännle HOTEL €€
(✆ 0931-541 56; www.winzermaennle.de; Domstrasse 32; s €60-80, d €90-110; 🅿🛜) This family-run converted winery is a feel-good retreat in the city's pedestrianised heart. Rooms are well furnished, if a little on the old-fashioned side; some among those facing the quiet courtyard have balconies. Communal areas are bright and often seasonally decorated. Breakfast costs €7.

Hotel Poppular HOTEL €€
(✆ 0931-322 770; www.hotelpoppular.de; Textorstrasse 17; r €70-100; 🅿🛜) Relatively basic, city-centre hotel above a wine restaurant where rooms have a vague Scandinavian feel about them and are immaculately kept. All in all an excellent deal for the location within suitcase-dragging distance of the Hauptbahnhof and often massively discounted on popular booking websites. For walkers-in reception closes at 10pm.

Hotel Rebstock HOTEL €€€
(✆ 0931-309 30; www.rebstock.com; Neubaustrasse 7; s/d from €115/250; ❄🛜) Würzburg's top digs, in a squarely renovated rococo townhouse, has 70 unique, stylishly finished rooms with the gamut of amenities, impeccable service and an Altstadt location. A pillow selection and supercomfy 'gel' beds should ease you into slumberland, perhaps after a fine meal in the dramatic bistro or the slick Michelin-star Kuno 1408 restaurant.

🍴 Eating

For a town of its size, Würzburg has an enticing selection of wine taverns, beer gardens, cafes and restaurants, with plenty of student hang-outs among them.

Juliusspital Bäckerei BAKERY €
(Juliuspromenade 19; snacks €2-5; ⊙ 5am-6pm Mon-Sat, 8am-5pm Sun) Würzburg has tens of cafe-bakeries, but this high-ceilinged, colourful affair within the Juliusspital is great for very early starters whose trains leave

before hotel breakfast is laid out. Seasonally decorated, it's warm and welcoming, though sells the same range of baked goods and sandwiches as every other place.

Uni-Café
CAFE €

(Neubaustrasse 2; snacks €4-8; ☉ 8am-1am Mon-Sat, from 9am Sun; ☏) Hugely popular contemporary cafe on two levels, with a student-priced, daily-changing menu of burgers, baguettes and salads plus a buzzy bar and much full-mouthed and animated waffling.

Capri & Blaue Grotto
ITALIAN €

(Elefantengasse 1; pizzas €7.50-9.50, other mains €4.50-13; ☉ 11.30am-2pm & 5-11pm Tue-Fri, evenings only Sat & Sun) This outpost of the *bel paese* has been plating up pronto pasta and pizza since 1952 – it was in fact Germany's first ever pizzeria.

★ Bürgerspital Weinstube
FRANCONIAN €€

(☑ 0931-352 880; www.buergerspital-weinstuben. de; Theaterstrasse 19; mains €7-25; ☉ 10am-midnight) If you are going to eat out just once in Würzburg, the aromatic and cosy nooks of this labyrinthine medieval place probably provide the top local experience. Choose from a broad selection of Franconian wines (some of Germany's best) and wonderful regional dishes and snacks, including *Most-suppe* (a tasty wine soup). Buy local whites in the adjoining wine shop.

Juliusspital
FRANCONIAN €€

(www.weinstuben-juliusspital.de; Juliuspromenade 19; mains €8-30; ☉ 11am-midnight) This attractive *Weinstube* (traditional wine tavern) features fabulous (if pricey) Franconian fish and even better wines. Ambient lighting, scurrying waiters and walls occupied by oil paintings make this the place to head to for a special do.

Backöfele
FRANCONIAN €€

(☑ 0931-590 59; www.backoefele.de; Ursuliner-gasse 2; mains €7-23; ☉ noon-midnight Mon-Thu, to 1am Fri & Sat, to 11pm Sun) This old-timey warren that has been serving hearty Franconian food for decades. Find a table in the cobbled courtyard or one of four historic rooms, each candlelit and uniquely furnished with local flair. Featuring schnitzel, snails, bratwurst in wine, wine soup with cinnamon croutons, venison, boar and other local favourites, the menu makes for mouth-watering reading. Bookings recommended.

Alte Mainmühle
FRANCONIAN €€

(☑ 0931-167 77; www.alte-mainmuehle.de; Mainkai 1; mains €11-23; ☉ 10am-midnight; ☏) Accessed straight from the old bridge, people cram into this old mill to savour modern twists on Franconian classics (including popular river fish). In summer the double terrace beckons – the upper one delivers pretty views of the bridge and Marienberg Fortress; in winter retreat to the snug timber dining room. Year-round guests spill out onto the bridge itself, Aperol spritz in hand.

☕ Drinking & Entertainment

Wine is the tipple of choice in Würzburg, much of it made with grapes from the surrounding hills. Juliusspital and Bürgerspital Weinstube are the best places to sample the local minerally whites. Meanwhile Sandstrasse is the place to head for a weekend night out for its gathering of studenty venues, live music, bars and kebab shops.

Sternbäck
PUB

(www.facebook.com/sternbaeck; Sterngasse 2; ☉ 9am-1am) This atmospheric, low-lit pub serves Distelhäuser beer and dishes up bratwurst and *Flammkuchen* (Alsatian pizza) under a modern fresco of fat-faced drinkers. It's an intimate and convivial place to enjoy a beer when you've had your fill of Würzburg's monastery-like wine taverns.

Kult
BAR

(Landwehrstrasse 10; ☉ 6pm-1am Mon, from 10am Tue-Sun) Enjoy a tailor-made breakfast, munch a cheap lunch or party into the wee hours at Würzburg's coolest cafe. The unpretentious interior, with its salvaged tables and old beige benches, hosts regular fancy-dress parties, table-football tournaments and other offbeat events. DJs take over at weekends.

MUCK
BAR

(www.cafe-muck.de; Sanderstrasse 29; ☉ 9am-1am) This very popular and long-established student cafe serves a hangover-busting breakfast and morphs into something of an informal party after nightfall.

Odeon Lounge
CLUB

(www.odeon-lounge.de; Augustinerstrasse 18; ☉ from 11pm Wed, Fri & Sat) Mainstream club in a former cinema at the heart of the Augustinerstrasse student nightlife district. Expect '90s parties, local DJs, R'n'B nights and a 'midlife' night you may, er, want to avoid.

Standard
LIVE MUSIC

(www.standard-wuerzburg.com; Oberthürstrasse 11a; ☉ 11.30am-1am Mon-Wed, to 3am Thu-Sat, 3pm-1am Sun) Soulful jazz spins beneath a corrugated-iron ceiling and stainless-steel fans, while bands and DJs play a couple of times a week in a second downstairs bar.

ℹ️ Information

Post Office (Paradeplatz 4; ⊙ 8.30am-6pm Mon-Fri, 9am-noon Sat)

Tourist Office (📞 0931-372 398; www.wuerz burg.de; Marktplatz 9; ⊙ 10am-6pm Mon-Fri, to 3pm Sat, to 2pm Sun May-Oct, closed Sun & slightly shorter hours Nov-Apr) Within the attractive Falkenhaus this efficient office can help you with room reservations and tour booking.

ℹ️ Getting There & Away

BUS

The Romantic Road Coach (p109) stops at the **main bus station** (Bahnhofplatz) next to the Hauptbahnhof, and at Residenzplatz. Budget coach company Flixbus (www.flixbus.de) links Würzburg with destinations across Germany and beyond including Nuremberg and Munich.

TRAIN

Train connections from **Würzburg train station** (Bahnhofplatz) include Bamberg (€22, one hour, twice hourly), Frankfurt (€20 to €36, one hour, hourly), Munich (€74, two hours, twice hourly) and Nuremberg (€20, one hour, twice hourly). For Rothenburg ob der Tauber (€15.70, one hour, hourly), change in Steinach.

Rothenburg ob der Tauber

📞 09861 / POP 11,100

A true medieval gem, Rothenburg ob der Tauber (meaning 'above the Tauber River') is a top tourist stop along the Romantic Road. With its web of cobbled lanes, higgledy-piggledy houses and towered walls, the town is the archetypal fairy-tale Germany. Urban conservation orders here are the strictest in Germany – and at times it feels like a medieval theme park – but all's forgiven in the evenings, when the lamplight casts its spell long after the last tour buses have left.

⊙ Sights

Mittelalterliches Kriminalmuseum
MUSEUM

(Medieval Crime & Punishment Museum; www.kriminalmuseum.eu; Burggasse 3; adult/concession €7/4; ⊙ 10am-6pm Apr-Oct, 1-4pm Nov-Mar) The star attractions at this gruesomely fascinating museum are medieval implements of torture and punishment. Exhibits include chastity belts, masks of disgrace for gossips, a cage for cheating bakers, a neck brace for quarrelsome women and a beer-barrel pen for drunks. You can even snap a selfie in the

stocks. The museum has 50,000 exhibits making it the biggest of its kind in Europe.

Jakobskirche
CHURCH

(Church of St Jacob; Klingengasse 1; adult/child €2.50/1.50; ⊙ 9am-5pm Apr-Oct, shorter hours Nov-Mar) One of the few places of worship in Bavaria to charge admission, Rothenburg's Lutheran parish church was begun in the 14th century and finished in the 15th. The building sports some wonderfully aged stained-glass windows but the top attraction is Tilman Riemenschneider's Heilig Blut Altar (Altar of the Holy Blood). The gilded cross above the main scene depicting the Last Supper incorporates Rothenburg's most treasured reliquary – a rock crystal capsule said to contain three drops of Christ's blood.

Deutsches Weihnachtsmuseum
MUSEUM

(Christmas Museum; 📞 09861-409 365; www.weihnachtsmuseum.de; Herrngasse 1; adult/child/family €4/2.50/7; ⊙ 10am-5pm Easter-Christmas, shorter hours Jan-Easter) If you're glad Christmas comes but once every 365 days, then stay well clear of the Käthe Wohlfahrt Weihnachtsdorf (p117), a Yuletide superstore that also houses this Christmas Museum. This repository of all things 'Ho! Ho! Ho!' traces the development of various Christmas customs and decorations, and includes a display of 150 Santa figures, plus lots of retro baubles and tinsel .

Stadtmauer
HISTORIC SITE

(Town Wall) With time and fresh legs, a 2.5km circular walk around the unbroken ring of town walls gives a sense of the importance medieval people placed on defending their settlements. A great lookout point is the eastern tower, the **Röderturm** (Rödergasse; adult/child €2/1; ⊙ 9am-5pm Mar-Oct & Dec), but for the most impressive views head to the western side of town, where a sweeping view of the Tauber Valley includes the Doppelbrücke, a double-decker bridge.

Reichsstadtmuseum
MUSEUM

(www.reichsstadtmuseum.rothenburg.de; Klosterhof 5; adult/child €6/5; ⊙ 9.30am-5.30pm Apr-Oct, 1-4pm Nov-Mar) Highlights of the Reichsstadtmuseum, housed in a former Dominican convent, include the *Rothenburger Passion* (1494), a cycle of 12 panels by Martinus Schwarz, and the oldest convent kitchen in Germany, as well as weapons and armour. Outside the main entrance (on your right as you're facing the museum), you'll see a spinning barrel, where the nuns distributed

Rothenburg ob der Tauber

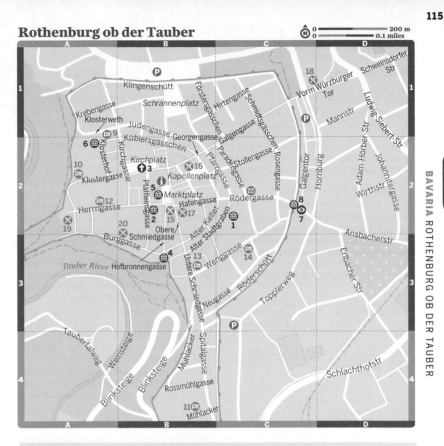

Rothenburg ob der Tauber

⊙ Sights
1 Alt-Rothenburger Handwerkerhaus C2
2 Deutsches Weihnachtsmuseum B2
3 Jakobskirche...B2
4 Mittelalterliches Kriminalmuseum B3
5 Rathausturm..B2
6 Reichsstadtmuseum A2
7 Röderturm...C2
8 Stadtmauer...C2

⊜ Sleeping
9 Altfränkische Weinstube A1
10 Burg-Hotel...A2
11 DJH Hostel B4
12 Hotel Herrnschlösschen A2

13 Hotel Raidel B3
14 Kreuzerhof Hotel Garni C3

⊗ Eating
15 Diller's Schneeballen B2
16 Gasthof Butz B2
17 Gasthof Goldener Greifen.................... B2
18 Mittermeier C1
19 Weinstube zum Pulverer A2
20 Zur Höll... B2

⊟ Shopping
Käthe Wohlfahrt
Weihnachtsdorf ....(see 2)

bread to the poor – and where women would leave babies they couldn't afford to keep.

Alt-Rothenburger
Handwerkerhaus   HISTORIC BUILDING
(www.alt-rothenburger-handwerkerhaus.de; Alter Stadtgraben 26; adult/child €3/1.50; ⊙11am-5pm Mon-Fri, from 10am Sat & Sun Easter-Oct, 2-4pm daily Dec) Hidden down a little alley is the Alt-Rothenburger Handwerkerhaus, where numerous artisans – including coopers, weavers, cobblers and potters – have their workshops today, and mostly have had for

BOTTOMS UP FOR FREEDOM

In 1631 the Thirty Years' War – pitching Catholics against Protestants – reached the gates of Rothenburg ob der Tauber. Catholic General Tilly and 60,000 of his troops besieged the Protestant market town and demanded its surrender. The town resisted but couldn't stave off the onslaught of marauding soldiers, and the mayor and other town dignitaries were captured and sentenced to death.

And that's about where the story ends and the legend begins. As the tale goes, Rothenburg's town council tried to sate Tilly's bloodthirstiness by presenting him with a 3L pitcher of wine. Tilly, after taking a sip or two, presented the councillors with an unusual challenge, saying, 'If one of you has the courage to step forward and down this mug of wine in one gulp, then I shall spare the town and the lives of the councilmen!' Mayor Georg Nusch accepted – and succeeded! And that's why you can still wander though Rothenburg's wonderful medieval lanes today.

It's pretty much accepted that Tilly was really placated with hard cash. Nevertheless, local poet Adam Hörber couldn't resist turning the tale of the Meistertrunk (champion drinker) into a play, which, since 1881, has been performed every Whitsuntide (Pentecost), the seventh Sunday after Easter. It's also re-enacted several times daily by the clock figures on the tourist office building.

the house's more than 700-year existence. It's half museum, half active workplace and you can easily spend an hour or so watching the artisans at work.

Rathausturm HISTORIC BUILDING
(Town Hall Tower; Marktplatz; adult/child €2/0.50; ⊘9.30am-12.30pm & 1-5pm Apr-Oct, 10.30am-2pm & 2.30-6pm Sun-Thu, to 7pm Fri & Sat Dec, noon-3pm Sat & Sun Jan-Mar & Nov) The Rathaus on Marktplatz was begun in Gothic style in the 14th century and was completed during the Renaissance. Climb the 220 steps of the medieval town hall to the viewing platform of the Rathausturm to be rewarded with widescreen views of the Tauber.

✨ Festivals & Events

Historisches Festspiel 'Der Meistertrunk' THEATRE
(www.meistertrunk.de; ⊘late May) Takes place on Whitsuntide, with parades, dances and a medieval market. The highlight is the re-enactment of the mythical *Meistertrunk* story. The *Meistertrunk* play itself is performed three more times: once during the Reichsstadt-Festtage (early September), when the city's history is re-enacted in the streets, and twice during the Rothenburger Herbst, an autumn celebration (October).

Historischer Schäfertanz DANCE
(Historical Shepherds' Dance; www.schaefertanz rothenburg.de; Marktplatz) Involving colourfully dressed couples, Historischer Schäfertanz is a less-than-spectacular traditional dance

event takes places on Marktplatz several times between April and October.

Christmas Market CHRISTMAS MARKET
(www.rothenburg.de; ⊘Advent) The Rothenburger Reiterlesmarkt as it's officially known is the town's Christmas market, one of the most romantic in Germany. It's set out around the central Marktplatz during Advent.

🛏 Sleeping

Hotel Raidel HOTEL €
(⊋09861-3115; www.gaestehaus-raidel.de; Wenggasse 3; s/d €45/70; 🕸) With 500-year-old exposed beams studded with wooden nails, antiques throughout and a welcoming owner, as well as musical instruments for the guests to play, this is the place to check in if you're craving some genuine romance on the Romantic Road.

DJH Hostel HOSTEL €
(⊋09861-941 60; www.rothenburg.jugend herberge.de; Mühlacker 1; dm from €23; 🕸) Rothenburg's youth hostel occupies two enormous old buildings in the south of town. It's agreeably renovated and extremely well equipped, but you can sometimes hear the screams of noisy school groups from outside.

Kreuzerhof Hotel Garni GUESTHOUSE €€
(⊋09861-3424; www.kreuzerhof-rothenburg.de; Millergasse 2-6; s €55-65, d €75-110; 🕸) Away from the tourist swarms, this quiet family-run B&B has charming, randomly furnished rooms with antique touches in a medieval townhouse and annexe. There's free tea and

coffee and the generous breakfast is really an energy-boosting set-up for the day.

Altfränkische Weinstube HOTEL €€
(☑ 09861-6404; www.altfraenkische.de; Klosterhof 7; d €80-130; 🛜) This very distinctive, 650-year-old inn has eight wonderfully romantic, realistically priced rural-style rooms with exposed half-timber, bath-tubs and most with four-poster or canopied beds. From 6pm onwards, the tavern serves up sound regional fare with a dollop of medieval cheer.

⭐**Hotel Herrnschlösschen** HOTEL €€€
(☑ 09861-873 890; www.hotel-rothenburg.de; Herrngasse 20; r from €225; 🛜) Occupying a 900-year-old mansion, this top-class hotel is a blend of ancient and new, with Gothic arches leaping over faux-retro furniture and ageing oak preventing ceilings from crashing down onto chic 21st-century beds. The hotel's restaurant has established itself as one of the town's most innovative dining spots and there's an exquisite baroque garden out back for a spot of R&R.

⭐**Burg-Hotel** HOTEL €€€
(☑ 09861-948 90; www.burghotel.eu; Klostergasse 1-3; s €100-135, d €125-195; 🅿️ ❄️ 🛜) Each of the 17 elegantly furnished guest rooms at this boutique hotel built into the town walls has its own private sitting area. The lower floors shelter a decadent spa with tanning beds, saunas and rainforest showers, and a cellar with a Steinway piano; while phenomenal valley views unfurl from the breakfast room and stone terrace.

The owners also run the hotel across the road where there are 14 more modern rooms and a restaurant. There is parking (€10 per day) and bikes for rent (€7.50 per day).

🍴 Eating

Gasthof Goldener Greifen FRANCONIAN €€
(☑ 09861-2281; www.gasthof-greifen-rothenburg.de; Obere Schmiedgasse 5; mains €8-17; ⏱ 11.30am-10pm; 🛜) Erstwhile home of Heinrich Toppler, one of Rothenburg's most famous medieval mayors (the dining room was his office), the 700-year-old Golden Griffin is the locals' choice in the touristy centre. A hearty menu of Franconian favourites is served in an austere semimedieval setting and out back in the sunny and secluded garden. There's also a long kids' menu, a rarity in Bavaria.

Weinstube zum Pulverer FRANCONIAN €€
(☑ 09861-976 182; Herrngasse 31; mains €8-15; ⏱ 5pm-late Wed-Fri, from noon Sat & Sun) The ornately carved timber chairs in this ancient wood-panelled wine bar (allegedly Rothenburg's oldest) are works of art. The simple but filling dishes, like soup in a bowl made of bread, gourmet sandwiches and cakes, are equally artistic. There's also a piano for postprandial self-expression.

Zur Höll FRANCONIAN €€
(☑ 09861-4229; www.hoell.rothenburg.de; Burggasse 8; mains €7-20; ⏱ 5-11pm Mon-Sat) This medieval wine tavern is in the town's oldest original building, with sections dating back to AD 900. The menu of regional specialities is limited but refined, though it's the superb selection of Franconian wines that people really come for.

Gasthof Butz GERMAN €€
(☑ 09861-2201; Kapellenplatz 4; mains €7-16; ⏱ 11.30am-2pm & 6-9pm Fri-Wed; 🛜) For a quick, no-nonsense goulash, schnitzel or roast pork, lug your weary legs to this locally adored, family-run inn in a former brewery. In summer two flowery beer gardens beckon. It also rents a dozen simply furnished rooms.

⭐**Mittermeier** BAVARIAN, INTERNATIONAL €€€
(☑ 09861-945 430; www.villamittermeier.de; Vorm Würzburger Tor 7; mains €10-30; ⏱ 6-10.30pm Tue-Sat; 🅿️🛜) Supporter of the slow food movement and a regular in the Michelin Guide, this hotel restaurant pairs punctilious artisanship with top-notch ingredients, sourced regionally whenever possible. There are five different dining areas including a black-and-white tiled 'temple', an alfresco terrace and a barrel-shaped wine cellar. The wine list is one of the best in Franconia. Book ahead.

🛍 Shopping

Käthe Wohlfahrt Weihnachtsdorf CHRISTMAS DECORATIONS
(www.wohlfahrt.com; Herrngasse 1; ⏱ 10am-5pm Mon-Sat) With its mind-boggling assortment of Yuletide decorations and ornaments, this huge shop lets you celebrate Christmas every day. Many of the items are handcrafted with

---

SNOWBALLS

Rothenburg's most obvious speciality is Schneeballen, ribbons of dough loosely shaped into balls, deep-fried then coated in icing sugar, chocolate and other dentist's foes. Some 27 different types are produced at **Diller's Schneeballen** (Hofbronnengasse 16; ⏱ 10am-6pm). A more limited range is available all over town.

amazing skill and imagination; prices are correspondingly high. This is the original shop of a chain that has spread across Rothenburg and all of Germany.

ℹ Information

Post Office (Rödergasse 11; ⊙ 9am-1pm Mon-Fri, to noon Sat, plus 2-5.30pm Mon, Tue, Thu & Fri)

Tourist Office (✆ 09861-404 800; www.touris mus.rothenburg.de; Marktplatz 2; ⊙ 9am-6pm Mon-Fri, 10am-5pm Sat & Sun May-Oct, 9am-5pm Mon-Fri, 10am-1pm Sat Nov-Apr) Helpful office offering free internet access.

ℹ Getting There & Away

BUS

The Romantic Road Coach (p109) stops in the main bus park at the Hauptbahnhof and on the more central Schrannenplatz.

TRAIN

You can go anywhere by train from Rothenburg, as long as it's Steinach. Change there for services to Würzburg (€15.70, one hour and 10 minutes). Travel to and from Munich (from €29, three to four hours) can involve up to three different trains, making a day trip from the capital unfeasible.

ℹ Getting Around

The city has five car parks right outside the walls. The town centre is essentially closed to nonresident vehicles, though hotel guests are exempt.

Dinkelsbühl

✆ 09851 / POP 11,600

Some 40km south of Rothenburg, immaculately preserved Dinkelsbühl proudly traces its roots to a royal residence founded by Carolingian kings in the 8th century. Saved from destruction in the Thirty Years' War and ignored by WWII bombers, this is arguably the Romantic Road's quaintest and most authentically medieval halt. For a good overall impression of the town, walk along the fortified walls with their 18 towers and four gates.

◉ Sights

Haus der Geschichte   MUSEUM
(House of History; www.hausdergeschichte-din kelsbuehl.de; Altrathausplatz 14; adult/child €4/2; ⊙ 9am-6pm Mon-Fri, 10am-5pm Sat & Sun May-Oct, 10am-5pm Nov-Apr) Dinkelsbühl's history comes under the microscope at the Haus der Geschichte, which occupies the 14th-century former town hall. Highlights include an interesting section on the Thirty Years' War and a

gallery with paintings depicting Dinkelsbühl at the turn of the century. Audioguides are included in the ticket price.

Münster St Georg   CHURCH
(www.st-georg-dinkelsbuehl.de; Marktplatz 1; ⊙ 9am-7pm) Standing sentry over the heart of Dinkelsbühl is one of southern Germany's purest late-Gothic hall churches. Rather austere from the outside, the interior stuns with an incredible fan-vaulted ceiling. A curiosity is the Pretzl Window donated by the bakers' guild; it's located in the upper section of the last window in the right aisle.

Museum of the 3rd Dimension   MUSEUM
(✆ 09851-6336; www.3d-museum.de; Nördlinger Tor; adult/child €10/6; ⊙ 11am-5pm daily May-Jun & Sep-Oct, Sat & Sun Nov-Mar, 10am-6pm daily Jul-Aug) Located just outside the easternmost town gate, this is an engaging place to entertain young minds, bored with the Romantic Road's twee medieval pageant. Inside there are three floors of holographic images, stereoscopes and attention-grabbing 3D imagery. The slightly inflated admission includes a pair of red-green-tinted specs.

★ Festivals & Events

Kinderzeche   CULTURAL
(www.kinderzeche.de; ⊙ mid-Jul) In the third week of July, the 10-day Kinderzeche celebrates how, during the Thirty Years' War, the town's children persuaded the invading Swedish troops to spare Dinkelsbühl from a ransacking. The festivities include a pageant, re-enactments in the festival hall, lots of music and other merriment.

🛏 Sleeping

Campingpark
'Romantische Strasse'   CAMPGROUND €
(✆ 09851-7817; www.campingplatz-dinkelsbuehl. de; Kobeltsmühle 6; per tent/person €9.30/4.40) This camping ground is set on the shores of a swimmable lake 1.5km northeast of the Wörnitz Tor.

DJH Hostel   HOSTEL €
(✆ 09851-555 6417; www.dinkelsbuehl.jugendher berge.de; Koppengasse 10; dm from €26; 🛜) Dinkelsbühl's renovated 25-room hostel in the western part of the Altstadt occupies a beautiful 15th-century half-timbered granary.

★ Dinkelsbühler
Kunst-Stuben   GUESTHOUSE €€
(✆ 09851-6750; www.kunst-stuben.de; Segringer Strasse 52; s €65, d €80-90, ste €100; 🅿@🛜)

Personal attention and charm by the bucket-load make this guesthouse, situated near the westernmost gate (Segringer Tor), one of the best on the entire Romantic Road. Furniture (including the four-posters) is all handmade by Voglauer, the cosy library is perfect for curling up in with a good book, and the suite is a matchless deal for travelling families. The artist owner will show his Asia travel films if enough guests are interested.

Deutsches Haus HOTEL €€
(☑ 09851-6058; www.deutsches-haus.net; Weinmarkt 3; r from €105; ☎) Concealed behind the town's most ornate and out-of-kilter facade, the 19 elegant rooms at this central inn opposite the Münster St Georg flaunt antique touches and big 21st-century bathrooms. Downstairs Dinkelbühl's hautiest restaurant serves game and fish prepared according to age-old recipes.

Gasthof Goldenes Lamm HOTEL €€
(☑ 09851-2267; www.goldenes.de; Lange Gasse 26-28; s €55-70, d €80-105; P ☎) Operated by the same family for four generations, this stress-free, bike-friendly oasis has pleasant rooms at the top of a creaky staircase, plus a rooftop garden deck with plump sofas. The attached wood-panelled restaurant plates up Franconian-Swabian specialities, including a vegetarian selection.

✖ Eating

Haus Appelberg FRANCONIAN, INTERNATIONAL €€
(☑ 09851-582 838; www.haus-appelberg.de; Nördlinger Strasse 40; dishes €6-12; ☺ 6pm-midnight Mon-Sat; ☎) At this 40-cover wine restaurant owners double up as cooks to keep tables supplied with traditional dishes such as local fish, Franconian sausages and *Maultaschen* (pork and spinach ravioli). On warm days swap the rustic interior for the secluded terrace, a fine spot for some evening idling over a Franconian white.

The eight rooms upstairs are of a very high standard with antique touches.

Weib's Brauhaus PUB FOOD €€
(www.weibsbrauhaus.de; Untere Schmiedgasse 13; mains €5.90-18.50; ☺ 11am-1am Thu-Mon, 6pm-1am Wed; ☎) A female brewer presides over the copper vats at this half-timbered pub-restaurant, which has a good-time vibe thanks to its friendly crowd of regulars. Many dishes are made with the house brew, including the popular *Weib's Töpfle* ('woman's pot') – pork in beer sauce with croquettes.

ⓘ Information

Tourist Office (☑ 09851-902 440; www.tourismus-dinkelsbuehl.de; Altrathausplatz 14; ☺ 9am-6pm Mon-Fri, 10am-5pm Sat & Sun May-Oct, 10am-5pm Nov-Apr) Located in the Haus der Geschichte. Lots of brochures available for download from the website.

ⓘ Getting There & Away

Despite a railway line cutting through the town, Dinkelsbühl is not served by passenger trains. Regional bus 501 to Nördlingen (50 minutes, eight daily) stops at the ZOB Schwedenwiese bus station. Reaching Rothenburg is a real test of patience without your own car. Change from bus 805 to a train in Ansbach, then change trains in Steinach. The Europabus stops right in the Altstadt at Schweinemarkt.

Nördlingen
☑ 09081 / POP 20,000

Delightfully medieval, Nördlingen receives slightly fewer tourists than its better-known neighbours and manages to retain an air of authenticity, which is a relief after some of the Romantic Road's kitschy extremes. The town lies within the Ries Basin, a massive impact crater gouged out by a meteorite more than 15 million years ago. The crater – some 25km in diameter – is one of the best preserved on earth, and has been declared a special 'geopark'. Nördlingen's 14th-century walls, all original, mimic the crater's rim and are almost perfectly circular.

Incidentally, if you've seen the 1970s film *Willy Wonka and the Chocolate Factory*, you've already looked down upon Nördlingen from a glass elevator.

⊙ Sights

You can circumnavigate the entire town in around an hour on top of the walls. Access points are near the old gates into the old town.

St Georgskirche CHURCH
(www.kirchengemeinde-noerdlingen.de; Marktplatz; tower adult/child €3.50/2.50; ☺ 9am-5pm Easter-Oct, 10.30am-12.30pm Tue-Sat, 9.30am-12.30pm Sun rest of the year, tower at least 10am-4pm daily) Dominating the heart of town, the immense late-Gothic St Georgskirche got its baroque mantle in the 18th century and seems to have been under restoration ever since. To truly appreciate Nördlingen's circular shape and the dished-out crater in which it lies, scramble up the 350 steps of the church's 90m-tall Daniel Tower, by far the town's tallest structure.

Bayerisches Eisenbahnmuseum   MUSEUM

(www.bayerisches-eisenbahnmuseum.de; Am Hohen Weg 6a; adult/child €6/3; ⊙noon-4pm Tue-Sat, 10am-5pm Sun May-Sep, noon-4pm Sat, 10am-5pm Sun Oct-Mar) Half museum, half junkyard retirement home/graveyard for locos that have long puffed their last, this trainspotter's paradise occupies a disused engine depot across the tracks from the train station (no access from the platforms). The museum runs steam and old diesel trains up to Dinkelsbühl, Feuchtwangen and Gunzenhausen several times a year; see the website for details.

Rieskrater Museum   MUSEUM

(www.rieskrater-museum.de; Eugene-Shoemaker-Platz 1; adult/child €4.50/2.50, ticket also valid for Stadtmuseum; ⊙10am-4.30pm Tue-Sun, closed noon-1.30pm Nov-Mar) Situated in an ancient barn, this unique museum explores the formation of meteorite craters and the consequences of such violent collisions with Earth. Rocks, including a genuine moon rock (on permanent loan from NASA), fossils and other geological displays shed light on the mystery of meteors.

Stadtmuseum   MUSEUM

(Vordere Gerbergasse 1; adult/child €4.50/2.50, ticket also valid for Rieskrater Museum; ⊙1.30-4.30pm Tue-Sun Apr-early Nov) Nördlingen's worthwhile municipal museum covers an ambitious sweep of human existence on the planet, from the early Stone Age to 20th-century art, via the 1634 Battle of Nördlingen during the Thirty Years' War, Roman endeavours in the area and the town's once-bustling mercantile life.

Stadtmauermuseum   MUSEUM

(An der Löpsinger Mauer 3, Löpsinger Torturm; adult/child €2/1.40; ⊙10am-4.30pm Tue-Sun Apr-Oct) Head up the spiral staircase of the Löpsinger Torturm for an engaging exhibition on the history of the town's defences, an apt place to kick off a circuit of the walls.

★ Festivals & Events

Nördlinger Pfingstmesse   FAIR

(Kaiserwiese; ⊙Jun) The largest annual celebration is the 10-day Nördlinger Pfingstmesse (or often just Nördlinger Messe) that starts two weekends after Whitsuntide (Pentecost). It takes place at the Kaiserwiese to the north of the town and involves 200 stalls and countless fairground attractions.

🛏 Sleeping

Kaiserhof Hotel Sonne   HOTEL €€

(☎09081-5067; www.kaiserhof-hotel-sonne.de; Marktplatz 3; s €55-75, d €80-120; P🐾) Right on the main square, Nördlingen's most famous digs once hosted crowned heads and their entourages, but they have quietly gone to seed in the past two decades. However, rooms are still packed with character, mixing 20th-century comforts with traditional charm, and the atmospheric regional restaurant downstairs is definitely worth a shot.

Art Hotel Ana Flair   DESIGN HOTEL €€

(☎09081-290 030; www.ana-hotels.com; Bürgermeister-Reiger-Strasse 14; s/d from €65/85; 🐾) One of the few hotels outside the historical walls, the crisply contemporary Ana Flair, right opposite the train station, is the latest addition to the town's hotel scene. The 39 rooms blend retro-styling with 21st-century layouts and materials, the communal areas throw a little bit of Swabian tradition into the mix and there's a reasonably priced restaurant for lazy evenings.

Breakfast is normally included making this a pretty good deal all round.

Jugend & Familengästehaus   GUESTHOUSE €€

(JUFA; ☎09081-290 8390; www.jufa.eu; Bleichgraben 3a; s/d from €55/75; P@🐾) Located just outside the town walls, this shiny, 186-bed hotel-hostel-guesthouse is spacious and clean-cut. There are two- to six-bed rooms, ideal for couples or families, and facilities include bicycle hire and a cafe. Unless you are travelling with an entire handball team in tow, staff are not permitted to sell beds in dorms to individual travellers, no matter how hard you plead.

🍴 Eating

La Fontana   ITALIAN €

(Bei den Kornschrannen 2; mains €7-10.50; ⊙11am-11pm Tue-Sun; 🐾) Nördlingen's most popular restaurant is this large Italian pizza-pasta place occupying one end of the terracotta Kornschrannen building as well as tumbling tables out onto Schrannenstrasse. The menu is long, the service swift and when the sun is shining there's no lovelier spot to fill the hole.

Cafe-buch.de   CAFE €

(Weinmarkt 4; snacks from €2; ⊙10am-6pm Mon, Tue & Thu-Sat, from 11am Sun, from noon Wed) That winning combination of coffee, cakes and secondhand books makes this cafe a pleasing midstroll halt for literary types and a nice break from the medieval onslaught for everyone else.

Café Radlos
CAFE €€

(www.cafe-radlos.de; Löpsinger Strasse 8; mains €5.50-16; ☺11.30am-2pm & 5pm-1am Wed-Mon; 🛜🖉) More than just a place to tuck into tasty pizzas and pastas, this convivially random cafe, Nördlingen's coolest haunt, parades cherry-red walls that showcase local art and photography exhibits. Kids have their own toy-filled corner, while you relax with board games, soak up the sunshine in the beer garden or surf the web.

ℹ️ Information

Geopark Ries Information Centre (www.geopark-ries.de; Eugene-Shoemaker-Platz; ☺10am-4.30pm Tue-Sun) Has a free exhibition on the Ries crater.

Tourist Office (☏04081-841 16; www.noerdlingen.de; Marktplatz 2; ☺9am-6pm Mon-Thu, to 4.30pm Fri, 10am-2pm Sat Easter-Oct, plus 10am-2pm Sun Jul & Aug, closed Sat & Sun rest of year) Staff sell the Nördlinger TouristCard (€12.50) that saves you around €8 if you visit everything in town.

ℹ️ Getting There & Away

The Europabus stops at Schäfflesmarkt not far from the St Georgskirche. Bus 501 runs to Dinkelsbühl from the new bus station (50 minutes, seven daily).

Train journeys to and from Munich (€30, two hours) and Augsburg (€16, 1¼ hours) require a change in Donauwörth.

Donauwörth

☏0906 / POP 19,750

Sitting pretty at the confluence of the Danube and Wörnitz rivers, Donauwörth rose from its humble beginnings as a 5th-century fishing village to its zenith as a Free Imperial City in 1301. Three medieval gates and five town wall towers still guard it today, and faithful rebuilding – after WWII had destroyed 75% of the medieval old town – means steep-roofed houses in a rainbow of colours still line its main street, Reichstrasse.

Reichstrasse is around 10 minutes' walk north of the train station. Turn right onto Bahnhofstrasse and cross the bridge onto Ried Island.

◎ Sights

Liebfraukirche
CHURCH

(Reichstrasse) At the western end of Reichstrasse rises this 15th-century Gothic church with original frescos and a curiously sloping floor that drops 120cm. Swabia's largest church bell (6550kg) swings in the belfry.

Käthe-Kruse-Puppenmuseum
MUSEUM

(www.kaethe-kruse.de; Pflegstrasse 21a; adult/child €2.50/1.50; ☺11am-6pm Tue-Sun May-Sep, 2-5pm Thu-Sun Oct-Apr) This nostalgia-inducing museum fills a former monastery with old dolls and dollhouses by world-renowned designer Käthe Kruse (1883–1968). Donauwörth is home to the Käthe Kruse doll factory, so many of the 150 exhibits you see here were made locally.

Rathaus
HISTORIC BUILDING

(Rathausgasse) Work on Donauwörth's landmark town hall began in 1236, but it has seen many alterations and additions over the centuries. At 11am and 4pm daily, the carillon on the ornamented step gable plays a composition by local legend Werner Egk (1901–83) from his opera *Die Zaubergeige* (The Magic Violin). The building also houses the tourist office.

Heilig-Kreuz-Kirche
CHURCH

(Heilig-Kreuz-Strasse) Overlooking the grassy banks of the shallow River Wörnitz, this soaring baroque confection has for centuries lured the faithful to pray before a chip of wood, said to come from the Holy Cross, installed in the ornate-ceilinged Gnadenkappelle (Grace Chapel).

🛏️ Sleeping & Eating

Drei Kronen
HOTEL €€

(☏09851-706 170; www.hotel3kronen.com; Bahnhofstrasse 25; s/d €85/120, apt per person €90; 🅿🛜) Situated opposite the train station a little way along Bahnhofstrasse, the 'Three Crowns' has the town's most comfortable, if slightly cramped, rooms and a lamplit restaurant. There's also an apartment with kitchen.

Posthotel Traube
BAVARIAN €€

(Kapellstrasse 14-16; mains €5-17; ☺11am-2pm & 5-10pm Mon-Fri & Sun, closed Sat) Choose from a cafe, coffeehouse, restaurant or beer garden at this friendly, multitasking hotel where Mozart stayed as a boy in 1777. The schnitzel, cordon bleu and local carp in beer sauce are where your finger should land on the menu.

Cafe Rafaello
ITALIAN €€

(www.raffaello-donauwoerth.de; Fischerplatz 1; mains €7-25; ☺10am-midnight) On Ried Island, this Italian job specialising in seafood uses Apennines kitsch to recreate *la dolce vita* to

HARBURG

Looming over the Wörnitz River, the medieval covered parapets, towers, turrets, keep and red-tiled roofs of the 12th-century **Schloss Harburg** (www.burg-harburg.de; Burgstrasse 1; courtyard admission €3, tour €4; ☉10am-5pm mid-Mar–Oct) are so perfectly preserved they almost seem like a film set. Tours tell the building's long tale and evoke the ghosts that are said to use the castle as a hang-out.

The walk to Harburg's cute, half-timbered Altstadt from the castle takes around 10 minutes, slightly more the other way as you're heading uphill. A fabulous panorama of the village and castle can be admired from the 1702 Stone Bridge spanning the Wörnitz.

One of the most truly romantic places to stay on the RR, part of Harburg Castle has been transformed into a very comfortable **hotel** (☑09080-968 60; d from €85; ℗☎) that combines the ancient architecture of this millennium-old burg with antique furniture and 21st-century plumbing. All of the rooms are different and some have idyllic views of the castle courtyard and the surrounding hills.

The Europabus stops in the village (outside the Gasthof Grüner Baum) but not at the castle. Hourly trains run to Nördlingen (€4.90, 15 minutes) and Donauwörth (€4, 12 minutes). The train station is about a 30-minute walk from the castle.

southern German tastes. The endless menu has something for everyone.

❶ Information

Tourist Office (☑09851-789 151; www.donauwoerth.de; Rathausgasse 1; ☉9am-noon & 1-6pm Mon-Fri, 3-5pm Sat & Sun May-Sep, shorter hours Mon-Fri, closed Sat & Sun Oct-Apr)

❶ Getting There & Away

The Romantic Road Coach (p109) stops by the Liebfraukirche.

Train connections from Donauwörth include Augsburg (€7, 30 minutes, twice hourly), Harburg (€4, 11 minutes, twice hourly), Ingolstadt (€12.90, 45 minutes, hourly) and Nördlingen (€7.20, 30 minutes, hourly).

Augsburg

☑0821 / POP 289,600

The largest city on the Romantic Road (and Bavaria's third largest), Augsburg is also one of Germany's oldest, founded by the step-children of Roman emperor Augustus over 2000 years ago. As an independent city state from the 13th century, it was also one of its wealthiest, free to raise its own taxes, with public coffers bulging on the proceeds of the textile trade. Banking families such as the Fuggers and the Welsers even bankrolled entire countries and helped out the odd skint monarch. However, from the 16th century, religious strife and economic decline plagued the city. Augsburg finally joined the Kingdom of Bavaria in 1806.

Shaped by Romans, medieval artisans, bankers, traders and, more recently, industry

and technology, this attractive city of spires and cobbles is an easy day trip from Munich or an engaging stop on the Romantic Road, though one with a grittier, less quaint atmosphere than others along the route.

◉ Sights

Fuggerei   HISTORIC SITE
(www.fugger.de; Jakober Strasse; adult/concession €4/3; ☉8am-8pm Apr-Sep, 9am-6pm Oct-Mar) The legacy of Jakob Fugger 'The Rich' lives on at Augsburg's Catholic welfare settlement, the Fuggerei, which is the oldest of its kind in existence. Around 200 people live here today and their rent remains frozen at 1 Rhenish guilder (now €0.88) per year, plus utilities and three daily prayers. Residents wave to you as you wander through the car-free lanes of this gated community flanked by its 52 pin-neat houses (containing 140 apartments) and little gardens.

To see how residents lived before running water and central heating, one of the apartments now houses the **Fuggereimuseum** (Mittlere Gasse 14; admission incl with entry to the Fuggerei; ☉9am-8pm Mar-Oct, to 6pm Nov-Apr), while there's a modern apartment open for public viewing at Ochsengasse 51. Interpretive panels are in German but you can ask for an information leaflet in English or download it from the website before you arrive.

St Anna Kirche   CHURCH
(Im Annahof 2, off Annastrasse; ☉noon-6pm Mon, 10am-12.30pm & 3-6pm Tue-Sat, 10am-12.30pm & 3-5pm Sun May-Oct, slightly shorter hours Nov-Apr) **FREE** Often regarded as the first Renaissance

church in Germany, the rather plain-looking (and well-hidden) St Anna Kirche is accessed via a set of cloisters lined with tombstones. The church contains a bevy of treasures, as well as the sumptuous Fuggerkapelle, where Jacob Fugger and some of his relatives lie buried, and the lavishly frescoed Goldschmiedekapelle (Goldsmiths' Chapel; 1420). The church played an important role during the Reformation. In 1518 Martin Luther, in town to defend his beliefs before the papal legate, stayed at what was then a Carmelite monastery. His rooms have been turned into the Lutherstiege, a very informative exhibition about the Reformation and Luther's life.

Brechthaus   MUSEUM
(☑0821-324 2779; Auf dem Rain 7; adult/concession €3.50/2.50; ☉10am-5pm Tue-Sun) Opened in 1998 to celebrate local boy Bertolt Brecht's 100th birthday, this house museum is the birthplace of the famous playwright and poet, where he lived for the first two years of his life (from 1898 to 1900) before moving across town. Among the displays are old theatre posters and a great series of life-size chronological photos, as well as his mother's bedroom.

Maximilianmuseum   MUSEUM
(☑0821-324 4102; www.kunstsammlungen-museen. augsburg.de; Philippine-Welser-Strasse 24; adult/ child €7/free; ☉10am-5pm Tue-Sun) The Maximilianmuseum occupies two patrician townhouses joined by a statue-studded courtyard covered by a glass-and-steel roof. Highlights include a fabulous collection of Elias Holl's original wooden models for his architectural creations, and a collection of gold and silver coins. However, the real highlights here are the expertly curated temporary exhibitions on a variety of Bavarian themes.

Dom Mariä Heimsuchung   CHURCH
(Hoher Weg; ☉7am-6pm) Augsburg's cathedral has its origins in the 10th century but was Gothicised and enlarged in the 14th and 15th centuries. The star treasures here are the so-called 'Prophets' Windows'. Depicting David, Daniel, Jonah, Hosea and Moses, they are among the oldest figurative stained-glass windows in Germany, dating from the 12th century. Look out for four paintings by Hans Holbein the Elder, including one of Jesus' circumcision.

Rathausplatz   SQUARE
The heart of Augsburg's Altstadt, this large, pedestrianised square is anchored by the Augustusbrunnen, a fountain honouring the Roman emperor; its four figures represent the Lech River and the Wertach, Singold and Brunnenbach brooks.

Rising above the square are the twin onion-domed spires of the Renaissance **Rathaus** (Rathausplatz), built by Elias Holl from 1615 to 1620 and crowned by a 4m-tall pine cone, the city's emblem (also an ancient fertility symbol). Upstairs is the **Goldener Saal** (Golden Hall; adult/child €2.50/1.50; ☉10am-6pm), a huge banquet hall with an amazing gilded and frescoed coffered ceiling.

For panoramic views over Rathausplatz and the city, climb to the top of the **Perlachturm** (adult/child €2/1; ☉10am-6pm Apr-Nov), a former guard tower, and also an Elias Holl creation.

Jüdisches Kulturmuseum   MUSEUM
(☑0821-513 658; www.jkmas.de; Halderstrasse 6-8; adult/child €4/2; ☉9am-6pm Tue-Thu, to 4pm Fri, 10am-5pm Sun) About 300m east of the main train station, as you head towards the Altstadt, you'll come to the Synagoge Augsburg, an art nouveau temple built between 1914 and 1917 and housing a worthwhile Jewish museum. Exhibitions here focus on Jewish life in the region, presenting religious artefacts collected from defunct synagogues across Swabia.

🛏 Sleeping

As you might expect for a city of Augsburg's size, you can find every type of accommodation here, even a large hostel. The city could be used as an alternative base for Oktoberfest, though hotel owners pump up their prices just as much as their Munich counterparts do.

Übernacht   HOSTEL €
(☑0821-4554 2828; www.uebernacht-hostel.de; Karlstrasse 4; dm/d from €19/50; ☏) Professionally run, 21st-century operation spread over three floors of a former office block with a wide selection of bright dorms, doubles and apartments, some en suite, some with shared facilities. Amenities are hotel standard and there's a superb kitchen for guest use. Book ahead in summer and during Oktoberfest.

Gästehaus SLEPS   GUESTHOUSE €
(☑0821-780 8890; www.sleps.de; Unterer Graben 6; s/d from €42/65; ☏) The SLEPS is simply the singles and doubles at Augsburg's youth hostel (*Jugendherberge*), rebranded as a guesthouse. Rooms still have that whiff of institutional occupation about them but are

bright, clean and quiet. For these prices the decent buffet breakfast is a real bonus these days.

★Dom Hotel
HOTEL €€

(☑ 0821-343 930; www.domhotel-augsburg.de; Frauentorstrasse 8; s €80-150, d €100-180; P ⊝ 🛜 🛎) Augsburg's top choice packs a 500-year-old former bishop's guesthouse (Martin Luther and Kaiser Maxmilian I stayed here) with 57 rooms, all different but sharing a stylishly understated air and pristine upkeep; some have cathedral views. The big pluses here, however, are the large swimming pool and fitness centre. Parking is an extra €6.

Hotel am Rathaus
HOTEL €€

(☑ 0821-346 490; www.hotel-am-rathaus-augsburg.de; Am Hinteren Perlachberg 1; s €70-105 d €105-145; 🛜) With a central location just steps from Rathausplatz and Maximilianstrasse, this boutique hotel has 31 rooms with freshly neutral decor and a sunny little breakfast room. Attracts a business-oriented clientele, so watch out for special weekend deals (almost a third off normal rates).

Steigenberger Drei Mohren Hotel
HOTEL €€€

(☑ 0821-503 60; www.augsburg.steigenberger.de; Maximilianstrasse 40; r from €150; P ⊝ ❄ @ 🛜) Proud dad Leopold Mozart stayed here with his prodigious offspring in 1766 and it remains by far Augsburg's oldest and grandest hotel. The punctiliously maintained rooms are the last word in soothing design and come with marble bathrooms and original art. Dine in-house at the gastronomic extravaganza that is Maximilians, a great place to swing by for Sunday brunch.

✖ Eating

In the evening, Maximilianstrasse is the place to tarry, with cafes tumbling out onto the pavements and Augsburg's young and beautiful watching the world go by. Fast-food joints gather around the Königsplatz and along Frauenstrasse.

Anno 1578
CAFE €

(Fuggerplatz 9; mains €5-11; ⊙ 9am-7pm Mon-Sat; 🛜) Munch on blockbuster breakfasts, lunchtime burgers and sandwiches, or just pop by for a cappuccino or ice cream at this trendy cafe under ancient neon-uplit vaulting. The central table, a huge chunk of timber, is a great place to meet locals and other travellers.

★Perlacht Acht
MEDITERRANEAN €€

(☑ 0821-2480 5265; www.perlachacht.de; Am Perlachberg 8; mains €10-17; ⊙ noon-11pm Mon-Fri, 9.30am-11pm Sat & Sun; 🛜) Run by a young local couple, this superb restaurant has its focus firmly on light, flavoursome dishes with a sunny Mediterranean bent. Take a seat at one of the hefty olive-wood tables to enjoy handmade pastas, tomato risotto with smoked mozarella and crispy pork belly with orange, fennel and gnocchi.

Antico Duomo
ITALIAN €€

(www.antico-duomo.de; Frauentorstrasse 2; mains €7-26; ⊙ 11am-11pm; 🛜) This Italian job opposite the cathedral has a pink Vespa scooter in the window, attractively laid tables and leathery chairs, seated on which you can enjoy something tasty from the *bel paese*. The menu runs the full gamut of Italian cuisine and there's plenty of prosecco and Valpolicella to wash it all down.

Bauerntanz
GERMAN €€

(Bauerntanzgässchen 1; mains €8-20; ⊙ 11am-11.30pm) Belly-satisfying helpings of creative Swabian and Bavarian food – *Spätzle* (local pasta) and more *Spätzle* – are plated up by friendly staff at this prim Alpine tavern with lace curtains, hefty timber interior and chequered fabrics. When the sun makes an appearance, everyone bails for the outdoor seating.

★August
INTERNATIONAL €€€

(☑ 0821-352 79; Johannes-Haag-Strasse 14; dinner €169; ⊙ from 7pm Wed-Sat) Most Augsburgers have little inkling their city possesses two Michelin stars, both of which belong to chef Christian Grünwald. Treat yourself to tasty smears and blobs that make up some of Bavaria's most innovative cooking, served in the beautifully renovated dining room of a small mansion east of the city centre. Reserve well ahead.

🍷 Drinking & Nightlife

City Club
CAFE

(www.cityclub.name; Konrad-Adenauer-Allee 9; ⊙ from 2pm Tue-Sun) For some grungy student drinking action, head to this cafe near the tram interchange with its mismatched furniture, vegie pizzas and almost nightly DJs.

Thing
BEER GARDEN

(www.mein-thing.de; Vorderer Lech 45; ⊙ 6pm-1am Mon-Thu, to 2am Fri & Sat, 5pm-midnight Sun) Augsburg's coolest beer garden sports totem poles and often gets crowded in the evenings. Serves great burgers and beer.

DON'T MISS

WIESKIRCHE

Located in the village of Wies, just off the B17 between Füssen and Schongau, the Wieskirche (☑ 08862-932 930; www.wieskirche.de; ☺ 8am-8pm Apr-Oct, to 5pm Nov-Mar) is one of Bavaria's best-known baroque churches and a Unesco World Heritage Site. About a million visitors a year flock to see its pride and joy, the monumental work of the legendary artist-brothers Dominikus and Johann Baptist Zimmermann.

In 1730, a farmer in Steingaden, about 30km northeast of Füssen, witnessed the miracle of his Christ statue shedding tears. Pilgrims poured into the town in such numbers over the next decade that the local abbot commissioned a new church to house the weepy work. Inside the almost circular structure, eight snow-white pillars are topped by gold capital stones and swirling decorations. The unsupported dome must have seemed like God's work in the mid-17th century, its surface adorned with a pastel ceiling fresco celebrating Christ's resurrection.

From Füssen, regional RVO bus 73 (www.rvo-bus.de) makes the journey six times daily. The Romantic Road Coach (p109) also stops here long enough in both directions to have a brief look round then get back on. By car, take the B17 northeast and turn right (east) at Steingaden.

☆ Entertainment

Augsburger Puppenkiste   THEATRE
(☑ 0821-450 3450; www.augsburger-puppenkiste. de; Spitalgasse 15; tickets from €9.50) The celebrated puppet theatre holds performances of modern and classic fairy tales that even non–German speakers will enjoy. Advance bookings essential.

❶ Information

Post Office (Halderstrasse 29; ☺ 8am-6.30pm Mon-Fri, 9am-1pm Sat) At the Hauptbahnhof.
Tourist Office (☑ 0821-502 0723; www. augsburg-tourismus.de; Rathausplatz; ☺ 8.30am-5.30pm Mon-Fri, 10am-5pm Sat, 10am-3pm Sun Apr-Oct, slightly shorter hours Mon-Fri Nov-Mar) This office multitasks as a citizen's advice point so staff can be slightly distracted.

❶ Getting There & Away

The Romantic Road Coach (p109) stops at both the Hauptbahnhof and the Rathaus.

Augsburg has rail connections with Donauwörth (€13, 20 to 40 minutes, three hourly), Munich (€14.60 to €20, 30 to 50 minutes, three hourly), Nuremberg (€19 to €62, one to two hours, hourly) and Ulm (€20 to €25.50, 45 minutes to one hour, three hourly). Direct services go to Füssen (€22, two hours, every two hours), otherwise change in Buchloe.

❶ Getting Around

From the train station take tram 3, 4 or 6 (€1.80) to the central interchange at Königsplatz where all Augsburg's tram routes converge. Trams 1 and 2 run from there to Ratshausplatz.

Landsberg am Lech

☑ 08191 / POP 28,800

Lovely Landsberg am Lech is often overlooked by Romantic Road trippers on their town-hopping way between Füssen to the south and Augsburg to the north. But it's for this very absence of tourists and a less commercial ambience that this walled town, prettily set on the River Lech, is worth a halt, if only a brief one.

Landsberg can claim to be the town where one of the German language's best-selling books was written. Was it a work by Goethe, Remarque, Brecht? No, unfortunately, it was Hitler. It was during his 264 days of incarceration in a Landsberg jail, following the 1923 beer-hall putsch, that Adolf penned his hate-filled *Mein Kampf,* a book that sold an estimated seven million copies when published. The jail later held Nazi war criminals and is still in use.

☉ Sights

Landsberg's hefty medieval defensive walls are punctuated by some beefy gates, the most impressive of which are the 1425 Bayertor to the east and the Renaissance-styled Sandauer Tor to the north. The tall Schmalztor was left centrally stranded when the fortifications were moved further out and still overlooks the main square and the 500 listed buildings within the town walls.

Johanniskirche   CHURCH
(Vorderer Anger 215) If you've already seen the Wieskirche to the south, you will instantly

recognise this small baroque church as a creation by the same architect, Dominikus Zimmermann, who lived in Landsberg and even served as its mayor.

Stadtpfarrkirche Mariä Himmelfahrt
CHURCH

(Georg-Hellmair-Platz) This huge 15th-century church with its slender bell tower was built by Matthäus von Ensingen, architect of Bern Cathedral. The barrel nave is stuccoed to baroque perfection, while a cast of saints populates columns and alcoves above the pews. Gothic-era stained glass casts rainbow hues on the church's most valuable work of art, the 15th-century *Madonna with Child* by local sculptor Lorenz Luidl.

Heilig-Kreuz-Kirche
CHURCH

(Von-Helfenstein-Gasse) Head uphill from the Schmalztor to view this beautiful baroque Jesuit church, the interior of which is a hallucination in broodily dark gilding and glorious ceiling decoration.

Neues Stadtmuseum
MUSEUM

(www.museum-landsberg.de; Von-Helfenstein-Gasse 426; adult/child €3/1.50; ⊙2-5pm Tue-Fri, from 11am Sat & Sun May-Jan, closed Feb-Apr) Housed in a former Jesuit school, Landsberg's municipal museum chronicles the area's past from prehistory to the 20th century, and displays numerous works of local art, both religious and secular in nature.

🛏 Sleeping & Eating

Stadthotel Augsburger Hof
HOTEL €€

(☑08191-969 596; www.stadthotel-landsberg.de; Schlossergasse 378; s €45-70, d €90; 🅿🛜) The 15 en suite rooms at this highly recommended traditional inn are a superb deal, and have chunky pine beds and well-maintained bathrooms throughout. The owners and staff are a friendly bunch, and the breakfast is a filling set-up for the day. Cycle hire and cycle-friendly.

Weidekind
INTERNATIONAL €€

(☑08191-979 7083; www.weidekind-landsberg.de; Bahnhofsplatz 1; mains €7-15; ⊙7am-6pm Mon, to 10pm Tue-Thu, to 11.30pm Fri, 5.30-11.30pm Sat, 10am-6pm Sun; 🛜) Arguably Landsberg's best eatery is in the *Bürgerbahnhof,* the publicly owned train station. Savour imaginative dishes, stylishly served in the 21st-century interior, all bare lamp bulbs and exposed brick walls, as you watch people buy their tickets for the next train. The building has a great vibe (Deutsche Bahn would have replaced

it with a ticket machine) and it's well worth stopping by.

Lechgarten
BAVARIAN €€

(www.lechgarten.de; Hubert-von-Herkomer-Strasse 73; mains €5-11; ⊙3-11pm Mon-Fri, noon-11pm Sat & Sun Apr-Oct) Lansberg's top beer garden on the tree-shaded banks of the River Lech has 250 seats, beer from Andechs Monastery and hearty beer-garden fare. Live music summer weekends, pretty river views any time.

ⓘ Information

Tourist Office (☑08191-128 246; www.landsberg.de; Hauptplatz 152; ⊙9am-12.30pm & 1.30-6pm Mon-Fri, 11.30am-5pm Sat & Sun May-Oct, shorter hours Nov-Apr) Within the wonderfully stucco'ed Rathaus.

ⓘ Getting There & Away

The Romantic Road Coach (p109) stops on the Hauptplatz.

The **train station** (Bahnhofsplatz) is just across the Lech from the historical centre. Landsberg has connections to Augsburg (€9.70, 50 minutes, hourly), Füssen (€17.80, 1½ hours, every two hours), with a change at Kaufering, and Munich (€14.60, 55 minutes, twice hourly), with a change at Kaufering.

NUREMBERG & FRANCONIA

Somewhere between Ingolstadt and Nuremberg, Bavaria's accent mellows, the oompah bands play that little bit quieter and wine competes with beer as the local tipple. This is Franconia (Franken) and, as every local will tell you, Franconians, who inhabit the wooded hills and the banks of the Main River in Bavaria's northern reaches, are a breed apart from their brash and extroverted cousins to the south.

In the northwest, the region's winegrowers produce some exceptional whites, sold in a distinctive teardrop-shaped bottle called the *Bocksbeutel*. For outdoor enthusiasts, the Altmühltal Nature Park offers wonderful hiking, biking and canoeing. But it is Franconia's old royalty and incredible cities – Nuremberg, Bamberg and Coburg – that draw the biggest crowds.

ⓘ Getting There & Away

The region has excellent rail links with the rest of Bavaria and neighbouring *Länder*. Nuremberg Airport (p138) handles flights from tens of destinations around Europe.

Nuremberg

0911 / POP 511,600

Nuremberg (Nürnberg), Bavaria's second-largest city and the unofficial capital of Franconia, is an energetic place where the nightlife is intense and the beer is as dark as coffee. As one of Bavaria's biggest draws it is alive with visitors year-round, but especially during the spectacular Christmas market.

For centuries, Nuremberg was the undeclared capital of the Holy Roman Empire and the preferred residence of most German kings, who kept their crown jewels here. Rich and stuffed with architectural wonders, it was also a magnet for famous artists, though the most famous of all, Albrecht Dürer, was actually born here. 'Nuremberg shines throughout Germany like a sun among the moon and stars,' gushed Martin Luther. By the 19th century, the city had become a powerhouse in Germany's industrial revolution.

The Nazis saw a perfect stage for their activities in working class Nuremberg. It was here that the fanatical party rallies were held, the boycott of Jewish businesses began and the infamous Nuremberg Laws outlawing German citizenship for Jewish people were enacted. On 2 January 1945, Allied bombers reduced the city to landfill, killing 6000 people in the process.

After WWII the city was chosen as the site of the war crimes tribunal, now known as the Nuremberg Trials. Later, the painstaking reconstruction – using the original stone – of almost all the city's main buildings, including the castle and old churches in the Altstadt, returned the city to some of its former grandeur.

◎ Sights

Most major sights are within the Altstadt and can be covered on foot. Only a few, such as the Reichsparteigelände and the Memorium Nuremberg Trials exhibition, require a trip by public transport.

★ **Kaiserburg**   CASTLE

(Imperial Castle; ☎0911-244 6590; www.kaiser burg-nuernberg.de; Auf der Burg; adult/child incl Sinwell Tower €7/free, Palas & Museum €5.50/free; ☺9am-6pm Apr-Sep, 10am-4pm Oct-Mar) This enormous castle complex above the Altstadt poignantly reflects Nuremberg's medieval might. The main attraction is a tour of the renovated residential wing (Palas) to see the lavish Knights' and Imperial Hall, a Romanesque double chapel and an exhibit on the inner workings of the Holy Roman Empire. This segues to the Kaiserburg Museum, which focuses on the castle's military and building history. Elsewhere, enjoy panoramic views from the Sinwell Tower or peer 48m down into the Deep Well.

For centuries the castle, which has origins in the 12th century, also sheltered the crown jewels (crown, sceptre, orb etc) of the Holy Roman Empire, which are now kept at Hofburg palace in Vienna. It also played a key role in the drawing up of Emperor Charles IV's Golden Bull, a document that changed the way Holy Roman Emperors were elected. The exhibition contains an original statue taken from Prague's Charles Bridge of Charles IV who spent a lot of time in both Bohemia and Franconia during his reign.

★ **Deutsche Bahn Museum**   MUSEUM

(☎0800-3268 7386; www.dbmuseum.de; Lessingstrasse 6; adult/child €6/3; ☺9am-5pm Tue-Fri, 10am-6pm Sat & Sun) Forget Dürer and wartime rallies, Nuremberg is a railway town at heart. Germany's first passenger trains ran between here and Fürth, a fact reflected in the unmissable German Railways Museum. which explores the history of Germany's legendary rail system. The huge exhibition that continues across the road is one of Nuremberg's top sights, especially if you have a soft spot for things that run on rails.

If you have tots aboard, head straight for KIBALA (Kinder-Bahnland, Children's Railway World), a section of the museum where lots of hands-on, interactive choo-choo-themed attractions await. There's also a huge model railway, one of Germany's largest, set in motion every hour by a uniformed controller.

The main exhibition charting almost two centuries of rail history starts on the ground floor and continues with more recent exhibits on the first. Passing quickly through the historically inaccurate beginning (as every rail buff knows, the world's first railway was the Stockton–Darlington, not the Liverpool–Manchester), highlights include Germany's oldest railway carriage dating from 1835 and lots of interesting Deutsche Reichsbahn paraphernalia from the former East Germany.

However, the real meat of the show is the two halls of locos and rolling stock. The first hall contains Ludwig II's incredible rococo rail carriage, dubbed the 'Versailles of the rails', as well as Bismarck's considerably less ostentatious means of transport. There's also Germany's most famous steam loco,

Nuremberg

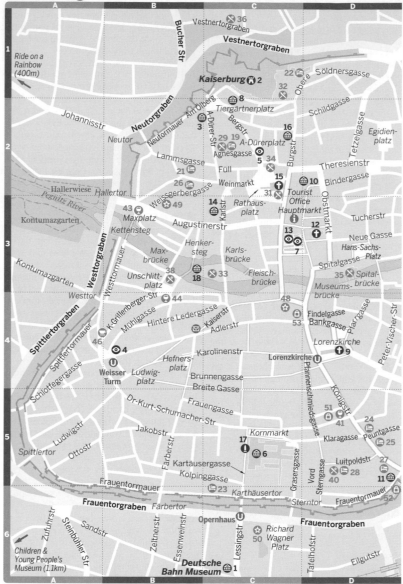

the Adler, built by the Stephensons in Newcastle-upon-Tyne for the Nuremberg–Fürth line. The second hall across the road from the main building houses some mammoth engines, some with their Nazi or Deutsche Reichsbahn insignia still in place.

Germanisches Nationalmuseum

MUSEUM

(German National Museum; ☑ 0911-133 10; www.gnm.de; Kartäusergasse 1; adult/child €8/5; ☉10am-6pm Tue & Thu-Sun, to 9pm Wed) Spanning prehistory to the early 20th century,

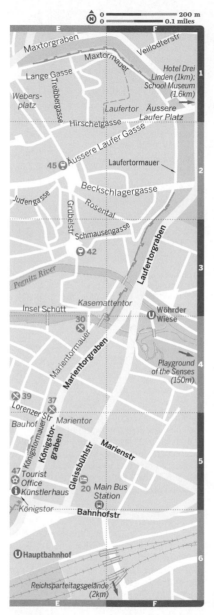

this museum is the German-speaking world's biggest and most important museum of Teutonic culture. It features works by German painters and sculptors, an archaeological collection, arms and armour, musical and scientific instruments, and toys.

Highlights of the eclectic collection include Dürer's anatomically detailed *Hercules Slaying the Stymphalian Birds* and the world's oldest terrestrial globe and pocket watch as well as 20th-century design classics and baroque dollhouses.

Reichsparteitagsgelände HISTORIC SITE

(Luitpoldhain; ☑ 0911-231 7538; www.museen.nuern berg.de/dokuzentrum; Bayernstrasse 110; grounds free, Documentation Centre adult/child incl audioguide €6/1.50; ⊙ grounds 24hr, Documentation Centre 9am-6pm Mon-Fri, 10am-6pm Sat & Sun) If you've ever wondered where the infamous B&W images of ecstatic Nazi supporters hailing their Führer were taken, it was here in Nuremberg. Much of the grounds were destroyed during Allied bombing raids, but enough remain to get a sense of the megalomania behind it, especially after visiting the excellent Dokumentationszentrum (Documentation Centre). It's served by tram 8 from the Hauptbahnhof.

In the north wing of the partly finished Kongresshalle (Congress Hall), the Documentation Centre examines various historical aspects, including the rise of the NSDAP, the Hitler cult, the party rallies and the Nuremberg Trials.

East of here is the Zeppelinfeld, where most of the big Nazi parades, rallies and events took place. It is fronted by a 350m-long grandstand, the Zeppelintribüne, where you can still stand on the very balcony from where Hitler incited the masses. It now hosts sporting events and rock concerts, though this rehabilitation has caused controversy.

The grounds are bisected by the 2km-long and 40m-wide Grosse Strasse (Great Road), which was planned as a military parade road. Zeppelinfeld, Kongresshalle and Grosse Strasse are all protected landmarks for being significant examples of Nazi architecture.

The Reichsparteitagsgelände is about 4km southeast of the city centre.

Memorium Nuremberg Trials MEMORIAL

(☑ 0911-3217 9372; www.memorium-nuremberg. de; Bärenschanzstrasse 72; adult/child incl audio guide €6/1.50; ⊙ 9am-6pm Mon & Wed-Fri, 10am-6pm Sat & Sun Apr-Oct, slightly shorter hours Nov-Mar) Göring, Hess, Speer and 21 other Nazi leaders were tried for crimes against peace and humanity by the Allies in Schwurgerichtssaal 600 (Court Room 600) of this still-working courthouse. Today the room forms part of an engaging exhibit detailing the background, progression and impact of the trials using film, photographs, audiotape

BAVARIA NUREMBERG

Nuremberg

and even the original defendants' dock. To get here, take the U1 towards Bärenschanze and get off at Sielstrasse.

The initial and most famous trial, held from 20 November 1945 until 1 October 1946, resulted in three acquittals, 12 sentences to death by hanging, three life sentences and four long prison sentences. Hermann Göring, the Reich's field marshall, famously cheated the hangman by taking a cyanide capsule in his cell hours before his scheduled execution.

Although it's easy to assume that Nuremberg was chosen as a trial venue because of its sinister key role during the Nazi years, it was actually picked for practical reasons since the largely intact Palace of Justice was able to accommodate lawyers and staff from all four Allied nations.

Note that Court Room 600 is still used for trials and may be closed to visitors.

Spielzeugmuseum   MUSEUM
(Toy Museum; Karlstrasse 13-15; adult/child €6/1.50; ⊙10am-5pm Tue-Fri, to 6pm Sat & Sun) Nuremberg

has long been a centre of toy manufacturing, and the large Spielzeugmuseum presents toys in their infinite variety – from innocent hoops to blood-and-guts computer games, historical wooden and tin toys to Barbie et al. Kids and kids at heart will delight in the imaginatively designed play area.

Way of Human Rights   MONUMENT
(Kartäusergasse) Next to the Germanisches Nationalmuseum, 30 austere, 8m-tall concrete columns, each bearing one article of the Universal Declaration of Human Rights in a different language (plus German), run the entire length of Kartäusergasse. This spectacle is the work of Israeli artist Dani Karavan and is even more relevant in today's central Europe than it was when he won the competition to design the look of the street in the early 1990s.

Albrecht-Dürer-Haus   MUSEUM
(📞0911-231 2568; Albrecht-Dürer-Strasse 39; adult/child €6/1.50; ⊙10am-5pm Tue, Wed & Fri, to 8pm Thu, to 6pm Sat & Sun, to 5pm Mon Jul-Sep)

Dürer, Germany's most famous Renaissance draughtsperson, lived and worked at this site from 1509 until his death in 1528. Enjoy the slightly OTT multimedia show before embarking on an audioguide tour of the four-storey house narrated by 'Agnes', Dürer's wife. Highlights are the hands-on demonstrations in the recreated studio and print shop on the 3rd floor and, in the attic, a gallery featuring copies and originals of Dürer's work. The museum gift shop across the street is a source of original, highbrow souvenirs.

Ehekarussell Brunnen   FOUNTAIN

(Am Weissen Turm) At the foot of the fortified Weisser Turm (White Tower; now the gateway to the U-Bahn station of the same name) stands this large and startlingly grotesque sculptural work depicting six interpretations of marriage (from first love to quarrel to death-do-us-part), all based on a verse by Hans Sachs, the medieval cobbler-poet. You soon realise why the artist faced a blizzard of criticism when the fountain was unveiled in 1984; it really is enough to put anyone off tying the knot.

Sachs' poem can be found chiselled into a large pink marble heart on the tower side of the fountain.

St Sebalduskirche   CHURCH

(www.sebalduskirche.de; Winklerstrasse 26; ⊙ 9.30am-4pm Jan-Mar, to 6pm Apr-Dec) Nuremberg's oldest church was hoisted skywards in rusty pink-veined sandstone in the 13th century. Its exterior is replete with religious sculptures and symbols; check out the ornate carvings over the Bridal Doorway to the north, showing the Wise and Foolish Virgins. Inside, the bronze shrine of St Sebald (Nuremberg's own saint) is a Gothic and Renaissance masterpiece that took its maker, Peter Vischer the Elder, and his two sons more than 11 years to complete (Vischer is in it, too, sporting a skullcap).

Lorenzkirche   CHURCH

(Lorenzplatz; ⊙ 9am-5pm Mon-Sat, 1-4pm Sun, guided tours in German 11am & 2pm Mon-Sat, 2pm Sun) FREE Dark and atmospheric, the Lorenzkirche has dramatically downlit pillars, taupe stone columns, sooty ceilings and many artistic highlights. Check out the 15th-century tabernacle in the left aisle – the delicate carved strands wind up to the vaulted ceiling. Remarkable also are the stained glass (including a rose window 9m in diameter) and Veit Stoss' *Engelsgruss* (Annunciation), a wooden carving with life-size figures

suspended above the high altar. Some of the free German-language tours climb the tower, normally out of bounds to visitors.

Stadtmuseum Fembohaus   MUSEUM

(☑ 0911-231 2595; Burgstrasse 15; adult/child €6/1.50; ⊙ 10am-5pm Tue-Fri, to 6pm Sat & Sun) Offering an entertaining overview of the city's history, highlights of the Stadtmuseum Fembohaus include the restored historic rooms of this 16th-century merchant's house. Other sections look at aspects of Nuremberg's past and the 'A Crown – Power – History' exhibition gives you a potted history of the city in 30 minutes in the company of a special audioguide, an excellent and commendably digestable idea.

Neues Museum   MUSEUM

(☑ 0911-240 269; www.nmn.de; Luitpoldstrasse 5; adult/child €6/5; ⊙ 10am-6pm Fri-Wed, to 8pm Thu, closed Mon) The aptly named New Museum showcases contemporary art and design from the 1950s onwards, with resident collections of paintings, sculpture, photography and video art complemented by world-class travelling shows. Equally stunning is the award-winning building itself, with a dramatic 100m curved glass facade that, literally and figuratively, reflects the stone town wall opposite.

Jüdisches Museum Franken   JEWISH, MUSEUM

(☑ 0911-977 4853; www.juedisches-museum.org; Königstrasse 89; adult/child €3/free; ⊙ Tue-Sun 10am-5pm) A quick U-Bahn ride away in the adjoining town of Fürth is the Jüdisches Museum Franken. Fürth once had the largest Jewish congregation of any city in southern Germany, and this museum chronicles the history of Jewish life in the region from Middle Ages to today. To reach the museum, take the U1 to the Rathaus stop in Fürth.

Felsengänge   HISTORIC SITE

(Underground Cellars; www.historische-felsengaenge. de; Bergstrasse 19; tours adult/concession/child under 7 €7/6/free; ⊙ tours hourly 11am-5pm Mon-Fri, 10am-5pm Sat & Sun) Deep beneath the Albrecht Dürer Monument on Albrecht-Dürer-Platz lurks the chilly Felsengänge. Departing from the brewery shop at Bergstrasse 19, tours descend to this four-storey subterranean warren, which dates from the 14th century and once housed a brewery and a beer cellar. During WWII, it served as an air-raid shelter. Tours take a minimum of three people and last 60 to 70 minutes. Take a jacket against the damp chill.

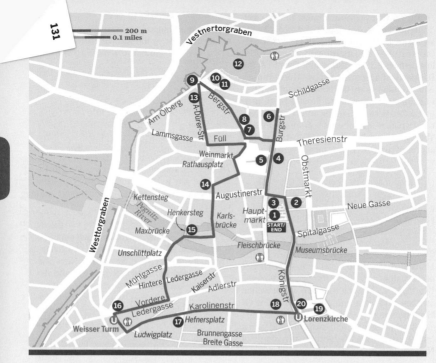

🏃 Walking Tour
Nuremberg Altstadt

START HAUPTMARKT
END HAUPTMARKT
LENGTH 2.5KM, TWO HOURS

This leisurely circuit covers the historic centre's key sights, taking as long as you like.

Start at the **❶ Hauptmarkt** (p133), the main square. At the eastern end is the ornate Gothic **❷ Pfarrkirche Unsere Liebe Frau** (p133), also called the Frauenkirche. Nearby the **❸ Schöner Brunnen** (p133) fountain rises from the cobblestones. Walk north to the **❹ Altes Rathaus**, the old town hall, with its Lochgefängnisse (medieval dungeons). Opposite is the 13th-century **❺ St Sebalduskirche** (p131), with the bronze shrine of St Sebald inside. Just up Burgstrasse, the **❻ Stadtmuseum Fembohaus** (p131) covers the highs and lows of Nuremberg's past. Backtrack south and turn right into Albrecht-Dürer-Platz, with the **❼ Albrecht Dürer Monument**. Directly beneath are the **❽ Felsengänge** (p131), tunnels once used as beer cellars and an air-raid shelter.

Moving up Bergstrasse, you'll reach the massive **❾ Tiergärtnertor**, a 16th-century tower. Nearby is the half-timbered **❿ Pilatushaus**. A few steps east is the **⓫ Historischer Kunstbunker** (p133) where precious art was stored in WWII. Looming over the whole scene is the **⓬ Kaiserburg** (p127). Go south to the **⓭ Albrecht-Dürer-Haus** (p130), where the Renaissance genius lived and worked. Continue south along Albrecht-Dürer-Strasse, turn left around behind Sebalduskirche to Karlsstrasse, to reach the **⓮ Spielzeugmuseum**, with generations of nostalgia-inducing playthings.

Cross the Karlsbrücke to enjoy a view of the **⓯ Weinstadl** (p133). Continue across the Henkersteg and south to Vordere Ledergasse, leading to the amazing **⓰ Ehekarussell Brunnen** (p131). Head east on Ludwigplatz past the **⓱ Peter-Henlein-Brunnen**, with a statue of the first watchmaker, and along Karolinenstrasse to the city's oldest house, **⓲ Nassauer Haus**, at No 2, and the massive **⓳ Lorenzkirche** (p131), with a 15th-century tabernacle with a suspended carving of the Annunciation. The **⓴ Tugendbrunnen** (Fountain of the Seven Virtues) is on the northern side of the church.

Historischer Kunstbunker
HISTORIC BUILDING

(Historical Art Shelter; ☑911-2360 2731; www.
felsengaenge-nuernberg.de; Obere Schmiedgasse 52; adult/concession/child under 7 €7/6/
free; ☉tours 2.30pm daily, plus 5.30pm Fri & Sat,
11.30am Sun) The Historischer Kunstbunker
is a climate-controlled bomb shelter deep
under the Burgberg that was used to pro-
tect art treasures during WWII. Priceless
masterpieces by Albrecht Dürer, sculptor
Veit Stoss and Martin Behaim, the maker
of a bafflingly accurate 15th-century globe,
were kept safe here from the Allied bombs
raining down on the city. The 75-minute
tour tells the story of how the bunker was
created from old beer cellars long before the
war began and which treasures were kept
safe down there.

Schöner Brunnen
FOUNTAIN

(Beautiful Fountain; Hauptmarkt) Standing like
a space probe on the northwestern corner
of the square is the 19m (62ft) Schöner
Brunnen. A replica of the late 14th-century
original, it is a stunning golden vision of 40
electors, religious heroes and other allegorical figures. The original, made of badly erod-
ed sandstone, stands in the Germanisches
Nationalmuseum.

Pfarrkirche Unsere Liebe Frau
CHURCH

(Frauenkirche; Hauptmarkt) At the eastern end
if the Hauptmarkt stands this ornate Gothic
church, also called the Frauenkirche. Its clock's
figures spring into action every day at noon.

Weinstadl & Henkersteg
HISTORIC BUILDING

On the northern side of the Pegnitz, near
the Karlsbrücke, is the impressive half-
timbered Weinstadl, an old wine depot with
two half-timbered storeys jutting out over
the river. It's had a storied life, ranging from
lepers' refuge to student dorm. Crossing
the river is the covered timber Henkersteg
(Hangman's Bridge), built to keep the hangman's exposure to disease to a minimum.

Mittelalterliche Lochgefängnisse
HISTORIC BUILDING

(Medieval Dungeons; ☑0911-2312690; https://mus
euun.nuernberg.de/lochgefaengnisse; adult/child
€3.50/1.50; ☉tours 10am-4.30pm Tue-Sun) Beneath the Altes Rathaus (1616–22), a hulk of
a building with lovely Renaissance-style interiors, you'll find the macabre Mittelalter-
liche Lochgefängnisse. This 12-cell death
row and torture chamber must be seen on
a guided tour (held every half-hour) and
might easily put you off lunch.

Hauptmarkt
SQUARE

(Hauptmarkt) This bustling square in the heart
of the Altstadt is the site of daily markets
as well as the famous *Christkindlsmarkte*
(Christmas markets). At the eastern end is
the ornate Gothic Frauenkirche (church).
Daily at noon crowds crane their necks to
witness the clock's figures enact a spectacle
called the Männleinlaufen (Little Men Dancing). Rising from the square like a Gothic
spire is the sculpture-festooned Schöner
Brunnen (Beautiful Fountain). Touch the
golden ring in the ornate wrought-iron gate
for good luck.

⛹ Tours

Geschichte für Alle
CULTURAL

(☑0911-307 360; www.geschichte-fuer-alle.de;
adult/concession €8/7) An intriguing range of
themed English-language tours by a non-
profit association. The 'Albrecht Durer' and
'Life in Medieval Nuremberg' tours come
highly recommended.

Old Town Walking Tours
WALKING

(☑0170-141 1223; www.nuernberg-tours.de; tour
€10; ☉1pm May-Oct) English-language Old
Town walking tours are run by the tourist
office – tours leave from the Hauptmarkt
branch and take two hours.

Nuremberg Tours
WALKING

(www.nurembergtours.com; adult/concession €22/
19; ☉11.15am Mon, Wed & Sat Apr-Oct) Four-hour
walking and public transport tours taking
in the city centre and the Reichsparteitagsgelände (p129). Groups meet at the entrance
to the Hauptbahnhof.

⭐ Festivals & Events

Christkindlesmarkt
CHRISTMAS MARKET

(www.christkindlesmarkt.de) From late November to Christmas Eve, the Hauptmarkt is tak-
en over by what most regards as Germany's
top Christmas market. Yuletide shoppers descend on the 'Christmas City' from all over
Europe to seek out unique gifts at the scores
of colourful timber trinket stalls that fill the
square.

🛏 Sleeping

Five Reasons
HOSTEL €

(☑0911-9928 6625; www.five-reasons.de; Frauen-
tormauer 42; dm/d from €18/50; @🛜) This crisp,
21st-century 90-bed hotel-hostel boasts spotless dorms, the trendiest hostel bathrooms
you are ever likely to encounter, premade
beds, card keys, fully equipped kitchen, a

small bar and very nice staff. Breakfast is around €5 extra depending on what option you choose. Overall a great place to lay your head in a very central location.

Probst-Garni Hotel
PENSION €

(☑0911-203 433; www.hotel-garni-probst.de; Luitpoldstrasse 9; s/d €55/70; ☎) A creaky lift from street level takes you up to this realistically priced, centrally located guesthouse, run for over 70 years by three generations of Probsts. The 33 gracefully old-fashioned rooms are multihued and high-ceilinged but some are more renovated than others. Breakfast is an extra €6.50.

Knaus-Campingpark
CAMPGROUND €

(☑0911-981 2717; www.knauscamp.de; Hans-Kalb-Strasse 56; per tent/person €7/8.70; ☎) A camping ground near the lakes not far from the Dokumentationszentrum Reichsparteitagsgelände, southeast of the city centre. Take the S-Bahn to Nürnberg Frankenstadion.

DJH Hostel
HOSTEL €

(☑0911-230 9360; www.nuernberg.jugendherberge.de; Burg 2; dm from €35) Open year-round, this impressive youth hostel is one of Germany's best and a real trip-stopper with a standard of facilities many four-star hotels would envy. Fully revamped a decade ago, the ancient Kornhaus is a dramatic building itself, but now flaunts crisply designed corridors, well-maintained dorms with super-modern bathrooms, a canteen, bar and very helpful staff.

★Hotel Deutscher Kaiser
HOTEL €€

(☑0911-242 660; www.deutscher-kaiser-hotel.de; Königstrasse 55; s/d from €90/110; ☎) Aristocratic in its design and service, this centrally located treat of a historic hotel has been in the same family since the turn of the 20th century. Climb the castle-like granite stairs to find rooms of understated simplicity, flaunting oversize beds, Italian porcelain, silk lampshades and real period furniture (*Biedermeier* and *Jugendstil*).

Agneshof
HOTEL €€

(☑0911-214 440; www.agneshof-nuernberg.de; Agnesgasse 10; s/d from €85/105; P☎) Tranquilly located in the antiques quarter near the St Sebalduskirche, the Agneshof's public areas have a sophisticated, artsy touch. The 74 box-ticking rooms have whitewashed walls and standard hotel furniture; some at the top have views of the Kaiserburg. There's a state-of-the-art wellness centre, and a pretty summer courtyard garden strewn with deckchairs.

Hotel Victoria
HOTEL €€

(☑0911-240 50; www.hotelvictoria.de; Königstrasse 80; s/d from €80/100; P☎) A hotel since 1896, the Victoria is a solid option in a central location. With its early-21st-century bathrooms and now ever so slightly dated decor, the price is about right. Popular with business travellers. Parking costs €14.

Hotel Elch
HOTEL €€

(☑0911-249 2980; www.hotel-elch.com; Irrerstrasse 9; s/d from €55/70; ☎) Occupying a 14th-century, half-timbered house near the Kaiserburg, the Elch has a boutique wing and a 21st-century reception and restaurant giving you the choice between fairy-tale 'historic' and slick 'boutique', the latter of which costs a bit more.

Burghotel
HOTEL €€

(☑0911-238 890; www.burghotel-nuernberg.de; Lammsgasse 3; s/d from €65/85; @☎▣) The mock-Gothic reception area and lantern-lit corridors (watch your head) indicate you're in for a slightly different hotel experience here. The small singles and doubles have strange '50s-style built-in timber furniture reminiscent of yesteryear train carriages, old-fashioned bedhead radios and chunky TVs, while some much larger 'comfort' rooms under the eaves have spacious sitting areas and more up-to-date amenities.

Art & Business Hotel
HOTEL €€

(☑0911-232 10; www.art-business-hotel.com; Gleissbühlstrasse 15; s/d from €60/90; ☎) No need to be an artist or a businessperson to sleep at this up-to-the-minute place, a short amble from the Hauptbahnhof. From the trendy bar to the latest in slate bathroom styling, design here is bold, but not overpoweringly so. From reception follow the cool carpeting to your room, a well-maintained haven unaffected by traffic noise despite the city-centre frenzy outside.

Hotel Drei Raben
BOUTIQUE HOTEL €€€

(☑0911-274 380; www.hoteldreiraben.de; Königstrasse 63; s/d from €100/160; P✳☎) The design of this classy charmer builds upon the legend of the three ravens perched on the building's chimney stack, who tell stories from Nuremberg lore. Art and decor in the 'mythical theme' rooms reflect a particular tale, from the life of Albrecht Dürer to the first railway.

NUREMBERG FOR KIDS

No city in Bavaria has more for kids to see and do than Nuremberg. Every two months the region even produces a thick 'what's on' magazine called Frankenkids (www.frankenkids.de) focusing specifically on things to do with children. Keeping the little ones entertained in these parts really is child's play.

Museums

Children & Young People's Museum (☎ 0911-600 040; www.kindermuseum-nuernberg.de; Michael-Ende-Strasse 17; adult/family €7.50/19.50; ⏱ 2-5.30pm Sat, 10am-5.30pm Sun Sep-Jun) Educational exhibitions and lots of hands-on fun – just a pity it's not open more often.

School Museum (☎ 0911-530 2574; Äussere Sulzbacher Strasse 62; adult/child €6/1.50; ⏱ 9am-5pm Tue-Fri, 10am-6pm Sat & Sun) Recreated classroom plus school-related exhibits from the 17th century to the Third Reich.

Deutsche Bahn Museum (p127) Feeds the kids' obsession for choo-choos.

Play

Playground of the Senses (www.erfahrungsfeld.nuernberg.de; Wöhrder Wiese; adult/child €8.50/7; ⏱ 9am-6pm Mon-Fri, 1-6pm Sat, 10am-6pm Sun May–mid-Sep) Some 80 hands-on 'stations' designed to educate children in the laws of nature, physics and the human body. Take the U2 or U3 to Wöhrder Wiese.

Toys

Playmobil (☎ 0911-9666 1700; www.playmobil-funpark.de; Brandstätterstrasse 2-10; admission €11.90; ⏱ 10am-6pm mid-Feb–Mar, 9am-6pm Apr, 9am-7pm May–mid-Sep) This theme park has life-size versions of the popular toys. It's located 9km west of the city centre in Zirndorf; take the S4 to Anwanden, then change to bus 151. Free admission if it's your birthday. Special 'Kleine Dürer' (Little Dürer; €2.99) figures are on sale here and at the tourist office.

Käthe Wohlfahrt Christmas shop (p137) The Nuremberg branch of this year-round Christmas shop.

Spielzeugmuseum (p130) Some 1400 sq metres of Matchbox, Barbie, Playmobil and Lego, plus a great play area.

Germanisches Nationalmuseum (p128) Has a toy section and holds ocassional tours for children.

🍴 Eating

Café am Trödelmarkt　　　　　CAFÉ €
(Trödelmarkt 42; dishes €4-10; ⏱ 9am-6pm Mon-Sat, 10am-6pm Sun) A gorgeous place on a sunny day, this multilevel waterfront cafe overlooks the covered Henkersteg bridge. It's especially popular for its continental breakfasts, and has fantastic cakes, as well as good blackboard lunchtime specials between 11am and 2pm.

Naturkostladen Lotos　　ORGANIC, BUFFET €
(www.naturkostladen-lotos.de; Am Unschlittplatz 1; dishes €4-9; ⏱ 9am-6.30pm Mon-Fri, to 5pm Sat; 🌱) Unclog arteries and blast free radicals with a blitz of grain burgers, spinach soup or vegan pizza at this strictly bio health-food shop. The fresh bread and cheese counter is a treasure chest of nutritious picnic supplies.

Suppdiwupp　　　　　　CAFETERIA €
(Lorenzer Strasse 27; soups & mains €4-7; ⏱ 11am-6pm Mon-Thu, to 4pm Fri, noon-5pm Sat) This fragrantly spicy lunch stop has outdoor seating, a weekly changing menu and a choice of nonliquid mains (sandwiches, salads) if you don't fancy one of the 16 types of broth. Very popular early afternoon so get there early.

Wurst Durst　　　　　　GERMAN €
(Luitpoldstrasse 13; dishes €3.50-6; ⏱ 11am-6pm Tue-Thu, to 5am Fri & Sat) Wedged in between the facades of Luitpoldstrasse, this tiny snack bar offers some munchies relief in the form of Belgian fries, sausages and trays of *Currywurst*.

American Diner
AMERICAN €

(Gewerbemuseumsplatz 3; burgers €6-11; ⊙ 11.30am-11.30pm Sun-Thu, to 12.30am Fri & Sat) This retro diner is one of several eateries within the Cinecitta Cinema complex, Germany's biggest multiplex. It serves filling prefilm burgers.

★ Albrecht Dürer Stube
FRANCONIAN €€

(✐ 0911-227 209; www.albrecht-duerer-stube.de; cnr Albrecht-Dürer-Strasse & Agnesgasse; mains €6-15.50; ⊙ 6pm-midnight Mon-Sat plus 11.30am-2.30pm Fri & Sun) This unpretentious and intimate restaurant has a Dürer-inspired dining room, prettily laid tables, a ceramic stove keeping things toasty and a menu of Nuremberg sausages, steaks, sea fish, seasonal specials, Franconian wine and *Landbier* (regional beer). Booking ahead at weekends is highly recommended, as there aren't many tables.

Goldenes Posthorn
FRANCONIAN €€

(✐ 0911-225 153; Glöckleinsgasse 2, cnr Sebalder Platz; mains €6-14; ⊙ 11.30am-11.30pm) Push open the heavy copper door to find a real culinary treat that has hosted royals, artists and professors (including Albrecht Dürer) since 1498. You can't go wrong sticking with the miniature local sausages, but the pork shoulder and also the house speciality – vinegar-marinated ox cheeks – are all good value for money.

Heilig-Geist-Spital
BAVARIAN €€

(✐ 0911-221 761; www.heilig-geist-spital.de; Spitalgasse 16; mains €7-18; ⊙ 11.30am-11pm) Lots of dark carved wood, a herd of hunting trophies and a romantic candlelit half-light make this former hospital, suspended over the Pegnitz, one of the most atmospheric dining rooms in town. Sample the delicious, seasonally changing menu inside or out in the pretty courtyard, a real treat if you are looking for somewhere traditional to dine.

Bratwursthäusle
FRANCONIAN €€

(http://die-nuernberger-bratwurst.de; Rathausplatz 1; meals €7.50-11.50; ⊙ 11am-10pm) Seared over a flaming beech-wood grill, the little links sold at this rustic inn next to the Sebalduskirche arguably set the standard across the land. You can dine in the timbered restaurant or on the terrace with views of the Hauptmarkt. Service can be flustered at busy times and it's cash only when the bill comes.

Hexenhäusle
GERMAN €€

(✐ 0911-4902 9095; www.hexenhaeusle-nuernberg.com; Vestnertorgraben 4; mains €7-12; ⊙ 5-11pm Tue-Thu, 11am-11pm Fri & Sat, 11am-9pm Sun) The half-timbered 'Witches' Hut' ranks among Nuremberg's most enchanting inns and beer gardens. Tucked next to a sturdy town gate at the foot of the castle, it serves the gamut of grilled fare, dumplings and other Franconian rib-stickers with big mugs of local Zirndorfer and Tucher beer. Also has a small beer garden.

Marientorzwinger
GERMAN €€

(www.wirtshaus-marientorzwinger.de; Lorenzer Strasse 33; mains €7-17; ⊙ 11.30am-1am) The last remaining *Zwinger* eatery (a tavern built in a *Zwinger*, a narrow space between two defensive walls) in Nuremberg is an atmospheric place to chomp on a mixed bag of sturdy regional specials in the simple wood-panelled dining room or the leafy beer garden. Fürth-brewed Tucher is the ale of choice here.

Burgwächter
FRANCONIAN, INTERNATIONAL €€

(✐ 0911-2348 9844; www.burgwaechter-nuernberg.de; Am Ölberg 10; mains €9-20; ⊙ 11am-10pm; ✐) Refuel after a tour of the Kaiserburg with prime steaks, bratwurst with potato salad, and vegetarian-friendly Swabian filled pastas and salads, as you feast your eyes on the best terrace views from any Nuremberg eatery or drinking spot. With kiddies in tow, ask for *Kloss* (a simple dumpling with sauce for €3.90).

◉ Drinking & Nightlife

Cafe Katz
BAR

(Hans-Sachs-Platz 8; ⊙ 11am-1am Sun-Thu, to 2am Fri & Sat) From the outside this place looks like a secondhand furniture shop, the vitrines packed with 1970s coffee tables, old school desks and 1980s high-back chairs. But the La Marzocco espresso machine gives the game away as this is one of Nuremberg's coolest cafes, an on-trend spot to see, be seen and enjoy a drink and/or a vegie or vegan meal amid retro furnishings.

Kloster
PUB

(Obere Wörthstrasse 19; ⊙ 5pm-1am) One of Nuremberg's best drinking dens is all dressed up as a monastery replete with ecclesiastic knick-knacks including coffins emerging from the walls. The monks here pray to the god of *Landbier* (regional beer) and won't be up at 5am for matins, that's for sure.

Kettensteg
BEER GARDEN

(Maxplatz 35; ⊙ 11am-11pm) At the end of the chain bridge and in the shadow of the Halletor you'll find this classic Bavarian beer garden complete with its gravel floor, folding slatted chairs, fairy lights, tree shade and river views. Zirndorfer, Lederer and Tucher beers are on tap and some of the food comes on heart-shaped plates.

Treibhaus CAFE
(Karl-Grillenberger-Strasse 28; light meals €6-10; ⊘9am to last customer; ⊚) Off the path of most visitors, this bustling cafe is a Nuremberg institution and one of the most happening places in town. Set yourself down in the sun on a yellow director's chair out front or warm yourself with something strong around the huge zinc bar inside. Visitors heap praise on the big breakfasts served here.

Meisengeige BAR
(Am Laufer Schlagturm 3; ⊘3.30pm-midnight Mon-Wed, to 1am Thu, to 2am Fri & Sat, 1.30pm-midnight Sun) The pub attached to a small foreign- and art-film cinema of the same name is a characterful old place (bentwood chairs, potted plants and big mirrors) for an evening beer, even if you aren't going to see a film. Located right by the Laufer Schlagturm, one of the medieval gates into the city.

Barfüsser Brauhaus BEER HALL
(Königstrasse 60; ⊘11am-1am Mon-Fri, to 2am Sat) This cellar beer hall deep below street level is a popular spot to hug a mug of site-brewed ale, bubbling frothily in the copper kettles that occupy the cavernous vaulted interior. The traditional trappings of the huge quaffing space clash oddly with the polo shirts of the swift-footed waiting staff, but that's our only criticism.

☆ Entertainment

Mata Hari Bar LIVE MUSIC
(www.mataharibar.de; Weissgerbergasse 31; ⊘from 8pm Wed-Sun) This bar with live music and DJ nights is a Nuremberg institution. After 9pm it's usually standing room only and the party goes on well into the early hours.

Staatstheater THEATRE
(☑0911-231 3808; www.staatstheater-nuernberg.de; Richard-Wagner-Platz 2) Nuremberg's magnificent state theatre serves up an impressive mix of dramatic arts. The renovated art nouveau opera house presents opera and ballet, while the Kammerspiele offers a varied program of classical and contemporary plays. The Nürnberger Philharmoniker also performs here.

Filmhaus CINEMA
(www.kunstkulturquartier.de; Königstrasse 93) This small indie picture house, part of the large Cultural Quarter complex, shows foreign-language movies, plus reruns of cult German flicks and films for kids.

Hirsch LIVE MUSIC
(☑0911-429 414; www.der-hirsch.de; Vogelweiherstrasse 66) This converted factory, 2.5km south of the Hauptbahnhof, hosts live alternative music almost daily, both big-name acts and local names. Take the U1 or U2 to Plärrer, then change to tram 4, alighting at Dianaplatz.

Mach1 CLUB
(☑0911-246 602; www.macheins.club; Kaiserstrasse 1-9; ⊘from 10pm Fri & Sat) This centrally located temple to dance has been around for decades, but is still one of the most popular venues at weekends. Mostly mainstream music and a young crowd.

🛍 Shopping

Käthe Wohlfahrt Christmas Shop CHRISTMAS DECORATIONS
(www.wohlfahrt.com; Königstrasse 8; ⊘10am-6pm Mon-Sat) The Nuremberg branch of Germany's chain of Christmas shops selling pricey Yuletide decorations 365 days a year.

Bier Kontor ALCOHOL
(An der Mauthalle 2; ⊘11am-2pm & 2.30-7pm Mon-Sat) This small shop just off the tourist drag stocks a whopping 350 types of beer, from local Franconian suds to Hawaiian ales, fruity Belgian concoctions to British porters. And staff really know their stuff when it comes to the amber nectar.

Handwerkerhof MARKET
(www.handwerkerhof.de; Am Königstor; ⊘9am-6.30pm Mon-Fri, 10am-4pm Sat Apr-Dec, shorter hours Jan-Mar) A recreation of an old-world Nuremberg crafts quarter, the Handwerkerhof is a walled tourist market by the Königstor. If you're in the market for souvenirs you may find some decent merchandise here such as gingerbread wooden toys and traditional ceramics, and there is plenty of bratwurst to go round, too.

ℹ Information

Post Office (Josephsplatz 3; ⊘9am-6.30pm Mon-Fri, to 2pm Sat)
ReiseBank (Hauptbahnhof; ⊘8am-9pm Mon-Fri, 8am-12.30pm & 1.15-4pm Sat & Sun)

Convenient place to change money at the Hauptbahnhof.

Tourist Office Hauptmarkt (☑ 0911-233 60; www.tourismus.nuernberg.de; Hauptmarkt 18; ⊙ 9am-6pm Mon-Sat, 10am-4pm Sun) Hauptmarkt branch of the tourist office. Has extended hours during Christkindlesmarkt that takes place on its doorstep.

Tourist Office Künstlerhaus (☑ 0911-233 60; www.tourismus.nuernberg.de; Königstrasse 93; ⊙ 9am-7pm Mon-Sat, 10am-4pm Sun) Publishes the excellent *See & Enjoy* booklet, a comprehensive guide to the city.

ⓘ Getting There & Away

AIR

Nuremberg's **Albrecht Dürer Airport** (NUE; ☑ 0911-937 00; www.airport-nuernberg.de; Flughafenstrasse), 5km north of the centre, is served by regional and international carriers, including Ryanair, Lufthansa, Air Berlin and Air France.

BUS

Buses to destinations across Europe leave from the **main bus station** (ZOB) near the Hauptbahnhof. There's a Touring/Eurolines office nearby. Flixbus (www.flixbus.com) links Nuremberg with countless destinations in Germany and beyond. Special Deutsche Bahn express coaches to Prague (from €10, 3½ hours, seven daily) leave from the ZOB.

TRAIN

Nuremberg is connected by train to Berlin (from €80, three to 3½ hours, hourly), Frankfurt (€30 to €60, 2¼ hours, at least hourly), Hamburg (from €80, 4½ hours, hourly) and Munich (€40 and €60, one hour, twice daily). Services also go to Cheb (€34, 1¾ hours, every two hours), for connections to Prague, and Vienna (from €90, four to 5½ hours, every two hours).

ⓘ Getting Around

TO/FROM THE AIRPORT

U-Bahn 2 runs every few minutes from the Hauptbahnhof to the airport (€2.75, 13 minutes). A taxi to the airport will cost about €20.

BICYCLE

Nuremberg has ample bike lanes along busy roads and the Altstadt is pretty bike friendly. For bike hire, try the excellent **Ride on a Rainbow** (☑ 0911-397 337; www.ride-on-a-rainbow.de; Adam-Kraft-Strasse 55; per day from €9).

PUBLIC TRANSPORT

The best transport around the Altstadt is at the end of your legs. Timed tickets on the VGN bus, tram and U-Bahn/S-Bahn networks cost from €1.30. A day pass costs €8.10. Passes bought on Saturday are valid all weekend.

Bamberg

☑ 0951 / POP 75,800

A disarmingly beautiful architectural masterpiece with an almost complete absence of modern eyesores, Bamberg's entire Altstadt is a Unesco World Heritage Site and one of Bavaria's unmissables. Generally regarded as one of Germany's most attractive settlements, the town is bisected by rivers and canals and was built by archbishops on seven hills, earning it the inevitable sobriquet of 'Franconian Rome'. Students inject some liveliness into its streets, pavement cafes, pubs and no fewer than 10 breweries cooking up Bamberg's famous smoked beer, but it's usually wide-eyed tourists who can be seen filing through its narrow medieval streets. The town can be tackled as a day trip from Nuremberg, but, to really do it justice and to experience the romantically lit streets once most visitors have left, consider an overnight stay.

⊙ Sights

★ **Bamberger Dom**   CATHEDRAL

(www.erzbistum-bamberg.de; Domplatz; ⊙ 9.30am-6pm Apr-Oct, to 5pm Nov-Mar) Beneath the quartet of spires, Bamberg's cathedral is packed with artistic treasures, most famously the slender equestrian statue of the Bamberger Reiter (Bamberg Horseman), whose true identity remains a mystery. It overlooks the tomb of cathedral founders, Emperor Heinrich II and his wife Kunigunde, splendidly carved by Tilmann Riemenschneider. The marble tomb of Clemens II in the west choir is the only papal burial site north of the Alps. Nearby, the Virgin Mary altar by Veit Stoss also warrants closer inspection.

Founded by Heinrich II in 1004, the cathedral's current appearance dates to the early 13th century and is the outcome of a Romanesque-Gothic duel between church architects after the original and its immediate successor

Bamberg

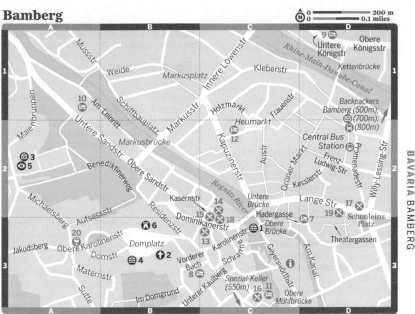

Bamberg

burnt down in the 12th century. The pillars
have the original light hues of Franconian
sandstone thanks to Ludwig I, who eradicat-
ed all postmedieval decoration in the early
19th century.

Altes Rathaus HISTORIC BUILDING
(Old Town Hall; Obere Brücke; adult/child €6/5;
◷10am-4.30pm Tue-Sun) Like a ship in dry
dock, Bamberg's 1462 Old Town Hall was
built on an artifical island in the Regnitz
River, allegedly because the local bishop had
refused to give the town's citizens any land
for its construction. Inside you'll find the
Sammlung Ludwig, a collection of precious
porcelain, but even more enchanting are the
richly detailed frescos adorning its facades –
note the cherub's leg cheekily protruding
from the eastern facade.

Historisches Museum MUSEUM
(☏0951-519 0746; www.museum.bamberg.de;
Domplatz 7; adult/child €7/1; ◷10am-5pm Tue-Sun
May-Oct) Bamberg's main museum fills the
Alte Hofhaltung (old court hall), a former
prince-bishops' palace near the cathedral,
with a mixed bag of exhibits. These include
a model of the pilgrimage church Vierzehn-
heiligen and the Bamberger Götzen, ancient
stone sculptures found in the region. Often

of greater interest are the expertly curated special exhibitions, which examine aspects of the region's past in more detail.

In winter the museum is often only open for special exhibitions.

Neue Residenz   PALACE

(New Residence; ☑0951-519 390; Domplatz 8; adult/child €4.50/free; ☉ 9am-6pm Apr-Sep, 10am-4pm Oct-Mar) This splendid episcopal palace gives you an eyeful of the lavish lifestyle of Bamberg's prince-bishops who, between 1703 and 1802, occupied its 40-odd rooms that can only be seen on guided 45-minute tours (in German). Tickets are also good for the Bavarian State Gallery, with works by Lucas Cranach the Elder and other Old Masters. The baroque Rose Garden delivers fabulous views over the town.

Fränkisches Brauereimuseum   MUSEUM

(☑0951-530 16; www.brauereimuseum.de; Michaelsberg 10f; adult/concession €4/3.50; ☉1-5pm Wed-Fri, 11am-5pm Sat & Sun Apr-Oct) Located in the Kloster St Michael, this comprehensive brewery museum exhibits over 1000 period mashing, boiling and bottling implements, as well as everything to do with local suds, such as beer mats, tankards, enamel beer signs and lots of photos and documentation. If the displays have left you dry mouthed, quench your thirst in the small pub.

Kloster St Michael   MONASTERY

(Franziskanergasse 2; ☉ 9am-6pm Apr-Oct) Above Domplatz, at the top of Michaelsberg, is the Benedictine Kloster St Michael, a former monastery and now an aged people's home. The monastery church is essential Bamberg viewing, both for its baroque art and the meticulous depictions of nearly 600 medicinal plants and flowers on the vaulted ceiling. The manicured garden terraces behind the church – former monastical vineyards – provide splendid city panoramas.

The entire complex was completely under wraps at the time of research as it underwent thorough renovation work that may take a number of years.

👉 Tours

BierSchmecker Tour   WALKING

(www.bier.bamberg.info; adult €22.50) Possibly the most tempting tour of the amazingly varied offerings at the tourist office is the self-guided BierSchmecker Tour. The price includes entry to the Fränkisches Brauereimuseum (depending on the route taken), plus five beer vouchers valid in five pubs and breweries, an English information booklet, a route map and a souvenir stein. Not surprisingly, it can take all day to complete the route.

🛏 Sleeping

Alt Bamberg   HOTEL €

(☑0951-986 150; www.hotel-alt-bamberg.de; Habergasse 11; s/d from €45/65; 🛜) Often heavily discounted on popular booking websites, the no-frills rooms at this well-located, old-school hotel are digs of choice for euro-watching nomads. Some rooms share showers, the breakfast is an ample spread and there's a well-respected Greek restaurant downstairs. Reception closes between 11am and 3pm.

Backpackers Bamberg   HOSTEL €

(☑0951-222 1718; www.backpackersbamberg.de; Heiliggrabstrasse 4; dm €17-20, s/d €30/45; 🛜) Bamberg's backpacker hostel is a well-kept affair, with clean dorms, a fully functional kitchen and a quiet, family-friendly atmosphere (staff stress this is not a party hostel). Make sure you let the hostel know when you're arriving, as it's left unstaffed for most of the day. It's located 400m north along Luitpoldstrasse from the Luitpoldbrücke.

Campingplatz Insel   CAMPGROUND €

(☑0951-563 20; www.campinginsel.de; Am Campingplatz 1; tents €4-8, adult/car €7/4; 🛜) If rustling nylon is your abode of choice, this well-equipped site, in a tranquil spot right on the river, is the sole camping option. Take bus 918 to Campingplatz.

★Hotel Sankt Nepomuk   HOTEL €€

(☑0951-984 20; www.hotel-nepomuk.de; Obere Mühlbrücke 9; s/d from €90/130; 🅿🛜) Aptly named after the patron saint of bridges, this is a classy establishment in a half-timbered former mill right on the Regnitz. It has a superb restaurant (mains €15 to €30) with a terrace and 24 new-fangled rooms of recent vintage. Breakfast is an extra €5.

Hotel Residenzschloss   HOTEL €€

(☑0951-609 10; www.residenzschloss.com; Untere Sandstrasse 32; r from €100; 🅿🛜) Bamberg's grandest digs occupy a palatial building formerly used as a hospital. But have no fear, as the swanky furnishings – from the Roman-style steam bath to the flashy piano bar – have little in common with institutional care. High-ceilinged rooms are business standard though display little historical charm. Take bus 916 from the ZOB.

Hotel Wohnbar BOUTIQUE HOTEL €€
(✆0951-5099 8844; www.wohnbar-bamberg.de; Stangsstrasse 3; s/d from €60/80; 🅿🛜) 'Carpe Noctem' (Seize the Night) is the motto of this charming 10-room retreat with boldly coloured, contemporary rooms near the university quarter. Those in the 'economy' category are a very tight squeeze. Parking costs €10 per day, breakfast €8.50.

Barockhotel am Dom HOTEL €€
(✆0951-540 31; www.barockhotel.de; Vorderer Bach 4; s/tw from €85/100; 🅿🛜) The sugary facade, a sceptre's swipe from the Dom, gives a hint of the baroque heritage and original details within. The 19 rooms have sweeping views of the Dom or the roofs of the Altstadt, and breakfast is served in a 14th-century vault.

Hotel Europa HOTEL €€
(✆0951-309 3020; www.hotel-europa-bamberg. de; Untere Königstrasse 6-8; d from €105; 🛜) This spick-and-span but unfussy affair just outside the Altstadt gets kudos for its friendliness, comfy beds and opulent breakfast, served in the winter garden or sunny courtyard. Rooms at the front are noisier but may overlook the cathedral and the red-tiled roofs of the Altstadt. Some are a bit small.

✕ Eating

★**Schlenkerla** GERMAN €
(✆0951-560 60; www.schlenkerla.de; Dominikanerstrasse 6; mains €7-13; ⊙9.30am-11.30pm) Beneath wooden beams as dark as the superb *Rauchbier* poured straight from oak barrels, locals and visitors gather around a large ceramic stove to dig into scrumptious Franconian fare at this legendary flower-festooned tavern. Staff will pass beers through a tiny window in the entrance for those who just want to taste a beer but not sit.

★**Klosterbräu** PUB FOOD €
(Obere Mühlbrücke 1-3; mains €7-13; ⊙11.30am-10pm Mon-Sat, to 2pm Sun) This beautiful half-timbered brewery is Bamberg's oldest. It draws *Stammgäste* (regulars) and tourists alike who wash down filling slabs of meat and dumplings with its excellent range of ales in the unpretentious dining room.

Zum Sternla FRANCONIAN €
(✆0951-287 50; www.sternla.de; Lange Strasse 46; mains €5-12; ⊙4-11pm Tue, 11am-11pm Wed-Sun) Bamberg's oldest *Wirtshaus* (inn; established 1380) bangs out bargain-priced staples including pork dishes, steaks, dumplings and

---

KLEIN VENEDIG

A row of diminutive, half-timbered cottages once inhabited by fisherfolk (hence the street's name meaning 'fishery') comprises Bamberg's Klein Venedig (Little Venice), which hems the Regnitz's east bank between Markusbrücke and Untere Brücke. The little homes balance on poles set right into the water and are fronted by tiny gardens and terraces (wholly unlike Venice, but who cares), the river flowing sluggishly past just centimetres below ground level.

Klein Venedig is well worth a stroll but looks at least as pretty from a distance, especially in summer when red geraniums spill from flower boxes. Good vantage points include the Untere Brücke near the Altes Rathaus, and Am Leinritt on the opposite bank.

---

sauerkraut, as well as specials, but it's a great, nontouristy place for a traditional *Brotzeit* (snack), or just a pretzel and a beer. The menu is helpfully translated from Franconian into German.

Spezial-Keller GERMAN €
(✆0951-548 87; www.spezial-keller.de; Sternwartstrasse 8; dishes €6-14; ⊙3pm-late Tue-Fri, from noon Sat, from 10.30am Sun) The walk into the hills past the cathedral to this delightful beer garden is well worth it, both for the malty *Rauchbier* and the sweeping views of the Altstadt. In winter the action moves into the cosy, wood-panelled tavern warmed by a traditional wood-burning tiled stove.

Bäckerei Seel BAKERY €
(Dominikanerstrasse 8; snacks from €1.50; ⊙6am-6pm Mon-Fri, 7am-4pm Sat) This old town bakery is the place to go for early starters who need breakfast at 6am. It stocks a delicious range of pastries and sandwiches, but if you want to eat on the premises it's standing only.

Alt Ringlein FRANCONIAN €€
(www.altringlein.com; Dominikanerstrasse 9; mains €7-20; ⊙11am-11pm; 🛜) Serving gourmet-ish takes on the most traditional of Franconian fare, this bastion of beer, meat and *Kloss* (Franconian dumplings) has one of the most impressive dining rooms in town, all chunky

carved wood chairs and dark-wood panelling. Service is swift and polite and there's a beer garden out back for summertime sipping.

Messerschmidt
FRANCONIAN €€

(☑ 0951-297 800; Lange Strasse 41; mains €12-25; ⊙ 11am-10pm; 🐾) This stylish gourmet eatery may be ensconced in the house where aviation engineer Willy Messerschmidt was born, but there's nothing 'plane' about dining here. The place oozes old-world charm, with dark woods, white linens and traditionally formal service. Sharpen your molars on platters of roast duck and red cabbage out on the alfresco terrace overlooking a pretty park, or in the attached wine tavern.

Ambräusianum
PUB FOOD €€

(☑ 0951-509 0262; Dominikanerstrasse 10; mains €9-14; ⊙ 11am-11pm Tue-Sat, to 9pm Sun) Bamberg's only brewpub is, as you might expect, a traditional affair and does a killer schnitzel plus pork knuckle and *Flammkuchen* (Alsatian pizza) that'll have you waddling out the door. Many just come for the home-brewed beer, but if you're not into downing tankards you can just have a taster rack for €3.

🍷 Drinking & Nightlife

Torschuster
BAR

(Obere Karolinenstrasse 10; ⊙ 7.30-1pm) Amid the palaces and ecclesiastic institutions of the Domberg stands this small pub serving beers from all of Bamberg's breweries and a good selection of whisky. Old enamel advertising signs decorate the walls but the main attraction here is the friendly owner Thomas' eclectic vinyl collection that doesn't go much past the mid-80s. All in all an after-dark antidote to medieval tavern life. Take bus 910 to Torschuster.

ⓘ Information

Post Office (Ludwigstrasse 25; ⊙ 9am-6pm Mon-Fri, to 12.30pm Sat)
Tourist Office (☑ 0951-297 6200; www.bamberg.info; Geyerswörthstrasse 5; ⊙ 9.30am-6pm Mon-Fri, to 4pm Sat, to 2.30pm Sun) Large professional office with parking, toliets and a children's playground all nearby. Staff sell the Bambergcard (€14.90), valid for three days of free bus rides and free museum entry.

ⓘ Getting There & Around

Bamberg has rail connections to Berlin (from €60, 2¾ hours, hourly), Munich (€25, two hours, every two hours or change in Nuremberg),

Nuremberg (€20, 40 minutes, up to four hourly) and Würzburg (€22, one hour, twice hourly).

Several buses, including 901, 902 and 931, connect the train station with the **central bus station** (ZOB; Promenadestrasse), which has a handy 12-hour left-luggage facility. Bus 910 goes from the ZOB to Domplatz.

Bayreuth
☑ 0921 / POP 73,000

Even without its Wagner connections, Bayreuth would still be an interesting detour from Nuremberg or Bamberg for its streets of sandstone baroque architecture and impressive palaces. But it's for the annual Wagner Festival that 60,000 opera devotees make a pilgrimage to this neck of the *Wald*.

Bayreuth's glory days began in 1735 when Wilhelmine, sister of King Frederick the Great of Prussia, was forced to marry stuffy Margrave Friedrich. Bored with the local scene, the cultured Anglo-oriented Wilhelmine invited the finest artists, poets, composers and architects in Europe to court. The period bequeathed some eye-catching buildings, still on display for all to see.

ⓞ Sights

★ Markgräfliches Opernhaus
THEATRE

(Opernstrasse 14; adult/child €8/free; ⊙ 9am-6pm Apr-Sep, 10am-4pm Oct-Mar) Designed by Giuseppe Galli Bibiena, a famous 18th-century architect from Bologna, Bayreuth's opera house is one of Europe's most stunningly ornate baroque theatres. Germany's largest opera house until 1871, it has a lavish interior smothered in carved, gilded and marbled wood. However, Richard Wagner considered it too modest for his serious work and conducted here just once.

This grand old dame spent most of the past decade under wraps, receiving a multimillion euro facelift but reopened its door in early 2018. It was declared a Unesco World Cultural Heritage Site in 2012.

Richard Wagner Museum
MUSEUM

(Haus Wahnfried; ☑ 0921-757 2816; www.wagnermuseum.de; Richard-Wagner-Strasse 48; adult/child €8/free; ⊙ 10am-6pm Jul & Aug, to 5pm Tue-Sun Sep-Jun) In the early 1870s King Ludwig II, Wagner's most devoted fan, gave the composer the cash to build Haus Wahnfried, a pleasingly symmetrical minimansion on the northern edge of the Hofgarten. The building now houses the Richard Wagner Museum, Ludwig's bronze bust stand-

BAYREUTH'S FAMOUS WAGNER FESTIVAL

The **Wagner Festival** (www.bayreuther-festspiele.de; ⊙ late Jul & Aug) has been a summer fixture in Bayreuth for over 140 years and is generally regarded as the top Wagner event anywhere in the world. The festival lasts for 30 days, with each performance attended by an audience of just over 1900. Demand is insane, with an estimated 500,000 fans vying for less than 60,000 tickets.

The vast majority of tickets go onto the open market in an online free-for-all. Every ticket is snapped up in seconds, a fact that has angered many a Wagner society, which used to get preferential treatment. Alternatively, it is still possible to lay siege to the box office 2½ hours before performances begin in the hope of snapping up cheap returned tickets, but there's no guarantee you'll get in.

ing prominently outside. Crisply renovated in the early part of the decade, the bulk of the exhibition looks at Wagner's life and work. Another section in the new building examines the history of the Bayreuth Wagner Festival.

Behind the house, hidden behind a ring of rhododendron bushes, lies the completely unmarked, ivy-covered tomb containing Wagner and his wife Cosima. The sandstone grave of his loving canine companion Russ stands nearby.

Festspielhaus
THEATRE

(✍ 0921-787 80; www.bayreuth.de; Festspielhügel 1-2; adult/concession €7/5; ⊙ tours 2pm Nov-Apr, 10am & 2pm Sep & Oct, no tours May-Aug) North of the Hauptbahnhof, the main venue for Bayreuth's annual Wagner Festival is the Festspielhaus, constructed in 1872 with King Ludwig II's backing. The structure was specially designed to accommodate Wagner's massive theatrical sets, with three storeys of mechanical works hidden below stage. It's still one of the largest opera venues in the world. To see inside you must join the daily tour. Take bus 305 to Am Festspielhaus.

Neues Schloss
PALACE

(✍ 0921-759 690; Ludwigstrasse 21; adult/child €5.50/free; ⊙ 9am-6pm Apr-Sep, 10am-4pm Oct-Mar) Opening into the vast Hofgarten, the Neues Schloss lies a short distance south of the main shopping street, Maxmilianstrasse. A riot of rococo style, the margrave's residence after 1753 features a vast collection of 18th-century Bayreuth porcelain. The annual VIP opening of the Wagner Festival is held in the Cedar Room. Also worth a look is the Spiegelscherbenkabinett (Broken Mirror Cabinet), which is lined with irregular shards of broken mirror – supposedly Margravine Wilhelmine's response to the vanity of her era.

Eremitage
PARK

(Eremitagestrasse) Around 6km east of the centre lies the Eremitage, a lush park girding the **Altes Schloss** (adult/child €4.50/free; ⊙ 9am-6pm Apr-Sep), the summer residence that belonged to 18th-century margrave Friedrich and his wife Wilhelmine. Visits to the palace are by guided tour only and take in the Chinese Mirror room where Countess Wilhelmine penned her memoirs. Also in the park is horseshoe-shaped Neues Schloss (not to be confused with the one in town), which centres on the amazing mosaic Sun Temple with gilded Apollo sculpture. Take bus 302 from the Hauptbahnhof.

Maisel's Bier-Erlebnis-Welt
BREWERY, MUSEUM

(✍ 0921-401 234; www.maisel.com/museum; Kulmbacher Strasse 40; tours adult/concession €8/5; ⊙ tours 2pm & 6pm) For a fascinating look at the brewing process, head to this enormous museum next door to the brewery of one of Germany's top wheat-beer producers – Maisel. The one-hour guided tour takes you into the bowels of the 19th-century plant, with atmospheric rooms filled with 4500 beer mugs and amusing artefacts. Visits conclude with a glass of sweet-cloudy Weissbier (wheat beer).

🛏 Sleeping

DJH Hostel
HOSTEL €

(✍ 0921-764 380; www.bayreuth.jugendherberge. de; Universitätsstrasse 28; dm from €23; 🛜) This excellent 140-bed hostel near the university has comfortable, fresh rooms, a relaxed atmosphere and heaps of guest facilities such as a multipurpose sports ground and beach volleyball court.

Goldener Löwe
HOTEL €€

(✍ 0921-746 060; www.goldener-loewe.de; Kulmbacher Strasse 30; s €40-105, d €75-140; P 😊 🛜) Outside the summer months (rates increase

(Continued on page 146)

1. Würzburg Residenz (p109), Würzburg 2. Schloss Linderhof (p97) 3. Kaiserburg (p127), Nuremberg

Romantic Residences

Think Southern Germany and the Alps, think story-book castles and noble palaces, hilltop ruins and Renaissance splendour – few places on earth boast such a treasure trove of medieval and aristocratic architecture and visiting these stately piles is a key part of any visit to the region.

Schloss Neuschwanstein

One of the world's most romantic castles (p92), King Ludwig II's 19th-century folly inspired Walt Disney's citadel as well as millions of tourists to visit this corner of the Alps. All turrets and pointed towers rising dreamily from the alpine forests, if Bavaria has a single unmissable sight, this is it.

Würzburg Residenz

Würzburg's Unesco-listed palace (p109) is one of the country's most exquisite chunks of aristocratic baroque, built by a stellar name of the period, Balthasar Neumann. The highlight of the huge building is without doubt the Grand Staircase whose ceiling boasts the world's largest fresco.

Schloss Linderhof

Another of Ludwig II's wistful follies, this lavish though compact palace (p97) was the only one of his creations he saw finished. The remote location in the foothills of the Alps only heightens the effect of the eye-pleasing symmetry of the outside and the quirkiness of the interior.

Kaiserburg

One of Bavaria's most historically significant fortresses, Nuremberg's Kaiserburg (p127) lords it over the old town of the state's second city. A tour takes you back to medieval times when Nuremberg was one of the key cities in the Holy Roman Empire, the castle was used as a safe box for the empire's trinkets.

(Continued from page 143)

considerably mid-July to end of August) this is a great little deal within easy walking distance of the sights. Rooms are tiny but impeccably kept, the Michelin-reviewed restaurant downstairs is tempting and there's free parking. The owners seem to have a bit of a jam fetish, every guest receiving a free jar.

Hotel Goldener Hirsch   HOTEL €€
(☑ 0921-1504 4000; www.bayreuth-goldener-hirsch.de; Bahnhofstrasse 13; s €65-85, d €85-110; P ⊜ 🖙) Just across from the train station, the 'Golden Reindeer' looks a bit stuffy from the outside, but once indoors you'll discover crisp, well-maintained rooms with contemporary furniture and unscuffed, whitewashed walls. Some of the 40 rooms have baths. Parking is free and the price includes breakfast.

Hotel Goldener Anker   HOTEL €€€
(☑ 0921-787 7740; www.anker-bayreuth.de; Opernstrasse 6; s €100-140, d €170-235; P ⊜ 🖙) Bayreuth's top address since 1753 stands just a few metres from the opera house and oozes refined elegance, with many of the rooms decorated in traditional style with heavy curtains, dark woods and antique touches. There's a swanky restaurant at ground level, the service is impeccable and there is fresh fruit waiting for you on arrival.

🍴 Eating

Kraftraum   CAFE €
(Sophienstrasse 16; mains €5.50-11; ⊙ 8am-1am Mon-Fri, from 9am Sat & Sun; ☑) This vegetarian eatery has plenty to tempt even the most committed meat eaters, including pastas, jacket potatoes, soups and huge salads. The retro-ish, shabby-chic interior empties on sunny days when everyone plumps for the alfresco seating out on the cobbles. Tempting weekend brunches (€15.50) always attract a large crowd.

Hansl's Wood Oven Pizzeria   PIZZA €
(www.hansls-holzofenpizzeria.de; Friedrichstrasse 15; pizzas €5.20-11; ⊙ 10am-10.30pm) The best pizza in town is found at this tiny place tucked away in a corner of the square near the Stadthalle. There's next to no chance of a seat at mealtimes, so grab a takeaway.

Torten Schmiede   CAFE €
(Ludwigstrasse 10; ⊙ 12.30-6pm Tue-Fri & Sun, 10am-6pm Sat) Bayreuth has lots of cafes, but with its car-boot sale of retro furniture,

homemade cakes and 'street art' on the walls, this tiny cafe is something that's a bit different. Enjoy your shot of caffeine and cake on a 1960s living room chair, or trendily streetside on a cushioned pallet.

Rosa Rosa   BISTRO €
(Von-Römer-Strasse 2; mains €4-11; ⊙ 5pm-1am; ☑) Join Bayreuth's chilled crowd at this alternatively minded bistro-cum-pub for belly-filling portions of salad, pasta and vegie fare, as well as seasonal dishes from the big specials board, or just a Frankenwälder beer in the evening. The poster-lined walls keep you up to date on the latest acts to hit town.

Oskar   FRANCONIAN, BAVARIAN €€
(Maximilianstrasse 33; mains €6-15; ⊙ 8am-1am Mon-Sat, from 9am Sun; 🖙) At the heart of the pedestrianised shopping boulevard, this multitasking, open-all-hours bar-cafe-restaurant is Bayreuth's busiest eatery. It's good for a busting Bavarian breakfast, a light lunch in the covered garden cafe, a full-on dinner feast in the dark-wood restaurant, or a *Landbier* (regional beer) and a couple of tasty Bayreuth bratwursts anytime you feel.

🍷 Drinking & Nightlife

Brauhaus Schinner   PUB
(www.buergerbraeu-schinner.de; Richard-Wagner-Strasse 38; ⊙ 5pm-midnight Tue-Sat, 10.30am-2pm Wed-Sat) The pub belonging to Bayreuth's Schinner brewery is a reassuringly old-fashioned affair with great, fresh-tasting beer but slightly pricey food. The speciality here is Braunbier, a dark bitter brew specific to Bayreuth.

ℹ Information

The **Bayreuth Card** (72hr €12.90) is good for unlimited trips on city buses, entry to eight museums and a two-hour guided city walk (in German). The card covers one adult and up to two children under 15.

Post Office (Hauptbahnhof, Bürgerreutherstrasse 1; ⊙ 8am-6.30pm Mon-Fri, 8.30am-1pm Sat)

Tourist Office (☑ 0921-885 88; www.bayreuth-tourismus.de; Opernstrasse 22; ⊙ 9am-7pm Mon-Fri, to 4pm Sat, plus 10am-2pm Sun May-Oct) Has a train ticket booking desk and a worthwhile gift shop. Also sells the Bayreuth Card (72 hours €12.90) that is good for unlimited trips on city buses and entry to eight museums.

ℹ Getting There & Away

Most rail journeys between Bayreuth and other towns in Bavaria require a change in Nuremberg

(€12, one hour, twice hourly), including Munich (€30 to €71, two hours, twice hourly). There are direct services to Bamberg (€22, 1½ hours, twice hourly) or change in Lichtenfels

Coburg

✆ 09561 / POP 41,000

If marriage is diplomacy by another means, Coburg's rulers were masters of the art. Over four centuries, the princes and princesses of Saxe-Coburg wed themselves into the dynasties of several European states, most prominently, Great Britain. In 1840, Albert of Saxe-Coburg-Gotha took his vows with first cousin Queen Victoria, founding the present British royal family. The British royals quietly adopted the less-German name of Windsor during WWI.

With its Victoria connections and cosy, small-town atmosphere, Coburg makes for an enjoyable escape from Nuremberg and other big cities. Also, if you've developed a taste for Franconian sausages, Coburg has one of the best.

◎ Sights

★ **Veste Coburg** FORTRESS

(www.kunstsammlungen-coburg.de; adult/concession €8/6; ⊙9.30am-5pm daily Apr-Oct, 1-4pm Tue-Sun Nov-Mar) Towering above Coburg's centre is a story-book medieval fortress, the Veste Coburg. With its triple ring of fortified walls, it's one of the most impressive fortresses in Germany, though it attracts few foreign visitors. It houses the vast collection of the Kunstsammlungen, with works by star painters such as Rembrandt, Dürer and Cranach the Elder. The elaborate Jagdintarsien-Zimmer (Hunting Marquetry Room) is a superlative example of carved woodwork.

Protestant reformer Martin Luther, hoping to escape an imperial ban, sought refuge at the fortress in 1530. His former quarters have a writing desk and, in keeping with the Reformation, a rather plain bed.

★ **Schloss Ehrenburg** CASTLE

(www.schloesser-coburg.de; Schlossplatz; adult/child €4.50/free; ⊙tours at least hourly 9am-6pm Tue-Sun Apr-Sep, 10am-4pm Tue-Sun Oct-Mar) The erstwhile residence of the Coburg dukes, Ehrenburg is a must for fans of the British monarchy – it was here that Prince Albert spent his childhood and Queen Victoria made several long visits. She stayed in a room with Germany's first flushing toilet

(1860, suitably illuminated) and the bed she slept in is still present. Another highlight is the splendid Riesensaal (Hall of Giants), which has a baroque ceiling supported by 28 statues of Atlas.

It was in the Riesensaal that Queen Vic met up with Emperor Franz Joseph. Depictions of Britain's most famous monarch, who once declared that Coburg would have been her natural choice of home had she not become queen, can be found throughout the lavish building. Tours take 45 minutes and are in German only but info sheets are provided in other languages.

Marktplatz SQUARE

Coburg's epicentre is the magnificent Markt, a beautifully renovated square radiating a colourful, aristocratic charm. The fabulous Renaissance facades and ornate oriels of the Stadthaus (townhouse) and the Rathaus vie for attention, while a greening bronze of Prince Albert, looking rather more flamboyant and Teutonically medieval than the Brits are used to seeing Queen Victoria's husband, calmly surveys the scene.

Coburger Puppenmuseum MUSEUM

(www.coburger-puppenmuseum.de; Rückerstrasse 2-3; adult/child €4/2; ⊙11am-4pm Apr-Oct, closed Mon Nov-Mar) Filling a huge townhouse, this delightfully old-fashioned museum boasts a huge nostalgia-inducing collection. The downstairs section is like a museum of German childhood with lots of different toys from the late 19th and early 20th centuries. Upstairs you'll find the collection of dolls, dollhouses, miniature kitchens and chinaware, some from as far away as Japan. Aptly named 'Hallo Dolly', the stylish cafe next door is ideally situated for restoring calm after all those eerie glass eyes.

⚜ Festivals & Events

Samba Festival DANCE

(www.samba-festival.de; ⊙mid-Jul) Believe it or not, Coburg hosts Europe's largest Samba Festival every year, an incongruous venue if ever there was one. This orgy of song and dance attracts almost 100 bands and up to 200,000 scantily clad, bum-wiggling visitors, many from the Portuguese-speaking world.

🛏 Sleeping & Eating

Hotelpension Bärenturm GUESTHOUSE €€

(✆09561-318 401; www.baerenturm-hotelpension. de; Untere Anlage 2; s/d from €75/90; 🅿🛜) For those who prefer their complimentary pillow pack of gummy bears served with a touch of history, Coburg's most characterful digs started life as a defensive tower that was expanded in the early 19th century to house Prince Albert's private tutor. Each of the 15 rooms is a gem boasting squeaky parquet floors, antique-style furniture and regally high ceilings.

The Square
HOTEL €€

(☑ 09561-705 8520; www.hotelthesquare.com; Ketschangasse 1; s/d from €75/85; P ☎) What The Square lacks in character it more than makes up for in space and facilities. Each room has a kitchen, or corridor access to one, some have baths and the three large apartments cost the same as a double. You can also choose your view – the Prince Albert bronze out front on the Marktplatz or the pretty Stadtkirche out back.

Café Prinz Albert
CAFE €

(Ketschengasse 27; snacks & cakes €2-5; ⊙ 7.30am-6pm Mon-Fri, from 8am Sat) This long-established cafe on Albertsplatz is a good snack stop mid-sightseeing. The breakfast menu has a historical theme – the 'Martin Luther' (€3.20) is a sober, modest affair compared to the more lavish 'Prinz Albert' (€8.90).

Tie
VEGETARIAN €€

(Leopoldstrasse 14; mains €10-20; ⊙ from 5pm Tue-Sun; ☑) A five-minute walk east of the Marktplatz, this vegetarian restaurant plates up imaginative food crafted from fresh organic ingredients. Dishes range from vegetarian classics to Asian inspirations, with the odd fish or meat dish for the unconverted. Seasonally set tables and temporary art exhibitions on the walls add colour to the simple decor.

ⓘ Information

Tourist Office (☑ 09561-898 000; www.coburg-tourist.de; Herrngasse 4; ⊙ 9am-5pm Mon-Fri, 10am-2pm Sat & Sun) Helpful office where staff sell the CObook (€14.90), a five-day ticket good for 13 sights in Coburg and around as well as local public transport. English audioguides (€3.50) to the city are also available here.

ⓘ Getting There & Around

Coburg has rail connections to Bamberg (€12.90, one hour, hourly), Bayreuth (€20.10, 1½ hours, hourly) and Nuremberg (€22, 1¾ hours, hourly).

The **Veste-Express** (www.geckobahn.de; one-way/return €3.50/5; ⊙ 10am-5pm Apr-Oct) tourist train leaves the tourist office every 30 minutes for the Veste Coburg. Otherwise it's a steep, 3km climb.

Altmühltal Nature Park

The Altmühltal Nature Park is one of Germany's largest nature parks and covers some of Bavaria's most eye-pleasing terrain. The Altmühl River gently meanders through a region of little valleys and hills before joining the Rhine-Main Canal and eventually emptying into the Danube. Outdoor fun on well-marked hiking and biking trails is the main reason to head here, but the river is also ideal for canoeing. There's basic camping in designated spots along the river, and plenty of accommodation in the local area.

The park takes in 2900 sq km of land southwest of Regensburg, south of Nuremberg, east of Treuchtlingen and north of Eichstätt. The eastern boundaries of the park include the town of Kelheim.

North of the river, activities focus around the towns of Kipfenberg, Beilngries and Riedenburg.

☂ Activities

Canoeing & Kayaking

The most beautiful section of the river is from Treuchtlingen or Pappenheim to Eichstätt or Kipfenberg, about a 60km stretch that you can do lazily in a kayak or canoe in two to three days. There are lots of little dams along the way, as well as some small rapids about 10km northwest of Dollnstein, so make sure you are up for little bits of portaging. Signs warn of impending doom, but locals say that, if you heed the warning to keep to the right, you'll be safe.

You can rent canoes and kayaks in just about every town along the river. Expect to pay about €15/25 per day for a one-/two-person boat, more for bigger ones. Staff will sometimes haul you and the boats to or from your embarkation point for a small fee.

You can get a full list of boat-hire outlets from the Informationszentrum Naturpark Altmühltal.

San-Aktiv Tours
CANOEING

(☑ 09831-4936; www.san-aktiv-tours.com; half-/full-day tour €22/28) San-Aktiv Tours is the largest and best-organised of the canoe-hire companies in the park, with a network of vehicles to shuttle canoes, bicycles and people around the area. Trips through the park run from April to October, and you can canoe alone or join a group. Packages generally include the canoe, swim vests, maps, instructions and transfer back to the embarkation point.

Cycling & Hiking

With around 3000km of hiking trails and 800km of cycle trails criss-crossing the landscape, foot and pedal are the best ways to strike out into the park. Cycling trails are clearly labelled and have long rectangular brown signs bearing a bike symbol. Hiking-trail markers are yellow. The most popular cycling route is the Altmühltal Radweg, which runs parallel to the river for 166km. The Altmühltal-Panoramaweg, stretching 200km between Gunzenhausen and Kelheim, is a picturesque hiking route, which crosses the entire park from west to east.

You can rent bikes in almost every town within the park, and prices are more or less uniform. Most bike-hire agencies will also store bicycles. Ask for a list of bike-hire outlets at the Informationszentrum Naturpark Altmühltal.

Located in Eichstätt, **Kanuuh** (🗷 08421-2110; www.kanuuh.de; Am Graben 22) will bring the bikes to you, or take you and the bikes to anywhere in Altmühltal Nature Park for an extra fee.

Rock Climbing

The worn cliffs along the Altmühl River offer some appealing terrain for climbers of all skill levels. The medium-grade 45m-high rock face of Burgsteinfelsen, located between the towns of Dollnstein and Breitenfurt, has routes from the fourth to eighth climbing levels, with stunning views of the valley. The Dohlenfelsen face near the town of Wellheim has a simpler expanse that's more suitable for children. The Informationszentrum Naturpark Altmühltal can provide more details on the region's climbing options.

ℹ️ Information

The park's main information centre is in Eichstätt, a charmingly historic town at the southern end of the park that makes an excellent base for exploring.

Informationszentrum Naturpark Altmühltal (🗷 08421-987 60; www.naturpark-altmuehltal. de; Notre Dame 1, Eichstätt; ☺ 9am-5pm Mon-Sat, 10am-5pm Sun Apr-Oct, 8am-noon & 2-4pm Mon-Thu, 8am-noon Fri Nov-Mar) Has information on Altmühltal Nature Park and can help with planning an itinerary. The website has

tons of information on every aspect of the park, including activities and accommodation.

ℹ️ Getting There & Away

There are bus and train connections between Eichstätt and all the major milestones along the river including, from west to east, Gunzenhausen, Treuchtlingen and Pappenheim.

BUS

From mid-April to October the FreizeitBus Altmühltal-Donautal takes passengers and their bikes around the park. Buses normally run three times a day from mid-April to early October. Route 1 runs from Regensburg and Kelheim to Riedenburg on weekends and holidays only. Route 2 travels between Eichstätt, Beilngries, Dietfurt and Riedenburg, with all-day service on weekends and holidays and restricted service on weekdays. All-day tickets, which cost €11 for passengers with bicycles and €8 for those without (or €25/18 per family with/without bicycles) are bought from the driver.

TRAIN

Hourly trains run between Eichstätt Bahnhof and Treuchtlingen (€7.10, 25 minutes), and between Treuchtlingen and Gunzenhausen (€4.50, 15 minutes). RE trains from Munich that run through Eichstätt Bahnhof also stop in Dollnstein, Solnhofen and Pappenheim.

Eichstätt

🗷 08421 / POP 13,500

Hugging a tight bend in the Altmühl River, Eichstätt radiates a tranquil Mediterranean-style flair with cobbled streets meandering past elegantly Italianate buildings and leafy piazzas. Italian architects, notably Gabriel de Gabrieli and Maurizio Pedetti, rebuilt the town after Swedes razed the place during the Thirty Years' War (1618–48) and it came through WWII virtually without a graze. Since 1980 many of its baroque facades have played host to faculties belonging to Germany's sole Catholic university.

Eichstätt is pretty enough, but is really just a jumping off and stocking up point for flits into the wilds of Altmühltal Nature Park. You'll be chomping at the bit, eager to hit a trail or grab a paddle, if you stay more than a day.

⊙ Sights

Dom   CHURCH
(www.bistum-eichstaett.de/dom; Domplatz; ☺ 7.15am-7.30pm) Eichstätt's centre is dominated by the richly adorned Dom. Standout features include an enormous 16th-century stained-glass window by Hans Holbein the

Elder, and the carved sandstone Pappenheimer Altar (1489–97), depicting a pilgrimage from Pappenheim to Jerusalem. The seated statue is of St Willibald, the town's first bishop. The adjoining Domschatzmuseum includes the robes of 8th-century English-born bishop St Willibald and baroque Gobelin tapestries.

Willibaldsburg   CASTLE
(⌨ 08421-4730; Burgstrasse 19; adult/child €4.50/ free; ⊙ 9am-6pm Tue-Sun Apr-Oct, 10am-4pm Tue-Sun Nov-Mar) The walk or drive up to the hill-top castle of Willibaldsburg (1355) is worth it for the views across the valley from the formally laid-out Bastiongarten; many locals also head up here on sunny days for the near-by beer garden. The castle itself houses two museums, the most interesting of which is the Jura-Museum, specialising in fossils and containing a locally found archaeopteryx (the oldest-known fossil bird), as well as aquariums with living specimens of the fossilised animals.

Domschatzmuseum   MUSEUM
(Cathedral Treasury Museum; ⌨ 08421-507 42; www.dioezesanmuseum-eichstaett.de; Residenzplatz 7; adult/concession €3/1.50, Sun €1; ⊙ 10.30am-5pm Wed-Fri, 10am-5pm Sat & Sun Apr-Nov) The worthwhile Domschatzmuseum includes the robes of 8th-century English-born bishop St Willibald and baroque Gobelin tapestries illustrating scenes from the life of St Walburga. There's lots of church silver and gold to admire and religious paintings galore.

Fürstbischöfliche Residenz   PALACE
(Residenzplatz 1; admission €1; ⊙ 7.30am-noon Mon-Fri, 2-4pm Mon-Wed, 2-5.30pm Thu) The prince-bishops lived it up at the baroque Residenz, built between 1725 and 1736 by Gabriel de Gabrieli. Inside, the stunning main staircase and a hall of mirrors stick in the mind. In the square outside rises a late 18th-century golden statue of the Madonna atop a 19m-high column.

Kloster St Walburga   CONVENT
(www.abtei-st-walburg.de; Westenstrasse) The final resting place of St Willibald's sister, the Kloster St Walburga is a popular local pilgrimage destination. Every year between mid-October and late February, water oozes from Walburga's relics in the underground chapel and drips down into a catchment. The nuns bottle diluted versions of the so-called *Walburgaöl* (Walburga oil) and give it away to the faithful.

A staircase from the lower chapel leads to an off-limits upper chapel where you can catch a glimpse through the grill of beautiful ex-voto tablets and other trinkets left as a thank you to the saint. The main St Walburga Church above has a glorious rococo interior.

🛏 Sleeping & Eating

DJH Hostel   HOSTEL €
(⌨ 08421-980   410;   www.eichstaett.jugend herberge.de; Reichenaustrasse 15; dm from €21; 🛜) This comfy 122-bed youth hostel provides pretty views of the Altstadt, and is peddle- and paddle-friendly.

Municipal Camping Ground   CAMPGROUND €
(⌨ 08421-908 147; www.eichstaett.de; Pirkheimerstrasse; per campsite €10; ⊙ Apr-Oct) This basic camping ground is on the northern bank of the Altmühl River, 1km southeast of the town centre.

★ Hotel Adler   HOTEL €€
(⌨ 08421-6767; www.adler-eichstaett.de; Marktplatz 22; s €60-65, d €85-110; 🅿🛜) A superb ambience reigns in this ornate 300-year-old building, Eichstätt's top digs. Sleeping quarters are bright and breezy, and the generous breakfast buffet is a proper set up for a day on the trail or river. Despite the posh feel, this hotel welcomes hiker and bikers.

Fuchs   HOTEL €€
(⌨ 08421-6789;   www.hotel-fuchs.de;   Ostenstrasse 8; s €45-70, d €75-85; 🅿🛜) This central, family-run hotel, with underfloor heating in the bathrooms, adjoins a cake shop with a sunny dining area. It's convenient to a launch ramp on the river where you can put in, and you can lock your canoe or kayak in the garage.

★ Gasthof Krone   BAVARIAN €€
(www.krone-eichstaett.de; Domplatz 3; mains €6.50-18.50; ⊙ 10am-midnight) The top place to source real local sustenance is this large, multilevel dining hall serving the best local food such as house sausages, river trout and seasonal salads. The local Hofmühl beer goes down a treat after a day on the water.

Trompete   BAVARIAN, ITALIAN €€
(⌨ 08421-981 70; www.braugasthof-trompete.de; Ostenstrasse 3; mains €5-16.50; ⊙ 7am-1am Mon-Fri, from 7.30am Sat & Sun) From breakfast to your last cocktail of the day, this friendly inn, just a short walk to the southeast of the centre, is a sure-fire option at any time of

day. The menu features some *echt*-Bavarian dishes such as Altmühltal trout and *Ochsenbraten* (roast beef) as well as a long list of pizzas and pastas.

🛈 Information

Post Office (Domplatz 7; ⏰ 9am-12.30pm & 1.30-5pm Mon-Fri, 9am-noon Sat)

Tourist Office (📞 08421-600 1400; www.eichstaett.de; Domplatz 8; ⏰ 10am-5pm Mon-Fri, to 4pm Sat, to 1pm Sun May-Sep, shorter hours & closed Sun rest of the year) Professionally run office with cycle hire and walking tours.

🛈 Getting There & Away

Eichstätt has two train stations. Main-line trains stop at the Bahnhof, 5km from the centre, from where coinciding diesel services shuttle to the Stadtbahnhof (town station). Trains run to Ingolstadt (€7, 25 minutes, hourly) and Nuremberg (€21.30, 1½ hours, every two hours).

REGENSBURG & THE DANUBE

The sparsely populated eastern reaches of Bavaria may live in the shadow of Bavaria's big-hitting attractions, but they hold many historical treasures to rival their neighbours. Top billing goes to Regensburg, a former capital, and one of Germany's prettiest and liveliest cities. From here the Danube gently winds its way to the Italianate city of Passau. Landshut was once the hereditary seat of the Wittelsbach family, and the region has also given the world a pope – Benedict XVI – who was born in Marktl am Inn. Away from the towns, the Bavarian Forest broods in semiundiscovered remoteness.

Regensburg

📞 0941 / POP 148,600

The capital of the Oberpfalz region of Bavaria, Regensburg dates back to Roman times and was the first capital of Bavaria. Two thousand years of history bequeathed the city some of the region's finest architectural heritage, a fact recognised by Unesco in 2006. Though big on the historical wow factor, today's Regensburg is a laid-back, studenty and unpretentious sort of place and its tangle of old streets is a joy to wander.

⊙ Sights

⭐ **Schloss Thurn und Taxis**   CASTLE
(www.thurnundtaxis.de; Emmeramsplatz 5; tours adult/child €13.50/11; ⏰ tours hourly 10.30am-

MUSEUM OF BAVARIAN HISTORY

Regensburg is set to acquire a major new attraction in mid-2019 – the Museum of Bavarian History. The architecturally striking building (other, less favourable, descriptions have been used) has been bolted together around 250m east of the Steinerne Brücke, altering the historical appearance of the riverfront. As well as the supercontemporary look of the structure, the wisdom of placing a major attraction in such a flood-prone location has also been questioned.

4.30pm late Mar-early Nov, to 3.30pm Sat & Sun Nov-Mar) In the 15th century, Franz von Taxis (1459–1517) assured his place in history by setting up the first European postal system, which remained a monopoly until the 19th century. In recognition of his services, the family was given the former Benedictine monastery St Emmeram, henceforth known as Schloss Thurn und Taxis. It was soon one of the most modern palaces in Europe and featured such luxuries as flushing toilets. Today it is the world's largest inhabited building.

The palace complex also contains the Schatzkammer (Treasury). The jewellery, porcelain and precious furnishings on display belonged, for many years, to the wealthiest dynasty in Germany. The fortune, administered by Prince Albert II, is still estimated at well over €1 billion.

⭐ **Dom St Peter**   CHURCH
(www.bistum-regensburg.de; Domplatz; ⏰ 6.30am-7pm Jun-Sep, to 6pm Apr, May & Oct, to 5pm Nov-Mar) It takes a few seconds for your eyes to adjust to the interior of Regensburg's soaring landmark, the Dom St Peter, one of Bavaria's grandest Gothic cathedrals with stunning kaleidoscopic stained-glass windows and an opulent, silver-sheathed main altar. The cathedral is home of the Domspatzen, a 1000-year-old boys' choir that accompanies the 10am Sunday service (only during the school year). The Domschatzmuseum (Cathedral Treasury) brims with monstrances, tapestries and other church treasures.

⭐ **Golf Museum**   MUSEUM
(📞 0941-510 74; www.golf-museum.com; Tändlergasse 3; adult/child €7.50/5; ⏰ 10am-6pm Mon-Sat) Claiming to be Europe's best golf museum

Regensburg

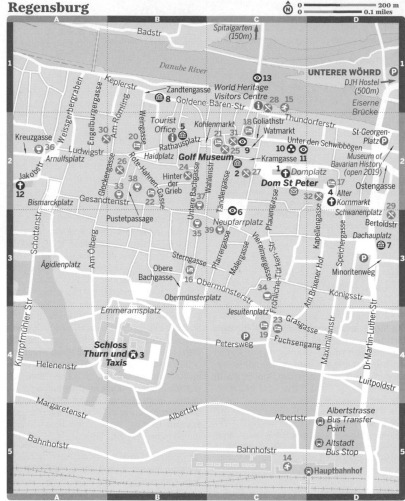

(not counting Scotland, home to the British Golf Museum), this fine repository of wooden clubs, ivory tees and yellowing score cards (including one belonging to King George V of England) backswings its way through golf's illustrious past – interesting, even if you think a green fee is something to do with municipal recycling. The entrance is in an antiques shop.

Altes Rathaus   HISTORIC BUILDING
(Old Town Hall; Rathausplatz; adult/child €7.50/4; ☺ tours in English 3pm Easter-Oct, 2pm Nov & Dec, in German every 30min) From 1663 to 1806,

the Reichstag (imperial assembly) held its gatherings at Regensburg's old town, an important role commemorated by an exhibit in today's Reichstagsmuseum. Tours take in the lavish assembly hall and the original torture chambers in the cellar. Buy tickets at the tourist office in the same building. Note that access is by tour only. Audioguides are available for English speakers in January and February.

Steinerne Brücke   BRIDGE
(Stone Bridge) An incredible feat of engineering for its day, Regensburg's 900-year-

Regensburg

old Stone Bridge was at one time the only fortified crossing of the Danube. Damaged and neglected for centuries (especially by the buses that once used it) the entire expanse has undergone renovation in recent years.

Schottenkirche St Jakob   CHURCH
(Jakobstrasse 3) The sooty 12th-century main portal of the Schottenkirche St Jakob is considered one of the supreme examples of Romanesque architecture in Germany. Its reliefs and sculptures form an iconography that continues to baffle the experts. Sadly it's protected from further pollution by an ageing glass structure that makes the whole thing an eyesore. However, this is more than made up for inside, where pure, tourist-free Romanesque austerity prevails.

Alte Kapelle   CHURCH
(Alter Kornmarkt 8) South of the Dom, the humble exterior of the graceful Alte Kapelle belies the stunning interior with its rich rococo decorations. The core of the church, however, is about 1000 years old, although the vaulted ceilings were added in the Gothic period. The church is open only during services but you can always peek through the wrought-iron grill.

Porta Praetoria   RUINS
(Unter den Schwibbögen) Just north of the Dom, the arched gate called Porta Praetoria is the most impressive reminder of Regensburg's Roman heritage. It was built in AD 179 by Emperor Marcus Aurelius as part of the Castra Regina. To see more remains of the Roman wall, stroll along Unter den Schwibbögen.

Document Neupfarrplatz   HISTORIC SITE
(☑ 0941-507 3417; Neupfarrplatz) Excavations in the mid-1990s revealed remains of Regensburg's once-thriving 16th-century Jewish quarter, along with Roman buildings, gold coins and a Nazi bunker. The subterranean Document Neupfarrplatz only provides access to a small portion of the excavated area, but tours feature a worthwhile multimedia presentation (in German) about the square's history. Back up above, on the square itself, a work by renowned Israeli artist Dani Karavan graces the site of the former synagogue. Contact the tourist office for tickets and tour details.

Historisches Museum   MUSEUM
(Dachauplatz 2-4; adult/child €5/2.50; ⊘10am-4pm Tue-Sun) A medieval monastery provides a suitably atmospheric backdrop for the city's history museum. The collections plot

the region's story from cave dweller to Roman, and medieval trader to 19th-century burgher.

Oskar Schindler Plaque   MEMORIAL

(Am Watmarkt 5) Oskar Schindler lived in Regensburg for years, and today one of his houses bears a plaque to his achievements, as commemorated in Steven Spielberg's epic dramatisation *Schindler's List*.

Roman Wall   HISTORIC SITE

The most tangible reminder of the ancient rectangular Castra Regina (Regen Fortress), where the name 'Regensburg' comes from, is the remaining Roman wall, which follows Unter den Schwibbögen and veers south onto Dr-Martin-Luther-Strasse. Dating from AD 179 the rough-hewn Porta Praetoria arch is the tallest Roman structure in all of Bavaria and formed part of the city's defences for centuries.

Kepler-Gedächtnishaus   MUSEUM

(Kepler Memorial House; Keplerstrasse 5; adult/child €2.20/1.10; ☉10.30am-4pm Sat & Sun) Disciples of astronomer and mathematician Johannes Kepler should visit the house he lived in while resident in Regensburg.

🏃 Activities

Schifffahrt Klinger   BOATING

(☎0941-521 04; www.schifffahrtklinger.de; cruises adult/child from €9/5.50; ☉Apr-late Oct) The name of the company's 50-minute Strudelfahrt river tour of the city may invoke a few giggles but is an enjoyable experience, as is the cruise to Walhalla.

Bikehaus   BICYCLE RENTAL

(☎0941-599 8194; www.fahrradverleih-regensburg.de; Bahnhofstrasse 18; bikes per day €15; ☉10am-7pm Mon-Sat) At Bikehaus you can rent anything from kiddies bikes to fully saddled tourers and tandems for a novel city tour. You'll need a €100 deposit which is returned when you give the bike back.

🎊 Festivals & Events

Dult   BEER

(www.r-dult.de; ☉May & Aug/Sep) Major Oktoberfest-style beer party with brewery tents, carousel rides, entertainment, sausages and vendors on the Dultplatz.

Weihnachtsmarkt   CHRISTMAS MARKET

(www.regensburg.de; ☉Dec) The Christmas market has stalls selling roasted almonds, gingerbread and traditional wooden toys.

Held at Neupfarrplatz and Schloss Thurn und Taxis during Advent.

🛏 Sleeping

Brook Lane Hostel   HOSTEL €

(☎0941-696 5521; www.hostel-regensburg.de; Obere Bachgasse 21; dm/s/d from €16/40/50, apt per person €55; ☜) Regensburg's only backpacker hostel has its very own convenience store, which doubles up as reception, but it isn't open 24 hours, so late landers should let staff know in advance. Dorms do the minimum required, but the apartments and doubles are applaudable deals, especially if you're travelling in a two- or more-some. Access to kitchens and washing machines throughout.

DJH Hostel   HOSTEL €

(☎0941-466 2830; www.regensburg.jugendherberge.de; Wöhrdstrasse 60; dm from €22; ☜) Regensburg's 190-bed DJH hostel occupies a beautiful old building on a large island about a 10-minute walk north of the Altstadt.

Hotel am Peterstor   HOTEL €

(☎0941-545 45; www.hotel-am-peterstor.de; Fröhliche-Türken-Strasse 12; s/d from €40/50; ☜) The pale-grey decor might be grim but the location is great, the price is right and staff go out of their way to assist. Make sure you get a nonsmoking room, as some still have a pong of secondhand smoke. Breakfast is an optional €5 extra, parking €8. Payment on arrival.

★ Elements Hotel   HOTEL €€

(☎941-2007 2275; www.hotel-elements.de; Alter Kornmarkt 3; d from €105; ☜) Four elements, four rooms, and what rooms they are! 'Fire' blazes in plush crimson; while 'Water' is a wellness suite with a jacuzzi; 'Air' is playful and light and natural wood; and stone and leather reign in colonial-inspired 'Earth'. Breakfast in bed costs an extra €10.

★ Hotel Orphée   HOTEL €€

(☎0941-596 020; www.hotel-orphee.de; Untere Bachgasse 8; s €40-120, d €80-155; ☜) Behind a humble door lies a world of genuine charm, unexpected extras and ample attention to detail. The striped floors, wrought-iron beds, original sinks and common rooms with soft cushions and well-read books give the feel of a lovingly attended home. Check-in and breakfast is nearby in the Cafe Orphée at Untere Bachgasse 8. Additional rooms are available above the cafe.

Hotel Goldenes Kreuz
HOTEL €€

(☑0941-558 12; www.hotel-goldeneskreuz.com; Haidplatz 7; s €90-135, d €110-160; ☎) Surely the best deal in town, the nine fairy-tale rooms each bear the name of a crowned head and are fit for a kaiser. Huge mirrors, dark antique and Bauhaus furnishings, four-poster beds, chubby exposed beams and parquet flooring produce a stylishly aristocratic opus in leather, wood, crystal and fabric. Breakfast is in the house chapel.

Zum Fröhlichen Türken
HOTEL €€

(☑0941-536 51; www.hotel-zum-froehlichen-tuerken.de; Fröhliche-Türken-Strasse 11; s/d €60/90; ☎) With its comfortable, clean quarters, unstinting breakfast and mild-mannered staff, the 'Jolly Turk' will bring a smile to any price-conscious traveller's face. The pricier rooms have private bathrooms.

Goliath Hotel
HOTEL €€

(☑0941-200 0900; www.hotel-goliath.de; Goliathstrasse 10; d from €135; P✳☎) Bang in the heart of Regensburg's historical core, the 41 rooms at the Goliath are all differently conceived and pristinely serviced. Some have little extras such as bathroom–bedroom windows and big baths. It's a cool pad, but doesn't go the whole boutique hog and staff are surprisingly old school.

Hotel Roter Hahn
HOTEL €€€

(☑0941-595 090; www.roter-hahn.com; Rote-Hahnen-Gasse 10; s/d from €110/140; P☎) A bulky beamed ceiling and a glassed-in Roman stone well (staff appear to be oblivious of its provenance) greet you in the lobby of the 'Red Rooster', contrasting with streamlined rooms offering freshly maintained amenities. The downside here is the extras – parking costs a hefty €20 a night, as does breakfast.

✖️ Eating

★Historische Wurstkuchl
GERMAN €

(☑0941-466 210; www.wurstkuchl.de; Thundorferstrasse 3; 6 sausages €9.60; ⊙9am-7pm) Completely submerged several times by the Danube's fickle floods, this titchy eatery has been serving the city's traditional finger-size sausages, grilled over beech wood and dished up with its own sauerkraut and sweet grainy mustard, since 1135 and lays claim to being the world's oldest sausage kitchen.

Spaghetteria Aquino
ITALIAN €

(www.spaghetteria-regensburg.de; Am Römling 12; dishes €6.50-11.50; ⊙5.30pm-midnight Mon-Fri, 11.30am-midnight Sat, 11.30am-3pm & 5.30pm-midnight Sun; ☎☑) Get carbed up at this former 17th-century chapel, where you can splatter six types of pasta with 24 types of sauce, and get out the door for the cost of a cocktail in Munich. The all-you-can-eat buffets (€7) are a cheap way to fill up at lunchtime. There are 14 different pizzas to choose from as well as vegan spaghetti dishes.

Dampfnudel Uli
CAFE €

(Watmarkt 4; dishes €5-8; ⊙10.01am-5.01pm Wed-Fri, to 3.01pm Sat) This quirkily old-fashioned little noshery serves a mean *Dampfnudel* (steamed doughnut) with custard in a Gothic chamber lined with photos of beer steins (tankards) at the base of the Baumburger Tower.

★Dicker Mann
BAVARIAN €€

(☑0941-573 70; www.dicker-mann.de; Krebsgasse 6; mains €9-21; ⊙9am-1am; ☎) The 'Chubby Chappy', a stylish, tranquil and very traditional inn, is one of the oldest restaurants in town, allegedly dating back to the 14th century. All the staples of Bavarian sustenance are plated up plus a few other dishes for good measure. On a balmy eve, be sure to bag a table in the lovely beer garden out back.

★Café Orphée
FRENCH €€

(Untere Bachgasse 8; mains €10-26; ⊙8am-1am) Claiming to be the Frenchiest bistro east of the Rhine – it really is like being teleported to 1920s Paris – this visually pleasing, always bustling eatery is bedecked in faded red velvet, dark wood and art nouveau posters. Light-lunch fare populates a handwritten menu of appetising Gallic favourites with slight Bavarian touches for sturdiness. Best breakfast menu in Bavaria.

Leerer Beutel
EUROPEAN €€

(☑0941-589 97; www.leerer-beutel.de; Bertoldstrasse 9; mains €12-28; ⊙6pm-1am Mon, 11am-1am Tue-Sat, 11am-3pm Sun) Subscriber to the slow food ethos, the cavernous restaurant at the eponymous cultural centre offers an imaginatively mixed menu of Bavarian, Tyrolean and Italian dishes, served indoors or out on the car-free cobbles. From Tuesday to Friday, clued-in locals invade for the two-course lunches for €7.20.

Haus Heuport
INTERNATIONAL €€

(www.heuport.de; Domplatz 7; mains €11.50-22; ⊙10am-midnight Mon-Fri, from 9am Sat & Sun; ☑) Enter an internal courtyard (flanked

WALHALLA

Modelled on the Parthenon in Athens, the Walhalla (www.walhalla-regensburg.de; Walhalla strasse 48, Donaustauf; adult/child €4/free; ⊙9am-6pm Apr-Oct, 10am-noon & 1-4pm Nov-Mar) is a breathtaking Ludwig I monument dedicated to the giants of Germanic thought and deed. Marble steps seem to lead up forever from the banks of the Danube to this dazzling marble hall, with a gallery of 127 heroes in marble.

The collection includes a few dubious cases, such as astronomer Copernicus, born in a territory belonging to present-day Poland. The most recent addition (2009) was romantic poet Heinrich Heine, whose works were set to music by Strauss, Wagner and Brahms.

To get here take the Danube Valley country road (unnumbered) 10km east from Regensburg to the village of Donaustauf, then follow the signs. Alternatively, you can take a two-hour boat cruise with Schifffahrt Klinger (p154), which includes a one-hour stop at Walhalla, or take bus 5 from Regensburg Hauptbahnhof.

by stone blocks where medieval torches were once extinguished) and climb up the grand old wooden staircase to this space-rich Gothic dining hall for eye-to-eye views of the Dom St Peter and an internationally flavoured culinary celebration. The Sunday breakfast buffet runs to a hangover-busting 2pm. Always busy.

Weltenburger am Dom BAVARIAN €€
(☑0941-586 1460; www.weltenburger-am-dom. de; Domplatz 3; dishes €7-20; ⊙11am-11pm; 🛜) Tightly packed gastropub with a mouth-watering menu of huge gourmet burgers, sausage dishes, beer hall and garden favourites such as *Obazda* (cream cheese on pretzels) and *Sauerbraten* (marinated roast meat), dark beer goulash and a few token desserts. Make sure you're hungry before you come as portions are huge.

★Storstad INTERNATIONAL €€€
(☑0941-5999 3000; www.storstad.de; Watmarkt 5; 3 courses from €40; ⊙noon-2pm, plus 6.30-9.30pm Tue-Thu, from 6pm Fri & Sat; 🛜) If you are looking for something a bit more creative on your plate than hunks of pork and dumplings, book a table at this 21st-century gourmet restaurant. The menus feature rare ingredients for Bavaria such as lamb, cod and mackerel, enjoyed paired with German and other European wine in the ultramodern, if rather overlit, dining room.

🍷 Drinking & Nightlife

★Cafebar BAR
(www.cafebar-regensburg.de; Gesandtenstrasse 14; ⊙8am-midnight Mon-Wed, to 1am Thu & Fri, 9am-1am Sat, 1pm-midnight Sun) This time-warped, tightly squeezed blast from the past in

Jugendstil tile, cast iron and stained glass has been filling with newspaper-reading caffeine fans at first rays and ethanol fans after sundown for over three decades.

Kneitinger PUB
(www.kneitinger.de; Arnulfsplatz 3; ⊙9am-midnight) Kneitinger is Regensburg's local beer and there's no better place to head in the city for some hearty home cooking, delicious house suds and outrageous oompah frolics than the brewery's own tavern. It's been in business since 1530.

Wirtshaus im Alten Augustiner Kloster BEER GARDEN
(www.hacker-pschorr-regensburg.de; Neupfarrplatz 15; ⊙10am-11.30pm) This popular fairy-lit beer garden and restaurant is ideally located in the heart of the city. Order a Munich-brewed Hacker-Pschorr lager and pack it away with some traditional south German fare in the sprawling garden or cavernous interior.

Félix CAFE
(www.cafefelix.de; Fröhliche-Türken-Strasse 6; ⊙9am-2am Sun-Thu, 10am-3am Fri & Sat) Early-bird's breakfast and after-dark trendoids leaf through the lengthy drinks menu behind the curvaceous neo-baroque frontage of this open-all-hours cafe with a welcoming air. You'd be lucky to get a seat here at lunchtime so arrive early.

Spitalgarten BEER GARDEN
(☑0941-847 74; www.spitalgarten.de; St Katharinenplatz 1; ⊙10am-11pm) A veritable thicket of folding chairs and slatted tables by the Danube, this is one of the best places in town for some alfresco quaffing. It claims to have

brewed beer (today's Spital) here since 1350, so it probably knows what it's doing by now.

Paletti BAR
(Gesandtenstrasse 6, Pustetpassage; ⊙ 8am-2am; 🔊) Tucked into a covered passageway off Gesandtenstrasse, this buzzy Italian cafe-bar that has not changed since the 1960s teleports you back to the postwar years when many Italian immigrants made Bavaria their home.

Hemingway's BAR
(www.hemingways.de; Obere Bachgasse 5; ⊙ 9am-1am Sun-Thu, to 2am Fri & Sat) Black wood, big mirrors and lots of photos of Papa himself add to the cool atmosphere of this swish, art-deco-style cafe-bar.

Moritz BAR
(www.cafemoritz.com; Untere Bachgasse 15; ⊙ 7.30am-1am Mon-Sat, from 9am Sun) Take some Gothic cross vaulting, paint it high-visibility tunnel orange, throw in some killer cocktails and invite a millennial crowd – and you've got Moritz!

ⓘ Information

Use the **Regensburg Card** (24/48hr €9/17) for free public transport and discounts at local attractions and businesses. Available at the tourist office.

Post Office (Domplatz; ⊙ 9.30am-noon & 2-6pm Mon-Fri, to noon Sat)

Tourist Office (🕿 0941-507 4410; https://tourismus.regensburg.de; Rathausplatz 4; ⊙ 9am-6pm Mon-Fri, to 4pm Sat, 9.30am-4pm Sun Apr-Oct, to 2.30pm Sun Nov-Mar; 🔊) In the historic Altes Rathaus. Sells tickets, tours, rooms and an audioguide for self-guided tours.

World Heritage Visitors Centre (🕿 0941-507 4410; www.regensburg-welterbe.de; Weisse-Lamm-Gasse 1; ⊙ 10am-7pm) Visitors centre by the Steinerne Brücke, focusing on the city's Unesco World Heritage Sites. Interesting interactive multimedia exhibits.

ⓘ Getting There & Away

TRAIN
Train connections from Regensburg:

Frankfurt am Main €70, three hours, every two hours

Landshut €14.50, 40 minutes, at least hourly

Munich €29.70, 1½ hours, hourly

Nuremberg €23.20, one to two hours, two hourly

Passau €26.40 to €31, one hour, every two hours or change in Plattling

ⓘ Getting Around

BICYCLE
Bikehaus (p154) rents anything from kiddies bikes to fully saddled tourers and tandems for a novel city tour. You'll need a €100 deposit that is returned when you give the bike back.

BUS
On weekdays the Altstadtbus (€1.10) somehow manages to squeeze its way through the narrow streets between the Hauptbahnhof and the Altstadt every 10 minutes between 9am and 7pm. The **bus transfer point** (Albertstrasse) is one block north of the Hauptbahnhof. Tickets for all city buses (except the Altstadtbus) cost €2.40 for journeys in the centre; an all-day ticket costs €5 at ticket machines.

Ingolstadt

🕿 0841 / POP 133,600

Even by Bavaria's high standards, Danube-straddling Ingolstadt is astonishingly affluent. Auto manufacturer Audi has its headquarters here, flanked by a clutch of oil refineries on the outskirts, but industry has left few marks on the medieval centre, with its cobblestone streets and historic, if slightly overrenovated, buildings. Ingolstadt's museum-church has the largest flat fresco ever made, and few people may know that its old medical school figured in the literary birth of Frankenstein, the monster by which all others are judged.

◉ Sights

Asamkirche Maria de Victoria CHURCH
(🕿 0841-305 1830; Neubaustrasse 11; adult/child €3/2; ⊙ 9am-noon & 12.30-5pm Tue-Sun Mar-Oct, plus Mon May-Sep, 1-4pm Tue-Sun Nov-Feb) The Altstadt's crown jewel is the Asamkirche Maria de Victoria, a baroque masterpiece designed by brothers Cosmas Damian and Egid Quirin Asam between 1732 and 1736. The church's mesmerising trompe l'oeil ceiling, painted in just six weeks in 1735, is the world's largest fresco on a flat surface.

Audi Factory FACTORY
(🕿 0800-283 4444; www.audi.com; Ettinger Strasse; adult/child €7/3.50; ⊙ 10.30am, 12.30pm & 2.30pm Mon-Fri in German, 11.30am Mon-Fri in English) Ingolstadt is home to the famous Audi factory that sprawls to the north of the city centre. The two-hour 'Production in a Nutshell' tours of the plant take you through

the entire Audi production process, from the metal press to the testing station.

Audi Forum – Museum Mobile MUSEUM
(☑0800-283 4444; www.audi.de/foren; Ettinger Strasse 40; adult/child €4/free; ⊗9am-6pm Mon-Fri, 10am-4pm Sat & Sun) The excellent Audi Forum exhibits on three floors chart Audi's humble beginnings in 1899 to its latest dream machines such as the R8. Some 50 cars and 20 motorbikes are on display, including prototypes that glide past visitors on an open lift. Take half-hourly bus 11 to the terminus from the Hauptbahnhof or Paradeplatz.

Liebfrauenmünster CHURCH
(Kreuzstrasse; ⊗8am-6pm) Ingolstadt's biggest church was established by Duke Ludwig the Bearded in 1425 and enlarged over the next century. This classic Gothic hall church has a pair of strangely oblique square towers that flank the main entrance. Inside, subtle colours and a nave flooded with light intensify the magnificence of the high-lofted vaulting and the blossoming stonework of several side chapels.

Museum für Konkrete Kunst MUSEUM
(Museum of Concrete Art; ☑0841-305 1875; www.mkk-ingolstadt.de; Tränktorstrasse 6-8; adult/concession €5/3; ⊗10am-5pm Tue-Sun) This unique art museum showcases works and installations from the Concrete Movement, all of a bafflingly abstract nature and certainly an acquired taste. The movement was defined and dominated by interwar artists Max Bill and Theo van Doesburg whose works make up a large share of the collections.

Lechner Museum MUSEUM
(☑0841-305 2250; www.lechner-museum.de; Esplanade 9; adult/concession €5/3; ⊗11am-5pm Thu-Sun) This unusual art museum highlights works cast in steel, a medium that's more expressive than you might think. Exhibits are displayed in a striking glass-covered factory hall dating from 1953.

Deutsches Medizinhistorisches Museum MUSEUM
(German Museum of Medical History; ☑0841-305 2860; www.dmm-ingolstadt.de; Anatomiestrasse 18-20; adult/concession €3/2; ⊗10am-5pm Tue-Sun) Located in the stately Alte Anatomie (Old Anatomy) at the university, this sometimes rather gory museum chronicles the evolution of medical science as well as the many (scary) instruments and techniques used. Unless you are, or have been, a medical student, pack a strong stomach for the visit.

Closed for renovations until 2020.

Neues Schloss PALACE
(New Palace) The ostentatious Neues Schloss was built for Duke Ludwig the Bearded in 1418. Fresh from a trip to wealth-laden France, Ludwig borrowed heavily from Gallic design and created a residence with 3m-thick walls, Gothic net vaulting and individually carved doorways. One guest who probably didn't appreciate its architectural merits was future French president Charles de Gaulle, held as a prisoner of war here during WWI.

Today the building houses the **Bayerisches Armeemuseum** (Bavarian Military Museum; ☑0841-937 70; www.armeemuseum.de; Paradeplatz 4; adult/concession €3.50/3, Sun €1; ⊗9am-5.30pm Tue-Fri, 10am-5.30pm Sat & Sun) with exhibits on long-forgotten battles, armaments dating back to the 14th century and legions of tin soldiers filling the rooms.

The second part of the museum is in the **Reduit Tilly** across the river. This 19th-century fortress has an undeniable aesthetic, having been designed by Ludwig I's chief architect. It was named after Johann Tilly – a field marshal of the Thirty Years' War, who was known as the 'butcher of Magdeburg' –

THE BIRTH OF FRANKENSTEIN

Mary Shelley's *Frankenstein*, published in 1818, set a creepy precedent in the world of monster fantasies. The story is well known: young scientist Viktor Frankenstein travels to Ingolstadt to study medicine. He becomes obsessed with the idea of creating a human being and goes shopping for parts at the local cemetery. Unfortunately, his creature is a problem child and sets out to destroy its maker.

Shelley picked Ingolstadt because it was home to a prominent university and medical faculty. In the 19th century, a laboratory for scientists and medical doctors was housed in the Alte Anatomie (now the Deutsches Medizinhistorisches Museum). In the operating theatre, professors and their students carried out experiments on corpses and dead tissue, though perhaps one may have been inspired to work on something a bit scarier...

and features exhibits covering the history of WWI and post-WWI Germany.

The museum complex also houses the **Bayerisches Polizeimuseum** (Donaulände 1; adult/concession €3.50/3, Sun €1; ⊙9am-5.30pm Tue-Fri, 10am-5.30pm Sat & Sun), which lives in the Turm Triva, built at the same time as the Reduit Tilly. Exhibitions trace the story of Bavarian police and their role in various episodes of history such as the Third Reich and the Cold War.

A combined ticket is available at each museum that covers entry to all three museums (adult/concession €7/5).

Kreuztor   HISTORIC BUILDING
(Kreuzstrasse) The Gothic Kreuztor (1385) was one of the four main gates into the city until the 19th century and its redbrick fairytale outline is now the emblem of Ingolstadt. This and the main gate within the Neues Schloss are all that remain of the erstwhile entrances into the medieval city, but the former fortifications, now flats, still encircle the centre.

🛏 Sleeping

Ingolstadt has lots of hotels aimed at business travellers, which can be an advantage at weekends when rates tumble.

DJH hostel   HOSTEL €
(☑0841-305 1280; www.ingolstadt.jugendherberge.de; Friedhofstrasse 4; dm from €20) This beautiful, cheap, well-equipped and wheelchair-friendly hostel crams 84 beds into a renovated redbrick fortress (1828), about 150m west of the Kreuztor.

★Kult Hotel   DESIGN HOTEL €€
(☑0841-95100; www.kult-hotel.de; Theodor-Heuss-Strasse 25; d from €130; P🖭🖘) The most eye-catching feature of rooms at this exciting design hotel, 2km northeast of the city centre, is the painted ceilings, each one a slightly saucy work of art. Otherwise fittings and furniture come sleek, room gadgets are the latest toys, and the restaurant constitutes a study in cool elegance.

Bayerischer Hof   HOTEL €€
(☑0841-934 060; www.bayerischer-hof-ingolstadt. de; Münzbergstrasse 12; s €70-85, d €85-100; 🖘) Located around a Bavarian eatery, the 34 rooms here are filled with hardwood furniture, TVs and modern bathrooms. Rates come down at weekends making it a good deal for lone travellers as almost half the rooms are business-traveller-oriented singles.

Hotel Anker   HOTEL €€
(☑0841-300 50; www.hotel-restaurant-anker. de; Tränktorstrasse 1; s/tw €70/90; 🖘) Bright rooms, a touch of surrealist art and a commendably central location make this family-run hotel a good choice. When checking in, try to avoid arriving at meal times, when staff are busy serving in the traditional restaurant downstairs.

Enso Hotel   HOTEL €€€
(☑0841-885 590; www.enso-hotel.de; Bei der Arena 1; s/d from €100/130; P🖘) Located just across the Danube from the city centre, the 176 business-standard rooms here come in bold dashes of lip-smacking red and soot black, with acres of retro faux veneer. Traffic noise is barely audible despite the location at a busy intersection. Amenities include a commendable Italian restaurant-bar and a fitness room.

🍴 Eating & Drinking

Local drinkers are proud that Germany's Beer Purity Law of 1516 was issued in Ingolstadt, the 500th anniversary of which the city celebrated in 2016. Herrnbräu, Nordbräu or Ingobräu are the excellent local brews.

Weissbräuhaus   PUB FOOD €€
(☑0841-328 90; Dollstrasse 3; mains €7-19; ⊙11am-midnight) This beer hall with a modern feel plates up standard Bavarian fare as well as the delicious signature *Weissbräupfändl* (pork fillet with homemade noodles). The beer garden with a charming fountain out back is a pleasant place to while away a balmy evening.

Zum Daniel   BAVARIAN €€
(☑0841-352 72; Roseneckstrasse 1; mains €8-17; ⊙9am-midnight Tue-Sun) In a wonderfully Bavarian step-gabled townhouse, Ingolstadt's oldest inn is a lovingly run, Michelin-reviewed local institution serving what many claim to be the town's best pork roast and seasonal specials.

Stella D'Oro   ITALIAN €€€
(☑0841-794 3737; www.stelladoro.de; Griesbadgasse 2; mains €15-30; ⊙11.30am-2.30pm & 5.30-11pm Mon-Sat) Ingolstadt has more Italian eateries than some Italian towns, so if you're going for *la dolce vita,* you might as well go for the best. The brief menu at this smart Italian job features a well-curated selection of meat, fish and pasta, though a starter here costs the same as a main elsewhere.

Kuchlbauer
PUB

(☑ 0841-335 512; www.zum-kuchlbauer-ingolstadt. de; Schäffbräustrasse 11a; ⊙ 11.30am-11pm Sun-Fri, to 1am Sat) This unmissable brewpub is half museum, half tavern with oodles of brewing knick-knacks lining the walls. The house beer comes in wheat, dark and Helles varieties.

Neue Galerie Das MO
BAR

(☑ 0841-339 60; www.dasmo.de; Bergbräustrasse 7; ⊙ 10.30am-midnight Sun-Wed, to 2am Thu-Sat; 🛜) This trendy haunt puts on occasional art exhibitions, but it's the walled beer garden in the shade of mature chestnut trees that punters really come for. The international menu offers everything from grilled meats to schnitzel and *Obazda*. Vegetarians are well catered for.

❶ Information

Post Office (Am Stein 8; ⊙ 8.30am-6pm Mon-Fri, 9am-1pm Sat)

Tourist Office Hauptbahnhof (☑ 0841-305 3005; www.ingolstadt-tourismus.de; Elisabeth-strasse 3; ⊙ 8.30am-6.30pm Mon-Fri, 9.30am-1pm Sat) Branch of the tourist office at the main train station.

Tourist Office Rathausplatz (☑ 0841-305 3030; www.ingolstadt-tourismus.de; Moritzstrasse 19; ⊙ 9am-6pm Mon-Fri, 10am-2pm Sat & Sun, shorter hours & closed Sun Nov-Mar) Centrally located visitors centre next to the Rathaus.

❶ Getting There & Around

When arriving by train from the north (from Eichstätt and Nuremberg), **Ingolstadt Nord station** (Am Nordbahnhof) is nearer to the historical centre than the Hauptbahnhof. Trains from the south arrive at the **Hauptbahnhof** (Elisabethstrasse). Ingolstadt has connections to Munich (€20, 40 minutes to one hour, twice hourly), Nuremberg (€20 to €33, 30 to 45 minutes, half-hourly) and Regensburg (€16.60, one hour, hourly).

Buses 10, 11 and 18 run every few minutes between the city centre and the Hauptbahnhof, 2.5km to the southeast.

Freising

☑ 08161 / POP 47,900

For 1000 years Freising was the spiritual and cultural epicentre of southern Bavaria. Now the nearest town to the airport, it's become something of a bedroom community for Munich but retains the feel of a traditional market town. In 1821 the bishop bowed to the inevitable and moved his seat to Munich. Freising sank in the ecclesiastical ranking but hung onto its religious gems, the main reasons to visit today. The town was a major way station in the life of Pope Benedict, who studied and taught at the university, was ordained here as a priest and later became archbishop here.

◉ Sights

Dom St Maria und St Korbinian
CATHEDRAL

(www.freisinger-dom.de; Domberg; ⊙ 8am-6pm Fri-Wed, from 2pm Thu) Looming over the old town is the Domberg, a hub of religious power with the twin-towered Dom St Maria und St Korbinian as its focal point. The restored church interior in whitewash, ochre and delicate rose is a head-turning stucco masterpiece by the Asam brother megastars, whose baroque frescos grace the most pious ceilings of Bavaria. Remnants from the Gothic era include the choir stalls and a *Lamentation of Christ* painting in the left aisle.

The altar painting by Rubens is a copy of the original in the Alte Pinakothek museum in Munich.

Don't miss the crypt, not so much to view Korbinian's mortal remains as to admire the forest of pillars, no two of which are carved alike. The Bestiensäule (Beast Pillar) features an epic allegory of Christianity fighting the crocodile-like monsters of evil.

East of the Dom are the cloisters, where the halls drip with fancy stucco and 1000 years' homage in marble plaques to the bishops of Freising. The baroque hall of the cathedral library was designed by none other than François Cuvilliés, of Cuvilliés-Theatre fame.

Diözesan Museum
MUSEUM

(www.dimu-freising.de; Domberg 21; adult/concession €6/4; ⊙ 10am-5pm Tue-Sun May-Oct) At the western end of the Domberg you'll find Germany's largest ecclesiastical museum. The building contains a Fort Knox–worthy collection of bejewelled gold vessels, reliquaries and ceremonial regalia, as well as some exquisite nativity scenes. Pride of place goes to the *Lukasbild,* a 12th-century Byzantine icon set in its own diminutive silver altar. Rubens and other masters await upstairs.

☞ Tours

Staatsbrauerei Weihenstephan
BREWERY

(www.weihenstephaner.de; Alte Akademie 2; tours with/without beer tasting €11/8; ⊙ 10am Mon-Wed & 1.30pm Tue) Southwest of the Domberg, a former Benedictine monastery hosts, among other university faculties, a respected college of beer brewing. Also here is the Staatsbrauerei Weihenstephan, a brewery founded in 1040, making it the world's oldest still in operation. Guided tours trace a millenium of brewery history in the museum, which is followed by a behind-the-scenes spin around the hallowed halls and concluded with a beer tasting (if you've paid extra). Tours must be booked ahead online.

ℹ️ Information

Tourist Office (☏ 08161-544 4111; www.frei sing.de; Rindermarkt 20; ⊙ 9am-6pm Mon-Fri, to 1pm Sat) For information, visit the tourist office, from which staff run a range of guided tours in English, including airport tours for kids, beer tours, and a tour that follows in the steps of Pope Benedict.

ℹ️ Getting There & Away

Freising is about 35km northeast of Munich at the northern terminus of the S1 (€8.70, 40 minutes) and is also frequently served by faster regional trains (€8.70, 25 minutes). The Domberg and Altstadt are a 10-minute walk from the train station.

Landshut

📞 0871 / POP 62,000

A worthwhile halfway halt between Munich and Regensburg, or a place to kill half a day before a flight from nearby Munich Airport, Landshut (pronounced 'Lants-hoot') was the hereditary seat of the Wittelsbach family in the early 13th century, and capital of the Dukedom of Bavaria-Landshut for over a century. Apart from a brief episode as custodian of the Bavarian University two centuries ago, Landshuters have since been busy retreating into provincial obscurity, but the town's blue-blooded past is still echoed in its grand buildings, a historical pageant with a cast of thousands and one seriously tall church.

⦿ Sights

Burg Trausnitz   CASTLE
(☏ 0871-924 110; www.burg-trausnitz.de; adult/child €5.50/free; ⊙ tours 9am-6pm Apr-Sep, 10am-4pm Oct-Mar) Roosting high above the Altstadt is Burg Trausnitz, Landshut's star attraction. The 50-minute guided tour (in German with English text) takes you through the Gothic and Renaissance halls and chambers, ending at an alfresco party terrace with bird's-eye views of the town below. The tour

includes the Kunst- und Wunderkammer (Room of Art and Curiosities), a typical Renaissance-era display of exotic curios assembled by the local dukes.

St Martin Church   CHURCH
(www.st.martin-landshut.de; Altstadt; ⊙ 7.30am-6pm Apr-Sep, to 5pm Oct-Mar) Rising in Gothic splendour at the southern end of the Altstadt is Landshut's record-breaking St Martin Church: its spire is the tallest brick structure in the world at 130.6m and took 55 years to build. It's by far Bavaria's tallest church with Regensburg's Dom a full 25m shorter.

Stadtresidenz   PALACE
(Altstadt 79; adult/child €3.50/free; ⊙ tours in German hourly 9am-6pm Apr-Sep, 10am-4pm Oct-Mar, closed Mon) Gracing the Altstadt is the Stadtresidenz, a Renaissance palace built by Ludwig X that hosts temporary exhibitions on historical themes. Admission is by guided tour only.

⭐ Festivals & Events

Landshuter Hochzeit   FESTIVAL
(www.landshuter-hochzeit.de; ⊙ Jul) Every four years, the town hosts the Landshuter Hochzeit (next held in 2021 and 2025), one of Europe's biggest medieval bashes. It commemorates the marriage of Duke Georg der Reiche of Bavaria-Landshut to Princess Jadwiga of Poland in 1475.

🛏️ Sleeping

DJH Hostel   HOSTEL €
(☏ 0871-234 49; www.landshut.jugendherberge. de; Richard-Schirrmann-Weg 6; dm from €22; 🛜) This clean, well-run 100-bed hostel occupies an attractive old villa up by the castle, with views across town.

Goldene Sonne   HOTEL €€
(☏ 0871-925 30; www.goldenesonne.de; Neustadt 520; s/d from €70/90; 🅿🛜) True to its name, the 'Golden Sun' fills a magnificently gabled, six-storey townhouse with light. Rooms sport stylishly lofty ceilings, ornate mirrors and renovated bathrooms. There's a fancy Bavarian restaurant on-site.

Zur Insel   HOTEL €€
(☏ 0871-923 160; www.insel-landshut.de; Badstrasse 16; s/d from €70/85; 🛜) Housed in a former mill on a large island in the Isar, this is a good-value place to kip with 15 simple folksy rooms and a wood-panelled restaurant.

✗ Eating

Tigerlilly Supperclub
ITALIAN €€

(www.tigerlilly-supperclub.com; Altstadt 362; mains €7-18; ⊘10am-midnight Mon, Wed & Thu, to 2am Fri & Sat, 11am-10pm Sun; 🤶) With its retro-styling, long communal benches and happy staff, Tigerlilly is a breath of trendy air in conservative Landshut. The menu has a definite Italian leaning with well-executed pizzas, salads and pastas galore.

Augustiner an der St Martins Kirche
BAVARIAN €€

(www.landshut-augustiner.de; Kirchgasse 251; mains €5-17; ⊘10am-midnight) This dark-wood tavern at the foot of the St Martin's spire is the best place in town to down a meat-dumpling combo, washed along with a frothy Munich wet one. It also does a mean Nuremberg Bratwurst.

Alt Landshut
BAVARIAN €€

(Isarpromenade 3; mains €6-15; ⊘11am-11pm) Sunny days see locals linger over an Augustiner and some neighbourhood nosh outside by the Isar. In winter you can retreat to the simple whitewashed dining room.

❶ Information

Tourist Office (☑ 0871-922 050; www.land shut.de; Altstadt 315; ⊘9am-6pm Mon-Fri, 10am-4pm Sat Apr-Oct, 9am-5pm Mon-Fri, 10am-2pm Sat Nov-Feb)

❶ Getting There & Away

TO/FROM THE AIRPORT
The airport bus (€13, 45 minutes) leaves hourly from near the tourist office and the train station between 3am and 10pm.

TRAIN
Landshut is a fairly major stop on the Munich–Regensburg main-line. Services include Munich (€17.30, one hour, twice hourly), Passau (€22, 1½ hours, hourly) and Regensburg (€14.50, 40 minutes, at least hourly).

Passau

☑ 0851 / POP 51,100

The power of flowing water has quite literally shaped the picturesque town of Passau on the border with Austria. Its Altstadt is stacked atop a narrow peninsula that jabs its sharp end into the confluence of three rivers: the Danube, the Inn and the Ilz. The rivers brought wealth to Passau, which for centuries was an important trading centre, especially for Bohemian salt, central Europe's

'white gold'. Christianity, meanwhile, generated prestige as Passau evolved into the largest bishopric in the Holy Roman Empire. The Altstadt remains pretty much as it was when the powerful prince-bishops built its tight lanes, tunnels and archways with an Italianate flourish, but the western end (around Nibelungenplatz) has received a modern makeover with shopping malls centred on the hang-glider-shaped central bus station (ZOB).

Passau is a Danube river-cruise halt and is often bursting with day visitors. It's also the convergence point of several long-distance cycling routes.

◉ Sights

Dom St Stephan
CHURCH

(www.bistum-passau.de; Domplatz; ⊘6.30am-7pm) There's been a church on this spot since the late 5th century, but what you see today is much younger thanks to the fire of 1662, which ravaged much of the medieval town, including the cathedral. The rebuilding contract went to a team of Italians, notably the architect Carlo Lurago and the stucco master Giovanni Battista Carlone. The result is a top-heavy baroque interior with a posse of saints and cherubs gazing down at the congregation from countless cornices and capitals.

The building's acoustics are perfect for its main attraction, the world's largest organ, which perches above the main entrance. This monster of a wind instrument contains an astonishing 17,974 pipes and it's an amazing acoustic experience to hear it in full puff. Half-hour organ recitals take place at noon daily Monday to Saturday (adult/child €5/2) and at 7.30pm on Thursday (adult/child €10/5) from May to October and for a week around Christmas. Show up at least 30 minutes early to ensure you bag a seat.

Dreiflusseck
LANDMARK

(Three River Corner) The very nib of the Altstadt peninsula, the point where the rivers merge, is known as the Dreiflusseck. From the north the little Ilz sluices brackish water down from the peat-rich Bavarian Forest, meeting the cloudy brown of the Danube as it flows from the west and the pale snow-melt jade of the Inn from the south to create a murky tricolour. The effect is best observed from the ramparts of the Veste Oberhaus.

Veste Oberhaus
FORTRESS

(☑0851-396 800; www.oberhausmuseum.de; adult/child €5/4; ⊘9am-5pm Mon-Fri, 10am-6pm

Sat & Sun mid-Mar–mid-Nov) A 13th-century defensive fortress, built by the prince-bishops, Veste Oberhaus towers over Passau with patriarchal pomp. Not surprisingly, views of the city and into Austria are superb from up here. Inside the bastion is the Oberhausmuseum, a regional history museum where you can uncover the mysteries of medieval cathedral building, learn what it took to become a knight and explore Passau's period as a centre of the salt trade. Displays are labelled in English.

Passauer Glasmuseum
MUSEUM

(☑0851-350 71; www.glasmuseum.de; Schrottgasse 2, Hotel Wilder Mann; adult/child €7/5; ☺9am-5pm) Opened by Neil Armstrong, of all people, Passau's warren-like glass museum is filled with some 30,000 priceless pieces of glass and crystal from the baroque, classical, art nouveau and art deco periods. Much of what you see hails from the illustrious glassworks of Bohemia, but there are also works by Tiffany and famous Viennese producers. Be sure to pick up a floor plan as it's easy to get lost.

Altes Rathaus
NOTABLE BUILDING

(Old Town Hall; Rathausplatz 2) An entrance in the side of the Altes Rathaus flanking Schrottgasse takes you to the Grosser Rathaussaal (Great Assembly Room; adult/child €2/1.50; ☺8am-noon Mon-Fri, plus 1-4pm Mon & Tue, 1-5pm Thu), where large-scale paintings by 19th-century local artist Ferdinand Wagner show scenes from Passau's history with melodramatic flourish. You can also sneak into the adjacent Small Assembly Room for a peek at the ceiling fresco, which features allegories of the three rivers.

The rest of the Rathaus is a grand Gothic affair topped by a 19th-century painted tower. A carillon chimes several times daily (hours are listed on the wall, alongside historical flood-level markers).

Museum Moderner Kunst
MUSEUM

(☑0851-383 8790; www.mmk-passau.de; Bräugasse 17; adult/child €6/4; ☺10am-6pm Tue-Sun, to 4pm Mon Jun-Sep) Gothic architecture contrasts with 20th- and 21st-century artworks at Passau's Modern Art Museum. The rump of the permanent exhibition is made up of cubist and expressionist works by Georg Philipp Wörlen, who died in Passau in 1954 and whose architect son, Hanns Egon Wörlen, set up the museum in the 1980s. Temporary exhibitions normally showcase big-hitting German artists and native styles and personalities from the world of architecture.

Römermuseum
MUSEUM

(☑0851-347 69; www.stadtarchaeologie.de; Lederergasse 43; adult/child €4/2; ☺10am-4pm Tue-Sun Mar–mid-Nov) Roman Passau can be viewed from the ground up at this Roman fort museum. Civilian and military artefacts unearthed here and elsewhere in Eastern Bavaria are on show and the ruins of Kastell Boiotro, which stood here from AD 250 to 400, are still in situ; some of the towers are still inhabited. There's a castle-themed kids' playground nearby.

Tours

Wurm + Köck
BOATING

(☑0851-929 292; www.donauschiffahrt.de; Höllgasse 26; city tour €8.90) From March to early November, Wurm + Köck operates cruises to the Dreiflusseck from the docks near Rathausplatz, as well as a whole host of other sailings to places along the Danube. The most spectacular vessel in the fleet is the sparkling *Kristallschiff* (Crystal Ship), decorated ostentatiously inside and out with Swarovski crystals.

Sleeping

Pension Rössner
GUESTHOUSE €

(☑0851-931 350; www.pension-roessner.de; Bräugasse 19; s/d €35/60; P 🖘) This immaculate place, in a restored mansion near the tip of the peninsula, offers great value for money and a friendly, cosy ambience. Each of the 16 rooms is uniquely decorated and many overlook the fortress. There's bike hire (€10 per day) and parking (€5 per day). Breakfast can be taken on the terrace overlooking the Danube for €7 extra. Booking recommended.

DJH Hostel
HOSTEL €

(☑0851-493 780; www.passau.jugendherberge.de; Oberhaus 125; dm from €23; 🖘) Beautifully renovated 129-bed hostel and one of Bavaria's best DJHs, right in the fortress.

HendlHouseHotel
HOTEL €

(☑0851-330 69; www.hendlhouse.com; Grosse Klingergasse 17; s/d €50/70; 🖘) With their light, unfussy decor and well-tended bathrooms, the 15 pristine rooms at this Altstadt hotel offer a high quality-to-price ratio. Buffet breakfast is served in the downstairs restaurant.

Camping Passau
CAMPGROUND €

(☑0851-414 57; www.camping-passau.de; Halser Strasse 34; per person €9.50; ☺May-Sep) Tent-only camping ground idyllically set on

WORTH A TRIP

MARKTL AM INN

On a gentle bend in the Inn River, some 60km southwest of Passau, sits the drowsy settlement of Marktl am Inn. Few outside Germany (or indeed Bavaria) had heard of it before 19 April 2005, the day when its favourite son, Cardinal Joseph Ratzinger, was elected Pope Benedict XVI. Literally overnight the community was inundated with reporters, devotees and the plain curious, all seeking clues about the pontiff's life and times. It's for these papal associations that people still flock to Marktl, though not in the numbers they once did.

Geburtshaus (☑ 08678-747 680; www.papsthaus.eu; Marktplatz 11; adult/child €3.50/free; ☺ 10am-noon & 2-6pm Tue-Fri, 10am-6pm Sat & Sun Easter-Oct), the simple but pretty Bavarian home where Cardinal Joseph Ratzinger (Pope Benedict XVI) was born in 1927 and lived for the first two years of his life before his family moved to Tittmoning, now houses an exhibition dedicated to the ex-pope. Things kick off with a film (in English) tracing the pontiff's early life, career and the symbols he selected for his papacy. You then head into the house proper, where exhibits expand on these themes. The modest room where Ratzinger came into the world is on the upper floor.

The **Heimatmuseum** (☑ 08678-8104; Marktplatz 2; adult/child €2/1.50) is in possession of a golden chalice and a skullcap that was used by Pope Benedict XVI in his private chapel in Rome. It is only open to groups of five or more by prior arrangement; visitors should call the **tourist office** (☑ 08678-748 820; www.marktl.de; Marktplatz 1; ☺ 10am-noon & 1-3pm) at least a day ahead to arrange entry. His baptismal font can be viewed at the **Pfarrkirche St Oswald** (Marktplatz 6), which is open for viewing except during church services.

Marktl is a very brief stop on an Inn-hugging branch line of the train service between Simbach and the junction at Mühldorf (€6.90, 20 minutes), from where there are regular direct connections to Munich, Passau and Landshut.

the Ilz River, 15 minutes' walk from the Altstadt. Catch bus 1 or 2 to Ilzbrücke.

Pension Vicus   GUESTHOUSE €
(☑ 0851-931 050; www.pension-vicus.de; Johann-Bergler-Strasse 2; s €45-50, d €65-80; [P][🛜]) A bright, colour-splashed, family-run pension on the southern side of the Inn. Rooms have small kitchenettes and there's a supermarket next door. Breakfast is an extra €7. Take frequent bus 3 or 4 from the ZOB to the Johann-Bergler-Strasse stop.

★**Hotel Schloss Ort**   BOUTIQUE HOTEL €€
(☑ 0851-340 72; www.hotel-schloss-ort.de; Im Ort 11; s/d from €70/90; [P][🛜]) The most characterful place to sleep in Passau, this 800-year-old medieval palace by the Inn River conceals a tranquil boutique hotel, stylishly done with polished timber floors, crisp white cotton sheets and wrought-iron bedsteads. Many of the 18 rooms enjoy river views and breakfast is served in the vaulted restaurant.

Hotel König   HOTEL €€
(☑ 0851-3850; www.hotel-koenig.de; Untere Donaulände 1; s €70-95, d €90-140; [P][🛜]) This riverside property puts you smack in the heart of the Altstadt and near all the sights. The

41 timber-rich rooms – many of them enormous – spread out over two buildings and most come with views of the Danube and fortress. Parking is €10 a night.

Hotel Wilder Mann   HOTEL €€
(☑ 0851-350 71; www.wilder-mann.com; Höllgasse 1; s €60-150, d €95-220; [P][🛜]) Sharing space with the Glasmuseum (p163), this historic hotel boasts former guests ranging from Empress Elisabeth (Sisi) of Austria to Yoko Ono. In the rooms, folksy painted furniture sits incongrously with 20th-century telephones and 21st-century TVs. The building is a warren of staircases, passageways and linking doors, so make sure you remember where your room is.

Guests receive a miserly discount to the museum but breakfast is normally included.

✗ Eating

Cafe Greindl   CAFE €
(www.greindl-passau.de; Wittgasse 8; light meals €6-10; ☺ 7am-6pm Mon-Sat, from 11am Sun) The affluent *Kaffee-und-Torte* society meet daily at this bright, flowery cafe that oozes Bavarian *Gemütlichkeit*. The staff pride themselves on their seasonal decor and the

service is excellent. The early opening makes this a sure-fire breakfast option.

Café Kowalski
CAFE €

(☑ 0851-2487; www.cafe-kowalski.de; Oberer Sand 1; mains €8-18; ⊘ 9.15am-1am Mon-Sat, 10am-midnight Sun; 🛜) Chat flows as freely as the wine and beer at this cool, retro-furnished cafe, a kicker of a nightspot. The giant burgers, schnitzels and big breakfasts are best consumed on the terrace overlooking the Ilz River.

★Culinarium Passau
MEDITERRANEAN €€

(☑ 0851-9890 8270; www.culinarium-passau.de; Lederergasse 16; mains €14-24, 3-/4-course menu €37/46; ⊘ 5-11pm Tue-Sat) Choose between seasonal and Mediterranean menus with paired wine and a regularly changing à la carte menu at this gourmet, evening-only restaurant with leaping brick vaulting on the southern side of the Inn. Diners rave about the service and laud praise on the standard of the dishes.

★Heilig-Geist-Stifts-Schenke
BAVARIAN €€

(☑ 0851-2607; www.stiftskeller-passau.de; Heilig-Geist-Gasse 4; mains €10-20; ⊘ 11am-midnight, closed Wed; 🛜) Not only does this historical inn have a succession of walnut-panelled ceramic-stove-heated rooms, a candlelit cellar (from 6pm) and a vine-draped garden, but the food is equally inspired. Amid the river fish, steaks and seasonal dishes there are quite gourmet affairs such as beef fillet in flambéed cognac sauce. Help it all along with one of the many Austrian and German wines in stock.

Diwan
CAFE €€

(☑ 0851-490 3280; Niebelungenplatz 1, 9th fl, Stadtturm; mains €6-14; ⊘ 9am-7pm Mon-Sat, 1-6pm Sun) It's all aboard the high-speed lift from street level to this trendy, high-perched cafe-lounge at the top of the Stadtturm, with by far the best views in town. From the tangled rattan and plush cappuccino-culture sofas you can see it all – the Dom St Stephan, the rivers, the Veste Oberhaus – while you tuck into the offerings of the changing seasonal menu.

🍸 Drinking & Nightlife

Andorfer Weissbräu
BEER GARDEN

(☑ 0851-754 444; Rennweg 2; ⊘ 9.30am-midnight Tue-Sun) High on a hill 1.5km north of the Altstadt, this rural beer garden attached to the Andorfer brewery serves filling Bavarian favourites, but the star of the show is the outstanding *Weizen* (wheat beer) and *Weizenbock* (strong wheat beer) brewed

metres away. Take bus 7 from the ZOB to Ries-Rennweg.

Caffè Bar Centrale
CAFE

(Rindermarkt 7; ⊘ 8am-10pm) Venetian bar that has to spill out onto the cobbles of the Rindermarkt as it's so tiny inside. It may be small, but there's a huge drinks menu and it's a fine place to head for a first or last drink. The Italian soundtrack fits nicely with the Italianate surroundings.

ℹ Information

Post Office (Bahnhofstrasse 1; ⊘ 9.30am-8pm Mon-Sat)

Tourist Office (☑ 0851-955 980; www.tourism. passau.de; Rathausplatz 3; ⊘ 8.30am-6pm Mon-Fri, 9am-4pm Sat & Sun Easter–mid-Oct, shorter hours mid-Oct–Easter) Passau's main tourist office is located in the Altstadt. There's another smaller office opposite the **Hauptbahnhof** (Bahnhofstrasse 28; ⊘ 9am-5pm Mon-Thu, to 4pm Fri, 10.30am-3.30pm Sat & Sun Easter-Sep, shorter hours Oct-Easter). Both branches sell the PassauCard.

ℹ Getting There & Away

BUS
A lonely bus leaves at 3.45am for the Czech border village of Železná Ruda (2¾ hours), though it arrives too late for connections to Prague. However, you can reach Pilsen.

TRAIN
Rail connections from Passau include Munich (€38.70, 2¼ hours, hourly), Nuremberg (€50, two hours, every two hours), Regensburg (€26.40 to €31, one hour, every two hours), or change in Plattling, and Vienna (€58, 2¾ hours, every two hours).

ℹ Getting Around

Central Passau is sufficiently compact to explore on foot. The CityBus links the Bahnhof with the Altstadt (€1) up to four times an hour. Longer trips within Passau cost €2; a day pass costs €4.50.

The walk up the hill to the Veste Oberhaus or the DJH Hostel, via Luitpoldbrücke and Ludwigsteig path, takes about 30 minutes. From April to October, a shuttle bus operates every 30 minutes from Rathausplatz (€2).

There are several public car parks near the train station, but only one in the Altstadt at Römerplatz.

Bavarian Forest

Together with the Bohemian Forest on the Czech side of the border, the Bavarian Forest (Bayerischer Wald) forms the largest continuous woodland area in Europe. This inspiring landscape of peaceful rolling hills and rounded tree-covered peaks is interspersed with seldom-disturbed valleys and stretches of virgin woodland, providing a habitat for many species long since vanished from the rest of Central Europe. A large area is protected as the surprisingly wild and remote Bavarian Forest National Park (Nationalpark Bayerischer Wald).

Although incredibly good value, the region sees few international tourists and remains quite traditional. A centuries-old glass-blowing industry is still active in many of the towns along the Glasstrasse (Glass Road), a 250km holiday route connecting Waldsassen with Passau. You can visit the studios, workshops, museums and shops, and stock up on traditional and contemporary designs.

The centrally located town of Zwiesel is a natural base, but other settlements along the Waldbahn such as Frauenau and Grafenau are also worth considering if relying on public transport.

◉ Sights

Bavarian Forest National Park
NATIONAL PARK

(Nationalpark Bayerischer Wald; www.national park-bayerischer-wald.de) A thickly wooded paradise for lovers of fresh air, the Bavarian Forest National Park extends for around 24,250 hectares along the Czech border, from Bayerisch Eisenstein in the north to Finsterau in the south. Its thick forest, most of it mountain spruce, is criss-crossed by hundreds of kilometres of marked hiking, cycling and cross-country skiing trails, some of which now link up with a similar network across the border. The region is home to deer, wild boar, fox, otter and countless bird species.

Around 1km northeast of the village of Neuschönau stands the **Hans-Eisenmann-Haus** (☑ 08558-961 50; www.nationalpark-bayer ischer-wald.de; Böhmstrasse 35; ⊙ 9am-6pm May-Nov, to 5pm Dec-Apr), the national park's main visitors centre. The free exhibition has displays designed to shed light on topics such as pollution and tree growth. There's also a children's discovery room, shop and library.

Museumsdorf Bayerischer Wald
MUSEUM

(☑ 08504-8482; www.museumsdorf.com; Am Dreiburgensee, Tittling; adult/child €7/5; ⊙ 10am-6pm Apr-Oct) On the southern edge of the Bavarian Forest is Tittling, home to this 20-hectare open-air museum displaying 150 typical Bavarian Forest timber cottages and farmsteads from the 17th to the 19th centuries. Exhibitions inside the various buildings range from clothing and furniture to pottery and farming implements. Take frequent RBO bus 6124 to Tittling from Passau Hauptbahnhof.

Glasmuseum
MUSEUM

(☑ 09926-941 020; www.glasmuseum-frauenau. de; Am Museumspark 1, Frauenau; adult/child €5/free; ⊙ 9am-5pm Tue-Sun) Frauenau's dazzlingly modern Glasmuseum covers four millennia of glass-making history, starting with the ancient Egyptians and ending with modern glass art from around the world. Demonstrations and workshops for kids are regular.

Gläserne Wald
PUBLIC ART

(Glass Forest; www.glaeserner-wald.de; Weissenstein, Regen) One of the more unusual sights along the Glass Route is the Gläserne Wald near the small town of Regen. Here glass artist Rudolf Schmid has created a forest of glass trees, some up to 8m tall. The trees, in a number of transparent shades, are set in a flowery meadow next to Weissenstein Castle and are an intriguing sight.

JOSKA Bodenmais
CULTURAL CENTRE

(☑ 09924-7790; www.joska.com; Am Moosbach 1, Bodenmais; ⊙ 9.30am-6pm Mon-Fri, to 5pm Sat year-round, 10am-5pm Sun May-Oct) **FREE** The glass highlight of the small town of Bodenmais is JOSKA Bodenmais, a crystal theme park complete with crystal shops, public artworks, beer garden, year-round Christmas market, crystal gallery and a workshop where visitors can try their hand at glass-blowing.

Waldmuseum
MUSEUM

(☑ 09922-503 706; www.waldmuseum.zwiesel.de; Kirchplatz 3, Zwiesel; adult/child €6/1; ⊙ 10am-4pm Thu-Mon) Housed in a former brewery, Zwiesel's 'Forest Museum' has exhibitions on local customs, flora and fauna, glass-making and life in the forest.

🏃 Activities

Two long-distance hiking routes cut through the Bavarian Forest: the European Distance Trails E6 (Baltic Sea to the Adriatic Sea) and E8 (North Sea to the Carpathian Mountains). There are mountain huts all along the way. Another popular hiking trail is the Gläserne Steig (Glass Trail) from Lam to Grafenau.

WEIDEN

A worthwhile trip from Regensburg and one of the largest towns in the Oberpfalz region in northeast Bavaria, sleepy Weiden sees few visitors save for the odd Czech coming over the border to shop. The pleasantly historical town centre is an easygoing stroll but the star attraction is the International Ceramics Museum (www.dnstdm.de; Luitpoldstrasse 25; adult/child €4/3; ⊙10am-1.30pm & 2-4.30pm), housed in a spare baroque monastery building right in the town centre. The permanent exhibition covers eight millennia of pottery, porcelain and faience including ancient Chinese and Egyptian artefacts. The temporary exhibitions here are selected from only top-notch travelling shows from around the world.

The train station (Bahnhofstrasse) is 800m southwest of the centre. Weiden has connections to Nuremberg (€22.60, 70 minutes, hourly), Regensburg (€20.50, 70 minutes, at least hourly) and Munich (€43.30, 2¾ hours, every 2 hours or change in Regensburg).

BAVARIA BAVARIAN FOREST

Whatever route you're planning, maps produced by Kompass – sheets 185, 195 and 197 – are invaluable companions. They are available from tourist offices, some bookshops and the park visitors centre.

The Bavarian Forest has seven ski areas, but downhill skiing is low-key, even though the area's highest mountain, the Grosser Arber (1456m), occasionally hosts European and World Cup ski races. The major draw here is cross-country skiing, with over 2000km of prepared routes through the ranges.

🛏 Sleeping

DJH Hostel HOSTEL €
(☎08553-6000; www.waldhaeuser.jugendherberge.de; Herbergsweg 2, Neuschönau; dm from €23; 🛜) The Bavarian Forest National Park's sole hostel is an ideal base for hikers, bikers and cross-country skiers.

★Das Reiners HOTEL €€
(☎08552-964 90; www.dasreiners.de; Grüb 20, Grafenau; r from €105; 🅿🛜⊕) This elegant hotel in Grafenau is good value for the weary traveller. The stylish rooms are spacious and most have balconies. Guests are treated to a pool and sauna, and scrumptious buffet meals. Half-board and other deals are available.

Hotel Zur Waldbahn HOTEL €€
(☎09922-8570; www.zurwaldbahn.de; Bahnhofplatz 2, Zwiesel; s €65-70, d €90-110; 🅿🛜) Many of the rooms at this characteristic inn, opposite Zwiesel train station, run by three generations of the same family, open to balconies with views over the town. The breakfast buffet is an especially generous spread and even includes homemade jams. The restaurant

serves traditional local fare and is probably the best in town.

Ferienpark Arber HOLIDAY PARK €€
(☎09922-802 595; www.ferienpark-arber.de; Waldesruhweg 34, Zwiesel; cabin from €100) This convenient and well-equipped camping ground around 500m north of Zwiesel train station has cabins for rent. The tariff includes service charges and a hefty €39 cleaning fee so it's best for those looking to stay at least a week, making this their base.

🍴 Eating & Drinking

Dampfbräu BAVARIAN €€
(☎09922-4737; Stadtplatz 6, Zwiesel; mains €6-15; ⊙11.30am-11.30pm; 🛜) The best place for some substantial East Bavarian fare and excellent 'steam' beer is this brewpub right in the centre of Zwiesel near the bridge. The traditional woodclad interior, dumpling-and-meat-heavy menu and pleasant countryside service make this a superb place to end a day in the Bavarian Forest.

Gasthaus Mühlhiasl BAVARIAN €€
(Museumsdorf Bayerischer Wald, Am Dreiburgensee, Tittling; mains €7-19; ⊙10am-6pm Apr-Oct) The rustic restaurant at the Museumsdorf Bayerischer Wald in Tittling sports traditionally laid tables under some of the chunkiest beams you'll ever see. The menu is east Bavarian to the core with lots of forest inhabitants, mushrooms and dumplings to choose from.

ⓘ Information

Tourist Office Grafenau (☎08552-962 343; www.grafenau.de; Rathausgasse 1, Grafenau; ⊙8am-5pm Mon-Thu, to 1pm Fri, 10-11.30am & 3-5pm Sat, 9.30-11.30am Sun)

Tourist Office Zwiesel (☑ 09922-500 1692; www.zwiesel.de; Stadtplatz 27, Zwiesel; ⊙ 8.30-11.30am & 1.30-4pm Mon-Thu, 8.30am-noon Fri)

ℹ Getting There & Around

From Munich, Regensburg or Passau, Zwiesel is reached by rail via Plattling (55 minutes, hourly); most trains continue to Bayerisch Eisenstein on the Czech border, with connections to Prague. The scenic Waldbahn shuttles directly between Zwiesel and Bodenmais, and Zwiesel and Grafenau.

There's also a tight network of regional buses, though service can be infrequent. The Igel-Bus, operated by Ostbayernbus (www.ostbayernbus. de), navigates around the national park on three routes. A useful one is the Lusen-Bus (€5/12.50 per one/three days), which leaves from Grafenau Hauptbahnhof and travels to the Hans-Eisenmann-Haus, the DJH Hostel and the Lusen hiking area.

The best value is usually the Bayerwald-Ticket (€9), a day pass good for unlimited travel on bus and train across the forest area. It's available from the park visitors centre, stations and tourist offices throughout the area.

Straubing

☑ 09421 / POP 47,100

Located approximately 30km southeast of Regensburg, Danube-straddling Straubing enjoyed a brief heyday as part of a wonky alliance that formed the short-lived Duchy of Straubing-Holland. As a result, the centre is chock-a-block with historical buildings that opened new horizons in a small town. In August, the demand for folding benches soars during the Gäubodenfest.

◉ Sights

Ursulinenkirche CHURCH
(www.kloster.ursulinen-straubing.de; Burggasse 40) The interior of the Ursulinenkirche was designed by the Asam brothers in their final collaboration. Its ceiling fresco depicts the martyrdom of St Ursula surrounded by allegorical representations of the four continents known at the time.

Gäubodenmuseum MUSEUM
(☑ 09421-9446 3222; www.gaeubodenmuseum.de; Frauenhoferstrasse 23; adult/child €4/1; ⊙ 10am-

4pm Tue-Sun) This intimate museum is one of Germany's most important repositories of Roman treasure. Displays include imposing armour and masks for both soldiers and horses, probably plundered from a Roman store.

St Jakobskirche CHURCH
(www.st-jakob-straubing.de; Pfarrplatz) St Jakobskirche is a late-Gothic hall church with original stained-glass windows, but also a recipient of a baroque makeover, courtesy of the frantically productive Asam brothers.

✯ Festivals & Events

Gäubodenfest FESTIVAL
(www.gaeubodenvolksfest-straubing.de; ⊙ mid-Aug) The Gäubodenfest is a 10-day blow-out that once brought together grain farmers in 1812, but today draws over 20,000 drinkers.

🛏 Sleeping & Eating

Asam Hotel HISTORIC HOTEL €€
(☑ 09421-788 680; www.hotelasam.de; Wittelsbacherhöhe 1; s/d from €90/115; 🅿 🛜) This four-star treat a few streets south of the train station is Straubing's top address with sleek, 21st century rooms and a fine-dining restaurant.

Weissbierhaus BAVARIAN €
(Theresienplatz 32; mains €6-15; ⊙ 9am-11pm) Simple, cosy and friendly, this authentic little place on the main square, with views from the outdoor seating of Straubing's grand architecture, is the place to enjoy a meat and dumpling combination and a local beer.

ℹ Information

Tourist Office (☑ 09421-9446 0199; www.straubing.de; Fraunhoferstrasse 27; ⊙ 9am-5pm Mon-Wed & Fri, to 6pm Thu, 10am-2pm Sat)

ℹ Getting There & Away

Surprisingly, Straubing has no direct train connections to Regensburg. First take the train to Radldorf then change to connecting bus (€10.50, 45 minutes, hourly). For Passau (€17.50, one hour, hourly) and Munich (€29, two hours, hourly) change at Plattling or Neufahrn.

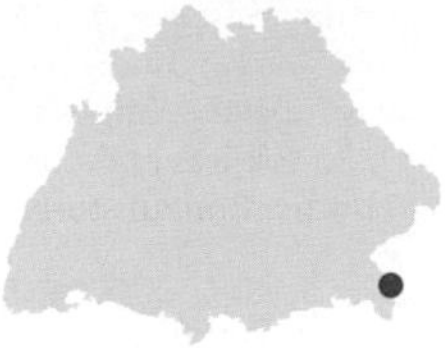

Salzburg & Around

☑ 0662 / POP 150,887

Best Places to Eat

➡ Esszimmer (p187)

➡ Bärenwirt (p186)

➡ Green Garden (p186)

➡ Magazin (p187)

➡ Triangel (p186)

➡ Cook&Wine (p185)

Best Places to Stay

➡ Hotel Schloss Mönchstein (p184)

➡ Hotel Stein (p183)

➡ Villa Trapp (p183)

➡ Gästehaus im Priesterseminar (p182)

➡ Haus Ballwein (p180)

Why Go?

The joke 'If it's baroque, don't fix it' is a perfect maxim for Salzburg: the story-book Altstadt (old town) burrowed below steep hills looks much as it did when Mozart lived here, 250 years ago. Standing beside the fast-flowing Salzach River, your gaze is raised inch by inch to graceful domes and spires, the formidable clifftop fortress and the mountains beyond. It's a backdrop that did the lordly prince-archbishops and Maria proud.

Beyond Salzburg's two biggest money-spinners – Mozart and *The Sound of Music* – hides a city with a burgeoning arts scene, wonderful food, manicured parks, quiet side streets where classical music wafts from open windows, and concert halls that uphold musical tradition 365 days a year. Everywhere you go, the scenery, the skyline, the music and the history send your spirits soaring higher than Julie Andrews' octave-leaping vocals.

When to go

Salzburg is in full bloom in March and April. Snow dusts the Alps and Easter brings classical music concerts. Summer is a time for open-air festivals, theatre and music.

Christmas transforms Salzburg into a winter wonderland. The first skiing of the season is possible on nearby peaks.

Salzburg Highlights

1 Festung Hohensalzburg (p171) Getting an eyeful of Salzburg from the city's whopping 900-year-old fortress.

2 Mozart (p181) Following in the footsteps of Salzburg's musical wunderkind.

3 Sound of Music (p178) Waltzing among the locations from the 1965 Hollywood film, while yodelling Maria-style at the top of your voice.

4 Salzburg Festival (p182) Timing your visit to catch a summer's worth of opera, theatre and music.

5 Untersberg (p193) Getting high on views of the Austrian and Bavarian Alps at this 1853m peak.

6 Augustiner Bräustübl (p188) Sipping steins of potent monk-made ales in this cavernous brewpub and beer garden.

7 DomQuartier (p176) Bingeing on baroque finery in the cathedral, abbey and lavish former palace of the prince-archbishops.

8 Museum der Moderne (p175) Tuning into Salzburg's contemporary art scene at this hilltop gallery.

History

Salzburg had a tight grip on the region as far back as 15 BC, when the Roman town Iuvavum stood on the site of the present-day city. This Roman stronghold came under constant attack from warlike Celtic tribes and was ultimately destroyed or abandoned due to disease.

St Rupert established the first Christian kingdom and founded St Peter's church and monastery in around AD 700. As centuries passed, the successive archbishops of Salzburg gradually increased their power and eventually were given the grandiose titles of Princes of the Holy Roman Empire.

Wolf Dietrich von Raitenau, Salzburg's most influential prince-archbishop from 1587 to 1612, spearheaded the total baroque makeover of the city, commissioning a large number of its most beautiful churches, palaces and gardens. He fell from power after losing a fierce dispute over the salt trade with the powerful rulers of Bavaria, and died a prisoner.

Another of the city's archbishops, Paris Lodron (1619–53), managed to keep the principality out of the Europe-wide Thirty Years' War. Salzburg also remained neutral during the War of the Austrian Succession a century later, but bit by bit the province's power waned and Salzburg came under the thumb of France and Bavaria during the Napoleonic Wars. In 1816 Salzburg became part of the Austrian Empire and was on the gradual road to economic recovery.

The early 20th century saw population growth and the founding of the prestigious

Salzburg Festival in 1920. Austria was annexed to Nazi Germany in 1938 and during WWII some 40% of the city's buildings were destroyed by Allied bombings. These were restored to their former glory, and in 1997 Salzburg's historic Altstadt (old town) became a Unesco World Heritage site.

◎ Sights

★ **Festung Hohensalzburg** FORT
(www.salzburg-burgen.at; Mönchsberg 34; adult/child/family €9.40/5.40/20.90, incl funicular €12.20/7/27.10; ⊙9.30am-5pm Oct-Apr, 9am-7pm May-Sep) Salzburg's most visible icon is this mighty, 900-year-old clifftop fortress, one of the biggest and best preserved in Europe. It's easy to spend half a day up here, roaming the ramparts looking for far-reaching views over the city's spires, the Salzach River and the mountains. The fortress is a steep 15-minute walk from the centre or a speedy ride up in the glass **Festungsbahn** (Festungsgasse 4; one way/return adult €6.90/8.60, child €3.70/4.70; ⊙9am-8pm May-Sep, to 5pm Oct-Apr) funicular.

The fortress began life as a humble bailey, built in 1077 by Gebhard von Helffenstein at a time when the Holy Roman Empire was at loggerheads with the papacy. The pres-ent structure, however, owes its grandeur to spendthrift Leonard von Keutschach, prince-archbishop of Salzburg from 1495 to 1519 and the city's last feudal ruler.

Highlights of a visit include the **Golden Hall** – where lavish banquets were once held – with a gold-studded ceiling imitating a starry night sky. Your ticket also gets you into the **Marionette Museum**, where skeleton-in-a-box Prince-Archbishop Wolf Dietrich steals the (puppet) show, and the **Fortress Museum**, which showcases a 1612 model of Salzburg, as well as medieval instruments, armour and some pretty gruesome torture devices.

The Golden Hall is the backdrop for year-round **Festungskonzerte** (fortress concerts), which often focus on Mozart's works. See www.mozartfestival.at for times and prices.

★ **Salzburg Museum** MUSEUM
(www.salzburgmuseum.at; Mozartplatz 1; adult/child €8.50/3; ⊙9am-5pm Tue-Sun; 🚇) Housed in the baroque Neue Residenz palace, this flagship museum takes you on a fascinating romp through Salzburg past and present. Ornate rooms showcase everything from Roman excavations to royal portraits.

SALZBURG & AROUND SIGHTS

SALZBURG IN...

Two Days

Get up early to see **Mozart's Geburtshaus** (p176) and boutique-dotted Getreidegasse (p191) before the crowds. Take in the baroque grandeur of **Residenzplatz** (p175) and the stately **Residenz** (p174) palace. Coffee and cake in the decadent **Café Tomaselli** (p188) fuels an afternoon absorbing history at the hands-on **Salzburg Museum** (p171) or monastic heritage at **Erzabtei St Peter** (p176). Toast your first day with homebrews in the beer garden at **Augustiner Bräustübl** (p188).

Begin day two with postcard views from the ramparts of **Festung Hohensalzburg** (p171), or absorbing cutting-edge art at **Museum der Moderne** (p175). Have lunch at **Afro Café** (p186) or bag goodies at the **Grünmarkt** (p185) for a picnic in the gardens of **Schloss Mirabell** (p176). Chamber music in the palace's **Marble Hall** (p190) or enchanting puppetry at **Salzburger Marionettentheater** (p189) rounds out the day nicely.

Four Days

On day three, you can join a Mozart or *Sound of Music* **tour** (p179). Hire a bike to pedal along the Salzach's villa-studded banks to summer palace **Schloss Hellbrunn** (p192). Dine in old-world Austrian style at **Bärenwirt** (p186) before testing the right-bank nightlife.

The fun-packed salt mines of **Hallein** (p194) and the Goliath of ice caves, **Eisriesenwelt** (p195) in Werfen, both make terrific day trips for your fourth day. Alternatively, grab your walking boots or skis and head up to the 1853m peak of **Untersberg** (p193).

Salzburg

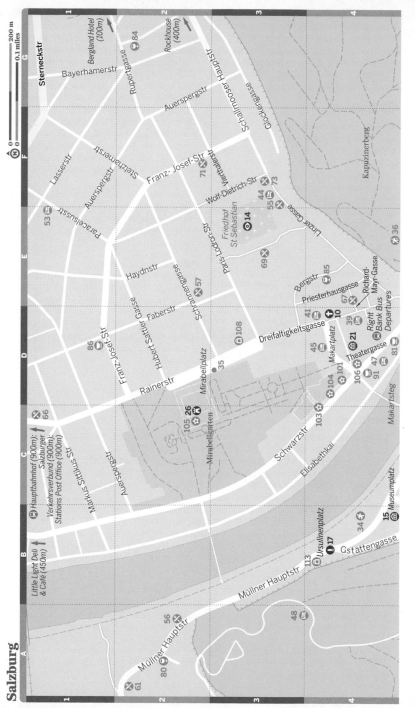

Sterneckstr

Bayerhamerstr

Bergland Hotel (100m)

Rockhouse (400m)

84

Rupertgasse

Auerspergstr

Schallmooser Hauptstr

Glockengasse

Kapuzinerberg

Lasserstr

Steinhamerstr

Auerspergstr

Franz-Josef-Str

71

Wolf-Dietrich-Str

44

55

73

Linzer Gasse

Paracelsusstr

53

Auerspergstr

Pals-Lodron-Str

Friedhof St Sebastian

14

69

36

Haydnstr

Schrannengasse

57

85

Bergstr

Priesterhausgasse

67

Hubert-Sattler Gasse

Faberstr

108

Dreifaltigkeitsgasse

41

10

39

Richard-Mayr-Gasse

Right Bank Bus Departures

Franz-Josef-Str

86

Rainerstr

Mirabellplatz

35

45

101

104

21

106

Makartplatz

Theatergasse

91

47

81

Markus Sittikus Str

66

105 26

Mirabellgarten

103

Schwarzstr

Makartsteg

Hauptbahnhof (900m); Salzburger Verkehrsverbund (900m); Stations Post Office (900m)

Little Light Deli & Café (450m)

Auerspergstr

Elisabethkai

Museumplatz

Ursulinenplatz

113

17

34

15

Gstättengasse

Müllner Hauptstr

Müllner Hauptstr

48

56

80

61

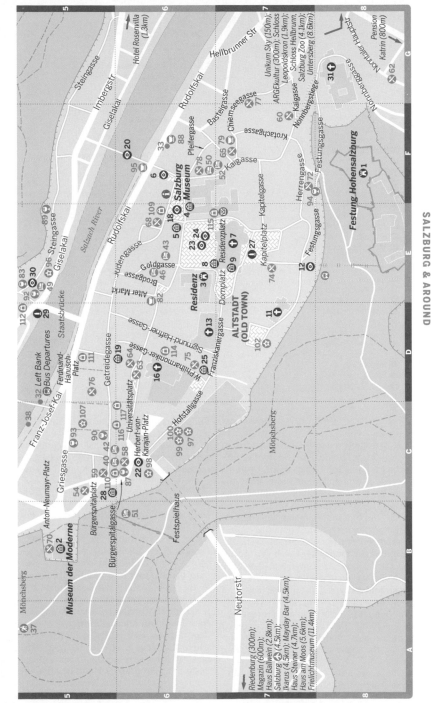

Salzburg

There are free **guided tours** at 6pm every Thursday.

A visit starts beneath the courtyard in the strikingly illuminated **Kunsthalle**, presenting rotating exhibitions of art. Upstairs, prince-archbishops glower down from the walls at **Mythos Salzburg**, which celebrates the city as a source of artistic and poetic inspiration. Showstoppers include Carl Spitzweg's renowned painting *Sonntagsspaziergang* (Sunday Stroll; 1841), the portrait-lined **prince-archbishop's room** and the **Ständesaal** (Sovereign Chamber), an opulent vision of polychrome stucco curling around frescoes depicting the history of Rome according to Titus Livius. The early 16th-century Millefiori tapestry, Prince Archbishop Wolf Dietrich's gold-embroidered pontifical shoe, and Flemish tapestries are among the many other attention-grabbing pieces.

The **Panorama Passage** also provides some insight into Salzburg's past, with its Roman walls, potter's kiln and models of the city at different points in history.

Salzburg's famous 35-bell **glockenspiel**, which chimes daily at 7am, 11am and 6pm, is on the western flank of the Neue Residenz.

★**Residenz**   PALACE
(www.domquartier.at; Residenzplatz 1; DomQuartier ticket adult/child €12/5; ⊙10am-5pm Wed-Mon Sep-Jun, 10am-5pm Thu-Tue, to 8pm Wed Jul & Aug) The crowning glory of Salzburg's DomQuartier, the Residenz is where the prince-archbishops held court until Salzburg became part of the Habsburg Empire in the 19th century. An audio-guide tour takes in the exuberant **state rooms**, lavishly adorned with tapestries, stucco and frescoes by Johann Michael Rottmayr. The 3rd floor is given over to the **Residenzgalerie**, where the focus is on Flemish and Dutch masters. Must-sees include Rubens' *Allegory on Emperor Charles V* and Rembrandt's chiaroscuro *Old Woman Praying*.

★**Museum der Moderne**　　　GALLERY
(www.museumdermoderne.at; Mönchsberg 32; adult/child €8/6; ⊙10am-6pm Tue-Sun, to 8pm Wed; ⊕) Straddling Mönchsberg's cliffs, this contemporary glass-and-marble oblong of a gallery stands in stark contrast to the fortress, and shows first-rate temporary exhibitions of 20th- and 21st-century art. The works of Alberto Giacometti, Dieter Roth, Emil Nolde and John Cage have previously been featured. There's a free guided tour of the gallery at 6.30pm every Wednesday. The Mönchsberg Lift (p179) whizzes up to the gallery year-round.

Dom　　　CATHEDRAL
(Cathedral; ☑0662-804 77 950; www.salzburger-dom.at; Domplatz; ⊙8am-7pm Mon-Sat, from 1pm Sun May-Sep, shorter hours Oct-Apr) Gracefully crowned by a bulbous copper dome and twin spires, the Dom stands out as a masterpiece of baroque art. Bronze portals symbolising faith, hope and charity lead into the cathedral. In the nave, both the intricate stucco and Arsenio Mascagni's ceiling frescoes recounting the Passion of Christ guide the eye to the polychrome dome.

Italian architect Santino Solari redesigned the cathedral during the Thirty Years' War and it was consecrated in 1628. Its origins date to an earlier cathedral founded by Bishop Virgil in 767.

For more on the history, hook onto one of the free guided tours, offered 2pm Monday to Friday in July and August.

Residenzplatz　　　SQUARE
With its horse-drawn carriages, palace and street entertainers, this stately baroque square is the Salzburg of a thousand postcards. Its centrepiece is the Residenzbrunnen, an enormous marble fountain. The plaza is the late 16th-century vision of Prince-Archbishop Wolf Dietrich, who, inspired by Rome, enlisted Italian architect Vincenzo Scamozzi to design it.

DOMQUARTIER

Salzburg's **DomQuartier** (www.dom
quartier.at) showcases the most fabulous baroque monuments and muse-
ums in the historic centre. A single ticket
(adult/child €12/5) gives you access
to the Residenz (p174) state rooms and
gallery, the upper galleries of the Dom
(p175), the Dommuseum (p178) and
Erzabtei St Peter. The free multilingual audio guide whisks you through the
quarter in 90 minutes, though you could
easily spend half a day absorbing all of
its sights. For an insight into the Dom-
Quartier's history and architecture, you
can download the audio guide to your
phone, tablet or PC from the website
before you visit.

Mozart's Geburtshaus   MUSEUM

(Mozart's Birthplace; www.mozarteum.at; Getreidegasse 9; adult/child €11/3.50; ⊘8.30am-7pm
Jul & Aug, 9am-5.30pm Sep-Jun) Wolfgang Amadeus Mozart, Salzburg's most famous son,
was born in this bright yellow townhouse in
1756, and spent the first 17 years of his life
here. Today's museum harbours a collection
of instruments, documents and portraits.
Highlights include the mini-violin he played
as a toddler, plus a lock of his hair and but-
tons from his jacket.

Mozart-Wohnhaus   MUSEUM

(Mozart's Residence; www.mozarteum.at; Makartplatz 8; adult/child €11/3.50; ⊘8.30am-7pm
Jul & Aug, 9am-5.30pm Sep-Jun) Tired of the
cramped living conditions on Getreidegasse, the Mozart family moved in 1773 to
this roomier abode, where the prolific Wolfgang composed works such as the *Shepherd
King* (K208) and *Idomeneo* (K366). Emanuel Schikaneder, a close friend of Mozart
and the librettist of *The Magic Flute*, was
a regular guest here. An audio guide accompanies your visit, serenading you with
opera excerpts. Alongside family portraits
and documents, you'll find Mozart's original
fortepiano.

Erzabtei St Peter   MONASTERY

(St Peter's Abbey; www.stift-stpeter.at; Sankt-Peter-
Bezirk 1-2; catacombs adult/child €2/1.50; ⊘church
8am-noon & 2.30-6.30pm, cemetery 6.30am-7pm,
catacombs 10am-6pm) A Frankish missionary
named Rupert founded this abbey-church

and monastery in around 700, making it
the oldest in the German-speaking world.
Though a vaulted Romanesque portal remains, today's church is overwhelmingly baroque, with rococo stucco, statues – including
one of archangel Michael shoving a crucifix
through the throat of a goaty demon – and
striking altar paintings by Martin Johann
Schmidt.

Take a stroll around the **cemetery**,
where the graves are miniature works of
art with intricate stonework and filigree
wrought-iron crosses. Composer Michael
Haydn (1737–1806), opera singer Richard
Mayr (1877–1935) and renowned Salzburg
confectioner Paul Fürst (1856–1941) all lie
buried here; the last is watched over by
skull-bearing cherubs.

The cemetery is home to the **catacombs** –
cave-like chapels and crypts hewn out of the
Mönchsberg cliff face.

Schloss Mirabell   PALACE

(Mirabellplatz 4; ⊘Marble Hall 8am-4pm Mon,
Wed & Thu, from 1pm Tue & Fri, gardens 6am-dusk)
FREE Prince-Archbishop Wolf Dietrich
built this splendid palace in 1606 to impress his beloved mistress, Salome Alt. It
must have done the trick because she went
on to bear the archbishop some 15 children
(sources disagree on the exact number –
poor Wolf was presumably too distracted
by spiritual matters to keep count). Johann Lukas von Hildebrandt, of Schloss
Belvedere fame, remodelled the palace in
baroque style in 1721. The lavish interior,
replete with stucco, marble and frescoes, is
free to visit.

The **Marmorsaal** (Marble Hall) provides
a sublime backdrop for evening chamber
concerts (p190).

The flowery parterres, rose gardens and
leafy arbours are less crowded first thing in
the morning and early evening. The lithe
Tänzerin (dancer) sculpture is a great spot
to photograph the gardens with the fortress
as a backdrop. *The Sound of Music* fans will
of course recognise the Pegasus statue, the
steps and the gnomes of the Zwerglgarten
(Dwarf Garden), where the mini von Trapps
practised their 'Do-Re-Mi'.

Stift Nonnberg   CONVENT

(Nonnberg Convent; Nonnberggasse 2; ⊘7am-
dusk) **FREE** A short climb up the Nonnberg-
stiege staircase from Kaigasse or along
Festungsgasse brings you to this Benedictine convent, founded 1300 years ago and

made famous as the nunnery in *The Sound of Music*. You can pay a visit the beautiful rib-vaulted church, but the rest of the convent is off-limits. Take €0.50 to switch on the light that illuminates the beautiful Romanesque frescoes.

Rupertinum
GALLERY

(www.museumdermoderne.at; Wiener-Philharmoniker-Gasse 9; adult/child/family €6/4/8; ⊙10am-6pm Tue & Thu-Sun, to 8pm Wed) In the heart of the Altstadt, the Rupertinum is the sister gallery of the Museum der Moderne (p175) and is devoted to rotating exhibitions of modern art. There is a strong emphasis on graphic works and photography.

Steingasse
HISTORIC SITE

On the right bank of the Salzach River, this narrow, cobbled lane was, incredibly, the main trade route to Italy in medieval times. Look out for the 13th-century **Steintor** gate and the house of **Joseph Mohr**, who wrote the lyrics to the all-time classic Christmas carol 'Silent Night', composed by Franz Xaver Gruber in 1818. The street is at its most photogenic in the late morning, when sunlight illuminates its pastel-coloured townhouses.

Christmas Museum
MUSEUM

(☑0662-84 35 23; Mozartplatz 2; adult/child €6/3; ⊙10am-6pm Wed-Sun) If you wish it could be Christmas every day, swing on over to this museum. The private collection brings festive sparkle in the form of advent calendars, hand-carved cribs, baubles and nutcrackers.

Pferdeschwemme
FOUNTAIN

(Horse Trough; Herbert-von-Karajan-Platz) Designed by Fischer von Erlach in 1693, this is a horse-lover's delight, with rearing equine pin-ups surrounding Michael Bernhard Mandl's statue of a horse tamer.

Franziskanerkirche
CHURCH

(Franziskanergasse 5; ⊙6.30am-7.30pm) A real architectural hotchpotch, Salzburg's Franciscan church has a Romanesque nave, a Gothic choir with rib vaulting and a baroque marble altar (one of Fischer von Erlach's creations).

Dreifältigkeitskirche
CHURCH

(Church of the Holy Trinity; Dreifaltigkeitsgasse 14; ⊙6.30am-6.30pm) Baroque master Johann Bernhard Fischer von Erlach designed this graceful church on the city's right bank. It's famous for Johann Michael Rottmayr's dome **fresco of the Holy Trinity**.

Domgrabungsmuseum
MUSEUM

(Cathedral Excavations Museum; ☑0662-62 08 08 131; www.salzburgmuseum.at; Residenzplatz; adult/child €3/1; ⊙9am-5pm Jul & Aug, by request Sep-Jun) Map out the city's past with a look at the rocks in this subterranean archaeology museum beside the Dom (p175). Particularly of interest are fragments of Roman mosaics, a milestone hewn from Untersberg marble and the brickwork of the former Romanesque cathedral.

SALZBURG & AROUND SIGHTS

WALK OF MODERN ART

Eager to slip out of its baroque shoes and show the world that it can do cutting edge, too, Salzburg commissioned a clutch of public artworks between 2002 and 2011, many of which can be seen on a wander through the Altstadt. Internationally renowned artists were drafted to create contemporary sculptures that provide striking contrast to the city's historic backdrop.

On Mönchsberg you will find Mario Merz' 21 neon-lit **Numbers in the Woods** and James Turrell's elliptical **Sky Space** (⊙10am-8pm Apr-Oct, to 6pm Nov-Mar), the latter creating a play of light and shadow at dawn and dusk. Back in town, you will almost certainly stroll past Stephan Balkenhol's **Sphaera** on Kapitelplatz, a huge golden globe topped by a startlingly realistic-looking man. Tucked away on Ursulinenplatz is Markus Lüpertz' **Mozart – Eine Hommage**, an abstract, one-armed bronze sculpture of the genius, sporting trademark pigtail and the torso of a woman. Another tribute to Mozart stands across the river on Schwarzstrasse in the shape of Marina Abramovic's **Spirit of Mozart**, a cluster of chairs surrounding a 15m-high chair, which, as the name suggests, is said to embody the spirit of the composer.

For more, visit the **Salzburg Foundation** (www.salzburgfoundation.at), the driving force behind this display of open-air art installations and sculpture.

Spielzeugmuseum
MUSEUM

(Toy Museum; www.spielzeugmuseum.at; Bürgerspitalgasse 2; adult/child/family €4.50/2/9; ⊗9am-5pm Tue-Sun; ♠) On the arcaded Bürgerspitalplatz, the Spielzeugmuseum takes a nostalgic look at toys, with its collection of dolls' houses and Steiff teddies. There's also dress-up fun, marble games and a little builder's dream of a Bosch workshop. Parents can hang out in the 'adult parking areas' and at the free tea bar while the little ones let off excess energy.

Friedhof St Sebastian
CEMETERY

(Linzer Gasse 41; ⊗9am-6.30pm) Tucked in behind the baroque Sebastianskirche (St Sebastian's Church), the peaceful St Sebastian cemetery and its cloisters were designed by Andrea Berteleto in Italianate style in 1600. Mozart family members and well-known 16th-century physician Paracelsus are buried here, but out-pomping them all is Prince-Archbishop Wolf Dietrich von Raitenau's mosaic-tiled mausoleum, an elaborate memorial to himself.

Dommuseum
MUSEUM

(www.domquartier.at; Domplatz; DomQuartier ticket adult/child €12/5; ⊗10am-5pm Wed-Mon) The Dommuseum is a treasure trove of sacred art. A visit whisks you past a cabinet of Renaissance curiosities crammed with crystals, coral and oddities such as armadillos and pufferfish, through rooms showcasing gem-encrusted monstrances, stained glass and altarpieces, and into the **Long Gallery**, which is graced with 17th- and 18th-century paintings, including Paul Troger's chiaroscuro *Christ and Nicodemus* (1739).

Haus der Natur
MUSEUM

(www.hausdernatur.at; Museumsplatz 5; adult/child/family €8.50/6/21.50; ⊗9am-5pm; ♠) Kids can bone up on dinosaurs and alpine crystals in Haus der Natur's natural history rooms, gawp at snakes and crocs in the reptile enclosure, and spot piranhas and coral reefs in the aquarium; blink-and-you'll-miss-them baby clownfish splash around in the 'Kinderstube'. There's also a science museum, where budding scientists

---

DIY SOUND OF MUSIC TOUR

Do a Julie Andrews and sing as you stroll on a self-guided tour of *The Sound of Music* film locations. Let's start at the very beginning:

The Hills Are Alive Cut! Make that *proper* mountains. The opening scenes were filmed around the jewel-coloured Salzkammergut lakes. Maria makes her twirling entrance on Alpine pastures just across the border in Bavaria.

A Problem Like Maria Nuns waltzing on their way to mass at Benedictine Stift Nonnberg (p176) is fiction, but it's fact that the real Maria von Trapp intended to become a nun here before romance struck.

Have Confidence Residenzplatz (p175) is where Maria belts out 'I Have Confidence' and playfully splashes the spouting horses of the Residenzbrunnen fountain.

So Long, Farewell The grand rococo palace of Schloss Leopoldskron (p179), a 15-minute walk from Festung Hohensalzburg, is where the lake scene was filmed. Its Venetian Room was the blueprint for the Trapps' lavish ballroom, where the children bid their farewells.

Do-Re-Mi The Pegasus fountain, the steps with fortress views, the gnomes...the Mirabellgarten at Schloss Mirabell (p176) might inspire a rendition of 'Do-Re-Mi' – especially if there's a drop of golden sun.

Sixteen Going on Seventeen The loved-up pavilion of the century hides out in Hellbrunn Park (p192), where you can act out those 'Oh, Liesl'/'Oh, Rolf' fantasies.

Edelweiss & Adieu The Felsenreitschule (p191) is the dramatic backdrop for the Salzburg Festival in the movie, where the Trapp Family Singers win the audience over with 'Edelweiss' and give the Nazis the slip with 'So Long, Farewell'.

Climb Every Mountain To Switzerland, that is. Or content yourself with Alpine views from Untersberg (p193), which appears briefly at the end of the movie when the family flees the country.

can race rowboats, take a biological tour of the human body and – literally – feel Mozart's music by stepping into a giant violin case.

Freilichtmuseum   MUSEUM
(www.freilichtmuseum.com; Hasenweg 1, Grossgmain; adult/child/family €11/5.50/22; ⊗9am-6pm Tue-Sun mid-Mar–early Nov; 🚹) Outside Salzburg, near Untersberg, the open-air Freilichtmuseum harbours approximately 100 archetypal Austrian farmhouses, evoking the crafts and trades of yore. It has tractors to clamber over, goats to feed, a butterfly-watching area and a huge adventure playground. It's 21km southwest of Salzburg via the A1. Bus 180 comes here, running every two hours from Salzburg Hauptbahnhof (€3.60, 35 minutes).

Schloss Leopoldskron   NOTABLE BUILDING
(www.schloss-leopoldskron.com; Leopoldskronstrasse 56-58) The grand rococo palace of Schloss Leopoldskron is where the lake scene was filmed in *The Sound of Music*. Its Venetian Room was the blueprint for the Trapps' lavish ballroom, where the children bid their farewells. It's now a plush hotel, but you can still admire it from the outside.

🏃 Activities

Salzburg's rival mountains are 540m Mönchsberg and 640m Kapuzinerberg – locals used to bigger things call them 'hills'. Both are thickly wooded and criss-crossed by walking trails, with photogenic views of the Altstadt.

There's also an extensive network of cycling routes, from a gentle 6km trundle along the Salzach River to Hellbrunn, to the 450km Mozart Radweg through Salzburgerland and Bavaria.

Mönchsberg   WALKING
(🚹) Rising sheer and rugged above the city, Mönchsberg commands photogenic views over the domes and spires of the Altstadt on one side, and of the fortress perched high on the hill on the other. Trails head out in all directions.

Arguably the most scenic trail is the 4km panoramic walking track from Stift Nonnberg (p176) to Augustiner Bräustübl (p188), taking in Festung Hohensalzburg (p171) and Museum der Moderne (p175) en route and affording views deep into the Austrian and Bavarian Alps. This trail is gentle

enough to appeal to families, with ample shade in summer.

To get to the top, take the Mönchsberg Lift (Gstättengasse 13; one way/return €2.40/3.70, incl gallery entry €9.10/9.70; ⊗8am-11pm Jul & Aug, 8am-7pm Mon, to 9pm Tue-Sun Sep-Jun).

Kapuzinerberg   WALKING
Presiding over the city, the serene, thickly wooded 640m peak of Kapuzinerberg is criss-crossed by walking trails up to a viewpoint that gazes across the river to the castle-topped Altstadt. Note the six baroque Way of the Cross chapels as you make the short trek uphill.

👉 Tours

Fräulein Maria's
Bicycle Tours   CYCLING
(www.mariasbicycletours.com; Mirabellplatz 4; adult/child €30/18; ⊗9.30am Apr-Oct, plus 4.30pm Jun-Aug; 🚹) Belt out *The Sound of Music* faves as you pedal on one of these jolly 3½-hour bike tours, taking in locations from the film including the Mirabellgarten (p176), Stift Nonnberg (p176), Schloss Leopoldskron and Hellbrunn (p192). No advance booking is necessary; just turn up at the meeting point on Mirabellplatz.

Salzburg Schifffahrt   CRUISE
(📞0662-82 57 69 12; Makartsteg; adult/child €15/7.50; ⊗late Mar-Oct) A boat ride along the Salzach is a leisurely way to pick up Salzburg's sights. Hour-long cruises depart from Makartsteg bridge, with some of them chugging on to Schloss Hellbrunn (adult/child €18/10, not including entry to the palace).

Bob's Special Tours   BUS
(📞0662-84 95 11; www.bobstours.com; Rudolfskai 38; ⊙office 8.30am-5pm Mon-Fri, 1-2pm Sat & Sun) Minibus tours to *The Sound of Music* locations (€48), the Bavarian Alps (€48) and Grossglockner (€96). Prices include a free hotel pick-up for morning tours starting at 9am. Reservations essential.

Amphibious Splash Tours   CRUISE
(📞0662-82 57 69 12; www.amphibious-splash-tours.at; Makartsteg; ⊙late Mar-Oct; 🚢) Is it a boat? Is it a bus? No, it's an amphibious splash tour – a novel combination of the two and a cool new way to boat along the Salzach River. Tours last roughly 1½ hours, with several departures daily (see the website for exact times).

✵ Festivals & Events

Mozartwoche   MUSIC
(Mozart Week; www.mozarteum.at; ⊙late Jan-early Feb) World-renowned orchestras, conductors and soloists celebrate Mozart's birthday with an 11-day feast of his music in late January.

Osterfestspiele   MUSIC
(Easter Festival; www.osterfestspiele-salzburg.at; ⊙late Mar-early Apr) This springtime musical shindig brings orchestral highlights, under Christian Thielemann's sprightly baton, to the Festspielhaus (p189), as well as choral concerts and opera (*Tosca* was staged in 2018).

Jazz & the City   MUSIC
(www.salzburgjazz.com; ⊙Oct) Salzburg gets its groove on at some 100 free concerts in the Altstadt in late October, held at cafes, bars and hotels across town. See the website for venue details.

Christkindlmarkt   CHRISTMAS MARKET
(www.christkindlmarkt.co.at; ⊙Nov–26 Dec) Salzburg is at its story-book best during Advent, when Christmas markets bring festive sparkle and choirs to Domplatz and Residenzplatz, starting in late November.

🛏 Sleeping

Salzburg is pricey, but you can find deals if you're willing to go the extra mile; ask the tourist office (p192) for a list of private rooms and pensions. Medieval guesthouses, avant-garde design hotels and chilled-out hostels all huddle in the Altstadt.

Note that high-season prices jack up another 10% to 20% during the Salzburg Festival (p182). If Salzburg is booked solid, consider staying in Hallein or across the border in Bavaria.

★**Haus Ballwein**   GUESTHOUSE €
(📞0662-82 40 29; www.haus-ballwein.at; Moosstrasse 69a; s €55-65, d €72-85, tr €85-90, q €90-100; 🅿🚲) With its bright, pine-filled rooms, mountain views, free bike hire and garden, this place is big on charm. The largest, quietest rooms face the back and have balconies and kitchenettes. It's a 10-minute trundle from the Altstadt; take bus 21 to Gsengerweg. Breakfast is a wholesome spread of fresh rolls, eggs, fruit, muesli and cold cuts.

Haus Steiner   GUESTHOUSE €
(📞0662-83 00 31; www.haussteiner.com; Moosstrasse 156; s/d €35/55, apt €70-80; 🅿🚲) Good-natured Rosemarie runs a tight ship at this sunny yellow chalet-style guesthouse that's ablaze with flowers in summer. The pick of the petite rooms, furnished in natural wood, come with fridges, balconies and mood-lifting mountain views; the family-sized apartments have kitchenettes. As for the location, it's just a 15-minute ride away from the Altstadt on bus 21 (get off at Hammerauerstrasse).

Haus am Moos   GUESTHOUSE €
(📞0662-82 49 21; www.ammoos.at; Moosstrasse 186a; s/d €32/64; 🅿🚲🏊) This Alpine-style chalet offers a slice of rural calm just a 15-minute ride from town on bus 21. Many rooms have balconies with gorgeous mountain views, and some come with canopy beds. The breakfast of muesli, cold cuts, eggs and fresh breads gears you up for the day, and there's an outdoor pool for an afternoon dip.

Yoho Salzburg   HOSTEL €
(📞0662-87 96 49; www.yoho.at; Paracelsusstrasse 9; dm €20-26, d €70-88; @🚲) Free wi-fi, secure lockers, comfy bunks, plenty of cheap beer and good-value schnitzels – what more could a backpacker ask for? Except, perhaps, a merry singalong with *The Sound of Music* screened daily (yes, *every* day). The friendly crew can arrange tours, adventure sports such as rafting and canyoning, and bike hire.

Stadtalm   HOSTEL €
(📞0662-84 17 29; www.stadtalm.at; Mönchsberg 19c; dm €25) This turreted hostel plopped on top of Mönchsberg takes in the entire

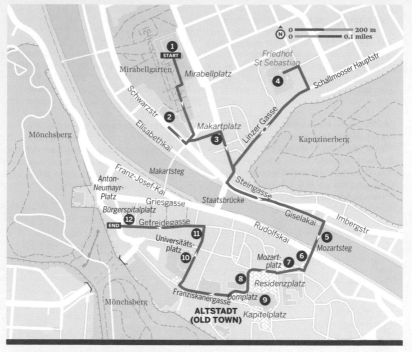

🏃 City Walk
In Mozart's Footsteps

START SCHLOSS MIRABELL
END FÜRST
LENGTH 3KM; 1½ HOURS

Mozart was the ultimate musical prodigy: he identified a pig's squeal as G-sharp when he was two years old, began to compose when he was five and first performed for Empress Maria-Theresia aged six. Follow in his footsteps on this classic walking tour.

Begin at baroque ❶ **Schloss Mirabell** (p176), where the resplendent Marmorsaal (Marble Hall) is often the backdrop for chamber concerts of Mozart's music. Stroll south through the gardens, passing the striking ❷ **Mozarteum** (p191), a foundation honouring Mozart's life and works, and the host of the renowned Mozartwoche festival. Around the corner on Makartplatz is the 17th-century ❸ **Mozart-Wohnhaus** (p176), where you can see how the Mozart family lived and listen to rare recordings of Mozart's symphonies. Amble north along Linzer Gasse to ❹ **Friedhof St Sebastian** (p178), the Italianate arcaded cemetery where Wolfgang's parents lie buried.

Retrace your steps towards the swiftly flowing Salzach River, turning left onto medieval Steingasse, then cutting through to Giselakai to cross the art nouveau ❺ **Mozartsteg** (Mozart Bridge). Look out for the ❻ **memorial plaque** at No 8, the house where Mozart's beloved Constanze died in 1842, as you approach ❼ **Mozartplatz**. On this elegant square, a coiffed, pensive Mozart rests in a bronze statue unveiled in 1842. Across the way is the ❽ **Residenz** (p174) palace where Mozart gave his first court concert at the ripe old age of six. Beside it is the baroque ❾ **Dom** (p175), where Mozart's parents were married in 1747 and Wolfgang was baptised in 1756; Mozart later composed music here and was cathedral organist. Follow Franziskanergasse to the ❿ **Kollegienkirche** on Universitätsplatz, where Mozart's D Minor Mass (K65) premiered in 1769. On Getreidegasse, stop to contemplate the birthplace of a genius at ⓫ **Mozart's Geburtshaus** (p176) and buy some famous chocolate *Mozartkugeln* (Mozart balls) at ⓬ **Fürst** (p191).

FESTIVAL TIME

In 1920, dream trio Hugo von Hofmannsthal, Max Reinhardt and Richard Strauss combined their creative forces and the Salzburg Festival (Salzburger Festspiele; www.salzburgerfestspiele.at; ⊘ Jul & Aug) was born. Now, as then, one of the highlights is the staging of Hofmannsthal's morality play *Jedermann* (Everyman) on Domplatz. A trilogy of opera, drama and classical concerts of the highest calibre have propelled the five-week summer festival to international renown, attracting some of the world's best conductors, directors, orchestras and singers.

Come festival time, Salzburg crackles with excitement, as a quarter of a million visitors descend on the city for some 200 productions. Theatre premieres, avant-garde works and the summer-resident Vienna Philharmonic performing works by Mozart are all in the mix. The Festival District on Hofstallgasse has a spectacular backdrop, framed by Mönchsberg's cliffs. Most performances are held in the cavernous Grosses Festspielhaus (p189), which accommodates 2179 theatregoers; the Haus für Mozart (p190) in the former royal stables; and the baroque Felsenreitschule (p191).

If you're planning to visit during the festival, do not leave *anything* to chance – book your flights, hotel and tickets months in advance. Sometimes last-minute tickets are available at the ticket office (☑ 0662-804 55 00; info@salzburgfestival.at; Herbert-von-Karajan-Platz 11; ⊘ 10am-6pm mid-Jul–Aug, 10am-12.30pm & 1-4.30pm Mon-Fri Sep–mid-Jul), but they're like gold dust. Book early to avoid disappointment. Ticket prices range from €11 to €430.

Salzburg panorama, from the city's spires and fortress to Kapuzinerberg. Digs are simple but you won't find them cheaper elsewhere. There's a good-value restaurant on-site.

★ Gästehaus im Priesterseminar GUESTHOUSE €€

(☑ 0662-877 495 10; www.gaestehaus-priesterseminar-salzburg.at; Dreifaltigkeitsgasse 14; s €67, d €120-134) Ah, the peace is heavenly at this one-time seminary tucked behind the Dreifältigkeitskirche. Its bright, parquet-floored rooms have received a total makeover, but the place still brims with old-world charm thanks to its marble staircase, antique furnishings and fountain-dotted courtyard. It's still something of a secret, though, so be sure to whisper about it quietly...

Pension Katrin PENSION €€

(☑ 0662-83 08 60; www.pensionkatrin.at; Nonntaler Hauptstrasse 49b; s €62-75, d €105-135, tr €145-179, q €165-199; P ⓢ) With its flowery garden, bright and cheerful rooms and excellent breakfasts, this pension is one of the homiest in Salzburg. The affable Terler family keeps everything spick and span, and nothing is too much trouble for them. They'll even help you upstairs with your luggage. Take bus 5 from the Hauptbahnhof to Wäschergasse.

Die Haslachmühle GUESTHOUSE €€

(☑ 0664-179 90 60; www.haslachmuehle.at; Mühlstrasse 18, Gnigl; d €112-162; P ⓢ) Sitting below Gaisberg and surrounded by attractive gardens and countryside, this charismatic B&B is lodged in a 17th-century flour mill. The family go out of their way to please, and the incredibly spacious, sunny, wood-floored rooms feature touches such as ceramic ovens, mountain views and Nespresso machines. It's a 15-minute ride from the Hauptbahnhof on bus 155 (Salzburg Kühberg stop).

Hotel Rosenvilla GUESTHOUSE €€

(☑ 0662-62 17 65; www.rosenvilla.com; Höfelgasse 4; s €74-120, d €120-180, ste €170-260; P ⓢ) This guesthouse goes the extra mile with its sharp-styled contemporary rooms, faultless service and incredible breakfasts, featuring spreads, breads, cereals, eggs and fruit to jump-start your day.

Arte Vida GUESTHOUSE €€

(☑ 0662-87 31 85; www.artevida.at; Dreifaltigkeitsgasse 9; d €110-145, apt €170-220; ⓢ) Arte Vida has the boho-chic feel of a Marrakech *riad,* with its lantern-lit salon, communal kitchen and serene garden. Asia and Africa have provided the inspiration for the rich colours and fabrics that dress the individually designed rooms. Affable hosts Herbert and Karoline happily give tips on Salzburg and its surrounds, and can arrange massages and private yoga sessions.

Hotel am Dom　　　　　BOUTIQUE HOTEL €€
(☑ 0662-84 27 65; www.hotelamdom.at; Goldgasse 17; s €109-219, d €149-349; ❄ ☎) Antique meets boutique at Hotel am Dom in the Altstadt. The original vaults and beams of the 800-year-old building contrast with razor-sharp design features. Artworks inspired by the musical legends of the Salzburg Festival grace the rooms, which sport caramel-champagne colour schemes, funky lighting, velvet throws and ultra-glam bathrooms.

Weisse Taube　　　　　HISTORIC HOTEL €€
(☑ 0662-84 24 04; www.weissetaube.at; Kaigasse 9; s/d/tr/q €143/155/281/324; ☎) Housed in a listed 14th-century building in a quiet corner of the Altstadt, the 'white dove' is a solid choice. Staff go out of their way to help and the warm-coloured rooms are well kept (some have fortress views). Breakfast is a generous spread.

Bergland Hotel　　　　BOUTIQUE HOTEL €€
(☑ 0662-87 23 18; www.berglandhotel.at; Rupertgasse 15; s €65-89, d €80-178, tr €120-198; ℗ @ ☎) Don't be fooled by the nondescript exterior. Belonging to the Kuhn family since 1912, the Bergland is ever so homey inside,

with art (courtesy of the owner) on the walls, touches such as traditional Austrian hats and painted furnishings in the rooms, and a handsome piano room. Breakfast will set you back an extra €9.50.

Hotel Amadeus　　　　HISTORIC HOTEL €€
(☑ 0662-87 14 01; www.hotelamadeus.at; Linzer Gasse 43-45; s €80-184, d €150-235, q €233-404; ☎) Centrally situated on the right bank, this 500-year-old hotel has a boutique feel, with bespoke touches such as chandeliers and four-poster beds in the vibrantly coloured rooms. Guests are treated to free tea or coffee in the afternoon.

★ **Hotel Stein**　　　　BOUTIQUE HOTEL €€€
(☑ 0662-874 34 60; www.hotelstein.at; Giselakai 3; d €229-483, ste €256-983, breakfast €28) Looking the business following a two-year makeover, Hotel Stein reopened its doors in 2018. In the rooms, a clean aesthetic combines with pops of bright colour, wall murals, contemporary furnishings and Saint Charles Apothecary cosmetics. With its stucco-bedecked ceiling, Venetian glass and claw-foot bathtub, the honeymoon suite is quite something.

★ **Villa Trapp**　　　　HOTEL €€€
(☑ 0662-63 08 60; www.villa-trapp.com; Traunstrasse 34; s €65-130, d €114-280, ste €290-580;

SALZBURG & AROUND SLEEPING

SALZBURG FOR CHILDREN

With dancing marionettes, chocolate galore and a giant fairy-tale fortress, Salzburg is kid nirvana. If the crowds prove unbearable with tots in tow, take them to the city's adventure **playgrounds** (there are 80 to pick from); the one on **Franz-Josef-Kai** (🖼) is centrally located.

Salzburg's sights are usually half-price for children, and most are free for kids under six years of age. Many galleries, museums and theatres also have dedicated programs for kids and families. These include the Museum der Moderne (p175), which has workshops for kids and teens, and the matinée performances at the enchanting Salzburger Marionettentheater (p189). The Salzburg Museum (p171) has lots of hands-on displays, from harp playing to old-fashioned writing with quills. Pick up 'Wolf' Dietrich's cartoon guide at the entrance.

Children will have a blast with natural history at the Haus der Natur (p178), with its fun facts on alpine crystals, dinosaurs, science and the human body. The highlight is the aquarium, with its clownfish and sharks.

Salzburg's very own toy story, the Spielzeugmuseum (p178) is a rambling attic of toys old and new. There are even 'adult parking areas' where grown-ups can hang out while tots play.

Take a whizz through Austrian farming life through the ages at the huge open-air Freilichtmuseum (p179), with animals to pet, crafts to explore and a big adventure playground to romp around in. For more animal-themed fun, head to the **Salzburg Zoo** (www.salzburg-zoo.at; Hellbrunnerstrasse 60, Anif; adult/child/family €11.50/5/26; ⏱ 9am-6.30pm Jun-Aug, shorter hours Sep-May; 🖼), near Schloss Hellbrunn.

P 🛜) Marianne and Christopher have transformed the original von Trapp family home into a beautiful guesthouse (for guests only, we might add). The 19th-century villa is elegant, if not *quite* as palatial as in the movie, with tasteful wood-floored rooms and a balustrade for sweeping down à la Baroness Schräder.

Family snapshots and heirlooms, including the baron's model ships and a photo of guest and Pink Floyd guitarist David Gilmour strumming 'Edelweiss', grace the dining room. From the main station, take a train or bus 160 to Aigen.

★ Hotel Schloss Mönchstein
HERITAGE HOTEL €€€

(📞 0662-848 55 50; www.monchstein.at; Mönchsberg Park 26; d €360-995, ste €695-2800; P ✳ 🛜) On a fairy-tale perch atop Mönchsberg and set in hectares of wooded grounds, this 16th-century castle is honeymoon (and second mortgage) material. Persian rugs, oil paintings and Calcutta marble finish the rooms to beautiful effect. A massage in the spa, a candlelit tower dinner for two with Salzburg views, a helicopter ride – just say the word.

Hotel Goldgasse
HISTORIC HOTEL €€€

(📞 0662-84 56 22; www.hotelgoldgasse.at; Goldgasse 10; s €139-186, d €227-342, ste €350-480, q €450-580; ✳ @ 🛜) Bang in the heart of the Altstadt, this 700-year-old townhouse has oodles of charm – some rooms have four-poster beds, while paintings of Emperor Franz Josef hang guard over others. The sunny terrace overlooks the rooftops of the old town.

Hotel Sacher
HERITAGE HOTEL €€€

(📞 0662-88 97 70; www.sacher.com; Schwarzstrasse 5-7; s €226-336, d €298-900, ste €502-3898; P ✳ @ 🛜) Tom Hanks, the Dalai Lama and Julie Andrews have all stayed at this 19th-century pile on the banks of the Salzach. Scattered with oil paintings and antiques, the rooms have gleaming marble bathrooms, and fortress or river views. Compensate for indulging on chocolate *Sacher Torte* in the health club.

Goldener Hirsch
LUXURY HOTEL €€€

(📞 0662-808 40; www.goldenerhirschsalzburg. com; Getreidegasse 37; r €195-813; P ✳ @ 🛜) A skylight illuminates the arcaded inner courtyard of this 600-year-old Altstadt pile, where famous past guests include Queen Elizabeth II and Pavarotti. Countess Harriet Walderdorff tastefully scattered the opulent rooms with objets d'art and hand-printed fabrics.

Hotel Bristol
LUXURY HOTEL €€€

(📞 0662-87 35 57; www.bristol-salzburg.at; Makartplatz 4; s €200-300, d €285-480, ste €430-1010; P ✳ 🛜) The Bristol transports you back to a more decadent era. Chandelier-lit salons, champagne at breakfast, exquisitely crafted furniture, service as polished as the marble – this is pure class. Even Emperor Franz Josef and Sigmund Freud felt at home here.

Arthotel Blaue Gans
BOUTIQUE HOTEL €€€

(📞 0662-84 24 91; www.blauegans.at; Getreidegasse 41-43; s €198-328, d €220-370, ste €449-579; ✳ 🛜) Contemporary design blends harmoniously with the original vaulting and beams of the 660-year-old Arthotel Blaue Gans. Rooms are pure and simple, with clean lines, lots of white and streamlined furnishings. The restaurant is well worth a visit too.

Hotel Wolf
HISTORIC HOTEL €€€

(📞 0662-843 45 30; www.hotelwolf.com; Kaigasse 7; s €98-138, d €148-248, ste €228-268; 🛜) Tucked in a quiet corner of Salzburg's Altstadt, Hotel Wolf occupies a lovingly converted 15th-century building. Uneven stone staircases and antique furnishings are a nod to its past, while the light, parquet-floored rooms range from modern to rustic.

🍴 Eating

Salzburg's eclectic dining scene skips from the traditional to the super-trendy to the downright touristy. This is a city where schnitzel is served with a slice of history in vaulted taverns; where you can dine in Michelin-starred finery or be serenaded by a warbling Maria wannabe. Save euros by taking advantage of the lunchtime *Tagesmenü* (fixed menu) served at most places.

Bistro de Márquez
INTERNATIONAL €

(📞 0680-236 96 64; www.bistrodemarquez.at; Schrannengasse 6; snacks €3-5.50, day special €6.90; ⏰ 3-7pm Tue-Fri, from 11.30am Sat) Piedad brings a little piece of her native Colombia to the table at this sweet, cosy bistro, where she cooks soul food including *arepas* (filled maize crêpes) to dip in salsas, and *pandebono* (Colombian cheese bread). It's all delicious, affordable and served with a smile.

Ludwig
BURGERS €

(☏0662-87 25 00; www.ludwig-burger.at; Linzer Gasse 39; burgers €7.40-13.60; ⊙11am-10pm Tue-Fri, from 9am Sat & Sun; ☏) Gourmet burger joints are all the rage in Austria and this hip restaurant fits the bill nicely, with its burgers made from organic, regional ingredients, which go well with hand-cut fries and homemade lemonade and shakes. It also rustles up superfood salads and vegan nutmushroom-herb burgers. An open kitchen is the centrepiece of the slick, monochrome interior.

Organic Pizza Salzburg
PIZZA €

(☏0664-597 44 70; www.organicpizza-salzburg.com; Franz-Josef-Strasse 24a; pizza €8.50-13.20; ⊙5-10pm Tue-Thu, from 2pm Fri & Sat) Good-natured staff, groovy music and awesome pizzas whipped up with super-fresh, organic ingredients make this a terrific choice. It's a tiny place so be prepared to wait at busy times – it's worth it.

Spicy Spices
INDIAN €

(☏0662-87 07 12; Wolf-Dietrich-Strasse 1; day special €8, with soup €9.50; ⊙noon-9pm; ☏) 'Healthy heart, lovely soul' is the mantra of this all-organic, all-vegetarian haunt. Service is slow but friendly. It's worth the wait, too, for the good-value *thali* (appetisers) and curries mopped up with *paratha* flatbread.

Imlauer Sky
AUSTRIAN €€

(☏0662-889 92; www.imlauer.com; Rainerstrasse 6, Imlauer Hotel Pitter; mains €20-29; ⊙11.30am-1.30am) From the lofty vantage point of this slickly modern, glass-fronted rooftop restaurant, Salzburg spreads out before you in all its glory – it's particularly spectacular after dark when the fortress lights up. Service is attentive and the menu swings from steaks and surf 'n' turf to well-executed classics such as Wiener schnitzel and *Tafelspitz* (braised beef with horseradish).

Johanneskeller im Priesterhaus
AUSTRIAN €€

(☏0662-26 55 36; www.johanneskeller.at; Richard-Mayr-Gasse 1; mains €10-20; ⊙5pm-midnight Tue-Sat) Full of cosy nooks and crannies, this brick-vaulted cellar is reached via a steep flight of stairs. The menu is succinct but well thought out, with mains swinging from classic Austrian – Styrian pork roast with dumplings and sauerkraut, say – to Mediterranean numbers such as gyros (rotisserie meat) with tzatziki. It's all bang on the money.

Cook&Wine
INTERNATIONAL €€

(☏0662-23 16 06; www.cookandwine.at; Kaigasse 43; mains €19-26.50; ⊙11.30am-11pm Tue-Sat) Highly regarded chef and food and wine connoisseur Günther Grahammer is the brains behind this slick operation. It combines a wine bar, a cookery school and a smart, bistro-style restaurant serving imaginative worldly dishes, such as steak tartare

DON'T MISS

TOP SNACK SPOTS

Want to grab a bite on the hoof or pick up some items for a nice picnic? Here's where to head:

Grünmarkt (Green Market; Universitätsplatz; ⊙7am-7pm Mon-Fri, to 3pm Sat) This market hums with hungry locals in search of fresh-made bread, regional cheeses, hams, fruit and enormous pretzels.

Stiftsbäckerei St Peter (Kapitelplatz 8; ⊙8am-5.30pm Mon & Tue, 7am-5.30pm Thu & Fri, 7am-1pm Sat) When you spy an old watermill you know you've arrived at this bakery. Since medieval times, it has been baking great sourdough loaves in a wood-fired oven.

Kaslöchl (Hagenauerplatz 2; ⊙9am-6pm Mon-Fri, 8am-1pm Sat; ☎) Blink and you'll miss this tiny shop jam-packed with cheeses – from fresh ones with herbs to tangy Alpine varieties.

IceZeit (Chiemseegasse 1; scoop €1.50; ⊙11am-8pm) This hole-in-the-wall ice-cream parlour does some of the finest gelato in town, with flavours such as chocolate-chilli and sour-cream-cranberry.

with wasabi cream, Asian-style bouillabaisse with lemongrass and chilli, and scallops with avocado-papaya salad.

Zum Zirkelwirt
AUSTRIAN €€

(☑0662-84 27 96; www.zumzirkelwirt.at; Pfeifergasse 14; mains €11.50-19; ⊙11am-midnight) A jovial inn serving good old-fashioned Austrian grub is what you get at Zum Zirkelwirt, which has a cracking beer garden on a tucked-away square and a cosy, wood-panelled interior for winter imbibing. Go straight for the classics including *Kaspressknödelsuppe* (cheese dumpling soup) and *Schweinsbraten im Weissbier-Kümmelsafterl* (pork roast in wheat beer and cumin sauce).

Green Garden
VEGETARIAN €€

(☑0662-84 12 01; www.thegreengarden.at; Nonntaler Hauptstrasse 16; mains €9.50-15; ⊙noon-2pm & 5.30-9pm Tue-Sat; ☑) ∅ The Green Garden is a breath of fresh air for vegetarians and vegans. Locavore is the word at this bright, modern cottage-style restaurant, pairing dishes such as wild herb salad, lemon-goat's-cheese tortellini and vegan burgers with organic wines in a totally relaxed setting.

Bärenwirt
AUSTRIAN €€

(☑0662-42 24 04; www.baerenwirt-salzburg.at; Müllner Hauptstrasse 8; mains €12-20; ⊙11am-11pm) Sizzling and stirring since 1663, Bärenwirt is Austrian through and through. Go for hearty *Bierbraten* (beer roast) with dumplings, locally caught trout or organic wild-boar bratwurst. A tiled oven warms the woody, hunting-lodge-style interior in winter, while the river-facing terrace is a summer crowd-puller. The restaurant is 500m north of Museumplatz.

Zwettler's
AUSTRIAN €€

(☑0662-84 41 99; www.zwettlers.com; Kaigasse 3; mains €11.50-18; ⊙11.30am-1am Tue-Sat, to midnight Sun) This gastro-pub has a lively buzz on its pavement terrace. Local grub such as schnitzel with parsley potatoes and venison ragout goes well with a cold, foamy Kaiser Karl wheat beer. The two-course lunch is a snip at €8.50.

K+K
AUSTRIAN €€

(☑0662-84 21 56; Waagplatz 2; lunch specials €11-13.50, mains €17-35; ⊙11am-11pm; ☑) This buzzy restaurant on the square is a warren of vaulted and wood-panelled rooms, with a lovely terrace for people-watching to boot.

Whether you go for Alpine salmon on a bed of spinach, saddle of venison in morel sauce or good old bratwurst with lashings of potatoes and cabbage, the food here hits the mark.

Triangel
AUSTRIAN €€

(☑0662-84 22 29; Wiener-Philharmoniker-Gasse 7; mains €12-38; ⊙11.30am-10pm Tue-Sat) The menu is market-fresh at this arty bistro, where the picture-clad walls pay tribute to Salzburg Festival luminaries. It does gourmet salads, a mean Hungarian goulash with organic beef, and delicious house-made ice cream. Lunch specials go for just €7.90.

Afro Café
INTERNATIONAL €€

(www.afrocafe.at; Bürgerspitalplatz 5; lunch €8.90, mains €14-19; ⊙9am-11pm Mon-Thu, to midnight Fri & Sat) Hot-pink walls, butterfly chairs and artworks made from beach junk...this Afro-chic cafe is totally groovy. Staff keep the good vibes and food coming – from breakfasts to ostrich burgers, and from samosas to steaks sizzling hot from the grill. It also does a good line in coffee, rooibos teas, juices and cakes.

Hagenauerstuben
AUSTRIAN €€

(☑0662-84 08 45; www.hagenauerstuben.at; Universitätsplatz 14; 2-course lunch €7.30, mains €11-18; ⊙10am-10pm Sun-Tue, to midnight Wed-Sat) You would be forgiven for thinking a restaurant tucked behind Mozart's Geburtshaus would have 'tourist trap' written all over it. Not so. The baroque-contemporary Hagenauerstuben combines a stylishly converted vaulted interior with a terrace overlooking the Kollegienkirche. Pull up a chair for good old-fashioned Austrian home cooking – spinach *Knödel* (dumplings), suckling pig with wild mushrooms, goulash and the like.

Paul Stube
INTERNATIONAL €€

(☑0662-84 32 20; Herrengasse 16; mains €11-22; ⊙5-11pm Mon-Sat) Up the cobbled Herrengasse lies this gloriously old-world tavern, with a dark-wood interior crammed with antique curios, which attracts a regular crowd of locals. In summer, guests spill out into the beer garden to dig into authentically prepared classics such as roast pork in wheat beer sauce.

Alter Fuchs
AUSTRIAN €€

(☑0662-88 20 22; www.alterfuchs.at; Linzer Gasse 47-49; lunch €6.90, mains €9.50-18;

⊙noon-midnight Mon-Sat; 🖉🖼) This sly old fox prides itself on no-nonsense Austrian fare – schnitzel, roast pork with dumplings, cordon bleu and the like. Bandana-clad foxes guard the bar in the vaulted interior, and there's a courtyard for good-weather dining. In the cosy *Stube* (parlour) out back, scribbling on the walls (chalk only, please) is positively encouraged. Service can be hit or miss.

Wilder Mann   AUSTRIAN €€

(🖉0662-84 17 87; Getreidegasse 20; mains €9-17; ⊙11am-9pm Mon-Sat) At this old-world Austrian tavern in the Altstadt, waitresses clad in traditional Dirndl bring goulash with dumplings, boot-sized schnitzels and other light and airy fare to the table.

★Esszimmer   FRENCH €€€

(🖉0662-87 08 99; www.esszimmer.com; Müllner Hauptstrasse 33; 3-course lunch €45, tasting menus €79-128; ⊙noon-2pm & 6.30 9.30pm Tue-Sat) Andreas Kaiblinger puts an innovative spin on market-driven French cuisine at Michelin-starred Esszimmer. Eye-catching art, playful backlighting and a glass floor revealing the Almkanal stream keep diners captivated, as do gastronomic show-stoppers such as Arctic char with calf's head and asparagus. Buses 7, 21 and 28 to Landeskrankenhaus stop close by.

★Magazin   GASTRONOMY €€€

(🖉0662-84 15 84; www.magazin.co.at; Augustinergasse 13a; mains €14-40; ⊙noon-2pm & 6-10pm Tue-Sat) In a courtyard below Mönchsberg's sheer rock wall, Magazin shelters a deli, wine store, cookery school and restaurant. The menus fizz with seasonal flavours – dishes such as *fregola* risotto with Dijon mustard and lemon oyster mushrooms, and miso-crusted salmon with algae – matched with wines from the 850-bottle cellar, and served alfresco or in the industrial-chic, cave-like interior.

Ikarus   GASTRONOMY €€€

(🖉0662-219 70; www.hangar-7.com; Wilhelm-Spazier-Strasse 7a, Salzburg Airport; lunch menu €58, tasting menus €135-185; ⊙noon-2pm & 7-10pm Thu-Sun, 7-10pm Mon-Wed; 🖉) At the space-age Hangar-7 complex at the airport, this glam two-Michelin-starred restaurant is the epitome of culinary globetrotting. Each month, Eckart Witzigmann and Martin Klein invite a world-famous chef to assemble an eight- to 12-course menu for a serious foodie crowd. There's also a gourmet vegetarian menu.

Blaue Gans Restaurant   AUSTRIAN €€€

(🖉0662-842 491 50; www.blauegans.at; Getreidegasse 43; lunch specials €9.90-12.90, mains €21-27; ⊙noon-10pm Mon-Sat) In the 650-year-old vaults of Arthotel Blaue Gans, this restaurant is a refined setting for regional cuisine, such as pike-perch with fennel compote, braised lamb shanks and *Marillenknödel* (apricot dumplings), all married with full-bodied wines. The olive-tree-dotted terrace is popular in summer.

Gasthof Schloss Aigen   AUSTRIAN €€€

(🖉0662-408 15 15; www.schloss-aigen.at; Schwarzenbergpromenade 37; mains €19.30-33.50, 4-course menu €62; ⊙11.30am-2pm & 5.30-9.30pm Thu & Fri, 11.30am-9.30pm Sat & Sun) A country manor with an elegantly rustic interior and a chestnut-shaded courtyard, Gasthof Schloss Aigen excels in Austrian home cooking. The Forstner family's house speciality is 'Wiener Melange', four different cuts of meltingly tender Pinzgauer beef, served with apple horseradish, chive sauce and roast potatoes, best matched with robust Austrian wines. Bus 7 stops at Bahnhof Aigen, a 10-minute stroll away.

Riedenburg   GASTRONOMY €€€

(🖉0662-83 08 15; www.riedenburg.at; Neutorstrasse 31; mains €20-34.50; ⊙noon-2pm & 6-10pm Tue-Sat) Helmut Schinwald works the stove at this gourmet restaurant with a romantic garden pavilion. His seasonally inflected flavours, such as homemade porcini ravioli with thyme butter and quail breast with pomegranate risotto, are expertly matched with top wines. The two-course lunch (€15) is a bargain.

Carpe Diem   FUSION €€€

(🖉0662-84 88 00; www.carpediemfinestfinger food.com; Getreidegasse 50; mains €29.50-42.50; ⊙8.30am-midnight) Avant-garde, Michelin-starred lounge-restaurant Carpe Diem has pride of place on Getreidegasse. A food-literate crowd flocks here for cocktails and finger-food cones, miniature season-inspired taste sensations with fillings including black cod, elderflower, basil and bell pepper, and *tagliolini* of cep mushrooms with blueberries and celery. Mains swing from Breton lobster with coriander and peach to quail with cardamom and stuffed courgette flowers.

CAFE CULTURE

You can make yourself pretty *gemütlich* (comfy) over coffee and people-watching in Salzburg's grand cafes. Expect to pay around €4 for a slice of cake and €8 for a daily special (more in fancy places). Here are five of our favourites:

Café Tomaselli (www.tomaselli.at; Alter Markt 9; ⊙ 7am-7pm Mon-Sat, from 8am Sun) Mozart once hung out at this Salzburg institution, where cakes (including a mean strudel) and elaborate coffees are brought to marble-topped tables.

Sacher (www.sacher.com; Schwarzstrasse 5-7; ⊙ 7.30am-11pm) Dig into *Sacher Torte* (iced dark-chocolate sponge with a layer of apricot jam) in refined, chandelier-lit surrounds. The terrace overlooks the Salzach River.

Fingerlos (www.cafe-fingerlos.at; Franz-Josef-Strasse 9; ⊙ 7.30am-7.30pm Tue-Sun) A lovely old-school cafe that is still frequented mostly by locals. Come for the pastries, delectable tortes and strong coffee.

Café Bazar (www.cafe-bazar.at; Schwarzstrasse 3; ⊙ 7.30am-7.30pm Mon-Sat, 9am-6pm Sun) A blast of a more decadent past, this river-facing coffee house is a terrific pick for breakfast, cake or a light lunch.

Kaffee Alchemie (www.kaffee-alchemie.at; Rudolfskai 38; ⊙ 7.30am-6pm Mon-Fri, from 10am Sat & Sun) This retro riverfront cafe has elevated coffee making to an art form. The beans are fair-trade, the cakes homemade and the espresso second to none.

Drinking & Nightlife

★**Augustiner Bräustübl** BREWERY
(www.augustinerbier.at; Augustinergasse 4-6; ⊙ 3-11pm Mon-Fri, from 2.30pm Sat & Sun) Who says monks can't enjoy themselves? Since 1621, cheery, monastery-run Augustiner Bräustübl brewery has served potent homebrews in beer steins, in the vaulted hall and beneath the chestnut trees of the 1000-seat beer garden. Get your tankard filled at the foyer pump and visit the snack stands for hearty, beer-swigging grub including *Stelzen* (ham hock), pork belly and giant pretzels.

★**Herbert's Bar** COCKTAIL BAR
(www.facebook.com/herbertsbarsalzburg; Herbert-von-Karajan Platz 1; ⊙ 5pm-midnight Tue-Thu, to 2am Sat & Sun) It's time to slip down the rabbit hole...unless you're already too late for that very important date. Welcome to Salzburg's bonkers – yet very, very cool – bar with an *Alice in Wonderland* theme. You'll find things getting curiouser and curiouser in the vaulted cellar, where mad hatters are served highballs from the great heights of fancy teapots.

One too many of those and you'll leave grinning like the Cheshire Cat...

★**Enoteca Settemila** WINE BAR
(www.facebook.com/enotecasettemila; Bergstrasse 9; ⊙ 5-11pm Wed-Sat) This bijou wine shop and bar brims with the enthusiasm and passion of Rafael Peil and Nina Corti. Go to sample their well-curated selection of wines, including Austrian, organic and biodynamic ones, with *taglieri* – sharing plates of cheese and *salumi* (salami, ham, prosciutto and the like) – from small Italian producers.

★**220 Grad** CAFE
(www.220grad.com; Chiemseegasse 5; ⊙ 9am-7pm Tue-Fri, to 6pm Sat; 🐾) In a tucked-away corner of the Altstadt, this retro-cool cafe is up there with the best for its freshly roasted coffee, breakfasts and decked terrace (always rammed in summer). Its name alludes to the perfect temperature for roasting beans, and the skilled baristas make a terrific single-origin espresso and house blends, which pair with cakes including sweet potato with lime cream.

Darwin's COCKTAIL BAR
(www.darwins-salzburg.at; Steingasse 1; ⊙ 9am-midnight Sun-Thu, to 2am Fri & Sat) Darwin himself might well have been partial to an expertly mixed cocktail or two at this glam vaulted bar, while dreaming up his theory of evolution or pondering the origin of the species. The great man himself is portrayed as an ape-man alongside other doodles of globes and quotes. It makes a mean espresso martini.

We Love Coffee
COFFEE

(www.we-love-coffee.at; Mozartsteg; ⊘ 7.30am-5pm Mon-Fri, from 9am Sat & Sun) For a caffeine fix on the hoof, you can't beat this cute cafe in a converted Piaggio Ape, which parks up next to Mozartsteg. It makes a mean espresso, chai latte and flat white.

Die Weisse
PUB

(www.dieweisse.at; Rupertgasse 10; ⊘ pub 10am-2am Mon-Sat, bar from 5pm) The cavernous brewpub of the Salzburger Weissbierbrauerei, this is the place to guzzle cloudy wheat beers in the wood-floored pub and the shady beer garden out the back. DJs work the decks in Sudwerk bar, especially at the monthly Almrausch, when locals like to party in skimpy Dirndls and strapping Lederhosen.

StieglKeller
BEER HALL

(www.restaurant-stieglkeller.at; Festungsgasse 10; ⊘ 11.30am-10pm) For a 365-day taste of Oktoberfest, try this cavernous, Munich-style beer hall, which shares the same architect as Munich's Hofbräuhaus (p76). It has an enormous garden above the city's rooftops and a menu of meaty mains (€13 to €25) such as fat pork knuckles and schnitzel. Beer is cheapest from the self-service taps outside.

Mayday Bar
COCKTAIL BAR

(www.hangar-7.com; Wilhelm-Spazier-Strasse 7a, Salzburg Airport; ⊘ noon-midnight Sun-Thu, to 1am Fri & Sat) Peer down at the Flying Bulls aviation enthusiasts' rare historical aircraft through the glass walls at this crystalline bar, part of the airport's futuristic Hangar-7 complex. Strikingly illuminated by night, it's a unique place for a fresh fruit cocktail or 'smart food' appetisers served in Bodum glasses.

Sternbräu
BEER GARDEN

(www.sternbrauerei.com; Griesgasse 23; ⊘ 9am-midnight; ♿) While it's quite firmly on the tourist trail, this massive beer garden remains a decent place to guzzle homebrews and people-watch in the Altstadt. It has been going strong since 1542. Skip the average food and go for a beer.

Little Grain
COCKTAIL BAR

(www.facebook.com/littlegrain1920; Getreidegasse 34; ⊘ 5pm-midnight Tue-Sat) Blink and you really will miss Little Grain, an intimate cocktail bar under the arcades, with a speakeasy vibe. The stone-vaulted bar is all soft lighting, flickering shadows and classy mixology. Name your poison.

Unikum Sky
CAFE

(☎ 0662-80 44 69 11; Unipark Nonntal; ⊘ 10am-7pm Mon-Fri, to 6pm Sat) For knockout fortress views and a full-on Salzburg panorama, head up to this sun-kissed terrace atop the Unipark Nonntal campus, 300m south of Schanzlgasse in the Altstadt. It's a relaxed spot to chill over drinks and inexpensive snacks.

Seven Senses
COCKTAIL BAR

(www.7-senses.at; Giselakai 3, Hotel Stein; ⊘ 7am-2am) Hotel Stein's chichi 7th-floor terrace bar attracts Salzburg's Moët-sipping socialites and anyone who loves a good view. It isn't cheap, but it's the best spot to see the Altstadt light up against the theatrical backdrop of the fortress.

Köchelverzeichnis
WINE BAR

(www.facebook.com/koechelverzeichnis; Steingasse 27; ⊘ 5-11pm Mon-Sat) This is a real neighbourhood bar with jazzy music, antipasti and a great selection of wines. Taste citrusy Grüner Veltliners and Rieslings from the family's vineyards in the Wachau.

☆ Entertainment

For a city of its size, Salzburg packs a mighty cultural punch, especially when the Salzburg Festival (p182) comes to town. You'll find everything from alternative arts to classical opera, including live jazz, rock and pop, puppet theatre, Mozart concerts, ballet and more. Advance booking is highly advisable.

★ Salzburger Marionettentheater
PUPPETRY

(☎ 0662-87 24 06; www.marionetten.at; Schwarzstrasse 24; tickets €20-37; ♿) The red curtain goes up on a miniature stage at this marionette theatre, a lavish stucco, cherub and chandelier-lit affair founded in 1913. The repertoire star is *The Sound of Music,* with a life-sized Mother Superior and a marionette-packed finale. Other enchanting productions include Mozart's *The Magic Flute* and Tchaikovsky's *The Nutcracker.* All have multilingual surtitles.

The theatre is a Unesco World Heritage site, proclaimed in 2017.

Grosses Festspielhaus
THEATRE

(☎ 0662-804 50; Hofstallgasse 1) Designed by architect Clemens Holzmeister in 1956 and

RETURN OF THE TRACHT

Ever thought about purchasing a tight-fitting Dirndl or a pair of strapping Lederhosen? No? Well, Salzburg might just change your mind with its *Trachten* (traditional costume) stores that can add Alpine oomph to your wardrobe. If you have visions of old maids in gingham and men in feathered hats, you might be surprised. Walk the streets where twenty-somethings flaunt the latest styles or hit the dance floor at Die Weisse's Almrausch club night (p189) and you'll see that hem lines have risen and necklines have plunged over the years. Young Salzburgers are reinventing the style by teaming Lederhosen with T-shirts and trainers, or pairing slinky off-the-shoulder numbers with ballet pumps. Their message? *Trachten* can be cool, even sexy.

Ploom (www.ploom.at; Ursulinenplatz 5; ⊘11am-6pm Thu & Fri, to 5pm Sat) Tanja Pflaum's sassy interpretations of the Dirndl are the ultimate in Alpine chic.

Lanz Trachten (www.lanztrachten.at; Schwarzstrasse 4; ⊘9am-6pm Mon-Fri, to 5pm Sat) This highly regarded tailor shop has been trading in quality Dirndls and Lederhosen since the 1920s.

Stassny (www.stassny.at; Getreidegasse 30; ⊘9.30am-6pm Mon-Fri, to 5pm Sat) You might pay a smidgen more for your Dirndl here, but it will be top-notch – and they come in myriad fabrics and colours.

Forstenlechner (www.salzburg-trachtenmode.at; Mozartplatz 4; ⊘9.30am-6pm Mon-Fri, to 5pm Sat) *Trachten* here are a mix of classic and contemporary styles in a veritable rainbow of colours. Prices hover around the midrange mark.

Wenger (www.wenger.at; Getreidegasse 29; ⊘10am-6pm Mon-Fri, to 5pm Sat) Has a melange of coquettish Dirndl and Lederhosen for ladies – some in styles that would make the grandparents blush. Most have a modern twist.

built into the sheer sides of the Mönchsberg, the cavernous Grosses Festspielhaus stages the majority of Salzburg Festival (p182) performances and can accommodate 2179 theatregoers.

Schlosskonzerte CLASSICAL MUSIC
(www.schlosskonzerte-salzburg.at; ⊘concerts 8pm) A fantasy of coloured marble, stucco and frescoes, the baroque Marmorsaal (Marble Hall) at Schloss Mirabell (p176) is the exquisite setting for chamber-music concerts. Internationally renowned soloists and ensembles perform works by Mozart and other well-known composers such as Haydn and Chopin. Tickets costing between €32 and €38 are available online or at the **box office** (☑0662-84 85 86; Theatergasse 2; ⊘10am-3pm Mon-Fri, to 1pm Sat).

ARGEkultur LIVE MUSIC
(www.argekultur.at; Ulrike-Gschwandtner-Strasse 5) This alternative cultural venue was born out of protests against the Salzburg Festival in the 1980s. Today it's a bar and performance hybrid. Traversing the entire arts spectrum, the line-up features concerts, cabaret, DJ nights, dance, poetry slams and world music. It's at the Unipark Nonn-

tal campus, a five-minute walk east of the Altstadt.

Landestheater THEATRE
(☑0662-87 15 12; www.salzburger-landestheater. at; Schwarzstrasse 22; tickets €11-70; ⊘box office 9am-5pm Mon-Fri, to 1pm Sat; ☖) Opera, operetta, ballet and musicals dominate the stage at this elegant 18th-century playhouse. There's a strong emphasis on Mozart's music, with the Mozarteum Salzburg Orchestra often in the pit. There are dedicated performances for kids, and *The Sound of Music* musical is a winner with all ages.

Rockhouse LIVE MUSIC
(www.rockhouse.at; Schallmooser Hauptstrasse 46) Salzburg's hottest live-music venue, Rockhouse presents first-rate rock, pop, jazz, folk, metal and reggae concerts – see the website for details. There's also a tunnel-shaped bar that has DJs (usually free) and bands. Rockhouse is 1km northeast of the Altstadt; take bus 4 to Canavalstrasse.

Haus für Mozart THEATRE
(House for Mozart; ☑0662-804 55 00; www.salz burgerfestspiele.at; Hofstallgasse 1) Housed in the former royal stables, the Haus für Mo-

zart (also known as the Kleines Festspiel-haus) is one of the venues of the Salzburg Festival (p182).

Felsenreitschule THEATRE
(Summer Riding School; Hofstallgasse 1) One of the premier venues of the Salzburg Festival (p182), the baroque Felsenreitschule was built in 1693 and designed by the architect of the age, Johann Bernhard Fischer von Erlach.

Mozart Dinner LIVE PERFORMANCE
(✆ 0662-82 86 95; www.mozart-dinner-concert-salzburg.com; Sankt-Peter-Bezirk 1; adult/child €63/40; ⊕ 7.30pm) You'll love or hate this themed dinner, with Mozart music, costumed performers and (mediocre) 18th-century-style food. It's held in Stiftskeller St Peter restaurant's lavish baroque hall.

Sound of Salzburg Show PERFORMING ARTS
(✆ 0662-231 058 00; www.soundofsalzburg.info; Griesgasse 23, Sternbräu; adult/child €39/20; ⊕ show 8pm) This all-singing show at Sternbräu (p189) beer garden is a triple bill of Mozart, The Sound of Music and operetta faves performed in traditional costume. Kitschy but fun.

Mozarteum CLASSICAL MUSIC
(✆ 0662-87 31 54; www.mozarteum.at; Schwarzstrasse 26; ⊕ box office 10am-3pm Mon-Fri) Opened in 1880 and revered for its supreme acoustics, the Mozarteum highlights the life and works of Mozart through chamber music (October to June), concerts and opera. The annual highlight is **Mozart Week** in January.

Das Kino CINEMA
(www.daskino.at; Giselakai 11) Shows independent and art-house films from Austria and across the globe in their original language. The cinema hosts the Bergfilmfestival, zooming in on adventure in the mountains, in November.

🛍 Shopping

Whether you're after a bottle of Mozart eau de toilette or a pair of yodelling Lederhosen, Getreidegasse is your street. Traditional wrought-iron signs hang above the shops, which sell everything from designer fashion to hats. Goldgasse, where goldsmiths once plied their trade, has accessories, antiques and porcelain. A popular street for shopping and strolling is Linzer Gasse.

★ Fürst CHOCLATE
(www.original-mozartkugel.com; Getreidegasse 47; ⊕ 10am-6.30pm Mon-Sat, noon-5pm Sun) Pistachio, nougat and dark-chocolate dreams, the Mozartkugeln (Mozart balls) here are still handmade to Paul Fürst's original 1890 recipe. Other specialities include cube-shaped Bach Würfel – coffee, nut and marzipan truffles dedicated to yet another great composer.

Spirituosen Sporer WINE
(Getreidegasse 39; ⊕ 9.30am-7pm Mon-Fri, 8.30am-5pm Sat) In Getreidegasse's narrowest house, family-run Sporer has been intoxicating local folk with Austrian wines, herbal liqueurs and famous Vogelbeer (rowan berry) schnapps since 1903.

Bottle Shop FOOD & DRINKS
(www.beerbottle.eu; Mirabellplatz 7; ⊕ 10am-6pm Mon-Fri, to 1pm Sat) A real delight for craft beer and cider lovers, this tucked-away shop does a creative line in ales, porters, stouts and ciders, all set under atmospheric vaults.

Salzburger Heimatwerk GIFTS & SOUVENIRS
(www.salzburgerheimatwerk.at; Residenzplatz 9; ⊕ 9am-6pm Mon-Fri, to 5pm Sat) As well as knocking fine fabrics into Dirndls and dapper traditional costumes, Salzburger Heimatwerk does a fine line in local handicrafts, schnapps, preserves and honeys.

Salzburg Salz GIFTS & SOUVENIRS
(Wiener-Philharmoniker-Gasse 6; ⊕ 10am-6pm Mon-Sat) Pure salt from Salzburgerland and the Himalayas, herbal salts and rock-salt tea lights are among the high-sodium wonders here.

ⓘ SALZBURG CARD

If you're planning on doing lots of sightseeing, save by buying the **Salzburg Card** (1-/2-/3-day card €28/37/43). The card gets you entry to all of the major sights and attractions, unlimited use of public transport (including cable cars) and numerous discounts on tours and events. The card is half-price for children and €3 cheaper in the low season.

The card can be purchased at the airport, the tourist office and most hotels, or online at www.salzburg.info.

ℹ Information

POST

Main Post Office (Residenzplatz 9; ⊘8am-6pm Mon-Fri)
Station Post Office (Südtiroler Platz 1; ⊘8am-7pm Mon-Fri, to 1pm Sat)

TOURIST INFORMATION

The main **tourist office** (📞0662-88 98 73 30; www.salzburg.info; Mozartplatz 5; ⊘9am-6pm Apr-Sep, 9am-6pm Mon-Sat Oct-Mar) has stacks of information about the city and its immediate surrounds. There's a ticket-booking agency (www.salzburgticket.com) in the same building.

For information on the rest of the province, visit **Salzburgerland Tourismus** (📞0662-668 80; www.salzburgerland.com; Wiener Bundesstrasse 23, Hallwang bei Salzburg; ⊘8am-5.30pm Mon-Thu, to 5pm Fri), 6.5km north of Salzburg.

ℹ Getting There & Away

AIR

Salzburg Airport (📞0662-858 00; www.salzburg-airport.com; Innsbrucker Bundesstrasse 95; 📶) is a 20-minute bus ride from the city centre and has regular scheduled flights to destinations all over Austria and Europe. Low-cost flights from the UK are provided by **Ryanair** (www.ryanair.com) and **EasyJet** (www.easyjet.com). Other airlines include **British Airways** (www.britishairways.com) and **Jet2** (www.jet2.com).

BUS

Salzburger Verkehrsverbund (📞24hr hotline 0662-63 29 00; www.svv-info.at) makes it easy to reach the province's smaller villages. Buses depart from just outside the Hauptbahnhof on Südtiroler Platz, where timetables are displayed. Bus information and tickets are available from the information points on the main station concourse.

For more information on buses in and around Salzburg and an online timetable, see www.postbus.at.

TRAIN

Salzburg has excellent rail connections with the rest of Austria from its recently revamped **Hauptbahnhof**.

Trains leave frequently for Vienna (€54.10, 2½ to three hours) and Linz (€27.50, 1¼ hours). There is a two-hourly express service to Klagenfurt (€41.20, three hours).

The quickest way to get to Innsbruck is by the 'corridor' train through Germany; trains depart at least every two hours (€47.20, two hours) and stop at Kufstein. Direct trains run at least hourly to Munich (€32, 1½ to two hours); some of these continue on to Karlsruhe via Stuttgart.

There are also several trains daily to Berlin (€150, five to 8½ hours), Budapest (€93.80, 5¼ hours), Prague (€98.90 to €125.60, 7½ hours) and Venice (€59, six to nine hours).

For timetables, see www.svv-info.at.

ℹ Getting Around

TO/FROM THE AIRPORT

The city's airport is around 5.5km west of the centre along Innsbrucker Bundesstrasse. Buses 2, 10 and 27 (€2.60, 19 minutes) depart from outside the terminal roughly every 10 to 15 minutes and make several central stops near the Altstadt; buses 2 and 27 terminate at the Hauptbahnhof. Services operate roughly from 5.30am to 11pm. A taxi between the airport and the city centre costs €15 to €20.

BICYCLE

Salzburg is one of Austria's most bike-friendly cities. It has an extensive network of scenic cycling trails heading off in all directions, including along the banks of the Salzach River. See www.movelo.com for a list of places renting out electric bikes (e-bikes).

A Velo (📞0676-435 59 50; Mozartplatz; bicycle rental half-day/full day/week €12/18/55, e-bike €18/25/120; ⊘9.30am-5pm Apr-Jun & Sep, to 7pm Jul & Aug) Just across the way from the tourist office.

BUS

Bus drivers sell single (€2.60), 24-hour (€5.70) and weekly tickets (€16). Single tickets bought in advance from machines are slightly cheaper. If you're planning on making several trips, tickets are cheaper still (€1.90 each), but only in units of five. Kids under six travel for free, while all other children pay half-price.

Bus routes are shown at bus stops and on some city maps; buses 1 and 4 start from the Hauptbahnhof and skirt the pedestrian-only Altstadt.

Information and timetables are available at www.salzburg-verkehr.at.

BUS TAXI

'Bus taxis' operate from 11.30pm to 1.30am (to 3am on weekends) on fixed routes, dropping off and picking up along the way, for a cost of €4.50. Ferdinand-Hanusch-Platz is the departure point for suburban routes on the left bank, and Theatergasse for routes on the right bank.

CAR & MOTORCYCLE

Parking places are limited and much of the Altstadt is only accessible on foot, so it's easier to leave your car at one of three park-and-ride points to the west, north and south of the city. The largest car park in the centre is the Altstadt Garage under Mönchsberg (€22 per day); some restaurants in the centre will stamp your ticket for a reduction. Rates are lower on streets with automatic ticket machines (blue zones); a three-hour maximum applies (€4.50, or €0.70 for 28 minutes) from 9am to 7pm on weekdays.

For car rental in Salzburg, options include **Avis** (www.avis.com; Ferdinand-Porsche-Strasse 7), **Europcar** (www.europcar.com; Gniglerstrasse 12) or **Hertz** (www.hertz.com; Ferdinand Porsche-Strasse 7).

AROUND SALZBURG

Schloss Hellbrunn

A prince-archbishop with a wicked sense of humour, Markus Sittikus, built Schloss Hellbrunn (www.hellbrunn.at; Fürstenweg 37; adult/child/family €12.50/5.50/26.50, gardens free; ⊗9am-9pm Jul & Aug, to 5.30pm Apr-Jun, Sep & Oct; ⊞) in the early 17th century as a summer palace and an escape from his functions at the Residenz (p174). The Italianate villa became a beloved retreat for rulers of state, who flocked here to eat, drink and make merry. It was a Garden of Eden to all who beheld its exotic fauna, citrus trees and trick fountains – designed to sober up the clergy without dampening their spirits.

Domenico Gisberti, poet to the court of Munich, once gushed: 'I see the epitome of Venice in these waters, Rome reduced to a brief outline.'

While the whimsical palace interior – especially the Oriental-style Chinese Room and frescoed Festsaal – is worth a peek, the eccentric Wasserspiele (trick fountains) are the big draw in summer. Be prepared to get soaked in the mock Roman theatre, the shell-clad Neptune Grotto and the twittering Bird Grotto. No statue here is quite as it seems, including the emblematic tongue-poking-out Germaul mask (Sittikus' answer to his critics). The tour rounds out at the 18th-century water-powered Mechanical Theatre, where 200 limewood figurines depict life in a baroque city. Tours run every 30 minutes.

Studded with ponds, sculptures and leafy avenues, the palace gardens are free and open until dusk year-round. Here you'll find

Salzburg & Salzburgerland

the *Sound of Music* pavilion of 'Sixteen Going on Seventeen' fame.

🛈 Getting There & Away

Hellbrunn is 4.5km south of Salzburg, a scenic 20-minute bike ride (mostly along the Salzach River) or a 12-minute ride on Bus 25 (€2, every 20 minutes), departing from Mozartsteg/Rudolfskai in the Altstadt.

Untersberg

Rising above Salzburg and straddling the German border is the rugged 1853m peak of Untersberg (www.untersbergbahn.at; cable car up/down/return €15/13.50/23.50, free with Salzburg Card; ⊗cable car 8.30am-5.30pm Jul-Sep, shorter hours Oct & mid-Dec–Jun, closed Nov–mid-Dec). Spectacular views of the city, the Rositten Valley and the Tyrolean, Salzburg and Bavarian Alpine ranges unfold from the summit. The mountain is a magnet to local skiers in winter, and hikers, climbers and paragliders in summer. From the cable car's top station, short, easy trails lead to nearby viewpoints at Geiereck (1805m) and Salzburg Hochthron (1853m), while others take you deeper into the Alps.

Temperatures can feel significantly cooler up here than down in the valley and trails are loose underfoot, so bring a fleece or jacket and sturdy footwear if you plan on doing some walking.

A cable car runs every half-hour to the peak. To reach the cable-car valley station, take bus 25 from Salzburg's Hauptbahnhof or Mirabellplatz to St Leonhard and the valley station.

Hallein & Bad Dürrnberg

📋 06245 / POP 20,769

Too few people visit Hallein in their dash west to Bavaria or north to Salzburg, but those who do are pleasantly surprised. Beyond its industrial outskirts lies a pristine late-medieval town, where narrow lanes are punctuated by courtyards, art galleries and boho cafes. Hallein's major family attraction, the Salzwelten salt mine, is actually located in Bad Dürrnberg, 6km southwest of town.

⊙ Sights

★ Salzwelten   MINE
(www.salzwelten.at; Ramsaustrasse 3, Bad Dürrnberg; adult/child/family €21/10.50/44; ⊘9am-5pm; ⊕) During Salzburg's princely heyday, the sale of salt filled its coffers. Today, at Austria's biggest show mine, you can slip into a boilersuit to descend to the bowels of the earth. The tour aboard a rickety train passes through a maze of claustrophobic passageways, over the border to Germany and down a 27m slide – don't brake, lift your legs and ask the guide to wax the slide for extra speed!

After crossing a salt lake on a wooden raft, a 42m slide brings you to the lowest point (210m underground) and back to good old Austria. Guided 70-minute tours depart every half-hour. Bus 41 runs from Hallein train station hourly on weekdays, less often at weekends.

Keltenmuseum   MUSEUM
(Celtic Museum; www.keltenmuseum.at; Pflegerplatz 5; adult/child €7.50/2.50; ⊘9am-5pm; ⊕) Overlooking the Salzach, the glass-fronted Keltenmuseum runs chronologically through the region's heritage in a series of beautiful vaulted rooms. It begins with Celtic artefacts, including *Asterix*-style helmets, an impressively reconstructed chariot and a selection of bronze brooches, pendants and buckles.

The 1st floor traces the history of salt extraction in Hallein, featuring high points such as a miniature slide and the mummified Mannes im Salz (Man in Salt) unearthed in 1577. There is a pamphlet with English explanations.

🎎 Festivals & Events

Halleiner Festwochen   PERFORMING ARTS
(www.forum-hallein.at; ⊘late Jul-Aug) First-rate musicians and artists draw crowds to the Halleiner Festwochen. The festival is one of the headliners on the summer events program in Salzburgerland, with everything from classical concerts to live jazz, plus theatre, comedy acts, readings and exhibitions.

🛏 Sleeping

Hotels are cheaper and less sought-after here than in Salzburg, a 25-minute train ride away – a point worth considering during the Salzburg Festival. The tourist office (p195) can help book holiday apartments.

Pension Hochdürrnberg   GUESTHOUSE €
(📋06245-751 83; www.hochduerrnberg.at; Rumpelgasse 14, Bad Dürrnberg; s/d/tr/q €50/60/70/100; ℗) Surrounded by meadows, this farmhouse in Bad Dürrnberg has countrified rooms with warm pine furnishings and downy bedding. The furry residents (rabbits, sheep and cows) will keep children amused.

Hotel Auwirt   HOTEL €€
(📋06245-804 17; www.auwirt.com; Salzburgerstrasse 42; camp sites per adult/child/tent €10/7/6.50, s €60-95, d €90-165, q €149-255; ℗⧖) Auwirt's light-filled, wood-floored, Alpine-trimmed rooms are spacious and comfy; some superior rooms come with balconies. The hotel is a good family base, with a tree-shaded garden and playground. You can also pitch a tent here.

Kranzbichlhof   HOTEL €€
(📋06245-737 720; www.kranzbichlhof.net; Hofgasse 12, Bad Dürrnberg; s €78-92, d €124-144, f €180-195; ℗⧖⊠) In a serene location backing onto woods, this glorious rambling chalet has spacious, light, pine-clad rooms done out in contemporary style (many featuring balconies). There's also a lovely garden, natural outdoor pool, and a spa offering everything from Ayurvedic treatments to yoga and even craniosacral therapy.

ℹ Information

Tourist Office (☑ 06245-853 94; www.hallein.com; Mauttorpromenade 6; ⊙ 8.30am-5pm Mon-Fri) Hallein's tourist office is a good first port of call for information on the town and its surrounds.

ℹ Getting There & Away

Hallein is close to the German border, 18km south of Salzburg via the B150 and A10/E55 in the direction of Graz/Villach. It's a 25-minute train journey from Salzburg, with departures roughly every 30 minutes (€4.70, 15 to 24 minutes).

Werfen

☑ 06468 / POP 2975

The world's largest accessible ice caves, the soaring limestone turrets of the Tennengebirge range and a formidable medieval fortress are but the tip of the superlative iceberg in Werfen. Such salacious natural beauty hasn't escaped Hollywood producers – Werfen stars in WWII action film *Where Eagles Dare* (1968) and makes a cameo appearance in the picnic scene of *The Sound of Music*.

Both the fortress and the ice caves can be squeezed into a day trip from Salzburg; start early, visit the caves first and be at the fortress for the last falconry show.

◉ Sights & Activities

★ **Eisriesenwelt**   CAVE
(www.eisriesenwelt.at; Eishohlenstrasse 30; adult/child €12/7, incl cable car €24/14; ⊙ 8am-4pm Jul & Aug, to 3pm May, Jun, Sep & Oct) Billed as the world's largest accessible ice caves, Eisriesenwelt is a glittering ice empire spanning 30,000 sq metres and 42km of narrow passages burrowing deep into the heart of the mountains. A tour through these Narnia-esque chambers of blue ice is a unique experience. As you climb up wooden steps and down pitch-black passages, with carbide lamps aglow, otherworldly ice sculptures shaped like polar bears and elephants, frozen columns and lakes emerge from the shadows.

A highlight is the cavernous **Eispalast** (ice palace), where the frost crystals twinkle when a magnesium flare is held up to them. A womb-like tunnel leads to a flight of 700 steps, which descends back to the entrance. Even if it's hot outside, entering the caves in any season is like stepping into a deep freeze – be sure to bring warm clothing and sturdy footwear.

In summer, minibuses (return adult/child €7/5) run at 8.18am, 10.18am, 12.18pm and 2.18pm from Werfen train station to Eisriesenwelt car park, which is a 20-minute walk from the bottom station of the cable car. The last return bus departs at 4.32pm. Allow roughly three hours for the return trip (including the tour). You can walk the whole route, but it's a challenging four-hour ascent, rising 1100m above the village.

Burg Hohenwerfen   CASTLE
(Hohenwerfen Fortress; www.salzburg-burgen.at; adult/child/family €12/6.50/28.50, incl lift €16/9/38; ⊙ 9am-5pm May-Sep, shorter hours Mar-Apr & Oct; 🚗) Slung high on a wooded clifftop and cowering beneath the majestic peaks of the Tennengebirge range, Burg Hohenwerfen is visible from afar. For 900 years this fortress has kept watch over the Salzach Valley; its current appearance dates to 1570. The big draw is the far-reaching view over Werfen from the 16th-century belfry, though the **dungeons** (displaying the usual nasties such as the iron maiden and thumb screw) are also worth a look.

🛏 Sleeping

Camping Vierthaler   CAMPGROUND €
(☑ 06468-565 70; www.camping-vierthaler.at; Reitsam 8; camp sites per adult/child/tent €6/3/6.50, bungalows d/tr/q €29/38/47; ⊙ mid-Apr–Sep) This lovely campground on the bank of the Salzach River has a back-to-nature feel. Facilities include a snack bar and playground. Bungalows with kitchenettes, patios and barbecue areas are also available.

Landgasthof Reitsamerhof   GUESTHOUSE €
(☑ 06468-5379; www.reitsamerhof.at; Reitsam 22, Werfen-Imlau; s €55-60, d €74-80, tr €96-108, f €118-120; 🅿 🛜) Bedecked with lovely geraniums in summer, this sunny yellow Landgasthof Reitsamerhof sits just south of Werfen and commands rousing views of the limestone spires of the Tennengebirge. Decorated in modern rustic style, most of the parquet-floored, pine-clad rooms open onto balconies, and the restaurant (mains €10 to €27) plays up Austrian classics such as schnitzel and *Zwiebelrostbraten* (onion roast).

✗ Eating

Oedlhaus AUSTRIAN €€
(www.oedlhaus.at; Eishöhlenstrasse 30; snacks
€3.50-8, mains €8-12.50; ⊙9am-3.45pm May,
Jun, Sep & Oct, to 4.45pm Jul & Aug) Next to
Eisriesenwelt cable-car top station, this
woodsy hut at 1574m fortifies walkers with
mountain grub such as *Gröstl* (pan-fried potatoes, pork and onions topped with a fried
egg). The terrace has views to rave about:
you can see across the Salzach Valley to the
chiselled limestone peaks of the Hochkönig
range.

★ Obauer EUROPEAN €€€
(⌨06468-52 12; www.obauer.com; Markt 46;
3-course lunch €38, dinner menus €50-135;
⊙noon-2pm & 7-9pm Wed-Sun; ⊛) Culinary
dream duo Karl and Rudi Obauer run the
show at this highly regarded, ingredient-
focused restaurant. Sit in the rustic-chic
restaurant or out in the garden, where most
of the fruit and herbs are grown. Signature
dishes, such as meltingly tender Werfen
lamb and flaky trout strudel, are complemented by the finest Austrian wines.

ℹ Information

Tourist Office (⌨06468-53 88; www.werfen.
at; Markt 24; ⊙9am-noon & 1-6pm Mon-Fri)
Hands out information and maps, and makes
hotel bookings free of charge.

ℹ Getting There & Away

Werfen is 45km south of Salzburg on the A10/
E55 motorway. Trains run frequently to Salzburg
(€8.80, 40 minutes).

Stuttgart & the Black Forest

POP 12.6 MILLION

Best Places to Eat

➡ Restaurant Bareiss (p230)

➡ Schwarzwaldstube (p230)

➡ Rebers Pflug (p214)

➡ Olivo (p205)

➡ Café Schäfer (p247)

Best Places to Stay

➡ Hotel Belle Epoque (p224)

➡ Glückseligkeit Herberge (p254)

➡ Hotel Oberkirch (p239)

➡ Brickstone Hostel (p217)

➡ Hotel Scholl (p213)

Why Go?

If one word could sum up Germany's southwesternmost region, it would be 'inventive'. Baden-Württemberg gave the world relativity (Einstein), DNA (Miescher) and the astronomical telescope (Kepler). It was here that Bosch invented the spark plug; Gottlieb Daimler the gas engine; and Count Ferdinand the zeppelin. And where would we be without Black Forest gateau, cuckoo clocks and the ultimate beer food, the pretzel?

Beyond the high-tech urban pleasures of 21st-century Stuttgart lies a region still ripe for discovery. On the city fringes, country lanes roll into vineyards and lordly baroque palaces, spa towns and castles steeped in medieval myth. Swinging south, the Black Forest (*Schwarzwald* in German) looks every inch the Grimms' fairy-tale blueprint. Wooded hills rise sharply above church steeples, looming over half-timbered villages and a crochet of tightly woven valleys. It is a perfectly etched picture of sylvan beauty, a landscape refreshingly oblivious to time and trends.

When to Go

Snow dusts the heights from January to late February, attracting downhill and cross-country skiers to the higher peaks in the Black Forest. In late February, around Shrove Tuesday, pre-Lenten *Fasnacht* parades bring carnival shenanigans and elaborate costumed characters to the region's towns and villages.

Enjoy cool forest hikes, riverside bike rides, splashy fun on lakes Constance and Titisee, lazy afternoons in beer gardens and open-air festivals galore during summer.

From late September to October the golden autumn days can be spent rambling in woods, mushrooming and snuggling up in Black Forest farmhouses.

Stuttgart & the Black Forest Highlights

1 **Stuttgart** (p198) Tuning into modern-day Germany in this city of high culture, fast cars and beer festivals.

2 **Baden-Baden** (p220) Wallowing in thermal waters and art nouveau grandeur in the belle of the Black Forest.

3 **Lake Constance** (p250) Kayaking, hiking or cycling between Swiss, German and Austrian borders.

4 **Ulm** (p214) Being wowed by the world's tallest cathedral steeple in Einstein's home town.

5 **Triberg** (p246) Going cuckoo for clocks, Black Forest gateau and Germany's highest waterfall.

6 **Black Forest** (p220) Striding into thickly wooded hills and valleys on mile after glorious mile of walking trails.

7 **Tübingen** (p210) Rowing your boat merrily along the Neckar River and living it up, Goethe-style, in this student town.

8 **Schauinsland Peak** (p242) Hitching a ride above the treetops to this peak for rousing views over the forest to the not-so-distant Alps.

STUTTGART

☑ 0711 / POP 628,032

Ask many Germans their opinion of Stuttgarters and they'll have plenty of things to say: they are road hogs, speeding along the autobahn; they are sharp-dressed executives with a Swabian drawl; they are tight-fisted homebodies who slave away to *schaffe, schaffe, Häusle baue* (work, work, build a house).

So much for the stereotypes: the real Stuttgart is less superficial than legend would have it. True, some good-living locals like their cars fast and their restaurants fancy, but most are just as happy getting their boots dirty in the surrounding vine-clad hills and hanging out with friends in the rustic confines of a *Weinstube* (wine tavern) or a tree-shaded *Biergarten*. In the capital of Baden-Württemberg, city slickers and country kids walk hand in hand, with no need to compromise.

History

Whether with trusty steeds or turbocharged engines, Stuttgart was born to ride – it was founded as the stud farm Stuotgarten around AD 950. Progress was swift: by the 12th century Stuttgart was a trade centre, by the 13th century a blossoming city and by the early 14th century the seat of the Württemberg royal family. Count Eberhard im Bart added sheen to Swabian suburbia by introducing the *Kehrwoche* in 1492, the communal cleaning rota still revered today.

The early 16th century brought hardship, peasant wars, plague and Austrian rulers (1520–34). A century later, the Thirty Years' War devastated Stuttgart and killed half its population.

In 1818, King Wilhelm I launched the first Cannstatter Volksfest to celebrate the end of a dreadful famine. An age of industrialisation dawned in the late 19th and early 20th centuries, with Bosch inventing the spark plug and Daimler pioneering the gas engine. Heavily bombed in WWII, Stuttgart was painstakingly reconstructed and became the capital of the new state of Baden-Württemberg in 1953. Today it is one of Germany's greenest and most affluent cities.

◎ Sights

Stuttgart's main artery is the shopping boulevard Königstrasse, running south from the Hauptbahnhof (p208). Steep grades are common on Stuttgart's hillsides: more than 500 city streets end in *Stäffele* (staircases).

★ **Staatsgalerie Stuttgart** GALLERY
(☑0711-470 400; www.staatsgalerie.de; Konrad-Adenauer-Strasse 30-32; adult/concession €7/5; ☺10am-6pm Tue, Wed & Fri-Sun, to 8pm Thu; Ⓤ Staatsgalerie) Neoclassical meets contemporary at the Staatsgalerie, which bears British architect James Stirling's curvy, colourful imprint. Alongside big-name exhibitions, the gallery harbours a stellar collection of European art from the 14th to the 21st centuries, and American post-WWII avant-gardists. Highlights include works by Miró, Picasso,

Matisse, Kandinsky and Klee. Special billing goes to masterpieces such as Dalí's *The Sublime Moment* (1938), Rembrandt's pensive, chiaroscuro *Saint Paul in Prison* (1627), Max Beckmann's utterly compelling, large-scale *Resurrection* (1916) and Monet's diffuse *Fields in the Spring* (1887).

Schlossplatz SQUARE
(Ⓤ Schlossplatz) Stuttgart's pride and joy is this central square, dominated by the exuberant three-winged Neues Schloss, an impressive, Versailles-inspired baroque palace that houses government ministries. In summer, the square plays host to open-air concerts and festivals, such as the **Sommerfest** (www.stuttgarter-sommerfest.de; ☺early Aug); in winter it twinkles with its Christmas market (p203).

Schloss Solitude PALACE
(☑0714-118 6400; www.schloss-solitude.de; Solitude 1; adult/concession €4/2; ☺10am-5pm Tue-Sun Apr-Oct, 1.30-4pm Tue-Sat & 10am-4pm Sun Nov-Mar; Ⓢ Feuersee) Domed Schloss Solitude, perched above Stuttgart, was built in 1763 for Duke Karl Eugen of Württemberg as a hunting palace and summer residence. Blending rococo and neoclassical styles, it's a lavish confection, with an opulently frescoed, chandelier-lit, gilded interior: top billing goes to the pearly white, stucco-encrusted Weisse Saal (White Hall).

Kunstmuseum Stuttgart GALLERY
(☑0711-2161 9600; www.kunstmuseum-stuttgart.de; Kleiner Schlossplatz 1; adult/concession €6/4; ☺10am-6pm Tue-Thu, Sat & Sun, to 9pm Fri; Ⓤ Schlossplatz) Occupying a shimmering glass cube, this gallery presents high-calibre special exhibits alongside a permanent gallery filled with a prized collection of works by Otto Dix, Willi Baumeister and Stuttgart-born abstract artist Alfred Hölzel. For far-reaching views over the city, head up to the Cube (p206) cafe and restaurant.

Schlossgarten GARDENS
(Ⓤ Neckartor) A terrific park for a wander right in the heart of the city, Stuttgart's sprawling Schlossgarten threads together the **Mittlerer Schlossgarten** (Middle Palace Garden), with its fine beer garden for summer imbibing, the sculpture-dotted **Unterer Schlossgarten** (Lower Palace Garden; Ⓤ Stöckach), and the **Oberer Schlossgarten** (Upper Palace Garden; Ⓤ Charlottenplatz), home to stately landmarks such as the Staatstheater (p207) and the glass-fronted **Landtag** (State Parliament; Ⓤ Charlottenplatz).

Stuttgart

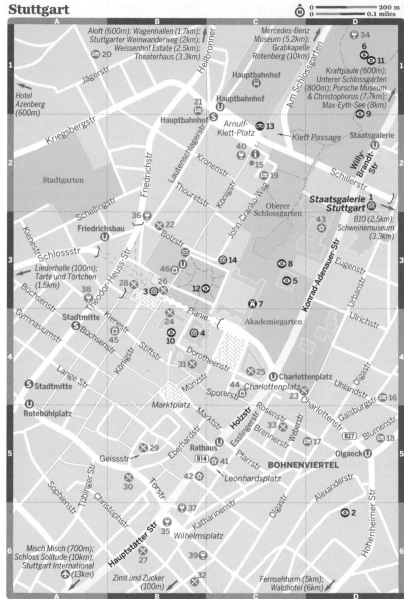

Weissenhof Estate   MUSEUM
(📞0711-257 9187; www.weissenhofmuseum.de;
Rathenaustrasse 1-3; adult/concession €5/2, guided tours €5/4; ⏰11am-6pm Tue-Fri, 10am-6pm
Sat & Sun, guided tours 3pm Tue-Sat, 11am & 3pm
Sun; Ⓤ Killesberg) Architecture enthusiasts
are thrilled by the recent opening of the
Weissenhof Estate, following many years of
restoration. Built in 1927 for the Deutscher
Werkbund exhibition, the estate showcases
the pioneering modern architecture of the
age, bearing the clean aesthetic imprint of 17
prominent architects, among them Ludwig
Mies van der Rohe, Le Corbusier and Walter

Stuttgart

Gropius. Two of Le Corbusier's residential units have received Unesco World Heritage status. Guided tours are in German only.

Fernsehturm TOWER
(☑ 0711-9291 4743; www.fernsehturm-stuttgart. de; Jahnstrasse 120, Stuttgart-Degerloch; adult/ concession €7/4; ⊙ 10am-11pm Mon-Thu, 9am-11pm Fri & Sat; Ⓤ Ruhbank (Fernsehturm)) Whether you think it a marvel or a monstrosity, the 217m-high Fernsehturm is one of Stuttgart's most visible landmarks, with its needle-thin concrete spire poking up above the city. Built in 1956, it was the world's first TV tower and the prototype for all to come. It goes without saying that the 360° views from the lookout platform and panoramic cafe are a knock-out, reaching over the city (particularly impressive when illuminated) to the Swabian Alps beyond.

Mercedes-Benz Museum MUSEUM
(☑ 0711-173 0000; www.mercedes-benz.com; Mercedesstrasse 100; adult/concession €10/5; ⊙ 9am-6pm Tue-Sun, last admission 5pm; Ⓢ Neckarpark) A futuristic swirl on the cityscape, the

Mercedes-Benz Museum takes a chronological spin through the Mercedes empire. Look out for legends such as the 1885 Daimler Riding Car (the world's first gasoline-powered vehicle) and the record-breaking Lightning Benz that hit 228km/h at Daytona Beach in 1909.

Porsche Museum MUSEUM
(☑ 0711-9112 0911; www.porsche.com/museum; Porscheplatz 1; adult/concession €8/4; ⊙ 9am-6pm Tue-Sun; Ⓢ Neuwirtshaus) Looking like a pearly white spaceship preparing for lift-off, the barrier-free Porsche Museum is a car-lover's dream. Audioguides race you through the history of Porsche from its 1948 beginnings. Stop to glimpse the 911 GT1 that won Le Mans in 1998. Call ahead for details of the factory tours that can be combined with a museum visit.

Turmforum VIEWPOINT
(www.s21erleben.de; Im Hauptbahnhof; ⊙ 9am-7pm Mon-Wed & Fri, 10am-9pm Thu, 10am-6pm Sat & Sun; Ⓤ Hauptbahnhof) **FREE** Some of the best views of Stuttgart are from the top of the tower jutting out from the main train station. A free lift (elevator) deposits you right

DON'T MISS

STUTTGARTER WEINWANDERWEG

To taste the region's fruity Trollingers and citrusy Rieslings, factor in a stroll through the vineyards surrounding Stuttgart. The **Stuttgarter Weinwanderweg** (www.stuttgarter -weinwanderweg.de; U Maybachstrasse) comprises several walking trails that thread through winegrowing villages. One begins at Pragsattel station (on the U5 or U6 line) and meanders northeast to Max-Eyth-See, affording fine views from Burgholzhofturm. Visit the website for alternative routes, maps and distances.

From October to March, look out for a broom above the door of Besenwirtschaften (Besa for short). Run by winegrowers, these rustic boltholes are atmospheric places to chat with locals while sampling the latest vintage and Swabian home cooking. Some operate every year but most don't. Check the Besen Kalender website (www.besenkalender. de) during vintage season.

below the revolving Mercedes star. You also get a bird's-eye view of 'Stuttgart 21', a huge – and controversial – revamp of the main train station. Exhibits on floors 3, 5 and 7a explain the details.

Landesmuseum Württemberg   MUSEUM
(☑0711-8953 5111; www.landesmuseum-stuttgart. de; Schillerplatz 6, Altes Schloss; ⊙10am-5pm Tue-Sun; U Charlottenplatz) FREE An archway leads to the turreted 10th-century Altes Schloss, where this museum features regional archaeology and architecture. The historic booty includes Celtic jewellery, neolithic pottery, diamond-encrusted crown jewels and rare artefacts. Time your visit to see, from the arcaded courtyard, the rams above the clock tower lock horns on the hour. Entry to the permanent collection is free.

Wilhelma Zoologisch-Botanischer Garten   ZOO
(www.wilhelma.de; Rosensteinpark; adult/ concession €16/8, after 4pm & Nov-Feb €11/5.50; ⊙8.15am-6pm, to 4pm in winter; U Wilhelma) Wilhelma Zoologisch-Botanischer Garten is a quirky mix of zoo and botanical gardens. Kid magnets include semistriped okapis, elephants, penguins and a petting farm. Greenhouses sheltering tree ferns, camellias and Amazonian species are among the botanical highlights. Sniff out the gigantic bloom of the malodorous titan arum in the Moorish Villa.

Württembergischer Kunstverein   GALLERY
(☑0711-223 370; www.wkv-stuttgart.de; Schlossplatz 2; adult/concession €5/3; ⊙11am-6pm Tue & Thu-Sun, to 8pm Wed; U Schlossplatz) Identified by its copper cupola, this gallery stages thought-provoking contemporary art exhibitions. There are free guided tours (in German) at 3pm on Sundays.

Planetarium Stuttgart   PLANETARIUM
(☑0711-216 890; www.planetarium-stuttgart.de; Willy-Brandt-Strasse 25; adult/concession €8/5; ⊙Tue-Sun; U Staatsgalerie) This pyramid-shaped planetarium uses up-to-the-minute technology to virtually propel you into outer space, with highly realistic projections of constellations and planets, plus plenty of background on astronomy. There are a number of different shows, many with fancy laser and music displays. Show times vary; check the website for latest listings. English audioguides are available.

Grabkapelle Rotenberg   CHAPEL
(www.grabkapelle-rotenberg.de; Württembergstrasse 340; adult/child €4/2; ⊙10am-5pm Tue-Sat, to 6pm Sun Apr-Nov; ☐61) When King Wilhelm I of Württemberg's beloved wife Katharina Pavlovna, daughter of a Russian tsar, died at the age of 30 in 1819, the king tore down the family castle and built this burial chapel. The king was also interred in the neoclassical Russian Orthodox chapel decades later. Modelled on the Pantheon, no less, and built from local sandstone, its pure-white interior is striking, with pillars and statues of the four evangelists lifting visitors' gaze to the dome.

Schweinemuseum   MUSEUM
(☑0711-6641 9600; www.schweinemuseum.de; Schlachthofstrasse 2a; adult/concession €5.90/5; ⊙11am-7.30pm; U Schlachthof) Billing itself as the world's biggest pig museum, the Schweinemuseum is one heck of a pigsty: 50,000 paintings, lucky trinkets, antiques, cartoons, piggy banks and a veritable mountain of cuddly toys cover the entire porcine spectrum. Since opening in the city's century-old former slaughterhouse, the kitsch-cool museum has drawn crowds to its exhibits spotlighting everything from pig worship to wild-boar hunting rituals.

🚶 Tours

CityTour Stuttgart
BUS

(adult/concession €15/12; ☺ blue tour 10am-4pm year-round, green tour 11am-4.40pm Apr-Oct; Ⓤ Hauptbahnhof) Departing roughly hourly from the tourist office (p208), the blue tour trundles through the city centre past icons such as Schlossplatz (p199) and the Mercedes-Benz Museum (p201). The new green tour takes in lesser-known corners in the south and west of Stuttgart.

Neckar-Käpt'n
BOATING

(www.neckar-kaeptn.de; Wilhelma; Ⓤ Wilhelma) From early May to late October, Neckar-Käpt'n runs cruises on the Neckar River, departing from its dock at Wilhelma in Bad Cannstatt on the U14.

✨ Festivals & Events

Christopher Street Day
LGBT

(www.csd-stuttgart.de; ☺ mid Jul) Held over the course of two weeks, Christopher Street Day is southern Germany's biggest gay and lesbian festival, with concerts, gala dinners, club nights, events and a huge (and hugely flamboyant) parade. The parade begins on Erwin-Schoettle-Platz and makes its way through the centre.

Weindorf
WINE

(www.stuttgarter-weindorf.de; ☺ late Aug-early Sep) A 12-day event where winemakers sell the year's vintages from hundreds of booths, accompanied by Swabian grub, cultural events, live music and kids' activities. Some 500 wines hailing from the vines in Baden-Württemberg are there for the sniffing, swirling and tasting. Begins on the last weekend in August; held in Schillerplatz, Kirchstrasse and Marktplatz.

Cannstatter Volksfest
BEER

(www.cannstatter-volksfest.de; Cannstatter Wasen; ☺ late Sep–mid-Oct; Ⓤ Cannstatter Wasen) Stuttgart's answer to Oktoberfest, Cannstatter Volksfest is a beer-guzzling bash held over three consecutive weekends from late September to mid-October. It lifts spirits with oompah music, fairground rides and fireworks. In 2018, the festival pulled out the stops for its 200th anniversary.

Weihnachtsmarkt
CHRISTMAS MARKET

(www.stuttgarter-weihnachtsmarkt.de; ☺ late Nov-late Dec) One of Germany's biggest Christmas markets brings festive twinkle to Marktplatz, **Schillerplatz** (Ⓤ Schlossplatz) and Schlossplatz (p199).

🛌 Sleeping

Hostel Alex 30
HOSTEL €

(☎ 0711-838 8950; www.alex30-hostel.de; Alexanderstrasse 30; dm €25-29, s/d €43/64; Ⓟ 🛜; Ⓤ Olgaeck) Fun-seekers on a budget should thrive at this popular hostel within walking distance of the city centre. Rooms are kept spic and span, and the bar, sun deck and communal kitchen are ideal for swapping stories with fellow travellers. Light sleepers might want to pack earplugs for thin walls and street noise. Breakfast costs €8.

Aloft
DESIGN HOTEL €€

(☎ 0711-8787 5000; www.aloftstuttgarthotel.com; Milaneo Shopping Mall, Heilbronner Strasse 70; d €95-293; 🛜; Ⓤ Stadtbibliothek) It looks pretty nondescript from outside but don't be fooled – this newcomer to Stuttgart's hotel scene is a slick, open-plan design number, with lots of retro-cool touches, pops of colour and terrific views. Rooms ramp up the modern-living factor with creature comforts from Bliss Spa toiletries to coffee-making facilities.

Hotel Azenberg
HOTEL €€

(☎ 0711-225 5040; www.hotelazenberg.de; Seestrasse 114-116; s €85-135, d €100-160; Ⓟ 🛜 🏊; 🚌 43) This family-run choice has individually designed quarters with themes swinging from English country manor to Picasso. There's a pool, tree-shaded garden and little spa for relaxing moments. Breakfast will set you back an extra €11.50. Take bus 43 from Stadtmitte to Hölderlinstrasse.

City Hotel
HOTEL €€

(☎ 0711-210 810; www.cityhotel-stuttgart.de; Uhlandstrasse 18; s €87-109, d €101-139; Ⓟ 🛜; Ⓤ Olgaeck) Eschew the anonymity of Stuttgart's cookie-cutter chains for this intimate hotel just off Charlottenplatz. Rooms are light, clean and modern, if slightly lacklustre. Breakfast on the terrace in summer is a bonus.

Steigenberger Graf Zeppelin
HOTEL €€€

(☎ 0711-204 80; www.stuttgart.steigenberger.de; Arnulf-Klett-Platz 7; d €180-282, ste €260-4000; Ⓟ ❄ 🛜 🏊; Ⓤ Hauptbahnhof) While its concrete facade won't bowl you over, inside is a different story. This five-star pad facing the Hauptbahnhof (p208) is luxury all the way with stylish rooms, Zen-style spa and the Michelin-starred restaurant, Olivo (p205).

Waldhotel
HOTEL €€€

(☎ 0711-185 720; www.waldhotel-stuttgart.de; Guts-Muths-Weg 18; s €126-185, d €145-300, ste €260-362; Ⓟ 🛜; Ⓤ Waldau) A serene hideaway just a short U-Bahn hop from the centre, the Waldhotel snuggles up to the forest on the fringes of Stuttgart. Many of the bright, contemporary, parquet-floored rooms open onto balconies or terraces, and there's a spa for postsightseeing chilling. It's a five-minute stroll to the iconic Fernsehturm (p201).

Kronenhotel   HOTEL €€€
(☑0711-225 10; www.kronenhotel-stuttgart.de; Kronenstrasse 48; s €115-125, d €160-190; P❄@🛜; ⒰Hauptbahnhof) A 1km walk north of central Königstrasse, this hotel outclasses most in the city with its terrific location, good-natured staff, well-appointed rooms and sauna. Breakfast is above par, with fresh fruit, eggs and bacon, smoked fish and pastries.

Der Zauberlehrling   BOUTIQUE HOTEL €€€
(☑0711-237 7770; www.zauberlehrling.de; Rosenstrasse 38; s €160-250, d €180-420; P🛜; ⒰Olgaeck) The dreamily styled rooms at the 'Sorcerer's Apprentice' offer soothing quarters after a day on the road. Each one interprets a different theme (Mediterranean siesta, sunrise, *1001 Nights*), through colour, furniture and features such as canopy beds, clawfoot tubs, tatami mats or fireplaces. Breakfast costs €19.

Ochsen Hotel   HISTORIC HOTEL €€€
(☑0711-407 0500; www.ochsen-online.de; Ulmer Strasse 323; s €92-143, d €124-175; P🛜; ⒰Inselstrasse) It's worth going the extra mile to this charismatic 18th-century hotel. At the pricier end of the spectrum, the spacious, warm-hued rooms have whirlpool tubs for a postsightseeing bubble. The wood-panelled restaurant dishes up appetising Swabian grub (mains €10 to €18) from *Maultaschen* (pork and spinach ravioli) to pork with *Spätzle* (egg noodles).

Hotel am Schlossgarten   HOTEL €€€
(☑0711-202 60; www.hotelschlossgarten.com; Schillerstrasse 23; d €160-250, ste €240-620; P❄🛜; ⒰Hauptbahnhof) Sidling up to the Schloss, this Hotel am Schlossgarten has handsome, park-facing rooms flaunting the luxuries that justify the price tag. Book a table at Michelin-starred Zirbelstube (tasting menus €109 to €139) for classy French dining in subtly lit, pine-panelled surrounds.

🍴 Eating

Stuttgart has raised the bar in the kitchen, with chefs putting an imaginative spin on local, seasonal ingredients. The city boasts a half-dozen Michelin-starred restaurants.

Zimt und Zucker   CAFE €
(www.zimtundzucker-stuttgart.de; Weissenburgstrasse 2c; cake & light meals €3.50-12; ⊙10am-5.30pm Tue-Sun; ⒰Österreichischer Platz) Cheerily decorated with cartoon murals and candy-bright colours that make it look like a kid has been let loose on the interior design, this laid-back cafe is filled with sugar, spice and all things nice. It serves speciality teas, delectable cakes and tortes, as well as great breakfasts (pancakes, muesli, fruit bowls) and daily lunch specials (Tuesday to Friday).

Super Jami   VEGAN €
(☑0711-3209 9749; www.super-jami.de; Bopserstrasse 10; snacks & light mains €5-10.50; ⊙11.30am-4pm Mon-Wed, 11.30am-4pm & 5.30-9.30pm Thu & Fri; ⒰Österreichischer Platz) Comic-strip murals bring a splash of colour to this cool, laid-back vegan deli. Great-value day specials such as Sri Lankan hoppers filled with *thel dala* (spicy devilled potatoes) go for €9.70 a pop, but there's more besides – superfood salads, wraps, chilli sin carne, Belgian waffles and the like.

Platzhirsch   INTERNATIONAL €
(☑0711-76162508;www.facebook.com/Platzhirsch. Stuttgart; Geissstrasse 12; mains €6.20-11.80; ⊙11am-2am Mon-Thu, 11am-3am Fri & Sat, 2pm-1am Sun; ⒰Rathaus) Combining a breath of country air with a pinch of urban cool, wood-panelled Platzhirsch always has a good buzz and, in summer, a packed terrace. Dig into mains such as parmesan *Knödel* (dumplings) in thyme-honey sauce, and saffron risotto with prawns. Lunch specials go for a wallet-friendly €6.90 to €7.80.

Tarte und Törtchen   DESSERTS €
(www.tarteundtoertchen.de; Gutbrodstrasse 1; sweets & breakfast €2.50-13.50; ⊙7am-6pm Tue-Fri, 9am-5pm Sat, 10am-5pm Sun; ⒰Schwab-/Bebelstrasse) For desserts that are edible works of art, it's worth the short U-Bahn ride out of town to this rather fabulous patisserie. The cakes and pastries are decadent indeed: from fruit tarts to zingy citrus mousses and millefeuilles. And it's a petite, elegant space for a leisurely breakfast, with its white walls, chandeliers and mishmash of vintage furniture.

Stuttgarter Markthalle   MARKET €
(Market Hall; www.markthalle-stuttgart.de; Dorotheenstrasse 4; ⊙7am-6.30pm Mon-Fri, 7am-5pm Sat; ⒰Charlottenplatz) Olives, cheeses, spices, patisserie, fruit and veg, wine and tapas – it's all under one roof at this large art nouveau market hall, which also has snack stands.

Reiskorn INTERNATIONAL €€
(☑0711-664 7633; www.das-reiskorn.de; Tor-
strasse 27; mains €11-15.50; ◎5-10pm Tue-Sat; ☑;
Ⓤ Rathaus) With a bamboo-green retro interior and an easygoing vibe, this imaginative
culinary globetrotter serves everything from
celery schnitzel with mango-gorgonzola
cream to meltingly tender beef braised in
chocolate-clove sauce, and banana and yam
curry. There are plenty of vegetarian and vegan choices. It's always busy.

Academie der
Schönsten Künste INTERNATIONAL €€
(☑0711-242 436; www.academie-der-schoensten-
kuenste.de; Charlottenstrasse 5; mains €11-24;
◎8am-midnight Mon-Sat, to 8pm Sun; Ⓤ Charlottenplatz) A breakfast institution since the
1970s, the Academy has evolved into a darling French-style bistro where dishes revolve
around market-fresh fare but also include
such tried-and-true classics as schnitzel with
pan-fried potatoes and *Flammekuchen* (Alsatian pizza). Sit inside among bright canvases or in the charismatic courtyard.

Ochs'n'Willi GERMAN €€
(☑0711-226 5191; www.ochsn-willi.de; Kleiner
Schlossplatz 4; mains €12-30; ◎11am-11.30pm;
Ⓤ Börsenplatz) A warm, woody hunter's
cottage restaurant just this side of twee,
Ochs'n'Willi delivers gutsy portions of Swabian and Bavarian fare. Dig into pork knuckles with lashings of dumplings and kraut,
spot-on *Maultaschen* (pasta pockets) or
rich, brothy *Gaisburger Marsch* (beef stew).
There's a terrace for warm-weather dining.

Amadeus INTERNATIONAL €€
(☑0711-292 678; http://amadeus-stuttgart.de;
Charlottenplatz 17; mains €12-30; ◎11.30am-11pm
Mon-Fri, 9am-11pm Sat, 10am-10pm Sun; Ⓤ Charlottenplatz) Once an 18th-century orphan-
age dishing up gruel, this chic, bustling,
bistro-style restaurant now serves glorious
Swabian food such as *Maultaschen* (pork
and spinach ravioli) and Riesling-laced *Ku-
tteln* (tripe), as well as salads and international dishes from wok noodles to burritos.
The terrace is a big draw in summer. Lunch
specials go for between €8 and €11.

Alte Kanzlei GERMAN €€
(☑0711-294 457; www.alte-kanzlei-stuttgart.de;
Schillerplatz 5a; mains €12-25; ◎9.30am-11.30pm
Mon-Fri, 9am-11.30pm Sat & Sun; Ⓤ Schlossplatz)
Empty tables are rare as gold dust at this
convivial, high-ceilinged restaurant, with
a terrace spilling out onto Schillerplatz

> **DON'T MISS**
>
> **BEAN DISTRICT**
> ···
> To really slip under Stuttgart's skin, mo-
> sey through one of the city's lesser-
> known neighbourhoods. Walk south to
> Hans-im-Glück Platz, centred on a foun-
> tain depicting the caged Grimms' fairy-
> tale character Lucky Hans, and you'll
> soon reach the boho-flavoured **Bohnen-**
> **viertel** (Bean District; www.bohnenviertel.
> net; Ⓤ Rathaus). A facelift has restored the
> neighbourhood's cobbled lanes and ga-
> bled houses, which harbour idiosyncratic
> galleries, workshops, bookshops, wine
> taverns and cafes.

(p203). Feast on Swabian favourites such as
Spanferkel (roast suckling pig) and *Flädle-
suppe* (pancake soup), washed down with
regional tipples.

Weinhaus Stetter GERMAN €€
(☑0711-240 163; www.weinhaus-stetter.de; Rosenstrasse 32; mains €10-17; ◎3-11pm Mon-Fri, noon-
3pm & 5.30-11pm Sat; Ⓤ Charlottenplatz) This
traditional wine tavern in the Bohnenviertel quarter serves up no-nonsense Swabian
cooking, including flavoursome *Linsen und
Saiten* (lentils with sausage), beef roast with
onion and *Kässpätzle* (eggy pasta topped
with onions and cheese) in a convivial atmosphere. The attached shop sells around
500 different wines.

★**Weinstube am Stadtgraben** GERMAN €€€
(☑0711-567 006; www.weinstube-stadtgraben.
de; Am Stadtgraben 6, Stuttgart-Bad Cannstatt;
4-course menu €45; ◎6-10pm; Ⓤ Daimlerplatz)
The Swabian food served at this warm,
rustic, wood-beamed wine tavern in Bad
Cannstatt is the real deal, albeit with a refined touch. Expect dishes that go with the
seasons – be it spot-on suckling pig in dark
beer sauce, fresh fish with pumpkin purée or
duck breast with red cabbage and spinach
dumplings. The wines hail from local vines.

★**Olivo** MODERN EUROPEAN €€€
(☑0711-204 8277; www.olivo-restaurant.de; Arnulf-
Klett-Platz 7; mains around €40, 4-course lunch/
dinner €98/132; ◎noon-1.30pm & 6.30-9.30pm
Wed-Fri, 6.30-9.30pm Tue & Sat; Ⓤ Hauptbahnhof)
Young, sparky chef Nico Burkhardt works
his stuff at Steigenberger's minimalist-chic,
Michelin-starred restaurant. Olivo is lauded
for its exquisitely presented, French-inspired
specialities such as Périgord goose liver with

STUTTGART & THE BLACK FOREST STUTTGART

sheep's milk yoghurt, brioche crumble and woodruff, or beautifully cooked Breton turbot with ricotta and wild garlic.

5   GASTRONOMY €€€
(☑0711-6555 7011; www.5.fo; Bolzstrasse 8; 3- to 8-course menus €84-176; ☺restaurant 6.30-9.30pm Mon-Sat, lounge bar 9am-11pm Mon-Thu, to 1am Fri & Sat, to 10pm Sun; Ⓤ Börsenplatz) This glossy, nouveau-chic restaurant and lounge walks the culinary high wire with a Michelin star and chef Claudio Urru presiding over the stove. Food is masterful, clever and presented in the newfangled, ingredient-listed style: dandelion with radish, wasabi and sesame; textures of *skrei* (Arctic cod) with shallots and spiced nuts; or figs with sorrel, acacia honey, bergamot and cacao.

Christophorus   GASTRONOMY €€€
(☑0711-9112 1911; www.porsche.com/museum; Porscheplatz 5, Porsche Museum; mains €35-65, 4-/5-course menu €82/105; ☺11.30am-3pm & 5.30pm-midnight Tue-Sat; Ⓢ Neuwirtshaus) Not only the cars at the Porsche Museum have va-va-voom. Christophorus is a sophisticated, grown-up affair, with red leather banquettes and linen-draped tables. Prime cuts of US beef grilled to perfection and more refined Med-style dishes, such as pickled char with asparagus panna cotta, and lamb with olive polenta, are paired with top-notch wines, served with finesse.

Cube   INTERNATIONAL €€€
(☑0711-280 4441; www.cube-restaurant.de; Kleiner Schlossplatz 1; mains €19-30; ☺noon-5pm & 6pm-midnight; Ⓤ Schlossplatz) The food is stellar but it actually plays second fiddle to the dazzling decor, refined ambience and stunning views at this glass-fronted cube atop the Kunstmuseum (p199). Lunches are perky, fresh and international, while dinners feature more Asian-inspired cuisine: red Thai curry, duck cooked two ways and yellowfin tuna with bean risotto. Lunch specials are a steal at €9.95.

Délice   GASTRONOMY €€€
(☑0711-640 3222; www.restaurant-delice.de; Hauptstätter Strasse 61; 5-course tasting menu €109; ☺7pm-midnight Mon-Fri; Ⓤ Österreichischer Platz) Natural, integral flavours sing in specialities such as red shrimp with tomato, wild herbs and sesame, and saddle of lamb with fennel, avocado and Roman-style dumplings at this incredibly intimate, barrel-vaulted Michelin-starred restaurant. It's the combined vision of chef Andreas Hettinger and passionate sommelier Evangelos Pattas, who will talk you through the award-winning Riesling selection.

🍸 Drinking & Nightlife

★**Schwarz Weiss Bar**   COCKTAIL BAR
(www.schwarz-weiss-bar.de; Wilhelmstrasse 8a; ☺7pm-3am Sun-Thu, to 5am Fri & Sat; Ⓤ Österreichischer Platz) Jazz creates a mellow mood at this slinky little cocktail bar, with barrel-vaulted ceilings, stone walls and dim lighting. The mixologists seem to put a pinch of magic into the succinct, everchanging list of cocktails – from 'The Maker' (bourbon, elderberry, Madeira, ginger, bergamot and bitters) to 'Naschi-Äffle' (Monkey 47 gin with pear juice, lavender, honey and ginger).

★**Kraftpaule**   MICROBREWERY
(www.kraftpaule.de; Nikolausstrasse 2; ☺4-10pm Tue-Fri, 11am-10pm Sat; Ⓤ Stöckach) Competition is stiff but for our money this might just be Stuttgart's coolest new-wave craft microbrewery and bar. The bartenders really know their stuff, the selection of beers – from IPAs to stouts, single hop brews and wheat beers – is *wunderbar,* and the vibe easygoing in the bare-wood-tabled and terracotta-tiled interior. Check the website for details on tastings.

Misch Misch   COFFEE
(www.misch-misch.de; Tübinger Strasse 95; ☺8am-6pm Mon-Thu, 8am-7pm Fri, 10am-7pm Sat; Ⓤ Marienplatz) If you're serious about your beans, this new retro-flavoured cafe just south of the centre is surely a little slice of heaven. As tiny and well loved as your own living room, here you can sip a mighty fine espresso, mocha or cold brew – and perhaps nibble on delicious carrot cake. If you like the house blend, you can buy the beans to take home.

Sky Beach   BAR
(www.skybeach.de; Königstrasse 6, top fl Galeria Kaufhof; ☺noon-12.30am Mon-Sat, 1-11.30pm Sun Apr-Sep; Ⓤ Hauptbahnhof) When the sun comes out, Stuttgarters live it up at this urban beach, complete with sand, cabana beds, DJs spinning mellow lounge beats and grandstand city views. It's on the top floor of the department store Galeria Kaufhof.

Wagenhallen   CLUB
(www.wagenhallen.de; Innerer Nordbahnhof 1; Ⓤ Wagenhallen Nordbahnhof) Swim away from the mainstream at this postindustrial space 2km north of the centre, where club nights, gigs and workshops skip from Balkan-beat parties to poetry slams. There's a relaxed

beer garden for summertime quaffing. Undergoing renovation at the time of writing, the Wagenhallen reopened in late 2018.

Biergarten im Schlossgarten   BEER GARDEN
(www.biergarten-schlossgarten.de; Am Schlossgarten 18; ☺10.30am-1am May-Oct; 🔊; Ⓤ Hauptbahnhof) Toast to summer with beer and pretzels at Stuttgart's best-loved, 2000-seat beer garden in the green heart of the Schlossgarten (p199). Regular live music on Sundays gets steins a-swinging.

Palast der Republik   BEER GARDEN
(☑0711-226   4887;   www.facebook.com/Palast Stuttgart; Friedrichstrasse 27; ☺11am-2am Mon-Thu, 11am-3am Fri & Sat, 3pm-2am Sun; Ⓤ Börsenplatz) Once a public toilet, this not-so-very-palatial kiosk-bar now offers a very different kind of piss-up. Everyone from students to bankers has a soft spot for *the* local hot spot for chilling under the trees and meeting friends, cold beer in hand.

Ciba Mato   LOUNGE
(Wilhelmsplatz 11; ☺5pm-1am Sun-Thu, to 3am Fri & Sat; Ⓤ Österreichischer Platz) There's more than a hint of Buddha Bar about this scarlet-walled, Asia-infused space. It's a slinky spot to sip a gingertini or pisco punch, or to hang out Bedouin-style in the *shisha* tent and nibble on fusion food. The terrace deck is a summertime magnet.

Paul & George   COCKTAIL BAR
(www.paulandgeorge.de; Weberstrasse 3; ☺6pm-1.30am; Ⓤ Rathaus) Housed in a building dating to 1889 and exuding its very own brand of old-school glamour and boho flair, Paul & George is named after the architects of this one-time tavern on Weberstrasse. With Thonet-style Bentwood chairs, bare brick walls and bow-tied waiters, it's an intimate spot for a craft gin, beer or highball.

Ribingurūmu   BAR
(Theodor-Heuss-Strasse 4; ☺3pm-2am Mon-Thu, to 3am Fri & Sat, to midnight Sun; Ⓤ Börsenplatz) A chilled-out crowd hangs out over jam-jar cocktails in Ribingurūmu, which exudes an 'old-skool' vibe with its vintage furnishings.

☆ Entertainment

For the low-down on events, grab a copy of German-language monthly *Lift Stuttgart* (www.lift-online.de) from the tourist office (p208) or news kiosks, or listings magazine *Prinz* (www.prinz.de/stuttgart). Events tickets can be purchased at the tourist office.

Liederhalle   CONCERT VENUE
(☑0711-202   7710;   www.liederhalle-stuttgart.de; Berliner Platz 1; Ⓤ Berliner Platz) Jimi Hendrix and Sting are among the stars who have performed at this culture and congress centre. The 1950s venue stages big-name classical and pop concerts, cabaret and comedy.

Staatstheater   PERFORMING ARTS
(☑0711-202   090;   www.staatstheater-stuttgart.de; Oberer Schlossgarten 6; Ⓤ Schlossplatz) Stuttgart's grandest theatre presents a top-drawer program of ballet, opera, theatre and classical music.

Kiste   JAZZ
(☑0711-1603 4970; www.kiste-stuttgart.de; Hauptstätter Strasse 35; ☺6pm-2am Mon-Thu, 7pm-3am Fri & Sat; Ⓤ Rathaus) Jam-packed at weekends, this hole-in-the-wall bar is Stuttgart's leading jazz venue, with nightly concerts starting at 9pm or 10pm.

Bix Jazzclub   LIVE MUSIC
(☑0711-2384 0997; www.bix-stuttgart.de; Leonhardsplatz 28; ☺7pm-1am Tue-Thu, to 2am Fri & Sat; Ⓤ Rathaus) Suave chocolate-gold tones and soft lighting set the scene for first-rate jazz acts at Bix, swinging from big bands to soul and blues.

Theaterhaus   THEATRE
(☑0711-402 0720; www.theaterhaus.com; Siemensstrasse 11; Ⓤ Maybachstrasse) This dynamic theatre stages live rock, jazz and other music genres, as well as theatre and comedy performances.

🛍 Shopping

Mooch around plane-tree-lined Königstrasse, Germany's longest shopping mile, or Königsbau Passagen on Schlossplatz (p199) and the Dorotheen Quartier for high-street brands, design and department stores. Calwer Strasse channels boutique shopping, Stifftstrasse designer labels. The casual Bohnenviertel (p205) is the go-to quarter for antiques, art galleries, vintage garb and Stuttgart-made crafts and jewellery.

Dorotheen Quartier   MALL
(www.dorotheen-quartier.de; Holzstrasse; ☺10am-8pm Mon-Fri, 9.30am-8pm Sat; Ⓤ Rathaus) A good one for rainy-day shopping, this architecturally striking new mall houses a host of design, high-street and fashion stores such as Diesel, American Vintage, Gant, MaxMara and BoConcept, as well as cafes, a bakery and a sushi bar and grill.

STUTTGART & THE BLACK FOREST STUTTGART

🛈 DISCOUNT CARD

Get a **StuttCard** (24/48/72 hours without VVS – public transport – ticket €15/20/25, with VVS ticket €25/35/45) for free entry to most museums, plus discounts on events, activities and guided tours. Sold at the tourist office and some hotels.

Feinkost Böhm   FOOD & DRINKS
(www.feinkost-boehm.de; Kronprinzstrasse 6; ⊘10am-8pm Mon-Thu, 9am-8pm Fri & Sat; Ⓤ Schlossplatz) Böhm is a foodie one-stop shop with regional wine, beer, chocolate and preserves, and an appetising deli.

Königsbau Passagen   SHOPPING CENTRE
(Königstrasse 26; ⊘10am-8pm Mon-Sat; Ⓤ Schlossplatz) Overlooking Schlossplatz (p199) is the classical, colonnaded Königsbau, reborn as an upmarket shopping mall, the Königsbau Passagen.

🛈 Information

Airport Tourist Office (☑ 0711-222 8100; Stuttgart Airport; ⊘8am-7pm Mon-Fri, 9am-1pm & 1.45-4.30pm Sat, 10am-1pm & 1.45-5.30pm Sun) The tourist office branch at Stuttgart Airport is situated in Terminal 3, Level 2 (Arrivals).

Post Office (Bolzstrasse 3; ⊘10am-8pm Mon-Fri, 9am-4pm Sat) Just northwest of the Schlossplatz.

Stuttgart Tourist Office (☑ 0711-222 80; www.stuttgart-tourist.de; Königstrasse 1a; ⊘9am-8pm Mon-Fri, to 6pm Sat, 10am-5pm Sun) The staff can help with room bookings (for a €3 fee) and public transport enquiries. Also has a list of vineyards open for tastings.

🛈 Getting There & Away

AIR

Stuttgart Airport (SGT; ☑ 0711-9480; www.stuttgart-airport.com), a major hub for Eurowings, is 13km south of the city. There are four terminals, all within easy walking distance of each other.

TRAIN

Long-distance IC and ICE destinations departing from **Stuttgart Hauptbahnhof** include Berlin (€130 to €154, 5½ hours), Frankfurt (€50 to €66, 1¼ hours) and Munich (€54, 2¼ hours). There are frequent regional services to Tübingen (€15.10, 43 minutes to one hour), Schwäbisch Hall (€16.60, 70 minutes) and Ulm (€21.90 to €27, one hour).

🛈 Getting Around

TO/FROM THE AIRPORT

Very frequent S2 and S3 trains take about 30 minutes from the airport to the **Hauptbahnhof** (€4.20).

PUBLIC TRANSPORT

From slowest to fastest, Stuttgart's VVS (www.vvs.de) public transport network consists of a Zahnradbahn (rack railway), buses, the Strassenbahn (tramway), Stadtbahn lines (light-rail lines beginning with U; underground in the city centre), S-Bahn lines (suburban rail lines S1 through to S6) and RegionalBahn lines (regional trains beginning with R). On Friday and Saturday there are night buses (beginning with N) with departures from Schlossplatz at 1.11am, 2.22am and 3.33am.

For travel within the city, single tickets are €2.50 and four-ride tickets (4er-Ticket) cost €9.70 for one zone. For short hops of three stops or less, a *Kurzstrecken* ticket (€1.40) suffices. A day pass, good for two zones (including, for instance, the Mercedes-Benz and Porsche Museums), is better value at €7 for one person and €12.30 for a group of between two and five.

LUDWIGSBURG

☑ 07141 / POP 92,973
This neat, cultured town was the childhood home of the dramatist Friedrich Schiller. Duke Eberhard Ludwig put it on the global map in the 18th century by erecting a chateau to out-pomp them all – the sublime, Versailles-inspired Residenzschloss. With its whimsical palaces and gardens, Ludwigsburg is baroque in overdrive and a flashback to when princes wore powdered wigs and lords went a-hunting.

⊙ Sights & Activities

★ **Residenzschloss**   PALACE
(☑ 07141-186400; www.schloss-ludwigsburg.de; Schlossstrasse 30; tour adult/concession €7/3.50, museums incl audioguide €3.50/1.80; ⊘10am-5pm daily mid-Mar–mid-Nov, 10am-5pm Tue-Sun mid-Nov–mid-Mar) Nicknamed the 'Swabian Versailles', the Residenzschloss is an extravagant 452-room baroque, rococo and Empire affair. The 90-minute chateau tours (in German) leave every half-hour; there are English tours at 1.15pm and 3.15pm daily.

The 18th-century feast continues with a spin around the staggeringly ornate scarlet-and-gold Karl Eugen Apartment, and three museums showcasing everything from exquisite baroque paintings to fashion accessories and majolica.

The Residenzschloss, on Schlossstrasse (the B27), lies 400m northeast of the central Marktplatz.

Blühendes Barock
GARDENS

(www.blueba.de; Mömpelgardstrasse 28; adult/concession €9/4.50; ☉ 7.30am-8.30pm, closed early Nov–mid-Mar) Appealing in summer is a fragrant stroll amid the herbs, rhododendrons and gushing fountains of the Blühendes Barock gardens. Admission includes entry to the Märchengarten.

Marktplatz
SQUARE

Dominated by a twin-spired, powderpuff-pink church and rimmed by arcaded houses, Ludwigsburg's striking market square was laid out in the 18th century in the baroque style by the Italian architect of the age, Donato Giuseppe Frisoni.

Schloss Favorite
PALACE

(www.schloss-favorite-ludwigsburg.de; Favoritepark 1) Sitting in parkland a five-minute walk north of the Residenzschloss is the petite baroque palace Schloss Favorite, built between 1717 and 1723 for Duke Eberhard Ludwig. It was mostly used as a hunting palace and summer residence. The interior of the palace is largely neoclassical in style and graced with Empire-style furniture.

The palace was undergoing extensive restoration at the time of writing and is set to reopen in mid 2019.

Märchengarten
AMUSEMENT PARK

(☑ 07414-910 2252; Mömpelgardstrasse 28; adult/concession €9/4.50; ☉ 9am-6pm, closed early Nov–mid-Mar) Kids drag their parents to this fairy-tale theme park to visit the witch with a Swabian cackle at the gingerbread house and admire themselves in Snow White's magic mirror. Should you want Rapunzel to let down her hair, get practising: *Rapunzel, lass deinen Zopf herunter.* (The gold-tressed diva only understands well-pronounced German!) Admission includes entry to the Blühendes Barock.

 Eating & Drinking

Alte Sonne
ALSATIAN €€

(☑ 07141-643 6480; http://alte-sonne.de; Bei der Katholischen Kirche 3; mains €17-30; ☉ noon-2.30pm & 6-10.30pm Wed-Sun; ☑) The most refined address in Ludwigsburg is the Alte Sonne, where the menu plays up regional, seasonal ingredients in attractively presented dishes that are a nod to the chef's native Alsace, be it leek and Riesling soup, cod in a speck crust with orange, celery, walnuts and smoked trout ravioli, or blueberry sorbet laced with Alsatian Muscat wine.

Ludwigsburger Brauhaus
BEER GARDEN

(www.brauhaus-ludwigsburg.de; Bahnhofstrasse 17; ☉ 11am-11pm) On Solitudeplatz, this brewpub serves home brews (by the glass, litre or metre) in cosy, wood-panelled surrounds in winter and in its popular beer garden in summer.

❶ Information

Ludwigsburg Tourist Office (☑ 07141-910 2252; www.mik-ludwigsburg.de; Eberhardtstrasse 1; ☉ 10am-6pm) Ludwigsburg's tourist office has excellent material in English on lodgings, festivals and events such as the baroque Christmas market.

❶ Getting There & Around

S-Bahn trains (local trains operating within a city and its suburban area) from Stuttgart serve the Hauptbahnhof, 750m southwest of the centre.

Stuttgart's S4 and S5 S-Bahn lines go directly to Ludwigsburg's Hauptbahnhof (€3.97, 10 minutes), 750m southeast of the centre. There are frequent links to the Residenzschloss on buses 421, 425 and 427. On foot, the chateau is 1km from the train station.

SWABIAN ALPS REGION

Often eclipsed by the Black Forest to the west and the Bavarian Alps to the southeast, the Swabian Alps (*Schwäbische Alb* in German) are wholly deserving of more attention. Ulm, where the Danube swiftly flows, forms the boundary in the south, while the Neckar runs past half-timbered towns, limestone crags, beech woods, juniper-cloaked heaths, hilltop ducal castles and robber-knight ruins further north.

The region is a geologist's dream – 200 million years ago it had more volcanoes than almost anywhere else on earth; today it holds Unesco World Heritage Geopark status. The karst landscape is riddled with caves, where rare fossils and ice age art (including the 30,000-year-old *Löwenmensch* on display in Museum Ulm; p215) have been discovered.

In 2017, the Swabian Jura Caves and ice age art received Unesco World Heritage status for having some of the world's oldest figurative art, dating from 43,000 to 33,000 years ago.

Tübingen

📞 07071 / POP 87,464

Liberal students and deeply traditional *Burschenschaften* (fraternities) singing ditties for beloved Germania, ecowarriors, artists and punks – all have a soft spot for this bewitchingly pretty Swabian city, where cobbled lanes lined with half-timbered townhouses twist up to a turreted castle. It was here that Joseph Ratzinger, now Pope Benedict XVI, lectured on theology in the late 1960s; that Friedrich Hölderlin studied stanzas, Johannes Kepler planetary motions, and Goethe the bottom of a beer glass.

The finest days unfold slowly in Tübingen: lingering in Altstadt cafes, punting on the plane-tree-lined Neckar River and pretending, as the students so diligently do, to work your brain cells in a chestnut-shaded beer garden.

◉ Sights & Activities

★ **Schloss Hohentübingen** CASTLE

(📞07071-297 7579; www.unimuseum.uni-tue bingen.de; Burgsteige 11; guided tour of wine cellar adult/concession €5/3; ◷10am-6pm Wed-Sun May-Sep, to 5pm Oct-Apr) FREE On its perch above Tübingen, this turreted 16th-century castle has a terrace overlooking the Neckar River, the Altstadt's triangular rooftops and the vine-streaked hills beyond. An ornate Renaissance gate leads to the courtyard and the laboratory where Friedrich Miescher discovered DNA in 1869.

Besides a clutch of museums, the finest of which is the **Museum Alte Kulturen** (adult/concession €5/3; ◷10am-5pm Wed, Fri-Sun, to 7pm Thu), the castle's highlights include the immense, 84,000-litre *Grosse Fass* wine vat – one of the world's oldest, dating to 1564 – which can only be visited on guided tours at 2pm, 3pm, 4pm and 5pm (book ahead online).

Am Markt SQUARE

Half-timbered townhouses frame the Altstadt's main plaza Am Markt, a much-loved student hang-out. Rising above it is the 15th-century Rathaus (town hall), which is opposite the Neptunbrunnen. Keep an eye out for No 15, where a white window frame identifies a secret room where Jews hid in WWII.

Kloster Bebenhausen MONASTERY

(www.kloster-bebenhausen.de; adult/concession €5/2.50, incl guided tour €7/3.50, audioguide €2; ◷9am-6pm Apr-Oct, 10am-noon & 1-5pm Tue-Sun Nov-Mar, guided tours 2pm & 3pm Sat & Sun Apr-

Oct) Founded in 1183 by Rudolph I, Count Palatine of Tübingen, Kloster Bebenhausen is one of southern Germany's finest medieval Cistercian monasteries. Beautifully situated on the wooded fringes of Naturpark Schönbuch, it became a royal hunting retreat post-Reformation. A visit takes in the intricately frescoed summer refectory, the Gothic abbey church and intricate star vaulting and half-timbered facades in the cloister. The monastery interior can only be visited by guided tour.

Bebenhausen is 7km north of Tübingen via the L1208. Buses run at least twice hourly (€2.30, 15 minutes).

Rathaus LANDMARK

(Am Markt 1) Drawing the gaze high above Am Markt, Tübingen's 15th-century Rathaus sports a riotous, exuberantly frescoed baroque facade and an astronomical clock.

Stiftskirche St Georg CHURCH

(Am Holzmarkt; ◷9am-4pm) FREE The late-Gothic Stiftskirche shelters the tombs of the Württemberg dukes and some dazzling late-medieval stained-glass windows.

Cottahaus LANDMARK

(Münzgasse 15) The Cottahaus is the one-time home of Johann Friedrich Cotta, who first published the works of Schiller and Goethe. A bit of a lad, Goethe conducted detailed research on Tübingen's pubs during his weeklong stay in 1797. The party-loving genius is commemorated by the plaque '*Hier wohnte Goethe*' (Goethe lived here). On the wall of the grungy student digs next door is perhaps the more insightful sign '*Hier kotzte Goethe*' (Goethe puked here).

Kunsthalle GALLERY

(📞07071-969 10; www.kunsthalle-tuebingen. de; Philosophenweg 76; adult/concession €7/5; ◷11am-7pm Tue, to 6pm Wed-Sun) The streamlined Kunsthalle stages first-rate exhibitions of mostly contemporary art; in recent times, everything from Post-Minimalist art to hyper realistic sculpture has been thrown into the spotlight. Buses 5, 13 and 17 run from central Tübingen to the Kunsthalle stop.

Hölderlinturm MUSEUM

(Bursagasse 6) You can see how the dreamy Neckar views from this silver-turreted tower fired the imagination of Romantic poet Friedrich Hölderlin, resident here from 1807 to 1843. It now contains a museum tracing his life and work. Due to extensive renovation work, the museum is closed until late 2019.

NATURPARK SCHÖNBUCH

For back-to-nature hiking and cycling, make for this 156-sq-km, lushly forested **nature reserve** (www.naturpark-schoenbuch.de; Kloster Bebenhausen; ⊙ information centre 9am-5pm Tue-Fri, 10am-5pm Sat & Sun). It's interwoven with 560km of marked trails. With a bit of luck and a pair of binoculars, you might catch a glimpse of black woodpeckers and yellow-bellied toads. The nature reserve's beech and oak woods fringe the village of Bebenhausen and its well-preserved Cistercian abbey (p210).

Bebenhausen, 7km north of Tübingen via the L1208, is the gateway to Naturpark Schönbuch. Buses run at least twice hourly (€2.30, 15 minutes).

Wurmlinger Kapelle — WALKING

(⊙ chapel 10am-4pm May-Oct) A great hike is the *Kreuzweg* (way of the cross) to the 17th-century Wurmlinger Kapelle, perched atop a 475m hill, about 6km southwest of Tübingen. A footpath loops up through well-tended vineyards to the whitewashed pilgrimage chapel, from where there are long views across the Ammer and Neckar valleys. The tourist office (p212) has leaflets (€1).

⭐ Festivals & Events

Stocherkahnrennen — SPORTS

(http://stocherkahnrennen.germania-strassburg.de; ⊙ late May) Students in fancy dress do battle on the Neckar at May's hilarious Stocherkahnrennen punt race, where jostling, dunking and even snapping your rival's oar are permitted. The first team to reach the Neckarbrücke wins the race, the title and as much beer as they can sink. The losers have to down half a litre of cod liver oil. Arrive in good time to snag a prime spot on **Platanenallee**.

🛏 Sleeping

Hotel am Schloss — HISTORIC HOTEL €€

(📞 07071-929 40; www.hotelamschloss.de; Burgsteige 18; s €99, d €128-148, tr/q €225/290; 🅿 🛜) So close to the castle you can almost touch it, this flower-bedecked hotel has dapper rooms ensconced in a 16th-century building. The hotel's cosy Mauganeschtle restaurant excels in hearty Swabian grub.

Hotel Krone — HOTEL €€

(📞 07071-133 10; www.krone-tuebingen.de; Uhlandstrasse 1; s €109, d €139-169, ste €189-239, f €204-229; 🛜) Occupying a late-9th-century house right in the heart of Tübingen, this four-star hotel has been given a contemporary facelift, but some original features remain, such as the stained-glass windows in the open fire-warmed lobby. Muted colours and clean lines define the spacious rooms, and

the plush top-floor spa has a sauna, infrared cabins and a roof terrace.

Hotel La Casa — HOTEL €€€

(📞 07071-946 66; www.lacasa-tuebingen.de; Hechinger Strasse 59; s €186-205, d €215-289, ste €269-400; 🛜 🛋) Tübingen's swishest hotel is a 15-minute stroll south of the Altstadt. Contemporary rooms designed with panache come with welcome tea, coffee and soft drinks. Breakfast is a smorgasbord of mostly organic goodies. The crowning glory is the top-floor spa with tremendous city views.

🍴 Eating

Kornblume — VEGETARIAN €

(📞 07071-920 9317; Haaggasse 15; snacks & light meals €3-8; ⊙ 8.30am-6pm Mon-Fri, to 3pm Sat; 🍴) Vegetarians and health-conscious locals squeeze into this hobbit-like cafe for wholesome soups, freshly squeezed juice, organic salads by the scoopful and day specials such as rye pancakes with vegetables, and sweet potato-chard curry.

Meze Akademie — MEZE €€

(📞 07071-938 7746; http://mezeakademie.com; Hechinger Strasse 67; meze €7.50-18; ⊙ noon-2.30pm & 5.30-11pm Mon-Fri, noon-2.30pm & 3.30-11pm Sat) Creative riffs on Greek meze (small dishes to share) take centre stage at this slick restaurant, with an open-plan design and bistro-style seating at bare wood tables. The menu seesaws with the seasons, so expect anything from wild boar sausage with caramelised onion and poached egg to more classic *dolmadakia* (stuffed vine leaves) and baked feta with tomato marmalade.

Mauganeschtle — GERMAN €€

(📞 07071-929 40; www.hotelamschloss.de; Burgsteige 18, Hotel am Schloss; mains €12-26.50; ⊙ noon-2.30pm & 6pm-midnight) It's a stiff climb up to this restaurant at Hotel am Schloss, but worth every step. Suspended above the rooftops of Tübingen, the terrace

MESSING ABOUT ON THE RIVER

There's nothing like a languid paddle along the sun-dappled Neckar River in summer. Hire a row boat, canoe, pedalo or punt at **Bootsvermietung Märkle** (Eberhardsbrücke 1; ⊘11am-6pm Apr-early Oct, to 9pm Jul & Aug), or sign up at the tourist office for **punting** (adult/child €7/5; ⊘1pm daily, plus 5pm Sat May-Sep) around the Neckarinsel. The summer's most hilarious fest is the Stocherkahn-rennen (p211) punt race, where students in fancy dress paddle hell for leather to be the first to the bridge.

is a scenic spot for the house speciality, *Maultaschen* (pasta pockets), with fillings such as lamb, trout, porcini and veal.

Neckarmüller   PUB FOOD €€
(⌧07071-278 48; www.neckarmueller.de; Garten-strasse 4; mains €7.50-15; ⊘10am-1am Mon-Sat, to 11.45pm Sun) Overlooking the Neckar, this cavernous microbrewery is a summertime magnet for its chestnut-shaded beer garden. Come for home brews by the metre and beer-laced dishes from (tasty) Swabian roast to (interesting) tripe stew. Day specials go for €6.50.

🍷 Drinking & Nightlife

Weinhaus Beck   BAR
(www.weinhaus-beck.de; Am Markt 1; ⊘8am-11pm) There's rarely an empty table at this wine shop and tavern beside the Rathaus (p210). It's a convivial place to enjoy regional and international wines (choose from 600 different varieties) or coffee and cake.

Kuckuck   BAR
(www.kuckuck-bar.de; Fichtenweg 5; ⊘8pm-2am Mon-Thu, to 5pm Fri & Sat, to 1am Sun) 'Cuckoo' is the name of this upbeat, student-driven bar and club, with plenty of good vibes and a young, fun crowd. The drinks are insanely cheap – €1.50 for a beer and €3 for a cocktail. It's a 3km trek north of town so hop in a taxi if you don't fancy the walk.

Bartista   COCKTAIL BAR
(www.bartista.de; Kirchgasse 19; ⊘6pm-1am Mon-Thu, to 3am Fri & Sat, 8pm-1am Sun) A pinch of 1920s flair goes a long way at this stylish little bar with red walls, candelabra and cosy armchairs for conversing. Cocktails are what it's all about here, such as the house special Tübingen Gardens – a zesty blend of lemon juice, elderflower syrup, lavender-infused gin and soda.

Schwärzlocher Hof   BEER GARDEN
(www.hofgut-schwaerzloch.de;Schwärzloch1; ⊘11am-10pm Wed-Sun) Scenically perched above the Ammer Valley, a 2km trudge west of town, this farmhouse is famous for its beer garden and home-pressed *Most* (cider).

Storchen   CAFE
(Ammergasse 3; ⊘3pm-1am Mon-Thu & Sun, to 2am Fri, 11am-2am Sat) Mind your head climbing the stairs to this easygoing student hangout, serving enormous mugs of milky coffee and cheap local brews under wooden beams.

ℹ Information

Post Office (Beim Nonnenhaus 14; ⊘9am-7pm Mon-Fri, to 6pm Sat) In the Altstadt.
Tübingen Tourist Office (⌧07071-913 60; www.tuebingen-info.de; An der Neckarbrücke 1; ⊘9am-7pm Mon-Fri, 10am-4pm Sat, plus 11am-4pm Sun May-Sep)

ℹ Getting There & Away

Tübingen is an easy train ride from Stuttgart (€15.10, one hour, at least two per hour) and Ulm (€26.50 to €37, two hours, roughly twice hourly). Trains depart from the **Hauptbahnhof**, 500m south of the Altstadt on the opposite side of the Neckar River.

Burg Hohenzollern

Rising dramatically from an exposed crag, with its medieval battlements and riot of towers and silver turrets often veiled in mist, Burg Hohenzollern (www.burg-hohenzollern. com; tour adult/concession €12/8, grounds admission without tour adult/concession €7/5; ⊘tours 10am-5.30pm mid-Mar–Oct, to 4.30pm Nov–mid-Mar) is darned impressive from a distance, but up close it looks more contrived. Dating to 1867, this neo-Gothic castle is the ancestral seat of the Hohenzollern family, the first and last monarchical rulers of the short-lived second German Empire (1871–1918).

History buffs should take a 35-minute German-language tour, which takes in towers, overblown salons replete with stained glass and frescos, and the dazzling *Schatz-kammer* (treasury). The grounds command tremendous views over the Swabian Alps.

Frequent trains link Tübingen, 28km distant, with Hechingen, about 4km northwest of the castle.

Schwäbisch Hall

📞 0791 / POP 38,827

Out on its rural lonesome near the Bavarian border, Schwäbisch Hall is an unsung gem. This medieval time capsule of higgledy-piggledy lanes, soaring half-timbered houses built high on the riches of salt, and covered bridges that criss-cross the Kocher River is story-book stuff.

Buzzy cafes and first-rate museums add to the appeal of this town, known for its rare black-spotted pigs and the jangling piggy banks of its nationwide building society.

◉ Sights

★ Kunsthalle Würth   GALLERY

(www.kunstwuerth.com; Lange Strasse 35; ⊙ 10am-6pm daily, guided tours 11.30am & 2pm Sun) FREE The brainchild of industrialist Reinhold Würth, this contemporary gallery is housed in a striking limestone building that preserves part of a century-old brewery. Stellar temporary exhibitions have recently spotlighted hidden treasures from the Academy of Fine Arts in Vienna including masterpieces by Dürer, Botticelli, Rembrandt, Rubens, Klimt and Hundertwasser. Guided tours (in German) and audioguides cost €6.

Am Markt   SQUARE

On Am Markt square, your gaze is drawn to the ornate Rathaus (Town Hall) and to the terracotta-hued Widmanhaus at No 4, a remnant of a 13th-century Franciscan monastery. It's also presided over by the late-Gothic Kirche St Michael (⊙ noon-5pm Mon, 10am-5pm Tue-Sat, 11.30am-5pm Sun) FREE and Gotischer Fischbrunnen.

Neubau   LANDMARK

Towering above Pfarrgasse is the steep-roofed, 16th-century Neubau, built as an arsenal and granary and now used as a theatre. Ascend the stone staircase for dreamy views over red-roofed houses to the former city fortifications, the covered Roter Steg bridge and the Henkerbrücke (Hangman's Bridge).

Hohenloher Freilandmuseum   MUSEUM

(📞 0791-971 010; www.wackershofen.de; Wackershofen; adult/concession €8/6; ⊙ 9am-6pm May-Sep, 10am-5pm Tue-Sun rest of year) One

place you can be guaranteed of seeing a black-spotted pig is this open-air farming museum, a sure-fire hit with the kids with its traditional farmhouses, orchards and animals. It's 6km northwest of Schwäbisch Hall and served by bus 7.

Hällisch-Fränkisches Museum   MUSEUM

(📞 0791-751 360; Keckenhof 6; ⊙ 10am-5pm Tue-Sun) FREE This well-curated museum traces Schwäbisch Hall's history with a collection of shooting targets, Roman figurines and rarities including an exquisite hand-painted wooden synagogue interior from 1738 and a 19th-century mouse guillotine.

🛏 Sleeping & Eating

★ Hotel Scholl   HOTEL €€

(📞 0791-975 50; www.hotel-scholl.de; Klosterstrasse 2-4; d €89-149; 🛜) A charming pick behind Am Markt, this family-run hotel has rustic-chic rooms with parquet floors and granite or marble bathrooms. Most striking of all is the attic penthouse with its beams, free-standing shower and far-reaching views over town. Breakfast is a fine spread of cold cuts, fruit and cereals.

Der Adelshof   HISTORIC HOTEL €€

(📞 0791-758 90; www.hotel-adelshof.de; Am Markt 12; s €95-100, d €125-225; 🅿🛜) This centuries-old pad is as posh as it gets in Schwäbisch Hall, with a wellness area and plush quarters, from the red-walled romance of the Chambre Rouge to the four-poster Turmzimmer. Its beamed Ratskeller restaurant (mains €18 to €27) knocks up spot-on local specialities such as saddle of veal with mushrooms, and pork tenderloin with lentils and Spätzle (egg noodles).

Entenbäck   BISTRO €€

(📞 0791-9782 9182; Steinerner Steg 1; mains €12-32; ⊙ 5-11pm Tue, 11am-2.30pm & 5-11pm Wed-Sat; 🚸) This inviting bistro receives high praise for its Swabian-meets-Mediterranean menu, from cream of Riesling soup to duck-filled Maultaschen (pasta pockets) and roast beef with onions and Spätzle. There's also a succinct vegetarian menu.

Schwein & Weinbar   GERMAN €€

(📞 0791-931 230; www.rebers-pflug.de; Weckriedener Strasse 2; €9.50-24.50; ⊙ 6.30-9pm Mon & Tue, noon-2pm & 6-9pm Wed-Sat) A relaxed and more reasonably priced alternative to the Michelin-starred finery of Rebers Pflug, this chic wine-bar/bistro under the same roof has a highly decent selection of light meals – all expertly prepared – from dry-aged beef burgers to *Gaisburger Marsch* (Swabian beef stew). There are some excellent regional wines represented.

Brauerei-Ausschank
Zum Löwen PUB FOOD €€
(☑ 0791-204 1622; Mauerstrasse 17; mains €10-17; ☺ 11.30am-2pm & 5.30-11pm Fri-Tue) Down by the river, this brewpub attracts a jovial bunch of locals who come for freshly tapped Haller Löwenbrauerei brews and hearty nosh such as Swabian *Maultaschen* (pasta pockets) topped with a fried egg, and pork cooked in beer-cumin sauce.

★**Rebers Pflug** INTERNATIONAL €€€
(☑ 0791-931 230; www.rebers-pflug.de; Weckrieden-er Strasse 2; mains €18.50-42, 3- to 7-course menu €65-115; ☺ 6.30-9pm Mon & Tue, noon-2pm & 6-9pm Wed-Sat; ☑) Hans-Harald Reber presides over the stove at this 19th-century country house, one of Schwäbisch Hall's Michelin-starred haunts. He puts an imaginative spin on seasonal, regional numbers such as local venison with chanterelles and parsley root *Spätzle* (egg noodles), and suckling pig cooked two ways with plum jus and sweet-potato cream. Vegetarians are also well catered for.

ℹ Information

Schwäbisch Hall Tourist Office (☑ 0791-751 246; www.schwaebischhall.de; Am Markt 9; ☺ 9am-6pm Mon-Fri, 10am-3pm Sat & Sun May-Sep, 9am-5pm Mon-Fri Oct-Apr) On the Altstadt's main square.

ℹ Getting There & Away

There are two train stations here. Trains from Stuttgart (€16.60, one hour, hourly) arrive at **Hessental**, on the right bank about 7km south of the centre and linked to the Altstadt by bus 1. Trains from Heilbronn go to the left-bank **Bahnhof Schwäbisch Hall**, a short walk along Bahnhofstrasse from the centre.

Ulm
☑ 0731 / POP 122,636
Starting with the statistics: Ulm has the crookedest house (as listed in *Guinness World Records*) and one of the narrowest (4.5m wide), the world's oldest zoomorphic sculpture (aged 30,000 years), tallest cathedral steeple (161.5m high), and is the birthplace of the physicist, Albert Einstein.

This idiosyncratic city will win your affection with everyday encounters, particularly in summer as you pedal along the Danube and the Fischerviertel's beer gardens hum with animated chatter. One *Helles* (pale lager) too many and you may decide to impress the locals by attempting the tongue twister: 'In Ulm, um Ulm, und um Ulm herum' ('In Ulm, around Ulm and all around Ulm').

◉ Sights

★**Ulmer Münster** CATHEDRAL
(www.ulmer-muenster.de; Münsterplatz; organ concerts adult/concession €8/4, tower adult/concession €5/3.50; ☺ 9am-7pm Apr-Sep, 10am-5pm Oct-Mar) FREE 'Ooh, it's so big'... First-time visitors gush as they strain their neck muscles gazing

---

SWABIAN MENU DECODER

As the Swabian saying goes: *Was der Bauer net kennt, frisst er net* (What the farmer doesn't know, he doesn't eat) – so find out before you dig in:

Bubespitzle Officially called *Schupfnudeln,* these short, thick potato noodles – vaguely reminiscent of gnocchi – are browned in butter and tossed with sauerkraut. Sounds appetising until you discover that *Bubespitzle* means 'little boys' penises'.

Gaisburger Marsch A strong beef stew served with potatoes and *Spätzle*.

Maultaschen Giant ravioli pockets, stuffed with leftover ground pork, spinach, onions and bread mush. The dish is nicknamed *Herrgottsbeschieserle* (God trickster) because it was a sly way to eat meat during Lent.

Saure Kuddle So who is for sour tripe? If you don't have the stomach, try the potato-based, meat-free *saure Rädle* (sour wheels) instead.

Spätzle Stubby egg-based noodles. These are fried with onions and topped with cheese in the calorific treat *Käsespätzle*.

Zwiebelkuche Autumnal onion tart with bacon, cream and caraway seeds, which pairs nicely with *neuer Süsser* (new wine) or *Moschd* (cider).

up to the Münster. It is. And rather beautiful. Celebrated for its 161.5m-high steeple, this Goliath of cathedrals, the world's tallest, took 500 years to build from the first stone laid in 1377. Note the hallmarks on each stone, inscribed by cutters who were paid by the block. Those intent on cramming the Münster into one photo, filigree spire and all, should lie on the cobbles.

Only by puffing up 768 spiral steps to the tower's 143m-high viewing platform can you appreciate the Münster's dizzying height. There are terrific views of the Black Forest and, on cloud-free days, the Alps.

The Israelfenster, a stained-glass window above the west door, commemorates Jews killed during the Holocaust. The Gothic-style wooden pulpit canopy eliminates echoes during sermons. Biblical figures and historical characters such as Pythagoras embellish the 15th-century oak choir stalls. The Münster's regular organ concerts are a musical treat.

Museum Ulm   MUSEUM
(☎0731-161 4330; www.museumulm.de; Marktplatz 9; adult/concession €8/6; ⊙11am-5pm Tues, Wed, Fri-Sun, to 8pm Thu) This museum is a fascinating romp through ancient and modern art, history and archaeology. Standouts include the 20th-century Kurt Fried Collection, starring Klee, Picasso and Lichtenstein works shown in rotating exhibitions. Archaeological highlights are tiny Upper Palaeolithic figurines unearthed in caves in the Swabian Alps, including the 30,000-year-old ivory *Löwenmensch* (lion man), the world's oldest zoomorphic sculpture. There's free entry on the first Friday of the month.

Marktplatz   SQUARE
Lording it over the square, the 14th-century **Rathaus** (Town Hall; 7am-6pm Mon-Thu, to 2pm Fri) FREE sports a step-gabled, lavishly frescoed Renaissance facade. Out front is the **Fischkastenbrunnen**, where fishmongers once dumped their catch to be sold at market. The Rathaus' architectural antithesis is the cutting-edge glass pyramid of the **Stadtbibliothek**, the city's main library.

Fischerviertel   AREA
The charming Fischerviertel, Ulm's old fishers' and tanners' quarter, is slightly southwest of the centre. Beautifully restored half-timbered houses huddle along the two channels of the Blau River. Harbouring art galleries, rustic restaurants, courtyards and the crookedest house in the world – as well

as one of the narrowest – the cobbled lanes are ideal for a leisurely saunter.

Stadtmauer   AREA
South of the Fischerviertel, along the Danube's north bank, runs the red-brick Stadtmauer (city wall), the height of which was reduced in the 19th century after Napoleon decided that a heavily fortified Ulm was against his best interests. Walk it for fine views over the river, the Altstadt and the slightly off-centre **Metzgerturm** (Butcher's Tower; Unter der Metzig).

Einstein Fountain & Monument   FOUNTAIN
(Zeughausgasse 15) A nod to Ulm's most famous son, this fiendishly funny bronze fountain by Jürgen Goertz shows a wild-haired, tongue-poking-out Albert Einstein, who was born in Ulm but left when he was one year old. Standing in front of the 16th-century **Zeughaus** (Arsenal; Am Zeughaus), the rocket-snail creation is a satirical play on humanity's attempts to manipulate evolution for its own self-interest. Nearby, at Zeughaus 14, is a single stone bearing the inscription *Ein Stein* (One Stone).

Synagogue   SYNAGOGUE
(Weinhof 2) Fitting neatly into Ulm's ensemble of eye-catching contemporary architecture, this free-standing synagogue was built for the Jewish community and completed in 2012. The architecturally striking edifice sits on the Weinhof, close to the former synagogue that was destroyed during Kristallnacht in 1938. At night its main window shimmers with the Star of David pattern.

Kunsthalle Weishaupt   GALLERY
(www.kunsthalle-weishaupt.de; Hans-und-Sophie-Scholl-Platz 1; adult/concession €6/4; ⊙11am-5pm Tues, Wed, Fri-Sun, to 8pm Thu) The glass-fronted Kunsthalle Weishaupt contains the private collection of Siegfried Weishaupt, which is presented in rotating exhibitions. The accent is on modern and pop art, with bold paintings by Klein, Warhol and Haring.

Stadthaus   LANDMARK
(www.stadthaus.ulm.de; Münsterplatz 50) Designed by Richard Meier, the contemporary aesthetic of the concrete-and-glass Stadthaus is a dramatic contrast to the Münster. The American architect caused uproar by erecting the postmodern building alongside the city's Gothic giant but the result is striking. The Stadthaus stages exhibitions and events, houses the tourist office (p219) and a **cafe** (www.cafe-restaurant-stadthaus.de;

Ulm

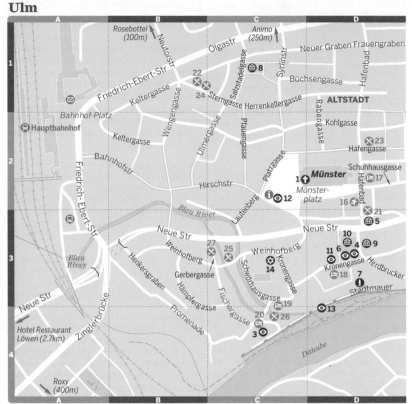

Ulm

◉ Top Sights
1 Münster C2

◉ Sights
2 Einstein Fountain & Monument F1
3 Fischerviertel C4
4 Fischkastenbrunnen D3
5 Kunsthalle Weishaupt D3
6 Marktplatz D3
7 Metzgerturm D3
8 Museum der Brotkultur C1
9 Museum Ulm D3
10 Rathaus D3
11 Stadtbibliothek D3
12 Stadthaus C2
13 Stadtmauer D4
14 Synagogue C3
15 Zeughaus F1

◉ Activities, Courses & Tours
16 Ulm Stories D2

◉ Sleeping
17 Becker's Boutique Hotel D2
18 Hotel am Rathaus & Hotel
   Reblaus D3
19 Hotel Schiefes Haus C3
20 Hotel Schmales Haus C4

◉ Eating
21 Barfüsser D3
22 Da Franco B1
23 Dean & David D2
24 Fräulein Lecker B1
25 Gerberhaus C3
26 Zunfthaus der Schiffleute C4
   Zur Forelle .... (see 20)
27 Zur Lochmühle C3

◉ Drinking & Nightlife
28 Café im Kornhauskeller E2
   Café im Stadthaus .... (see 12)
29 Naschkatze E4

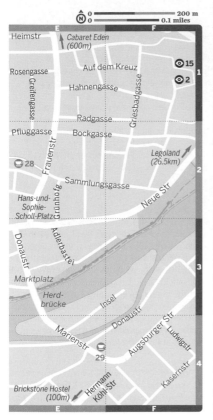

cariously close to the Münster's (p214) spires and the rooftops of the Altstadt.

Legoland
AMUSEMENT PARK

(www.legoland.de; Legoland-Allee 1, Günzburg; adult/concession €45.50/40.50; ⊙10am-6pm late Mar-early Nov) A sure-fire kid-pleaser, this pricey Lego-themed amusement park has shows, splashy rides and a miniature world built from 25 million Lego bricks. Note that it's around 20% cheaper to purchase tickets online in advance. Legoland is in Günzburg, 37km east of Ulm, just off the A8.

🛏 Sleeping

Brickstone Hostel
HOSTEL €

(☑ 0731-708 2559; www.brickstone-hostel.de; Schützenstrasse 42, Neu-Ulm; dm €19-21, s/d €32/46; 🛜) We love the homely vibe at this beautifully restored art nouveau house in Neu-Ulm. The high-ceilinged rooms are kept spotless and backpacker perks include a self-catering kitchen with free coffee and tea, plus an honesty bar, bike rental and a cosy lounge with book exchange. Bed linen costs an extra €3. Take bus 7 to Schützenstrasse from the Hauptbahnhof (p220).

⭐ Hotel Schiefes Haus
B&B €€

(☑ 0731-967 930; www.hotelschiefeshausulm.de; Schwörhausgasse 6; s €125, d €148-160; 🛜) There was a crooked man and he walked a crooked mile...presumably to the world's most crooked hotel. Fear not – this early 16th-century, half-timbered rarity is not about to topple into the Blau. Up those creaking wooden stairs, in your snug, beamed room, you won't have to buckle yourself to the bed thanks to spirit levels and specially made height adjusters.

Hotel Restaurant Löwen
HOTEL €€

(☑ 0731-388 5880; www.hotel-loewen-ulm.de; Klosterhof 41; s €91, d €126-136, ste €138; 🅿🛜) It's amazing what you can do with a former monastery and an eye for design. Exposed beams and stone add an historical edge to streamlined rooms with parquet floors. Breakfast is a hearty spread of homemade jam, eggs, freshly baked bread and cold cuts. Take tram 1 from central Ulm to Söflingen.

Hotel Schmales Haus
B&B €€

(☑ 0731-6027 2595; www.hotelschmaleshaus. de; Fischergasse 27; s/d €119/149, ste €183-229; 🅿) Measuring a mere 4.5m across, this half-timbered 'narrow house' is a one-off. The affable Heides have transformed the slender 16th-century pad into a gorgeous

⊙8am-midnight Mon-Thu, 8am-1am Fri & Sat, 9am-midnight Sun).

Museum der Brotkultur
MUSEUM

(www.museum-brotkultur.de; Salzstadelgasse 10; adult/concession €4/3; ⊙10am-5pm) How grain grows, what makes a good dough and other bread-related mysteries are unravelled at the Museum of Bread Culture. The collection celebrates bread as the staff of life over millennia and across cultures, displaying curios from mills to Egyptian corn mummies.

🏃 Activities

Ulm Stories
AMUSEMENT PARK

(www.ulmstories.de; Kramgasse 3; flight €5; ⊙10am-6pm Tue-Sat) Ever dreamt of flying? Then you're going to love Ulm Stories, a new full-body flight simulator where you can get a virtual sparrow's-eye view of the cityscape as it would have looked in 1890, darting pre-

DON'T MISS

SPOT THE SPARROW

You can't move for *Spatzen* (sparrows) in the German language. You can eat like one *(essen wie ein Spatz)* and swear like one *(schimpfen wie ein Rohrspatz)*; there are *Spatzenschleuder* (catapults), *Spätzles* (little darlings) and *Spatzenhirne* (bird brains). Nicknamed *Spatzen*, Ulm residents are, according to legend, indebted to the titchy bird for the construction of their fabulous Münster (p214).

The story goes that the half-baked builders tried in vain to shove the wooden beams for the minster sideways through the city gate. They struggled, until a sparrow fluttered past with straw for its nest. Enlightened, the builders carried the beams lengthways, completed the job and placed a bronze statue of a sparrow at the top to honour the bird.

Today there are sparrows everywhere in Ulm: on postcards, in patisseries, at football matches (team SSV Ulm are dubbed 'die Spatzen') and, above all, in the colourful sculptures dotting the Altstadt.

B&B, with exposed beams, downy bedding and wood floors in the three rooms.

Hotel am Rathaus & Hotel Reblaus   HOTEL €€

(☑0731-968 490; www.rathausulm.de; Kronengasse 10; s €78-125, d €98-140, q €149-175, s/d without bathroom €66/76; 🛜) Just paces from the Rathaus (p215), these family-run twins ooze individual charm in rooms with flourishes including stucco and Biedermeier furnishings. Light sleepers take note: the walls are thin and the street can be noisy.

Becker's Boutique Hotel   BOUTIQUE HOTEL €€€

(☑0731-3885 0250; www.beckershotel.de; Münsterplatz 24; d €149-179; 🛜) The Münster (p214) bells are your wake-up call at this supercentral new boutique hotel. There are just seven rooms, tastefully done out in crisp whites, blues and greens, with luxurious fabrics, parquet floors and walk-in rain showers. Lots of thought has gone into little details, including express app check-ins, generous made-to-order breakfasts, and toiletries hailing from a local soap factory.

✗ Eating

Fräulein Lecker   GERMAN €

(☑0731-3996 6494; https://fraeuleinlecker.de; Sterngasse 14; tasting plates €6-10, sushi set €7.90; ⊙4-11pm Mon-Thu, to midnight Fri & Sat) Almost Scandi in style with its clean-lined simplicity, this wine-store-bar-bistro lit by funky bottle lights is a great place to try (and buy) local wines with region-driven snacks – from tasting platters of cheeses and hams to *Dinnete* (a Swabian take on tarte flambée) and German sushi (substituting pearl barley for rice). As the name suggests, it's all *lecker* (yum).

Dean & David   DELI €

(☑0731-1439 3174; https://deananddavid.de; Hafengasse 3; snacks & light meals €5-13; ⊙9.30am-9pm Mon-Sat; ✍) This is a great find for vegetarians, vegans and frankly anyone looking for a healthy bite while exploring central Ulm. The slickly modern deli-cafe rustles up interesting salads (from mango prawn to vegan superfood and grilled veggie), sandwiches, curries, soups, freshly squeezed juices and green smoothies at wallet-friendly prices. Allergies are catered for.

Animo   CAFE €

(☑0731-964 2937; www.cafe-animo.de; Syrlinstrasse 17; day specials around €7; ⊙7.30am-6pm Tue-Fri, 9am-6pm Sat & Sun; ✍) Snuggled away in a *Topferei* (potter's workshop), Animo is a relaxed cafe, with homemade cakes and vegetarian specials (creative salads, pasta, risotto and the like) – all served in beautifully detailed porcelain. Also hosts regular cultural events.

★ Zur Forelle   GERMAN €€

(☑0731-639 24; www.ulmer-forelle.de; Fischergasse 25; mains €17.50-27.50; ⊙11.30am-2.30pm & 5pm-midnight Mon-Fri, 11am-midnight Sat, 11am-10pm Sun) Since 1626, this low-ceilinged tavern has been convincing wayfarers (Einstein included) of the joys of seasonal Swabian cuisine. Ablaze with flowers in summer, this wood-panelled haunt by the Blau prides itself on its namesake *Forelle* (trout), kept fresh under the bridge and served in a number of different guises alongside menu staples such as schnitzel and beef roulade.

Gerberhaus   MEDITERRANEAN €€

(☑0731-175 5771; www.gerber-haus.de; Weinhofberg 9; mains €10-29; ⊙11.30am-2.30pm & 5.30-10pm) This warm, inviting woodcutter's cottage hits the mark with its delicious mix of Swabian and Italian-inspired dishes. Plump for a river-facing table and sample clean, bright flavours such as home-smoked salmon carpaccio, or Swabian old favourites including *Kässpätzle* and *Maultaschen* (regional take on ravioli). Day specials cost as little as €7.

Zunfthaus der Schiffleute
GERMAN €€
(📱 0731-644 11; www.zunfthaus-ulm.de; Fischergasse 31; mains €10-28.50; ⏲ 11.30am-midnight; 📶) Looking proudly back on a 600-year tradition, this timber-framed restaurant sits by the river. The menu speaks of a chef who loves the region, with Swabian favourites such as *Katzagschroi* (beef, onions, egg and fried potatoes) and meaty one-pot *Schwäbisches Hochzeitssüppchen*.

Zur Lochmühle
GERMAN €€
(📱 0731-673 05; www.lochmuehle.com; Gerbergasse 6; mains €12.50-24; ⏲ 11am-midnight) The watermill has been churning the Blau since 1356 at this rustic half-timbered pile. Plant yourself in the riverside beer garden for Swabian classics such as crispy roast pork, *Schupfnudeln* (potato noodles) and brook trout with lashings of potato salad.

Barfüsser
PUB FOOD €€
(📱 0731-602 1110; Neue Strasse 87-89; mains €8-23; ⏲ 9am-1am Sun-Thu, to 2am Fri & Sat) Hearty fare such as *Käsespätzle* (cheese noodles) and pork roast soak up the prize-winning beer, microbrewed in Neu-Ulm, at this brewpub. There are also some excellent craft beers to sample. The lunch special goes for €6.90.

Da Franco
ITALIAN €€€
(📱 0731-305 85; www.da-franco.de; Neuer Graben 23; mains €23-29; ⏲ 10.30am-midnight Tue-Sun) If you fancy a break from the norm, give this little Italian place a whirl. There is a seasonal touch to authentic dishes such as swordfish with clams, and veal escalope with asparagus, all cooked and presented with style.

🍷 Drinking & Entertainment

Rosebottel
BAR
(www.rosebottel.de; Zeitblomstrasse 21; ⏲ 8pm-1am Mon-Sat) Ranked in the *Mixology Bar Guide* as one of Germany's best bars, Rosebottel time-warps you back to a more decadent age with its dark wood panelling, antique furniture and cosy, candlelit nooks. Come for the creative cocktails and impressive array of gins mixed with Rosebottel's own small-batch lemonades infused with ginger, fruits and botanicals.

Naschkatze
CAFE
(http://cafenaschkatze.de; Marienstrasse 6, Neu-Ulm; ⏲ 8am-7pm Mon-Fri, 9am-6pm Sat, 10am-6pm Sun) Naschkatze, or 'sweet-toothed', is a fitting name for this vintage-cool cafe, where Ulmers come to lap up the retro vibe, coffee and homemade cakes.

Cabaret Eden
CLUB
(http://cabareteden.de; Karlstrasse 71; ⏲ 7pm-1am Thu, 11pm-5am Fri & Sat) Once a striptease bar, Cabaret Eden has reinvented itself as an alternative club, with everything from DJs spinning hip-hop and drum 'n' bass to yoga nights where asanas (postures) are practised to electronica beats. It's close to Ulm Ost station.

Café im Kornhauskeller
CAFE
(Hafengasse 19; ⏲ 8am-midnight Mon-Sat, 9am-10pm Sun) Arty cafe with an inner courtyard for coffee, breakfast, light bites or ice cream. It's also a chilled spot for a beer or glass of wine in the evening.

Roxy
CONCERT VENUE
(📱 0731-968 620; www.roxy.ulm.de; Schillerstrasse 1) This huge cultural venue, housed in a former industrial plant 1km south of the Hauptbahnhof (p220), has a concert hall, cinema, disco, bar and special-event forum. Take tramline 1 to Ehinger Tor.

ℹ️ Information

Post Office (Bahnhofplatz 2; ⏲ 8.30am-6.30pm Mon-Fri, 9am-1pm Sat) To the left as you exit the **Hauptbahnhof** (p220).

Ulm Tourist Office (📱 0731-161 2830; www.tourismus.ulm.de; Münsterplatz 50, Stadthaus; ⏲ 9am-6pm Mon-Sat, 11am-3pm Sun Apr-Dec, 9.30am-6pm Mon-Fri, to 4pm Sat Jan-Mar) Ulm's main tourist office has plenty of info on the city and its surrounds. It can help book rooms and arrange guided tours.

ℹ️ CITY SAVER

If you're planning on ticking off most of Ulm's major sights, consider investing in a good-value **UlmCard** (1/2 days €12/18), available at the tourist office, which covers public transport in Ulm and Neu-Ulm, a free city tour or rental of the itour audioguide, entry to all museums, plus numerous other discounts on tours, attractions and restaurants.

❶ Getting There & Away

Ulm is about 90km southeast of Stuttgart and 150km west of Munich, near the intersection of the north–south A7 and the east–west A8.

Ulm is well-served by ICE and EC trains; major destinations include Stuttgart (€21.90 to €27, one hour, several hourly) and Munich (€34 to €40, 1¼ hours, several hourly).

Ulm's **bus station** (Friedrich-Ebert-Strasse) is near the **Hauptbahnhof** (Bahnhofplatz).

❶ Getting Around

Ulm's ecofriendly trams run on renewable energy. There's a **local transport information counter** (www.swu-verkehr.de; Neue Strasse 79; ⊙ 9am-6pm Mon-Fri, to 2pm Sat) in the centre of town. A single/day ticket for the bus and tram network in Ulm and Neu-Ulm costs €2.20/4.40.

Should you wish to zip around on two wheels, you can hire sturdy city bikes from the tourist office (p219) for €12 per day.

THE BLACK FOREST

As deep, dark and delicious as its famous cherry gateau, the Black Forest gets its name from its canopy of evergreens. With deeply carved valleys, thick woodlands, luscious meadows, stout timber farmhouses and wispy waterfalls, it looks freshly minted for a kids' bedtime story. Wandering on its many miles of forest trails, you half expect to bump into a wicked witch or huntsman, and might kick yourself for not bringing those breadcrumbs to retrace your tracks...

Measuring 160km from top to bottom, the Black Forest is a ludicrously lovely expanse of hills, lakes and forest, topping out at 1493m Feldberg. It reaches from the spa town of Baden-Baden to the Swiss border, and from the Rhine almost to Lake Constance. This corner of the country is made for slow touring: on foot, by bicycle or behind the wheel of a car on one of many twisty roads with sensational views.

Baden-Baden

☑ 07221 / POP 54,160

Baden-Baden's curative waters and air of old-world luxury have attracted royals, the rich and celebrities over the years – Barack Obama and Bismarck, Queen Victoria and Victoria Beckham included. This Black Forest town boasts grand colonnaded buildings and whimsically turreted art nouveau villas

spread across the hillsides and framed by forested mountains.

The bon vivant spirit of France, just across the border, is tangible in the town's open-air cafes, chic boutiques and pristine gardens fringing the Oos River. And with its temple-like thermal baths – which put the *Baden* (bathe) in Baden – and palatial casino, the allure of this grand dame of German spa towns is as timeless as it is enduring.

◉ Sights

★**Museum Frieder Burda**　　　　GALLERY
(☑ 07221-398 980; www.museum-frieder-burda.de; Lichtentaler Allee 8b; adult/concession €13/11; ⊙ 10am-6pm Tue-Sun) A Joan Miró sculpture guards the front of this architecturally innovative gallery, designed by Richard Meier. The star-studded collection of modern and contemporary art features Picasso, Gerhard Richter and Jackson Pollock originals; these are complemented by temporary exhibitions. There are free short guided tours at noon, 2pm and 4pm on Saturdays.

Casino　　　　HISTORIC BUILDING, CASINO
(☑ 07221-302 40; www.casino-baden-baden.de; Kaiserallee 1; admission €5, guided tour €7; ⊙ 2pm-2am Sun-Thu, to 3.30am Fri & Sat, guided tours 9.30-11.45am Apr-Oct, 10am-11.30am Nov-Mar) The sublime casino seeks to emulate – indeed, outdo – the gilded, chandelier-lit splendour of Versailles. Marlene Dietrich called it 'the most beautiful casino in the world'. Gents must wear a jacket and tie. If you're not much of a gambler and want to simply marvel at the opulence, hook onto a 40-minute guided tour.

Lichtentaler Allee　　　　GARDENS
This 2.3km ribbon of greenery, threading from Goetheplatz to Kloster Lichtenthal, is quite a picture: studded with fountains and sculptures and carpeted with flowers (crocuses and daffodils in spring, magnolias, roses and azaleas in summer). Shadowing the sprightly Oosbach River, its promenade and bridges are made for aimless ambling. The avenue concludes at the Kloster Lichtenthal.

Trinkhalle　　　　LANDMARK
(Pump Room; Kaiserallee 3; ⊙ 10am-5pm Mon-Sat, 2-5pm Sun) Standing proud above a manicured park, this neoclassical pump room was built in 1839 as an attractive addition to the Kurhaus (p223). The 90m-long portico is embellished with 19th-century frescos of local legends. Baden-Baden's elixir of youth, some say, is the free curative mineral water

The Black Forest

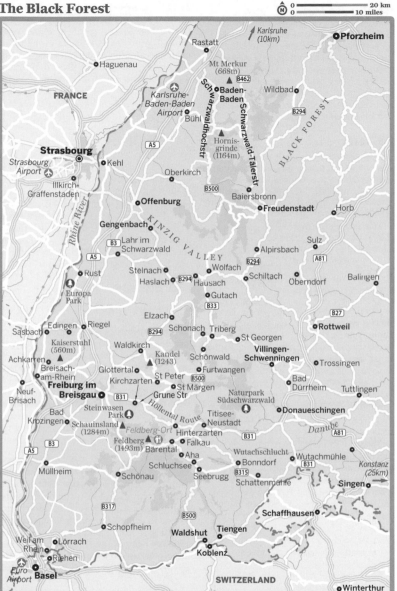

that gushes from a faucet linked to the Friedrichsbad spring.

Staatliche Kunsthalle GALLERY
(📞 07221-3007 6400; www.kunsthalle-baden-baden.
de; Lichtentaler Allee 8a; adult/concession €7/5, Fri
free; ⊙10am-6pm Tue-Sun) Sidling up to the
Museum Frieder Burda is this gallery, which
showcases rotating exhibitions of contemporary art in neoclassical surrounds. Previous
exhibitions include the works of Nigerian artist Emeka Ogboh and the experimental creations of Chinese artist Liang Shuo.

Baden-Baden

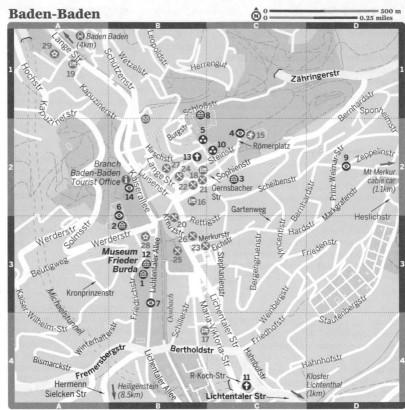

Baden-Baden

Fabergé Museum
MUSEUM

(☑07221-970 890; www.faberge-museum.de; Sophienstrasse 30; adult/concession €18/12; ☺10am-6pm) Admittedly it's not everyone's cup of tea, but if you happen to find Fabergé fascinating, you're going to love this museum devoted to its impossibly ornate imperial Easter eggs, jewellery and gem-encrusted animals made for Russian tsars in the late 19th and early 20th centuries.

Florentinerberg
RUINS

(Höllengasse) The Romans used to cool off at this hill; check out the ruins of the original baths at its foot. Nowadays, on the same site, the serene botanical gardens nurture wisteria, cypress trees, orange and lemon groves.

Paradies am Annaberg
GARDENS

(Das Paradies) These Italianate gardens are the perfect spot to unwind, with their soothing fountains and waterfalls. There are fine views of the Altstadt and wooded hills from these heights. Bus 205 to Friedrichshöhe runs nearby.

Mt Merkur
VIEWPOINT

(funicular one-way/return €2/4; ☺10am-10pm) Though modest in height, the 668m Mt Merkur commands widescreen views of Baden-Baden and the Murg Valley. It's a popular spot for paragliding, gentle hiking and family picnics. Buses 204 and 205 stop near the funicular, which has been trundling to the top since 1913.

Kurhaus
LANDMARK

(www.kurhaus-baden-baden.de; Kaiserallee 1) Corinthian columns and a frieze of mythical griffins grace the belle époque facade of the Kurhaus, which towers above well-groomed gardens. An alley of chestnut trees, flanked by two rows of boutiques, links the Kurhaus with Kaiserallee.

Stiftskirche
CHURCH

(Marktplatz; ☺8am-6pm) **FREE** The centrepiece of cobbled Marktplatz is this pink church, a hotchpotch of Romanesque, late Gothic and, to a lesser extent, baroque styles. Its foundations incorporate some ruins of the former Roman baths. Come in the early afternoon to see its stained-glass windows cast rainbow patterns across the nave.

Römische Badruinen
RUINS

(Römerplatz; adult/child €2.50/1; ☺11am-noon & 3-4pm mid-Mar–mid-Nov) The beauty-conscious Romans were the first to discover the healing properties of Baden-Baden's springs in the city

they called Aquae Aureliae. Slip back 2000 years at one of the oldest and best-preserved Roman bathing complexes in the country. Multilingual audioguides are available.

Russische Kirche
CHURCH

(Russian Church; Lichtentaler Strasse 76; admission €1; ☺10am-6pm) Beautiful, if a little incongruous, Baden-Baden's Byzantine-style 1882 Russian church is lavishly adorned with frescos and topped with a brilliantly golden onion dome.

Neues Schloss
HISTORIC BUILDING

(Schlossstrasse) Vine-swathed steps lead from Marktplatz to the 15th-century Neues Schloss, the former residence of the Baden-Baden margraves, which is set to reopen at some point in the distant future. The lookout is still accessible, and affords far-reaching views over Baden-Baden's rooftops and spires to the Black Forest beyond.

🏃 Activities

⭐ Friedrichsbad
SPA

(☑07221-275 920; www.carasana.de; Römerplatz 1; 3hr ticket €25, incl soap-&-brush massage €37; ☺9am-10pm, last admission 7pm) If it's the body of Venus and the complexion of Cleopatra you desire, abandon modesty to wallow in thermal waters at this palatial 19th-century marble-and-mosaic-festooned spa. As Mark Twain said, 'after 10 minutes you forget time; after 20 minutes, the world', as you slip into the regime of steaming, scrubbing, hot-cold bathing and dunking in the Roman-Irish bath.

Panoramaweg
HIKING

If you want to appreciate Baden-Baden and the northern Black Forest from its most photogenic angles, walk all or part of the 40km Panoramaweg, a high-level ridge trail weaving through orchards and woodlands past waterfalls and viewpoints. The five-stage hike begins at the Bernharduskirche, close to the centre of town. For details and maps, visit the tourist office's (p225) website.

Caracalla Spa
SPA

(☑07221-275 940; www.carasana.de; Römerplatz 11; 2/3hr €16/19, day ticket €23; ☺8am-10pm, last admission 8pm) This modern, glass-fronted spa has a cluster of indoor and outdoor pools, grottoes and surge channels, making the most of the mineral-rich spring water. For those who dare to bare, saunas range from the rustic 'forest' to the roasting 95°C 'fire' variety.

🛏 Sleeping

Hotel am Sophienpark
HISTORIC HOTEL €€

(☑ 07221-3560; www.hotel-am-sophienpark.de; Sophienstrasse 14; s €99-140, d €150-160, ste €300, f €150-199; P 🛜) Overlooking attractively tended gardens right in the heart of Baden-Baden, this hotel has retained all the grace and character of the belle époque, with Juliet balconies and a mansard roof. The interior brims with period features, such as the impressive wrought-iron staircase, which sweeps up to generously sized rooms that swing from contemporary to romantic and chandelier-lit in style.

Hotel am Markt
HISTORIC HOTEL €€

(☑ 07221-270 40; www.hotel-am-markt-baden.de; Marktplatz 18; s €65-88, d €105-128, apt €110-138; P 🛜) Sitting pretty in front of the Stiftskirche (p223), this hotel, which is almost three centuries old, has 23 homely, well-kept rooms. It's quiet up here apart from your wake-up call of church bells, but then you wouldn't want to miss out on the great breakfast.

Rathausglöckel
HOTEL €€

(☑ 07221-906 10; www.rathausgloeckel.de; Steinstrasse 7; s €80-100, d €115-139, ste €135-300; P 🛜) Right in the thick of things, this friendly family-run hotel occupies a 16th-century townhouse. The attractively renovated rooms (some with rooftop views) are dressed in muted tones with pine furniture – those on the 3rd floor command the best views over Baden-Baden's rooftops. Breakfast is a generous spread of fresh bread, fruit and pastries, homemade jam and bacon and eggs.

Heiligenstein
HOTEL €€

(☑ 07221-961 40; www.hotel-heiligenstein.de; Heiligensteinstrasse 19a; s €90-95, d €122-145; P) It's worth going the extra mile (or seven) to this sweet hotel overlooking vineyards. Pared-back, earthy-hued rooms come with balconies, and guests can put their feet up in the spa and gardens. The highly regarded restaurant (mains €16 to €27) serves local, seasonally inspired fare, from freshly caught trout to venison with blackcurrant sauce and asparagus.

Schweizer Hof
HOTEL €€

(☑ 07221-304 60; www.schweizerhof.de; Lange Strasse 73; s €69-89, d €99-145, ste €135-185; P 🛜) Sitting on one of Baden-Baden's smartest streets, this above-par hotel is a real find, with 40 dapper, recently updated rooms, chandelier-lit spaces, and a garden with sun lounges for chilling. The buffet breakfast is a rich affair.

Hotel Belle Epoque
LUXURY HOTEL €€€

(☑ 07221-300 660; www.hotel-belle-epoque.de; Maria-Viktoria-Strasse 2c; s €170-185, d €240-305, ste €389-685; 🛜) Nestling in manicured parkland, this neo-Renaissance villa is one of Baden-Baden's most characterful five-star pads. Antiques lend a dash of old-world opulence to the individually designed rooms. Rates include afternoon tea, with scones, cakes and fine brews served on the terrace or by the fireplace.

🍴 Eating

Café König
CAFE €

(Lichtentaler Strasse 12; cake €3.50-5, lunch specials €11-19; ⊗ 8.30am-6.30pm) Liszt and Tolstoy once sipped coffee at this venerable cafe, which has been doing a brisk trade in Baden-Baden's finest cakes, tortes, pralines and truffles for over 250 years. Black Forest gateau topped with clouds of cream; fresh berry tarts; or moist nut cakes – oh, decisions!

Kaffeehaus Baden-Baden
CAFE €

(Gernsbacher Strasse 24; snacks €3-6; ⊗ 9.30am-6pm Mon-Fri, 10.30am-6pm Sat, 1-6pm Sun) The aroma of freshly roasted coffee fills this artsy cafe, a laid-back spot for an espresso or chai latte and a slice of freshly baked cake. Its shop sells speciality teas, coffees, chocolate, organic preserves and handmade ceramics.

Weinstube im Baldreit
GERMAN €€

(☑ 07221-231 36; Küferstrasse 3; mains €12.50-19; ⊗ 5-10pm Tue-Sat) Well hidden down cobbled lanes, this wine-cellar restaurant is tricky to find, but worth looking for. Baden-Alsatian fare such as *Flammkuchen* (Alsatian pizza) topped with Black Forest ham, Roquefort and pears is expertly matched with local wines. Eat in the ivy-swathed courtyard in summer, and the vaulted interior in winter.

Monte Christo
TAPAS €€

(☑ 07221-393 434; http://monte-christo-baden-baden.de; Eichstrasse 5; tapas €6-17, mixed tapas plate €20; ⊗ 6pm-1am Tue-Sat) Bare wood tables, soft lighting and decorative tiles create a cosy feel at this tapas bar, where punchy Spanish flavours – from baked sheep's cheese with olives, garlic and rosemary to sweet-potato chips with fig aioli – are served with generosity, panache and fine Riojas. There's always a buzz – even after most restaurants in town have closed – and for good reason.

La Casserole
FRENCH €€

(☑07221-222 21; Gernsbacher Strasse 18; mains €16-21; ⊘11.30am-3pm & 5-10pm Thu-Sat, 5-10pm Mon-Wed) Lace curtains, cheek-by-jowl tables and flickering candles create the classic bistro tableau at intimate La Casserole. Go for satisfying Alsatian specialities such as beef cheeks braised in Pinot Noir until tender, served with *Spätzle* (thick egg-based noodles).

★ Nigrum
GASTRONOMY €€€

(☑07221-397 9008; www.restaurant-nigrum. de; Baldreitstrasse 1; 3 /5 /8 course menu €65/85/115; ⊘6pm-midnight Tue-Sat) This dark, seductive, gold-kissed glamour puss of a restaurant has insiders whispering Michelin star. Profound, season-driven flavours here are presented in the new-fangled way according to primary ingredients. The tasting menus don't disappoint – be it braised, meltingly soft Iberian pork cheek or salmon confit with octopus. It's all beautifully cooked and served with flair.

Schneider's Weinstube & Vinothek
GERMAN €€€

(☑07221-976 6929; www.schneiders-weinstube. de; Merkurstrasse 3; mains €20-29; ⊘5-11pm Mon-Sat) A charmingly old-school choice, Schneider's brings you the best of Badisch food and Pinot wines to the table. You'll receive a heartfelt welcome in the warmly lit space, where the menu swings with the seasons – from pike-perch with potato salad to braised wild boar with cranberry sauce. Check out the day specials on the blackboard.

Rizzi
INTERNATIONAL €€€

(☑07221-258 38; www.rizzi-baden-baden.de; Augustaplatz 1; mains €16-38; ⊘noon-1am) Book well ahead to snag a table at this insanely popular restaurant, housed in a pastel-pink villa overlooking the Lichtentaler Allee (p220). In summer, the tree-shaded patio is the place to sip excellent wines while tucking into choice steaks. Other menu favourites include organic schnitzels, pepped-up pastas and homemade burgers. Lunch specials go for between €8 to €14.

☆ Entertainment

Festspielhaus
CONCERT VENUE

(☑07221-301 3101; www.festspielhaus.de; Beim Alten Bahnhof 2, Robert-Schuman-Platz) Ensconced in an historical train station and fabled for its acoustics, the Festspielhaus is Europe's second-biggest concert hall, seating 2500 theatregoers, and a lavish tribute to

TEN YEARS YOUNGER
....
Rheumatism, arthritis, respiratory complaints, skin problems – all this and a host of other ailments can, apparently, be cured by Baden-Baden's mineral-rich spring water. If you'd rather drink the stuff than bathe in it, head to the **Fettquelle** (Römerplatz; ⊘24hr) fountain at the base of a flight of steps near Römerplatz, where you can fill your bottle for free. It might taste like lukewarm bathwater but if it makes you feel 10 years younger, who cares?

Baden-Baden's musical heritage. Under the direction of Andreas Mölich-Zebhauser, the grand venue hosts a world-class program of concerts, opera and ballet.

Baden-Badener Philharmonie
CLASSICAL MUSIC

(☑07221-932 791; www.philharmonie.baden-baden.de; Solmsstrasse 1) The revered Philharmonie Baden-Baden frequently performs in the Kurhaus (p223).

Baden-Baden Theater
THEATRE

(☑07221-932 700; www.theater.baden-baden.de; Goetheplatz) The Baden-Baden Theater is a neo-baroque confection of white-and-red sandstone with a frilly interior that looks like a miniature version of the Opéra-Garnier in Paris. It forms the gateway to Lichtentaler Allee (p220) and stages an eclectic line-up of German-language productions.

❶ Information

Branch Baden-Baden Tourist Office (Kaiserallee 3; ⊘10am-5pm Mon-Sat, 2-5pm Sun; 🔊) In the Trinkhalle (p220). Sells events tickets. Free wi-fi.

Main Baden-Baden Tourist Office (☑07221-275 200; www.baden-baden.com; Schwarzwaldstrasse 52, B500; ⊘9am-6pm Mon-Sat, to 1pm Sun) Situated 2km northwest of the centre. If you're driving from the northwest (from the A5) this place is on the way into town. Sells events tickets.

Post Office (Lange Strasse 44; ⊘9am-7pm Mon-Fri, to 2pm Sat) Located inside Kaufhaus Wagener.

❶ Getting There & Around

Karlsruhe-Baden-Baden Airport (Baden Airpark; ☑07229-662 000; www.badenairpark.de), 15km west of Baden-Baden, serves destinations

---

DON'T MISS

SILENT HEIGHTS

Escape the crowds and enjoy the view at these Baden-Baden lookouts and trails.

Neues Schloss (p223) A stately 15th-century residence with views over the rooftops of Baden-Baden to the dark woods of the Black Forest.

Mt Merkur (p223) Hiking and picnicking high above Baden-Baden at this lookout, reached by funicular.

Florentinerberg (p223) Uplifting views over city and forest-draped hill from these former Roman baths and botanical gardens.

Paradies am Annaberg (p223) Landscaped gardens in the Italian style, with falls and far-reaching forest views.

Panoramaweg (p223) A 40km hike starting in Baden-Baden, which dips into the most scenic bits of the northern Black Forest.

---

including London Stansted, Edinburgh, Rome and Malaga by Ryanair.

Buses to Black Forest destinations depart from the bus station, next to the **Hauptbahnhof** (Ooser Bahnhofstrasse).

Baden-Baden is on a major north–south rail corridor. Twice-hourly destinations include Freiburg (€23.70 to €40, 45 to 90 minutes) and Karlsruhe (€11 to €16, 15 to 30 minutes).

Local buses run by **Stadtwerke Baden-Baden** (www.stadtwerke-baden-baden.de; Waldseestrasse 24) cost €2/6.40 for a single/24-hour ticket. A day pass for up to five people is €10.60. Bus 201 (every 10 minutes) and other lines link the Bahnhof with Leopoldsplatz. Bus 205 runs roughly hourly between the Bahnhof and the airport (p225) from Monday to Friday, less frequently at weekends.

Karlsruhe

📱 0721 / POP 307,755

When planning this radial city in 1715, the margraves of Baden placed a mighty baroque palace smack in the middle – an urban layout so impressive it became the blueprint for Washington, DC.

Laid-back and cultured, Karlsruhe grows on you the longer you linger, with its rambling parks and museums crammed with futuristic gizmos and French Impressionist paintings. The suburbs dotted with art nouveau town-

houses are a reminder that France is just 15km away. Some 43,000 students keep the beer cheap and the vibe upbeat in the pubs, and the wheels of innovation in culture and technology turning.

⊙ Sights

★ **Schloss** PALACE
(Schlossbezirk 10) From the baroque-meets-neoclassical Schloss, Karlsruhe's 32 streets radiate like the spokes of a wheel. Karl Wilhelm, margrave of Baden-Durlach, named his epicentral palace Karlsruhe (Karl's retreat) when founding the city in 1715. Destroyed during WWII, the grand palace was sensitively rebuilt. In warm weather, locals play *pétanque* on the fountain-strewn Schlossplatz parterre. The palace harbours the Badisches Landesmuseum.

Edging north, the Schlossgarten is a relaxed spot for walks and picnics.

Badisches Landesmuseum MUSEUM
(📱0721-926 6514; www.landesmuseum.de; Schlossbezirk 10; adult/concession €4/3, after 2pm Fri free; ⊙10am-5pm Tue-Thu, to 6pm Fri-Sun) The treasure-trove Badisches Landesmuseum, inside the Schloss, shelters the jewel-encrusted crown of Baden's grand-ducal ruling family, and spoils of war from victorious battles against the Turks in the 17th century. Scale the tower for a better look at Karlsruhe's circular layout and for views stretching to the Black Forest.

Kunsthalle Karlsruhe GALLERY
(📱0721-926 3359; www.kunsthalle-karlsruhe.de; Hans-Thoma-Strasse 2-6; adult/concession €12/9; ⊙10am-6pm Tue & Wed & Fri-Sun, to 9pm Thu) The outstanding State Art Gallery presents a world-class collection, from the canvases of late-Gothic German masters such as Matthias Grünewald and Lucas Cranach the Elder to Impressionist paintings by Degas, Monet and Renoir. Step across to the Orangerie to view works by German artists including Georg Baselitz and Gerhard Richter.

Kloster Maulbronn MONASTERY
(Maulbronn Monastery; www.kloster-maulbronn.de; Maulbronn; adult/concession/family €7.50/3.80/18.80; ⊙9am-5.30pm Mar-Oct, 9.30am-5pm Tue-Sun Nov-Feb) Billed as the best-preserved medieval monastery north of the Alps, this one-time Cistercian monastery was founded by Alsatian monks in 1147. It was born again as a Protestant school in 1556 and designated a Unesco World Heritage Site in

1993. Its famous graduates include the astronomer Johannes Kepler. Aside from the Romanesque-Gothic portico in the monastery church and the weblike vaulting of the cloister, it's the insights into monastic life that make this place so culturally stimulating.

Maulbronn is 37km east of Karlsruhe, near the Pforzheim Ost exit on the A8. From Karlsruhe, take the S4 to Bretten Bahnhof and from there bus 700.

Zentrum für Kunst und Medientechnologie
MUSEUM

(ZKM; ☎ 0721-810 00; www.zkm.de; Lorenzstrasse 19; adult/concession €6/4; ⊗ 10am-6pm Wed-Fri, 2-6pm Sat, 11am-6pm Sun) Set in a historical munitions factory, the ZKM is a mammoth exhibition and research complex fusing art and emerging electronic media technologies. The interactive Medienmuseum has media art displays, including a computer-generated 'legible city' and real-time bubble simulations. The Museum für Neue Kunst hosts first-rate temporary exhibitions of post-1960 art. Served by tram 2, the ZKM is 2km southwest of the Schloss and a similar distance northwest of the Bahnhof (p228).

Marktplatz
SQUARE

The grand neoclassical Marktplatz is dominated by the Ionic portico of the 19th-century **Evangelische Stadtkirche** and the dusky-pink **Rathaus**. The iconic red-stone **pyramid** is an incongruous tribute to Karl Wilhelm, margrave of Baden-Durlach, and marks his tomb.

Museum beim Markt
MUSEUM

(☎ 0721-926 6578; Karl-Friedrich-Strasse 6; adult/concession €4/3; ⊗ 11am-5pm Tue-Thu, 10am-6pm Fri-Sun) At the northern tip of Marktplatz, Museum beim Markt presents an intriguing stash of post-1900 applied arts, from art nouveau to Bauhaus.

🛏 Sleeping

bbKarlsruhe Hostel
HOSTEL €

(☎ 015 785 073 050; www.bbkarlsruhe.de; Karlstrasse 132a; dm/s/d €30/50/64) Artsy, individually decorated rooms with a retro feel and paintings on the walls make this one of Karlsruhe's most enticing budget picks. Bathrooms are shared, as is the kitchen. It's a 10-minute walk northwest of the Bahnhof (p228). The nearest tram stop is Kolpingplatz.

Hotel Rio
HOTEL €€

(☎ 0721-840 80; www.hotel-rio.de; Hans-Sachs-Strasse 2; s €78-119, d €86-132; P 🛜) Service can be brusque but this is still one of your best bets for spotless, contemporary quarters in Karlsruhe. Breakfast is worth the extra €6 – eggs, salmon, the works. Take the tram to Mühlburger Tor.

Acora Hotel
HOTEL €€

(☎ 0721-850 90; www.acora.de; Sophienstrasse 69-71; s €80-121, d €100-152; P 🛜) Chirpy staff make you feel at home at this apartment-hotel, featuring bright, modern rooms equipped with kitchenettes.

🍴 Eating & Drinking

Vogelbräu
PUB FOOD €

(☎ 0721-377 571; www.vogelbraeu.de/karlsruhe/lokal.html; Kapellenstrasse 50; mains €7-10; ⊗ 10am-midnight) Quaff a cold one with regulars by the copper vats or in the leafy beer garden of this microbrewery. The unfiltered house pils washes down hale and hearty food such as goulash, dumplings and bratwurst with beer sauce. The tram to Durlacher Tor stops close by.

DeliBurgers
BURGERS €

(☎ 0721-6699 1055; www.deliburgers.de; Akademiestrasse 39; burgers €7-10; ⊗ 11.30am-9.30pm) DeliBurgers does what it says on the tin: top-quality beef burgers, grilled to your taste, with gourmet toppings and organic buns. Everything is made right here – from the sauces to the fluffy hand-cut fries. It's near the Europaplatz tram stop.

Casa do José
PORTUGUESE €€

(☎ 0721-9143 8018; www.casadojose.de; Kriegsstrasse 92; mains €14-24.50; ⊗ 5-11pm Tue-Fri, 11.30am-11pm Sat & Sun) A slice of Portugal in the heart of Karlsruhe, Casa do José extends a heartfelt *bemvindo* (welcome). The look is modern-rustic, with beams suspended above bistro tables in a light interior. *Petiscos* (Portuguese tapas) such as salt-cod fritters and fried garlic sausage are an appetising prelude to dishes such as *cataplana de peixe e marisco* (paprika-spiked fish and shellfish stew).

Kommödchen
INTERNATIONAL €€€

(☎ 0721-350 5884; www.kommoedchen-ka.de; Marienstrasse 1; mains €20-30; ⊗ 6pm-midnight Tue-Sun) A drop of good old-fashioned sophistication in Karlsruhe's southern Südstadt neighbourhood, Kommödchen keeps things cosy with soft lamplight, bistro seating, portraits festooning the walls and warm service. Matched with great wines, the menu has Mediterranean and Asian overtones in dishes such as red tuna carpaccio with lemon-herb dressing, and grilled tiger prawns with mango-coconut sauce.

Oberländer Weinstuben   GERMAN €€€
(📞 0721-250 66; www.oberlaender-weinstube.de; Akademiestrasse 7; 3-course lunch/dinner €30/51, mains €19-26; ⊗ noon-3pm & 6pm-midnight Tue-Sat) This highly atmospheric pick brings together an elegant wood-panelled tavern and a flowery courtyard. Fine wines marry perfectly with seasonal winners such as slow-cooked ox cheeks, goose ravioli with salsify and nut-butter foam, and rack of venison with pumpkin – all cooked with flair and served with finesse.

Phono   CRAFT BEER
(http://phono.bar; Karl-Wilhelm-Strasse 6; ⊗ 6pm-11.45pm Mon, to 1am Tue-Wed, to 2am Thu-Fri, 8pm-2am Sat) This vintage-cool craft beer bar in Karlsruhe's Oststadt hums with folk thirsty for unusual brews – and here there are 70 to try from all over the world. Phono also hosts events from tastings to DJ sets. Take the tram to Durlacher Tor. From here it's a 300m walk northeast.

ℹ️ Information

Karlsruhe Tourist Office (📞 0721-3720 5383; www.karlsruhe-tourismus.de; Bahnhof-platz 6; ⊗ 8.30am-6pm Mon-Fri, 9am-1pm Sat) Sells the Karlsruhe Card (24/48/72hr card €18.50/22.50/26.50) offering free or discounted entry to museums and other attractions as well as unlimited use of public transport. A cheaper version of the card (24/48/72hr card €12.50/16.50/20.50) excludes public transport.

Post Office (Poststrasse 3; ⊗ 9am-6.30pm Mon-Fri, 9.30am-1pm Sat) East of the **Bahnhof**.

ℹ️ Getting There & Around

Destinations well-served by train from the **Bahnhof** include Baden-Baden (€11.50 to €16.50, 15 minutes) and Freiburg (€29 to €37, one hour).

The **Bahnhof** is linked to the **Marktplatz** (p227), 2km north, by tram and light-rail lines 2, 3, S1, S11, S4 and S41. Single tickets cost €2.50; a 24-Stunden-Karte (24-hour unlimited travel card) costs €6.40 (€10.60 for up to five people).

Freudenstadt

📞 07441 / POP 22,579

Duke Friedrich I of Württemberg built a new capital here in 1599, which was bombed to bits in WWII. The upshot is that Freudenstadt's centre is underwhelming, though its magnificent setting in the Black Forest is anything but.

Freudenstadt marks the southern end of the Schwarzwaldhochstrasse (Black Forest Highway) and is a terminus for the gorgeous Schwarzwald-Tälerstrasse (Black Forest Valley Road), which runs from Rastatt via Alpirsbach.

⊙ Sights

Stadtkirche   CHURCH
(Marktplatz; ⊗ 10am-5pm) **FREE** In the southwest corner of Marktplatz looms the 17th-century red-sandstone Stadtkirche, with an ornate 12th-century Cluniac-style baptismal font, Gothic windows, Renaissance portals and baroque towers. The two naves are at right angles to each other, an unusual design by the geometrically minded Duke Friedrich I.

Marktplatz   SQUARE
Lovers of statistics will delight in ticking off Germany's biggest square (216m by 219m, for the record), dislocated by a T-junction of heavily trafficked roads. At the heart of Freudenstadt, it harbours rows of shops, cafes with alfresco seating and a playground.

🏃 Activities

While you won't linger for Freudenstadt's sights, the deep forested valleys on its fringes are worth exploring. Scenic hiking trails include a 12km uphill walk to **Kniebis** (www.kniebis.de) on the **Schwarzwaldhochstrasse**, where there are superb Kinzig Valley views. Ask the tourist office (p230) for details.

Jump on a mountain bike to tackle routes such as the 85km **Kinzigtal-Radweg**, taking in dreamy landscapes and half-timbered villages, or the 60km **Murgtal-Radweg** over hill and dale to Rastatt. Both valleys have bike trails and it's possible to return to Freudenstadt by train.

Pfau Schinken   FOOD
(📞 07445-6482; www.pfau-schinken.de; Alte Post-strasse 17, Herzogsweiler; ⊗ 7.30am-12.30pm & 2-6pm Mon-Fri, 7.30am-12.30pm Sat, guided tours 2.30pm & 4.30pm Tue, 11.30am Sat) When you smell the tantalising aroma of *Schwarzwälder Schinken* (Black Forest ham), you know you've arrived at Pfau, which lends insight into the curing and smoking process on its guided tours. It's a 10-minute drive north of Freudenstadt on the B28.

Panorama-Bad   SWIMMING
(www.panorama-bad.de; Ludwig-Jahn-Strasse 60;
adult/concession 3hr pass €7.30/6.20; ⊙9am-
10pm Mon-Sat, to 8pm Sun) The glass-fronted
Panorama-Bad is a relaxation magnet with
pools, steam baths and saunas.

🛏 Sleeping

Camping Langenwald   CAMPGROUND €
(☑07441-2862; www.camping-langenwald.de;
Strasburger Strasse 167; per person/tent €8.60/10;
⊙Easter-Oct; ▧) This leafy site has a so-
lar-heated pool and a nature trail. There's
plenty to keep the kids amused, including a
playground, table football and volleyball. It's
served by bus 12 to Kniebis.

Warteck   HOTEL €€
(☑07441-919 20; www.warteck-freudenstadt.
de; Stuttgarter Strasse 14; s €70-82, d €81-114,
tr €146-178; ▣🛜) In the capable hands of
the Glässel family since 1894, this hotel
sports modern, gleamingly clean rooms.
The real draw here, however, is the elegant
wood-panelled restaurant (mains €14.50 to
€39), which serves market-fresh fare such
as beetroot tortellini and rack of venison
with wild mushrooms.

Hotel Adler   HOTEL €€
(☑07441-915 252; www.adler-fds.de; Forststrasse
15-17; s €70-105, d €100-130, ste €150; ▣🛜) This
family-run hotel near the Marktplatz has
well-kept, recently renovated rooms with
parquet floors, transparent bathroom par-
titions and pops of lime green. The restaurant (mains €12 to €17) dishes up appetising

regional grub such as *Zwiebelrostbraten*
(roast beef with onions).

Hotel Grüner Wald   SPA HOTEL €€€
(☑07441-860 540; www.gruener-wald.de; Kinzig-
talstrasse 23, Lauterbad; s €92-102, d €174-210, ste
€220-304; ▣🛜▧) Nuzzling between forest
and meadows, this eco-conscious spa hotel
in Lauterbad, 2km south of Freudenstadt,
is a terrific pick for a relaxing break, with
warm-toned, country-style rooms done
out in wood and natural fabrics, affording
knock-out views from their balconies. The
spa has an indoor pool, relaxation area with
waterbeds, saunas and steam room. There's
a pretty garden with hammocks.

🍴 Eating

Speckwirt   GERMAN €
(☑07441-919 5680; www.speckwirt-fds.de; Marktplatz 45; mains €7.50-13.50, lunch special €7.90;
⊙9am-10pm; 🛜🚼) Speckwirt has winged
Black Forest tradition into the 21st century with its new-wave-rustic decor of basket
lights, forest murals on the wall and chunky
pine trappings. Come for good old-fashioned
grub along the lines of *Maultasche* (Swabian-
style ravioli) in speck sauce to a *Vesperbrett*
(sharing platter) of Black Forest ham and sausage. Children's menus (€4.50 to €6.50) are
available.

Turmbräu   GERMAN €€
(www.turmbraeu.de; Marktplatz 64; mains €8-28;
⊙11am-midnight Sun-Thu, to 3am Fri & Sat) For a
lively night out in Freudenstadt, this is your
place, with a microbrewery that doubles as a

HIKING THE BLACK FOREST

As locals will tell you, you need to hit the trails to really see the Black Forest. From gentle
half-day strolls to multiday treks, we've cherry-picked the region for a few of our favourites. Local tourist offices can help out with more info and maps, or check out the free
tour planner at www.wanderservice-schwarzwald.de.

It's also worth checking out the Schwarzwaldverein (www.schwarzwaldverein.de),
where well-marked paths criss-cross the darkest depths of the Black Forest.

The ultimate long-distance trail is the 280km **Westweg**, marked with a red diamond,
stretching from Pforzheim in the northern Black Forest to Basel in Switzerland. Highlights feature the steep Murg Valley, Titisee and 1493m Feldberg. But if you have less
time (and energy), these shorter hikes are terrific alternatives:

➡ Panoramaweg (p223)

➡ Gütenbach-Simonswäldertal (p247)

➡ Wutachschlucht (p245)

➡ Feldberg–Steig (p243)

➡ Martinskapelle (p248)

beer garden. Pull up a chair in ye-olde barn to munch hearty grub such as goulash, stubby pork knuckles with sauerkraut, and *Bierkrustenbraten* (pork roast with beer sauce) while guzzling Turmbräu brews – a 5L barrel costs €39.

★ **Schwarzwaldstube** MODERN EUROPEAN €€€
(☑ 07442-4920; www.traube-tonbach.de; Tonbachstrasse 237, Baiersbronn-Tonbach; tasting menus €180-225, cookery courses around €200; ⊙ 7pm-midnight Wed, noon-2pm & 7-9pm Thu-Sun) Schwarzwaldstube commands big forest views from its rustically elegant dining room. Head chef Torsten Michel performs culinary magic, carefully sourcing ingredients and presenting with an artist's flair. The tasting menu goes with the seasons, but might begin with a palate-awakening confit of Arctic cod with red-bell pepper ginger crust, followed by suckling veal with smoked bone marrow and Périgord truffle.

If you fancy getting behind the stove, sign up for one of the cookery classes, which revolve around a theme or techniques including pasta-making and preparing pâtés. The website has details and dates.

Schwarzwaldstube has three Michelin stars. It's located in the village of Tonbach, 11km north of Freudenstadt.

★ **Restaurant Bareiss** MODERN EUROPEAN €€€
(☑ 07442-470; www.bareiss.com; Hermine-Bareiss-Weg 1, Baiersbronn-Mitteltal; lunch menu €105, dinner menus €185-225; ⊙ noon-2pm & 7-9.30pm Wed-Sun) Claus-Peter Lumpp has consistently won plaudits for his brilliantly composed, French-inflected menus at Restaurant Bareiss. On paper, dishes such as sautéed langoustine with almond cream, and fried fillet of suckling calf and sweetbreads with chanterelles seem deceptively simple; on the plate they become things of beauty, rich in textures and aromas and presented with an artist's eye for detail.

Restaurant Bareiss has three Michelin stars. It's situated 11km north of Freudenstadt.

❶ Information

Freudenstadt Tourist Office (☑ 07441-864 730; www.freudenstadt.de; Marktplatz 64; ⊙ 9am-6pm Mon-Fri, 10am-3pm Sat, 10am-1pm Sun; ☎) Hotel reservations are free.

❶ Getting There & Away

Freudenstadt's focal point is the Marktplatz (p228) on the B28. The town has two train stations: the *Stadtbahnhof*, five minutes' walk north

of Marktplatz, and the Hauptbahnhof, 2km southeast of Marktplatz at the end of Bahnhofstrasse.

Trains on the Ortenau line, serving Offenburg and Strasbourg, depart hourly from the Hauptbahnhof and are covered by the 24-hour Europass. The pass represents excellent value at €11.90 for individuals and €19 for families. Trains go roughly hourly to Karlsruhe (€19.60, 1½ to two hours) from the *Stadtbahnhof* and Hauptbahnhof.

Kinzigtal

Shaped like a horseshoe, the Kinzigtal (Kinzig Valley) begins south of Freudenstadt and shadows the babbling Kinzig River south to Schiltach, west to Haslach and north to Offenburg. Near Strasbourg, 95km downriver, the Kinzig is swallowed up by the mighty Rhine. The valley's inhabitants survived for centuries on mining and shipping goods by raft.

This Black Forest valley is astonishingly pretty, with hills brushed with thick larch and spruce forest or ribboned with vines; its half-timbered villages look every inch the Grimms' fairy tale. For seasonal colour, come in autumn (for foliage) or spring (for fruit blossom).

❶ Getting There & Away

The B294 follows the Kinzig from Freudenstadt to Haslach, from where the B33 leads north to Offenburg. If you're going south, pick up the B33 to Triberg and beyond in Hausach.

An hourly train line links Freudenstadt with Offenburg (€16.20, 1¼ hours), stopping in Alpirsbach (€3.95, 16 minutes), Schiltach (€6.80, 26 minutes), Hausach (€9.60, 42 minutes), Haslach (€11.30, 50 minutes) and Gengenbach (€14.80, one hour). From Hausach, trains run roughly hourly southeast to Triberg (€6.70, 21 minutes), Villingen (€12.90, 44 minutes) and Konstanz (€31.60, two hours). For Konstanz, it's cheaper to buy the Baden-Württemberg Ticket (€24).

Alpirsbach

☑ 07444 / POP 6337
Nudging the wooded hills of the Upper Kinzigtal, Alpirsbach is presided over by a splendid Benedictine monastery. Lore has it that the town itself is named after a quaffing cleric who, when a glass of beer slipped clumsily from his hand and rolled into the river, exclaimed: *All Bier ist in den Bach!* (All the beer is in the stream!). A prophecy, it seems, as today Alpirsbacher Klosterbräu is brewed from pure spring water.

◎ Sights

★Monkey 47 DISTILLERY
(☑ 07455-946 870; www.monkey47.com; Äusserer
Vogelsberg 7, Lossburg) **FREE** Embracing the
global craft gin craze, Monkey 47 has scooped
awards for its batch-distilled, handcrafted
dry gin, with piney, peppery notes. Distillery
tours are free, but the early monkey gets the
banana – it's by appointment only. See the
website for details. The distillery is 11km
north of Alpirsbach on the L408.

Kloster Alpirsbach MONASTERY
(www.kloster-alpirsbach.de; Klosterplatz 1; adult/
concession €6/3; ⊙ 10am-5.30pm Mon-Sat, 11am-
5.30pm Sun) All the more evocative for its
lack of adornment, this 11th-century former
Benedictine monastery effectively conveys
the simple, spiritual life in its Romanesque
three-nave church, spartan cells and Gothic
cloister, which hosts candlelit concerts from
June to August. It's amazing what you can
find under the floorboards, as the museum
reveals with its stash of 16th-century clothing, caricatures (of artistic scholars) and
lines (of misbehaving ones).

Alpirsbacher Klosterbräu BREWERY
(☑ 07444-670; www.alpirsbacher.com; Marktplatz
1; tours €7-12.20; ⊙ tours 2.30pm) Alpirsbacher Klosterbräu is brewed from pure spring
water. Brewery tours at 2.30pm, taking a
behind-the-scenes peek at the brewing process, are in German, though guides may
speak English. Two beers are thrown in for
the price of a €7 ticket, while more expensive €12.20 tickets include bratwurst and a
glass of beer schnapps.

⌷ Sleeping & Eating

Hotel Rössle HISTORIC HOTEL €€
(☑ 07444-956 040; www.roessle-alpirsbach.de;
Aischbachstrasse 5; s €58, d €88-98, tr €120, f €170;
P 🛜) This welcoming family-run number
lodges in a half-timbered house a couple of
minutes' stroll from the monastery. Light,
spacious rooms are done out in modern
Black Forest style, with pale wood, forest-
green tones and stag-embossed cushions.
Connecting rooms are available for families.
There's a highly regarded, region-focused
restaurant (mains €19 to €26) and a lounge
warmed by an open fire.

Muggelcaf CAFE €
(☑ 07444-956 5970; http://muggelcaf.com; Marktstrasse 10; light bites €6.50-13; ⊙ 11am-10pm Sun-
Thu, to 1am Fri & Sat) *Harry Potter* fans might

like the name of this cheery, central cafe-bar,
housed in a half-timbered building. Come for
light meals including salads, burgers and tarte
flambée, and Alpirsbacher Klosterbräu brews.

ⓘ Information

Alpirsbach Tourist Office (☑ 07444-951 6281;
www.stadt-alpirsbach.de; Krähenbadstrasse 2;
⊙ 9-11.30am Mon, Wed & Fri, 2-5.30pm Tue &
Thu) The tourist office can supply hiking maps
and, for cyclists, information on the 85km
Kinzigtalradweg from Offenburg to Lossburg.

Schiltach

☑ 07836 / POP 3803
Sitting snugly at the foot of wooded hills and
on the banks of the Kinzig and Schiltach rivers, medieval Schiltach looks too ludicrously
pretty to be true. The meticulously restored
half-timbered houses, which once belonged
to tanners, merchants and raft builders, are
a riot of crimson geraniums in summer.

Being at the confluence of the two rivers,
logging was big business here until the 19th
century and huge rafts were built to ship
timber as far as the Netherlands. The willow-fringed banks now attract grey herons
and kids who come to splash in the shallow
waters when the sun's out.

◎ Sights

Marktplatz SQUARE
Centred on a trickling fountain, the sloping, triangular Marktplatz is Schiltach at
its picture-book best. The frescoes of its
step-gabled 16th-century Rathaus depict
scenes from local history.

Schlossbergstrasse STREET
Clamber south up Schlossbergstrasse, paus-
ing to notice the plaques that denote the
trades of one-time residents, such as the
Strumpfstricker (stocking weaver) at No 6,
and the sloping roofs where tanners once
dried their skins. Up top there are views
over Schiltach's red rooftops.

Museum am Markt MUSEUM
(Marktplatz 13; ⊙ 11am-5pm Apr-Oct, Sat & Sun only
Nov-Mar) **FREE** Museum am Markt is crammed
with everything from antique spinning wheels
to Biedermeier costumes. Highlights include
the cobbler's workshop and an interactive display recounting the tale of the devilish Teufel
von Schiltach, who, as local lore has it, was responsible for the raging fire that reduced the
town to ashes in the 16th century.

(Continued on page 234)

STUTTGART & THE BLACK FOREST KINZIGTAL

CANADASTOCK/SHUTTERSTOCK ©

Dramatic Landscapes

From the high Alps to the Black Forest, the low dark hills of eastern Bavaria to the glassy mountain lakes of the Alpine foothill region, southern Germany has a photogenic menu of landscapes to suit every taste.

Mountains

Bavaria enjoys only a sliver of Europe's premier mountain range, the Alps, but it certainly packs a lot into its slice. Take a ride high into the thinning air in one of the region's countless cable cars, snap on skis, lace up hiking boots or just enjoy the views with a beer in hand.

Forests

Though there are plenty of trees in between, Southern Germany is a tale of two forests, one Bavarian in the east one Black in the west. The former is a dark, mysterious, sparsely populated area that spills over into neighbouring Czech Republic, the latter the location of Germany's newest national park.

1. Maria Gern and Watzmann mountain, Berchtesgaden National Park (p106) **2.** Lake Constance (p250) and Meersburg (p256) **3.** Bavarian Forest National Park (p166)

Lakes

From soothing Lake Constance in the west to Munich's watery playground Lake Starnberg, the Black Forest's Titisee to the drama of Berchtesgaden's Königsee, southern Germany's lakes serve up some of the region's most astounding scenery and most serene views plus lots of fun both in and on the water.

Rivers

One of the world's most famous rivers, the Danube is born in the Black Forest before cutting through Bavaria and Baden-Württemberg at the beginning of its long journey to the Black Sea. The lesser-known Altmühl is a more tranquil affair flowing through Franconia, an ideal waterway for a lazy kayak trip.

(Continued from page 231)

Schüttesäge Museum
MUSEUM

(Hauptstrasse 1; ⊙ 11am-5pm daily Apr-Oct) **FREE**
The riverfront Schüttesäge Museum focuses on Schiltach's rafting tradition with reconstructed workshops, a watermill generating hydroelectric power for many homes in the area and touchy-feely exhibits for kids, from different kinds of bark to forest animals.

🛏 Sleeping & Eating

Adler 1604
BOUTIQUE HOTEL €€

(☑ 07836-957 5800; http://adler1604.com; Hauptstrasse 20; s €90, d €120-130; 🅿 🛜) Occupying a lovingly converted half-timbered house, dating to (you guessed it!) 1604, this Schiltach newcomer has hit the ground running. In the capable hands of the Meiers, the boutique hotel keeps things intimate with eight newly renovated rooms, featuring perks including Nespresso makers, fresh fruit and honesty bars. Top billing goes to the romantic *Erker* (bay window) rooms.

Zur Alten Brücke
GUESTHOUSE €€

(☑ 07836-2036; www.altebruecke.de; Schramberger Strasse 13; s/d/apt €60/90/110; 🅿 🛜) You'll receive a warm welcome at this riverside guesthouse. The pick of the bright, cheery rooms overlook the Schiltach. Michael cooks up seasonal, regional fare in the kitchen and there's a terrace for summer imbibing.

Weysses Rössle
GUESTHOUSE €€

(☑ 07836-387; www.weysses-roessle.de; Schenkenzeller Strasse 42; s €62, d €86-98; 🅿 🛜) Rosemarie and Ulrich continue the tradition of 19 generations in this 16th-century inn. Countrified rooms decorated with rosewood and floral fabrics also feature stylish bathrooms and wi-fi. Its restaurant (menus €25 to €42) serves locally sourced, organic fare.

ℹ Information

Schiltach Tourist Office (☑ 07836-5850; www.schiltach.de; Marktplatz 6; ⊙ 9am-noon & 2-4pm Mon-Thu, 9am-noon Fri) The tourist office in the Rathaus can provide info and free internet access. Local hiking options are marked on an enamel sign just opposite.

Gutach

☑ 07831 / POP 2267

Slumbering at the foot of thickly wooded hills and identified by its rambling hip-roofed, shingle-clad farmhouses ablaze with geraniums in summer, little Gutach is a fine rural escape for hiking, cycling and family

holidays. It's in a side valley that forks south of the Kinzigtal.

One of the village's main claims to fame is that it's the original home of the Bollenhut bonnet.

◎ Sights

★ Vogtsbauernhof
MUSEUM

(Black Forest Open-Air Museum; ☑ 07831-935 60; www.vogtsbauernhof.org; Wählerbrücke 1, Gutach; adult/concession/child/family €10/9/5.50/28; ⊙ 9am-6pm late Mar-early Nov, to 7pm Aug, last entry 1hr before closing) The Schwarzwälder Freilichtmuseum spirals around the Vogtsbauernhof, a self-contained early-17th-century farmstead. Farmhouses shifted from their original locations here, using techniques such as thatching and panelling, to create this authentic farming hamlet and preserve age-old Black Forest traditions. There are free guided tours at 2.30pm daily in German, and at 1pm daily in July and August in English.

Duravit Design Centre
MUSEUM

(www.duravit.de; Werderstrasse 36, Hornberg; ⊙ 8am-6pm Mon-Fri, noon-4pm Sat) **FREE** If giant cuckoo clocks and Black Forest gateau no longer thrill, how about a trip to the world's largest loo? Drive on the B33 to Hornberg and there, in all its lavatorial glory, stands the titanic toilet dreamed up by designer Philippe Starck. Even if you have no interest in designer urinals or home jacuzzis, the centre's worth visiting for the tremendous view across the Black Forest from the 12m-high ceramic loo. The design centre is 3.5km south of Gutach.

🛏 Sleeping

Zur Mühle
CAMPGROUND €

(☑ 07834-775; www.camping-kirnbach.de; Talstrasse 79, Wolfach/Kirnbach; camping per adult/child/tent €4.90/3.50/7) A chilled spot to pitch a tent, with lovely views over wooded hills, this campground has plenty of shade, a stream where kids can paddle and walking trails heading off into the forest. It's 5.5km east of the Vogtsbauernhof.

Gasthaus zum Hirsch
GUESTHOUSE €

(☑ 07831-228; www.hirsch-gutach.de; Hirschgasse 2; s/d/f €47/69/95) This stout half-timbered house shelters simple pine-clad quarters, which are a little dated but perfectly comfortable. Spacious family rooms are available. The restaurant (mains €15 to €21) plays up Black Forest and Badisch flavours in dishes such as venison goulash with *Spätzle* (egg pasta) and whole-baked trout with almond butter. There's an appealing terrace in summer.

❶ Getting There & Away

Gutach is in the side valley that runs south of the Kinzigtal. The B33 runs through it, linking it to Triberg, 13.5km south.

From nearby Hausach there are regular trains to towns such as Gengenbach (€4.30, 18 minutes) and Triberg (€6.70, 21 minutes).

Haslach

☑ 07832 / POP 6934

An enticingly mellow little town with lanes stacked with medieval timber-framed houses, Haslach makes a laid-back base for dipping into the Kinzigtal on foot or by bike. Haslach's 17th-century former Capuchin monastery houses its pride and joy, the **Schwarzwälder Trachtenmuseum** (Black Forest Costume Museum; Klosterstrasse 1; adult/concession €3/2.50; ☺10am-12.30pm & 1.30-5pm Tue-Sun Apr-Oct, 10am-12.30pm & 1.30-5pm Tue-Fri Nov-Mar), showcasing flamboyant costumes and outrageous hats, the must-have accessories for the well-dressed Fräulein of the 1850s. Look out for the Black Forest Bollenhut, a straw bonnet topped with pom poms (red for unmarried women, black for married) and the Schäppel, a fragile-looking crown made from hundreds of beads and weighing up to 5kg.

Haslach is 18km south of Gengenbach via the B33 or by train (€4.30, 13 minutes). The centrally located Bahnhof is just on the northern edge of the Altstadt.

Gengenbach

☑ 07803 / POP 10,941

If ever a Black Forest town could be described as chocolate-box, it would surely be Gengenbach, with its scrumptious Altstadt of half-timbered townhouses framed by vineyards and orchards. It's fitting, then, that director Tim Burton made this the home of gluttonous Augustus Gloop in the 2005 blockbuster *Charlie and the Chocolate Factory* (though less so that he called it Düsseldorf).

◉ Sights & Activities

Marktplatz SQUARE

Between the town's two tower-topped gates sits the triangular Marktplatz, dominated by the Rathaus, an 18th-century pink-and-cream confection. The fountain bears a statue of a knight, a symbol of Gengenbach's medieval status as a Free Imperial City.

Engelgasse STREET

The best way to discover Gengenbach's historical centre is with a serendipitous mooch through its narrow backstreets, such as the gently curving Engelgasse, off Hauptstrasse, lined with listed half-timbered, shuttered houses draped in vines and bedecked with scarlet geraniums in summer.

Kloster Gengenbach MONASTERY

(Klosterstrasse 4; ☺dawn to dusk) FREE Amble along Klosterstrasse to check out the former Benedictine monastery. A calm *Kräutergarten* (herb garden), stippled with fragrant and medicinal herbs, can be visited behind its walls.

Weinpfad WALKING

Stop by the tourist office (p236) for info on the hour-long Weinpfad, a wine trail beginning in the Altstadt that threads through terraced vineyards to the Jakobskapelle, a 13th-century hilltop chapel commanding views as far as Strasbourg on clear days.

✪ Festivals & Events

★ **Gengenbach Advent Calendar** CHRISTMAS

(Rathaus, Marktplatz; ☺Dec) Every December, Gengenbach rekindles childhood memories of opening tiny windows when the Rathaus morphs into the world's biggest Advent calendar. At 6pm daily, one of 24 windows is opened to reveal a festive scene. Previously, the tableaux have been painted by well-known artists and children's-book illustrators including Marc Chagall, Andy Warhol and Tomi Ungerer.

🛏 Sleeping & Eating

DJH Hostel HOSTEL €

(☑0781-317 49; www.jugendherberge-schloss-ortenberg.de; Burgweg 21, Ortenberg; dm €22.50-29.50; P🐾) The Hogwarts gang would feel at home in the 12th-century Schloss Ortenberg, rebuilt in whimsical neo-Gothic style complete with lookout tower and wood-panelled dining hall. A staircase sweeps up to dorms with Kinzig Valley views. From Gengenbach station, take bus 7134 or 7160 to Ortenberg, and get off at the 'Schloss/Freudental' stop.

Weinhotel Pfeffer und Salz HOTEL €€

(☑07803-934 80; www.pfefferundsalz-gengenbach.de; Mattenhofweg 3; s/d/tr €60/90/122; P🐾) On a vineyard spreading just north of Gengenbach, Pfeffer und Salz is an appealingly converted Black Forest farmhouse with pretty gardens, views and a playground. The rooms are light, contemporary and decorated in warm colours – and above all supremely peaceful. Wine tastings can be arranged. Half board costs an extra €21.

Stadthotel Pfeffermühle HOTEL €€
(☑ 07803-933 50; www.stadthotel-gengenbach.de; Oberdorfstrasse 24; s/d €60/90; [P][☎]) In a snug half-timbered house dating to 1476, close to one of the Altstadt gate towers, this neat-and-tidy hotel is a bargain. Decorated with antique knick-knacks, the wood-panelled restaurant (mains €14 to €22) serves up regional favourites such as Black Forest trout and *Sauerbraten* (pot roast).

★**Die Reichsstadt** BOUTIQUE HOTEL €€€
(☑ 07803-966 30; www.die-reichsstadt.de; Engelgasse 33; d €160-194, ste €214-244; [P][☎]) This boutique stunner on Engelgasse wings you to story-book heaven. Its 16th-century exterior conceals a pure, contemporary aesthetic, where clean lines, natural materials and subtle cream-caramel shades are enlivened with eye-catching details. A spa, sparkling wine on arrival, free fruit in your room and one of the top restaurants in town complete this pretty picture.

Gasthof Hirsch GERMAN €€
(☑ 07803-3387; www.hirschgengenbach.de; Grabenstrasse 34; mains €18-23.50; ☺8am-2pm & 5-11pm Thu-Mon) This is a warm, woody tavern in the old-school mould, with black-and-white photos on the walls, soft lamplight and cheek-by-jowl tables. The kitchen reels out Badisch and Swabian soul food, from spinach *Knödel* (dumplings) to venison goulash with *Spätzle* (eggy pasta), matched with Pinot and Riesling wines from the region.

Zum Turm GERMAN €€
(☑ 07803-1496; www.zum-turm.de; Hauptstrasse 39; mains €9-15; ☺5pm-midnight Tue-Fri, 11am-1pm Sat, 11am-10pm Sun) Behind a pretty half-timbered facade, Zum Turm attracts a faithful crowd for the great beer on tap and by the bottle (including local Alpirsbacher brews), the warm, woody atmosphere and the menu of straightforward grub – *Flammkuchen* in many guises, steaks, salads and Badisch specialities such as crispy pork knuckles.

❶ Information

Gengenbach Tourist Office (☑ 07803-930 143; www.gengenbach.info; Im Winzerhof; ☺9am-12.30pm & 1.30-5pm Mon-Fri year-round, plus 10am-noon Sat May-Oct & Dec)

The tourist office is in a courtyard just off Hauptstrasse.

❶ Getting There & Away

Regular trains run from Gengenbach to Kinzigtal towns including Schiltach (€9.50, 35 minutes) as well as other destinations including Offenburg (€2.50, nine minutes), Freiburg (€16.20, one hour) and Villingen-Schwenningen (€17.30, one hour). The Bahnhof is a two-minute walk west of the Altstadt.

Freiburg

☑ 0761 / POP 226,393

Sitting plump at the foot of the Black Forest's wooded slopes and vineyards, Freiburg is a sunny, cheerful university town, its medieval Altstadt a story-book tableau of gabled townhouses, cobblestone lanes and cafe-rimmed plazas. Party-loving students spice up the local nightlife.

Blessed with 2000 hours of annual sunshine, this is Germany's warmest city. Indeed, while neighbouring hilltop villages are still shovelling snow, the trees in Freiburg are clouds of white blossom, and locals are already imbibing in canal-side beer gardens. This eco-trailblazer has shrewdly tapped into that natural energy to generate nearly as much solar power as the whole of Britain, making it one of the country's greenest cities.

◉ Sights

★**Freiburger Münster** CATHEDRAL
(Freiburg Minster; www.freiburgermuenster.info; Münsterplatz; tower adult/concession €2/1.50; ☺10am-5pm Mon-Sat, 1-7pm Sun, tower 9.30am-5pm Mon-Sat, 1-5pm Sun) With its lacy spires, cheeky gargoyles and intricate entrance portal, Freiburg's 11th-century minster cuts an impressive figure above the market square. It has dazzling kaleidoscopic stained-glass windows that were mostly financed by medieval guilds and a high altar with a masterful triptych by Dürer protégé Hans Baldung Grien. Square at the base, the tower becomes an octagon higher up and is crowned by a filigreed 116m-high spire. On clear days you can spy the Vosges Mountains in France.

Closer to the ground, near the main portal in fact, note the medieval wall measurements used to ensure that merchandise (eg loaves of bread) were the requisite size.

Note that the cathedral is closed for visits during services (exact times are available at the info desk inside).

Augustinermuseum   MUSEUM

(☑ 0761-201 2501; www.freiburg.de; Augustinerplatz 1; adult/concession/child €7/5/free; ◉ 10am-5pm Tue-Thu, Sat & Sun, to 7pm Fri) Dip into the past as represented by artists working from the Middle Ages to the 19th century at this superb museum in a sensitively modernised monastery. The Sculpture Hall on the ground floor is especially impressive for its fine medieval sculptures and masterpieces by Renaissance artists Hans Baldung Grien and Lucas Cranach the Elder. Head upstairs for eye-level views of mounted gargoyles.

Schlossberg   VIEWPOINT

(Schlossbergring; cable car one-way/return €3.30/5.50; ◉ 9am-10pm daily Mar-Oct, closed Tue Nov-Feb) The forested Schlossberg dominates Freiburg. Take the footpath opposite the Schwabentor, leading up through sun-dappled woods, or hitch a ride on the recently restored *Schlossbergbahn* cable car. For serious hikers, several trails begin here including those to St Peter (17km) and Kandel (25km).

Rathausplatz   SQUARE

(Town Hall Square) Join locals relaxing in a cafe by the fountain in chestnut-shaded Rathausplatz, Freiburg's prettiest square. Pull out your camera to snap pictures of the square's ox-blood-red 16th-century Altes Rathaus (Old Town Hall) that houses the tourist office (p241); the step-gabled 19th-century Neues Rathaus (New Town Hall); and the medieval Martinskirche church with its modern interior.

Schwabentor   GATE

(Schwabenring) The 13th-century Schwabentor, on the Schwabenring, is a massive city gate with a mural of St George slaying the dragon, and tram tracks running under its arches. It's one of two intact medieval gates in Freiburg.

Museum für Stadtgeschichte   MUSEUM

(☑ 0761-201 2515; Münsterplatz 30; adult/concession €3/2; ◉ 10am-5pm Tue-Sun) The sculptor Christian Wentzinger's baroque townhouse, east of the Historisches Kaufhaus, now shelters this museum, spelling out in artefacts Freiburg's eventful past. Inside, a wrought-iron staircase guides the eye to an elaborate ceiling fresco.

Archäologisches Museum   MUSEUM

(☑ 0761-201 2574; www.freiburg.de; Rotteckring 5; adult/concession €4/3; ◉ 10am-5pm Tue-Sun) This archaeology-focused museum is inside the neo-Gothic **Colombischlössle**. From the skylit marble entrance, a cast-iron staircase ascends to a stash of finds from Celtic grave offerings to Roman artefacts and Stone Age statuettes.

Museum für Neue Kunst   GALLERY

(☑ 0761-201 2583; Marienstrasse 10; adult/concession €3/2; ◉ 10am-5pm Tue-Sun) Across the Gewerbekanal from the Altstadt, this gallery highlights 20th-century Expressionist and abstract art, including emotive works by Oskar Kokoschka and Otto Dix.

Historisches Kaufhaus   HISTORIC BUILDING

(Münsterplatz) Facing the Münster's south side and embellished with polychrome tiled turrets is the arcaded brick-red Historisches Kaufhaus, an early 16th-century merchants' hall. The coats of arms on the oriels and the four figures above the balcony symbolise Freiburg's allegiance to the House of Habsburg.

👉 Tours

Freiburg Kultour   TOURS

(☑ 017 661 266 675; www.freiburg-kultour.com; adult/concession €10/8; ◉ 2.30-4pm Fri, 10.30am-noon Sat, 11.30am-1pm Sun) Kultour offers 1½-to two-hour walking tours of the Altstadt and the Münster in German and English. Book online or call ahead. The meeting point is on Rathausplatz. A number of self-guided tours are available to download on its website.

🛏 Sleeping

Black Forest Hostel   HOSTEL €

(☑ 0761-881 7870; www.blackforest-hostel.de; Kartäuserstrasse 33; dm €18-28, s/d €44/64, linen €4; ◉ reception 7am-1am; @) Boho budget digs with chilled common areas, a shared kitchen, bike rental, musical instruments and a ping-pong table. There's no wi-fi but you can check email using the internet terminals. It's a five-minute walk from the town centre.

COLD FEET OR WEDDED BLISS?

As you wander the Altstadt, watch out for the gurgling *Bächle*, streamlets once used to water livestock and extinguish fires. Today they provide welcome relief for hot feet on sweltering summer days. Just be aware that you could get more than you bargained for: legend has it that if you accidentally step into the *Bächle*, you'll marry a Freiburger or a Freiburgerin.

Freiburg

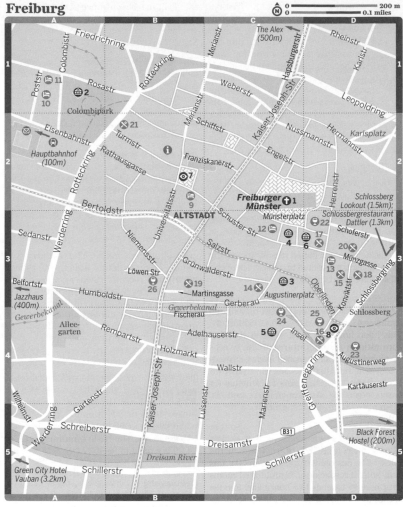

The Alex

BOUTIQUE HOTEL €€

(☎ 0761-296 970; www.the-alex-hotel.de; Rheinstrasse 29; d €94-148; P❄☎) The Alex stands head and shoulders above most hotels in town. Its clean, contemporary aesthetic includes lots of plate glass, blonde wood, natural materials and a muted palette of colours. Besides modern rooms with rain showers, there's a bar, Winery29, where you can try locally produced wines.

Green City Hotel Vauban

HOTEL €€

(☎ 0761-888 5740; http://hotel-vauban.de; Paula-Modersohn-Platz 5; d €96-116, apt €150; ☎) ∅ This ecofriendly hotel fits in neatly to Freiburg's Vauban neighbourhood, a shining model of sustainability with its PlusEnergy housing and car-free streets. The light, bright rooms are furnished with local woods and plump white bedding. The pick of the doubles have balconies. To reach it, take tram 3 from Freiburg Hauptbahnhof to Freiburg Paula-Modersohn-Platz.

Hotel Barbara

HISTORIC HOTEL €€

(☎ 0761-296 250; www.hotel-barbara.de; Poststrasse 4; s €80-98, d €114-156, apt €139-212; ☎) A grandfather clock, curvy staircases and high ceilings give this art nouveau townhouse a nostalgic feel. It's a homely, family-run place with

Freiburg

old-fashioned, pastel-hued rooms, homemade jams and eggs to order at breakfast. There's no lift so be prepared to lug your bags.

Hotel Schwarzwälder Hof   HOTEL €€
(☑ 0761-380 30; www.schwarzwaelder-hof.com; Herrenstrasse 43; s €70-85, d €99-120, f €150-180; ☞) This bijou hotel has an unrivalled style-for-euro ratio. A wrought-iron staircase sweeps up to stylish rooms furnished in classic, modern or traditional style. Some have postcard views of the Altstadt; others are suitable for families (cots are also available on request). There's also an on-site restaurant.

Hotel am Rathaus   HOTEL €€
(☑ 0761-296 160; www.am-rathaus.de; Rathausgasse 4-8; s €85-105, d €110-173; ℗☞) Right in the thick of things on Rathausplatz (p237), this neat hotel has spacious, neutral-toned rooms with homely touches like books and free tea and coffee in the lounge; ask for a rear-facing room if you're a light sleeper.

Hotel Minerva   HOTEL €€
(☑ 0761-386 490; www.minerva-freiburg.de; Poststrasse 8; s €65-99, d €133-155, tr €180; ☞) All curvaceous windows and polished wood, this art nouveau charmer is five minutes' trudge from the Altstadt. The sleek, contemporary rooms feature free wi-fi. Breakfast is a generous spread of fresh fruit, cold cuts, pastries, cereals and eggs.

★**Hotel Oberkirch**   HISTORIC HOTEL €€€
(☑ 0761-202 6868; www.hotel-oberkirch.de; Münsterplatz 22; s €119-139, d €159-199; ℗) Wake up to views of the Münster (p236) at this

green-shuttered hotel. The country-style rooms feature floral wallpaper, though some have recently been revamped. The dark-wood downstairs tavern (mains €17 to €25) does a roaring trade in hearty Badisch fare such as venison ragout with *Knödel* (dumplings).

🍴 Eating

Edo's Hummus Küche   VEGETARIAN €
(http://edoshummus.com; Atrium Augustinerplatz; light meals €2.50-8.50; ⊙11.30am-9pm Mon-Sat; ☞) Edo's pulls in the midday crowds with superb homemade hummus served with warm pitta, as well as lentils, fava bean salad and falafel. The basic hummus plate for €4.90 is a meal in itself.

Vegetage   VEGETARIAN €
(Rathausgasse 4, Bursengalerie; buffet €2.20 per 100g; ⊙11.30am-3pm Mon-Sat; ☞) For a quick, wholesome vegetarian lunch this buffet takes some beating. The freshly squeezed juices pack a vitamin punch. It's on the 1st floor of a little covered arcade just off central Rathausplatz (p237).

Markthalle   MARKET €
(www.markthalle-freiburg.de; Martinsgasse 235; light meals €4-8; ⊙8am-8pm Mon-Thu, to midnight Fri & Sat) Eat your way around the world – from curry to sushi, oysters to antipasti – at the food counters in this historical market hall, nicknamed 'Fressgässle'.

Gasthaus zum Kranz   GERMAN €€
(☑ 0761-217 1967; www.gasthauszumkranz.de; Herrenstrasse 40; mains €15-26; ⊙11.30am-3pm Mon,

---

DON'T MISS

EUROPE IN MINIATURE
....

Germany's largest theme park, **Europa-Park** (www.europapark.de; Europa-Park-Strasse 2, Rust; adult/concession €49.50/42.50; ⊙9am-6pm Apr-early Nov, to 8pm Aug–mid-Sep, 11am-7pm late Nov-early Jan), located 35km north of Freiburg near Rust, is Europe in miniature. Get soaked fjord-rafting in Scandinavia before nipping across to England to race at Silverstone, or Greece to ride the water roller coaster Poseidon. Aside from white-knuckle thrills, the park's Children's World amuses tots with labyrinths and Viking ships.

When Mickey waltzed off to Paris, Europa-Park even got its own mousy mascot, Euromaus.

Shuttle buses (hourly in the morning) link Ringsheim train station, on the Freiburg–Offenburg line, with the park. By car, take the A5 exit to Rust (57b).

11.30am-3pm & 5.30pm-midnight Tue-Sat, noon-3pm & 5.30pm-midnight Sun) There's always a good buzz at this rustic, quintessentially Badisch tavern. Pull up a hefty chair at one of the even heftier timber tables for well-prepared regional favourites such as roast suckling pig, *Maultaschen* (pork and spinach ravioli) and *Sauerbraten* (beef pot roast with vinegar, onions and peppercorns). Service can be hit-and-miss.

Englers Weinkrügle   GERMAN €€
(☑0761-383 115; Konviktstrasse 12; mains €9-19; ⊙11.30am-2pm & 5.30pm-midnight Tue-Sun) A warm, woody Baden-style *Weinstube* (wine tavern) with wisteria growing out front and regional flavours on the menu. The trout in various guises (for instance, with Riesling or almond butter sauce) is delicious.

Martin's Bräu   PUB FOOD €€
(☑0761-387 000; www.martinsbräu-freiburg.de; Martinsgässle; mains €9-18; ⊙11am-midnight Sun-Thu, to 1am Fri & Sat) Home-brewed pilsners and craft beers wash down meaty snacks from ox-tongue salad to suckling pig and enormous bratwursts. Copper vats gleam in the wood-panelled interior. You'll find it off Kaiser-Joseph-Strasse.

Enoteca Trattoria   ITALIAN €€
(☑0761-389 9130; www.enoteca-freiburg.de; Schwabentorplatz 6; mains €16-30; ⊙6pm-midnight Mon-Sat) This is the trattoria of the two Enoteca twins (the more formal restaurant is at Gerberau 21). The chef here always hits the mark with authentic Italian dishes such as *taleggio* ravioli with Frascati sauce and glazed pear.

★Kreuzblume   INTERNATIONAL €€€
(☑0761-311 94; www.hotel-kreuzblume.de; Konviktstrasse 31; mains €18-32, 3-course menu €42.50; ⊙6-11pm Wed-Sun; ☑) Situated on a flower-festooned lane, Kreuzblume is a pocket-sized restaurant with clever backlighting, slick monochrome decor and a menu fizzing with bright, sunny flavours. It attracts a rather food-literate clientele. Each dish combines just a few hand-picked ingredients in bold and tasty ways: apple, celery and chestnut soup, say, or roast duck breast with wild herb salad. Service is top notch.

★Wolfshöhle   MEDITERRANEAN €€€
(☑0761-303 03; www.wolfshoehle-freiburg.de; Konviktstrasse 8; mains €23-49, 3-course lunch/dinner €35/63; ⊙noon-2pm & 6-9.30pm Tue-Sat) With tables set up on a pretty square, Wolfshöhle is a summer-evening magnet. The menu whisks you off on a gastronomical tour of the Mediterranean, with well-executed, beautifully presented dishes listed in the modern, ingredient-driven way: Jerusalem artichoke with black truffle and hazelnut, for instance, or sea bass with saffron and clams. The €35, three-course lunch offers a good introduction.

Zirbelstube   GASTRONOMY €€€
(☑0761-210 60; www.colombi.de; Rotteckring 16; mains €34-48; ⊙noon-2pm & 7pm-midnight Tue-Sat) Freiburg's bastion of fine dining is this Michelin-starred restaurant, decorated in warm Swiss pine. Chefs of exacting standards allow each ingredient to shine in specialities such as glazed rack of venison with caramelised pineapple, and cod confit with cauliflower cooked three ways – all perfectly matched with quality wines.

Schlossbergrestaurant
Dattler   GERMAN €€€
(☑0761-137 1700; http://dattler.de; Am Schlossberg 1; mains €20-34; ⊙9.15am-11pm Wed-Sun; ☑) One for special occasions, this refined restaurant atop the Schlossberg (p237) has panoramic windows affording compelling surround views of Freiburg's spire-studded cityscape. The food is pretty impressive, with the chef keeping things regional in dishes

such as *Badisches Rahmtöpfle* (pork medallions with mushrooms and homemade *Spätzle)*. There's plenty to appeal to vegetarians and vegans.

🍸 Drinking & Entertainment

Schlappen PUB
(www.schlappen.com; Löwenstrasse 2; ⊗11am-1am Mon-Wed, to 2am Thu, to 3am Fri & Sat, 3pm-1am Sun) In historical digs and crammed with antiques and vintage theatre posters, this rocking, friendly boozer has made the magic happen for generations of students. The drinks – a good array of beers, gins, absinthes and whiskies – are affordable and the terrace heaves in summer.

Alte Wache WINE BAR
(www.alte-wache.com; Münsterplatz 38; ⊗10am-7pm Mon-Fri, to 4pm Sat) Right on the square, this 18th-century guardhouse serves local Müller-Thurgau and Pinot Noir wines at the tasting tables. See the website for details of the regular food and wine events.

Hausbrauerei Feierling MICROBREWERY
(www.feierling.de; Gerberau 46; ⊗11am-midnight Sun-Thu, 11am-1am Fri & Sat) This stream-side microbrewery and beer garden is a relaxed spot to quaff a cold one under the chestnut trees in summer or next to the copper vats in winter. Snacks including pretzels and sausages (snacks €3 to €9.50) soak up the malty, organic brews.

Greiffenegg-Schlössle BEER GARDEN
(Schlossbergring 3; ⊗11am-midnight Mar-Oct) All of Freiburg is at your feet from this chestnut-shaded beer garden atop Schlossberg (p237). Perfect sunset spot.

Juri's COCKTAIL BAR
(www.juris-bar.de; Schwabentorplatz 7; ⊗6pm-2am Wed-Sat & Mon) What a find this mulberry-hued wine and cocktail bar is, with its cushion-strewn nooks and candlelit tables. It does a head-spinning range of wines and cocktails from gin basil smashes (gin, basil, sugar and lemon) to Sloppy Joe mojitos made with mint rum.

Jazzhaus LIVE MUSIC
(☑0761-349 73; www.jazzhaus.de; Schnewlinstrasse 1) Under the brick arches of a wine cellar, this venue hosts first-rate jazz, rock and world music concerts at least a couple of nights a week (see the website for details). It morphs into a club from 11pm to 3am on Friday and Saturday nights.

ℹ️ Information

Available at the tourist office, the three-day **WelcomeKarte**, covering all public transport and the **Schauinslandbahn** (www.schauinslandbahn.de; Schauinslandstrasse, Oberried; return adult/child €12.50/8, one-way €9/6; ⊗9am-5pm Oct-Jun, to 6pm Jul-Sep) cable car, costs €26/16 per adult/child.

Freiburg Tourist Office (☑0761-388 1880; www.visit.freiburg.de; Rathausplatz 2-4; ⊗8am-8pm Mon-Fri, 9.30am-5pm Sat, 10.30am-3.30pm Sun Jun-Sep, 8am-6pm Mon-Fri, 9.30am-2.30pm Sat, 10am-noon Sun Oct-May) Pick up the three-day WelcomeKarte (€26).

Post Office (Eisenbahnstrasse 58-62; ⊗8.30am-6.30pm Mon-Fri, 9am-2pm Sat)

ℹ️ Getting There & Around

AIR
Freiburg shares **EuroAirport** (BSL; ☑France + 33 3 89 90 31 11; www.euroairport.com) with Basel (Switzerland) and Mulhouse (France); get there on the airport bus. The airport is 71km south of Freiburg via the A5 motorway. Low-cost airline easyJet and Ryanair fly from here.

BICYCLE
Bike paths run along the Dreisam River, leading westward to Breisach and then into France. **Freiburg Bikes** (☑0761-202 3426; www.freiburgbikes.de; Wentzingerstrasse 15; city bike 4hr/day €10/15, mountain/e-bike per day €22/30; ⊗9.30am-1pm & 2-7pm Mon-Sat, 10am-1pm & 2-6pm Sun Jun-Sep, reduced hours rest of year), across the bridge from the Hauptbahnhof, rents bikes and sells cycling maps.

BUS
The **airport bus** (☑0761 500 500; www.freiburger-reisedienst.de; one-way/return €19.90/39) goes hourly from Freiburg's bus station to EuroAirport. The journey takes roughly an hour.

Südbaden Bus (www.suedbadenbus.de) and RVF (www.rvf.de) operate bus and train links to towns and villages throughout the southern Black Forest. Single tickets for one/two/three zones cost €2.30/4/5.70; a 24-hour Regio24 ticket costs €5.80 for one person and €8.20 for two to five people. Buses depart from the Hauptbahnhof.

TRAIN
Freiburg is on a major north–south rail corridor, with frequent departures from the **Hauptbahnhof** for destinations such as Basel (€19.10 to €26.60, 45 minutes) and Baden-Baden (€23.70 to €40, 45 minutes to 1½ hours). There's a local connection to Breisach (€5.70, 26 minutes, at least hourly).

Schauinsland

One of the best vantage points in the Black Forest, with soul-stirring views reaching over forest, valley and to the Alps beyond on cloud-free days, the 1284m **peak** (www.bergwelt-schauinsland.de) of Schauinsland is an easy day trip from Freiburg, a mere cable car (p241) ride away. Up top, walking trails are plentiful and morph into cross-country ski tracks in winter. The peak is topped by a lookout tower commanding fabulous views to the Rhine Valley and Alps, plus walking, cross-country and cycling trails that allow you to capture the scenery from many angles. You can bounce downhill from Schauinsland on the 8km off-road **scooter track** (www.rollerstrecke.de; Schauinsland Peak; €25; ☉2pm & 5pm Sun May-Jun, Sat & Sun Jul, Sep & Oct, Wed-Sun Aug), one of Europe's longest; it takes around an hour from top to bottom station.

On a quiet perch above the rippling hills of the Black Forest, **Die Halde** (☑07602-944 70; www.halde.com; Oberried-Hofsgrund; d incl full board €280-304; [P][@][≋]) is a rustic-chic retreat, with an open fire crackling in the bar, calm rooms dressed in local wood and a glass-walled spa overlooking the valley. Martin Hegar cooks market-fresh dishes from trout to wild boar with panache in the wood-panelled restaurant (mains €24-35).

St Peter

☑07660 / POP 2583

As if cupped in celestial hands, the twin-spired baroque abbey church of St Peter thrusts up above meadows and hills plaited with dark-green spruce forest and interwoven with hiking trails.

In this serene, back-to-nature village on the southern slopes of Mt Kandel (1243m), folk are deeply committed to time-honoured traditions. On religious holidays, villagers from toddlers to pensioners still proudly don colourful, handmade *Trachten* (folkloric costumes).

The town's most outstanding landmark is this former **Benedictine abbey** (Klosterhof 11; guided tours adult/concession €6/2; ☉tours 11.30am Sun, 11am Tue, 2.30pm Thu), a rococo jewel designed by Peter Thumb of Vorarlberg. Many of the period's top artists collaborated on the sumptuous interior of the twin-towered red-sandstone church, including Joseph Anton Feuchtmayer, who carved the gilded Zähringer duke statues affixed to pillars. Guided tours (in German) to the monastery complex include the rococo library.

The **tourist office** (☑07652-120 60; www.hochschwarzwald.de; Klosterhof 11; ☉9am-noon & 3-5pm Mon-Fri; ☎) is under the archway leading to the Klosterhof (the abbey courtyard). A nearby information panel shows room availability.

St Peter is on the Schwarzwald Panoramastrasse, a 70km-long route from Waldkirch (17km northeast of Freiburg) to Feldberg with giddy mountain views.

By public transport, the best way to get from Freiburg to St Peter is to take the train to Kirchzarten (13 minutes, twice hourly) and then bus 7216 (23 minutes, twice hourly). Local public transport is free with the KONUS guest card.

Breisach

☑07667 / POP 15,500

Rising above vineyards and the Rhine, Breisach is where the Black Forest spills into Alsace. Given its geographical and cultural proximity to France, it's little surprise that the locals share their neighbours' passion for a good bottle of plonk.

From the cobbled streets lined with pastel-painted houses you'd never guess that 85% of the town was flattened in WWII, so successful has been the reconstruction.

⊙ Sights & Activities

St Stephansmünster　　　　　　CHURCH
(Münsterplatz; ☉9am-5pm Mon-Sat) [FREE]
Plonked on a hill above the centre for all to behold in wonder, the Romanesque and Gothic St Stephansmünster shelters a faded fresco cycle, Martin Schongauer's *The Last Judgment* (1491), and a magnificent altar triptych (1526) carved from linden wood. From the tree-shaded square outside, the Schänzletreppe steps lead down to the Gutgesellentor, the gate where Pope John XXIII was scandalously caught fleeing the Council of Constance in 1415.

Neuf-Brisach　　　　　　　　　FORTRESS
Vauban's French fortified town of Neuf-Brisach (New Breisach), a Unesco World Heritage Site, sits 4km west of Breisach. Shaped like an eight-pointed star, the town was commissioned by Louis XIV in 1697 to strengthen French defences and prevent

the area from falling to the Habsburgs. It was conceived by Sébastien Le Prestre de Vauban (1633–1707). Take bus 1076 from Breisach station to get here.

BFS BOATING
(www.bfs-info.de; Rheinuferstrasse; ☉Apr-Sep) Boat excursions along the Rhine are run by BFS. A one-hour harbour tour costs €12.

🛏 Sleeping

DJH Hostel HOSTEL €
(☑07667-7665; www.jugendherberge-breisach.de; Rheinuferstrasse 12; dm €23.90-30.40; P☎) On the banks of the Rhine, this hostel has first-rate facilities, including a barbecue hut, volleyball court and access to the swimming pool next door.

ℹ Information

Breisach Tourist Office (☑07667-940 155; http://tourismus.breisach.de; Marktplatz 16; ☉9am-12.30pm & 1.30-6pm Mon-Fri, 10am-3pm Sat) The tourist office can advise on wine tasting and private rooms in the area.

ℹ Getting There & Around

Breisach's train station, 500m southeast of Marktplatz, serves Freiburg (€5.70, 26 minutes, at least hourly) and towns in the Kaiserstuhl. Buses go to Colmar, 22km west.

Breisach is a terrific base for free-wheeling over borders. Great rides include crossing the Rhine to the delightful French town of Colmar, or pedalling through terraced vineyards to Freiburg. Hire an e-bike from the centrally located **Fahrradverleih Breisach** (☑07667-287 1183; http://fahrrad verleih-breisach.de; Fischerhalde 5a; per half-/full day €25/30; ☉10am-2pm & 5-7pm Mon-Sat).

Feldberg

☑07655, 07676, 07652 / POP 1880
At 1493m, Feldberg is the Black Forest's highest mountain, and one of the few places here with downhill skiing. The actual mountaintop is treeless and not particularly attractive but on clear days the view southward towards the Alps is mesmerising.

Feldberg is also the name given to a cluster of five villages, of which Altglashütten is the hub.

Feldberg-Ort is around 9km west of Altglashütten, right in the heart of the 42-sq-km nature reserve that covers much of the mountain. Most of the ski lifts are here, including the scenic *Feldbergbahn* chairlift to the Bismarckdenkmal (Bismarck monument).

◉ Sights & Activities

Todtnauer Wasserfall WATERFALL
(Todtnau; adult/concession €2/1; ☉daylight hours) Head south on the Freiburg–Feldberg road and you'll glimpse the roaring Todtnauer Wasserfall. While the 97m falls are not as high as those in Triberg (p246), they're every bit as spectacular, tumbling down sheer rock faces and illuminating the velvety hills with their brilliance. Hike the zigzagging 9km trail to Aftersteg for views over the cataract. Take care on paths in winter when the falls often freeze solid. The waterfall's car park is on the L126.

Feldbergbahn CABLE CAR
(www.feldbergbahn.de; Dr-Pilet-Spur 17; adult/concession return €9.50/6.60; ☉9am-5pm Jul-Sep, to 4.30pm May, Jun & Oct) A cable car whisks you to the 1493m summit of Feldberg in minutes. The panorama unfolding at the top reaches across the patchwork meadows and woods of the Black Forest all the way to the Vosges and Swiss and French Alps on clear days.

Feldberg–Steig HIKING
Orbiting the Black Forest's highest peak, the 1493m Feldberg, this 12km walk traverses a nature reserve that's home to chamois and wildflowers. On clear days, the views of the Alps are glorious. It's possible to snowshoe part of this route in winter.

Haus der Natur HIKING
(☑07676-933 630; www.naturpark-suedschwarz wald.de; Dr-Pilet-Spur 4; ☉10am-5pm) The eco-conscious Haus der Natur can advise on the area's great hiking opportunities, including the rewarding 12km Feldberg–Steig to the Feldberg summit. In winter, Feldberg's snowy heights are ideal for a stomp through twinkling woods. Strap on snowshoes for the 3km Seebuck-Trail or more challenging 9km Gipfel-Trail. The Haus der Natur rents snowshoes for €10/5 per day for adults/children.

🛏 Sleeping & Eating

Naturfreundehaus HOSTEL €
(☑07676-336; www.naturfreundehaus-feldberg. de; Am Baldenweger Buck; dm €15.50) ✔ In a Black Forest farmhouse a 30-minute walk from Feldberg's summit, this back-to-nature hostel uses renewable energy and serves fair-trade and organic produce at breakfast (€6). Surrounding views of wooded hills and comfy, pine-clad dorms make this a great spot for hiking in summer, and skiing and snowshoeing in winter.

WORTH A TRIP

KAISERSTUHL

Squeezed between the Black Forest and the French Vosges, the low-lying volcanic hills of the Kaiserstuhl in the Upper Rhine Valley yield highly quaffable wines, including fruity *Spätburgunder* (Pinot Noir) and *Grauburgunder* (Pinot gris) varieties.

The grapes owe their quality to a unique microclimate, hailed as Germany's sunniest, and fertile loess (clay and silt) soil that retains heat during the night. Nature enthusiasts should look out for rarities including sand lizards, praying mantis and European bee-eaters.

The Breisach tourist office (p243) can advise on cellar tours, wine tastings, bike paths such as the 55km Kaiserstuhl-Tour circuit, and trails such as the Winzerweg (Wine Growers' Trail), an intoxicating 15km hike from Achkarren to Riegel.

The *Kaiserstuhlbahn* does a loop around the Kaiserstuhl. Stops (where you may have to change trains) include Sasbach, Endingen, Riegel and Gottenheim. The area is 15km northeast of Breisach.

Landhotel Bierhäusle　　　GUESTHOUSE €€
(🖉 07655-306; www.bierhaeusle-feldberg.de; Orts-strasse 22, Feldberg-Falkau; d €99-120, tr €118-138; 🅿 🛜 🐾) A winner for families, this enticing chalet-style guesthouse has dreamy views over forested hills, and immaculate country-style rooms done out in florals and pine. The best open onto balconies. For kids, there are games, a playground, trampoline and animals (goats, rabbits and guinea pigs) to pet. Breakfast is a good spread of bread, cold cuts, homemade jam, eggs and fruit.

Schwarzwaldhaus　　　　　　GERMAN €€
(🖉 07655-933 833; www.das-schwarzwaldhaus. com; Falkauer Strasse 3, Feldberg-Altglashütten; mains €11-21, 2-course lunch €10.90; ⊙ 11am-3pm & 6-10pm Fri-Tue, 6-10pm Thu; 🖉 🖶) With dark wood panelling, low beams, banquette seating and a *Kachelofen* (ceramic tiled oven), the Schwarzwaldhaus is a rustic tavern in the traditional Black Forest mould. Mains swing from perfectly crisp schnitzel to venison goulash with bread dumplings, with half portions and specials for kids and vegetarians available.

ℹ Information

Feldberg Tourist Office (🖉 07652-120 60; Kirchgasse 1, Altglashütten; ⊙ 9am-noon & 1-5pm Mon-Fri; 🛜) Altglashütten's Rathaus harbours the tourist office, with stacks of info on activities, plus rucksacks, pushchairs and GPS devices for hire from €2 to €5 per day.

ℹ Getting There & Away

Bärental and Altglashütten are stops on the *Dreiseenbahn*, linking Titisee with Seebrugg (Schluchsee). From the train station in Bärental, bus 7300 makes trips at least hourly to Feldberg-Ort (€2.25, 21 minutes).

From late December until the end of the season, shuttle buses run by Feldberg SBG link Feldberg and Titisee with the ski lifts (free with a lift ticket or Gästekarte).

Titisee-Neustadt

🖉 07651 / POP 12,083

Titisee is a cheerful summertime playground with a name that makes English-speaking travellers giggle. The iridescent blue-green glacial lake, rimmed by forest, has everyone diving for their cameras or into the ice-cool water. Though a tad on the touristy side in the peak months, a quick stroll along these shores brings you to quiet bays and woodland trails that are blissfully crowd-free.

🏃 Activities

Seepromenade　　　　WALKING, WATER SPORTS
Wander along the flowery Seestrasse promenade and you'll soon leave the crowds and made-in-China cuckoo clocks behind to find secluded bays ideal for swimming and picnicking. A lap of the lake is 7km. Hire a rowing boat or pedalo at one of the set-ups along the lake front; expect to pay around €12 per hour.

Strandbad Titisee　　　　　　SWIMMING
(Strandbadstrasse 1; ⊙ 9am-7pm Jun-Sep) FREE
This lake-front lido has a pool and children's pool, a slide, floating raft and a volleyball area, as well as lawns for sunbathing. Action Forest rents kayaks and stand-up paddle boards here for €10/18 per half/full hour.

Badeparadies　　　　　　　　　SPA
(www.badeparadies-schwarzwald.de; Am Badeparadies 1; 3hr €20, incl sauna complex €24; ⊙ 10am-10pm Mon-Thu, to 11pm Fri, 9am-10pm Sat & Sun) This huge, glass-canopied leisure

and wellness centre is a year-round draw. You can lounge, cocktail in hand, by palm-fringed lagoons in Palmenoase, race down white-knuckle slides with gaggles of overexcited kids in Galaxy, or strip off in themed saunas with waterfalls and Black Forest views in the adults-only Wellnessoase.

Bootsvermietung Titisee BOATING
(www.boote-titisee.de; Seestrasse 37; €26/49 per half-hour/hour) For a novel way to paddle across the lake, rent one of the so-called 'donuts', giant rings with space for the whole family. It also rents out electric boats.

🛏️ Sleeping & Eating

Neubierhäusle PENSION €€
(☎07651-8230; www.neubierhaeusle.de; Neustädter Strasse 79; d €85-95, apt €148-178; P🖘) Big forest views, piny air and pastures on the doorstep – this farmhouse is the perfect country retreat. Dressed in local wood, the light-filled rooms are supremely comfy, while apartments have space for families. Your hosts lay on a hearty breakfast (included in the room rate), and you can help yourself to free tea and fruit throughout the day.

Action Forest Active Hotel GUESTHOUSE €€
(☎07651-825 60; www.action-forest-hotel.de; Neustädter Strasse 41; s €55-60, d €100-110, tr €120-140, q €140-170; P🖘) You can't miss this green-fronted guesthouse, snuggled up against the forest. It's run by a friendly family and contains spacious, light-filled rooms (including generously sized triples and quads for families), fitted out with country-style pine furnishings.

Bergseeblick PENSION €€
(☎07675-929 4440; https://bergseeblick.com; Erlenweg 3; s €40, d €75-95, tr €95, f €125; P🖘) But a two-minute stroll from the shores of Titisee, this family-friendly guesthouse has recently modernised rooms – some big enough for families – done out in neutral colours and chunky pine furnishings. The lounge with complimentary drinks and snacks is a nice touch, and the generous breakfast includes fresh rolls, pastries, fruit, cold cuts and cooked options.

Hotel Bären HOTEL €€€
(☎07651-8060; www.baeren-titisee.de; Neustädter Strasse 35; d €182-252; P🖘🏊) Run by the welcoming Sauter family, this streamlined hotel fuses contemporary living with traditional local materials (note the wood shingling on the facade). The bright, spacious rooms have warm tones and ultramodern bathrooms, and open onto balconies with fine Black Forest views. There's an impressive spa area with an indoor pool, sauna and steam room and barefoot path.

Villinger Feinkost DELI €
(☎07651-1401; www.feinkost-villinger.de; Hauptstrasse 6, Neustadt; lunch €9.50-14; ⊙7.30am-9pm Mon-Wed, to 10.30pm Thu-Sat) Market-fresh food prepared in creative ways, local sourcing and a nicely chilled setting make this upbeat bistro and deli one of the best picks in town. Lunch specials swing from brook trout with polenta to *Käsespätzle* (cheese-topped noodles) and beef bourguignon – all tasty and cracking value.

ℹ️ Information

Titisee-Neustadt Tourist Office (☎07652-120 60; www.hochschwarzwald.de; Strandbadstrasse 4; ⊙9am-5pm Mon-Fri; 🖘) The tourist office stocks walking and cycling maps, and has pushchairs and backpacks available to hire (€3 to €5). Free wi-fi.

ℹ️ Getting There & Around

While the *Höllentalbahn* undergoes extensive restoration work in 2018, there is a restricted train service. From Titisee train station, there are frequent services on bus 7257 to Schluchsee (40 minutes) and bus 7300 to Feldberg–Bärental (13 minutes). The train station in Titisee is just 200m north of the lake.

Local public transport is free with the KONUS guest card.

Ski-Hirt (☎07651-922 80; Titiseestrasse 28, Neustadt; ⊙9am-6.30pm Mon-Fri, to 4pm Sat) rents reliable bikes and ski equipment, and can supply details on local cycling options.

Schluchsee
☎07656 / POP 2440

Photogenically poised above its namesake lake – the Black Forest's largest – and rimmed by forest, Schluchsee tempts you outdoors with pursuits such as swimming, windsurfing, hiking, cycling and, ahem, skinny-dipping from the secluded bays on the western shore. The otherwise sleepy resort jolts to life with sunseekers in summer and cross-country skiers in winter.

🥾 Activities & Tours

Wutachschlucht HIKING
(www.wutachschlucht.de) This wild gorge, carved out by a fast-flowing river and flanked by

near-vertical rock faces, lies near Bonndorf, close to the Swiss border and 20km east of Schluchsee. The best way to experience its unique microclimate, where you might spot orchids, ferns, rare butterflies and lizards, is on this 13km trail leading from Schattenmühle to Wutachmühle.

Aqua Fun Strandbad
SWIMMING

(Freiburger Strasse 16; adult/concession €4/2.70; ⏰9am-7pm May-Sep) Popular with families, this lake-front lido has a heated pool, water slide and rapid river, a sandy beach and a volleyball court.

MS Schluchsee
BOATING

(www.seerundfahrten.de; Freiburger Strasse; ⏰10.30am-4.45pm late Apr-Oct) Boat tours around Schluchsee make stops in Aha, Seebrugg and the Strandbad. A 75-minute round trip costs €10/5 for adults/children. You can hire rowing boats and pedalos for €6/10 per half/full hour.

🛏 Sleeping & Eating

Gasthof Hirschen
GUESTHOUSE €€

(☑07656-989 40; www.hirschen-fischbach.de; Schluchseestrasse 9, Fischbach; s €65-70, d €136; 🅿🛜) It's worth going the extra mile to this farmhouse, prettily perched on a hillside in Fischbach, 4km north of Schluchsee. The simple, quiet rooms are a good-value base for summer hiking and modest winter skiing. There's also a sauna, playground and a restaurant (mains €13 to €21) dishing up regional fare.

Heger's Parkhotel Flora
SPA HOTEL €€€

(☑07656-974 20; www.parkhotel-flora.de; Sonnhalde 22; s €160 d €240-256, ste €266-342; 🅿🛜🏊) This luxe spa hotel has beautiful views of the wooded hills from its gardens and outdoor pool, a lounge warmed by an open fire and modern, generously sized rooms. After a day's hiking in the hills, the spa area, with its salt inhalation room and anti-ageing vinotherapy treatments is just the ticket. There's also a refined restaurant.

Parkhotel Flora
EUROPEAN €€

(☑07656-974 20; www.parkhotel-flora.de; mains €18.50-32.50; ⏰6-9.30pm Mon-Fri, noon-1.30pm & 6-9.30pm Sat & Sun; 🍴) At the hotel of the same name, this elegant restaurant majors in well-executed regional and international dishes, from Black Forest trout in almond butter to rabbit ragout with Pinot blanc. These are married with Kaiserstuhl wines from the family vineyard. In summer, try to wangle a table on the garden terrace. The menu caters for allergies and vegetarians.

Seehof
INTERNATIONAL €€

(☑07656-988 9965; http://seehof-schluchsee.de; Kirchsteige 4; mains €14.50-27; ⏰11.30am-10.30pm) Seehof is an inviting spot for a bite to eat, with a terrace overlooking the lake. Its menu is packed with local fish and meat mains, salads, pizzas and ice cream.

ℹ Information

Schluchsee Tourist Office (☑07652-120 60; www.schluchsee.de; Fischbacher Strasse 7, Haus des Gastes; ⏰9am-4pm Mon-Fri) Schluchsee's tourist office hands out maps and has info on activities and accommodation.

ℹ Getting There & Around

Bus 913 runs regularly to Feldberg–Altglashütten (10 minutes) and Titisee (29 minutes). Bus 7257 links Schluchsee three or four times daily with the Neustadt and Titisee train stations (40 minutes). Local public transport is free with the KONUS guest card.

City, mountain and e-bikes can be rented for €13/14/25 per day at **Müllers** (www.staumauer-schluchsee.de; An der Staumauer 1; ⏰10am-6pm Apr-Oct). An hour's pedalo/rowing boat/motor boat hire costs €8/8/17.

Triberg
☑07722 / POP 4787

Home to Germany's highest waterfall, heir to the original 1915 Black Forest gateau recipe, and nesting ground of the world's biggest cuckoos, Triberg leaves visitors reeling with superlatives. It was here that in bleak winters past folk huddled in snowbound farmhouses to carve the clocks that would drive the world cuckoo, and here that in a flash of brilliance the waterfall was harnessed to power the country's first electric street lamps in 1884.

◎ Sights & Activities

⭐Triberger Wasserfälle
WATERFALL

(adult/concession €5/4.50) Niagara they ain't but Germany's highest waterfalls do exude their own wild romanticism. The Gutach River feeds the seven-tiered falls, which drop a total of 163m and are illuminated until 10pm. A paved trail accesses the cascades. Pick up a bag of peanuts at the ticket counter to feed the tribes of inquisitive red squirrels. Entry is cheaper in winter. The falls are located in central Triberg.

Stöcklewaldturm
TOWER

(www.stoecklewaldturm.de; admission €0.50; ⊙10am-8pm Wed-Sun May-Sep, 11am-7pm Wed-Sun Oct-Apr) A steady and attractive 6.5km walk through spruce forest and pastures from Triberg's waterfall brings you to this 1070m-high 19th-century lookout tower, where the 360° views stretch from the Swabian Alps to the snowcapped Alps. The car park on the L175 is a 10-minute stroll from the tower. Footpaths head off in all directions from the summit, one of which leads to a woodsy cafe (snacks €2.50-7).

Eble Uhren–Park
LANDMARK

(www.uhren-park.de; Schonachbach 27; adult/child €2/free; ⊙9am-6pm Mon-Sat, 10am-6pm Sun) The *Guinness World Records*–listed world's largest cuckoo clock occupies an entire house, but is mostly a gimmick to lure shoppers inside a large clock shop. It's still interesting to get a glimpse of its supersized mechanism and hear the call of the whopping 4.5m cuckoo.

Haus der 1000 Uhren
MUSEUM

(House of 1000 Clocks; ☑07722-963 00; www.hausder1000uhren.de; Hauptstrasse 79; ⊙9.30am-6pm May-Sep, 10am-5pm Oct-Apr) A glockenspiel bashes out melodies and a cuckoo greets his fans with a hopelessly croaky squawk on the hour at the kitschy House of 1000 Clocks, a wonderland of clocks from traditional to trendy. The latest quartz models feature a sensor that sends the cuckoo to sleep after dark!

Weltgrösste Kuckucksuhr
LANDMARK

(First World's Largest Cuckoo Clock; www.dold-urlaub.de; Untertalstrasse 28, Schonach; adult/child €2/1; ⊙10am-noon & 1-5pm Tue-Sun) A rival to the hotly contested giant-cuckoo-clock crown, the so-called 'world's oldest-largest cuckoo clock' kicked into gear in 1980 and took local clockmaker Joseph Dold three years to build by hand. A Dold family member is usually around to explain the mechanism.

Gütenbach-Simonswäldertal
HIKING

Gütenbach, 22km south of Triberg, is the trailhead for one of the Black Forest's most beautiful half-day hikes. It leads to Simonswäldertal, 13km distant. A forest trail threads to Balzer Herrgott, where a tree has grown into a sandstone figure of Christ. Walking downhill from here to Simonswälder Valley, fir-draped hills rise like a curtain before you.

Sanitas Spa
SPA

(☑07722-860 20; www.sanitas-spa.de; Gartenstrasse 24; 2hr pass €15, half day €26-30, full day €45-50; ⊙10am-10pm) Fronted by wraparound windows overlooking Triberg's forested hills, Parkhotel Wehrle's day spa is gorgeous. This is a serene spot to wind down in, with its spacily lit kidney-shaped pool, exquisitely tiled hammams, steam rooms, whirlpool and waterbed meditation room. Treatments vary from *rhassoul* clay wraps to reiki. Admission is cheaper on weekdays. Towel and robe hire is available for €8.

Sleeping & Eating

Gasthaus Staude
GUESTHOUSE €€

(☑07722-4802; http://gasthaus-staude.com; Obertal 20, Triberg-Gremmelsbach; s €55, d €86-104; 🅿🛜) A beautiful example of a 17th-century Black Forest farmhouse, with its hip roof, snug timber-clad interior and wonderfully rural setting in the forest, Gasthaus Staude is worth going the extra mile for. The rooms are silent and countrified, with chunky wood furnishings – the most romantic one has a four-poster bed. It's a 15-minute drive east of town on the B500.

Parkhotel Wehrle
HISTORIC HOTEL €€€

(☑07722-860 20; www.parkhotel-wehrle.de; Gartenstrasse 24; s €95-115, d €159-265; 🅿🛜🌊) Standing proud on Triberg's main drag for the past 400 years, this historical hotel has quarters with a baroque or Biedermeier touch, some beautifully furnished with antiques and the best with Duravit whirlpool tubs. The hotel's restaurant is highly regarded. Guests have entry to the fabulous Sanitas Spa.

★Café Schäfer
CAFE €

(☑07722-4465; www.cafe-schaefer-triberg.de; Hauptstrasse 33; cakes €3-4; ⊙9am-6pm Mon, Tue, Thu & Fri, 8am-6pm Sat, 11am-6pm Sun) Confectioner Claus Schäfer uses the original 1915 recipe for Black Forest gateau to prepare this sinful treat that layers chocolate cake perfumed with cherry brandy, whipped cream and sour cherries and wraps it all in more cream and shaved chocolate. Trust us, it's worth the calories.

Parkhotel Wehrle Restaurant
GERMAN €€€

(www.parkhotel-wehrle.de; Gartenstrasse 24; mains €15-24; ⊙6-9pm daily, noon-2pm Sun) Hemingway once waxed lyrical about the trout he ordered at this venerable restaurant.

ⓘ Information

Triberg's main drag is the B500, which runs more or less parallel to the Gutach River. The town's focal point is the Marktplatz, a steep 1.2km uphill walk from the Bahnhof.

Triberg Tourist Office (07722-866 490; www.triberg.de; Wallfahrtstrasse 4; 9am-5pm Mon-Fri, 10am-5pm Sat & Sun) Inside the Schwarzwald-Museum. Stocks walking (€3), cross-country ski trail (€2) and mountain bike (€6.90) maps.

ℹ Getting There & Away

From the Bahnhof, 1.5km north of the centre, the *Schwarzwaldbahn* train line loops southeast to Konstanz (€27.50, 1½ hours, hourly), and northwest to Offenburg (€13.50, 46 minutes, hourly).

Bus 7150 travels north through the Gutach and Kinzig valleys to Offenburg; bus 7265 heads south to Villingen via St Georgen. Buses also depart from the Bahnhof.

Martinskapelle

A road twists scenically up a remote valley to **Martinskapelle** at 1085m, so named because of the little whitewashed chapel that has stood here in some shape or form since around AD 800. A beautiful swath of forest, interwoven with marked walking trails in summer and cross-country ski tracks in winter, unfolds at the top. It's a serene place for slipping away from the crowds.

A scenic and easygoing 10km loop walk begins at the Martinskapelle. The well-marked path wriggles through forest to tower-topped Brendturm (1149m), which affords views from Feldberg to the Vosges and the Alps on cloud-free days. Continue via Brendhäusle and Rosseck for a stunning vista of overlapping mountains and forest.

It's worth spending the night up here at the **Kolmenhof** (07723-931 00; www.kolmenhof.de; An der Donauquelle; s/d €55/115; P 🤖) to appreciate the total sense of calm, early morning forest walks and views. The closest town of real note is Triberg, where there are more accommodation choices.

Bus 7270 runs roughly hourly from the Marktplatz in Triberg to Escheck (€2.30, 20 minutes); from here it's a 4.5km walk to Martinskapelle.

Villingen-Schwenningen

07721 / POP 84,674

Villingen and Schwenningen trip simultaneously off the tongue, yet each town has its own flavour and history. Villingen once belonged to the Grand Duchy of Baden and Schwenningen to the duchy of Württemberg, conflicting allegiances that apparently can't be reconciled. Villingen, it must be said, is the more attractive of the twin towns.

Encircled by impenetrable walls that look as though they were built by the mythical local giant, Romäus, Villingen's Altstadt is a late-medieval time capsule, with cobbled streets and handsome patrician houses. Though locals nickname it the *Städtle* (little town), the name seems inappropriate during February's mammoth week-long *Fasnacht* (carnival) celebrations.

◉ Sights & Activities

Upper Danube Valley
Nature Reserve   NATURE RESERVE
(Naturpark Obere Donau; www.naturpark-obere-donau.de) Theatrically set against cave-riddled limestone cliffs, dappled with pine and beech woods that are burnished gold in autumn, and hugging the Danube's banks, this reserve bombards you with rugged splendour. Stick to the autobahn, however, and you'll be none the wiser. To fully explore the nature reserve, slip into a bicycle saddle or walking boots, and hit the trail.

One of the finest stretches is between Fridingen and Beuron, a 12.5km ridge-top walk of three to four hours. The sign-posted, easy-to-navigate trail runs above ragged cliffs, affording eagle's-eye views of the meandering Danube, which has almost 2850km to go before emptying into the Black Sea. The vertigo-inducing outcrop of Laibfelsen is a great picnic spot. From here, the path dips in and out of woodlands and meadows flecked with purple thistles. In Beuron the big draw is the working Benedictine abbey, one of Germany's oldest, dating to 1077. The lavish stuccoed-and-frescoed church is open to visitors: see www.beuron.de for details.

Fridingen and Beuron lie on the L277, 45km east of Villingen.

Franziskaner Museum   MUSEUM
(www.franziskanermuseum.de; Rietgasse 2; adult/concession €5/3; 1-5pm Tue-Sat, 11am-5pm Sun) Next to the 13th-century Riettor gate tower and occupying a former Franciscan monastery, the Franziskaner Museum skips merrily through Villingen's history and heritage. Standouts include Celtic artefacts unearthed at Magdalenenberg, 30 minutes' walk south of Villingen's centre.

Münsterplatz   SQUARE
The Münsterplatz is presided over by the
step-gabled Altes Rathaus (Old Town Hall)
and Klaus Ringwald's Münsterbrunnen,
a bronze fountain and a tongue-in-cheek
portrayal of characters that have shaped Villingen's history. The square throngs with activity on Wednesday and Saturday mornings
when market stalls are piled high with local
bread, meat, cheese, fruit and flowers.

Münster   CATHEDRAL
(Münsterplatz; ⊘9am-6pm) `FREE` The main
crowd-puller in Villingen's Altstadt is the
red-sandstone, 12th-century Münster with its
disparate spires: one overlaid with coloured
tiles, the other spiky and festooned with gargoyles. The Romanesque portals with haut-
relief doors depict dramatic biblical scenes.

Kneippbad   SWIMMING
(Am Kneippbad 1; adult/concession €4.50/3;
⊘6.30am-8pm Mon-Fri, 8am-8pm Sat & Sun mid-
May–early Sep) If the sun's out, take a 3km
walk northwest of the Altstadt to this forest
lido, a family magnet with its outdoor pools,
slides and volleyball courts.

🛏 Sleeping & Eating

Rindenmühle   HOTEL €€€
(☑07721-886 80; www.rindenmuehle.de; Am
Kneippbad 9; s €94-120, d €160-185; P�) This
converted watermill houses one of Villingen's smartest hotels, with forest walks
right on its doorstep and a recently added
spa and fitness area. Rooms are slick and
decorated in muted hues. In the restaurant
(mains €19 to €32), Martin Weisser creates
award-winning flavours using home-grown
organic produce, including chickens, geese
and herbs from his garden.

OM   VEGETARIAN €
(☑07721-204 3690; www.om-cafe.de; Obere Strasse
12; lunch special €6.90; ⊘noon-2.30pm Mon, noon-
8pm Tue-Sat; 🖉) Doubling up as a yoga studio and boutique, this cafe brings the warm
colours and boho flavour of India to central
Villingen. On the lunch menu are healthy,
vegetarian dishes from curries and stir-fries
to soups, salads and spicy lentil dishes.

Gasthaus Löwen   ITALIAN €€
(☑07721-404 1926; www.loewenvillingen.de; Obere
Strasse 10; mains €14-24; ⊘10.30am-2.30pm &
6-10.30pm Tue-Sat; 🖉) This German-Italian
bistro creates a modern mood with its brick
floor, bare wood tables, globe lights and
moulded chairs. Hailing originally from Venice, the friendly owners are firm believers in
slow food and organic ingredients, so expect
such season-driven taste sensations as homemade gnocchi with artichokes, and tuna
sashimi with beetroot sorbet. Day specials
are chalked up on a blackboard.

ℹ Information

Villingen Tourist Office (☑07721-822 340;
www.wt-vs.de; Rietgasse 2; ⊘10am-5pm Mon-
Sat, 11am-5pm Sun) In the Franziskaner Museum. E-bikes are available for rent for €10/20
per half/full day.

ℹ Getting There & Around

Villingen's Bahnhof, situated on the eastern
edge of the Altstadt, is on the scenic train line
from Konstanz (€22.20, 70 minutes) to Triberg
(€6.50, 23 minutes) and Offenburg (€20.30, 70
minutes). Trains to Stuttgart (€29.90 to €31.50,
two hours) involve a change in Rottweil, and to
Freiburg (€21.30 to €31.60, two hours) a change
in Donaueschingen.

From Villingen Bahnhof, buses 7265 and 7270
make regular trips north to Triberg. Frequent
buses (eg line 1) link Villingen with Schwenningen.

Rottweil

☑0741 / POP 24,915
Baden-Württemberg's oldest town is the
Roman-rooted Rottweil, founded in AD 73.
But a torrent of bad press about the woofer
with a nasty nip means that most folk readily associate the town with the Rottweiler,
which was indeed bred here as a hardy
butchers' dog until recently. Fear not, the
Rottweiler locals are much tamer. And the
town is something of an unsung beauty,
with its medieval Altstadt buttressed by
towers and lined with gabled houses.

⊙ Sights

★**Testturm**   TOWER
(Berner Feld 60; adult/concession €9/5; ⊘10am-
6pm Fri & Sun, to 8pm Sat) Sticking out above
Rottweil like a sore thumb, the futuristic,
environmentally progressive Testturm is the
brainchild of steel-engineering giant Thys-
senkrupp, who aims to speed up skyscraper
construction. At a whopping 246m high, it's
the tallest elevator test tower in the world. At
the time of research, it was open to the public, with Germany's highest visitor platform
(232m) commanding staggering 360° views
of the Black Forest, Swabian Alps and – on
clear days – the Swiss Alps .

Schwarzes Tor
GATE

(Schwarzer Graben) The sturdy 13th-century Schwarzes Tor is the gateway to Hauptstrasse and the well-preserved Altstadt, a cluster of red-roofed, pastel-painted houses. The town gate is the starting point for the pre-Lenten *Fasnacht* celebrations.

Sidling up to it, the curvaceous Hübschen Winkel townhouse will make you look twice with its 45° kink.

Münster Heilig-Kreuz
CATHEDRAL

(Münsterplatz; ⊙9am-7pm) **FREE** Standing proud on Münsterplatz, the late-Romanesque, three-aisled Münster-Heiliges-Kreuz features some striking Gothic stonework and cross-ribbed vaulting. The cathedral reopened in late 2017 following extensive renovation work.

🛏 Sleeping & Eating

Hotel Bären
HOTEL €€

(🖉0741-174 600; Hochmaurenstrasse 1; s €83-108, d €120-135; 🅿🛜) Standing head and shoulders above most hotels in town, the Bären extends a *herzlich Willkommen* (warm welcome). Its spacious contemporary rooms, most recently revamped, are done out in blonde wood, clean lines and pops of colour. Breakfast is a highly decent spread of fresh breads and fruits, cold cuts and cereals.

Wandelbar
CAFE €

(🖉0741-3488 6724; www.wandel-bar.com; Neckartal 67; light bites €6-10; ⊙11.30am-7pm Tue & Wed, 11.30am-1am Thu & Fri, 2pm-1am Sat, 2-7pm Sun) Wandelbar is one of Rottweil's coolest haunts, with a high-ceilinged, stone-walled, gallery-style interior, retro furniture and bold art on the walls. It takes you through from morning espresso to afternoon *Kaffee und Kuchen* (with delicious homemade cakes) and evening cocktails. Or go for snacks such as tapas, paninis and tarte flambée.

ℹ Information

Rottweil Tourist Office (🖉0741-494 280; www.rottweil.de; Hauptstrasse 21; ⊙9.30am-5.30pm Mon-Fri, to 12.30pm Sat) Can advise on accommodation, tours and biking the Neckartal-Radweg.

ℹ Getting There & Away

Rottweil is just off the A81 Stuttgart–Singen motorway. Trains run at least hourly to Stuttgart (€25.50, 1½ hours) and Villingen (€3.80, 30 minutes) from the Bahnhof, 1.2km southeast of the Altstadt.

Unterkirnach
🖉07721 / POP 2534

Nuzzling among velvety green hills, low-key Unterkirnach is a winner with families and anyone into their outdoor sports. In summer, the village is a terrific starting point for forest hikes, with 130km of marked walking trails, while in winter there are 50km of *Loipen* (cross-country ski tracks) and some terrific slopes to sledge.

Kids can slide and climb to their heart's content at the all-weather **Spielscheune** (www.spielscheune-unterkirnach.de; Schlossbergweg 4; admission €4.50; ⊙2-6pm Mon & Wed-Fri, 11am-6pm Sat & Sun; 👪), or toddle uphill to the farm to meet inquisitive goats and Highland cattle (feeding time is 3pm).

When you stay overnight, you'll automatically receive the KONUS guest card, which means the indoor pool, Spielscheune, play barn, guided walks (ask the **tourist office** (🖉07721-800 837; www.unterkirnach.de; Villinger Strasse 5; ⊙9am-12.30pm & 2-5pm Mon-Fri) for details), ski lifts (in winter) and local transport are free.

Unterkirnach is on a minor road that runs just south and parallel of the B33 between Triberg and Villingen.

Bus 61 runs roughly one an hour between Unterkirnach and Villingen (€3.50, 16 minutes).

LAKE CONSTANCE

Nicknamed the *schwäbische Meer* (Swabian Sea), Lake Constance – Central Europe's third-largest lake – straddles three countries: Germany, Austria and Switzerland. Formed by the Rhine Glacier during the last ice age and fed and drained by that same sprightly river today, this whopper of a lake measures 63km long by 14km wide and up to 250m deep. There is a certain novelty in the fact that this is the only place in the world where you can wake up in Germany, cycle across to Switzerland for lunch and make it to Austria in time for afternoon tea, strudel and snapshots of the Alps.

Taking in meadows and vineyards, orchards and wetlands, beaches and Alpine foothills, the lake's landscapes are like a 'greatest hits' of European scenery. Culture? It's all here, from baroque churches to Benedictine abbeys, Stone Age dwellings to Roman forts, and medieval castles to zeppelins.

Lake Constance

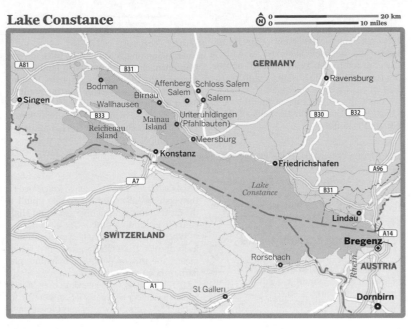

ℹ️ Getting There & Around

The most enjoyable way to cross the lake is by ferry. **Konstanz** is the main hub but Meersburg and Friedrichshafen also have ferry options.

Although most towns have a train station (Meersburg is an exception), in some cases buses provide the only land connections. **Bodensee Ticket** (www.bodensee-ticket.com), which groups all Lake Constance-area public transport, publishes a free *Fahrplan* (timetable) with schedules for all train, bus and ferry services. A day pass (€18.50/26 for one/all zones) gets you access to land transport around Lake Constance, including areas in Austria and Switzerland. It's sold at train stations and ferry docks. Children pay half price.

CAR FERRY

The roll-on roll-off **Konstanz–Meersburg car ferry** (www.sw.konstanz.de; car up to 4m incl driver/bicycle/pedestrian €9.40/5.30/3) runs 24 hours a day, except when high water levels prevent it from docking. The ferry runs every 15 minutes from 5.35am to 8.50pm, every 30 minutes from 8.50pm to midnight and every hour from midnight to 5.35am. The crossing, affording superb views from the top deck, takes 15 minutes.

The car ferry dock in Konstanz, served by local bus 1, is 4km northeast of the centre along Mainaustrasse. In Meersburg, car ferries leave from a dock 400m northwest of the old town.

PASSENGER FERRY

The most useful lines are run by German **BSB** (☑ 07531-364 00; www.bsb-online.com; Hafenstrasse 6, Konstanz) and Austrian **Vorarlberg Lines** (www.vorarlberg-lines.at; Seestrasse 4, Bregenz). BSB ferries link Konstanz with ports such as Meersburg (€6.10, 30 minutes), Friedrichshafen (€13.30, 1¾ hours), Lindau (€17.30, three hours) and Bregenz (€18.60, 3½ hours); children aged six to 15 years pay half price. The website lists timetables in full.

Der Katamaran (☑ 07531-363 9320; www.der-katamaran.de; Passenger Ferry Dock, Konstanz; adult/6-14yr €10.50/5.70) is a sleek passenger service that takes 50 minutes to make the Konstanz–Friedrichshafen crossing. It runs hourly from 6am to 7pm, plus hourly from 8pm to midnight on Fridays and Saturdays from mid-May to early October.

Konstanz

☑ 07531 / POP 82,859

Sidling up to the Swiss border, bisected by the Rhine and outlined by the Alps, Konstanz sits prettily on the northwestern shore of Lake Constance. Roman emperors, medieval traders and the bishops of the 15th-century Council of Constance have all left their mark on this alley-woven town, mercifully spared from the WWII

Konstanz

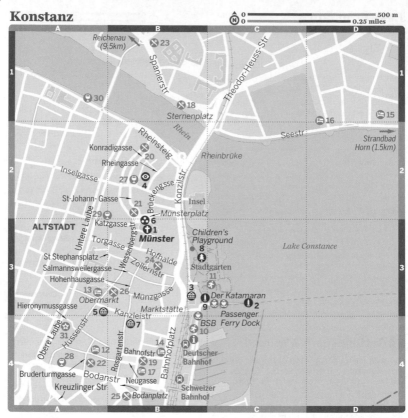

N 0 500 m
0 0.25 miles

Konstanz

bombings that obliterated other German cities.

⊙ Sights

★ Münster
CATHEDRAL

(Münsterplatz 1; tower adult/child €2/1; ⊙10am-6pm, tower 10am-5pm Mon-Sat, 12.30-5.30pm Sun) Crowned by a filigreed spire and looking proudly back on 1000 years of history, the sandstone Münster was the church of the Diocese of Konstanz until 1821. Its interior is an architectural potpourri of Romanesque, Gothic, Renaissance and baroque styles. Standouts include the 15th-century Schnegg, an ornate spiral staircase in the northern transept, to the left of which a door leads to the 1000-year-old crypt. From the crypt's polychrome chapel, you enter the sublime Gothic cloister.

Mainau
GARDENS

(www.mainau.de; adult/concession €21/12 summer, €10/6 winter; ⊙10am-7pm late Mar-late Oct, to 5pm rest of year) Jutting out over the lake and bursting with flowers, the lusciously green islet of Mainau is a 45-hectare Mediterranean garden dreamed up by the Bernadotte family, relatives of the royal house of Sweden.

Around two million visitors flock here every year to admire sparkly lake and mountain views from the baroque castle, and wander sequoia-shaded avenues and hothouses bristling with palms and orchids.

Römersiedlung
RUINS

(Münsterplatz; tour €1; ⊙tours 6pm Sun) The glass pyramid in front of the Münster shelters the Römersiedlung, the 3rd-century-AD remains of the Roman fort Constantia that gave the city its name. You'll only get a sneak peek from above, so join one of the guided tours that begin at the tourist office (p256) for a touch of magic as a staircase opens from the cobbles and leads down to the ruins.

Rathaus
HISTORIC BUILDING

(City Hall; Kanzleistrasse) Slightly south of the Münster, the flamboyantly frescoed Renaissance Rathaus occupies the former linen weavers' guildhall. Behind it you'll find a peaceful arcaded courtyard.

Niederburg
AREA

Best explored on foot, Konstanz' cobbled heart Niederburg stretches north from the Münster to the Rhine. The twisting lanes lined with half-timbered townhouses are the place to snoop around galleries and antique shops.

Imperia
STATUE

At the end of the pier, giving ferry passengers a come-hither look from her rotating pedestal, stands *Imperia*. Peter Lenk's 9m-high sculpture of a buxom prostitute, said to have plied her trade in the days of the Council of Constance, was inspired by a short story by Honoré de Balzac, *La Belle Impéria*. In her clutches are hilarious sculptures of a naked (and sagging) Pope Martin V and Holy Roman Emperor Sigismund, symbolising religious and imperial power.

Rosgartenmuseum
MUSEUM

(www.rosgartenmuseum-konstanz.de; Rosgartenstrasse 3-5; adult/concession €3/1.50, 1st Sun of the month & after 2pm Wed free; ⊙10am-6pm Tue-Fri, to 5pm Sat & Sun) The one-time butchers' guildhall now harbours the Rosgartenmuseum, spotlighting regional art and history, with an emphasis on medieval panel painting and sculpture. Most of the information is given in German only.

Konzilgebäude
HISTORIC BUILDING

(Council Building; Konzilstrasse) Look out for the white, dormered Konzilgebäude, built in 1388, which served as a granary and warehouse before Pope Martin V was elected here in 1417. Today it's a conference and concert hall.

Stadtgarten
PARK

With its landscaped flower beds, plane trees and children's playground, the Stadtgarten is a fine place to kick back and enjoy dreamy views out over Lake Constance.

Zeppelin Monument
MONUMENT

(Stadtgarten) The Zeppelin Monument shows airship inventor Count Ferdinand von Zeppelin in an Icarus-like pose. He was born in 1838 on the Insel islet.

Reichenau
ISLAND

(www.reichenau-tourismus.de) In AD 724 a missionary named Pirmin founded a Benedictine monastery on Reichenau, a 4.5km-by-1.5km island (Lake Constance's largest) about 11km west of Konstanz. During its heyday, from 820 to 1050, the so-called Reichenauer School produced stunning illuminated manuscripts and vivid frescos. Today, three surviving churches provide silent testimony to Reichenau's Golden Age. Thanks to them, this fertile islet of orchards and wineries was declared a Unesco World Heritage Site in 2000.

Strandbad Horn
BEACH

(Eichhornstrasse 100; ☺mid-May–Sep; 🚼) FREE
This lake-front beach, 4km northeast of the centre, has sunbathing lawns, a kiddie pool, playground, volleyball courts and a naturist area.

🏃 Activities

La Canoa
CANOEING

(www.lacanoa.com; Robert-Bosch-Strasse 4; canoe/kayak/SUP 3hr €15/20/30, per day €25/30/45; ☺10am-12.30pm & 2-6pm Tue-Fri, 10am-4pm Sat) La Canoa has canoe, kayak and SUP rental points in all major towns on the lake; see the website for details.

Bootsvermietung Konstanz
BOATING

(Stadtgarten; per hour €12-32; ☺11am-7pm Easter–mid-Oct) This boat rental in the Stadtgarten (p253) has pedalos for trundling across the lake.

🛌 Sleeping

Glückseeligkeit Herberge
GUESTHOUSE €

(☑07531-902 2075; www.herberge-konstanz.de; Neugasse 20; s €40-60, d €60-80; 🛜) What a sweet deal this little guesthouse is. Housed in a period building in the Altstadt, it shelters petite but attractively decorated rooms. The attic room has direct access to the roof terrace, which peers over a jumble of rooftops to the cathedral spire. There's also a shared lounge, kitchen and patio. E-bikes are available for rental.

Hotel Halm
HOTEL €€

(☑07531-1210; www.hotel-halm-konstanz.de; Bahnhofplatz 6; s €70-120, d €90-140; 🛜) A joyous hop and skip from the lake and Altstadt, this late-19th-century pile has warm, elegantly furnished rooms with marble bathrooms; upgrade if you want a balcony with a lake view. Its pride and joy is its lavish Moorish Hall, serving Middle Eastern cuisine. There's also a small sauna for a postsightseeing steam.

Hotel Barbarossa
HISTORIC HOTEL €€

(☑07531-128 990; www.hotelbarbarossa.de; Obermarkt 8-12; s €70-90, d €115-170, f €180-200; 🛜) This 600-year-old patrician house features parquet-floored, individually decorated rooms, which are bright and appealing if a tad on the small side. The terrace has views over Konstanz' rooftops and spires. The first-floor Weinstube restaurant (mains €20 to €24) serves food with a Mediterranean slant in a historic, wood-panelled parlour.

Villa Barleben
HISTORIC HOTEL €€€

(☑07531-942 330; www.hotel-barleben.de; Seestrasse 15; s €76.50-165, d €100-325; 🅿🛜) Gregariously elegant, this 19th-century villa's sunny rooms and corridors are sprinkled with antiques and ethnic art. The rambling lakefront gardens are ideal for dozing in a *Strandkorb* (wicker beach lounger), G&T in hand, or enjoying lunch on the terrace.

Viva Sky
HOTEL €€€

(☑07531-692 3620; www.hotel-viva-sky.de; Sigismundstrasse 19; s €90-150, d €129-179, apt €149-169, f €179-199, ste €179-219; 🅿🛜) An arresting panorama of Konstanz' Altstadt spreads out before you from the top floor of this stylish newcomer. It might look nondescript from outside, but inside, rooms are very comfortable, with parquet floors and themed touches. The pick of them have balconies with fine views, while the top suite ups the romance with a whirlpool bath and four-poster bed.

Riva
BOUTIQUE HOTEL €€€

(☑07531-363 090; www.hotel-riva.de; Seestrasse 25; s €110-230, d €200-320, ste €320-660; 🅿🛜🏊) This ultrachic contender has crisp white spaces, glass walls and a snail-like stairwell. Zen-like rooms with hardwood floors feature perks such as free minibars. A rooftop pool, spa area and gym, and a gourmet restaurant and terrace overlooking the lake, seal the deal.

🍴 Eating

★ Voglhaus
CAFE €

(☑07531-918 9520; www.das-voglhaus.de; Wessenbergstrasse 8; light meals €5-9.50; ☺9am-6.30pm Mon-Sat, 11am-6pm Sun; 🍴) Locals flock to the 'bird house' for its chilled vibe and contemporary wood-and-stone interior, warmed by an open fire in winter. Wood-oven bread with spreads, wholegrain bagels, wraps and cupcakes pair nicely with smoothies and speciality coffees such as the Hansel and Gretel (with gingerbread syrup). Day specials swing from yellow curry to pasta bowls.

Ess Bar
INTERNATIONAL €

(☑07531-804 3475; www.essbar-konstanz.de; Bahnhofstrasse 15; light meals €10-12; ☺noon-1am Tue-Thu, to 2am Fri & Sat) The packed tables speak volumes at this minimalist-chic, monochrome-toned bistro, with banquette seating and a pavement terrace for summer-day dining. The menu packs flavour punches in tapas-style dishes including Asian-style oysters with chilli, lime and ginger; spinach risotto with parmesan; and pulled pork with miso aioli – all bang on the money. Order a few – sharing is the way to go.

Sol
VEGETARIAN €

(☑ 07531-936 4990; www.sol-konstanz.de; Ebertplatz 4; snacks & mains €4-10; ⊗ 10am-10pm; ☑) Over the Rhine just north of the Altstadt, this cool and wholesome cafe has a chilled vibe, with exposed stone walls and an open deli kitchen. The menu plays up regional and organic ingredients in bites including quinoa burgers, falafel, homemade cake, vegan ice cream and smoothies. Go easy on the spicy sauce, though – it's seriously hot stuff.

Tamara's Weinstube
GERMAN €

(☑ 07531-284 318; http://tamaras-weinstube.de; Zollernstrasse 6-8; light bites & meals €5-13.50; ⊗ 4pm-midnight Mon-Sat) With stone walls, low wood beams, soft lighting and a traditional *Kachelofen* (tiled oven), this wine bar is as cosy as they come. It's a terrific spot for an evening of Badisch wines and regional grub such as ox salad with onions and gherkins, homemade potato salad, pork knuckles and farm-fresh bratwurst.

Constanzer Wirtshaus
GERMAN €€

(☑ 07531-363 0130; www.constanzer-wirtshaus.de; Spanierstrasse 3; mains €10-19; ⊗ 11am-midnight; ⋈) On the banks of the Rhine where it flows into Lake Constance, this delightfully old-school tavern has bags of character, with its vaulted interior and waterfront terrace. Classic German food such as veal goulash, *Schweinebraten* (regional pork roast with bread dumplings) and *Kässpätzle* (noodles topped with cheese and fried onions) marry well with the house brews and Lake Constance wines.

Münsterhof
GERMAN €€

(☑ 07531-363 8427; Münsterplatz 3; mains €11-20; ⊗ 11.30am-1am Sun-Fri, to 3am Sat; ☑) Tables set up in front of the Münster (p253), a slick bistro interior and a lunchtime buzz have earned Münsterhof a loyal local following. Dishes from cordon bleu with pan-fried potatoes to asparagus-filled *Maultaschen* (pasta pockets) in creamy chive sauce are substantial and satisfying. The €8.40 lunch special is great value.

Tolle Knolle
INTERNATIONAL €€

(☑ 07531-175 75; Bodanplatz 9; mains €11.50-19; ⊗ 11am-midnight) On a fountain-dotted square with alfresco seating, this art-slung restaurant lives up to its 'great potato' mon-

iker. Potatoes come in various guises: with *Wiener Schnitzel*, beer-battered fish and on the signature pizza.

La Bodega
TAPAS €€

(☑ 07531-277 88; Schreibergasse 40; tapas €5-10.50; ⊗ 5pm-1am Tue-Sat) Squirrelled away in Niederburg, this candy-bright bodega with a pocket-sized terrace whips up tapas from *papas canarias* (Canarian potatoes) to stuffed calamari.

San Martino Gourmet
GASTRONOMY €€€

(☑ 07531-284 5678; www.san-martino.net; Bruderturmgasse 3; mains €42-56, 5-course menu €160; ⊗ 6-10pm Tue-Sat) A class act with space for just 16 lucky diners, this Michelin-starred restaurant rests against the old city walls. Jochen Fecht's season-inspired food allows each ingredient to shine in dishes such as wood sorrel with Monkey 47 gin and bergamot, and nose-to-tail veal with soubise and Shimeji mushrooms.

🍸 Drinking & Entertainment

Klimperkasten
BAR

(Bodanstrasse 40; ⊗ 6pm-1am Mon-Thu, to 3am Fri & Sat) Indie kids, garage and old-school fans all hail this retro cafe, which gets clubbier after dark when DJs work the decks. Occasionally hosts gigs.

Schwarze Katz
BAR

(Katzgasse 8; ⊗ 6pm-1am Tue-Thu & Sun, to 2am Fri & Sat) Found the Black Cat? You're in luck. A relaxed mood, friendly crowd and reasonably priced drinks (including Black Forest Alpirsbacher beer) make this a Konstanz favourite.

Strandbar Konstanz
BAR

(http://strandbar-konstanz.de; Webersteig 12; ⊗ noon-11pm Apr & May, noon-midnight Jun-Aug, 2-10pm Sep) Konstanz gets its summer groove on down at this beach bar, with sand, deckchairs, DJ beats, long drinks and good vibes on the banks of the Rhine.

Brauhaus Johann Albrecht
PUB

(http://konstanz.brauhaus-joh-albrecht.de; Konradigasse 2; ⊗ 11.30am-midnight) This stepgabled microbrewery is a relaxed haunt for quaffing craft beers. There's a terrace for summer imbibing.

K9
CULTURAL CENTRE

(www.k9-kulturzentrum.de; Hieronymusgasse 3) Once a medieval church, this is now Konstanz' most happening cultural venue, with a line-up skipping from salsa nights and film screenings to gigs, club nights and jive nights. See the website for schedules.

❶ Information

Konstanz Tourist Office (☏ 07531-133 030; www.konstanz-tourismus.de; Bahnhofplatz 43, Hauptbahnhof; ☻9am-6.30pm Mon-Fri, 9am-4pm Sat, 10am-1pm Sun Apr-Oct, 9.30am-6pm Mon-Fri Nov-Mar) Located at the Hauptbahnhof. Inside you can pick up a walking-tour brochure (€1) and city map (€0.50); outside there's a hotel reservation board and free hotel telephone.

❶ Getting There & Away

Konstanz is the main ferry hub – for passengers and for cars (p251) – for Lake Constance.

Konstanz' **Hauptbahnhof** (Bahnhofplatz) is the southern terminus of the scenic *Schwarzwaldbahn*, which trundles hourly through the Black Forest, linking Offenburg with towns such as Triberg and Villingen. To reach Lake Constance's northern shore, you usually have to change in Radolfzell. The Schweizer Bahnhof has connections to destinations throughout Switzerland.

❶ Getting Around

The city centre is a traffic headache, especially on weekends. Your best bet is the free Park & Ride lot 3km northwest of the Altstadt, near the airfield on Byk-Gulden-Strasse, where your only outlay will be for a bus ticket.

Local buses cost €2.35 for a single ticket, and day passes are €4.60/7.90 for an individual/family; see www.sw.konstanz.de for timetables. Bus 1 links the Meersburg car-ferry dock with the Altstadt. If you stay in Konstanz for at least two nights, your hotelier will give you a Gästekarte entitling you to free local bus travel.

Bikes can be hired from **Kultur-Rädle** (☏ 07531-273 10; Bahnhofplatz 29; per day/week €13/70; ☻9am-12.30pm & 2.30-6pm Mon-Fri, 10am-4pm Sat year-round, plus 10am-12.30pm Sun Easter-Sep), close to the tourist office.

Meersburg

☏ 07532 / POP 5776

Tumbling down vine-streaked slopes to Lake Constance and crowned by a perkily turreted medieval castle, Meersburg lives up to all those clichéd knights-in-armour, damsel-in-distress fantasies. And if its tangle of cobbled lanes and half-timbered houses filled with jovial banter doesn't sweep you

off your feet, the local Pinot Noir served in its cosy *Weinstuben* (wine taverns) will.

◉ Sights & Activities

Burg Meersburg　　　　　　　　CASTLE
(Schlossplatz 10; adult/concession €12.80/10; ☻9am-6.30pm Mar-Oct, 10am-6pm Nov-Feb) Looking across Lake Constance from its lofty perch, Burg Meersburg is an archetypal medieval stronghold, complete with keep, drawbridge, knights' hall and dungeons. Founded by Merovingian king Dagobert I in the 7th century, the fortress is among Germany's oldest, no mean feat in a country with a *lot* of old castles. The bishops of Konstanz used it as a summer residence between 1268 and 1803.

Meersburg Therme　　　　　　　　SPA
(☏ 07532-440 2850; www.meersburg-therme.de; Uferpromenade 12; thermal baths 2hr adult/concession €9/8.50, incl sauna 3hr €18/17.50; ☻10am-10pm Mon-Thu, to 11pm Fri & Sat, 9am-10pm Sun) It's a five-minute walk east along the Uferpromenade to this lake-front spa, where the 34°C thermal waters, water jets and Swiss Alp views are soothing. Those who dare to bare all can skinny-dip in the lake and steam in saunas that are replicas of Unteruhldingen's Stone Age dwellings (p261).

Neues Schloss　　　　　　　　CASTLE
(www.neues-schloss-meersburg.de; Schlossplatz 13; adult/concession €5/2.50; ☻9.30am-6pm Apr-Oct, noon-5pm Sat & Sun Nov-Mar) In 1710 Prince-Bishop Johann Franz Schenk von Stauffenberg, perhaps tired of the dinginess and rising damp, swapped the Altes Schloss for the dusky-pink, lavishly baroque Neues Schloss. A visit to the now state-owned palace takes in the extravagant bishops' apartments replete with stucco work and frescos, Bathasar Neumann's elegant staircase, and gardens with inspirational lake views.

Lakefront　　　　　　　　HARBOUR
(Seepromenade) Stroll the harbour for classic snaps of Lake Constance or to hire a pedalo. On the jetty, you can't miss – though the pious might prefer to – Peter Lenk's satirical *Magische Säule* (Magic Column). The sculpture is a hilarious satirical depiction of characters who have shaped Meersburg's history, including buxom wine-wench Wendelgart and poet Annette von Droste-Hülshoff.

Vineum　　　　　　　　MUSEUM
(www.vineum-bodensee.de; Vorburggasse 13; adult/concession €5.50/3; ☻11am-6pm Tue-Sun Apr-Oct,

11am-6pm Sat & Sun Nov-Mar) Housed in the 400-year-old Heilig-Geist-Spital (Hospice of the Holy Spirit), this new museum presents an intriguing interactive romp through the history of winemaking in and around Meersburg – from sniffing the different aromas to tasting 16 locally produced wines in the Vinemathek.

🛏 Sleeping & Eating

Meersburg goes with the seasons, with most places closing from November to Easter.

Landhaus Ödenstein GUESTHOUSE €€
(☑ 07532-6142; www.oedenstein.de; Droste-Hülshoff-Weg 25; s €67-99, d €99-155; P 🛜) Spectacularly plonked on a hill above vine-cloaked slopes, this family-run guesthouse has knock-out views of Lake Constance and spotless, light-filled rooms with pine furnishings – the pick of which have balconies. A pretty garden, warm welcome and generous breakfasts sweeten the deal.

Gasthof zum Bären GUESTHOUSE €€
(☑ 07532-432 20; www.baeren-meersburg.de; Marktplatz 11; s €52, d €96-118; P 🛜) Straddling three 13th- to 17th-century buildings, this guesthouse receives glowing reviews for its classic rooms, spruced up with stucco work, ornate wardrobes and lustrous wood; corner rooms No 13 and 23 are the most romantic. The rustic tavern (mains €9 to €18) serves Lake Constance fare such as *Felchen* (whitefish).

**Romantik
Residenz am See** BOUTIQUE HOTEL €€€
(☑ 07532-800 40; www.hotel-residenz-meersburg. com; Uferpromenade 11; s €129-141, d €234-294, apt €344-384; P 🛜) Sitting with aplomb on the promenade, this romantic hotel is a class act. The higher you go, the better the view from the warm-hued rooms facing the vineyards or lake. All room rates include breakfast, minibar and a four-course dinner in Residenz restaurant. The hotel also houses the Michelin-starred Casala, offering sophisticated Mediterranean cuisine. Bikes/e-bikes can be rented for €12/25 per day.

Badische Weinstube GERMAN €€
(☑ 07532-496 42; www.badische-weinstube.com; Unterstadtstrasse 17; mains €14-28; ⊙ 5-11pm Wed-Sun) Close to the lake front, this wine tavern combines a mock-rustic interior with a pavement terrace. Try the homemade fish soup flavoured with saffron and garlic, followed by Lake Constance *Felchen* (white fish) in

almond butter or *Zwiebelrostbraten* (onion roast) with *Spätzle* (egg noodles).

Winzerstube zum Becher GERMAN €€
(☑ 07532-9009; www.winzerstube-zum-becher. de; Höllgasse 4; mains €10.50-26; ⊙ noon-2pm & 6-10pm Tue-Sun) Vines drape the facade of this wood-panelled bolthole, run by the same family since 1884. Home-grown Pinot Noirs accompany Lake Constance classics such as whitefish in almond-butter sauce. The terrace affords Altes Schloss views.

Casala MEDITERRANEAN €€€
(☑ 07532-800 40; www.hotel-residenz-meersburg. com; Uferpromenade 11; tasting menus €90-135; ⊙ 6.30-9pm Thu-Sun; ✍) At the Romantik Residenz am See hotel's Michelin-starred restaurant, chef Markus Philippi brings sophisticated Mediterranean cuisine to the table. One of the menus is vegetarian.

ⓘ Information

Meersburg Tourist Office (☑ 07532-440 400; www.meersburg.de; Kirchstrasse 4; ⊙ 9am-noon & 2-4.30pm Mon-Fri) Housed in a one-time Dominican monastery.

ⓘ Getting There & Away

Meersburg, which lacks a train station, is 18km west of Friedrichshafen.

From Monday to Friday, eight times a day, express bus 7394 makes the trip to Konstanz (€4, 40 minutes) and Friedrichshafen (€4.55, 30 minutes). Bus 7373 connects Meersburg with Ravensburg (€6, 40 minutes, four daily Monday to Friday, two Saturday). Meersburg's main bus stop is next to the Mariä-Heimsuchung church on Stettener Strasse (on the northern edge of the Altstadt).

ⓘ BODENSEE ERLEBNISKARTE

The three-day **Bodensee Erlebniskarte** (adult/child €74/37, not including ferries €41/21), available at area tourist and ferry offices from late March to mid-October, allows free travel on almost all boats and mountain cableways on and around Lake Constance (including its Austrian and Swiss shores). It also includes free entry to more than 160 tourist attractions and museums. There are also seven-day (adult/child €99/49) and 14-day (adult/child €144/72) versions.

STUTTGART & THE BLACK FOREST MEERSBURG

ONE LAKE, TWO WHEELS, THREE COUNTRIES

When the weather warms, there's no better way to explore Bodensee (Lake Constance) than with your bum in a saddle. The well-marked **Bodensee Radweg** (Bodensee Cycle Path; www.bodensee-radweg.com) is a 273km loop of Lake Constance, taking in vineyards, meadows, orchards, wetlands and historic towns. There are plenty of small beaches where you can stop for a refreshing dip in the lake. See the website for itineraries and maps.

Bike hire is available in most towns for between €10 and €20 per day. While the entire route takes roughly a week, ferries and trains also make it possible to cover shorter chunks, such as Friedrichshafen–Konstanz–Meersburg, in a weekend.

The 24-hour **Konstanz–Meersburg Car Ferry** (p251) leaves from a dock 400m northwest of the old town

Friedrichshafen

07541 / POP 59,108

Zeppelins, the cigar-shaped airships that first took flight in 1900 under the stewardship of high-flying Count Ferdinand von Zeppelin, will forever be associated with Friedrichshafen. An amble along the flowery lake-front promenade and a visit to the museum that celebrates the behemoth of the skies are the biggest draws of this industrial town, which was heavily bombed in WWII and rebuilt in the 1950s.

☉ Sights & Activities

★**Zeppelin Museum**   MUSEUM

(www.zeppelin-museum.de; Seestrasse 22; adult/concession €9/5; ☺9am-5pm daily May-Oct, 10am-5pm Tue-Sun Nov-Apr) Near the eastern end of Friedrichshafen's lake-front promenade is the Zeppelin Museum, housed in the Bauhaus-style former *Hafenbahnhof* (harbour station), built in 1932. The centrepiece is a full-scale mock-up of a 33m section of the *Hindenburg* (LZ 129), the largest airship ever built, measuring an incredible 245m long and outfitted as luxuriously as an ocean liner. The hydrogen-filled craft tragically burst into flames, killing 36, while landing in New Jersey in 1937.

Schlosskirche   CHURCH

(www.schlosskirche-fn.de; Schlossstrasse 2; ☺9am-6pm Easter-late Oct) **FREE** The western end of Friedrichshafen's promenade is anchored by the twin-onion-towered baroque Schlosskirche. It's the only accessible part of the Schloss and is still inhabited by the ducal family of Württemberg.

Zeppelin NT   SCENIC FLIGHTS

(☎07541-590 00; www.zeppelinflug.de; Messestrasse 132; 30/45/60/90/120-min flight €245/380/455/640/825) Real airship fans will justify the splurge on a trip in a high-tech, 12-passenger Zeppelin NT. Shorter trips cover lake destinations such as **Schloss Salem** (www.salem.de; Schlossbezirk 1; adult/concession €9/4.50; ☺9.30am-6pm Mon-Sat, 10.30am-6pm Sun Apr-Oct) and Lindau, while longer ones drift across to Austria or Switzerland. Take-off and landing are in Friedrichshafen.

🛏 Sleeping & Eating

Gasthof Rebstock   GUESTHOUSE €€

(☎07541-950 1640; www.gasthof-rebstock-fn.de; Werastrasse 35; s/d/tr/q €65/80/95/110; ☜) Geared up for cyclists and offering bike rental (€8 per day), this family-run hotel has a beer garden and humble but tidy rooms with pine furnishings. It's 750m northwest of the *Stadtbahnhof.*

Aika Seaside Living   BOUTIQUE HOTEL €€€

(☎07541-378 357; www.aika-cafe.de; Karlstrasse 38; d €139-219, ste €260-350; ☜) Well, it might not be the 'seaside' exactly, but Aika comes up trumps with its large, spacious, wood-floored rooms and slick, contemporary neutral-palette suites, which come with fabulous views of the lake. The cafe downstairs has one of the best terraces in town.

Aika   CAFE €

(www.aika-cafe.de; Karlstrasse 38; snacks €3-8; ☺8.30am-8pm Mon-Fri, 9am-8pm Sat, 9.30am-8pm Sun) Slick and monochrome, this deli-cafe has a lakeside terrace for lingering over a speciality coffee, breakfast, homemade ice cream, cake or sourdough sandwich.

Beach Club   CAFE €

(www.beachclub-fn.de; Uferstrasse 1; snacks €6-10; ☺9am-midnight Apr-Oct) This lake-front shack is the place to unwind on the deck, cocktail in hand, and admire the *Klangschiff* ('sound ship') sculpture and the not-so-distant Alps. Revive over salads, sandwiches, tarte flambée, tapas and ice cream.

s'Wirtshaus am See
GERMAN €€

(☎ 07541-388 5989; www.swirtshaus.de; Seestrasse 18; mains €13-26; ⏰9am-11pm; 🛜🪑) Right on the lake front, this restaurant goes in for the new-wave rustic look, with a sleek blonde-wood interior, contemporary fireplace and funky stag antler lights. The Swabian menu includes dishes such as *Allgäuer Käsesuppe* (cheese soup), bratwurst in dark beer sauce, and roast chicken with lashings of potato salad. Try to snag a table on the terrace in summer.

ℹ Information

Friedrichshafen Tourist Office (☎ 07541-2035 5444; www.friedrichshafen.info; Bahnhofplatz 2; ⏰9am-1pm & 2-6pm Mon-Fri, 9am-1pm Sat) On the square outside the *Stadtbahnhof*. Staff can book zeppelin flights.

ℹ Getting There & Around

Friedrichshafen's **airport** (☎ 07541-2840; www.bodensee-airport.eu; Am Flugplatz 64) is served by airlines including easyJet, British Airways and Lufthansa.

There are ferry options, including a catamaran to Konstanz. Sailing times are posted on the waterfront just outside the Zeppelin Museum.

From Monday to Friday, seven times a day, express bus 7394 makes the trip to Konstanz (1¼ hours) via Meersburg (30 minutes). Birnau and Meersburg are also served almost hourly by bus 7395.

Friedrichshafen is on the Bodensee (Lake Constance)–Gürtelbahn train line, which runs along the lake's northern shore from Radolfzell to Lindau. There are also regular services on the Bodensee-Oberschwaben-Bahn to Ravensburg (€6, 14 to 20 minutes).

Trains and buses depart from the Bahnhof, which is 500m west of the Altstadt.

Ravensburg

☎ 0751 / POP 49,830

Ravensburg has puzzled the world for the past 125 years with its jigsaws and board games. The medieval Altstadt has toy-town appeal, studded with turrets, robber-knight towers and gabled patrician houses. For centuries, dukes and wealthy merchants polished the cobbles of this Free Imperial City – now it's your turn.

◉ Sights & Activities

Museum Humpis-Quartier
MUSEUM

(www.museum-humpis-quartier.de; Marktstrasse 45; adult/concession €5/3; ⏰11am-6pm Tue, Wed & Fri-Sun, to 8pm Thu) Seven exceptional late-medieval houses set around a glass-covered courtyard shelter a permanent collection focusing on Ravensburg's past as a trade centre, based on the lives of four historic characters. Free audioguides provide some background.

Marienplatz
SQUARE

The heart of the Altstadt is the elongated, pedestrianised Marienplatz, framed by sturdy towers such as the round Grüner Turm, with its lustrous tiled roof, and frescoed patrician houses, such as the late-Gothic, step-gabled Waaghaus. The 15th-century Lederhaus, with its elaborate Renaissance facade, was once the domain of tanners and shoemakers.

Liebfrauenkirche
CHURCH

(Church of Our Lady; Kirchstrasse 18; ⏰9am-6pm) FREE Rising high above Marienplatz, the weighty, late-Gothic Liebfrauenkirche conceals some fine examples of 15th-century stained glass and a gilt altar.

Mehlsack
TOWER

(Mehlsackweg; ⏰11am-4pm Sat & Sun Aug-Sep) FREE The all-white Mehlsack (flour sack) is a tower marking the Altstadt's southern edge. A steep staircase leads up to the Veitsburg, a quaint baroque castle that now harbours a restaurant of the same name, with outlooks over Ravensburg's mosaic of red-tiled roofs.

Ravensburger Spieleland
AMUSEMENT PARK

(www.spieleland.de; Mecklenbeuren; adult/concession €34.50/32.50; ⏰10am-6pm Apr-Oct) Kids in tow? Take them to this board-game-inspired theme park, with attractions including giant rubber-duck racing, cow milking against the clock, rodeos and Alpine rafting. By car it's 10 minutes south of Ravensburg on the B467.

🛏 Sleeping & Eating

Hotel zum Engel
B&B €€

(☎ 0751-363 6130; www.engel-ravensburg.de; Marienplatz 71; s €90-107, d €120-156; 🛜) Following a recent makeover, the Engel (angel) is flying once again. The location on Marienplatz square is unbeatable, the welcome friendly and the rooms tastefully decorated, with wood floors, soft pastel hues and original features including exposed wood beams and vintage furnishings.

Gasthof Obertor
GUESTHOUSE €€

(📋0751-366 70; www.hotelobertor.de; Markt-strasse 67; s €78-98, d €126-136, f €196; 🅿🛜) The affable Rimpps take pride in their lem-on-fronted patrician house. Obertor stands head and shoulders above most Altstadt guesthouses, with spotless rooms, a sauna area and generous breakfasts.

Waldhorn
HISTORIC HOTEL €€€

(📋0751-361 20; http://waldhorn.de; Marienplatz 15; s €119-129, d €159-199; 🛜) The Waldhorn creaks with history and its light, appealingly restored rooms make a great base for exploring the Altstadt. Breakfast is served in the wood-beamed restaurant, lodged in the 15th-century vintners' guildhall.

Cafe Glücklich
CAFE €

(http://cafeglueecklich.com; Grüner-Turm-Strasse 25; light meals €6-12; ⊘9am-6pm Mon-Sat; 📋) *Glücklich* means 'happy' and most customers are that indeed at this sweet, easygoing cafe, decked out with floral wallpaper and mismatched vintage furniture. Nab a table for homemade treats prepared with regional ingredients – from breakfast burgers to green smoothies, vegan waffles, tortes, tarts and chai. The staff can advise on allergy-free options.

Mohren
INTERNATIONAL €

(📋0751-1805 4310; www.mohren-ravensburg.de; Marktstrasse 61; mains €9-22.50; ⊘10.30am-midnight Mon-Fri, 9.30am-midnight Sat) 'Contemporary rustic' best sums up Mohren, with its bright feel, exposed red brick and log piles. The menu wings you from antipasti to steaks, Swabian classics and Thai curries, all playfully presented and revealing the chef's pride in careful sourcing.

Gleis 9
INTERNATIONAL €€

(📋0751-3594 3720; http://gleis9-rv.de; Escher-Wyss-Strasse 9; mains €13-17; ⊘5pm-midnight Tue-Thu & Sun, to 3am Fri & Sat) In a warehouse right behind Ravensburg's main train station, on what was once platform 9, this industrial-cool pick has a cool backlit, red-brick, lounge-style interior. The menu stays on track with street food: goat's cheese with pesto, chicken gyros, pulled pork with slaw, sweet potato fries – you name it. DJ beats pick up as the night wears on.

ℹ️ Information

Ravensburg Tourist Office (📋0751-828 00; www.ravensburg.de; Lederhaus, Marienplatz 35; ⊘9am-5.30pm Mon-Fri, 9.30am-2pm Sat)

The office is located right in the heart of town on Marienplatz.

ℹ️ Getting There & Away

The train station is six blocks west of the tourist office along Eisenbahnstrasse. Ravensburg is on the train line linking Friedrichshafen (€6, 15 minutes, at least twice hourly) with Ulm (€20.10, 1¼ hours, at least hourly) and Stuttgart (€36.50, two hours, at least hourly).

Lindau

📋08382 / POP 25,249

Brochures rhapsodise about Lindau being Germany's 'Garden of Eden' and the 'Bavarian Riviera'. Paradise and southern France it ain't, but it is pretty special. Cradled in the southern crook of Lake Constance and almost dipping its toes into Austria, this is a good-looking, outgoing little town, with a candy-coloured postcard of an Altstadt, clear-day Alpine views and lake-front cafes that use every sunray to the max.

◎ Sights

Seepromenade
AREA

In summer the harbourside promenade has a happy-go-lucky air, with its palms, bobbing boats and folk sunning themselves in pavement cafes.

Out at the harbour gates, looking across to the Alps, is Lindau's signature 36m-high Neuer Leuchtturm and, just in case you forget which state you're in, a statue of the Bavarian lion. The square, tile-roofed 13th-century **Mangturm** (Old Lighthouse) guards the northern edge of the sheltered port.

Stadtmuseum
MUSEUM

(www.kultur-lindau.de; Marktplatz 6; adult/concession €8/3.50; ⊘10am-6pm) Lions and voluptuous dames dance across the trompe l'oeil facade of the flamboyantly baroque Haus zum Cavazzen, which contains this museum, showcasing a fine collection of furniture, weapons and paintings. The museum also hosts stellar temporary exhibitions; previous shows have included works by Picasso, Chagall, Matisse, Emil Nolde, Klee and August Macke.

Neuer Leuchtturm
VIEWPOINT

(New Lighthouse; Hafenplatz; adult/concession €1.80/0.70; ⊘10am-7.30pm) Climb 139 steps to the top of this 36m-high lighthouse for cracking views out over Lindau and Lake

Constance, especially on clear days when the Alps are visible on the horizon. The lighthouse shines at night.

Peterskirche
CHURCH

(Oberer Schrannenplatz; ⊘variable) FREE Looking back on a 1000-year history, this enigmatic church is now a war memorial, hiding exquisite time-faded frescoes of the Passion of Christ by Hans Holbein the Elder. The cool, dimly lit interior is a quiet spot for contemplation. Next door is the turreted 14th-century Diebsturm, once a tiny jail.

Altes Rathaus
LANDMARK

(Old Town Hall; Bismarckplatz 4) Lindau's biggest architectural stunner is the step-gabled Altes Rathaus, built in 1422 in flamboyant Gothic style. Decorated many centuries later in 1930, its facade is a frescoed frenzy of cherubs, merry minstrels, galleons, fishermen, farmers and sea monsters.

🛏 Sleeping

Hotel Anker
GUESTHOUSE €€

(⊘08382-260 9844; www.anker-lindau.com; Bindergasse 15; s €59-69, d €85-169; 🛜) Shiny parquet floors, citrus colours and artwork have spruced up the charming and peaceful rooms at this central guesthouse, tucked down a cobbled lane. Rates include a hearty breakfast. There is no lift.

Hotel Garni-Brugger
HISTORIC HOTEL €€

(⊘08382-934 10; www.hotel-garni-brugger.de; Bei der Heidenmauer 11; s €60-88, d €94-135, tr €118-148, q €128-165; 🛜) This 18th-century hotel has bright rooms done up in floral fabrics and pine, which are comfortable enough if nothing flash. The family go out of their way to please. Guests can unwind in the little spa with steam room and sauna (€10) in the cooler months.

Helvetia
BOUTIQUE HOTEL €€€

(⊘08382-9130; www.hotel-helvetia.com; Seepromenade; r €220-380; 🛜✷) With an unbeatable location right on the lake front with a stellar view of the lighthouse, Helvetia is a superchic boutique number, with a mix of highly stylish rooms with themes swinging from the Swiss Alps to Oriental Spa (with own sauna). Or you can notch up the fancy factor by staying the night in a private yacht in the harbour.

Hotel Alte Schule
HOTEL €€€

(⊘08382-911 4444; www.hotelalteschule-lindau.de; Alter Schulplatz 2; s €75-95, d €120-220, ste €180-

WORTH A TRIP

PFAHLBAUTEN
....

Awarded Unesco World Heritage status in 2011, the **Pfahlbauten** (Pile Dwellings; www.pfahlbauten.de; Strandpromenade 6, Unteruhldingen; adult/concession €10/8; ⊘9am-6.30pm Apr-Sep, to 5pm Oct, 9am-5pm Sat & Sun Nov) represent one of 11 prehistoric pile dwellings around the Alps. Based on the findings of local excavations, the carefully reconstructed dwellings catapult you back to the Stone and Bronze Ages, from 4000 to 850 BC. A spin of the lakefront complex takes in stilt dwellings that give an insight into the lives of farmers, fishers and craftspeople. Kids love the hands-on activities from axe-making to fire-starting using flints.

250; P🛜) A recent makeover has brought this hotel bang up to date. Housed in a listed 15th-century building, the themed rooms zoom in on different places around Lake Constance, from the flowery exuberance of Insel Mainau to the rustic-cool, mountain-themed Pfänder. Regional and organic produce incuding pastries, eggs to order and fresh orange juice, appear at breakfast.

Alte Post
HOTEL €€€

(⊘08382-934 60; www.alte-post-lindau.de; Fischergasse 3; s €75-95, d €140-190, f €180-210; 🛜) This 300-year-old coaching inn was once a stop on the Frankfurt–Milan mail run. Well-kept, light and spacious, the newly revamped rooms (including those suitable for families) have solid oak floors and furnishings. Downstairs is a beer garden and a highly regarded restaurant (mains €10 to €22).

🍴 Eating & Drinking

Engelstube
GERMAN €€

(⊘08382-5240; www.engel-lindau.de; Schafgasse 4; mains €14-21; ⊘11am-3pm & 5-11pm) Dark wood panelling and plenty of rustic touches keep the vibe cosy at this smart wine tavern, which looks proudly back on more than 600 years of history. Regional dishes such as Lake Constance fish with herbs, and roast Bavarian ox are cooked to a T. Try to snag a spot on the pavement terrace in summer.

Weinstube Frey
GERMAN €€

(⊘08382-947 9676; Maximilianstrasse 15; mains €16-22; ⊘11.30am-10pm) This 500-year-old

WORTH A TRIP

AFFENBERG SALEM

No zoo-like cages, no circus antics, just happy Barbary macaques free to roam in a near-natural habitat: that's the concept behind conservation-oriented **Affenberg Salem** (www.affenberg-salem.de; Mendlishauser Hof, Salem; adult/concession €9/6; ⊕9am-6pm mid-Mar-Oct). Trails interweave the 20-hectare woodlands, where you can feed tailless monkeys one piece of special popcorn at a time, observe their behaviour (you scratch my back, I'll scratch yours...) and get primate close-ups at hourly feedings. The park is also home to storks; listen for bill clattering and look out for their nests near the entrance.

wood-panelled wine tavern oozes Bavarian charm with its cosy nooks. Dirndl-clad waitresses serve up regional wines and fare such as Lake Constance whitefish with market veg, and *Zwiebelrostbraten* (onion beef roast). Sit out on the terrace when the sun's out.

Grosstadt CAFE €€
(☑08382-504 2998; www.grosstadt-lindau.de; In der Grub 27; light meals €6-16; ⊕9am-1am; 🛜🅿) There's always a good buzz at this retro-flavoured cafe, full of intimate nooks and crannies and with a terrace spilling out onto the cobbles. The menu is a winning mix of speciality coffees, wraps, soups, creative salads, bagels and deli-style dishes such as marinated feta with rocket, with vegan and gluten-free options. It morphs into a chilled bar by night.

Valentin MEDITERRANEAN €€€
(☑08382-504 3740; https://valentin-lindau.de; In der Grub 28; mains €20-31, day specials €11.50-13.50; ⊕6-11pm; 🅿) With a deft hand, the chef sources local, seasonal, largely organic ingredients to go into his Med-style dishes at this chic vaulted restaurant. Dishes such as ayurvedic spinach soup, octopus with chorizo, cabbage and sweet potato, and chocolate molten cake with pumpkin ice cream are beautifully prepared and presented. Vegetarians and vegans are well catered for.

37° CAFE
(Bahnhofplatz 1; ⊕10am-8pm Tue-Sun) Part boutique, part boho-chic cafe, 37° combines a high-ceilinged interior with a cracking lake-facing pavement terrace. Pull up a candy-coloured chair for cold drinks and light bites such as tapas, quiche and soups.

Kunst Café CAFE
(http://kunst-cafe.info; Maximilianstrasse 48; ⊕10am-6pm Mon-Sat, noon-6pm Sun) Eat and drink among art and antiques at this rather elegant cafe, where oil paintings festoon walls and chandeliers hang from stuccoed

ceilings. It's a nicely chilled choice for a beer, coffee and a slice of homemade cake or snacks such as tarte flambée.

🛈 Information

Post Office (Zeppelinstrasse 6, REWE Markt; ⊕7am-8pm Mon-Sat) Post office in REWE supermarket.

Lindau Tourist Office (☑08382-260 030; www.lindau.de; Alfred-Nobel-Platz 1; ⊕10am-noon & 2-5pm Mon-Fri, 10am-4pm Sat & Sun) Lindau's tourist office is handily situated near the main train station.

🛈 Getting There & Away

Lindau is on the B31 and connects to Munich by the A96. The precipitous Deutsche Alpenstrasse (German Alpine Rd), which winds giddily eastward to Berchtesgaden, begins here.

Lindau is at the eastern terminus of the Bodensee–Gürtelbahn train line, which goes along the lake's north shore via Friedrichshafen (€8, 18 to 35 minutes) westward to Radolfzell, and the southern terminus of the Südbahn to Ulm (€27.90, 1½ to two hours) via Ravensburg (€12.50, one hour).

The lake front **Hauptbahnhof** (Am Bahnhof 1) is right in the heart of the Altstadt.

🛈 Getting Around

The compact, walkable *Insel* (island), home to the town centre and harbour, is connected to the mainland by the Seebrücke, a road bridge at its northeastern tip, and by the Eisenbahndamm, a rail bridge open to cyclists and pedestrians. The **Hauptbahnhof** lies to the east of the island, a block south of the pedestrianised, shop-lined Maximilianstrasse.

Buses 1 and 2 link the Hauptbahnhof to the main bus hub, known as ZUP. A single ticket costs €2.20; a day pass is €4.40.

Bikes and tandems can be rented at **Unger's Fahrradverleih** (☑08382-943 688; www.fahrrad-unger.de; Inselgraben 14; per day bikes €6-12, tandems €18, electro-bikes €20; ⊕9am-1pm & 3-6pm Mon-Fri, 9am-1pm Sat & Sun Mar-Oct).

Understand Munich, Bavaria & the Black Forest

Munich, Bavaria & the Black Forest Today

A high-voltage economy and thigh-slapping traditions, green energy and the world's greatest luxury car industry, supermarkets of organic food and sausages and beer for breakfast – southern Germany's contradictions continue to baffle outsiders. But what is clear is that the whole caboodle is based on three sound principles – a Bavarian electorate that has returned the same conservative-minded party to power every time since 1958, a focus on manufacturing and respect for the traditions of yesteryear.

Best in Print

Massacre in Munich: Manhunt for the Killers Behind the 1972 Olympics Massacre (Michael Bar Bar-Zohar and Eitan Haber; 2005) The title says it all, really.

Lola Montez: A Life (Bruce Seymour; 1998) A superbly written account of the life of Bavaria's most outrageous courtesan who brought down a king.

Ludwig II of Bavaria (Martha Schad; 2001) One of the most readable and compact biographies of Bavaria's most flamboyant monarch and available throughout the state.

Best on Film

Sophie Scholl: The Final Days (Marc Rothmund; 2005) Extremely moving account of the capture, trial and execution of members of the White Rose anti-Nazi group.

Ludwig (Luchino Visconti; 1973) The reign of Ludwig II.

Hierankl (Hans Steinbichler; 2003) Family drama set against the backdrop of the Alps.

The Nasty Girl (Michael Verhoeven; 1990) A woman digging up her town's Nazi past gets more than she bargains for.

Business As Usual

In October 2018 Bavaria was due to hold its *Landtagswahl* (regional election), the Bavarian Christlich-Soziale Union (CSU) set to receive a mandate to govern for another five years with Ilse Aigner at the helm. While other regions of Germany, especially in the former GDR, face a growing populist threat from the AfD (Alternativ für Deutschland; Alternative for Germany), Bavaria is a bastion of stability, a solid core at the heart of Europe's steadiest country. In 2018 Bavaria also celebrated 100 years of the Free State and 200 years of its constitution, two dates that added to the feeling of continuity. So as southern Germany continues apace, you could say there's no better place to be. The hundreds of thousands of migrants from places such as Turkey, Syria and Afghanistan certainly seem to think so. Despite alarmist warnings from the populists following Chancellor Merkel's open-door immigration policy, mosques have not sprung up across the Free State despite the arrival of many Muslim migrants – another southern German success story of sorts.

It's the Economy, Stupid!

Even the most militant anti-capitalist might, just for a moment, agree that Bavaria is a rampant success story of postwar free enterprise. Just one stat says it all – if Bavaria was an independent country (and not a small number of locals secretly wish it were), its economy would be the world's 19th largest (equally affluent Baden-Württemberg would rank around 22nd), bigger than Sweden or Austria and more than twice the size of the neighbouring Czech Republic. Germany's economic powerhouse is cooking with gas, and probably on an ecofriendly stove of sturdy design, proudly stamped with 'Hergestellt in Bayern' (Made in Bavaria). As Germany becomes Europe's unopposed, post-Brexit superpower, the south is leading the economic charge.

So what underpins the south's economic triumph? Good 'ole manufacturing seems to be the 'secret', with a motor industry second to none leading the way. The most desirable names of the Teutonic luxury car world – BMW, Audi, Porsche and Mercedes – are all based in the south, pumping billions of euros into the economy and employing hundreds of thousands. With the Volkswagen emissions scandal still high up on the local news agenda, the south's automotive industry can only benefit.

Tourism also generates a small chunk of the south's wealth. In 2017 Munich alone saw well over three million foreign visitors crumple hotel bed sheets, and blockbuster sights such as Schloss Neuschwanstein and Regensburg's Unesco-listed city centre also attract millions. The overtourism and Airbnb/Uber rows that are plaguing other European destinations haven't yet arrived in Bavaria or Baden-Württemberg.

No, It's the Environment, Stupid!

With the south's countless factories boxing up everything from R8s to locos, you'd expect a toxic murk to envelope you at the plane door. But it doesn't. In fact, by 2025 Munich is aiming to become the world's first major city powered solely using renewable energy sources, and in the countryside some small towns look very different from one direction than from the other as south-facing roofs bear the weight of millions of solar panels (you see this odd phenomenon best from trains). Farmers have turned over considerable acreage to accommodate vast swathes of buzzing solar panels, wind turbines are a common sight and biking has been in fashion for decades. The plan to switch off Germany's nuclear power stations by 2022 is still on track, with Berlin's politicians seemingly still on board with the policy first drafted in 2011.

Traditional Success Story

How good it must feel to be a German from the south – a high-octane economy, sun and wind powering your latest gadgetry, the cultural and historic delights of Germany's secret capital (Munich) and an Alpine playground a swift train ride away; and your country heading the free world and the German Chancellor Merkel now the most powerful figure in Europe. So, why all the glum faces on the S-Bahn you may wonder? What do these people have to be grumpy about? As throughout the Western world, even flourishing southern Germany is not immune to an underlying angst about the future. But the difference here may be that on the evenings and weekends, locals retreat to the unglobalised world of thigh-slapping tradition – the beer hall, the Alpine tavern, a baroque theatre or a folk bash – to celebrate their astounding successes, whatever the future may bring.

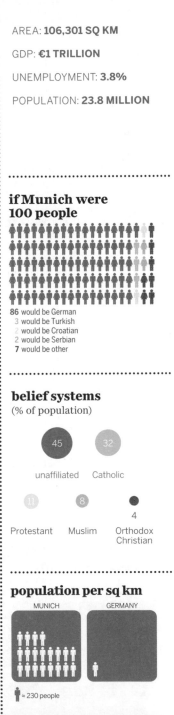

AREA: **106,301 SQ KM**

GDP: **€1 TRILLION**

UNEMPLOYMENT: **3.8%**

POPULATION: **23.8 MILLION**

if Munich were 100 people

86 would be German
3 would be Turkish
2 would be Croatian
2 would be Serbian
7 would be other

belief systems
(% of population)

45 unaffiliated

32 Catholic

11 Protestant

8 Muslim

4 Orthodox Christian

population per sq km

MUNICH

GERMANY

≈ 230 people

History

One of Europe's oldest states, with origins dating back to the 6th century, Germany's largest *Land*, Bavaria, has enjoyed a long and eventful past, populated by a weird-and-*wunderbar* cast of oddball kings, scandalous courtesans and infamous Nazis. It has suffered war and revolution, mad monarchs and even madder dictators, but you could say all's well that ends well, with Bavaria and southern Germany in general one of the world's most prosperous and peaceful places.

Tribal Melting Pot

The first recorded inhabitants of Bavaria were the Celts, who proved to be a pushover for the Romans who began swarming across the Alps in the 1st century AD. The invaders founded the province of Raetia with Augusta Vindelicorum (Augsburg) as its capital. By the 5th century the tables were turned on the Romans by marauding eastern Germanic tribes pushing up the Danube Valley in search of pastures new.

As with all central Europe's peoples, the precise origin of the Bavarian tribe is obscure, but it's widely assumed that it coalesced from the remaining Romans, Romanised Celts and the newcomers from the east. The name 'Bajuwaren' may be derived from 'men from Bohemia', the neighbouring region of today's Czech Republic.

The Franken began forming in the 3rd century AD from several western Germanic tribes who settled along the central and lower Rhine, on the border with the Roman Empire. The Schwaben, meanwhile, are a sub-tribe of the population group of the Alemannen (Alemannic tribes) who spread across the southwestern corner of Germany around the 2nd century AD. In the 3rd century they took on the Romans, eventually pushing as far east as the Lech River.

On Bavaria's coat of arms, 'Old Bavaria' is represented by a blue panther, the Franconians by a red-and-white rake, the Swabians by three black lions, and the Upper Palatinate (no longer part of today's Bavaria) by a golden lion.

Church Dominance

Religion, especially of the Roman Catholic variety, has shaped all aspects of Bavarian history and culture for nearly two millennia. Following the decline of the Roman Empire, missionaries from Ireland and Scotland swarmed across Europe to spread the gospel. They found open arms and

TIMELINE	15 BC	AD 555–788	7th–8th centuries
	Nero Claudius Drusus and Tiberius Claudius Nero, stepsons of Roman emperor Augustus, conquer the Celtic tribes north of the Alps, calling their new colony Raetia. Augusta Vindelicorum (today's Augsburg) is capital.	The Agilofinges dynasty founds the first Bavarian duchy with Garibald I (r 555–91) its first-known duke. It remains in power until absorbed into the Frankish Empire in 788 by Charlemagne.	Christianity takes hold as roving missionaries arrive in Bavaria from Ireland, Scotland and the Frankish Empire. In 738 St Boniface creates the dioceses of Salzburg, Freising, Passau and Regensburg.

minds among the Agilofinges, the dynasty who had founded the first Bavarian duchy in the 6th century. They adopted the faith eagerly and Christianity quickly took root. By 739 there were bishoprics in Regensburg, Passau, Freising and Salzburg, and monasteries had been founded in Tegernsee, Benediktbeuern, Weltenburg and several other locations.

For almost the next 800 years, the Church dominated daily life as the only major religion in the land. Until 1517, that is. That's when a monk and theology professor named Martin Luther sparked the Reformation with his 95 theses critiquing papal infallibility, clerical celibacy, selling indulgences and other elements of Catholic doctrine.

Despite the Church's attempt to quash Luther, his teachings resonated widely, especially in Franconia and Swabia, though not in Bavaria proper where local rulers instantly clamped down on anyone toying with conversion. They also encouraged the newly founded Jesuit order to make Ingolstadt the hub of the Counter-Reformation. The religious strife eventually escalated into the Thirty Years' War (1618–48), which left Europe's soil drenched with the blood of millions. During the conflict, Bavaria's Duke Maximilian I (r 1598–1651) fought firmly on the side of Catholic emperor Ferdinand II of Habsburg, who thanked him by expanding Max's territory and promoting him to *Kurfürst* (prince-elector). With calm restored in 1648 following the signing of the Peace of Westphalia, Bavaria – along with much of the rest of central Europe – lay in ruins.

The treaty permitted each local ruler to determine the religion of his territory and essentially put the Catholic and Lutheran churches on equal legal footing. Bavaria, of course, remained staunchly Catholic. In fact, if the baroque church-building boom of the 17th century is any indication, it seemed to positively revel in its religious zeal.

But beyond Bavaria times were a-changing. The Enlightenment spawned reforms throughout Europe, first leading to the French Revolution, then the Napoleonic Wars and ultimately to the demise of the Holy Roman Empire. The ancient Church structure collapsed along with it, prompting the secularisation of Bavarian monasteries after 1803 and, finally, religious parity. Although Ludwig I restored the monasteries, Protestants have since enjoyed equal rights throughout Bavaria, even though it remains predominantly Catholic to this day.

Much to the delight and pride of the population, Bavarian-born Joseph Cardinal Ratzinger was elected Pope Benedict XVI in 2005 (he resigned in early 2013). The last German pope was Adrian VI who ruled from 1522 to 1523.

For a comprehensive overview of Bavarian history (partly in English) see the website of the government-financed Haus der Bayerischen Geschichte at www.hdbg.de.

The most prominent Wittelsbach descendant is Prince Luitpold of Bavaria who runs his own brewery, the Schlossbrauerei Kaltenberg, and hosts a popular jousting tournament, the Kaltenberger Ritterturnier. Learn more at www.kaltenberg. com.

The Wittelsbachs

From 1180 to 1918, a single family held Bavaria in its grip: the House of Wittelsbach. Otto von Wittelsbach was a distant relative of Emperor

962	1158	1180	1214
The pope crowns the Saxon king Otto I Kaiser (emperor), marking the beginning of the Holy Roman Empire, which remains a major force in European history until 1806.	Duke Heinrich der Löwe establishes Munich as a market town in a bid to take control of the lucrative central European trade in salt, known then as 'white gold'.	The Wittelsbachs' 738-year reign begins with Otto von Wittelsbach's appointment as duke of Bavaria by Emperor Friedrich Barbarossa, marking the transition from tribal duchy to territorial state.	Emperor Friedrich II grants the fiefdom of the Palatinate along the Rhine River to Duke Otto II von Wittelsbach, thereby significantly enlarging the family's territory and increasing its power.

Friedrich Barbarossa who, in 1180, appointed him duke of Bavaria, which at that time was a fairly small and insignificant territory. Ensuing generations of Wittelsbachs focused on expanding their land – and with it their sphere of influence – through wheeling and dealing, marriage, inheritance and war.

Being granted the fiefdom of the Palatinate, an area along the Rhine River northwest of present-day boundaries, was a good start back in 1214, but the family's fortunes peaked when one of their own, Ludwig the Bavarian, became Holy Roman Emperor in 1328. As the first Wittelsbach on the imperial throne, Ludwig used his powerful position to bring various far-flung territories, including the March of Brandenburg (around Berlin), the Tyrol (part of today's Austria) and several Dutch provinces, under Bavarian control.

The Thirty Years' War brought widespread devastation but, by aligning themselves with Catholic emperor Ferdinand II, the Wittelsbachs managed not only to further expand their territory but to score a promotion from duchy to *Kurfürstentum* (electorate), giving them a say in the election of future emperors.

Not all alliances paid off so handsomely. In the 1680s Maximilian II Emanuel (r 1679–1726) – a man of great ambition but poor judgement – battled the Turks alongside the Habsburg Kaiser in an attempt to topple the Ottoman Empire. Much to his dismay, his allegiance did not lead to the rewards he had expected. So he tried again, this time switching sides and fighting with the French against Austria in the War of the Spanish Succession (1701–14). The conflict ended in a disastrous Franco-Bavarian loss and a 10-year occupation of Bavaria by Habsburg troops. Not only had Max Emanuel failed to achieve his personal goals, his flip-flop policies had also seriously weakened Bavaria's political strength.

Max Emanuel's son, Karl Albrecht (r 1726–45), was determined to avenge his father's double humiliation. Through some fancy political manoeuvring, he managed to take advantage of the confusion caused by the War of Succession and, with the backing of Prussia and France, ended up on the imperial throne as Karl VII in 1742. His triumph, however, was short-lived as Bavaria was quickly reoccupied by Austrian troops. Upon Karl Albrecht's death in 1745, his son Maximilian III Joseph (r 1745–77) was forced to renounce the Wittelsbachs' claims to the imperial crown forever.

The Accidental Kingdom

Modern Bavaria, more or less as we know it today, was established in the early 19th century by Napoleon. At the onset of the Napoleonic Wars (1799–1815), Bavaria initially found itself on the losing side against

---

Germany's first ever postage stamp was issued in Bavaria in November 1849 and was called the *Schwarze Einser* (Black Penny). Not as rare as Britain's Penny Black, a used copy only fetches a couple of thousand euros when auctioned.

Top Five Wittelsbach Residences

Schloss Neuschwanstein (p92)

Munich Residenz (p43)

Schloss Herrenchiemsee (p104)

Schloss Nymphenburg (p59)

Schloss Linderhof (p97)

1506	1516	1517	1555
To further prevent Bavaria from being split into ever-smaller territories, Duke Albrecht the Wise introduces the law of primogeniture. Possessions now pass automatically to first-born sons.	On 23 April the Reinheitsgebot (Purity Law) is passed in Ingolstadt, which limits the ingredients used in the production of beer to water, barley and hops.	Martin Luther splits the Christian church by kicking off the Reformation with his 95 theses posted on the door of the cathedral in the eastern German town of Wittenberg.	Emperor Karl V signs the Peace of Augsburg allowing each local ruler to decide which religion to adopt in their principality, ending decades of religious strife and officially recognising Lutherism.

France. Tired of war and spurred on by his powerful minister Maximilian Graf von Montgelas, Maximilian IV Joseph (r 1799–1825) decided to put his territory under Napoleon's protection.

In 1803, after victories over Austria and Prussia, Napoleon set about remapping much of Europe. Bavaria fared rather well, nearly doubling its size when it received control over Franconia and Swabia. In 1806

MILESTONES IN BLACK FOREST HISTORY

In the beginning the Black Forest was just that: a huge, dark, dense clump of trees so impenetrable that even the Romans didn't dare colonise it, although they couldn't resist taking advantage of the thermal mineral springs in Baden-Baden on the forest's edge. Around the 7th century, a band of intrepid monks took a stab at taming the area, but it would be another few centuries until the ruling Zähringer clan founded Freiburg in 1120. In order to solidify their claim on the land, they moved farmers into the valleys to clear the trees and create small settlements. This led to the discovery of natural resources and, up until the 15th century, the extraction of iron, zinc, lead and even silver were major industries.

While their feudal lords enjoyed the spoils of their subjects' labour, the lot of the miners and farmers steadily deteriorated. In the 16th century unrest fomenting in the Black Forest eventually grew into the Peasant Rebellion that swept through much of southern Germany. Poorly equipped and haphazardly organised, the farmers were, of course, no match for the authorities who brought the uprising to a bloody conclusion.

In the following centuries the people of the Black Forest experienced a series of hardships of Biblical proportions. The Thirty Years' War left about 70% of the population dead, and plague and crop failures did much the same for the rest. Unsurprisingly, many of the survivors left for greener pastures in other parts of Europe.

The Black Forest stayed out of the spotlight for well over a century until the Baden Revolution of 1848–49. Inspired by the democratic movement in France and the declaration of the French Republic in February 1848, local radical democratic leaders Friedrich Hecker and Gustav von Struve led an armed rebellion against the archduke of Baden in April 1848, demanding freedom of expression, universal education, popular suffrage and other democratic ideals. Struve was arrested and Hecker fled into exile, but their struggle inspired the population and spilled over into other parts of Germany. Eventually Prussian troops cracked down on the revolutionaries in a fiery showdown at Rastatt in July 1849.

Nearly 100 years later, Freudenstadt and Freiburg were among the regional cities bombed to bits during WWII. In 1952 the Black Forest became part of the newly formed German state of Baden-Württemberg. Although it's still largely agrarian, tourism is the single biggest source of income today.

1618–48	1806	1835	1848
The Thirty Years' War involves most European nations, but is fought mainly on German soil, bringing murder, starvation and disease, and decimating Europe's population from 21 million to 13.5 million.	Bavaria becomes a kingdom and nearly doubles its size when handed Franconia and Swabia. Sweeping reforms result in the passage of the state's first constitution in 1808.	Drawn by a steam locomotive called Adler (Eagle), Germany's first railway commences operations between Nuremberg and nearby Fürth, transporting newspapers, beer and people. It ploughs on until 1922.	A man with a weakness for the arts and beautiful women, King Ludwig I is forced to resign after his affair with Lola Montez causes a public scandal.

Napoleon created the kingdom of Bavaria and made Maximilian I his new best buddy.

Alas, keeping allegiances had never been Bavaria's strong suit and, in 1813, with Napoleon's fortunes waning, Montgelas shrewdly threw the new kingdom's support behind Austria and Prussia. After France's defeat, the victorious allies again reshaped European boundaries at the Con-

LOLA MONTEZ, FEMME FATALE

A whip-toting dominatrix and seductress of royalty, Lola Montez (1818–61) would show today's celebs what sex scandals are all about. Born as Eliza Gilbert in Ireland, to a young British army officer and a 13-year-old Creole chorus girl, Lola claimed to be the illegitimate daughter of poet Lord Byron (or, depending on her mood, of a matador). When her actual father died of cholera in India, her mother remarried and then shipped the seven-year-old Eliza off to Scotland. During her time in Scotland she was occasionally seen running stark naked through the streets. She then finished her schooling in Paris and after an unsuccessful stab at acting, reinvented herself as the Spanish dancer Lola Montez.

She couldn't dance either but her beauty fascinated men, who fell at her feet – sometimes under the lash of her ever-present riding crop. One time she fired a pistol at a lover who'd underperformed, but he managed to escape with his trousers around his knees.

Those succumbing to her charms included the tsar of Russia, who paid her 1000 roubles for a 'private audience'; novelist Alexandre Dumas; and composer Franz Liszt. Liszt eventually tired of Lola's incendiary temper, locked his sleeping mistress in their hotel room and fled – leaving a deposit for the furniture Lola would demolish when she awoke.

When fired by a Munich theatre manager, Lola took her appeal to the court of Ludwig I himself. As the tale goes, Ludwig asked casually whether her lovely figure was a work of nature or art. The direct gal she was, Lola seized a pair of scissors and slit open the front of her dress, leaving the ageing monarch to judge for himself. Predictably, she was rehired (and the manager sacked).

The king fell head over heels for Lola, giving her a huge allowance, a lavish palace and even the doubtful title of Countess of Landsfeld. Her ladyship virtually began running the country, too, and when Munich students rioted during the 1848 revolution, Lola had Ludwig shut down the university. This was too much for the townsfolk, who joined the students in revolt. Ludwig was forced to abdicate and Lola was chased out of town.

Lola cancanned her way around the world; her increasingly lurid show was very popular with gold miners in California and Australia. Next came a book of 'beauty secrets' and a lecture tour featuring topics such as 'Heroines of History and Strong-Minded Women'. She shed her Spanish identity, but in doing so, Lola – who had long publicly denied any link to her alter ego, Eliza – became a schizophrenic wreck. She spent her final two years as a pauper in New York, dying of pneumonia and a stroke aged 43.

1865	1869	1870–71	1886
Wagner's opera *Tristan und Isolde* is premieres at Munich's Nationaltheater on 10 June during the composer's 18 months in the city under the patronage of Ludwig II.	Building work on Schloss Neuschwanstein is begun by architect Eduard Riedel. Due to lack of funds work is halted in 1892 and Ludwig II's fairy-tale pile is never completed.	Through brilliant diplomacy and the Franco-Prussian War, Bismarck creates a unified Germany. However, Bavaria keeps much of its sovereignty and many of its own institutions.	King Ludwig II is declared mentally unfit and confined to Schloss Berg on Starnberger See where he drowns in mysterious circumstances in shallow water, alongside his doctor.

gress of Vienna (1814–15) and Bavaria got to keep most of the territory it had obtained with Napoleon's help.

Reluctant Reformers

During the 18th century, the ideas of the Enlightenment that had swept through other parts of Europe had largely been ignored in Bavaria. Until Elector Maximilian III Joseph (r 1745–77) arrived on the scene, that is. Tired of waging war like his predecessors, he made peace with Austria and busied himself with reforming his country from within. He updated the legal system, founded the Bavarian Academy of Sciences and made school attendance compulsory. Max Joseph's reign also saw the creation of the Nymphenburg porcelain factory and the construction of the Cuvilliés-Theater at the Munich Residenz.

Now that the reforms had begun, there was no going back, especially after Bavaria became a kingdom in 1806. The architect of modern Bavaria was King Maximilian I's minister, Maximilian Graf von Montgelas. He worked feverishly to forge a united state from the mosaic of 'Old Bavaria', Franconia and Swabia, by introducing sweeping political, administrative and social changes, including the secularisation of the monasteries. The reforms ultimately led to Bavaria's first constitution in 1808, which was based on rights of freedom, equality and property ownership, and the promise of representative government. Ten years later Bavaria got its first *Landtag* (two-chamber parliament).

Under Max I's son, Ludwig I (r 1825–48), Bavaria flourished into an artistic and cultural centre, an 'Athens on the Isar'. Painters, poets and philosophers gathered in Munich, where Leo von Klenze and Friedrich von Gärtner were creating a showcase of neoclassical architecture. Königsplatz with the Glyptothek and Propyläen, flashy Ludwigstrasse with the Siegestor triumphal arch, and the Ludwig Maximilian University were all built on Ludwig I's watch, as was the Alte Pinakothek. The king was also keen on new technology and heavily supported the idea of a nationwide railway. The first short line from Nuremberg to Fürth opened during his reign in 1835.

Politically, though, Ludwig I brought a return to authority from the top as revolutionary rumblings in other parts of Europe coaxed out his reactionary streak. An arch-Catholic, he restored the monasteries, introduced press censorship and authorised arrests of students, journalists and university professors whom he judged subversive. Bavaria was becoming restrictive, even as French and American democratic ideas flourished elsewhere in Germany.

On 22 March 1848 Ludwig I abdicated in favour of his son, Maximilian II (r 1848–64), who finally put into place many of the constitutional

Bavaria is made up of seven historical *Regierungsbezirken* (administrative areas) – Unterfranken, Oberfranken, Mittelfranken, Oberpfalz, Schwaben, Niederbayern and Oberbayern.

At economic odds at times recently, Bavaria and Greece once shared a ruler when Otto I of Bavaria became modern Greece's first monarch in 1832. The biggest headache of his reign: Greece's ailing economy.

HISTORY RELUCTANT REFORMERS

1914–18	1919	1923	1932
WWI: Germany, Austria, Hungary and Turkey go to war against Britain, France, Italy and Russia. Germany is defeated, the monarchy overthrown and Bavaria declared a 'free state'.	Left-leaning intellectuals proclaim the Münchner Räterepublik on 4 April, hoping to create a Soviet-style regime. The movement never spreads beyond Munich and is quashed by government forces on 3 May.	Hitler's failed putsch attempt lands him in jail where he takes just nine months to pen his vitriolic rant, *Mein Kampf* (My Struggle). It sells between eight and nine million copies.	Hitler and Churchill almost meet when the latter is researching his family history in Munich. Hitler calls off the meeting, considering a washed-up politician such as Churchill unworthy of his time.

reforms his father had ignored, such as abolishing censorship and introducing the right to assemble. Further progressive measures passed by his son Ludwig II (r 1864–86) early in his reign included welfare for the poor, liberalised marriage laws and free trade.

Ludwig, a 1973 flick directed by Luchino Visconti, is a lush, epic and sensitive Oscar-nominated portrayal of the life of Ludwig II, a highly emotional and tormented king out of step with his time.

The Mystique of Ludwig II

No other Bavarian king stirs the imagination quite as much as Ludwig II, the fairy-tale king so tragically at odds with a modern world that had no longer any use for an absolutist, if enlightened, monarch. Ludwig was a sensitive soul, fascinated by romantic epics, architecture and the music of Richard Wagner. When he became king at 18, he was at first a rather enthusiastic leader; however, Bavaria's days as a sovereign state were numbered. After it was absorbed into the Prussian-led German Reich in 1871, Ludwig became little more than a puppet king (albeit one receiving regular hefty allowances from Berlin).

Disillusioned, the king retreated to the Bavarian Alps to drink, draw castle plans, and enjoy private concerts and operas. His obsession with French culture and the Sun King, Louis XIV, inspired the fantastical palaces of Neuschwanstein, Linderhof and Herrenchiemsee (more were planned) – lavish projects that spelt his undoing.

In January 1886 several ministers and relatives arranged a hasty psychiatric test that diagnosed Ludwig as mentally unfit to rule. He was dethroned and taken to Schloss Berg on Starnberger See. Then, one evening, the dejected bachelor and his doctor took a lakeside walk and several hours later were found dead – mysteriously drowned in just a few feet of water.

No-one knows with certainty what happened that night. There was no eyewitness or proper criminal investigation. The circumstantial evidence was conflicting and incomplete. Reports and documents were tampered with, destroyed or lost. Conspiracy theories abound. That summer the authorities opened Neuschwanstein to the public to help pay off Ludwig's huge debts. King Ludwig II was dead, but a tourist industry was just being born.

Hitler called his regime the 'Third Reich' because he thought of the Holy Roman Empire and Bismarck's German empire as the first and second Reichs, respectively.

Nazi Legacy

If Berlin was the head of the Nazi government, its heartbeat was in Bavaria. This was the birthplace of the movement, born out of the chaos and volatility of a post-WWI Germany wracked by revolution, crippling reparations and runaway inflation. Right-wing agitation resonated especially among Bavarians who deeply resented losing much of their sovereignty to a centralised national government in Berlin.

In Munich, a failed artist and WWI corporal from Austria – Adolf Hitler – had quickly risen to the top of the extreme right-wing National-

1933	1938	1939–45	1943
Hitler becomes chancellor of Germany and creates a dictatorship, making Munich the 'capital of the movement' and Obersalzberg, near Berchtesgaden, a second seat of government.	The Munich Agreement allows Hitler to annex the Sudetenlands, a mostly German-speaking region of Czechoslovakia. British prime minister Neville Chamberlain declares there will be 'peace in our time'.	WWII: Hitler invades Poland; Britain, France and, in 1941, the US, declare war on Germany; Jews are murdered en masse in concentration camps throughout Eastern Europe during the Holocaust.	Members of the Nazi resistance group, Die Weisse Rose (The White Rose), are caught distributing anti-Nazi leaflets at Ludwig Maximilian University and executed a few days later, following a sham trial.

sozialistische Arbeiterpartei (NSDAP). On 8 November 1923 he led his supporters in a revolt aimed at overthrowing the central government following a political rally in the Bürgerbräukeller (near today's Gasteig arts centre). The so-called Beer Hall Putsch was an abysmal failure, poorly planned and amateurishly executed. The following day a ragtag bunch of would-be armed revolutionaries marched through Munich's streets but only got as far as the Feldherrnhalle where a shoot-out with police left 16 Nazis and four policemen dead.

The NSDAP was banned and Hitler was sentenced to five years in prison for high treason. While in Landsberg jail, west of Munich, he began work on *Mein Kampf* (My Struggle), dictated in extended ramblings to his secretary Rudolf Hess. Incredibly, Hitler was released after only nine months in 1924 on grounds of 'good behaviour'.

After Hitler took control of Germany in January 1933, Bavaria was assigned a special status. Munich was declared the 'Capital of the Movement' and Nuremberg became the site of the Nazi party's mass rallies. In 1935 the party brass enacted the Nuremberg Laws, which ushered in the systematic repression of the Jews. In Dachau, north of Munich, Germany's first concentration camp was built in 1933. In addition, many Nazi honchos hailed from Bavaria, including Sturmabteilung (SA) chief Ernst Röhm (later killed by Hitler), Heinrich Himmler and Hermann Göring. Hitler himself was born just across the border, in Austria's Braunau. The Nazis enjoyed almost universal support in Bavaria, but there were also some pockets of resistance, most famously the Munich-based group Die Weisse Rose (The White Rose).

In 1938 Hitler's troops met no resistance when they marched into Austria and annexed it to Nazi Germany. The same year, the UK's Neville Chamberlain, Italy's Benito Mussolini and France's Édouard Daladier, in an attempt to avoid another war, continued their policy of appeasement

Bavaria's Most Visited Nazi Sites

....

Eagle's Nest (p106), Berchtesgaden

....

Dachau concentration camp (p86)

....

Reichsparteitagsgelände (p129), Nuremberg

....

Nuremberg Trials courtroom (p129), Nuremberg

....

Dokumentation Obersalzberg (p106), Berchtesgaden

HISTORY NAZI LEGACY

INVENTIONS

Over the past five centuries, Bavaria has been a bit of a hotbed when it comes to inventors and inventions, giving the world some of its most essential gadgets and machines. If you've put on a pair of jeans, listened to an MP3 or driven a diesel-powered car recently – all are Bavarian inventions (Levi Strauss, Karlheinz Brandenburg and Rudolf Diesel respectively). The globe (Martin Daliaim in 1493), the watch (Peter Henlein in 1505) and the plane engine (Gustav Weisskopf in 1901) are other things we just couldn't imagine the world without. That may no longer be the case, however, with steerable oxcarts (Georg Lankensperger in 1816) and the board game Ludo (Josef Schmidt in 1908).

1945	1945–46	1958	1950s–80s
Hitler commits suicide in his Berlin bunker. A broken Germany surrenders to the Allies and is divided into four zones. Bavaria falls into the US Zone.	The Allies hold a series of trials against Nazi leaders accused of crimes against peace and humanity in a courthouse at Nuremberg. Ten of the accused are executed by hanging.	The Munich air disaster kills 23 of the Manchester United Busby Babes, journalists and supporters on a slushy runway at Riem airfield.	Bavaria leads the way in the nation's *Wirtschaftswunder* (economic miracle) with huge companies such as Adidas, Puma and Playmobil established in the state.

by handing Hitler control over large portions of Czechoslovakia in the Munich Agreement. Chamberlain's naive hope that such a move would bring 'peace in our time' was destroyed on 1 September 1939 when Nazi troops marched into Poland, kicking off WWII.

A State Apart

Modern Bavaria may be integrated thoroughly within the German political construct, but its people take great pride in their distinctiveness. Its history, traditions, attitudes, political priorities and culture are, in many ways, quite different from the rest of Germany. While seeing themselves as Germans, Bavarians are Bavarians first. This is not true over the 'border' in Baden-Württemberg.

After WWII Bavaria became part of the American occupation zone and was allowed to pass its own constitution in December 1946. In 1949 it became the only German state that didn't ratify the German constitution because, in its opinion, it put unacceptable limitations on state

Part travelogue, part history, *Germania* (2010), by Simon Winder, is arguably the most digestible account of Germany's past to be published in recent decades, a fair share of the book dealing with Bavaria.

WE ARE POPE!

'Habemus papam.' It was a balmy spring evening in Rome in April 2005 when the world – Catholics and non-Catholics – held its collective breath. Who would follow in the footsteps of the charismatic Pope John Paul II who had led the church for 27 years? The man was Cardinal Joseph Ratzinger, henceforth known as Benedict XVI and born on 16 April 1927 in Bavaria's Marktl am Inn. For the first time in nearly 500 years a German had been elected pope. The following day the headline of the tabloid German daily *Bild* screamed proudly: *'Wir sind Papst!'* (We are Pope!).

Ratzinger's election met with a mix of elation and disappointment. Those who had hoped for a more progressive and liberal church leader were stunned to find that the job had gone to this fierce and uncompromising cardinal who for 24 years had been John Paul II's enforcer of church doctrine. He was known to be opposed to abortion, homosexuality and contraception, and ruthless in his crackdowns on dissident priests. 'Panzer cardinal' and 'God's Rottweiler' were just two of his nicknames.

Yet, even his staunchest critics could not deny that Ratzinger was well prepared for the papal post. A distinguished theologian, he spoke seven languages and had written more than 50 books. He could look back on a long career as a university professor, archbishop of Freising and Munich, and 24 years as John Paul II's main man.

If Pope Benedict's election was a surprise, it was nothing compared to the way he left the papacy. In February 2013 he resigned citing old age, the first pope to do so in over 700 years. He was succeeded by Argentine Jesuit pope Francis, but many fretted that having two popes alive at the same time might cause problems. However, so far this has not proved to be the case.

1972	1974	2005	2006
Bavaria shows off its prosperity, friendliness and cutting-edge architecture during the Olympic Games, although the event is overshadowed by the so-called Munich Massacre, a deadly terrorist attack on Israeli athletes.	Just two years after the tragic events of the Munich Olympics, the city hosts the final of the FIFA World Cup. West Germany defeat Holland 2:1 at the Olympiastadion.	Cardinal Joseph Ratzinger, who was born in 1927 in the town of Marktl am Inn near the Austrian border, is elected Pope Benedict XVI.	Munich's new Allianz Arena hosts the first match of the FIFA World Cup soccer championships. Hosts Germany beat Costa Rica 4:2 in an exciting curtain-raiser.

powers. Bavaria did, however, agree to honour and abide by the federal constitution and has always done so. However, to underscore its independent streak it calls itself 'Freistaat' (free state) Bayern, even though this has no real political meaning.

Since 1946 a single party, the archconservative Christlich-Soziale Union (CSU; Christian Social Union) has dominated Bavarian politics at every level of government, from communal to state. Although peculiar to Bavaria, it is closely aligned with its national sister party, the Christlich-Demokratische Union (CDU; Christian Democratic Union).

Powerful CSU figures include Franz-Josef Strauss, who served as Bavarian *Ministerpräsident* (minister-president, ie governor) from 1978 until his death in 1988, and his protégé, Edmund Stoiber, who clung to the job from 1999 until 2007. Although hugely popular and successful in Bavaria, both failed in their attempts to become federal chancellor: Strauss when losing to Helmut Schmidt in 1980, and Stoiber when outmanoeuvred by Gerhard Schröder in 2002. Since October 2008, Bavaria has been led by Horst Seehofer.

No other German state has been more successful in its postwar economic recovery than Bavaria. Within decades, it transformed from an essentially agrarian society into a progressive, high-tech state. The upturn was at least in part fuelled by the arrival of two million ethnic German expellees mainly from the Sudetelands of Bohemia and Moravia, who brought much-needed manpower. Bavaria is now synonymous with state-of-the-art engineering, quality manufacturing and top-of-the-range cars. But much of the past lives on in its traditional ways and in the treasure trove of architecture bequeathed by its erstwhile rulers.

In 1923 a postage stamp cost 50 billion marks, a loaf of bread cost 140 billion marks and US$1 was worth 4.2 trillion marks. In November 1923, the new Rentenmark was traded in for one trillion old marks.

HISTORY A STATE APART

2007	2008–13	2016	2018
After 14 years, Edmund Stoiber steps down as minister-president of Bavaria and party chairman of the CSU, having seen his leadership skills called into question.	The CSU is forced into a coalition (with the FDP) for the first time since the early 1960s. Normality resumes in 2013 when the party regained its overall majority in the *Landtag*.	An Islamic terrorist kills nine and himself at a shopping mall near the Olympiapark.	Bavaria holds state elections to decide who will lead the region for the next five years.

People & Culture

The culture of southern Germany is truly a vibrant mixed bag. Where else on earth can you find beer-hall oompah bands alongside Gothic sculpture, or galleries of cutting-edge contemporary art next door to shops selling strapping folk costume (that people still actually wear). The ebb and flow of history has left many cultural tide marks here, some from the bucolic past, others from darker and more recent chapters in the region's history. Whatever cultural experience floats your boat, Bavaria is bound to intrigue.

Regional Identity

Few other states in Germany can claim as distinct an identity as Bavaria. The country's southernmost state has always been a crossroads of trading routes to the Mediterranean and southeast Europe, and as the Alps never formed a truly impassable barrier, Bavaria early on absorbed the influences of Mediterranean culture. This gave the Bavarian character an easygoing outlook but one tempered with a Germanic respect for law and order. Patriotic feeling runs high, and at any hint of an affront, Bavarians close ranks, at least until the next party or festival. People here claim to be Bavarians first, Germans second, though this feeling weakens the further north into Franconia you head.

Indigenous Bavarians still strongly identify with their tribal heritage and call everyone not born in this neck of the *Wald* a *Zuagroaste* ('newcomer' in Bavarian dialect).

For outsiders the marriage of traditional rural Bavaria with modern-day industrial efficiency and wealth are hard to see as one entity – the two just don't seem to fit together. A popular slogan once coined by the state government dubbed Bavaria 'the land of Lederhosen and laptops', conjuring up images of farmers and computer scientists happily working hand in virtual hand. Modern Bavaria is indeed the land of Oktoberfest, beer and tradition, but it's also about cutting-edge glass-and-steel architecture, bright-lights nightlife, hipster fashion, sophisticated dining and world-class sport. It's youthful, dynamic and with only a hint of the brooding introspection you may encounter elsewhere in Germany.

Only created in 1952 out of the small states of Württemberg-Baden, Württemberg-Hohenzollern and Baden, today's Baden-Württemberg has none of the national feeling of Bavaria. Region is more important there with Swabia and the Allgäu possessing their own traditions.

Lifestyle

So who exactly is the average inhabitant of Germany's south? Statistically speaking, they are in their early thirties, white and married, have at least some higher education and live in a 90-sq-metre rented apartment in a midsize town. They drive a midsize car, but use public transport to commute to work in the service industry, where they earn about €3500 per month. About 40% of that evaporates in tax and social security deductions. The average Bavarian or Baden-Württemberger tends to vote conservative, but would not rule out giving another party the nod. Sorting and recycling rubbish is done religiously and, speaking of religion, Bavarians tend to be Roman Catholic while those from Baden-Württemberg are more likely to be Lutherans, though neither are regular churchgoers. A southern German feels comfortable on the hiking trail and ski slopes,

The distinctive Bavarian flag is made up of at least 21 blue and white diamonds.

but is not fitness-obsessed and could actually lose a few pounds. When they decide to have a family, they will have exactly 1.38 children.

Religion

Bavaria is overwhelmingly Roman Catholic with more than 50% claiming to be followers of the Vatican. However, pockets of Lutherans can be found in cities such as Munich, Augsburg and Nuremberg, and in the Bavarian regions of Oberfranken and Mittelfranken they are marginally in the majority. Munich has a growing Jewish community of around 10,000 people, most of them arrivals from former Soviet republics from the last three decades. Muslims account for almost 5% of the population and this number is growing.

Baden-Württemberg is divided into the Lutheran north/middle and the Catholic south – the split between the two is around 50/50. Islam is the state's third religion with around 6% of the population claiming to be followers of the Prophet.

Conventions

Locals are generally accommodating and fairly helpful towards visitors, and many will volunteer assistance if you look lost. This politeness does not necessarily extend to friendliness, however, and in public, people usually maintain a degree of reserve towards strangers – you won't find many conversations striking up on the bus or in the supermarket checkout queue. On the other hand, in younger company it's easy to chat with just about anyone, particularly in studenty hang-outs.

Shaking hands is common among both men and women, as is a hug or a kiss on the cheek, especially among young people. When making a phone call, start by giving your name (eg 'Smith, *Grüss Gott*' – which means 'Hello' in southern Germany). Not doing so is considered impolite.

Importance is placed on the formal *'Sie'* form of address, especially in business situations. Among younger people and in social settings, though, people are much more relaxed about using *'Sie'* and *'du'*.

Sport

Football

Mention *Fussball* (football, soccer) in Bavaria and passions will flare. FC Bayern München has dominated the Bundesliga on and off for the past two decades and has won the German championship 21 times, most recently in 2017. It's also had some success in the UEFA Champion's League, reaching the final five times since 1999, but winning the competition only twice. The team packs plenty of actual and financial muscle and attracts some of Europe's best players.

Bayern may dominate proceedings but there are several other good teams in southern Germany. FC Augsburg and VfB Stuttgart currently play in the top flight; SpVgg Greuther Fürth and 1 FC Nürnberg play in the second tier.

In 2015 women's football came to the fore in Bavaria when Bayern Munich won the women's Bundesliga for the first time since 1976, a feat they repeated in 2016.

If you want to follow the thrills, spills and manager tantrums in Germany's top soccer league, it's all online at www.bundesliga.de (in English).

Bavarians have won over 40 gold medals in the modern Olympic era, more than Belgium, the Czech Republic and Greece.

MULTICULTURALISM

Despite a high level of tolerance, few groups mix on a day-to-day basis and racial tensions have increased, at least in the cities. Government 'integration courses' for immigrants on welfare payments have done little to break down barriers and neo-Nazism is on the rise with a growing number of cases of intimidation of non-white foreigners reported.

Bavarian flag

The football season runs from September to June, with a winter break from Christmas to mid-February.

Skiing

Bavarian slopes still lure the sport's elite to annual World Cup races held in such resorts as Garmisch-Partenkirchen, Reit im Winkl and Berchtesgaden. On New Year's Day, Garmisch-Partenkirchen is also a stop on the four-part Vierschanzen-Tournee, the World Cup ski-jumping competition. Famous female champions from Bavaria include Rosi Mittermaier, a two-time Olympic gold-medal winner in 1976, and more recently Martina Ertl and Hilde Gerg. In early 2005 Alois Vogl ended the men's drought by snagging the World Cup for slalom.

Arts

Literature

Germany's most successful golfer, Bernhard Langer, is the son of a Russian prisoner of war who jumped off a Siberia-bound train and settled in Bavaria.

Quite a few German writers of the 18th and 19th centuries, including Jean Paul and ETA Hoffmann, lived in southern Germany, but the golden age of Bavarian literature kicked off in the second half of the 19th century. Some of the finest writers of the time, Thomas Mann and Frank Wedekind (famous for his coming-of-age tale *Spring Awakening,* 1891) among them, contributed to *Simplicissimus,* a satirical magazine founded in 1896 with a cover bearing a trademark red bulldog. A few of its barbs about Emperor Wilhelm II were so biting that the magazine was censored and some of its writers (Wedekind among them) were sent to jail. During his 40 years in Munich, Thomas Mann wrote an entire bookcase of acclaimed works and picked up a Nobel prize in the process. His Bavarian gems include the short story *Gladius Dei* (1902), a clever parody of Munich's pretensions to being the Florence of Bavaria.

More contemporary names are/were an eclectic, label-defying bunch. Herbert Rosendorfer (1934–2012), a former Munich judge, has a long list of credits, including a legal satire, a history of the Thirty Years' War and travel guides. Anna Rosmus (b 1960) has turned her investigation of the Third Reich period in Passau, her birthplace, into several best-selling novels, including *Against the Stream: Growing Up Where Hitler Used to Live* (2002). Munich-based Patrick Süskind (b 1949) achieved international acclaim with *Das Parfum* (Perfume; 1985), his extraordinary tale of a psychotic 18th-century perfume-maker, which was made into a film by Tom Tykwer in 2006.

Although he lived mostly in Switzerland, Nobel Prize–winner Hermann Hesse (1877–1962) is originally a Black Forest boy whose most famous novels, *Siddhartha* and *Steppenwolf,* became hippie-era favourites. The philosopher Martin Heidegger (1889–1976), author of *Being and Time,* one of the seminal works of German existentialism, also hailed from the Black Forest, as did Hans Jacob Christoffel von Grimmelshausen (1622–76), a 17th-century literary genius and author of the earliest German adventure novel, *Simplicissimus* (Adventures of a Simpleton; 1668), which later inspired the name of the aforementioned satirical magazine.

Bavaria's greatest playwright of international stature was the ever-abrasive Bertolt Brecht (1898–1956) from Augsburg. After WWII, writers throughout Germany either dropped out of sight ('inner exile' was the favoured term) or, as Hans Carossa and Ernst Wiechert did, attempted some kind of political and intellectual renewal.

Cinema & Television

Germany's last true international success, the Oscar-winning *Das Leben der Anderen* (The Lives of Others; 2006), may have been filmed in Berlin, but Munich's Bavaria Film studio is no slouch in the movie scene. Successes cranked out this side of the millennium include Marc Rothemund's Oscar-nominated *Sophie Scholl: The Final Days* (2005) and Tom Twyker's *Perfume: Story of a Murderer* (2006).

The studio pegs its pedigree back to 1919 and has lured many well-known directors, including Alfred Hitchcock (*The Pleasure Garden;* 1925), Billy Wilder (*Fedora;* 1978), Rainer Werner Fassbinder (*Bolwieser;* 1977) and, most famously, Wolfgang Petersen (*Das Boot,* 1981, and *The Never-ending Story,* 1984). Many made-for-German-TV features, detective series such as *Polizeiruf 110* and popular soaps such as *Marienhof,* are also produced in Munich. Part of the studio complex is Bavaria Filmstadt, a

In Anna Rosmus' *Against the Stream: Growing Up Where Hitler Used to Live* (2002), a teenage girl writes an essay and uncovers shocking crimes in prewar Passau.

Catholic Bavaria has produced few Jewish writers of note. A major exception is Jakob Wassermann (1873–1934), a popular novelist of the early 20th century.

HEIMATFILM

Southern Germany's dreamy Alpine landscapes helped spawn the *Heimatfilm* (homeland film), the only film genre to have been created in Germany. It reached its zenith in the 1950s and helped spread many of today's cosy clichés about Bavaria.

Most *Heimatfilms* show a world at peace with itself, focusing on basic themes such as love, family and the delights of traditional rural life. An interloper, such as a priest, creates some kind of conflict for the main characters – perhaps a milkmaid and her boyfriend or a poacher fighting local laws – who then invoke traditional values to solve the problem. Stories are set in the mountains of Austria, Bavaria or Switzerland, with predictable plots and schmaltzy film scores.

If you'd like to experience the *Heimatfilm* genre, titles to look out for include *Die Fischerin vom Bodensee* (The Fisher Girl of Lake Constance; 1956), *Hoch Droben auf dem Berg* (High Up On the Mountain; 1957) and *Die Landärztin von Tegernsee* (Lady Country Doctor; 1958), though these often cheap flicks were made by the dozen.

Bavaria Filmstadt

Florian von Donnersmarck, celebrated director of the Oscar-winning *Das Leben der Anderen* (The Lives of Others; 2006), learned his craft at the Munich film school.

movie-themed film park with original sets and props from *Das Boot* and other famous flicks.

Music

Ironically, the composer most commonly associated with Bavaria didn't hail from Bavaria at all. Richard Wagner (1813–83) was born in Leipzig and died in Venice but his career took a dramatic turn when King Ludwig II became his patron in 1864 and financed the *Festspielhaus* (opera house) in Bayreuth, which was completed in 1872. Strongly influenced by Beethoven and Mozart, Wagner is most famous for his operas, many of which dealt with mythological themes (eg *Lohengrin* or *Tristan und Isolde*). His great achievement was a synthesis of visual, musical, poetic and dramatic components into a *Gesamtkunstwerk* (single work of art). Wagner's presence also drew other composers to Bayreuth, most notably Anton Bruckner and Franz Liszt, Wagner's father-in-law.

The Academy Award–nominated *Sophie Scholl: The Final Days* (2005) re-creates in harrowing detail the last six days in the life of this courageous Nazi resistance fighter, who was executed aged 21.

As the scores for symphonies became more complex, not the least thanks to Wagner, Bavarian composers hastened to join in. Richard Strauss (1864–1949), who hailed from Munich, created such famous symphonies as *Don Juan* and *Macbeth* but later focused on operas, including the successful *Der Rosenkavalier* (The Knight of the Rose).

Last but not least, there's Munich-born Carl Orff (1895–1982), who achieved lasting fame with just a single work: his life-embracing 1935 cantata *Carmina Burana,* a work characterised by simple harmonies, rhythms and hypnotic repetition. Kloster Andechs, where he is buried, holds an annual Orff festival.

The most illustrious name in music to emerge from just across the border in Austria was Wolfgang Amadeus Mozart, born in Salzburg in 1756. On their travels, the Mozart family visited several places in Bavaria and played at the court of the prince-elector Maximilian III in Munich

A traditional dance group perform at Oktoberfest (p28)

in 1762. Mozart's birthplace and his family house can both be visited in Salzburg.

First stop for fans of 'serious music' should be Munich where the Münchner Philharmoniker are the chart toppers thanks to music director Valery Gergiev. Equally respected is the Bayerische Staatsoper, currently helmed by Austrian Nikolaus Bachler. Nuremberg's highbrow scene perked up in 2005 when the Bavarian state government elevated the municipal theatre to the Staatstheater Nuremberg, whose opera, concert and ballet productions also get high marks.

Southern Germany maintains a busy festival schedule, but the granddaddy of them all is the Wagner Festival in Bayreuth. Opened by the maestro himself in 1876 with the *Ring des Nibelungen* opera marathon, it was run by the composer's grandson, Wolfgang Wagner, from 1951 until his death in 2010. Although it stagnated a bit under his leadership, it has now re-emerged as a major societal and artistic event.

One of the few Bavarian names to have made it in the pop era is Harold Faltermeyer, born in Munich in 1952. He is best known for composing the 'Axel F' theme tune for the 1984 film *Beverly Hills Cop* and the 'Top Gun Anthem', both of which earned him a Grammy. In the 1980s he worked as a session musician and producer with some of the biggest names of the era such as Billy Idol, Barbra Streisand and the Pet Shop Boys.

The Goethe Institut (www.goethe. de) website is a superb place to start for detailed info on all aspects of German culture.

Painting & Sculpture

Early Works

Frescos and manuscript illumination were early art forms popular between the 9th and 13th centuries. The oldest frescos in Bavaria are in the crypt of the Benedictine Abbey of St Mang in Füssen. Stained glass

VOLKSMUSIK

No other musical genre is as closely associated with Bavaria as *Volksmusik* (folk music). Every village has its own proud brass band or choir, and the state government puts serious euros into preserving this traditional music. More than 600,000 Bavarians, mostly lay musicians, belong to some 11,000 music groups, most of them in the Alpine regions. The basic musical form is the ¾-time *Landler,* which is also a dance involving plenty of hopping and stomping; men sometimes slap themselves on their knees in what is called *Platteln.* Typical instruments are the accordion and the zither and some songs end in a yodel. Popular performers of traditional *Volksmusik* are the Rehm Buam, Sepp Eibl and Ruperti Blech.

In the 1970s and '80s, small stages in Munich such as the Fraunhofer pub gave birth to a new style of *Volksmusik.* Performers infused the folklore concept with a political edge, freed it from conservative ideology and merged it with folk music from countries as diverse as Ireland and Ghana. Among the pioneers was the Biermösl Blosn, a band known for its satirical and provocative songs. Also keep an ear out for the Fraunhofer Saitenmusik, a chamber folk music ensemble that plays traditional tunes on acoustic instruments and which used to be the Fraunhofer pub's house band.

Since the '90s the scene has gone even further and now champions wacky crossovers of Bavarian folk with pop, rock, punk, hip-hop and techno in what has been dubbed 'Alpine New Wave'. Look for the folk rockers Hundsbuam, or the jazzy Munich trio Die Interpreten. Rudi Zapf uses the hammered dulcimer to take you on a musical journey around the world. The wildest band of them all is the hardcore folk-punk band Attwenger.

emerged around 1100; the 'Prophet's Windows' in Augsburg's cathedral are the earliest example in central Europe.

Gothic

Portraiture and altar painting hit the artistic stage around AD 1300. Top dog here was Jan Polack, whose work can be admired in such churches as Munich's Schloss Blutenburg.

A major Gothic sculptor was Erasmus Grasser, whose masterpieces include the St Peter altar in St Peterskirche in Munich and the *Morris Dancers* in the Munich Stadtmuseum. Another is Veit Stoss, a Franconian who imbued his sculptures with dramatic realism. In 1503 Stoss spent a stint in jail for forgery, but restored his reputation with the main altar in Bamberg's cathedral, his crowning achievement.

Renaissance

The Renaissance saw the rise of human elements in painting: religious figures were now depicted alongside mere mortals. The heavyweight – quite literally – in Germany was the Nuremberg-born Albrecht Dürer, who excelled both as a painter and graphic artist. His subjects ranged from mythology to religion to animals, all in fantastic anatomical detail, natural perspective and vivid colours. The Alte Pinakothek in Munich has several famous works, and Dürer's Nuremberg house is now a museum.

Dürer influenced Lucas Cranach the Elder, a major artist of the Reformation. Cranach's approach to landscape painting, though, grew out of the *Donauschule* (Danube School), an artistic movement based in Passau and Regensburg. The amazing details of these landscapes seethed with dark movement, making them the focal point of the painting rather than a mere backdrop.

The brightest of stars among Renaissance sculptors was Tilman Riemenschneider. His skills were formidable, allowing his stone to mimic wood and featuring compositions playing on light and shadow. Must-sees include the altars in the Jakobskirche in Rothenburg ob der Tauber and in the Herrgottskirche in Creglingen, both on the Romantic Road. The Mainfränkisches Museum in Würzburg also has an outstanding Riemenschneider collection.

Baroque & Rococo

The sugar-iced styles of the baroque and rococo periods left their mark throughout Bavaria, especially in church art. Illusionary effects and contrast between light and shadow are typical features, and surfaces are often bewilderingly ornate.

Arguably the finest and most prolific artists of the period, the brothers Cosmas and Egid Asam, were of a generation of Germans educated in Rome in the Italian baroque tradition. Their father, Hans Georg, was a master fresco artist who transformed the Basilika St Benedikt in Benediktbeuern. Word of their supreme talent, along with the family's connections in the Benedictine order, meant the duo were always swamped with work. Cosmas was primarily a fresco painter while Egid used his considerable talents as an architect and stucco sculptor. Examples of their brilliant collaboration can be found throughout Bavaria, most notably in the Asamkirche in central Munich and the Asamkirche Maria de Victoria in Ingolstadt.

Another set of brothers who dominated the baroque period was Dominikus and Johann Baptist Zimmermann, whose collaboration reached its pinnacle in the Unesco-listed Wieskirche, a short stop on the Romantic Road. Johann Baptist also worked on Munich's St Peterskirche and Schloss Nymphenburg. Both were members of the so-called Wessobrunner School, which counted architect and stucco artist Josef Schmuzer among its founding members. Schmuzer's work can be admired at Kloster Ettal and in the Alte St Martinskirche in Garmisch-Partenkirchen.

The 19th Century

Heart-on-your-sleeve Romanticism that drew heavily on emotion and a dreamy idealism dominated the 19th century. Austria-born Moritz von Schwind is noted for his moody scenes of German legends and fairy tales. His teacher, Peter Cornelius, was a follower of the Nazarenes, a group of religious painters who drew from the old masters for inspiration. There's a giant fresco of his in Munich's Ludwigskirche, although for the full survey of Romantic art you should swing by the nearby Sammlung Schack.

The website www. kulturportal-bayern.de is your guide to Bavarian culture, with sections on fine arts, film, museums, traditions and much more.

CORNELIUS GURLITT – NO ORDINARY ART COLLECTOR

Thousands of pieces of art were looted by the Nazis across Europe during WWII and many remain missing. However, the mystery of what happened to some of them was solved in March 2012 when almost 1400 works were discovered in the Schwabing apartment of Cornelius Gurlitt. This included some paintings by Chagall, Matisse, Dix and Lieberman among countless others. Cornelius was the son of art dealer and collector Hildebrand Gurlitt who had been responsible for selling art deemed degenerate by the Nazis for foreign currency. He was captured by the US Army with 20 boxes of artworks after WWII but released due to his Jewish heritage and the art returned to him. Hildebrand died in 1956 and Cornelius hid the works in his Munich flat, occasionally selling the odd painting abroad to make ends meet. It was on one of these sales trips that he was rumbled – German customs officers undertook a random inspection of a train crossing the Switzerland–Germany border and Cornelius was discovered with €9000 in readies. Suspicious of how the unemployed Bavarian could have so much cash, Munich's prosecutor ordered a search of his flat.

Romanticism gradually gave way to the sharp edges of realism and, later on, the meticulous detail of naturalism. Major practitioners were Wilhelm Leibl, who specialised in painting Bavarian country scenes, and Hans Thoma, who joined Leibl in Munich, but favoured the landscapes of his native Black Forest. Look for their works in Munich's Städtische Galerie im Lenbachhaus.

Munich Secession & Jugendstil

During the 1890s a group of about 100 artists shook up the art establishment when they split from Munich's *Künstlergesellschaft* (Artists' Society), a traditionalist organisation led by portrait artist Franz von Lenbach. Secessionists were not linked by a common artistic style, but by a rejection of reactionary attitudes towards the arts that stifled new forms of expression. They preferred scenes from daily life to historical and religious themes, shunned studios in favour of natural outdoor light and were hugely influential in inspiring new styles.

One of them was *Jugendstil* (art nouveau), inspired by printmaking and drawing on functional, linear ornamentation partly inspired by Japanese art. The term originated from the weekly trendsetting art-and-literature magazine *Die Jugend,* published in Munich from 1896 until 1940. In Munich the Neue Pinakothek is the place to head for some fine examples of this most elegant of styles.

The website www.theater paradies-deutschland.de (in German) is the ultimate thespian's portal with links to hundreds of theatres throughout the German-speaking world.

Expressionism

In the early 20th century German artists looked for a purer, freer approach to painting through abstraction, vivid colours and expression. In Bavaria the trailblazer was the artist group *Der Blaue Reiter* (The Blue Rider), founded by Wassily Kandinsky and Franz Marc in 1911, and joined later by Paul Klee, Gabriele Münter and other top artists. The Städtische Galerie im Lenbachhaus has the most comprehensive collection, much of it donated by Münter, who managed to hide her colleagues' paintings from the Nazis. A good selection of Münter's own paintings is on view at the Schlossmuseum of Murnau, a town in the Alps. At the Buchheim Museum on Starnberger See, the focus is on the equally avant-garde artist group called *Die Brücke* (The Bridge), founded in 1905 in Dresden by Ernst Ludwig Kirchner, Erich Heckel and Karl Schmidt-Rottluff.

Nazi Era

After the creative surge in the 1920s, the big chill of Nazi conformity sent Germany into an artistic deep freeze in the 1930s and '40s. Many internationally famous artists, including Paul Klee and Max Beckmann,

TRACHTEN

If the tourist bumf is to be believed, Bavaria is full of locals cavorting around in *Trachten* (folk costume), the men in Lederhosen, the women in figure-hugging, cleavage-baring, aproned dresses called Dirndl. You may not see many such exotic folk on the streets of Nuremberg, Ingolstadt or Passau, but travel to the Alpine region, and you'll be in cliché heaven. Many young Munich city dwellers own these traditional outfits, but most only leave the closet for Oktoberfest and special occasions, but things are different in rural areas, especially among older generations. If you want to see real *Trachten* on parade, go to any folk festival or even just a Sunday morning church service in Oberammergau or Berchtesgaden.

Munich has several *Trachten* emporia selling everything from the real hand-embroidered deal to made-heaven-knows-where imitations. Getting garbed up for a beer festival or a night in a beer hall is an essential part of the fun in the Bavarian capital.

MORE FAMOUS BAVARIANS

➡ Franz Beckenbauer (b 1945 in Munich) – 'Der Kaiser' is the Germany's most famous footballer and manager.

➡ Pope Benedict XVI (b 1927 in Marktl am Inn) – Served as pope from 2005 until his resignation in 2013.

➡ Edmund Stoiber (b 1941 in Oberaudorf) – The most influential politician in postwar Bavaria.

➡ Uschi Disl (b 1970 in Bad Tölz) – Bavaria's most successful Olympian with two golds, four silvers and three bronzes in the biathlon.

were classified as 'degenerate' and their paintings confiscated, sold off or burned.

Modern & Contemporary

Post-1945 creativity revived the influence of Nolde, Kandinsky and Schmidt-Rottluff, but also spawned a new abstract expressionism in the work of Willi Baumeister. The completely revamped and enlarged Franz Marc Museum in Kochel am See traces the evolution of pre- and post-WWII expressionism.

An edgy genre that has found major representation in Bavaria is concrete art, which emerged in the 1950s and takes abstract art to its extreme, rejecting any natural form and using only planes and colours. See what this is all about at the Museum für Konkrete Kunst in Ingolstadt and the Museum im Kulturspeicher in Würzburg.

The Bavarian photorealist Florian Thomas is among the influential artists whose work is now in the Museum Frieder Burda in Baden-Baden. Other good spots to plug into the contemporary art scene are the Neues Museum in Nuremberg, and the Pinakothek der Moderne and the superb Museum Brandhorst in Munich.

Theatre

Theatre in its various forms enjoys a wide following in Bavaria, especially in Munich, which has the famous Münchener Kammerspiele, but also in Nuremberg, Regensburg and Bamberg. Bavaria's longest-running drama is the *Passionsspiele* (Passion Play), which has been performed in Oberammergau once every decade since the 17th century.

For a dose of local colour, head to a *Bauerntheater* (literally, 'peasant theatre'), which usually presents silly and rustic tales in dialect so thick that it's basically incomprehensible to all non-Bavarians. But never mind, because the story lines are so simplistic, you'll probably be able to follow the plot anyway. The oldest *Bauerntheater* is in Garmisch-Partenkirchen.

If you're travelling with kids, don't miss one of the many excellent marionette theatres starring endearing and often handmade puppets. The most famous is the Augsburger Puppenkiste in Augsburg, but the Marionettentheater Bad Tölz and the Münchener Marionetten Theater will also take you on a magic carpet ride.

Stuttgart's Staatstheater hosts the Stuttgart Ballet, generally regarded as one of Europe's best companies.

Food & Drink

Sausages with foaming wheat beer in rollicking Munich beer halls, snowball-sized dumplings with an avalanche of sauerkraut and roast pork in the Alps, Black Forest gateau slathered in chocolate, cream and cherries – calorific excess still abounds in southern Germany. But while country menus revel in tradition, in the cities things have changed. Munich can easily switch from pig-trotter-chomping rusticity to the chic flavours of Michelin-starred fine dining. Meanwhile menus in Nuremberg and Freiburg go beyond the obvious, with a world of street food and new chefs wowing critics.

Regional & Seasonal

Classic Mains

Above Bratwurst

The Chinese say you can eat every part of the pig bar the 'oink', and Bavarian chefs seem to be in full agreement. No part of the animal is spared their attention as they cook up its *Schweinshaxe* (knuckles), *Rippchen* (ribs),

Züngerl (tongue) and *Wammerl* (belly). Pork also appears as *Schweine-braten* (roast pork) and the misleadingly named *Leberkäse* (liver cheese), a savoury meatloaf that contains neither liver nor cheese. The Black Forest contributes the famous *Schwarzwälder Schinken* – ham that's been salted, seasoned and cured for around two weeks.

Non-pork-based dishes include *Hendl* (roast chicken) and *Fleischpflanzerl*, the Bavarian spin on the hamburger. Fish is often caught fresh from the lakes. *Forelle* (trout) is especially popular in the Black Forest and served either *Forelle Müllerin* (baked), *Forelle Blau* (boiled) or *Räucherforelle* (smoked). In Bavarian beer gardens, you'll often find *Steckerlfisch* (skewers of grilled mackerel).

Originating in Swabia but now served throughout southern Germany are *Maultaschen* (ravioli-like stuffed pasta pockets), and *Küsspätzle* (stubby noodle-dumpling hybrids topped with melted cheese).

Eating Price Ranges

....

€ *less than €12*

....

€€ *€12 to €22*

....

€€€ *more than €22*

FOOD & DRINK REGIONAL & SEASONAL

Side Orders

The humble *Kartoffel* (potato) is 'Vegetable *Nummer Eins*' in any meat-and-three-veg dish and can be served as *Salzkartoffeln* (boiled), *Bratkartoffeln* (fried), *Kartoffelpüree* (mashed) or shaped into *Knödel* (dumplings). Dumplings can be made of bread *(Semmelknödel)* and there's also a meaty version made with liver *(Leberknödel)*. Pickled cabbage is another common vegetable companion and comes as either sauerkraut (white) or *Rotkohl* and *Blaukraut* (red). Rice is a semi-traditional side you might occasionally encounter.

Bavaria's Wunderful World of Wurst

While travelling around Bavaria you might find yourself thinking 'another town, another sausage' – it must be said that nowhere else on earth offers so much sausage variety as Bavaria does. Bavaria's flagship sausage is the veal Weisswurst (p290). In Eastern Bavaria and Franconia the smaller mildly spicy bratwurst rules. Nuremberg and Regensburg make the most famous versions: finger-sized and eaten by the half dozen or dozen – or ask for *'drei im Weggla'* (three in a bun). When it comes to size, Coburg has the king of the wurst, a 30cm affair, grilled over the embers of pine cones and served in a miniature airline-style bun with a dollop of mustard. Bayreuth also gets in on the act with its own bratwurst, as do many other small towns in Franconia.

Sausages that do not hail from southern Germany, but make for tasty snacks all the same, include the *Bockwurst,* a mixture of ground veal and pork flavoured with herbs; the Thüringer, a kind of large bratwurst with a lower fat content and PGI (protected geographical indication) status

If you want to train your tummy for your trip to Bavaria, try any of the recipes – roast pork to liver dumplings – detailed on www. bavariankitchen. com.

SEASON'S GREETINGS

Late April and May is peak season for *Spargel* (white asparagus), which is classically paired with boiled potatoes, hollandaise sauce and sometimes *Schinken* (smoked or cooked ham). In spring, look for *Bärlauch,* a wild-growing garlic that is often turned into a delicious pesto sauce. Wild mushrooms peak in late summer and early autumn when you find many dishes revolving around *Pfifferlinge* (chanterelles) and *Steinpilze* (cep or porcini). Other autumn delights include pumpkins, game and *Zwiebelkuchen* (onion tart), especially in rural Swabia, where it is paired with sweet *Neuer Süsser* (new wine) or *Most* (cider).

At Oktoberfest in September, between six and seven million partygoers wash down entire farms of pigs, oxen and chickens with *Mass* litres of beer. In March, the city throws festivals for pre-Lenten *Starkbier* (strong beer), where you can quaff the malty 7.5% brews that monks once dubbed *flüssiges Brot* (liquid bread).

Black Forest gateau

from the EU; and the Frankfurter, the Krakauer and the hot-dog-like Wiener.

Whatever shape of sausage arrives on your table or is handed to you in a flimsy napkin from a kiosk window, it will invariably be served with *Senf* (mustard). Even this comes in a number of varieties and pairing sausage to mustard in Bavaria is a bit like matching wines to food in France and Italy. *Weisswurst* is traditionally served with *süsser* (sweet whole-grain mustard), others normally come with *mittelscharfer Senf* (medium strength). English-style mustard is rare. Common side dishes that may come with your sausage are tangy sauerkraut, potato salad and/ or a simple slice of bread.

You can get a sausage at almost anywhere human beings gather in numbers across the south of Germany, but each town has its own kiosk, cafe or restaurant traditionally considered the best place to eat the local sausages. In Nuremberg this is the Bratwursthäusle (p136) and Goldenes Posthorn (p136), in Munich it's the Weisses Brauhaus (p70), and in Coburg and Bayreuth simple, unassuming kiosks on their main squares.

> Bavarians like to 'pig out' and the numbers prove it: of the 60kg of meat consumed by the average resident each year, about two-thirds are pork. Oink!

Just Desserts

You will never forget your first forkful of real *Schwarzwälder Kirschtorte* (Black Forest gateau): a three-layered chocolate sponge cake filled with cream, morello cherries and Kirsch (cherry liqueur). The real thing is nothing like the supermarket frozen versions you might have tried back home.

Usually served with a dollop of ice cream is *Apfelstrudel* (apple strudel), which actually originated in Austria but is now eaten all over southern Germany. Tasty alternatives include *Dampfnudeln* (steamed doughy dumplings drenched in custard sauce), and Allgäu's *Apfelkrap-fen* (sugar-sprinkled apple fritters). Nuremberg is famous for its *Leb-kuchen* (gingerbread) made with nuts, fruit peel, honey and spices, while in Rothenburg ob der Tauber, *Schneeballen* (snowballs) are spherical nests of linguine-like dough sprinkled with sugar and/or dipped in a variety of sweet flavourings. *Bayerische Creme* is a cream and gelatin custardy creation, flavoured with liqueur and normally served with strawberries or raspberries. *Prinzregententorte* from Munich has at least seven layers of sponge glued together with chocolate butter cream and iced with chocolate.

In beer halls and beer gardens it must be said that the desserts are a bit of an afterthought. The situation is slightly better in restaurants, but the sweet-toothed should really head to a cafe-bakery or coffee house to get their sugar high.

Ethnic Food

Munich is naturally the place where taking a break from beer and pork comes easiest. You don't have to be in the Bavarian metropolis long to realise the Bavarians are bonkers about Italian food. Italian *trattorie, ristoranti* and *pizzerie* are so common that in some parts of the city it's almost easier to get a lasagna than *Leberkäse!* Many of these places are Italian owned and the standard of food is high with ingredients shipped in from over the Alps. This may contribute to prices being higher than in the *bel paese*. French restaurants are also a feature of Munich's more gentrified neighbourhoods, while Thai, Korean and Indian food is becoming increasingly popular. One unusual culinary experience you can have in Munich is going Afghan – Munich has a large Afghan population and there are several Afghan restaurants in the city.

Cookery Schools

The region's fledgling cookery school scene has grown over the last decade or so. On average, anticipate paying between €140 and €240 for a day at the stove, which usually includes lunch and recipes to take home. We've picked three favourites, but you can search by region for a course to suit you on www.kochschule.de or www.die-kochschulen.de (both in German). The annual Munich restaurant review magazine *Munich Geht Aus* (Munich Goes Out) also has a comprehensive listings section for the Bavarian capital.

Schwarzwaldstube (p230) Three-Michelin–star legend in Baiersbronn in the Black Forest. Classes revolve around a theme such as cooking with asparagus or pasta making.

For an in-depth study of what's pouring at Munich's beer halls and gardens, Larry Hawthorne's *The Beer Drinker's Guide to Munich* is an indispensable tool that will take you far beyond the Hofbräuhaus.

In June 2015 *Obatzda* (soft cheese mixed with butter) was given Protected Geographical Indication (PGI) by the European Commission.

DARE TO TRY

Feeling daring? Why not give these three regional faves a whirl:

Sauere Kutteln/Nierle/Lüngerl (sour tripe/kidneys/lung) No beer fest would be complete without these offal faves, simmered in vinegar or wine, bay, laurel, juniper and spices.

Bubespitzle Otherwise known as *Schupfnudeln*, this Swabian dish's ingredients are innocuous: potato noodles tossed in butter, served with sauerkraut and speck. But the name (literally, 'little boys' penises') certainly isn't.

Leberknödelsuppe Hearty beef broth with beef, veal or pork liver dumplings, flavoured with onions, parsley and marjoram.

Wirthaus in der Au (☎089-448 14 00; www.wirtshausinderau.de; Lilienstrasse 51; ⌂Deutsches Museum) Munich's king of *Knödel* since 1901 runs an English-language dumpling-making workshop.

Magazin (p187) Hop over the border to Salzburg for hands-on, small-group classes spotlighting cookery themes from fish and crustaceans to Austrian desserts.

Grape & Grain

Here's to Beer!

The northern Bavarian region of Oberfranken has 163 breweries – that's three times more than the neighbouring Czech Republic.

Bavaria's beer consumption figures are simply astounding. The estimated per capita intake is around 170L per year, around 20L per person more than the neighbouring Czechs, who lead the world country rankings by around 50L (Austria is second, Germany third). Bavaria produces around 22.3 million hectolitres of *bier* every year, a certain share of which goes for export.

Beer Glossary

Alkoholfreies Bier – nonalcoholic beer

Bockbier/Doppelbock – strong beer (*doppel* meaning even more so), either pale, amber or dark in colour with a bittersweet flavour

Dampfbier (steam beer) – originating from Bayreuth, it's top-fermented (this means the yeast rises to the top during the fermentation process) and has a fruity flavour

Dunkles (dark lager) – a reddish-brown, full-bodied lager, malty and lightly hopped

Helles (pale lager) – a lightly hopped lager with strong malt aromas and a slightly sweet taste

Hofbräu – type of brewery belonging to a royal court

Klosterbräu – type of brewery belonging to a monastery

Malzbier – sweet, aromatic, full-bodied malt beer

Märzen – full bodied with strong malt aromas and traditionally brewed in March

Pils (pilsener) – a bottom-fermented lager with strong hop flavour

Rauchbier (smoke beer) – dark beer with a fresh, spicy or 'smoky' flavour, found mostly in Bamberg

Weissbier/Weizen (wheat beer) – wheat beers (around 5.4% alcohol) with fruity and spicy flavour, often recalling bananas and cloves; a cloudy *Hefeweizen* has a layer of still-fermenting yeast on the bottom of the bottle, whereas *Kristallweizen* is clearer with more fizz

For more information about German grape varieties, growing regions, wine festivals and courses, check out the German Wine Institute (www.deutsche weine.de).

If you want to go easy on the booze, order a sweetish *Radler,* which comes in half or full litres and mixes *Helles Lagerbier* and lemonade. A

WEISSWURST ETIQUETTE

Bavarians love sausage and there is no sausage more Bavarian than the *Weisswurst*. It's so Bavarian, in fact, that there's even an imaginary boundary – the *Weisswurst* equator – beyond which it is no longer served (ie roughly north of Frankfurt, though you'll rarely find it even in Franconia where the bratwurst rules supreme). Unlike most sausages, which are pork-based, this one's made from veal and pork fat and flavoured with onions and parsley, and sometimes lemon, mace, ginger and cardamom. Before refrigeration *Weisswurst* had to be eaten before noon to prevent them going off, but now they're available all day long. They're brought to the table still swimming in hot water. The way to eat them is to strip them of their skin and eat only with fresh pretzels, sweet mustard and, preferably, paired with a mug of *Weissbier* (wheat beer). This unlikely combination is a popular breakfast choice among those who rise at the crack of brunch. No preservatives are used in the production of Bavaria's oddest sausage, hence its white-ish grey hue.

DIE BESTEN! FREILAND EIER aus Olching

REINER ZIEGEN FRISCHKÄSE zart-cremig im Geschmack

EMPFEHLUNG ALS
SPARGELWEIN
WEISSBURGUNDER PFALZ · CAPSULA VIOLA TOSKANA

Top: Viktualienmarkt (p47)

Bottom: *Spätzle* (egg noodles)

Traditional Christmas biscuits

Russe (Russian) is generally a litre-sized concoction of *Helles Weissbier* and lemonade.

Riesling to Pinot

'Prost!' (with beer) or *'Zum Wohl!'* (with wine) are typical drinking toasts.

Bavaria's only wine-growing region is located in Franconia, in and around Würzburg. Growers here produce some exceptional dry white wines, which are bottled in distinctive green flagons called *Bocksbeutel*. If Silvaner is the king of the grape here, then Müller-Thurgau is the prince, and Riesling, Weissburgunder (Pinot grigio) and *Bacchus* the courtiers. The latter three thrive especially on the steep slopes flanking the Main River. Red wines play merely a supporting role. Nearly 80% of all wine produced is consumed within the region.

Kaiserstuhl is the major wine-growing area in the Black Forest. It produces mainly Spätburgunder (Pinot noir) and Grauburgunder (Pinot gris).

Kaffee und Kuchen

In Bavaria beer is officially defined not as alcohol but as a staple food, just like bread.

Anyone who has spent any length of time in Bavaria or the Black Forest knows the reverence bestowed on the three o'clock weekend ritual of *Kaffee und Kuchen* (coffee and cake). More than just a chance to devour delectable cakes and tortes – though it's certainly that, too – locals see it as a social event. You'll find *Cafe-Konditoreien* (cafe–cake shops) pretty much everywhere – in castles, in the middle of the forest, even plopped on top of mountains. Track down the best by asking sweet-toothed locals where the cake is *hausgemacht* (homemade). Coffee is usually brewed fresh and all the usual varieties are on offer, including cappuccinos, espressos and *Milchkaffee* (milky coffee).

Except in posh cafes, tea is usually a teabag in a glass or pot of hot water, served with a slice of lemon. If you want milk, ask for *Tee mit Milch*.

Festive Food

Major holidays are feast days and usually spent at home with family, gorging and guzzling way more than everyone knows is good for them. At Easter roast lamb is often the star of the show. Easter is preceded by Lent, a period of fasting when sweet dishes such as *Rohrnudeln* (browned yeasty buns served with plum compote and vanilla sauce) are enjoyed and fish replaces meat in Catholic households. Carp, served boiled, baked or fried, is popular at Christmas time, although more people roast a goose or a turkey as the main event. *Lebkuchen* (gingerbread) and *Spekulatius* (spicy cookies) are both sweet staples of *Advent* (the pre-Christmas season). For drinks, *Glühwein* (spicy mulled wine), best consumed at a Christmas market, is a favoured seasonal indulgence.

With roughly 14,000 distillers, the Black Forest has the highest density of schnapps makers in the world.

Where to Eat & Drink

Gastätte & Gasthöfe Rural inns with a laid-back feel, local crowd and solid menu of *gutbürgerliche Küche* (home cooking). There's sometimes a beer garden out the back.

Eiscafé Italian or Italian-style cafes, where you can grab an ice cream or cappuccino and head outside to slurp and sip.

Stehcafé A stand-up cafe with shared tables for coffee and snacks at speed and on the cheap – though these have become rare in recent years.

Cafe-Konditorei A traditional cake shop doubling as a cafe.

Ratskeller Atmospheric town-hall basement restaurant, generally more frequented by tourists than locals nowadays.

Restaurant These serve everything from informal meals to *gehobene Küche* (gourmet meals). The *Tagesmenü* (fixed daily menu) often represents good value.

Bierkeller & Weinkeller The emphasis is on beer and wine respectively, with a little food (sausages and pretzels, cold cuts etc) on the side.

Imbiss Handy speed-feed stops for savoury fodder from wurst-in-a-bun to kebabs and pizza, normally with no seating.

When to Eat

Traditionally *Frühstück* (breakfast) is a sweet and savoury smorgasbord of bread, cheese, salami, wurst, preserves, yoghurt and muesli. At weekends, it's an altogether more leisurely, family-oriented affair. Many cafes have embraced the brunch trend, serving all-you-can-eat buffets with fresh rolls, eggs, smoked fish, fruit salad and even prosecco. The ultimate Bavarian breakfast involves *Weisswurst,* pretzels and beer.

Freising's Weihenstephan Brewery claims to be the world's oldest having been pumping out ales since 1040. The millennium celebrations in 2040 promise to be quite a bash!

Traditionally, *Mittagessen* (lunch) has been the main meal of the day, but modern working practices have changed this considerably, at least in the cities. However, many restaurants still tout lunchtime dishes or a fixed lunch menu (*Mittagsmenü* or *Tagesmenü*), which can be an affordable way of dining even at moderately upscale restaurants.

DOS & DON'TS

➡ Do bring a small gift – flowers or a bottle of wine – when invited to a meal.

➡ Do say *'Guten Appetit!'* (*bon appetit!*) before starting to eat.

➡ Do offer to help with clearing the table and washing the dishes afterwards.

➡ Don't start eating until everyone has been served.

➡ Don't expect to get a glass of tap water at a restaurant.

➡ Don't assume you can pay by credit card when eating out.

➡ Do watch out for 'no prams' signs in Munich if travelling with kids.

Dinner is dished up at home around 7pm. For those who have already eaten heartily at noon, there is *Abendbrot* (bread with cold cuts). Bar the cities with their late-night dining scenes, Germans head to restaurants earlier than elsewhere in Europe, and many kitchens in rural areas stop serving around 9pm. At home, meals are relaxed and require few airs and graces beyond the obligatory *'Guten Appetit'* (literally 'good appetite'), exchanged before eating.

Dining Etiquette

On the Menu

English menus are not a given, even in big cities, though the waiter or waitress will almost invariably be able to translate for you. The more rural and remote you go, the less likely it is that the restaurant will have an English menu, or multilingual staff for that matter. It helps to know a few words of German. That said, a good share of Bavaria's waitstaff are not from Germany at all and might just know your language!

Paying the Bill

Sometimes the person who invites pays, but generally locals go Dutch and split the bill evenly between them. This might mean everyone chipping in at the end of a meal or asking to pay separately *(getrennte Rechnung)*. Buying rounds in bars British-style is not usually the done thing, though friends might buy each other the odd drink. In bars and beer halls, table service is still quite common and waiting staff often come around to *abkassieren* (cash up). Always make sure you can pay by card before you tuck in – most restaurants now take cards, but it's by no means a given.

Table Reservations

If you want to dine at formal or popular restaurants, it is wise to make table reservations a day or two ahead. Michelin-starred restaurants are often booked up weeks in advance, especially at weekends and some have a compulsory reservation policy. Most *Gasthöfe, Gaststätten,* cafes and beer halls should be able to squeeze you in at a moment's notice, except on Saturday nights when things are normally chock-a-block.

See www.bier gartenguide.com for a definitive guide to all of Munich's beer gardens. The printed version is available at bookshops across the state.

Though Germany is not thought of as a particularly strong coffee destination, per capita Germans actually drink more arabica than wine or beer.

BEER-GARDEN GRUB

In beer gardens, tables laid with a cloth and utensils are reserved for people ordering food. If you're only planning to down a mug of beer, or have brought along a picnic, don't sit there.

If you do decide to order food, you'll find very similar menus at all beer gardens. Typical dishes include roast chicken, spare ribs, *Schweinebraten* (roast pork) and schnitzel.

Radi is a huge, mild radish that's eaten with beer; you can buy a prepared radish or buy a radish at the market and a *Radimesser* at any department store; stick it down in the centre and twist the handle round and round, creating a radish spiral. If you do it yourself, smother the cut end of the radish with salt until it weeps to reduce the bitterness (and increase your thirst!).

Obatzda (oh-batsdah) is Bavarian for 'mixed up'. This cream-cheese-like speciality is made of butter, ripe Camembert, onion and caraway. Spread it on *Brezn* (a pretzel) or bread. It's a bit of an acquired taste for the uninitiated.

Presssack (yes, that triple 's' is correct) is ham and other cooked meat in aspic, served with horse radish and sliced onion. *Saure Zipfel* or *Blaue Zipfel* is bratwurst cooked in vinegar and spices and served with a pretzel. It's mostly found in Franconia.

Radi

Tipping

Tipping is quite an individual matter and you could easily get round the whole of Bavaria without giving a single one. As a rule of thumb, most Germans round up the bill to the nearest five or ten euros in restaurants, cafes and bars. Do whatever you're comfortable with, given the service and setting. Give any tip directly to the server when paying your bill. Say either the amount you want to pay, or *'Stimmt so'* if you don't want change. Only tip if you were really satisfied with the service and your server has gone out of his or her way to make the experience a pleasant one. Levels of service vary greatly across southern Germany.

Landscapes & Wildlife

From Alpine peaks to the Danube plain, from the Black Forest to the lakes of southern Bavaria, southern Germany provides diverse central-European vistas by the bucket and is a joy to explore. This diversity has also been recognised on a national level with three national parks functioning in the region, the most recent addition to the list being the Black Forest National Park in 2014. Germany's south also has some pretty accessible wild animal populations so get those binoculars and cameras ready.

The Land

Above Red deer

In Bavaria and the Black Forest nature has been as prolific and creative as Picasso in his prime. The most dramatic region is the Bavarian Alps, a phalanx of craggy peaks created by tectonic uplift some 770 million years ago and chiselled and gouged by glaciers and erosion ever since. Several limestone ranges stand sentinel above the rest of the land, including, west to east, the Allgäuer Alps, the glaciated Wetterstein/Karwendel Alps (with Germany's highest mountain, the Zugspitze at 2962m) and the Berchtesgadener Alps. Many peaks tower well above 2000m and are capped with a snowy mantle year-round.

North of here, the Alpine Foothills are a lush mosaic of moorland, rolling hills, gravel plains and pine forests dappled with glacial lakes, including the vast Chiemsee, Starnberger See and the Ammersee. The foothills are book-ended by Lake Constance in the west and the Inn and Salzach Rivers in the east.

The Bavarian Forest in Eastern Bavaria is a classic *Mittelgebirge,* a midsize mountain range, and one of Germany's greatest unknowns. Its highest peak, the Grosse Arber (1456m), juts out like the tall kid in your school photo. Much of it is blanketed by dark, dense forests that fade into the thinly populated Frankenwald and Fichtelgebirge areas further north. The forest thickens as it crosses the border with the Czech Republic.

The Black Forest, in Germany's southwestern corner, is another *Mittelgebirge,* a storied quilt that enwraps waterfalls, rolling hills, sparkling lakes, lush vineyards, and oak, pine and beech forests into one mystique-laden package. The little Kinzig River divides the north from the much higher south, where the Feldberg is the highest elevation at 1493m.

Much of Franconia and Swabia is a complex patchwork of low ranges, rifts and deep meandering valleys. A Jurassic limestone range is responsible for bizarre rock formations, such as those in the Franconian Switzerland region north of Nuremberg.

Southern Germany is traversed by several major rivers, of which the Danube, which originates in the Black Forest, and the Main are the longest. The Inn and the Isar flow down from the Alps into the Danube, the former at Passau, the latter near Deggendorf on the edge of the Bavarian Forest. Germany's main south–north river, the mighty Rhine, divides the Black Forest from France and Switzerland.

Wildlife

The most common large forest mammal is the red deer, a quick-footed fellow with skinny legs supporting a chunky body. Encounters with wild boar, a type of wild pig with a keen sense of smell but poor eyesight, are also possible, especially in the Bavarian Forest, though they tend to stay well clear of humans.

Beavers faced extinction in the 19th century not only because they were coveted for their precious pelts (beaver hats were all the rage), but also because they were cooked up in strict Catholic households each Friday since the good people considered them to be 'fish'. Reintroduced in the mid-1960s, beavers are thriving once again, especially along the Danube, between Ingolstadt and Kelheim, and its tributaries. Eating them is *verboten!*

Lynxes actually died out in Germany in the 19th century but in the 1980s Czech authorities released 17 lynxes in the Bohemian Forest, and a small group of brave souls have since tried their luck again in the Bavarian Forest right across the border. There have even been rare sightings around the Feldberg in the southern Black Forest.

In the Alps, the Alpine marmot, a sociable animal that looks like a fat squirrel, lives in burrows below the tree line, while wild goats make their home in the upper mountains. The snow hare, whose fur is white in winter, is also a common Alpine denizen. The endangered *Auerhuhn* (capercaillie), a grouselike bird, also makes its home here and in the Bavarian Forest. Lizards, praying mantids and European bee-eaters live in the sunny Kaiserstuhl area.

Some 58% of Bavaria's forest is in private hands, 30% belongs to the Freistaat Bayern and 2% to the federal authorities. The remaining 10% is common land.

LANDSCAPES & WILDLIFE WILDLIFE

The true king of the skies is the golden eagle. If you're lucky, you might spot one patrolling the mountain peaks in Berchtesgaden National Park.

Germany's 16 Unesco Biosphere Reserves include the Bavarian Forest, the Berchtesgaden Alps and the Swabian Alb. For the lowdown, visit www.unesco.org.

Local skies are home to over 400 bird species, from white-backed woodpeckers and pygmy owls to sparrowhawks, grey herons, European jays and black redstarts. The Wutach Gorge in the Black Forest is a unique habitat that supports such rare birds as treecreepers and kingfishers, as well as many species of butterflies, beetles and lizards.

Plants

Despite environmental pressures, southern German forests remain beautiful and commendably tranquil places to escape the crowds. At lower altitudes, they usually consist of a jumbled mix of beech, oak, birch, chestnut, lime, maple and ash that erupt into a riot of colour in autumn. Up at the higher elevations, fir, pine, spruce and other conifers are more prevalent. Canopies often shade low-growing ferns, heather, clover and foxglove.

NATIONAL & NATURE PARKS

PARK	FEATURES	ACTIVITIES	BEST TIME TO VISIT	WEBSITE
Bavarian Forest National Park	mountain forest, bogs, streams; deer, hazel grouse, fox, otter, pygmy owl, three-toe woodpecker; 243 sq km	hiking, mountain biking, cross-country skiing	year-round	www.nationalpark-bayerischer-wald.de
Berchtesgaden National Park	lakes, mixed forest, cliffs, meadows; eagle, chamois, marmot, blue hare, salamander; 210 sq km	hiking, skiing, wildlife-watching	year-round	www.nationalpark-berchtesgaden.de
Altmühltal Nature Park	mixed forest, streams, rock formations, Roman ruins; 2962 sq km	hiking, cycling, canoeing, kayaking, rock climbing, cross-country skiing, fossil digging	late spring to autumn	www.naturpark-altmuehltal.de
Bavarian Forest Nature Park	largest continuous forest in Germany (includes the smaller Nationalpark Bayerischer Wald), moorland, meadows, rolling hills; 3077 sq km	hiking, cycling, cross-country skiing, Nordic walking	late spring to autumn	www.naturpark-bayerwald.de
Central/North Black Forest Nature Park	mixed forest, deep valleys, lakes; deer, wild boar, raven, capercaillie; 3750 sq km	hiking, Nordic walking, mountain biking	late spring to autumn	www.naturpark schwarzwald.de
Southern Black Forest Nature Park	mixed forest, pastures, lake, moorland; capercaillie, deer, lynx; 3700 sq km	hiking, Nordic walking, snowshoeing, mountain biking	year-round	www.naturpark-sued schwarzwald.de
Black Forest Nature Park	mixed forest, moorland plateaux and lakes; 100 sq km	walking	year-round	www.schwarzwald-nationalpark.de

Pfifferlinge (chanterelles), the Black Forest (p220)

In spring, Alpine regions burst with wildflowers – orchid, cyclamen, gentian, pulsatilla, Alpine roses, edelweiss and buttercups – which brighten meadows. Minimise your impact by sticking to trails.

Wild Food

Bavaria and the Black Forest's woods brim with berries, herbs and mushrooms, a surprising number of which are perfectly edible. Summer and autumn yield rich forest pickings, with bilberries, raspberries, blackberries and wild strawberries; wild herbs like bear's garlic, dandelion, dill, buckhorn and sorrel fringe meadows and woodlands. The fungi-foraging season kicks off with apricot-hued, trumpet-shaped *Pfifferlinge* (chanterelles) in June/July, peaks with the prized *Steinpilz* (cep or porcini) around August and ends with autumnal delights like button-topped *Maronen* (Bay Bolete).

Tourist offices can point you towards local *Kräuterwanderungen* and *Pilzwanderung* (herb and mushroom walks), such as those run by the German Alpine Club (www.alpenverein.de) or Schwarzwaldverein (www.schwarzwaldverein.de); you'll need to join as a member first. A word of warning, however – several people die in southern Germany each year after consuming, and sometimes just touching, poisonous mushrooms. It's better to go mushrooming with a local first, one who knows what to pick and what to leave on the forest floor. Never let children touch any mushroom.

Of course many of the forest's inhabitants end up on restaurant plates. Venison and wild boar are common dishes, especially in Bavaria's east. Often a pricey meat in other countries, venison costs only a little bit more then beef and pork and tastes best with forest berry sauce and dumplings, an unmissable culinary experience in these parts.

Bavaria sprawls over 70,550 sq km, making it bigger than Ireland, Portugal or Denmark. The Black Forest is comparatively small at only 13,500 sq km.

Berchtesgaden National Park (p106)

National & Nature Parks

Bavaria is home to Germany's oldest national park, the Bavarian Forest National Park, which was founded in 1970. There is only one more of Germany's 16 national parks in Bavaria but it's a good one: the Berchtesgaden National Park on the Austrian border, a ravishing mountainscape of big-shouldered Alps and jewel-coloured, fjordlike lakes. Both parks preserve places of outstanding natural beauty, rare geographical features and various wildlife species.

Germany's newest national park was created in Baden-Württemberg – the Black Forest National Park – in 2014. At 100 sq km it's a small affair split into two parts roughly 3.5km apart. The creation of a national park here was opposed by logging companies, two of the state's big political parties, the CDU and the FDP, and many locals. The park represents just 0.7 % of the state's considerable forest, but an area now left entirely to nature.

The Black Forest also has two nature parks, which enjoy a lower degree of environmental protection and are essentially outdoor playgrounds. These are sprawling rural landscapes criss-crossed by roads and dotted with villages. Selective logging (no clear-cutting) and agriculture here is done in a controlled and environmentally friendly fashion.

The Black Forest straddles the Continental Divide. Water either drains into the north-flowing Rhine, which empties into the Atlantic Ocean, or into the east-flowing Danube, which empties into the Black Sea.

Survival Guide

Directory A–Z

Accessible Travel

Generally speaking, southern Germany caters well for people with disabilities, especially wheelchair users.

➡ You'll find access ramps and/or lifts in many public buildings, including train stations, museums, theatres and cinemas.

➡ New hotels and some renovated establishments have lifts and rooms with extra-wide doors and spacious, accessible bathrooms.

➡ Nearly all trains are accessible, and local buses and U-Bahns are becoming increasingly so. Seeing-eye dogs are allowed on all forms of public transport.

➡ Many local and regional tourism offices have special brochures for people with disabilities, although usually in German.

Resources

Deutsche Bahn Mobility Service Centre (☎0180 651 2512; www.bahn.com) Train access information and route planning assistance.

German National Tourism Office (www.germany.travel) Your first port of call, with inspirational information in English. Click on 'Discover Germany – Barrier Free'.

Munich for Physically Challenged Tourists (www.munich. de) Searching the official Munich tourism website will produce gigabytes of info on everything for travellers with disabilities from Oktoberfest to local clubs and organisations to special ride services.

Natko (www.natko.de) Central clearing house for enquiries about barrier-free travel in Germany.

Download Lonely Planet's free Accessible Travel guides from http://lptravel.to/AccessibleTravel.

Accommodation

Bavaria and the Black Forest offer all types of places to unpack your suitcase, from hostels, campsites and traditional taverns to chains, business hotels and luxury resorts. Reservations are a good idea between June and September, around major holidays and festivals and, in business-oriented cities, during trade shows.

Camping

Almost every town in southern Germany has a camping ground a short bus ride away. German camping grounds are normally well maintained and offer a wide range of facilities.

➡ The core season runs from May to September with only a few campsites open year-round. July and August are naturally the busiest months.

➡ There are usually separate charges per person, tent and car, and additional fees for resort tax, electricity and sewage disposal.

➡ A Camping Card International may yield some modest savings.

➡ The *ADAC Camping & Caravanning Führer*, available from bookshops, is a comprehensive camping guide, in German. Other handy sources include www.alanrogers.com and www.eurocampings.eu.

➡ It's a grey area, but wild camping in Germany is illegal. Farmers may be willing to let you camp on their land if you ask permission first.

Farm Stays

A holiday on a working farm is a big hit with kids who

BOOK YOUR STAY ONLINE

For more accommodation reviews by Lonely Planet authors, check out http://lonelyplanet.com/hotels/. You'll find independent reviews, as well as recommendations on the best places to stay. Best of all, you can book online.

love interacting with their favourite barnyard animals and helping with everyday chores. Accommodation ranges from bare-bones rooms with shared facilities to fully furnished holiday flats. Minimum stays of three days are common. For more information see www.land tourismus.de.

Hostels

Bavaria has many hostels of both the indie and youth varieties. While dorm rooms are the cheapest form of accommodation available (even cheaper than camping at certain times of the week/year), private rooms can cost the same or even more than midrange hotel rooms booked online or at the last minute.

➡ There are backpacker hostels across the region, though fewer in Baden-Württemberg than Bavaria. This type of hostel attracts a convivial, international crowd to mixed dorms and private rooms. Facilities usually include communal kitchens, lockers, internet access, laundry and a common room.

➡ Most hostels offer inexpensive sightseeing and themed tours.

➡ Classic Hostelling International–affiliated hostels are run by the Deutsches Jugendherbergswerk (DJH hostel; www.jugendherberge. de) and cater primarily to German school groups and families.

➡ Most DJH hostels have been modernised but can't quite shake that institutional feel. Some can be noisy with harried, grumpy staff.

➡ Rates in gender-segregated dorms or in family rooms range from roughly €20 to €30 per person, including linen and breakfast. People over 27 are charged an extra €4. In Bavaria, if space is tight, priority is given to people

Climate

Munich
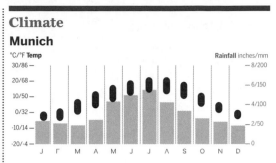

Salzburg
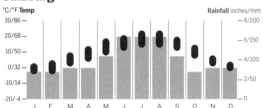

Zugspitze
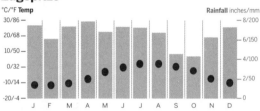

under 27, except for those travelling as a family.

➡ Unless you're a member of your home country's HI association, you either need to buy a Hostelling International Card for between €7 and €22.50 (valid for one year) depending on age. They are available at any DJH hostel.

➡ DJH hostels can be booked online.

Hotels

Hotels range from small family-run establishments to comfortable midsize properties to luxurious international chains. Expect even budget establishments to be well run and clean. In most older, privately run hotels rooms may vary dramatically in terms

of size, decor and amenities. The cheapest share bathroom facilities, while others may come with a shower cubicle installed but no private toilet; only pricier ones have en suite bathrooms. If possible, ask to see a couple of rooms before committing.

Top-end establishments offer deluxe amenities, perhaps a scenic location, special decor or historical ambience. Many also have pools, saunas, business centres and other upmarket facilities.

Standards of service across the board may be lower than those you are used to back home.

Pensions, Inns & Private Rooms

Pensionen (guesthouses) and *Gasthäuser* (inns) or

Gasthöfe are smaller, less formal and cheaper than hotels; the latter usually have a restaurant. You can expect clean rooms but only minimal amenities – maybe a radio, sometimes a small television, almost never a phone. Some facilities may be shared. What rooms lack in amenities, they often make up for in charm and authenticity.

Privatzimmer (essentially guest rooms in private homes) are ubiquitous in southern Germany and great for catching a glimpse into how locals live, although privacy seekers may find these places a little bit too close for comfort. Tourist offices list rooms available, or look around for *Zimmer Frei* (rooms available) signs in house or shop windows. Per person prices range from €25 to €40.

Booking Services

➜ The website www.sightsleeping.by is a booking portal for rooms in some of Bavaria's most magnificent properties such as castles, palaces and other historical buildings.

➜ Many tourist office and hotel websites let you check room availability and make reservations. Staff can also help you in person or, if you arrive after office hours, have vacancies posted in the window or a display case.

➜ Electronic reservation boards, especially common in the Alps, connect you directly to local properties for free, but don't always work reliably.

Customs Regulations

Most articles that you take into Germany for your personal use may be imported free of duty and tax. The following allowances apply to duty-free goods purchased in a non-EU country. In addition, you can bring in other products up to a value of €430, including tea, coffee and perfume. Bringing meat and milk, as well as products made from them, into the EU is prohibited.

Alcohol 1L of strong liquor or 2L of less than 22% alcohol by volume and 4L of wine

Tobacco 200 cigarettes or 100 cigarillos or 50 cigars or 250g of loose tobacco

Electricity

Type F
230V/50Hz

Type C
230V/50Hz

Embassies & Consulates

Most foreign embassies are in Berlin but many countries have consular offices in Munich (only Australia and New Zealand in the list below don't).

Austrian Consulate (☑089-998 150; Ismaninger Strasse 136; ⊜Bundesfinanzhof)

Belgian Honorary Consulate (☑089-242 188 529; Altheimer Eck 13; ⊜Karlsplatz, ⑤Karlsplatz, ⑪Karlsplatz)

Canadian Consulate (☑089-219 9570; Tal 29)

Czech Republic Consulate (☑089-9583 7232; Libellenstrasse 1; ⑪Freimann)

Dutch Consulate (☑089-206 026 710; Nymphenburgerstrasse 20a; ⑪Stiglmaierplatz)

French Consulate (☑089-419 4110; Heimeranstrasse 10; ⑪Schwanthalerhöhe)

Irish Honorary Consulate (☑089 2080 5990; Denninger Strasse 15; ⑪Richard-Strauss-Strasse)

Polish Consulate (☑089-418 6080; Röntgenstrasse 5; ⑪Böhmerwaldplatz)

UK Consulate (☎089 211 090; Möhlstrasse 5; 🚇Holbeinstrasse)

US Consulate (☎089-288 80; Königinstrasse 5; 🚌100 to Königinstrasse)

Health

Excellent healthcare is readily available and for minor illnesses such as colds pharmacists can provide advice and sell over-the-counter medication. They can also advise when more specialised help is required and point you in the right direction.

Before You Go

While Germany has excellent healthcare, some planning before departure, particularly for pre-existing illnesses, will be beneficial.

➡ Bring medications in their original, labelled, containers. A signed and dated letter from your physician describing your conditions and medications, including generic names, is a good idea.

➡ If carrying syringes or needles, be sure to have a physician's letter documenting their medical necessity.

➡ Carry a spare pair of contact lenses and glasses, and take your optical prescription with you.

Insurance

If you're an EU citizen, a European Health Insurance Card (EHIC) covers you for most medical care. An EHIC will not cover you for non-emergencies or emergency repatriation. Citizens from other countries should find out if there is a reciprocal arrangement for free medical care between their country and Germany. If you do need health insurance, make sure you get a policy that covers you for the worst possible case, such as an accident requiring an emergency flight home. Find out in advance if your insurance plan will make payments directly to providers or reimburse you later for overseas health expenditures.

Internet Access

Getting online is fairly easy, though as is the case across Europe internet cafes are almost a thing of the past.

➡ Public libraries offer free terminals and sometimes wi-fi access, but downsides may include time limits, reservation requirements and queues.

➡ Some tourist information centres have free web access.

➡ Internet access is sometimes available at slightly seedy telephone call shops, which cluster near train stations in big cities.

➡ Hotels and hostels often have high-speed access and wi-fi (W-LAN in German – the word wi-fi is not generally understood), which is usually free. At some business hotels you can pay for faster internet speed. The lower down the hotel food chain you go, the less likely it is that wi-fi will actually work or that signal will reach everywhere. Hostels, however, often have excellent wi-fi.

➡ Many cafes and pubs offer wi-fi access, often at no charge with purchase.

➡ There are some free hotspots in Germany's south but these often require pre-registration.

Language Courses

Several Munich schools offer quality German language courses.

DESK (☎089-263 334; www. desk-sprachkurse.de; Blumenstrasse 1; 🅂Marienplatz, 🇺Marienplatz) Tried and tested school with three decades of experience and a central location.

Deutschakademie (☎089-2601 8989; www.deutsch akademie.de; Sonnenstrasse

8) Small groups, and courses running throughout the day.

Inlingua (☎089-231 1530; www.inlingua-muenchen. de; Sendlinger-Tor-Platz 6; 🇺Sendlinger Tor) A national language-school chain serving a more corporate clientele.

Ludwig-Maximilians-Universität München (www.sprachenzentrum.uni-muenchen.de; Schellingstrasse 3; 🇺Universität) Summer and term-time courses.

Legal Matters

By law, you must, in theory, carry photo identification such as your passport or national identity card (a driving licence may or may not be acceptable to the police). If you are arrested, you have the right to make a phone call and are presumed innocent until proven guilty. If you don't know a lawyer, contact your nearest consulate for a referral.

LGBT+ Travellers

Homosexuality is legal in Bavaria and the Black Forest, but the scene, even in Munich, is tiny compared to, say, Berlin or Cologne. Nuremberg, Regensburg and Freiburg are a little more relaxed as well, but in rural areas gays and lesbians tend to keep a low profile. There are websites aplenty but most are in German only. Try www.gay-web.de or, for women, www.lesarion.de.

Maps

Most tourist offices distribute free (but often very basic) city maps, but for driving around you'll need a detailed road map or atlas such as those published by Falkplan, Freytag & Berndt, RV Verlag or ADAC. Look for them at bookshops, tourist offices, newsagents and petrol stations. Find downloadable maps and driving directions at www.viamichelin.com and www.stadtplandienst.de. For hiking maps Kompass and Fritsch print excellent and very detailed regional maps.

Money

→ Germany is one of the 17 countries in the EU that uses the euro as its national currency. No other currency is accepted.

→ Euros come in seven notes (five, 10, 20, 50, 100, 200 and 500 euros) and eight coins (one and two euro coins, and one, two, five, 10, 20 and 50 cent coins).

→ Exchange money at airports, some banks and currency exchange offices, such as Reisebank, American Express and TravelEx. In rural areas, such facilities are rare, so make sure you have plenty of cash.

ATMs & Credit Cards

ATMs widely available. Credit and debit cards accepted at most hotels and shops but not all restaurants.

A piece of plastic can be vital in emergencies and occasionally also useful for phone or internet bookings. Avoid getting cash on your credit card via ATMs since fees are steep and you'll be charged interest immediately (in other words, there's no grace period as with purchases). Report lost or stolen cards to the following:

American Express ☑069 9797 1000

MasterCard ☑0800 819 1040

Visa ☑0800 814 9100

Cash

Bavaria is still very much a cash culture and making sure you have ample supply of the stuff will avoid embarrassing situations, such as trying to pay for a beer in a pub or a sausage at the railway station with your credit card. Even at the supermarket cashiers (and the queue behind you) can still get a bit huffy if you

don't have readies, especially when spending small sums.

Opening Hours

Opening hours don't vary much across the year.

Banks 8.30am–4pm Mon–Fri, limited opening Sat

Restaurants 11am–11pm

Cafes 7.30am–7pm

Bars and clubs 6pm–1am minimum

Shops 9.30am–8pm Mon–Sat

Post

→ Germany's postal service is operated by Deutsche Post (www.deutschepost.de) and is very reliable.

→ Main post offices are often near train stations.

→ Busy offices often have a dedicated desk/window for letters and postcards, avoiding the need to stand in lengthy queues with locals paying bills etc.

Public Holidays

Businesses and offices are closed on the following public holidays:

Neujahrstag (New Year's Day) 1 January

Heilige Drei Könige (Epiphany) 6 January

Ostern (Easter) March/April; Good Friday, Easter Sunday and Easter Monday

Maifeiertag (Labour Day) 1 May

Christi Himmelfahrt (Ascension Day) 40 days after Easter

Pfingsten (Whitsun/Pentecost) mid-May to mid-June – Whit Sunday and Whit Monday

Fronleichnam (Corpus Christi) 10 days after Pentecost

Mariä Himmelfahrt (Assumption Day, Bavaria only) 15 August

Tag der Deutschen Einheit (Day of German Unity) 3 October

Weihnachtstag (Christmas Day) 25 December

Sankt Stephanstag (Boxing/St Stephen's Day) 26 December

Safe Travel

Bavaria has a very low crime rate and is a remarkably safe place to live and travel in.

→ Take all the usual precautions, such as locking hotel rooms and cars, not leaving valuables unattended, and keeping an eye out for pickpockets in crowds.

→ Bavaria has been hit by Islamic terrorism in recent years, and while your chances of becoming a victim are low, vigilance is advised.

→ In Munich and the Bavarian Alps, the *Föhn* (a warm, dry wind) is a local weather-related annoyance most common in autumn. It makes some cranky but also brings exquisitely clear views of the mountains.

Telephone
Mobile Phones

→ Mobile phones operate on GSM 900/1800. If your home country uses a different standard, you'll need a multiband GSM phone in Germany.

→ If you have an unlocked multiband phone, a prepaid rechargeable SIM card from a German telecom provider will always work out cheaper than using your own network. Cards are available at any mobile-phone store (eg T-Mobile, Vodafone, E-Plus or O2) and will give you a local number without signing a contract.

→ If you have a SIM card from anywhere in the EU you will be charged the same in Germany as you are at home (or wherever the SIM is from).

Phone Codes

German phone numbers consist of an area code, which starts with 0, and the local number. Area codes can be up to six numbers and local numbers up to nine digits long. If dialling from a landline within the same city, you don't need to dial the area code. If using a mobile, you must dial it.

➤ If calling Germany from abroad, first dial your country's international access code, then 49 (Germany's country code), the area code (dropping the initial 0) and the local number. Germany's international access code is 00.

➤ Numbers starting with 0800 are toll-free but numbers starting with 0190 or 900 are charged at exorbitant rates. Direct-dialled calls made from hotel rooms are also usually charged at a premium.

Time

Clocks in Germany are set to central European time (GMT/UTC plus one hour). Daylight-saving time kicks in at 2am on the last Sunday in March and ends on the last Sunday in October. The use of the 24-hour clock (eg where 6.30pm is 18.30) is common.

Toilets

➤ Men's toilets are marked 'Herren' (or just 'H'), the ladies' 'Damen' (or just 'D').

➤ Public toilets in southern Germany's city centres are almost non-existent. Use facilities in department stores, railway stations and other public places.

➤ Toilets are rarely free and those at large railway stations can charge €1 to spend a penny. At some facilities payment is by donation, thus you pay as much as you like. At others there's a price list.

➤ Sanifair toilets charge €0.70 but you receive a €0.50 voucher to spend in the establishment in which it is located. Annoyingly this type of facility has spread in recent years from motorway service stations to other

places such as department stores and railway stations.

Tourist Information

Every reasonable-sized town in southern Germany has a municipally funded tourist information centre, some of which are stand-alone operations, while others are twinned with a kind of local residents' information point. Only very occasionally will you come across staff who don't speak English and the vast majority of those charged with aiding tourists on their way are knowledgeable, friendly and efficient. Websites operated by tourist boards vary wildly in quality.

Good websites for your pre-trip research include www.bayern.by and www.germany-tourism.de.

Each region/product/ *Land* also has its own dedicated website:

Baden-Württemberg Tourist Association (www.tourism-bw.com)

Black Forest Tourism Association (www.schwarzwald-tourismus.info)

Eastern Bavarian Tourism Association (www.ostbayern-tourismus.de)

Romantic Road Tourism Association (www.romantische strasse.de)

Franconian Tourism Association (www.frankentourismus.org)

Tourism Association Allgäu-Bavarian Swabia (www.bavarian-alps.info)

Upper Bavarian Tourism Association (www.oberbayern-tourismus.de)

Visas

Most European Union nationals only need their national identity card or passport to enter, stay and work in Germany. Citizens of Australia, Canada, Israel, Japan, New Zealand and the US are among those countries that need only a valid passport (no visa) if entering as tourists for up to three months within a six-month period. Passports should be valid for at least another four months from the planned date of departure from Germany.

Nationals from other countries need a so-called Schengen Visa, named after the 1995 Schengen Agreement that enables passport controls between most countries in the European Union to be abolished (all except the UK and Ireland have signed up). For full details, see www.auswaertiges-amt.de or check with a German consulate in your country.

Transport

GETTING THERE & AWAY

If coming from anywhere in Europe, southern Germany's central position means excellent transport connections to the rest of the Continent. Air, rail and bus are all options and Germany's super-fast autobahn (motorways) make car journeys quick and relatively inexpensive when compared to other countries. From other continents, air is the best option with many big-name flag-carrier airlines operating in and out of Munich airport.

Flights, cars and tours can all be booked online at www.lonelyplanet.com/bookings.

Entering the Country

Entering Germany is normally a straightforward procedure. Citizens of most Western countries don't need a visa, but even if you do, you'll be through checks swiftly.

When arriving in Germany from any of the Schengen countries (all Germany's neighbours), you no longer have to go through passport and customs checks, regardless of your nationality.

Air

Airports

Southern Germany is served by several airports:

Flughafen München (MUC; ☑089-975 00; www.munich-airport.de) The main regional hub, 30km northeast of Munich's city centre.

Frankfurt Airport (FRA; www.frankfurt-airport.com; Hugo-Eckener-Ring; ☎; ☒Flughafen Regionalbahnhof) Although Munich is well served by transcontinental flights, most land in Frankfurt, which is closer to northern Bavaria and the beginning of the Romantic Road.

Salzburg Airport (☑0662-858 00; www.salzburg-airport.com; Innsbrucker Bundesstrasse 95; ☎) Convenient for the southeast of the region and the Alps.

Frankfurt-Hahn (HHN; www.hahn-airport.de; Lautzenhausen) Despite the name, this airport is about 100km west of Frankfurt – not at all convenient for southern Germany.

Nuremberg (NUE; ☑0911 93 700; www.airport-nuernberg.de; Flughafenstrasse) The main airport in Franconia.

Karlsruhe-Baden-Baden (Baden Airpark; ☑07229-662 000; www.badenairpark.de) Serves for the north of the Black Forest.

EuroAirport Basel-Mulhouse-Freiburg (BSL; ☑France + 33 3 89 90 31 11; www.euroairport.com) Serves Freiburg and the south of the Black Forest.

Allgäu Airport (FMM; ☑08331-984 2000; www.allgaeu-airport.de; Am Flughafen 35, Memmingen) Ryanair uses this airport

CLIMATE CHANGE & TRAVEL

Every form of transport that relies on carbon-based fuel generates CO_2, the main cause of human-induced climate change. Modern travel is dependent on aeroplanes, which might use less fuel per kilometre per person than most cars but travel much greater distances. The altitude at which aircraft emit gases (including CO_2) and particles also contributes to their climate change impact. Many websites offer 'carbon calculators' that allow people to estimate the carbon emissions generated by their journey and, for those who wish to do so, to offset the impact of the greenhouse gases emitted with contributions to portfolios of climate-friendly initiatives throughout the world. Lonely Planet offsets the carbon footprint of all staff and author travel.

125km west of Munich near the town of Memmingen.

Airlines

Lufthansa is the main airline serving Germany. It operates a huge network of domestic and international flights and the airline has an impeccable safety record. Munich is also a major hub for Eurowings. Many of the world's major national carriers fly into Munich while budget airlines prefer the region's smaller airports.

Tickets

➜ Bagging a flight any time around Oktoberfest (late September to early October) is nigh on impossible, even well in advance. Other busy times include late August, Christmas and New Year.

➜ When flights to Munich are unavailable or beyond budget, many travellers buy cheaper tickets to other airports such as Frankfurt, Salzburg or Nuremberg, then hop on a train to their final destination.

➜ Don't assume budget airline tickets to Germany will be cheaper than those offered by other airlines. Lufthansa often have some great deals.

➜ If travelling from North America, Australia or Asia via Frankfurt, save money (and time) and take the train south, rather than another domestic flight to Munich. Frankfurt airport has its own train station.

Land

Border Crossings

Germany is bordered (anticlockwise) by Denmark, the Netherlands, Belgium, Luxembourg, France, Switzerland, Austria, the Czech Republic and Poland. The Schengen Agreement abolished passport and customs formalities between Germany and all bordering countries.

Boat

The Romanshorn-Friedrichshafen ferry provides the quickest way across Lake Constance between Switzerland and Germany. Ferries operated by SBS Schifffahrt (www.sbsag.ch) take 40 minutes.

Bus

Eurolines (www.eurolines.com) The umbrella organisation of European coach operators, connecting over 500 destinations across Europe. Its website has links to each national company's site, with detailed fare and route information, promotional offers, contact numbers and, in many cases, an online booking system. In Germany, Eurolines is represented by Deutsche Touring. Eurolines have a number of passes that can save you money.

Flixbus (www.flixbus.com) A low-cost bus company that has presented Eurolines with some very stiff competition in recent years. It runs dozens of routes within Germany and links Bavaria to many other countries.

Busabout (www.busabout.com) A hop-on, hop-off service that runs coaches along several interlocking European loops between May and October. Six out of the seven loops include Munich and four take in Stuttgart and Salzburg.

Car & Motorcycle

➜ When bringing your own vehicle to Germany, you need a valid driving licence, your car registration certificate and proof of insurance.

➜ Foreign cars in Germany must display a nationality sticker unless they have official Euro-plates.

➜ Equipment you need to have in your car by law includes a first-aid kit, spare bulbs and a warning triangle.

➜ Between November and May, even away from the Alps, make sure your vehicle is fitted with winter tyres and carry snow chains in the boot. Spiked tyres are prohibited.

➜ Be aware that if driving to Germany via France, you must now have a breathalyser approved by the French authorities in the car, as well as other equipment not required in Germany. The Czech Republic also has some finicky requirements, so see www.theaa.com (click through to Driving, then Driving Abroad) for the full rundown.

Train

➜ Long-distance trains connecting major German cities with those in other countries are called EuroCity (EC) trains. Seat reservations are highly recommended, especially during the peak summer season and around major holidays.

➜ Linking the UK with continental Europe, the Eurostar (www.eurostar.com) takes less than three hours from London-St Pancras to Paris, where you can get a high-speed TGV service to Munich taking another six hours.

➜ There are direct overnight trains to Munich from Amsterdam, Copenhagen, Belgrade, Budapest, Bucharest, Florence, Milan, Rome, Venice and Vienna.

➜ Use the Deutsche Bahn website (www.bahn.de) or The Man in Seat 61 site (www.seat61.com) to plan your journey to southern Germany.

GETTING AROUND

Air

Although it is possible to fly, say, from Frankfurt to Munich or Salzburg, the time and cost involved don't make air travel a sensible way to get around southern Germany.

Unless you're travelling to Bavaria or the Black Forest from northern Germany, planes are only marginally faster than trains if you factor in the time it takes to travel to and from the airports. Lufthansa and Eurowings are among the airlines flying domestically.

Bicycle

Cycling is one of the most popular ways to get around for both locals and visitors, making southern Germany one of Europe's most bike-friendly regions.

➡ Cycling is allowed on all roads and highways but not on the autobahn (motorway). Cyclists must follow the same rules of the road as vehicles.

➡ Cycle paths are ubiquitous in large cities.

➡ Lights are compulsory but helmets aren't, not even for children. Wearing one is still a good idea, though.

➡ Bicycles may be taken on most trains but usually require a separate *Fahrradkarte* (bicycle ticket). However, they're not allowed on high-speed ICE trains. For specifics enquire at a local station or call Deutsche Bahn (DB) on the **DB Radfahrer-Hotline** (Bicycle Hotline; 📞0180-599 6633; ⏰8am-8pm).

➡ Many regional bus companies use vehicles with special bike racks. Bicycles are also allowed on

practically all lake and river boats.

➡ Around 250 train stations throughout the country hire bikes. All information can be found at www.bahn.de.

➡ Cycle hire centres are common – rates range between €10 and €25 per day.

➡ Spare parts and servicing are widely available – almost every town has a professionally run bike shop.

➡ Bett & Bike (Bed & Bike; www.bettundbike.de) lists accommodation with facilities for bikes (storage, tools, washing amenities).

Bus

Basically, wherever there is a train, take it. Buses are generally slower, less dependable and more polluting than trains, but in some rural areas they may be your only option. This is especially true of the Bavarian Forest and the Black Forest, sections of the Alpine foothills and the Alpine region. Separate bus companies, each with its own tariffs and schedules, operate in the different regions, but with a bit of practice all timetables and fares can be looked up using the Deutsche Bahn website (www.bahn.de).

In cities, buses generally converge at the *Busbahnhof* or *Zentraler Omnibus Bahnhof/ZOB* (central bus station), often near the Hauptbahnhof (central train station). The frequency of service varies from 'rarely' to 'constantly'. Commut-

er-geared routes offer limited or no service in the evenings and on weekends. It's always a good idea to ask about special fare deals, such as day or weekly passes or tourist tickets.

Car & Motorcycle

➡ German autobahns (motorways) are generally of a good standard, though they do possess some quirks such as excessively bendy slip roads and many two-lane sections.

➡ The extensive network of *Bundesstrassen* (secondary 'A' and 'B' roads) is also good, though perhaps not up to the standard you are used to back home.

➡ As yet no tolls are charged on public roads – an idea to charge foreigners for using motorways was quietly shelved.

➡ Traffic can be heavy on *Bundesstrassen* at busy times of the day.

➡ Up-to-the-minute travel and roadwork information in English is available at www.bayerninfo.de. Traffic reports on the radio (in German) usually follow on-the-hour news summaries and should trigger your car radio's TIM (Traffic Information Message) system.

➡ Well-equipped service areas appear every 40km to 60km on autobahns with petrol stations, toilet facilities and restaurants; some are open 24 hours. In between are *Rastplätze* (rest stops), which usually have picnic tables and free (if sometimes grotty) toilet facilities. Toilets at large service stations are never free and annoyingly you'll need change to access them.

Automobile Associations

Germany's main motoring organisation, the **Allgemeiner Deutscher**

ROMANTIC ROAD COACH

The **Romantic Road Coach** (www.romanticroadcoach.de) is geared towards individual travellers on the Romantic Road between Würzburg and Füssen from April to October.

There's one coach in either direction daily. Tickets can be purchased by phone or online and are available either for the entire distance or for segments between any of the stops. Various discounts are available.

Automobil-Club (General German Automobile Club; ✆for information 0800 510 1112, for roadside assistance from mobile 222 2222; www.adac.de) has offices in all major cities and many smaller ones.

Driving Licences

Drivers need a valid driving licence. International Driving Permits (IDP; issued by your local automobile association) for non-EU drivers are not compulsory but having one may help Germans make sense of your home licence (always carry that too) and may simplify the car hire process.

Hire

➜ Southern Germany has an excellent public transport system meaning car hire isn't absolutely necessary. One exception is the trip along the Romantic Road where a car makes travel a lot easier.

➜ As anywhere, rates for car hire vary quite considerably by model, pick-up date and location.

➜ Mini economy class vehicles start from around €35 per day, but expect surcharges for additional drivers and one-way hire.

➜ Prebooking through websites such as www.auto-europe.co.uk, www.rentalcars.com and www.holidayautos.com can bring daily rates down to less than €20 depending on how long you need the car.

➜ Child or infant seats are usually available for free or for a symbolic charge. Satellite-navigation units can be hired for a small fee per day. Both should be reserved at the time of booking.

➜ To pick up your car you'll probably need to be at least 21 years old with a valid driving licence as well as a major credit card.

➜ Taking your car into an Eastern European country,

such as the Czech Republic or Poland, is usually not allowed for insurance reasons. Check in advance if that's where you're heading.

➜ All the main international companies maintain branches at airports, major train stations and in large towns.

Insurance

➜ German law requires that all registered vehicles carry minimum third-party liability insurance. Don't even think of driving uninsured or under-insured.

➜ When hiring a vehicle, make sure your contract includes adequate liability insurance at the very minimum.

➜ Optional Collision Damage Waiver (CDW) for hire cars is extra and is charged when you pick up the vehicle.

Road Rules

➜ Driving is on the right-hand side of the road and standard international signs are in use. If you're unfamiliar with these, contact your local motoring organisation.

➜ Obey the road rules carefully: speed and red-light cameras are common and notices are sent to the car's registration address, wherever that may be. If you're renting a car, the police will obtain your home address from the rental agency and fines may be chased up by debt collectors where you live.

➜ There's a long list of other actions that may incur a fine, including using abusive language or gestures and running out of petrol on the autobahn.

➜ Speed limits are 50km/h in built up areas, 100km/h on highways and country roads and 130km/h on the autobahn unless otherwise indicated. There are sections of autobahn where there's no speed limit, but always keep an eye out for signs

indicating that slower speeds must be observed.

➜ Drivers unaccustomed to the high speeds on autobahns should be extra careful when passing another vehicle. It takes only seconds for a car in the rear-view mirror to close in at 200km/h. Pass as quickly as possible, then quickly return to the right lane.

➜ Ignore drivers who flash their headlights to make you drive faster and get out of the way. It's an illegal practice, as is passing on the right.

➜ If you break down, pull over to the side of the road immediately and set up your warning triangle about 100m behind the car. Emergency call boxes are spaced about 2km apart or, if you have a mobile phone, call the ADAC and wait for assistance.

➜ The highest permissible blood-alcohol level for drivers is 0.05%, which for most people equates to roughly one glass of wine or two small beers. The limit for drivers under 21 and for those who have held their license for less than two years is 0%.

➜ Pedestrians at crossings have right of way over all motor vehicles. Always watch out for cyclists when turning right; they too have the right of way. Right turns at a red light are only legal if there's also a green arrow pointing to the right.

Hitching

Trampen (hitching) is never entirely safe, and we don't recommend it. Travellers who hitch should understand that they are taking a small but potentially serious risk. That said, in some remote parts of Bavaria and the Black Forest – such as sections of the Alpine foothills and the Bavarian Forest – that are poorly served by public transport, you will very occasionally see people thumbing for a ride. Remember that it's safer to travel in pairs and be sure to let someone know where you're planning to go.

A safer and more predictable form of travelling is ride-shares, where you travel as a passenger in exchange for some petrol money. Most arrangements are now made via online ride-boards at www.blablacar.de or www.drive2day.de. You can advertise a ride yourself or link up with a driver going to your destination.

Local Transport

➔ Most towns have efficient public transport systems. Bigger cities, such as Munich and Nuremberg, integrate buses, trams, and U-Bahn (underground) and S-Bahn (suburban) trains into a single network.

➔ Tickets are generally bought in advance from ticket machines before boarding any mode of transport and must be stamped before or upon boarding in order to be valid.

➔ Fares are either determined by zones or time travelled, or sometimes by both. Tageskarten (day passes) generally offer better value than single-ride tickets.

➔ The fine if you're caught without a valid ticket is €40.

➔ Taxis are metered and charged at a base rate (flag fall) plus a per-kilometre fee. These are fixed but vary across cities. Some charge extra for bulky luggage or night-time rides. Rarely can you flag down a taxi. Rather, you board at a taxi rank or order one by phone.

Train

Southern Germany's rail system is mostly operated by Deutsche Bahn (www.bahn.com), though private operators such as BLB (www.blb.info), Meridian (www.der-meridian.de) and Agilis (www.agilis.de) oversee an ever-increasing number of lines. Deutsche Bahn operates a bamboozling 'alphabet soup' of train types serving just about every corner of the region and country. The system is efficient, but largely automated and unmanned. This can cause problems when things go wrong as there are often no staff members around to whom you can turn for information.

Long-distance trains are either called ICE (InterCity Express), which travel at high speeds, or the only slightly slower IC (InterCity) or EC (EuroCity) trains. Both run at hourly or bi-hourly intervals. Regional service is provided by the RE (Regional Express), the RB (RegionalBahn) and the S-Bahn.

Most train stations have coin-operated lockers charging from €1.50 to €4 for 24 hours.

Train Classes

German trains have 1st- and 2nd-class cars, both of them modern and comfortable. Seating is either in compartments of up to six people or in open-plan carriages with panoramic windows. Trains and most areas on platforms are completely nonsmoking. ICE, IC and EC trains are fully air-conditioned and have a restaurant or self-service bistro.

Tickets

➔ Large train stations have a Reisezentrum (travel centre) where staff sell tickets and can help you plan an itinerary (ask for an English-speaking agent). Smaller stations may only have a few ticket windows or no staff at all.

➔ Sometimes you will have no choice but to buy your ticket from a vending

SAMPLE TRAIN FARES

Permanent rail deals include the following:

TICKET	COST	VALIDITY
Bayern-Ticket	€25 + €6 per extra person	Mon-Fri 9am-3am, weekends midnight-3am of next day
Baden-Württemberg-Ticket	€24 + €6 per extra person	Mon-Fri 9am-3am, weekends midnight-3am of next day
Bayern-Ticket Nacht	€23 + €3 per extra person	6pm-6am
Baden-Württemberg-Ticket Nacht	€21 + €6 per extra person	6pm-6am

All of the above tickets are good for second-class travel on RE, RB and S-Bahn trains, as well as all public buses, trams, U-Bahns and privately run railways across the given Land for which they are valid. Always buy them from vending machines as there's a small surcharge if you purchase from a service desk. Remember, with the daytime tickets you can save tens of euros by putting off your journey until after 9am, especially when travelling long distances within Bavaria. The Bayern-Ticket is also valid as far as Salzburg Hauptbahnhof but not to Cheb in the Czech Republic.

machine. These are plentiful at staffed and unstaffed stations and convenient if you don't want to queue at a ticket counter. Instructions are in English and the ticket purchasing system has been greatly simplified though can still confuse the uninitiated.

➡ Both ticket windows and machines accept major credit cards, but machines don't take notes bigger than €50. Tickets sold on board (cash only) incur a service fee (€3 to €8) unless the station where you boarded was unstaffed or had a broken vending machine.

➡ Tickets are also available online up to 10 minutes before departure but need to be printed out.

➡ Tickets and passes are almost always checked. The fine for not holding a valid travel document is €40.

➡ Standard, non-discounted train tickets are expensive, but promotions, discount

TRAIN PASSES

If residing permanently outside Europe, you qualify for the **German Rail Pass** (www.germanrailpasses.com), which entitles you to unlimited travel for four to 10 days within a one-month period. Sample prices for 3/10/15 days of travel are €223/405/570 in 2nd class (half-price for children ages six to 11). The pass is valid on all trains within Germany, plus Salzburg and Basel as well as some river services, and entitles you to discounts on the Europabus along the Romantic Road and the Bayerische Zugspitzbahn.

The German Rail Youth Pass for people between 12 and 25, and the German Rail Twin Pass for two adults travelling together are variations on the scheme. If Bavaria is part of a wider European itinerary, look into a Eurail Pass (www.eurail.com).

A great resource for rail passes wherever you live is Rail Europe (www.raileurope-world.com), a major agency specialising in train travel around Europe.

tickets and special offers become available all the time. Check the website or ask at the train station.

RESERVATIONS

Seat reservations (€4.50 per person) for long-distance travel are recommended, especially on a Friday or Sunday afternoon, around holidays or in summer. They can be made up to 10 minutes before departure by phone, online or at ticket counters.

Language

German belongs to the West Germanic language family, with English and Dutch as close relatives, and has around 100 million speakers. It is commonly divided into two forms – Low German (*Plattdeutsch*) and High German (*Hochdeutsch*). Low German is an umbrella term used for the dialects spoken in Northern Germany. High German is considered the standard form and is understood throughout German-speaking communities; it's also the variety used in this chapter.

German is easy for English speakers to pronounce because almost all of its sounds are also found in English. If you read our coloured pronunciation guides as if they were English, you'll have no problems being understood. Note that kh is like the 'ch' in 'Bach' or the Scottish 'loch' (pronounced at the back of the throat, r is also pronounced at the back of the throat (almost like a g, but with some friction), zh is pronounced as the 's' in 'measure', and ü as the 'ee' in 'see' but with rounded lips. The stressed syllables are indicated with italics.

BASICS

Hello.	*Guten Tag.*	goo·ten tahk
Goodbye.	*Auf Wiedersehen.*	owf vee·der·zay·en
Yes./No.	*Ja./Nein.*	yah/nain
Please.	*Bitte.*	bi·te
Thank you.	*Danke.*	dang·ke
You're welcome.	*Bitte.*	bi·te

WANT MORE?

For in-depth language information and handy phrases, check out Lonely Planet's *German Phrasebook*. You'll find it at **shop.lonelyplanet.com**, or you can buy Lonely Planet's iPhone phrasebooks at the Apple App Store.

Excuse me.	*Entschuldigung.*	ent·shul·di·gung
Sorry.	*Entschuldigung.*	ent·shul·di·gung
How are you?		
	Wie geht es Ihnen/dir? (pol/inf)	vee gayt es ee·nen/deer
Fine. And you?		
	Danke, gut. Und Ihnen/dir? (pol/inf)	dang·ke goot unt ee·nen/deer
What's your name?		
	Wie ist Ihr Name? (pol)	vee ist eer nah·me
	Wie heißt du? (inf)	vee haist doo
My name is ...		
	Mein Name ist ... (pol)	main nah·me ist ...
	Ich heiße ... (inf)	ikh hai·se ...
Do you speak English?		
	Sprechen Sie Englisch? (pol)	shpre·khen zee eng·lish
	Sprichst du Englisch? (inf)	shprikhst doo eng·lish
I don't understand.		
	Ich verstehe nicht.	ikh fer·shtay·e nikht

ACCOMMODATION

campsite	*Campingplatz*	kem·ping·plats
guesthouse	*Pension*	pahng·zyawn
hotel	*Hotel*	ho·tel
inn	*Gasthof*	gast·hawf
room in a private home	*Privatzimmer*	pri·vaht·tsi·mer
youth hostel	*Jugendherberge*	yoo·gent·her·ber·ge

Do you have a ... room?	*Haben Sie ein ...?*	hah·ben zee ain ...
double	*Doppelzimmer*	do·pel·tsi·mer
single	*Einzelzimmer*	ain·tsel·tsi·mer
How much is it per ...?	*Wie viel kostet es pro ...?*	vee feel kos·tet es praw ...
night	*Nacht*	nakht
person	*Person*	per·zawn

Is breakfast included?
Ist das Frühstück ist das *frü*·shtük
inklusive? in·kloo·*zee*·ve

DIRECTIONS

Where's ...?
Wo ist ...? vaw ist ...

What's the address?
Wie ist die Adresse? vee ist dee a·*dre*·se

How far is it?
Wie weit ist es? vee vait ist es

Can you show me (on the map)?
Können Sie es mir *ker*·nen zee es meer
(auf der Karte) zeigen? (owf dair *kar*·te) *tsai*·gen

How can I get there?
Wie kann ich da vee kan ikh dah
hinkommen? *hin*·ko·men

Turn ...	*Biegen Sie ... ab.*	bee·gen zee ... ab
at the corner	*an der Ecke*	an dair *e*·ke
at the traffic lights	*bei der Ampel*	bai dair *am*·pel
left	*links*	lingks
right	*rechts*	rekhts

EATING & DRINKING

I'd like to reserve a table for ...	*Ich möchte einen Tisch für ... reservieren.*	ikh *merkh*·te *ai*·nen tish für ... re·zer·*vee*·ren
(eight) o'clock	*(acht) Uhr*	(akht) oor
(two) people	*(zwei) Personen*	(tsvai) per·*zaw*·nen

I'd like the menu, please.
Ich hätte gern die ikh *he*·te gern dee
Speisekarte, bitte. *shpai*·ze·kar·te *bi*·te

What would you recommend?
Was empfehlen Sie? vas emp·*fay*·len zee

What's in that dish?
Was ist in diesem vas ist in *dee*·zem
Gericht? ge·*rikht*

I'm a vegetarian.
Ich bin Vegetarier/ ikh bin ve·ge·*tah*·ri·er/
Vegetarierin. (m/f) ve·ge·*tah*·ri·e·rin

That was delicious.
Das hat hervorragend das hat her·*fawr*·rah·gent
geschmeckt. ge·*shmekt*

Cheers!
Prost! prawst

Please bring the bill.
Bitte bringen Sie *bi*·te bring·en zee
die Rechnung. dee *rekh*·nung

KEY PATTERNS

To get by in German, mix and match these simple patterns with words of your choice:

When's (the next flight)?
Wann ist (der van ist (dair
nächste Flug)? *naykhs*·te flook)

Where's (the station)?
Wo ist (der Bahnhof)? vaw ist (dair *bahn*·hawf)

Where can I (buy a ticket)?
Wo kann ich (eine vaw kan ikh (*ai*·ne
Fahrkarte kaufen)? *fahr*·kar·te *kow*·fen)

Do you have (a map)?
Haben Sie *hah*·ben zee
(eine Karte)? (*ai*·ne *kar*·te)

Is there (a toilet)?
Gibt es (eine Toilette)? gipt es (*ai*·ne to·a·*le*·te)

I'd like (a coffee).
Ich möchte ikh *merkh*·te
(einen Kaffee). (*ai*·nen ka·*fay*)

I'd like (to hire a car).
Ich möchte ikh *merkh*·te
(ein Auto mieten). (ain *ow*·to *mee*·ten)

Can I (enter)?
Darf ich darf ikh
(hereinkommen)? (her·*ein*·ko·men)

Could you please (help me)?
Könnten Sie *kern*·ten zee
(mir helfen)? (meer *hel*·fen)

Do I have to (book a seat)?
Muss ich (einen Platz mus ikh (*ai*·nen plats
reservieren lassen)? re·zer·*vee*·ren *la*·sen)

Key Words

bar (pub)	*Kneipe*	*knai*·pe
bottle	*Flasche*	*fla*·she
bowl	*Schüssel*	*shü*·sel
breakfast	*Frühstück*	*frü*·shtük
cold	*kalt*	kalt
cup	*Tasse*	*ta*·se
daily special	*Gericht des Tages*	ge·*rikht* des *tah*·ges
delicatessen	*Feinkost-geschäft*	*fain*·kost·ge·sheft
desserts	*Nachspeisen*	*nahkh*·shpai·zen
dinner	*Abendessen*	*ah*·bent·e·sen
drink list	*Getränke-karte*	ge·*treng*·ke·kar·te
fork	*Gabel*	*gah*·bel
glass	*Glas*	glahs
grocery store	*Lebensmittel-laden*	*lay*·bens·mi·tel·lah·den

hot (warm)	warm	warm
knife	Messer	me·ser
lunch	Mittagessen	mi·tahk·e·sen
market	Markt	markt
plate	Teller	te·ler
restaurant	Restaurant	res·to·rahng
set menu	Menü	may·nü
spicy	würzig	vür·tsikh
spoon	Löffel	ler·fel
with/without	mit/ohne	mit/aw·ne

Meat & Fish

beef	Rindfleisch	rint·flaish
carp	Karpfen	karp·fen
fish	Fisch	fish
herring	Hering	hay·ring
lamb	Lammfleisch	lam·flaish
meat	Fleisch	flaish
pork	Schweinefleisch	shvai·ne·flaish
poultry	Geflügelfleisch	ge·flü·gel·flaish
salmon	Lachs	laks
sausage	Wurst	vurst
seafood	Meeresfrüchte	mair·res·frükh·te
shellfish	Schaltiere	shahl·tee·re
trout	Forelle	fo·re·le
veal	Kalbfleisch	kalp·flaish

Fruit & Vegetables

apple	Apfel	ap·fel
banana	Banane	ba·nah·ne
bean	Bohne	baw·ne
cabbage	Kraut	krowt
capsicum	Paprika	pap·ri·kah
carrot	Mohrrübe	mawr·rü·be
cucumber	Gurke	gur·ke
fruit	Frucht/Obst	frukht/awpst

SIGNS

Ausgang	Exit
Damen	Women
Eingang	Entrance
Geschlossen	Closed
Herren	Men
Toiletten (WC)	Toilets
Offen	Open
Verboten	Prohibited

grapes	Weintrauben	vain·trow·ben
lemon	Zitrone	tsi·traw·ne
lentil	Linse	lin·ze
lettuce	Kopfsalat	kopf·za·laht
mushroom	Pilz	pilts
nuts	Nüsse	nü·se
onion	Zwiebel	tsvee·bel
orange	Orange	o·rahng·zhe
pea	Erbse	erp·se
plum	Pflaume	pflow·me
potato	Kartoffel	kar·to·fel
spinach	Spinat	shpi·naht
strawberry	Erdbeere	ert·bair·re
tomato	Tomate	to·mah·te
vegetable	Gemüse	ge·mü·ze
watermelon	Wassermelone	va·ser·me·law·ne

Other

bread	Brot	brawt
butter	Butter	bu·ter
cheese	Käse	kay·ze
egg/eggs	Ei/Eier	ai/ai·er
honey	Honig	haw·nikh
jam	Marmelade	mar·me·lah·de
pasta	Nudeln	noo·deln
pepper	Pfeffer	pfe·fer
rice	Reis	rais
salt	Salz	zalts
soup	Suppe	zu·pe
sugar	Zucker	tsu·ker

Drinks

beer	Bier	beer
coffee	Kaffee	ka·fay
juice	Saft	zaft
milk	Milch	milkh
orange juice	Orangensaft	o·rang·zhen·zaft
red wine	Rotwein	rawt·vain
sparkling wine	Sekt	zekt
tea	Tee	tay
water	Wasser	va·ser
white wine	Weißwein	vais·vain

EMERGENCIES

| Help! | | |
| Hilfe! | | hil·fe |

Go away!
Gehen Sie weg!   gay·en zee vek

Call the police!
Rufen Sie die Polizei!   roo·fen zee dee po·li·tsai

Call a doctor!
Rufen Sie einen Arzt!   roo·fen zee ai·nen artst

Where are the toilets?
Wo ist die Toilette?   vo ist dee to·a·le·te

I'm lost.
Ich habe mich verirrt.   ikh hah·be mikh fer·irt

I'm sick.
Ich bin krank.   ikh bin krangk

It hurts here.
Es tut hier weh.   es toot heer vay

I'm allergic to ...
Ich bin allergisch   ikh bin a·lair·gish
gegen ...   gay·gen ...

SHOPPING & SERVICES

I'd like to buy ...
Ich möchte ... kaufen.   ikh merkh·te ... kow·fen

I'm just looking.
Ich schaue mich nur um.   ikh show·e mikh noor um

Can I look at it?
Können Sie es mir   ker·nen zee es meer
zeigen?   tsai·gen

How much is this?
Wie viel kostet das?   vee feel kos·tet das

That's too expensive.
Das ist zu teuer.   das ist tsoo toy·er

Can you lower the price?
Können Sie mit dem   ker·nen zee mit dem
Preis heruntergehen?   prais he·run·ter·gay·en

There's a mistake in the bill.
Da ist ein Fehler   dah ist ain fay·ler
in der Rechnung.   in dair rekh·nung

ATM	*Geldautomat*	gelt·ow·to·maht
post office	*Postamt*	post·amt
tourist office	*Fremden-*	frem·den-
	verkehrsbüro	fer·kairs·bü·raw

TIME & DATES

What time is it? *Wie spät ist es?*   vee shpayt ist es

It's (10) o'clock. *Es ist (zehn) Uhr.*   es ist (tsayn) oor

At what time? *Um wie viel Uhr?*   um vee feel oor

At ... *Um ...*   um ...

morning	*Morgen*	mor·gen
afternoon	*Nachmittag*	nahkh·mi·tahk
evening	*Abend*	ah·bent

QUESTION WORDS

How?	*Wie?*	vee
What?	*Was?*	vas
When?	*Wann?*	van
Where?	*Wo?*	vaw
Who?	*Wer?*	vair
Why?	*Warum?*	va·rum

yesterday	*gestern*	ges·tern
today	*heute*	hoy·te
tomorrow	*morgen*	mor·gen
Monday	*Montag*	mawn·tahk
Tuesday	*Dienstag*	deens·tahk
Wednesday	*Mittwoch*	mit·vokh
Thursday	*Donnerstag*	do·ners·tahk
Friday	*Freitag*	frai·tahk
Saturday	*Samstag*	zams·tahk
Sunday	*Sonntag*	zon·tahk
January	*Januar*	yan·u·ahr
February	*Februar*	fay·bru·ahr
March	*März*	merts
April	*April*	a·pril
May	*Mai*	mai
June	*Juni*	yoo·ni
July	*Juli*	yoo·li
August	*August*	ow·gust
September	*September*	zep·tem·ber
October	*Oktober*	ok·taw·ber
November	*November*	no·vem·ber
December	*Dezember*	de·tsem·ber

TRANSPORT

Public Transport

boat	*Boot*	bawt
bus	*Bus*	bus
metro	*U-Bahn*	oo·bahn
plane	*Flugzeug*	flook·tsoyk
train	*Zug*	tsook

At what time's the ... bus?	*Wann fährt der ... Bus?*	van fairt dair... bus
first	*erste*	ers·te
last	*letzte*	lets·te

NUMBERS

1	eins	ains
2	zwei	tsvai
3	drei	drai
4	vier	feer
5	fünf	fünf
6	sechs	zeks
7	sieben	zee·ben
8	acht	akht
9	neun	noyn
10	zehn	tsayn
20	zwanzig	tsvan·tsikh
30	dreißig	drai·tsikh
40	vierzig	feer·tsikh
50	fünfzig	fünf·tsikh
60	sechzig	zekh·tsikh
70	siebzig	zeep·tsikh
80	achtzig	akht·tsikh
90	neunzig	noyn·tsikh
100	hundert	hun·dert
1000	tausend	tow·sent

A ... to (Berlin).	Eine ... nach (Berlin).	ai·ne ... nahkh (ber·leen)
1st-class ticket	Fahrkarte erster Klasse	fahr·kar·te ers·ter kla·se
2nd-class ticket	Fahrkarte zweiter Klasse	fahr·kar·te tsvai·ter kla·se
one-way ticket	einfache Fahrkarte	ain·fa·khe fahr·kar·te
return ticket	Rückfahrkarte	rük·fahr·kar·te

At what time does it arrive?
Wann kommt es an? van komt es an

Is it a direct route?
Ist es eine direkte ist es ai·ne di·rek·te
Verbindung? fer·bin·dung

Does it stop at (Freiburg)?
Hält es in (Freiburg)? helt es in (frai·boorg)

What station is this?
Welcher Bahnhof vel·kher bahn·hawf
ist das? ist das

What's the next stop?
Welches ist der vel·khes ist dair
nächste Halt? naykh·ste halt

I want to get off here.
Ich möchte hier ikh merkh·te heer
aussteigen. ows·shtai·gen

Please tell me when we get to (Kiel).
Könnten Sie mir bitte kern·ten zee meer bi·te
sagen, wann wir in zah·gen van veer in
(Kiel) ankommen? (keel) an·ko·men

Please take me to (this address).
Bitte bringen Sie mich bi·te bring·en zee mikh
zu (dieser Adresse). tsoo (dee·zer a·dre·se)

platform	Bahnsteig	bahn·shtaik
ticket office	Fahrkartenverkauf	fahr·kar·ten·fer·kowf
timetable	Fahrplan	fahr·plan

Driving & Cycling

I'd like to hire a ...	Ich möchte ein ... mieten.	ikh merkh·te ain ... mee·ten
4WD	Allradfahrzeug	al·raht·fahr·tsoyk
bicycle	Fahrrad	fahr·raht
car	Auto	ow·to
motorbike	Motorrad	maw·tor·raht

How much is it per ...?	Wie viel kostet es pro ...?	vee feel kos·tet es praw ...
day	Tag	tahk
week	Woche	vo·khe

bicycle pump	Fahrradpumpe	fahr·raht·pum·pe
child seat	Kindersitz	kin·der·zits
helmet	Helm	helm
petrol	Benzin	ben·tseen

Does this road go to ...?
Führt diese Straße fürt dee·ze shtrah·se
nach ...? nahkh ...

(How long) Can I park here?
(Wie lange) Kann ich (vee lang·e) kan ikh
hier parken? heer par·ken

Where's a petrol station?
Wo ist eine Tankstelle? vaw ist ai·ne tangk·shte·le

I need a mechanic.
Ich brauche einen ikh brow·khe ai·nen
Mechaniker. me·khah·ni·ker

My car/motorbike has broken down (at ...).
Ich habe (in ...) eine ikh hah·be (in ...) ai·ne
Panne mit meinem pa·ne mit mai·nem
Auto/Motorrad. ow·to/maw·tor·raht

I've run out of petrol.
Ich habe kein ikh hah·be kain
Benzin mehr. ben·tseen mair

I have a flat tyre.
Ich habe eine ikh hah·be ai·ne
Reifenpanne. rai·fen·pa·ne

Are there cycling paths?
Gibt es Fahrradwege? geept es fahr·raht·vay·ge

Is there bicycle parking?
Gibt es Fahrrad- geept es fahr·raht·
Parkplätze? park·ple·tse

GLOSSARY

(pl) indicates plural

Abtei – abbey
ADAC – Allgemeiner Deutscher Automobil Club (German Automobile Association)
Allee – avenue
Altstadt – old town
Apotheke – pharmacy
Ärzt – doctor
Ausgang – exit

Bad – spa, bath
Bahnhof – train station
Basilika – basilica
Bedienung – service; service charge
Berg – mountain
Bibliothek – library
Biergarten – beer garden
Bierkeller – cellar pub
Brauerei – brewery
Brotzeit – literally bread time, typically an afternoon snack featuring bread with cold cuts, cheeses or sausages
Brücke – bridge
Brunnen – fountain, well
Burg – castle
Busbahnhof – bus station

Christkindlmarkt – Christmas food and craft market; sometimes spelt *Christkindlesmarkt*

DB – Deutsche Bahn (German national railway)
Denkmal – memorial
Deutsche Reich – German empire; refers to the period 1871–1918
DJH – Deutsches Jugendherbergswerk (German youth hostel association)
Dom – cathedral
Dorf – village

Eingang – entrance

Fahrrad – bicycle
Ferienwohnung, Ferienwohnungen (pl) – holiday flat or apartment
Fest – festival
Flohmarkt – flea market
Flughafen – airport

Krankenhaus – hospital
Kunst – art
Kurhaus – literally spa house, but usually a spa towns central building, used for social gatherings and events
Kurort – spa resort
Kurtaxe – resort tax
Kurverwaltung – spa resort administration
Kurzentrum – spa centre

Land, Länder (pl) – state
Landtag – state parliament

Markgraf – margrave; German nobleman ranking above a count
Markt – market; often used instead of *Marktplatz*
Marktplatz – marketplace or square; often abbreviated to *Markt*
Mass – 1L tankard or stein of beer
Mensa – university cafeteria
Milchcafé – coffee with milk
Münster – minster, large church, cathedral

Nord – north
Notdienst – emergency service
NSDAP – National Socialist German Workers Party, Nazi party

Ost – east

Pension, Pensionen (pl) – inexpensive boarding house
Pfarrkirche – parish church
Platz – square
Postamt – post office

Radwandern – bicycle touring
Rathaus – town hall
Ratskeller – town hall restaurant
Reisezentrum – travel centre in train or bus stations
Ruhetag – rest day; closing day at a shop or restaurant

Saal, Säle (pl) – hall, room
Sammlung – collection
S-Bahn – *Schnellbahn*; suburban-metropolitan trains
Schatzkammer – treasury
Schloss – palace
Schnellimbiss – fast-food stall or restaurants
See – lake
Seilbahn – cable car
Speisekarte – menu
Stadt – city, town
Stadtbad, Stadtbäder (pl) – public pool
Staumauer – dam
Strasse – street; often abbreviated to Str
Süd – south

Tal – valley
Tor – gate
Tracht, Trachten (pl) – traditional costume
Turm – tower

U-Bahn – underground train

Verboten – forbidden
Viertel – quarter, district
Volksmusik – folk music

Wald – forest
Wasserfall – waterfall
Weg – way, path
Weinstube – traditional wine bar or tavern
West – west

Zimmer Frei – room available (for accommodation purposes)

Behind the Scenes

SEND US YOUR FEEDBACK

We love to hear from travellers – your comments keep us on our toes and help make our books better. Our well-travelled team reads every word on what you loved or loathed about this book. Although we cannot reply individually to your submissions, we always guarantee that your feedback goes straight to the appropriate authors, in time for the next edition. Each person who sends us information is thanked in the next edition – the most useful submissions are rewarded with a selection of digital PDF chapters.

Visit **lonelyplanet.com/contact** to submit your updates and suggestions or to ask for help. Our award-winning website also features inspirational travel stories, news and discussions.

Note: We may edit, reproduce and incorporate your comments in Lonely Planet products such as guidebooks, websites and digital products, so let us know if you don't want your comments reproduced or your name acknowledged. For a copy of our privacy policy visit lonelyplanet.com/privacy.

WRITER THANKS

Marc Di Duca

Huge thanks goes out to Robert Leckel of München Tourismus for his invaluable assistance and great ideas. I'd also like to thank all the staff of Bavaria's excellent tourist offices for their help, especially those in Landsberg, Nuremberg, Bamberg, Augsburg and Bayreuth. Finally many thanks to my wife for holding the fort while I was away in Bavaria.

Kerry Christiani

I'd like to say *vielen Dank* to all of the locals, travellers and tourism pros who made the road to research a pleasure. Particular thanks go to Andrea Mauch in Konstanz, Maren Schullerus in Baden-Baden, Anna Beyrer in Ulm, Yvonne Halmich in Karlsruhe, Christine Strecker in Freiburg, Sandra Nörpel in Stuttgart, and Stephanie Staudhammer in Salzburg.

ACKNOWLEDGEMENTS

Climate map data adapted from Peel MC, Finlayson BL & McMahon TA (2007) 'Updated World Map of the Köppen-Geiger Climate Classification', Hydrology and Earth System Sciences, 11, 163344.

Cover photograph: Rothenburg ob der Tauber, Francesco Carovillano/4Corners ©

THIS BOOK

This 6th edition of Lonely Planet's *Munich, Bavaria & the Black Forest* guide was researched and written by Marc Di Duca and Kerry Christiani, and curated by Marc. The previous edition was also written by Marc and Kerry. This guidebook was produced by the following:

Destination Editor Niamh O'Brien

Senior Product Editor Genna Patterson

Product Editors Shona Gray, Sandie Kestell

Senior Cartographer Valentina Kremenchutskaya

Book Designer Gwen Cotter

Assisting Editors James Bainbridge, Michelle Coxall, Samantha Forge, Victoria Harrison, Jennifer Hattam, Gabrielle Innes, Rosie Nicholson, Tamara Sheward, Gabrielle Stefanos, Simon Williamson

Cover Researcher Naomi Parker

Thanks to Martina Brunner, Heather Champion, Deniz Ozkan, Kathryn Rowan, Renata Willi

Index

Map Pages **000**
Photo Pages **000**

Map Legend

Sights

- Beach
- Bird Sanctuary
- Buddhist
- Castle/Palace
- Christian
- Confucian
- Hindu
- Islamic
- Jain
- Jewish
- Monument
- Museum/Gallery/Historic Building
- Ruin
- Shinto
- Sikh
- Taoist
- Winery/Vineyard
- Zoo/Wildlife Sanctuary
- Other Sight

Activities, Courses & Tours

- Bodysurfing
- Diving
- Canoeing/Kayaking
- Course/Tour
- Sento Hot Baths/Onsen
- Skiing
- Snorkelling
- Surfing
- Swimming/Pool
- Walking
- Windsurfing
- Other Activity

Sleeping

- Sleeping
- Camping
- Hut/Shelter

Eating

- Eating

Drinking & Nightlife

- Drinking & Nightlife
- Cafe

Entertainment

- Entertainment

Shopping

- Shopping

Information

- Bank
- Embassy/Consulate
- Hospital/Medical
- Internet
- Police
- Post Office
- Telephone
- Toilet
- Tourist Information
- Other Information

Geographic

- Beach
- Gate
- Hut/Shelter
- Lighthouse
- Lookout
- Mountain/Volcano
- Oasis
- Park
- Pass
- Picnic Area
- Waterfall

Population

- Capital (National)
- Capital (State/Province)
- City/Large Town
- Town/Village

Transport

- Airport
- Border crossing
- Bus
- Cable car/Funicular
- Cycling
- Ferry
- Metro station
- Monorail
- Parking
- Petrol station
- S-Bahn/Subway station
- Taxi
- T-bane/Tunnelbana station
- Train station/Railway
- Tram
- Tube station
- U-Bahn/Underground station
- Other Transport

Routes

- Tollway
- Freeway
- Primary
- Secondary
- Tertiary
- Lane
- Unsealed road
- Road under construction
- Plaza/Mall
- Steps
- Tunnel
- Pedestrian overpass
- Walking Tour
- Walking Tour detour
- Path/Walking Trail

Boundaries

- International
- State/Province
- Disputed
- Regional/Suburb
- Marine Park
- Cliff
- Wall

Hydrography

- River, Creek
- Intermittent River
- Canal
- Water
- Dry/Salt/Intermittent Lake
- Reef

Areas

- Airport/Runway
- Beach/Desert
- Cemetery (Christian)
- Cemetery (Other)
- Glacier
- Mudflat
- Park/Forest
- Sight (Building)
- Sportsground
- Swamp/Mangrove

Note: Not all symbols displayed above appear on the maps in this book

OUR STORY

A beat-up old car, a few dollars in the pocket and a sense of adventure. In 1972 that's all Tony and Maureen Wheeler needed for the trip of a lifetime – across Europe and Asia overland to Australia. It took several months, and at the end – broke but inspired – they sat at their kitchen table writing and stapling together their first travel guide, *Across Asia on the Cheap*. Within a week they'd sold 1500 copies. Lonely Planet was born. Today, Lonely Planet has offices in Franklin, London, Melbourne, Oakland, Dublin, Beijing and Delhi, with more than 600 staff and writers. We share Tony's belief that 'a great guidebook should do three things: inform, educate and amuse'.

OUR WRITERS

Marc Di Duca

Munich, Bavaria A travel author for over a decade, Marc has worked for Lonely Planet in Siberia, Slovakia, Bavaria, England, Ukraine, Austria, Poland, Croatia, Portugal, Madeira and on the Trans-Siberian Railway, as well as writing and updating tens of other guides for other publishers. When not on the road, Marc lives near Mariánské Lázně in the Czech Republic with his wife and two sons. Marc also wrote the Plan Your Trip, Understand and Survival Guide sections.

Kerry Christiani

Stuttgart & the Black Forest, Salzburg & Around Kerry is an award-winning travel writer, photographer and Lonely Planet author, specialising in Central and Southern Europe. Based in Wales, she has authored/co-authored more than a dozen Lonely Planet titles. An adventure addict, she loves mountains, cold places and true wilderness. She features her latest work at https://its-a-small-world.com and tweets @kerrychristiani.

Published by Lonely Planet Global Limited
CRN 554153
6th edition – March 2019
ISBN 978 1 78657 377 3
© Lonely Planet 2019   Photographs © as indicated 2019
10 9 8 7 6 5 4 3 2 1
Printed in China